ISRAEL'S DIVINE HEALER

Books in This Series

God at Sinai
God Is a Warrior
Grace in the End
Israel's Divine Healer
The Messiah in the Old Testament

STUDIES IN
OLD TESTAMENT BIBLICAL THEOLOGY

ISRAEL'S DIVINE HEALER

MICHAEL L. BROWN

ZONDERVAN™
GRAND RAPIDS, MICHIGAN 49530 USA

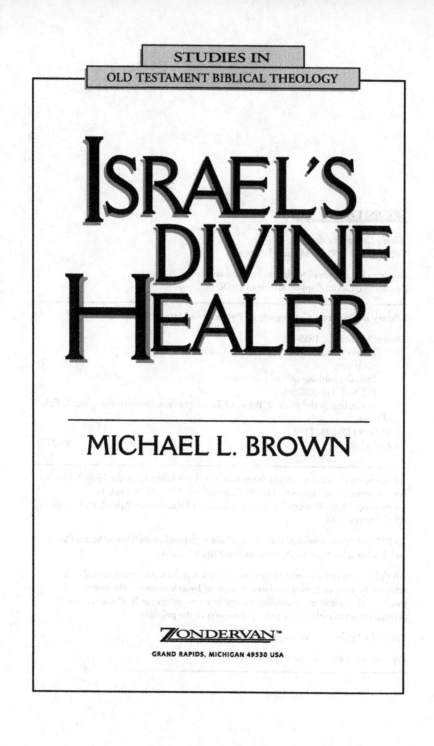

ZONDERVAN™

Israel's Divine Healer

Requests for information should be addressed to:
Zondervan, Grand Rapids, Michigan 49530

Library of Congress Cataloging-in-Publication Data

Brown, Michael L., 1955-
Israel's divine healer / by Michael L. Brown.
p. cm.
Includes bibliographical references.
ISBN: 0-310-20029-6
1. Healing in the Bible. 2. Bible. O.T.—Criticism, interpretation, etc. I. Title of Book.
BS1199.H39B76 1994
234'.13-dc 20 95-2139
CIP

Edited by Verlyn D. Verbrugge

Printed in the United States of America

◆ Contents ◆

◆ Preface to Series ◆

The editors are pleased to announce the "Studies in Old Testament Biblical Theology" series, with the hope that it contributes to the field of Old Testament theology and stimulates further discussion. If Old Testament theology is the queen of Old Testament studies, she is a rather neglected queen. To write in the area of Old Testament theology is a daunting proposition, one that leads many to hesitate taking on the task. After all, Old Testament theology presupposes an understanding of all the books of the Old Testament and, at least as conceived in the present project, an insight into its connection with the New Testament.

Another reason why theology has been neglected in recent years is simply a lack of confidence that the Old Testament can be summarized in one or even a number of volumes. Is there a center, a central concept, under which the entire Old Testament may be subsumed? Many doubt it. Thus, while a number of articles, monographs, and commentaries address the theology of a source, a chapter, or even a book, few studies address the Old Testament as a whole.

The editors of this series also believe it is impossible to present the entirety of the Old Testament message under a single rubric. Even as important a concept as the covenant fails to incorporate all aspects of the Old Testament (note especially wisdom literature). Thus, this series will present separate volumes, each devoted to a different theme, issue, or perspective of biblical theology, and will show its importance for the Old Testament and for the entire Christian canon.

One last word needs to be said about theological approach. Gone are the days when scholars, especially those who work in a field as ideologically sensitive as theology, can claim neutrality by hiding behind some kind of scientific methodology. It is, therefore, important to announce the approach taken in this series. Those who know the editors, authors, and publisher will not be surprised to learn that an evangelical approach is taken throughout this series. At the same time, however, we believe that those who do not share this starting point may still benefit and learn from these studies.

The general editors of this series, Willem A. VanGemeren and Tremper Longman III, wish to thank the academic publishing department of Zondervan, particularly Stan Gundry and Verlyn Verbrugge, who will be working most closely with the series.

Willem A. VanGemeren
Professor of Old Testament and Semitic Languages
Trinity Evangelical Divinity School

◆ Preface ◆

My interest in Israel's divine Healer is long-standing, both spiritually and academically. The origins of that interest, however, are unique and worth recounting. Raised in a Conservative Jewish home on Long Island, New York, I can only explain my teenage foray into the world of drugs and hard rock music as symptomatic of the times—those turbulent years of the late 60s and early 70s, the years of Woodstock idealism, the so-called Age of Aquarius. For me, a pleasure-seeking youth of just fifteen or sixteen, the rock/drug world was full of allure and temptation, and I plunged into that world with reckless abandon.

Little did I know that by the end of 1971, while still sixteen, I would experience a radical conversion in a small Italian Pentecostal church in Queens, New York. Drawn there with the sole purpose of pulling my two best friends (and fellow band members) out of the church and back to "reality," I was confronted instead with the love of God emanating from a sincere people who simply believed. Their testimony of God's life-changing power, their acceptance of this young, proud, stubborn rebel, and their eyewitness stories of miracles, healings, and deliverances seemed totally genuine. Soon enough, my resistance melted, faith came alive, and I surrendered. In a moment of time, I was free.

In the present context, there are two key events from those early days that are especially relevant. First, I experienced a sudden and dramatic healing of a bad and persistent case of hives, which had tormented me for days. The remission came in immediate answer to prayer after a frustrating week. Now I was an eyewitness. Second, at the behest of my dear father, I met the local rabbi. Pleased beyond words that I had given up my destructive ways, my father wanted me to "return" to my traditions. Although I did not take the route they had envisioned, the relationship formed with that rabbi has endured for almost twenty-five years, and it was in direct response to his persistent prodding that I began to study Hebrew in college. At that time, I had not the faintest inkling that those studies would lead to serious Semitic scholarship.

But that is only part of the story. Life was not always so simple in my Pentecostal church. Why were many prayers for the sick not answered? Why was it that the more I read and learned, the more I questioned some of our doctrinal distinctives? By 1977, a separation came, and I became active in a church that was theologically and academically much more broad-minded, albeit certainly lacking in terms of those early, miraculous testimonies of which I had by now become skeptical. Then, in 1982–83, I and many others in the congregation experienced a dramatic spiritual renewal, prompting me to reconsider the relevance of what was then my working dissertation topic, "Abbreviated Verbal Idioms in the Hebrew Bible." In the light of eternity, was such a project worth the time and effort?

Along with this was a new problem: People were getting healed again in answer to prayer, but their theology, so far as I could tell, was askew, and their use of Scripture to support their position seemed amiss. The same held true, I thought, in even more pronounced fashion among the leading figures in public healing ministry. How could this be? Was it my view that needed adjustment? Or was God simply honoring honest, trusting hearts in spite of doctrinal error?

I was determined to understand as best I could the biblical views of God as Healer, and as one specializing in Old Testament and Semitics, the study of the Hebrew root *rāpā'* seemed logical. Thus I began my exegetical and comparative philological study of *rāpā'*, completed as a New York University dissertation in 1985 under the tutelage of Baruch Levine. At the same time, I began to teach on the subject of healing in various popular and academic settings here and abroad, often praying for the sick as well. I can now add further eyewitness accounts of supernatural answers to prayer, along with some difficult stories of suffering, pain, and death, all in connection with seeking to minister to those in need.

In 1990, the idea of turning my rather technical (and not particularly edifying) dissertation into a book began to gel, and, at the request of a potential publisher, in 1991 I drafted a chapter on "Israel's Divine Healer in the Prophetic Books," greatly expanding and revising relevant portions of my thesis for a theological and biblical audience. It was to the credit of Len Goss at Zondervan Publishing House that the projected volume was deemed suitable for the nascent series, Studies in Old Testament Biblical Theology. The bulk of this present monograph was written from June 1992 to April 1994, with roughly 20 percent of the material drawn from my thesis. That which was used, of course, has been thoroughly reworked, and I am amazed to see just how much I have learned personally through a fresh, wide-ranging encounter with the biblical text. It is liberating to derive one's theology and beliefs from the Scriptures, without having a prefabricated mold into which every passage and book must be squeezed. The reader can make his or her own judgment as to how faithful I have been to the task of honest interpretation.

When preparing the chapter on the prophetic literature, I regularly used my own translations of the Hebrew text. This has been retained in what is now chapter 4. However, as the project wore on, I felt that, for the most part, my own renderings added little to the argument, hence my primary use of the NIV elsewhere. When appropriate, I have suggested corrections to the NIV, and for comparison, I have made reference in particular to the New Jewish Version, since its overall approach and methodology often vary greatly from "Christian" versions.

The nontechnical reader may want to skip section 0.3.1 ("The Root *rāpā'*: Lexical and Etymological Discussion") and proceed directly to 0.3.2 ("The Root *rāpā'*: Old Testament Usage and Meaning"). Also, for those put off by lengthy endnotes, it would be advisable to follow the main line of thought in the text before returning to a more careful perusal of both text and notes. However, while the primary purpose of the citations is, quite naturally, bibliographic documentation, the interested reader will also find some theological and exegetical tangents, which, I trust, will be of value. It is hoped that the reader will find the final chapter ("Conclusions and Reflections") refreshingly succinct as well as practical. As far as documentation is concerned, where possible, I have included works published up to the beginning of 1995.

The editors of this series, Tremper Longman III and Willem VanGemeren, have proven themselves to be both gentlemen and scholars of the first order. At their request, and with my complete agreement, special effort was made to include both the eschatological and New Testament dimensions of the subject of Israel's divine Healer. It has been a real pleasure to work with Tremper since the formal inception of this study in 1992. William Shea was kind enough to give me his helpful input on the first half of this study, and I benefited greatly from Mark Smith's critique of an early draft of chapter 4. My colleague and friend, Stephen Homcy, sharpened chapter 5, both in general and in detail. My appreciation is also owed to: Zondervan editor Verlyn Verbrugge, who saved me from several embarrassing oversights, challenging me at some points and causing me to clarify myself at many others; Ed van der Maas, Senior Acquisitions Editor, for accepting the final manuscript for publication, swollen as it was to twice the contracted length; Loren Mendelsohn, Chief of Public Services at the Cohen Library of the City College of New York, who tracked down some last minute bibliographical data that had eluded me for months; H. Y. Park, M.D., for introducing me to the work of the Department of Healing Ministry of the Asian Center for Theological Studies and Mission (ACTS) in Seoul. I hope also that my old friend, Rabbi William Berman, will see some fruit to his prodding of more than twenty years ago. For the many faults and imperfections that remain in this work, I alone am to blame.

Finally, my wife Nancy, and our two daughters, Jennifer and Megan, have endured with grace the seemingly endless process of completing this study, the burden of which was greatly intensified through a demanding national and international speaking schedule, coupled with some popular writing commitments. How often did I hear from my teenagers, "Dad, you're still not done with that book?" At last, I can answer in the affirmative. I deeply appreciate their standing with me at all times, and I thank God for each of them.

It is my fervent prayer, as one involved in both the worlds of scholarship and ministry, that the many hours invested in research and writing will lead to fertile academic discussion, fruitful theological debate, and, most of all, living faith. As one who has been confronted over and again with the debilitating effects of sickness and disease on our race—looking into the eyes of the mother of a severely handicapped child, praying at the bedside of a dying young father, holding the hand of a teenager racked with the agony of cancer in his bones—the subject of this book is far from a theological abstraction for me. I long for the day when sickness will be no more. Until then, I will greatly appreciate advances in the ministry of healing, as well as in the field of medicine. May the Lord, Israel's divine Healer, hailed by the rabbis as the reliable Physician (*rôpēʾ neʾemān*) and revered by the Syriac-speaking church in the person of Jesus, the Messiah, as the good Doctor (*ʾasyāʾ ṭābāʾ*), be glorified through this work.

◆ Abbreviations ◆

AB — Anchor Bible
ABRL — Anchor Bible Reference Library
ABD — *Anchor Bible Dictionary*
AfO — *Archiv für Orientforschung*
AHW — W. von Soden, *Akkadisches Handwörterbuch*
AION — *Annali dell'Istituto orientale di Napoli* (Nuova Serie)
AJBI — Annual for the Japanese Biblical Institute
AnBib — Analecta biblica
ANET — J. B. Pritchard, *Ancient Near Eastern Texts*
ANRW — *Aufstieg und Niedergang der römischen Welt*
AOAT — Alter Orient und Altes Testament
AOS — American Oriental Society
AS — Assyriological Studies
ASV — American Standard Version
ATD — Das Alte Testament Deutsch
ATR — *Anglican Theological Review*
AusBR — *Australian Biblical Review*
AUSS — *Andrews University Seminary Studies*
AV — Authorized Version (King James Version)
BA — *Biblical Archaeologist*
BAGD — Bauer, Arndt, Gingrich, Danker, *Greek English Lexicon of the New Testament*
BAR — *Biblical Archaeology Review*
BASOR — *Bulletin of the American Schools of Oriental Research*
BBB — Bonner biblische Beiträge
BBET — Beiträge zur biblischen Exegesis und Theologie
BDB — Brown, Driver, Briggs, *Hebrew and English Lexicon of the Old Testament*
BHS — *Biblia hebraica stuttgartensia*
BHK — R. Kittel, *Biblia hebraica*
Bib — *Biblica*
BibOr — Biblica et orientalia
BibRev — *Bible Review*
BibS — Biblische Studien
BK — *Bibel und Kirche*
BWL — W. G. Lambert, *Babylonian Wisdom Literature*
BN — *Biblische Notizen*

BRev	*Bible Review*
*BRL*²	K. Galling, ed., *Biblisches Reallexikon*
BSac	*Bibliotheca Sacra*
BT	*The Bible Translator*
BTB	*Biblical Theology Bulletin*
BurH	*Buried History*
BW	*Biblical World*
BWANT	Beiträge zur Wissenschaft vom Alten und Neuen Testament
BZ	*Biblische Zeitschrift*
BZAW	Beihefte zur *ZAW*
CAD	*The Assyrian Dictionary of the Oriental Institute of the University of Chicago*
CB	*Cultura biblica*
CBQ	*Catholic Biblical Quarterly*
CIS	*Corpus inscriptionum semiticarum*
CNT	Commentaire du Nouveau Testament
ConBOT	Coniectanea biblica, Old Testament
ConsJud	*Conservative Judaism*
CTA	A. Herdner, *Corpus des tablettes en cunéiformes alphabétiques*
CTh	*Cahiers théologiques*
DBSup	*Dictionnaire de la Bible, Supplément*
DISO	Jean and Hoftijzer, *Dictionnaire des inscriptions sémitiques de l'ouest*
DSS	Dead Sea Scrolls
EA	El Amarna
EBC	*Expositor's Bible Commentary*
EDNT	*Exegetical Dictionary of the New Testament*
EI	*Erets Israel*
EJ	*Encyclopedia Judaica*
EM	*Ensiqlopediyyah Miqra'it*
ERE	*Encyclopedia of Religion and Ethics*
EstBib	*Estudios biblicos*
EvQ	*Evangelical Quarterly*
EvT	*Evangelische Theologie*
ExpTim	*Expository Times*
FOTL	Forms of Old Testament Literature
FRLANT	Forschungen zur Religion und Literatur des Alten und Neuen Testaments
GKC	Gesenius's *Hebrew Grammar*, ed. E. Kautzsch, trans. E. Cowley
HALAT	W. Baumgartner, et al., *Hebräisches und aramäisches Lexikon zum Alten Testament*
HAR	*Hebrew Annual Review*
HAT	Handbuch zum Alten Testament
HBT	*Horizons in Biblical Theology*
Herm.	Hermenia
HS	*Hebrew Studies*

HSM Harvard Semitic Monographs
HSS Harvard Semitic Studies
HTR *Harvard Theological Review*
HUCA *Hebrew Union College Annual*
IBS *Irish Biblical Studies*
ICC International Critical Commentaries
IDB *Interpreter's Dictionary of the Bible*
Int *Interpretation*
ISBE *International Standard Bible Encyclopedia*
ITC International Theological Commentary
ITQ *Irish Theological Quarterly*
JAAR *Journal of the American Academy of Religion*
JANESCU *Journal of the Ancient Near Eastern Society of Columbia University*
JAOS *Journal of the American Oriental Society*
JB Jerusalem Bible
JBC *Jerome Biblical Commentary* (ed. R. E. Brown, et al.)
JBL *Journal of Biblical Literature*
JETS *Journal of the Evangelical Theological Society*
JJS *Journal of Jewish Studies*
JNSL *Journal for Northwest Semitic Languages*
JNES *Journal of Near Eastern Studies*
JQR *Jewish Quarterly Review*
JSJ *Journal for the Study of Judaism in the Persian, Hellenistic, and Roman Period*
JSNT *Journal for the Study of the New Testament*
JSNTSupp. Journal for the Study of the New Testament—Supplement series
JSOT *Journal for the Study of the Old Testament*
JSOTSupp. Journal for the Study of the Old Testament—Supplement series
JTS *Journal of Theological Studies*
KAI Donner and Rolling, *Kanaanäische und aramäische Inschriften*
KAT Kommentar zum Alten Testament
KBL L. Kohler and W. Baumgartner, *Lexicon in Veteris Testamenti libros*
KD Keil and Delitzsch commentary series
KHAT Kurzgefasstes exegetisches Handbuch zum Alten Testament
KTU M. Dietrich, O. Loretz, J. Sanmartín, *Die keilalphabetische Texte aus Ugarit*
LÄ *Lexikon der Ägyptologie*
LS *Louvain Studies*
LSJ Liddell, Scott, and Jones, *Greek-English Lexicon*
LTP *Laval théologique et philosophique*
LXX Septuagint
MM Moulton and Milligan, *The Vocabulary of the Greek Testament*
MT Masoretic Text
NAB New American Bible

NAC	New American Commentary
NASB	New American Standard Bible
NCB	New Century Bible commentary series
NEB	New English Bible
NICNT	New International Commentary on the New Testament
NICOT	New International Commentary on the Old Testament
NIDNTT	*New International Dictionary of New Testament Theology*
NIGTC	New International Greek Testament Commentary
NIV	New International Version
NJV	New Jewish Version
NovT	*Novum Testamentum*
NRSV	New Revised Standard Version
NT	New Testament
NTS	*New Testament Studies*
OBO	Orbis biblicus et orientalis
OBT	Overtures to Biblical Theology
OLZ	*Orientalische Literaturzeitung*
Or	*Orientalia* (Rome)
OrChr	*Oriens Christianus*
OT	Old Testament
OTL	Old Testament Library
OTP	James Charlesworth's *Old Testament Pseudepigrapha*
OTS	Oudtestamentische Studiën
PEQ	*Palestine Exploration Quarterly*
PPG	J. Friedrich, W. Röllig, *Phönizisch-punische Grammatik*
QD	Quaestiones disputatae
RA	*Revue archéologique*
RB	*Revue biblique*
REB	Revised English Bible
RevQ	*Revue de Qumran*
RHPhR	*Revue d'histoire et de philosophie religieuses*
RLA	*Reallexikon der Assyriologie*
RS	Ras Shamra
RSP	L. R. Fischer, S. Rummel, eds., *Ras Shamra Parallels*
RSR	*Recherches de science religieuse*
RSV	Revised Standard Version
RTL	*Revue théologique de Louvain*
RV	Revised Version
SBC	Student Bible Commentary
SBL	Society of Biblical Literature
SBLDS	Society of Biblical Literature Dissertation Series
SBLMS	Society of Biblical Literature Monograph Series
SBS	Stuttgarter Bibelstudien
SBT	Studies in Biblical Theology
ScEs	*Science et esprit*

Sem	*Semeia*
SJLA	Studies in Judaism in Late Antiquity
SJT	*Scottish Journal of Theology*
SLAG	*Schriften der Luther-Agricola Gesellschaft*
SNTSMS	Society for New Testament Studies Monograph Series
SOTBT	Studies in Old Testament Biblical Theology
ST	*Studia theologica*
Str-B	H. Strack and P. Billerbeck, *Kommentar zum Neuen Testament*
TBT	*The Bible Today*
TD	*Theology Digest*
TDNT	*Theological Dictionary of the New Testament*
TDOT	*Theological Dictionary of the Old Testament*
THAT	*Theologisches Handwörterbuch zum Alten Testament*
ThZ	*Theologische Zeitschrift*
ThLZ	*Theologische Literaturzeitung*
TJ	Targum Jonathan
TOTC	Tyndale Old Testament Commentaries
TQ	*Theologische Quartalschrift*
TrinJ	*Trinity Journal*
TS	*Theological Studies*
TTZ	*Trier theologische Zeitschrift*
TWAT	*Theologisches Wörterbuch zum Alten Testament*
TWOT	*Theological Wordbook of the Old Testament*
TynBul	*Tyndale Bulletin*
UBL	Ugarit and Bible Literature
UF	*Ugarit-Forschungen*
UT	Cyrus Gordon, *Ugaritic Textbook*
VoxEv	*Vox Evangelica*
VT	*Vetus Testamentum*
VTSupp.	Vetus Testamentum, Supplements
WBC	Word Biblical Commentaries
WEC	Wycliffe Exegetical Commentary
WMANT	Wissenschaftliche Monographien zum Alten und Neuen Testament
WTJ	*Westminster Theological Journal*
WzM	*Wege zum Menschen*
WZKM	*Wiener Zeitschrift für die Kunde des Morgenlandes*
ZAH	*Zeitschrift für Althebraistik*
ZÄS	*Zeitschrift für Ägyptienstudien*
ZAW	*Zeitschrift für die alttestamentliche Wissenschaft*
ZBK	Züricher Bibelkommentare
ZNW	*Zeitschrift für die neutestamentliche Wissenschaft*

◆ Introduction ◆

0.1. PURPOSE

This is a book about the divine Healer of Israel according to the testimony of the OT prophets and poets, psalmists and sages, historians and lawgivers. It does not attempt to study diachronically the concept of the Lord as Israel's *rôpē'* ("Healer") based on a critical reconstruction of the biblical sources,[1] nor does it attempt to determine empirically whether the miracles and healings of the Bible actually occurred.[2] Rather, this study seeks to analyze systematically the witness of the Hebrew Scriptures, the sacred text of synagogue and church for two millennia.

According to the OT record, what importance was attached to the Lord as *rôpē'*? How did this relate to the Sinaitic covenant, as well as to the battle for Israelite monolatry and/or monotheism? How was sickness perceived in the biblical world, and how were sickness and sin (and demonic powers) thought to be interrelated? Were handicapped Israelites viewed as unclean, inferior, or under divine judgment? Were physicians in Israel considered to be complementary to the Lord or in competition with him? Is there biblical evidence for popular or "official" fusions of magic, medicine, and religion? To what extent were the concepts of sickness and healing applied metaphorically by the prophets? What was the source of healing according to the wisdom literature? Does the OT "language of healing" reflect a decidedly holistic mentality? To what extent was the hope of a national (and even universal) profusion of divine healing eschatological? Is there a contrast between the OT and NT theology of divine healing? This is just a sampling of some of the issues that must be addressed.

It is striking to note, however, that while some of these themes have been treated individually and others touched on in a piecemeal fashion, to date no full-scale synthesis of the relevant material has been undertaken. The excellent treatment of J. Hempel, *Heilung als Symbol und Wirklichkeit im biblischen Schriftum*, runs less than eighty pages and is now more than thirty-five years old.[3] The important studies of K. Seybold focused primarily on sickness, and that in the Psalms.[4] K. Stendahl's survey of the root *rp'* does not, by and large, touch on the broader issues of sickness and divine healing.[5] The insightful sixty-page study of Exodus 15:26 by N. Lohfink principally treats literary-critical issues.[6] The recent articles of H. Niehr and H. Rouillard, reconstructing the history and origin of the concept of Yahweh the Physician, run less than fifteen and thirty pages respectively and cannot, therefore, offer more than brief, speculative outlines.[7] The monographs of W. Ebstein and A. Gemayel, along with the concise treatments of, *inter alios*, A. Lods, P. Humbert, C. Westermann, E. Neufeld, H. Weippert, W. Th. Im der Smitten, D. J. Simundson, D. W. Amundsen and G. B. Ferngren, G. F. Hasel, J. V. Kinnier-Wilson, and D. J. Wiseman deal mainly with sickness, medicine, and health from a biblical (primarily OT) perspective, although not without some theological reflection.[8] The wide-ranging studies of W. W. G. von Baudissin and W. A. Jayne on healing and/or resurrection deities, along with the work on Baal and the *rpum* as healer(s) by J. C. de Moor, allow for only limited (or no) interaction with the OT material.[9] Articles in biblical dictionaries and encyclopedias have generally focused on technical descriptions of diseases and/or *materia medica* attested in the Scriptures,[10] while entries in biblical Hebrew wordbooks and theological dictionaries have for the most part treated the OT material only as it intersects with the specific roots in question (primarily *rp'* and *ḥlh*).[11] Among OT theologies, G. von Rad's treatment of Yahweh as *rôpē'*, barely covering two (!) pages, actually *stands out* for its completeness.[12] The major OT anthropologies of L. Kohler and H. W. Wolff deal briefly—and almost exclusively—with the human dimensions of sickness and healing.[13] The influential works on Israelite religion of such scholars as Y. Kauffman, W. F. Albright, G. Fohrer, H. Ringgren, and W. H. Schmidt give surprisingly little (or no) attention to the subject at hand,[14] and even the recent major reconstructions of the rise of Yahwistic monotheism by de Moor and M. S. Smith make only passing reference to Yahweh as Healer.[15]

All this stands in contrast to: (1) the prominent role played by the Lord as Healer in the OT, of obvious importance to OT theology;[16](2) the fact that healing deities played a major role in the religious life of Israel's neighbors (and hence, by extension, in the religious conceptions of Israel);[17] (3) the importance attached to health and fertility by virtually every culture worldwide, both ancient and modern. Just consider the large proportion of prayers and petitions that contain requests for healing of physical maladies (including "opening" of wombs) as well as restoration of agricultural fecundity (especially in agrarian societies). These observations suggest that the systematic study of Yahweh the *rôpē'* has been unduly neglected.[18] It is also significant that one of the earliest assertions of the biblical authors (viz., Ex 15:26)[19]—and one that must have encountered a great amount of polytheistic resistance and competition[20]—was that the Lord *alone* was to be Israel's divine Healer. Hence, this subject can help shed light on the study of Israelite religion in its broader ancient Near Eastern context.

0.2. METHODOLOGY

The approach of this study can be characterized as comparative, canonical, and conservative. The first chapter, "Human Physicians and Healing Deities," provides a comparative survey of the relevant texts from ancient Mesopotamia, Egypt, and where available, Syria-Palestine. It considers the relationship between medicine, magic, and religion to ascertain the role of the physician (or physician-priest) in the society and culture of Israel's neighbors. In the ancient Near Eastern mind, religious beliefs and medical practices were thoroughly intertwined.[21] Thus the fact that there is considerable functional overlap between the Akkadian terms *asû* ("physician") and *āšipu* ("exorcist/magical-expert"),[22] or that ancient Near Eastern childbirth texts are often replete with both exorcism rites and supplications, occasions no surprise.[23] Moreover, there is a somewhat expected tension when the dual concepts of human healing and divine healing coexist within one society,[24] especially as that society develops in its scientific understanding of the causes and cures of disease.[25] In this broad ancient Near Eastern context, the (relatively limited) OT evidence for physicians and medical practices is discussed. Certain pivotal verses (e.g., 2Ch 16:12) are illuminated through comparative analysis. More importantly, the survey of ancient deities often supplicated or praised for their alleged healing prowess (including Marduk and Gula in Mesopotamia, Thoth and Sekhmet in Egypt, possibly Baal in Ugarit and Canaan, and at a later time, Asklepios/Aesculapius in Greece and Rome) sheds great light on the biblical witness of the Lord as Healer. Against this backdrop, passages such as Exodus 23:20–26 (esp. 25–26) and Deuteronomy 7:12–16 (esp. 14–15), not to mention much of the prophetic polemic, take on a new significance. In fact, the comparative survey of healing deities also provides important insights for the study of the NT miracles of Jesus and his disciples. On this point biblical scholars of all persuasions agree: Israelite, Judean, and early Christian culture and religion were not formed in a vacuum!

The approach of this work is canonical in that it seeks to treat the OT material as preserved, transmitted, and ultimately received by the believing Jewish and Christian communities, with attention to the final form of the text.[26] That is to say, while it may not be possible to date with precision the earliest substrata of a biblical poem or narrative, it *is* possible to observe the specific function of the final—and hence scriptural—version in its canonical context. Thus, scholars focusing on the source-critical analysis of Exodus 15:22–27, with suggested dates ranging from "ancient" to postexilic (see below, 2.2.1.), have sometimes failed to note the strategic location of this account in the book of Exodus: The revelation of Yahweh as Healer comes immediately after the Exodus from Egypt and the miracle at the Red Sea; it introduces the frequent motif of the Lord as Israel's all-sufficient Provider in the wilderness; and it both precedes and underscores the Sinaitic demand for allegiance to Yahweh alone. Thus, scripturally speaking, the Lord reveals himself as *rôpēʾ* with Egyptian polytheism in the background and Canaanite "paganism" in the foreground. This can be missed when the text in its current form is overly dissected. The comments of N. M. Sarna, who makes reference to "the coroner's approach, that is, dissecting a literary corpse," are relevant: "To be preoccupied with the smallest units of literary tradition may have its purposes; but the exercise is ultimately of limited value. A totality—things in combination—often possesses properties and engenders qualities neither carried by nor necessarily inherent in any of its discrete components."[27] Thus, while the building blocks of biblical theology are the elucidation of relevant passages, the exegesis of key verses, and the etymological analysis of central terms, these can only serve to give a clearer picture of the whole (theological) edifice.

In this study, it has been deemed fruitful to examine the OT material according to broad synchronic categories, viz., "Israel's Divine Healer in the Torah and Historical Books" (ch. 2), "Israel's Divine Healer in Poetry and Wisdom Literature" (ch. 3), and "Israel's Divine Healer in the Prophetic Books" (ch. 4).[28] While it was difficult to discern a clear diachronic development in the OT material,[29] the broad literary genres do present distinct insights into Israelite perceptions of sickness, healing, and faith. Chapter 5, "Israel's Divine Healer in the New Testament," examines the continuation, or, more precisely, the beginning of the *full realization* of the OT promise of divine healing in the ministry of Jesus and his disciples. Consideration is also given to the eschatological dimensions of the miracles of Jesus in the context of the inbreaking of the kingdom of God.

My approach is conservative in that it affirms the God of the Bible as the one true God, accepting what the scriptural authors and redactors declare about him as trustworthy. While questions of the editing and dating of the biblical material do not substantially affect the results of this study, the affirmation of the Scriptures as "the Word of God" do make for this distinctive: Even if one readily accepts that from a literary perspective, various OT descriptions, characteristics, and epithets of Yahweh developed out of convergence and conflict with the surrounding (and, all too often, native) polytheistic environment,[30] *when ultimately applied to the Lord*, they are true. Thus, as far as dating of texts is concerned, the Ugaritic epithet of Baal as *rkb 'rpt* ("rider on the clouds") predates the similar OT attribution to Yahweh (e.g., Ps 68:5[4] with v. 34[33]).[31] Yet from a conservative biblical viewpoint, it is not Baal who "rides the clouds/heavens"[32] but the Lord.[33] With regard to the designation of Yahweh as *rôpē'*, de Moor opines, "It is certainly not inconceivable that the Israelites borrowed the epithet *rp'*, 'Healer,' 'Saviour' from the cult of Ba'lu/Baal," adding, "Of course this involved a certain amount of polemic."[34] Seybold, with reference to de Moor and Hempel, is more dogmatic: "In [the] context [of Ex 15:26] it is highly significant that in the Canaanite environs the Ugarit[ic] equivalent (*rapi'u*, 'physician, healer, savior') was a title of honor for living kings such as Epitheton of the god Baal, *a title that Exodus 15 wrests from this deity and claims for Yahweh alone.*"[35]

For believers in the veracity of the Scriptures, the historical and comparative data presented in what follows should illumine faith without undermining it. For those who do not share my conservative presuppositions, this work may still be consulted with profit, since it does, in fact, seek to provide an in-depth analysis of what the authors of Israel's sacred literature believed—and wanted others to believe![36]—about Yahweh the *rôpē'*.

0.3. THE OLD TESTAMENT LANGUAGE OF HEALING

0.3.1. The Root *rāpā'*: Lexical and Etymological Discussion[37]

This root is central to the OT language of healing, occurring 67 times in verbal conjugations (38 Qal, 17 Niphal, 9 Piel, 3 Hitpael) and 19 times in derived nominal forms (*marpē'*—14;[38] *rᵉpû'â*—3, all pl.; *rip'ût*—1;[39] *tᵉrûpâ*—1[40]).[41] Outside of the OT, *rp'* is attested in Amorite, El Amarna Akkadian, Aramaic, Ugaritic, Phoenician-Punic, Old South Arabian, Arabic, and Ethiopic, although in some of these languages, the evidence is meager.[42] Scholars have generally posited: (1) a root meaning for *rp'* in Proto-Semitic[43] of "to bring together, draw near";[44] and (2) a fundamental meaning for *rp'* in Hebrew[45] of "to heal" (i.e., physical illness and disease).[46] However, the suggested root meanings for both Proto-Semitic and Hebrew are questionable and have themselves led to questionable renderings.

Of course, one might ask whether the very exercise of searching for a root's "original" or "fundamental" meaning is the real cause of both linguistic and interpretive errors. The writings of J. Barr and others on semantics have exposed what is called the "root fallacy,"[47] i.e., the pseudo-linguistic practice of imposing an alleged fundamental meaning of a root on all its varied conjugations and derivations. And, in fact, this has been done with *rāpā'*, either by superimposing one Hebrew meaning ("heal") over the varied biblical usages,[48] or by mishandling the cognate evidence—in which case unnatural meanings were also forced on the OT text. Yet, in spite of these caveats, it is often fruitful to seek one general sense that lies at the heart of the diverse nuances of the root in question, without in any way limiting the semantic range.[49] The multiplicity of the branches does not deny the unity of the trunk!

As Semitic studies—in particular biblical Hebrew studies—over the last twenty years have shifted more and more toward synchronic linguistic research,[50] and with a decided reaction against the hyperetymologizing of the past,[51] the importance now placed by scholars on a "root" or "etymological" meaning has greatly diminished. Yet this negative assessment in no way obviates the fact that in more cases than not, the common and obvious meaning of a root flows through the varied cognate languages, and that this meaning often underlies the specific nuances attested in the individual lexical stock of the particular language in question.[52] In fact, two of the more salient features of the Semitic language family are the tenacity of the root and the close interrelatedness of the different Semitic languages—features that by their very nature support, rather than argue against, the search for a root meaning.[53] Nonetheless, etymological studies still suffer from undisciplined and/or nonsystematic excesses.

With regard to the Proto-Semitic derivation of *rp'*, many scholars, generally adducing meanings found in Arabic and Ethiopic,[54] have argued that Hebrew *rôpē'* "originally meant 'mender, one who sews together,'"[55] since "the word's stem, *rp'*, now generally used in the sense 'to heal,' originally means to patch, to sew together, to unite."[56] Several problems with this line of reasoning surface, however. (1) There is little justification to begin with usage attested only in the "younger" Semitic languages (viz., classical Arabic and Ethiopic) and then to proceed backward to the "older" Semitic languages (viz.,

Canaanite [i.e., Hebrew and Phoenician], Ugaritic, El Amarna Akkadian, and probably Old Aramaic[57] and Amorite), suggesting that meanings found exclusively in the younger languages form the semantic base for different meanings attested in the older languages. Not only is this faulty linguistic logic, but it contradicts the evidence as well, since the oldest extant witness to *rf'* in South Semitic itself comes from Old South Arabian in the sense of "to heal."[58]

(2) While it is legitimate to proceed from a prehistoric *Grundbedeutung* of a root to a historically attested range of meanings,[59] it is somewhat dangerous to take the semantic development of a root in one language and superimpose it on the lexical stock of another language. In the case of *rp'* in biblical Hebrew, this has produced infelicitous renderings such as "stitchers of lies" (!) for *rōpᵉ'ê 'ᵉlil* (Job 13:4b).[60] It should also be pointed out that the South Semitic evidence itself can be utilized to argue *against* the likelihood that a *rôpē'* was so called because he "mended" and "stitched together" the human body,[61] since *rf'* was never used with regard to physical healing in classical Arabic, nor did it become the primary root for "heal, healer" in any well-attested South Semitic language.

(3) While it is possible to characterize an ancient Near Eastern physician as "one who sews together" or "patches up,"[62] I am not aware of one lexical citation in the whole gamut of the Hebrew language—ancient, medieval, or modern—where *rp'* is ever cited in the specific sense of "to stitch, patch, sew," nor are there any OT examples of medical sewing or stitching.[63] Thus the likelihood of the commonly proposed semantic development is open to serious objection.[64]

With regard to *rp'* in biblical Hebrew, scholars are virtually unanimous in their understanding that Hebrew *rp'* fundamentally means "to heal," tracing virtually all other semantic derivations back to this common (yet not primary) OT sense. This has produced: (1) forced translations (e.g., 2Ch 7:14: "I will *heal* their *land*"; 2Ki 2:21: "I have *healed* these *waters*"); (2) an exaggerated dichotomy between "literal" healing (i.e., of physical illness) and "figurative" healing (e.g., "the hurts of a nation"—as if individual healing were "literal" and national healing "figurative"); contributing to (3) a tendency to read the prophetic, often metaphorical usage, of *rp'* in overly spiritualized terms.[65]

The standard lexicon of Brown, Driver, and Briggs begins its entry on *rāpā'* with the Qal meaning of "*heal*: 1. lit.," citing instances of physical healings in the Bible. The second division is then "2. fig., *heal* hurts of nation."[66] Under the first Niphal meaning of "*be healed*"[67] the editors then group such diverse texts as Leviticus 13:18, 37; 14:3, 48, where the referents of *rp'* are skin disease and mildew; 2 Kings 2:22, where *rp'* has to do with the restoration of undrinkable salt waters; and Jeremiah 19:11, referring to a broken potter's vessel that could not be repaired. And once again, the second meaning of "fig., *be healed*: of national hurts," follows.[68] The important lexicon of Gesenius-Buhl, often surpassing BDB in its philological accuracy and insight, defines the Qal of *rp'* with "heilen (urspr.: Wunden)";[69] the first edition of the Koehler-Baumgartner *Lexicon* begins with the expected definition of "*heilen*, heal"[70] (this is unchanged in the third edition, completed by J. J. Stamm[71]); and E. Ben-Yehuda's *Thesaurus*, covering all phases of the Hebrew language, renders *rp'* with "*heilen*; *guerir*; to heal."[72]

Now if the basic meaning of *rāpā'* is "to heal," then all other meanings must flow from this one semantic stream. However, this is not in keeping with the biblical Hebrew usage.

0.3.2. The Root *rāpā'*: Old Testament Usage and Meaning

A careful analysis of the biblical material indicates that in every instance *rp'* is used with reference to *restoring* a wrong, sick, broken, or deficient condition to its original and proper state.[73] Consequently, I believe that "restore, make whole," not "heal," should be recognized as the common semantic denominator of biblical Hebrew *rp'*,[74] and that future biblical Hebrew lexicons should list "heal" as the first subheading, beginning their entries with the general definition of "restore, make whole."[75] All the semantic streams attested in the OT flow freely from this one source: the "healing" of a sick body (2Ki 20:5), the "repairing" of a broken down altar (1Ki 18:30), the "restoration" of a drought-stricken and locust-eaten land (2Ch 7:14), the "making wholesome" of undrinkable waters (2Ki 2:21–22), the "mending" of the earth's fissures (Ps 60:4[2]), the "fixing" of a smashed piece of pottery (Jer 19:11), and the "recovery" of a mildew infected house (Lev 14:48).[76]

This provides for several basic insights, also improving on the traditional etymological understanding.[77] (1) It has the linguistic merit of moving from the etymological "trunk" to the "branches," i.e., it proceeds from a meaning that can easily be posited as the common denominator of all other attested meanings. To begin with a meaning of "to heal," however, reverses the process (i.e., it proceeds from a branch to the trunk).[78] No compelling reason exists to argue that uses such as making undrinkable waters wholesome or fixing broken pottery derived from the concept of healing the human body. Moreover, postbiblical Hebrew usage of *rp'* falls almost exclusively within the semantic range of "heal,"[79] suggesting that meanings such as "fix, repair" represent more primitive, rather than later, derived meanings. Also, in light of the frequency of biblical Hebrew usage of *rp'* = "heal," one might question the traditional assumption that speakers and writers of biblical Hebrew would move with fluidity from associating *rp'* with "heal" to associating it with "repair, mend, etc.,"[80] if the Hebrew usage of *rp'* had not *originally* been broader.

(2) More importantly, the recognition that *rp'* fundamentally means "restore, make whole" provides insight into ancient

Israel's understanding of the Lord as *rôpē'*,[81] as well as into their concepts of "wholeness," since one and the same root was used for the "healing/making whole/restoring" of body and spirit, land and water, city and nation. The Lord as *rôpē'* could be supplicated to make infertile wombs fruitful, mend earthquake-torn lands, make poisonous waters wholesome, or restore an apostate people. There was great fluidity in this OT usage![82] In our twentieth-century ideological lexicon, we would have to use several different verbs to represent the Hebrew usage of *rp'*, such as "heal, fix, mend, restore, repair, remit, make wholesome/fresh," etc. And while it is true that regardless of a word's etymological and semantic development, it still has but one meaning in any given context, it is also true that the cumulative evidence of a word's usage must be taken into consideration. In this case, the fact that God revealed himself as *rôpē'* cannot be separated from the wide range of broken/sickly/deficient objects that he was expected to *rāpā'*. Thus Exodus 15:26—*'ᵃnî yhwh rōpᵉ'ekā* (best rendered as "I am the LORD your Healer"; see below, 2.2.1, n. 61)—fits quite naturally in a context that recounts (a) the Lord's making undrinkable waters wholesome (vv. 22–24), and (b) his promise to keep obedient Israel free of all the "sickness" (*maḥᵃlâ*) he inflicted on Egypt (including, presumably, making the Nile waters undrinkable, along with smiting Egypt's land, people, and cattle). Clearly, he was more than Israel's "Great Physician," in twentieth-century, Western terms. Rather, he was the Restorer, the One who made them whole. Thus, one reasons why I translate *yhwh rōpᵉ'ekā* as "the Lord your Healer" is that "Healer" conveys a wider range of meanings than do the terms *physician, doctor*, *Arzt* (German), or *médecin* (French).[83]

In our contemporary occidental mentality, we tend to separate the concepts of "healing" and "forgiveness."[84] Yet, when the psalmist prayed, "LORD, have mercy on me; *heal* me, for I have *sinned* against you" (Ps 41:4[5]), he recognized that his sin was the source of his sickness, and that God's "healing" would make him whole again in body *and* spirit (see below, 3.1.1–3.1.9). The "either physical or spiritual" dichotomy often seen in comments on OT verses with *rp'* is extremely faulty.[85] In fact, regardless of one's understanding of the etymological origin of Semitic *rp'*, OT usage insists that references to the Lord as Israel's *rôpē'* be taken in the broadest possible sense.

0.3.3. The Old Testament Language of Healing: Additional Vocabulary[86]

'sp. The basic meaning of *'sp*, a common verbal root in the OT (occurring 200 times) is "to gather, remove."[87] It is found four times in the context of healing, all with reference to Naaman the "leper" (*m*ᵉ*ṣōrā'*; cf. 2Ki 5:3, 6, 7, 11, and see below, 2.2.6), although the actual description of his healing reads: "and his flesh was restored [*wayyāšāb b*ᵉ*śārô*] and became clean [*wayyiṭhar*] like that of a young boy" (5:14; cf. vv. 10, 12).[88] Some have explained the atypical usage of *'sp* in this context as "perhaps an abbreviated expression for *ripp*ᵉ*'ô miṣṣāra'tô wa'*ᵃ*sāpô*, i.e., to heal a person of leprosy and so make it possible to mix with his fellows," understanding *'asāpô* in the sense of "collect, gather (persons) into a place" (e.g., Ge 42:17; Ps 27:10; 2Sa 11:27; or, alternatively, as in 2Ki 22:20).[89] Further support for this is found in Numbers 12:14, with reference to Miriam's leprosy: "The LORD replied to Moses [who had just prayed for his sister's healing], 'If her father had spit in her face, would she not have been in disgrace for seven days? Confine her outside the camp for seven days; after that she can be brought back [*tē'āsēp*; see also v. 15].'"[90]

This suggestion is certainly plausible, since the Hebrew syntax in 2 Kings 5 makes it difficult to render *'āsap* with "remove," seeing that the direct object of the verb is not the *ṣāra'at* but rather the *m*ᵉ*ṣōra'* (i.e., not the leprosy but the leper; cf. v. 3: *'āz ye'*ᵉ*sōp '<u>ōtô</u> <u>miṣṣāra'</u>tô*; or v. 6, *wa'*ᵃ*sap<u>tô</u>*

miṣṣāra'atô, where Naaman [direct object] is to be cured *of* his leprosy [indirect object]). Thus a meaning such as "cure" (as an ellipsis for "[cure him and, hence] regather him [to his people from his leprosy]") is required,[91] and, in fact, translating with "recover" would effectively convey some sense of the idiom to English readers.[92]

(*'lh*) *'ᵃrûkâ* (cf. *tᵉ'ālâ*). According to BDB, *'ᵃrûkâ* means "**healing** of a wound, **restoration** (properly the new flesh that grows at the wounded spot)," with reference to Arabic *arika*.[93] It is used three times in Jeremiah (8:22; 30:17; 33:6, always with *'lh*, and contextually coupled with *rp'*) and once in Isaiah (58:8, with *ṣmḥ*), always as a prophetic metaphor (the Jeremianic usage being particularly graphic).[94] *'ᵃrûkâ* is also used figuratively for the rebuilding of Jerusalem's walls (Ne 4:1) and the repairing of the temple (2Ch 24:13).[95] Related to the concept of *'lh 'ᵃrûkâ* is *tᵉ'alâ*, "healing, new skin," derived from *'lh*, viz., "the new skin which *rises* on a wound."[96] It occurs twice in Jeremiah (30:13; 46:11), both times with identical wording (*tᵉ'ālâ 'ên lāk*, immediately following *rᵉpū'ôt*).

***ghh*.** This root, which means "to free (from sickness), cure,"[97] occurs once verbally—in prophetic, metaphorical usage (Hos 5:13b, parallel with *rp'*: "he is not able to cure you [*lō' yûkal lirpō' lākem*] nor heal you of your sores [*wᵉlō'-yigheh mikem māzôr*])"[98]—and once nominally (*gēhâ*, Pr 17:22a: "A cheerful heart is good medicine [*lēb śāmēaḥ yêtib gēhâ*]").[99] Although *kēhâ*, not *gēhâ*, occurs in the Hebrew text of Nahum 3:19a, an emendation to *gēhâ* has been proposed,[100] based on LXX's *iasis* ("healing"; cf. BHS), as well as the overall context of the verse;[101] note also the nouns *šeber* ("break, injury," etc.; see below, 4.1.3) and *makkâ* ("wound") and the verb *ḥālâ* ("to be sick, weak"; cf. below, 0.4), all common in the OT vocabulary of sickness and healing and all found in Nahum 3:19.

***ḥbš*.** This root, with cognates in Aramaic, Arabic, Ethiopic, and Akkadian,[102] occurs 33 times in the OT, 31 verbal and 2 participial.[103] Its basic meaning is "to bind or tie on, up,"[104] as in "to saddle (a donkey)" (e.g., Ge 22:3; this is the most common usage of the root); "to tie around" (headgear, etc., e.g., Ex 29:9), "fetter" (possibly Job 40:13).[105] *ḥbš* occurs 10 times in the semantic range of healing (primarily in prophetic or metaphoric usage),[106] meaning "to bind up, bandage a wound" (Isa 1:6; Hos 6:1), "to bind up, set a fracture" (Eze 30:21[*bis*]; 34:4, 16; see also Isa 30:26, all with *šbr*), and, more generally, "to bind up, heal" (Job 5:18), even with regard to the "*broken*hearted" (again, *šbr*) who, figuratively speaking, also need to be "bound up" (Isa 61:1 [*nišbᵉrê lēb*]; see also Ps 147:3 [*hārōpē' lišbûrê lēb ûmᵉḥabbēš lᵉ'aṣṣᵉbôtām*]). The Qal participle, *ḥōbēš* (Isa 3:7), has been variously translated as "healer,"[107] "surgeon,"[108] "binder up,"[109] "dresser of wounds" (NJV), or, rather inaccurately, "master" (NEB). NIV is more free with "I have no remedy." However, in light of the foregoing discussion, the rendering of the NJV, viz., "dresser of wounds" is best, while "binder up" (Gray) is possible, although somewhat infelicitous.

ḥyh. Just as sickness is associated with death, so healing is associated with life, and life and death, healing and—sickness, are in God's hands. Thus Deuteronomy 32:39b states: "I put to death and bring to life [*wa'ᵃḥayyeh*], I have wounded and I will heal." And the king of Israel, when confronted with the request to heal Naaman, replies: "Am I God? Can I kill and bring back to life [*ûlᵉhaḥᵃyôt*]?" (2Ki 5:7). H. Ringgren is therefore correct in stating that "make alive" (or, "bring back to life") "is practically synonymous with 'cure disease.'"[110] It also is noteworthy that the primary Akkadian verb for healing is *bulluṭu*, the D-stem of *balāṭu*, "live, be alive (v.); life (n.),"[111] and that one of the common epithets of the Mesopotamian deities was *muballiṭ* (or, *muballiṭat*) *mīti*, lit., "he (or she) who gives life to the dead," but used with reference to healing the seriously ill (as opposed to resurrection of the dead).[112] Aramaic *ḥyh* is also, on occasion, used for healing.[113]

The semantic connection between "life" and "healing" in the Hebrew, Aramaic, and Akkadian usage is clear: Either the sick person is in danger of death—hence, being kept alive means being healed; or the sick person, because of his or her affliction, is not truly "living"—hence, to live, in the fullest sense of the word, one must be restored from his illness.[114] Thus, in some cases, it is difficult to determine whether to translate *ḥyh* with "live," "recover," or "be healed" (cf. the verses from Nu 21, 2Ki 2 and 8, cited below), since, for the seriously or terminally ill person, to be healed quite literally means to *continue living* (most graphically illustrated in Isa 38:1, 9, 21, summarized in v. 16b with *haḥᵃyēnî*).[115] Note also Genesis 20:7, where God says to Abimelech, king of Gerar, "Now return the man's wife [viz., Sarah], for he is a prophet, and he will pray for you and you *will live* [*weḥᵉyēh*]. But if you do not return her, you may be sure that you and all yours *will die,*" while verses 17–18 read, "Then Abraham prayed to God, and God healed Abimelech, his wife and his slave girls so they could have children again, for the LORD had closed up every womb in Abimelech's household because of Abraham's wife Sarah" (cf. also the usage in Nu 14:38).

Ringgren summarizes OT usage of *ḥyh* in the context of healing as follows:

> *Life as Health; Life to the Full.* The word *chayah* thus means not merely "be or stay alive," but also to enjoy a full, rich, and happy life. Often it simply means "be strong and healthy." The Israelites bitten by the serpents in the desert looked on the brazen serpent and "lived," i.e., were healed (Nu. 21:8f.) The men circumcised by Joshua remained in the camp until they were "healed." Samson, almost dying of thirst, "revives" and his spirit returns (*shûbh*), i.e., his strength is restored (Jgs. 15:19; cf. Gen. 45:27, where joy "revives" Jacob's spirit). Ahaziah sends to find out whether he will "recover" from his sickness (2 K. 1:2; similarly 2 K. 8:8–10, 14, of Ben-hadad, king of Damascus; 2 K. 20:1, 7 = Isa. 38:1, 9, 21, of Hezekiah).[116]

The Piel[117] of *ḥyh* in the Psalms[118] is to be understood against this backdrop: keeping alive, preserving life = delivering from trouble, sickness, death, the grave, etc. (e.g., Pss 143:11; 33:19; 41:3[2]; 30:4[3]).[119] Note also that *ḥyh* is sometimes parallel with *rp'* (cf. Pr 4:22: "[words of wisdom] are life [*ḥayyîm*] to those who find them and health [*marpē'*] to a man's whole body").[120]

ḥlm. In the sense of "to be[come] healthy, strong." *ḥlm* I (to be distinguished from *ḥlm* II, "to dream"[121]) occurs only at Job 39:4 and Isaiah 38:16 (Hiphil, "You restored me to health"—*taḥlîmēnî//haḥeyēnî*; see discussion of *ḥyh*, above).

khh. See above, under *ghh.*

meṯōm. Although the verbal root *tmm* ("to be complete, finished"), which occurs 63 times in the OT, is never related to healing or health, the derived nominal form *meṯōm* ("soundness") occurs three times in the context of health (Ps 38:3, 7[4, 8]; Isa 1:6), and always in the phrase *'ên meṯōm b-*, "there is no soundness in. . . ."[122]

šwb. This important root, which has been treated extensively,[123] basically means "to turn back." In the semantic domain of physical healing, it means "to restore [i.e., return, turn back] to the (previous) state of health," as in 2 Kings 5:14: "and his [i.e., Naaman's] flesh was restored [*wayyāšāb beśārô*] and became clean like that of a young boy" (see *'āsap,* above). The exact sense of *šwb* in 1 Kings 13:6, referring to Jeroboam's suddenly "shriveled hand" (NIV; or "rigid arm," NJV) is ambiguous. Does it mean, "'Intercede with the LORD your God and pray for me that my hand may be *restored* [*watāšōb yādî 'ēlāy*].' So the man of God interceded with the LORD, and the king's hand *was restored* [*watāšāb yad-hammelek*] and became as it was before" (NIV)? Or does the usage of *šwb* here hark back to verse 4: "the hand . . . shriveled up, so that he could not *pull it back*" (*lehăšîbāh 'ēlāyw*); hence, " . . . pray for me that I may be able to draw back my arm . . . and the king was able to draw his arm back" (NJV)? The specific wording, viz., *lehăšîbāh 'ēlāyw*

// *wᵉ tāšōb yādî 'ēlāy*, gives preference to the latter translation, although Holladay translates 1 Kings 13:6 with "return (to health = be restored)."[124]

When used with *nepeš*, the Hiphil of *šwb* can mean "to refresh, reinvigorate, keep alive" (e.g., Ru 4:15; Ps 19:8; Pr 25:13; La 1:11, 19; cf. also the Polel in Ps 23:3), or simply "to bring one back, rescue" (e.g., from *šaḥat*; cf. Job 33:30). Similarly, *šwb* with *rûaḥ* can mean "be refreshed" (cf. Jdg 15:19, with *ḥyh*), although it can simply mean "to catch one's breath" (Job 9:18).[125]

šlm. This root is related to healing in the sense of "wholeness, well-being." Thus the NIV translates *šālôm* in 1 Samuel 25:6 (*bis*) with "Good health" (following *ḥāy*, "Long life"), and in Isaiah 57:18–19, the divine pronouncement of *šālôm šālôm* falls in the context of "I have seen his ways, but I will heal him (*wa'erpā'ēhû*).... And I will heal them" (*ûrᵉpā'tîw*).[126] Also, more broadly, it was the false prophets who "superficially treated" the fractured state of God's people (*wayyᵉrappᵉ'û 'et-šeber 'ammî 'al nᵉqallâ*), claiming, "All is well! All is well!—when nothing was well" (*šālôm šālôm wᵉ'ên šālôm*; Jer 6:14, 8:11, my translation; the NIV reflects the more political context: "'Peace, peace,' they say, when there is no peace"). Generally speaking, however, it can be stated that *šlm* is rarely part of the OT vocabulary of healing; rather, to be healed/healthy was one of the necessary ingredients required for there to be a state of *šālôm*.[127]

0.4. THE OLD TESTAMENT TERMINOLOGY FOR SICKNESS

This vocabulary—especially *ḥlh*, "to be weak, debilitated; to be sick, suffer, feel pain"—has been treated elsewhere in depth, especially by Seybold,[128] who lists the primary word groups for sickness as derived from the following roots: (1) *ḥlh* (attested verbally in all stems and occurring in the nominal forms *ḥōlî, maḥ^a leh, maḥ^a lâ, maḥ^a lûyîm, taḥ^a lû'îm, maḥlôn* [?]); (2) *dwh*, "referring to an indisposition, specifically to menstruation, in most cases used metaphorically in a general sense in combination with *lēbh*"; (3) *k'b*, "to feel pain"; (4) "a series of rare verbs that are much harder to categorize," including *'ns* (2Sa 12:15), *nss* (Isa 10:18, "highly problematical"), and *mrṣ* (e.g., 1Ki 2:8; Mic 2:10), the most common Semitic root for sickness.[129]

0.5. A NOTE ON THE LITERATURE CITED

It is not only impossible to attain any semblance of "bibliographical completeness" in a wide-ranging study such as this,[130] it is not necessarily profitable to make the attempt. Salient interpretations would be lost in the maze of alternative scholarly views, and key monographs and articles would be swallowed up in the sea of unimportant or tangential literature.[131] In general, therefore, I have sought to adhere to the following guidelines: (1) Ancient Near Eastern texts are cited in their most accessible or accurate form (this applies to citations of both texts and translations). Original publication data are not listed, and references to secondary literature are given primarily when they shed further light on the specific discussion at hand.

(2) Only major works on subjects like the history of medicine or the phenomenology of disease are cited. The interested reader will find sufficient bibliographical data for further research in these works.

(3) When interpreting specific verses in the OT and NT, I have leaned heavily on the principal modern commentaries, reference works, and articles in major journals, listing more obscure and peripheral works only when particularly relevant.[132] Textual differences are acknowledged solely where pertinent; variations in the ancient versions are examined primarily when they aid exegetically or in the history of interpretation. Among

modern translations, non-English versions have generally not been utilized.

(4) Rabbinic literature has been used extensively, since this rich mine of tradition and interpretation is often untapped by Christian scholars of the OT. I have utilized both halakhic and haggadic midrashim, Talmudic exegesis and expositions of OT verses, classical rabbinic commentaries, and, where applicable, discussions from the law codes and responsa literature.

(5) I follow D. J. A. Clines in occasionally citing (and quoting) "sermons and works of popular devotion alongside vast works of erudition,"[133] since modern-day proponents (or opponents) of divine healing often provide a practical reading of the relevant biblical texts in a real-life context of sickness and recovery, despair and faith. Thus, just as students of OT prophetism have gained insight from comparative anthropological studies of ancient and contemporary "prophetism," spirit-possession, and shamanism,[134] so also students of divine healing in the OT can gain insight—by comparison and contrast—from the testimonies and accounts of ancient and modern "ministers of healing" (be they physician-priests of the Egyptian healing goddess Sekhmet, biblical miracle-workers like Elijah and Elisha, or charismatic missionaries praying for the sick today in Third World nations).[135]

◆ 1 ◆

Human Physicians and Healing Deities

1.1. INTRODUCTION AND GENERAL

As long as human beings have been on the earth, they have battled sickness, disease, accident, and calamity, ultimately succumbing to the inexorable power of death. Indeed, sickness and plague have left their mark on the history of our race, both nationally and individually;[1] and from the pains of childbirth to miscarriages and stillbirths,[2] from the perils of infancy[3] to the debilitating stages of old age,[4] from crippling disease to spreading epidemic,[5] humankind's struggle for health and longevity has been intense. It is only natural, then, that the earliest records of civilization already document responses to these universal afflictions, some spiritual and others natural. (1) The spiritual response to these strange and malevolent forces of sickness and disease was prayer and appeasement (to the God, gods, or human foe) and/or magical rites and incantations (to or against demonic, numinous powers). (2) The natural reaction took the form of basic medical care (e.g., treating wounds and setting broken bones), experimental remedies (e.g., various herbs and potions), and attempts at diagnosis and treatment.[6] Of course, both the spiritual and natural approaches were more often than not interrelated, and the desired success of the natural treatments was frequently tied into the real or imagined efficacy of the spiritual methods employed.[7]

Generally speaking, it appears that minor injuries such as cuts, bruises, and fractures were treated primarily by natural means, since the origin of these complaints was not hidden and the basic treatment could largely be determined by outward observation.[8] However, in the case of mysterious ailments such as fevers, internal disorders, and severe pain, the primary emphasis was on spiritual means, since an outside, apparently hostile force was attacking the body.[9] In the words of medical historian H. E. Sigerist: "When a man became sick, there was a reason for it; somewhere, somehow his vigilance had broken down and a stronger power was in command. A fellow man had bewitched him, or a spirit had taken possession of his body."[10] Disease was therefore perceived to be more than a merely biological process; and with regard to the OT vocabulary of sickness, Seybold has drawn attention to the "relative frequency of words formed from terms meaning 'hit or strike,'"[11] stating, "There is not one unambiguous example suggesting that sickness or disease were associated with one of the organs, or even with internal parts of the body. Sickness was viewed as blows or attacks by a higher power in analogy to bodily wounds."[12] Of related interest is the religious explanation of severe birth defects and deformities in terms of either polytheistic superstition or biblical monotheism. These tragic conditions were not simply natural, ordinary occurrences; they were caused by outside intervention and were often portentous in themselves.[13]

1.2. HUMAN PHYSICIANS

1.2.1. Human Physicians in Ancient Egypt and Mesopotamia[14]

Turning back to the world of the OT, the treatment of sickness was rarely conceptualized as a purely (or even primarily) physical affair. The general ancient Near Eastern pattern suggests that magical and superstitious healing methods precede more scientific methods; yet there is evidence that the reverse may have been true in Egypt,[15] where there is clear evidence of empirico-rational medicine dating back to the Old Kingdom.[16] Indeed, there are several eloquent testimonies to the reputation of Egypt's physicians. Writing in the fourteenth century B.C., Niqmaddu II of Ugarit requested that the pharaoh (probably Amenhopis IV, according to W. L. Moran) send "a palace attendant that is a physician. Here there is no physician."[17] O. Keel has provided a pictorial example of the difficulties that one might willingly endure so as to consult an Egyptian physician of renown.[18] At a later time, according to Homer (*Odyssey*, 4:231–32), "Egypt was so rich in medicines that everyone was a physician";[19] and in an oft-quoted comment, Herodotus observed the great specialization that was to be found among Egyptian physicians: "Egypt swarms with physicians, every single one a specialist."[20] He also praised them for their proficiency in healing disease (*History* 3:1, 132).

According to J. V. Kinnier-Wilson,

> medicine in Egypt was in the hands of two kinds of doctors.[21] There was the *heri-ha'ab* (written *ḫry-ḥ3b*), and the *seynu* (written *synw* [or, *swnw*]). The first of these means "carrier of the ritual book," by which is meant the book of magic or incantation, by means of which diseases might be countered magically. As such . . . the *heri-ha'ab* was the equivalent of the Akkadian *ašipu*, the "exorcist" or "incantation priest."[22] The *seynu*, on the other hand, was the practical physician or surgeon, and still today the Coptic *seyn* is the normal word for "doctor." He corresponds very largely to the Akkadian *asû*, usually translated "physician."[23]

The famous Egyptian medical papyri, dating in their current form to the second millennium B.C.,[24] reflect an advanced knowledge of anatomical science,[25] and they are in some cases surprisingly devoid of magical or religious jargon.[26] Moreover, the medical man, in and of his own right, often held a position of honor in the Pharaoh's court.[27] Nonetheless, a clear-cut distinction between magic, medicine, and religion is not to be found in ancient Egypt. Healing shrines were often the depositories of medical libraries,[28] and, as is often attested elsewhere, most of the medical men were priests.[29] Moreover, as would be expected, much healing was done under the patronage of a particular god or goddess (e.g., Sekhmet, Ptah's wife),[30] and sickness was frequently believed to be the work of malevolent demons from which even the gods were not immune.[31] Thus magical and superstitious rites were evoked on a fairly regular basis.[32]

Yet, in spite of the surprising *decline* in the purity of medical practice witnessed in the history of ancient Egypt (due, of course, to the corresponding increase in magical practices),[33] it must be said that many of the actual prescriptions themselves are, by and large, excellent examples of some of the earliest human efforts at empirico-rational observation, far different from the norm of crude and superstitious folk-medicine that ruled the day. Also, as Liebowitz has noted, it was only when these practical treatments were unsuccessful that one resorted to outright magic.[34]

The crude and superstitious pattern of medical practice was, however, the norm in ancient Mesopotamia, and it is well documented in hundreds of texts.[35] The only real deviation to this rule is in a lengthy text from Sumer that is completely devoid of any magical conjurations.[36] This is not to say, however, that the superstition and magic of the Akkadian medical texts preclude any type of order or method. Actually, Mesopotamian medicine evidences a highly developed internal system integrating folk-belief, religious ritual, and prescribed treatment,[37] most clearly seen in the twin professions of *ašipu* and *asû*, yielding the "sciences" of *ašiputu* and *asûtu*.[38] According to Ritter, the *ašipu* as healer "views disease as a particular expression of the wider beliefs that he holds, namely that a chain of events, initiated under the influence of 'supernatural' powers or forces, proceeds on a predetermined course to an outcome that can be predicted by the skillful reading of 'signs.'"[39] Conversely, the *asû*, "without reference to a more general system of notions, views disease as the complex of presenting symptoms and findings; by his 'practical grasp' (intuition plus accumulated experience) of the immediate situation he proceeds with treatment."[40]

Yet for all the "systematizing" of the Mesopotamian medical practice, it was thoroughly bankrupt in terms of scientific knowledge.[41] Thus, since the *asû* prescribed treatment based on the outward observation of symptoms only, he did not actually examine the patient. And the "signs" that guided the *ašipu* in determining his prognosis could often be as far-fetched as the observation of white pigs, black dogs, creaking doors, or croaking ravens.[42] In keeping with this picture, then, diagnoses were made: it was the hand of Adad, or Sin, or Shamash, etc.; or a demon had seized him; he would live, or have a relapse, or die (sometimes expressed as "Sign of Land-of-No-Return").[43] And as would be expected, the prescriptions were no more "scientific" than the diagnoses—either crude representations of folk-medicine or formulas for exorcism, or the like. Of special note, however, was the great dependence placed on different types of plants and herbs that were believed to have special medicinal or magical value,[44] since this characteristic healing practice was attributed to the gods as well.[45]

1.2.2. Human Physicians in Canaan and Israel[46]

There are no extant medical papyri or medical texts of any kind from ancient Israel (or Canaan),[47] and thus our knowledge of physicians is almost entirely dependent on the few scant references found in the Bible.[48] Moreover, the legislation concerning *ṣāraʿat*[49] in Leviticus 13–14 provides indirect evidence at best, since, as noted by Milgrom, "Israel's priest is a far cry from the pagan physician or magician,"[50] and the priest served more as an observer than as a healer.[51] Nonetheless, certain conclusions regarding the role of human physicians in ancient Israel (as well as certain aspects of the general practice of "medicine") may be drawn from the explicit statements and the implicit assumptions made in the Hebrew Scriptures.

1.2.2.1. References to Medical Practices in the Old Testament

There are several casual references to the basic treatments of wounds and broken bones, all of which underscore the fact that certain medical practices and treatments were normal and, from a religious standpoint, neutral:[52]

- Isaiah 1:5b–6: "Your whole head is injured, your whole heart afflicted. From the sole of your foot to the top of your head there is no soundness—only wounds and welts and open sores, not cleansed or bandaged, or soothed with oil" (*lō'-zōrû wᵉ lō' ḥubāšû wᵉ lō' rukkᵉ kâ baššāmen*). Although the figure is metaphorical, the physical image on which it is based graphically illustrates the expected medical treatment: cleansing, bandaging, and soothing with oil.[53]
- Jeremiah 8:22: "Is there no balm in Gilead? Is there no physician there? Why then is there no healing for the wound of my people?"[54] Several basic insights may be gleaned from this poetic, metaphorical cry: (1) The *rôpē'* was viewed positively. (2) His presence in a typical village/city was expected (unless, of course, Gilead was atypical, being the proverbial home of balm). (3) He was recognized as a "professional" (i.e., either as a known, practicing "folk-healer," or as a member of a professional class). (4) He was expected to promote the healing of wounds.[55] (5) Balm (*ṣᵒrî*) was commonly utilized in this process.[56]
- Jeremiah 46:11; 51:8: "Go up to Gilead and get balm, O Virgin Daughter of Egypt. But you multiply remedies in vain; there is no healing for you" (*laššawᵉ' hirbêt rᵉpū'ôt tᵉ 'ālâ 'ên lāk*);[57] "Babylon will suddenly fall and

be broken. Wail over her! Get balm for her pain (*qᵉḥû ṣºrî lᵉmak'ôbāh*); perhaps she can be healed." These verses, once again prophetic metaphors, imply that it was not uncommon to seek out various (apparently "nonreligious") cures for serious afflictions, that there were several—if not many—possible treatments that might be available, and that balm was also used to alleviate pain.

- Jeremiah 6:14: "For they superficially treat[58] the fracture of my people, saying 'All is well! All is well!'—when nothing is well" (my translation; cf. also 8:11). Although the context is decidedly prophetic and not medical, the verse indicates that setting of fractures was a known skill and one that could be performed in either a careful or careless fashion.
- Ezekiel 30:21 provides further details: "Son of man, I have broken the arm of Pharaoh king of Egypt. It has not been bound up for healing or put in a splint so as to become strong enough to hold a sword" (*ben-'ādām 'et-zᵉrô'a par'ô melek-miṣrayim šābartî wᵉhinneh lō'-ḥubbᵉšâ lātēt rᵉpū'ôt lāsûm ḥittûl lᵉḥobšah lᵉḥozqāh lit-pōs beḥāreb*).[59] Thus it was understood that binding up the break would promote healing (*lātēt rᵉpū'ôt*) without any needed recourse to divine or magical powers. In such cases, healing was primarily viewed as a natural process.[60]
- Ezekiel 34:4a; Zechariah 11:16 (speaking to the selfish shepherds): "You have not strengthened the weak or healed [or, "treated"] the sick or bound up the injured." "For I am going to raise up a shepherd over the land who will not care for the lost, or seek the young, or heal [or, "treat"] the injured, or feed the healthy, but will eat the meat of the choice sheep, tearing off their hoofs." The literal imagery behind these prophetic metaphors is that of a shepherd caring for his sheep.

While Akkadian texts make reference to a veterinarian (see *CAD* A, II, 347), the verses cited here indicate that, as a general rule, shepherds were expected to take care of the basic medical needs of the flock: strengthening the weak, treating (*rippē'*) the sick, and binding up the injured (*nišberet*, i.e., those with breaks or fractures).

1.2.2.2. Exodus 21:19

Even more instructive is the testimony of Exodus 21:19, the key verse cited in the rabbinic search for a scriptural mandate to practice medicine and/or consult a physician.[61] Beginning in 21:18, the text reads: "If men quarrel and one hits the other with a stone or with his fist and he does not die but is confined to bed, the one who struck the blow will not be held responsible if the other gets up and walks around outside with his staff; however, he must pay the injured man for his time [off] and see that he is completely healed." This reinforces what has been emphasized above, viz., that there can be no doubt that in ancient Israel, just as in any other ancient nation, there were fully accepted, religiously "neutral" medical practices, especially in cases such as the one mentioned here, where the injury was caused by a human (as opposed to a divine, angelic, or demonic) agent.[62] What is unique to Exodus 21:19 is that medical treatment is *mandated* in a divinely given ordinance.[63] Because the injured party would recuperate, his opponent was to be acquitted (*wᵉ niqqâ hammakkeh*); "he must only pay for his time off[64] and he must cause him to completely recover" (*wᵉ rappō' yᵉ rappē'*)—i.e., by paying out his medical expenses and/or insuring that he received proper treatment.[65] There is no tension here over the question of divine healing: One man injured another during a fight and, as a result, must see that the injured party receives all necessary treatment. The only "spiritual" issue is that this Torah precept was to be obeyed! Hammurabi's Code, 206, provides an important parallel: "If a seignior has struck a(nother) seignior in a brawl and has inflicted an injury on him, that seignior shall swear, 'I did not strike him deliberately'; and he shall also pay for the physician."[66]

Ibn Ezra, whose discussion of this verse was cited above (n. 8), offered a curious theological-linguistic remark on the usage of the Piel here. Whereas the Qal of *rp'* is used when God is the agent (because for him, healing is *qal*—"easy!"), the Piel is used when there is a human agent (i.e., because of the difficulty of the healing task!). But we should note that the Piel here is used in a causative sense.[67] Aside from this verse, there are no other clear instances where *rp'* in the Piel has this sense; it generally means "to treat" when used with reference to physical healing (although translating with "heal" cannot be excluded[68]).

1.2.2.3. **rōpᵉ'îm** *in the Old Testament (with Special Attention to 2 Chronicles 16:12)*

There are three additional references to physicians (*rōpᵉ'îm*) in the OT and one mention of the *ḥōbēš,* but aside from 2 Chronicles 16:12, none of the other verses is particularly instructive. The sarcastic and, therefore, idiomatic reference in Isaiah 3:7 (*lō'-'ehᵉyeh ḥōbēš*—"I'm no dresser of wounds!"; cf. NJV) suggests that *ḥōbēš* was a *terminus technicus* for one who "bandaged and bound up fractures and wounds."[69] Job's insulting reference to his friends as "quack doctors" (*rōpᵉ'ê 'ᵉlil,* Job 13:4b) provides no real information concerning ancient Israelite/ancient Near Eastern medical practice, aside from the fact that then, as now, there were incompetent men engaged in medical quackery to the point of infamous proverbial fame.[70]

Genesis 50:2 speaks of the Egyptian physicians (*rōpᵉ'îm; bis*)[71] who embalmed Jacob, and it has been clearly demonstrated by W. Spiegelberg "that the embalming business in Egypt was in the hands of the physicians."[72] The fact that the author of Genesis 50 used the word *rōpᵉ'îm* for the Egyptian embalmers proved to Spiegelberg "that the Yahwist was well oriented here also."[73] He further refers to a bilingual demotic papyrus[74] from Ptolemaic times that equates Greek *taricheutēs* (= *entaphiastēs*)[75] with Egyptian *sjn.w* ("Physicians").[76] Thus, the Hebrew usage of *rōpᵉ'îm* should be understood only as the natural Hebrew reflex of Egyptian "physician," in this case a physician who happened to be an embalmer.[77] It cannot be argued that *rp'* was used because of any specific understanding of the embalming process (e.g., *repairing* of the body after the initial "radical surgery," or *preserving* of the body from decay), nor can R. M. Good's viewpoint be accepted, viz., that in Genesis 50:2, "the verb 'to heal' is used with the technical meaning 'to prepare for burial.' Jacob's 'healers' (*rōpᵉ'îm*) are those who embalmed the patriarch."[78] Rather, the usage of *rōpᵉ'îm* in Genesis 50 tells us nothing about Hebrew or Canaanite medical practices, nor does it give insight into the usage of Hebrew *rp'* (in particular with regard to alleged chthonic meanings).[79] Based on Genesis 50:2, one can only state that in some cases in ancient Egypt the embalmers were physicians and that the Hebrew word for physician was *rōpē'*.

We are left then with 2 Chronicles 16:12, a text almost universally cited as evidence that the biblical faith stood in opposition to human physicians.[80] The following remarks are typical, representing, respectively, a medical historian, an OT scholar, a NT and history of religions scholar, and a twentieth-century minister of divine healing:

- A. S. Lyons: "Some passages in the Bible suggest that physicians were held in high esteem [citing Ecclus 38 from the Apocrypha] .... However, other statements in the Bible suggest that admiration was mixed at times with mockery. 'In his disease he sought not the Lord but went to the Physicians. And Asa slept with his fathers.'"[81]
- K. Seybold: "The Yahweh religion ... was ... critical of medicinal practices.... The late remark chastising one

for turning to the physicians instead of Yahweh in the case of foot trouble (2 Chron. 16:12), and the extensive argumentation with which Sirach 38 must try to justify the medical arts, both show that this was, and remained, a problem."[82]

- H. C Kee: "[Outside of Ge 50:1–3], in the prophetic, historical, and wisdom traditions ... physicians are portrayed in strictly negative terms.... In II Chron 16:11–12, Asa is denounced on the ground that, when he was stricken with a disease of the feet which increased in severity, he did not turn to Yahweh for help but to the physicians. The implication is that Asa got what he deserved by seeking medical rather than divine aid."[83]
- M. Woodworth-Etter groups 2 Chronicles 16:12 along with Job 13:4 and Mark 5:26—"(She) had suffered many things of many physicians, and had spent all that she had, and was nothing bettered, but rather grew worse" (AV)[84]—concluding: "These scriptures show that the Bible gives no very favorable recognition of physicians."[85]

To the contrary, however, it can be demonstrated that 2 Chronicles 16:12 has little to do with the issue of divine healing versus human healing, nor is it a critique of physicians in general.[86] Rather, it deals acutely with the issue of leaning on the arm of the flesh instead of leaning on the arm of the Lord, also providing evidence that there was magical or pagan medical practice that could readily be consulted.[87] These conclusions are based on the rather caustic wording of the text, "even in his sickness, he did not seek the LORD, but rather made [oracular] inquiry of the physicians" (my translation of *wᵉ gambᵉ ḥolyô lō'-dāraš 'e̲t-yhwh kî b̲ārōpᵉ'îm*) in light of the overall context of 2 Chronicles 14–16. We turn first to the context.

Early in Asa's reign[88] the Chronicler records, "He removed the foreign altars and the high places, smashed the sacred stones and cut down the Asherah poles. *He commanded*

Judah to seek the LORD [*wayyō'mer lîhûdâ lidrôš 'et-yhwh*], the God of their fathers, and to obey his laws and commands" (2Ch 14:3–4).[89] Then, confronted with a military crisis in which Judah was outnumbered, the king cried out, "Help us, O LORD our God, for we rely on you, and in your name we have come against this vast army. O LORD, you are our God; do not let man prevail against you" (14:11b). A great victory ensued, after which Azariah son of Oded prophesied, "Listen to me, Asa and all Judah and Benjamin. The LORD is with you when you are with him. *If you seek him* [*w*ᵉ*'im-tidr*ᵉ*šūhû*], he will be found by you, but if you forsake him, he will forsake you" (15:2; cf. also v. 4). Spurred on by this word, the king

> assembled all Judah and Benjamin and the people from Ephraim, Manasseh and Simeon who had settled among them, for large numbers had come over to him from Israel when they saw that the LORD his God was with him.... They entered into a covenant *to seek the* LORD [*lidrôš 'et-yhwh*], the God of their fathers, with all their heart and soul. *All who would not seek the* LORD [*w*ᵉ*kol 'ᵃšer lō'-yidroš layhwh*], the God of Israel, were to be put to death, whether small or great, man or woman.... All Judah rejoiced about the oath because they had sworn it wholeheartedly. *They sought God eagerly* [*ûb*ᵉ*kol-r*ᵉ*ṣônām biqšūhû*], and he was found by them. So the LORD gave them rest on every side. (15:9, 12–13, 15)

It is against this remarkable backdrop—a backdrop all the more remarkable when one considers how often it is ignored—that 2 Chronicles 16:12 must be evaluated.

Late in Asa's reign (viz., the thirty-sixth year), "Baasha king of Israel went up against Judah and fortified Ramah to prevent anyone from leaving or entering the territory of Asa king of Judah" (16:1). Amazingly enough, instead of turning to the Lord, Asa entered into a treaty with Ben-Hadad king of Aram, taking the silver and gold treasuries from the house of the Lord and his own palace to bribe Ben-Hadad to break his preexistent treaty with Baasha (16:2–6). This time the prophet Hanani came with a different pronouncement:

> Because you relied on the king of Aram and not on the LORD your God, the army of the king of Aram has escaped from your hand. Were not the Cushites and Libyans a mighty army with great numbers of chariots and horsemen? [cf. 14:9]. Yet when you relied on the LORD [cf. 14:11], he delivered them into your hand. (16:7b–8)

Enraged with the prophet who rebuked him for leaning on the arm of flesh, Asa put him in prison. "At the same time Asa brutally opressed some of the people" (16:10). At this point, then, the Scripture records: "In the thirty-ninth year of his reign Asa was afflicted with a disease in his feet" (16:12a). Thus the stage is set and the question is clear: Will Asa humble himself and repent? Will he cry out to the Lord for help? Will this terribly painful, life-threatening affliction[90] cause the king to once again *seek the Lord*?[91] The answer is forcefully concise: *wegam-bᵉḥolyô lō'-dāraš 'et-yhwh kî bārōpᵉ'îm*—"even in his sickness, he did not seek the LORD, but rather made [oracular] inquiry of the physicians" (my translation, as above).

The Hebrew idiom is unmistakable, yet the distinction between *dāraš 'et-* and (*dāraš*) *bᵉ-* has been almost universally missed by both ancient and modern versions, as well as by most commentaries.[92] Compare, e.g., the LXX., Peshitta, AV, RSV, NEB,[93] NIV, NASB, NAB, NJV, and the commentaries of E. L. Curtis and A. A. Madsen, Myers, and Dillard.[94] C. F. Keil correctly noted, "It is not the mere inquiring of the physicians which is here censured, but only the godless manner in which Asa trusted in the physicians,"[95] stressing that *daraš bᵉ* is always oracular or religious in nature (cf. 1Ch 10:13b–14, regarding Saul: *wᵉgam-liš'ôl ba'ôb lidrôš* [note "double-duty" *ba'ôb*] *wᵉlō'-dāraš bayhwh wayᵉmîtehû*—"he even consulted and inquired of a medium; but he didn't inquire of the LORD. So he put him to death" [my translation]). As to the specific meaning of *daraš . . . bārōpᵉ'îm,* W. Rudolph saw a clear reference to magical practices engaged in by the physicians; and H. J. Stoebe thought that the Hebrew usage clearly pointed to pagan physicians, comparing 2 Kings 1:2, "Go and consult Baal-Zebub,[96] the god of Ekron, to see if I will recover from this injury."[97] In a similar vein, the popular *Spirit-Filled Life Bible* comments, "The *physicians* were probably sorcerers or medicine-men who operated with curses and magic, which is why they should not have been sought. To his shame, Asa is remembered as one who *did not seek the Lord.*"[98] In light of the context, the precise Hebrew usage, and the magical/idolatrous/superstitious nature of most ancient Near Eastern medical practice,[99] a conclusion similar to those just cited is inescapable.[100]

There is no defense for M. Jastrow's proposal that "the rather absurd" *bārōpᵉʾîm* be corrected to *bārōʾîm* ("the seers"); nor is there justification for his more widely discussed second choice,[101] viz., emending the vowels to read *bārᵉpāʾîm* ("the shades") if *bārōʾîm* seemed "too radical."[102] Hempel found possible support for this revocalization in the LXX's rendering of Isaiah 26:14 and Psalm 88(87):11, where MT *rᵉpāʾîm* became Greek *iatroi* ("physicians"),[103] and, most recently, M. S. Smith opined, "It is difficult to criticize Asa for seeking medical aid unless the help was sought from theologically dangerous sources, such as the dead Rephaim."[104] However, in this case, the "theologically dangerous sources" *were* the *rōpᵉʾîm*—either pagan physician-priests or native Judean magician-physicians. The irony of this entire narrative is underscored when it is remembered that the name *ʾāsāʾ* might well have been a theophoric hypocoristicon meaning "God/Yah has healed."[105] He whose very name meant "(the LORD) healed," the godly king so renowned for his earnest seeking of Yahweh, ended his life refusing to seek the divine Healer—once again his only hope in time of extremity—trusting instead in the occult/oracular practices of (pagan?) physicians.[106]

Thus 2 Chronicles 16:12 provides further testimony to the existence of magical-medical practice in or around ancient Israel, without, however, censuring physicians in general.[107] Furthermore, if 2 Kings 1:2 is a representative example, overt consultation of pagan deities (presumably famed as healers) was not unknown.[108] Also, the fact that the inspection of *ṣāra'at* was under the jurisdiction of the Israelite priests,[109] coupled with the fact that the prophets were sometimes employed as healing "intermediaries,"[110] demonstrates the intimate ties that existed between Israelite religious faith and the healing art. However, it is likely that the battle for religious purity and monotheism militated against a thriving class of physicians in ancient Israel, given the idolatrous and magical nature of virtually all ancient Near Eastern medicine. It is also possible that, just as the priests could not ascend the altar by steps (so as not to expose their nakedness, thereby distancing themselves from the widespread fertility rites of pagan priests),[111] they could function only as observers and hygienists, *not* healers, thereby relegating all supernatural, religious healing to Yahweh's hand alone (again in contrast to the general ancient Near Eastern pattern, where, it was observed, the priests were often physicians).

1.3. HEALING DEITIES

1.3.1. Healing Deities in Ancient Egypt and Mesopotamia[112]

It is not only the processes of disease that are often mysterious, but the processes of healing as well, hence the involvement of the deity in the healing process was actively sought.[113] The battle with debilitating illness was too intense, too numinous, too devastating. If one lost one's health and vigor one became a burden to both family and society,[114] apparently suffering from divine disfavor as well. Thus it was crucial that the deity's favor be incurred and his or her help secured. *To the ancient Near Eastern—and biblical!—mind, it was impossible to countenance a major god/God who did not heal.* In our compartmentalizing Western mentalities we often make sharp distinctions between the care of the body and the care of the soul, and religious faith and scientific medical practice are frequently viewed as mutually exclusive categories.[115] Yet concepts such as these would be virtually unintelligible to the ancient Near Eastern/biblical mentality (see above, 1.2).[116] As surely as there were earthly healers whose help could be sought—in fact, even *more* surely—there were divine healers who could be supplicated. The earthly practitioners were ultimately dependent on their spiritual counterparts.[117] There is therefore little exaggeration to Sigerist's sweeping statement that in religious lore, "all ancient gods had the power of healing." His reference to Apollo is also instructive: "Apollo was considered the inventor of medicine: his healing functions were denoted by a great variety of attributes such as *akesios [healing]*, *alexikakos [warding off evil]*, *epikourios [helping]*, *iatros [physician]*, *iatromantis [physician-seer]*, *paion [healer]*, *soter [deliverer]*."[118] Such divine attributes were considered to be the norm; thus Baudissin, in his discussion of the healing gods of the Babylonians and West Semites, aptly noted that in all religions of the world, any deity might on occasion be seen as a dispenser of healing and health, even if he (or she) was not known primarily as a healing deity.[119] For the purposes of this study, however, it will be worthwhile to focus our attention on the deities that gained special repute for their healing prowess, especially as witnessed in their epithets.[120]

Baudissin claims that there is no specific Semitic deity that was known *primarily* as a healer, and Jayne has observed a similar situation in the Egyptian pantheon.[121] Thus, strictly speaking, an ancient Semitic Asklepios did not exist.[122] Nonetheless, there were many gods who were worshiped and supplicated as healers, and these are known to us primarily through the above-mentioned divine epithets, as well as through the panegyric literature and the expressions of prayer and supplication.

Surveying briefly the major deities of the Egyptian pantheon,[123] Amun is praised as "he who frees from evil and drives away suffering, a doctor who makes the eye healthy without medicine; who opens the eyes and cures squinting,"[124] while according to Eusebius, Apis, the "son" or "living replica" of Ptah, was credited with the origin of medicine.[125] Horus was the "chief physician in the house of Re,"[126] Imhotep, the deified former physician, became the god of the physicians,[127] while Isis, "great of magic," excelled in the treatment of children.[128] Khonshu's "soul energy" was able to cast out demons and heal diseases,[129] and Serapis, labeled by Jayne an "iatromantic" deity, was thought to work through dreams, oracles, magic, and other mystical means.[130]

As mentioned above (1.2.1), much healing was done under the patronage of Ptah's spouse Sekhmet. Their son, Nefertem, forming the third member of the triad, was eventually displaced by none other than Imhotep. Ptah's Memphis shrine was renowned for its great healings, and Ptah, designated as Ptah-Sotmu ("Ptah who hears"), was expected to respond to prayers during a period of incubation.[131] Thus, in the morning a healing remedy would be divined by the "Learned Men of the Magic Library," no doubt the physician-priests.[132] In fact, the priests of Sekhmet became famous for their medical skills, especially in the area of bone-setting.[133] All this shows how fundamentally important the role of the god as healer actually was, and it reminds us again of the basic mentality of the ancient world in which "spiritual" and "natural" care were so intimately interrelated.[134]

Out of the many deities praised for their healing deeds in the Babylonian and Assyrian pantheon,[135] special attention will be given to Marduk and Gula.[136] The latter was praised as *azugallatu*, "the great [lady] physician,"[137] and of herself she could say:

> Mention of me is sweet—men discourse on sound health and the healing touch.... I am a physician, I can heal, I carry around all [healing] herbs, I drive away disease, I gird myself with the leather bag containing health-giving incantations, I carry around texts which bring recovery, I

> give cures to mankind. My pure dressing alleviates the wound, my soft bandage relieves diseases. At the raising of my eyes the dead come back to life, at the opening of my mouth palsy disappears. I am merciful, I am compassionate. . . ."[138]

She is "the dispenser of life/health" (*qā'išat balāṭu*),[139] "whose 'sacred formula' [can] restore to health,"[140] and she gives life to the dead (i.e., heals the seriously ill).[141] As *mūdāt murṣi* she has intimate knowledge of sickness,[142] and as *muṭibat šīri*, she makes the flesh well.[143] Indeed, she is *šu'ētu balāṭi*, "the lady of life/health/vigor,"[144] so that her "mere looking [at a person] spells good health," and her "turning to [a person], well being."[145]

As for Marduk, while he was not preeminently a healer, as the chief god of the Babylonian pantheon he was often extolled for his healing powers.[146] If Gula was "the lady of life," then Marduk was *bēl balāṭi*, "the lord of life,"[147] who gives life and health to the gods (*nādin balaṭ ilani*).[148] He was both "expert physician"[149] and "lord of exorcism" (*bēl ašiputi*),[150] "he who has the incantation and the spittle of life/health,"[151] "he who loves to heal."[152] And in *Ludlul bēl nemēqi*, Marduk is hailed in terms that are extremely reminiscent of some biblical psalms:[153] "The Lord took hold of me, the Lord set me on my feet, the Lord gave me life, he rescued me [from the pit,] he summoned me [from destruction, . . .] he pulled me from the *Hubur* river. . . ."[154] Thus the onlookers' praises flow: "'Who but Marduk restores his dead to life? . . . Marduk can restore to life from the grave.'"[155] Thus it seems clear that, according to these words of adoration, whatever the need, however great the distress, it was believed that the healing god could deliver.[156]

Of special interest is the recurring phrase *muballiṭ mīti*, "he who gives life to the dead," cited above as a common epithet of the Babylonian gods (and coupled here with the related concept of "restoring to life from the grave"). As the context indicates, and as Baudissin has clearly shown, these words have nothing to do with a belief in the resurrection of the dead.[157] Actually, the vivid references to being lifted out of pits and rivers and being redeemed from *šaḥat*[158] illustrate the well-documented fact that "by the Babylonians and West Semites, sickness was universally regarded as a state of falling [*Verfallensein*] near death."[159] In fact, as Brunner has pointed out in a similar context in an Egyptian hymn,[160] the underworld "is the isolation of the individual from his surroundings, and above all sickness or living in a foreign land."[161]

1.3.2. Healing Deities in Ancient Syria-Canaan

Although our knowledge of religious beliefs in ancient Syria-Canaan has greatly increased in the last one hundred years, due especially to the texts from Ugarit (and now Ebla),[162] these texts have yielded surprisingly little concrete information regarding healing deities.[163] J. C. de Moor has sought to portray Baal as a West Semitic Asklepios,[164] equating him with the Ugaritic deity *rpu*,[165] but the available data does not support his conclusions, in spite of his erudite argumentation.[166] The Ugaritic texts hardly present Baal as a preeminent healer;[167] the extrabiblical evidence for Baal as healer is sparse, albeit informative; and the deity *rpu* (normally vocalized as an active participle, hence, *rāpiu*), even if he is to be equated with Baal, never heals anyone in the Ugaritic corpus.[168] Moreover, it is not absolutely certain that *rpu* should be translated as "healer" (although this is virtually a universal practice), since *rpu* is clearly related to the *rpum*, who just as clearly are etymologically equivalent to the Hebrew and Phoenician *rp'm* ("shades of the dead").[169] Thus, it is *possible* that Ugaritic *rpu* is to be derived from a putative *rp'*–II, and not from *rp'*–I, "make whole, heal."[170] If, however, the Ugaritic texts do provide evidence for a deity known as "healer" (even if this title/epithet reflects more of a historical development than the reality attested in the Ugaritic texts), this would be important for OT studies, since the equivalent participial form in Hebrew (*rôpē'*) was used in several key OT texts (esp. Ex 15:26) with reference to the Lord.

Outside of Ugaritic, Baal is scarcely mentioned in healing contexts,[171] although it would seem logical, based on the importance of the deity as healer in the ancient world, that he too had a reputation as a giver and restorer of life.[172] Thus, I differ with de Moor, *not* in theory, but based on the presently available data.[173]

The deity *ḥrn* is invoked in several Ugaritic texts for healing from snakebite and the like (nominal or verbal forms of *rp'* are not found), but he was not one of the central figures in the pantheon.[174] In the Pheonician-Punic pantheon, the key healing deity is Eshmun, equated later by the Egyptians with Thoth, Ptah, or Imhotep, and by the Greeks with Asklepios.[175] Jayne notes that "his special healing function is asserted by all classical authors who refer to him,"[176] although the earliest primary witness to his healing acts is a trilingual text (Punic, Greek, and Latin) from Sardinia, c. 180 B.C. The inscription was written by a grateful worshiper in honor of *'šmn m'rḥ* ("Eshmun the Leader"[?]),[177] because *šm[' q]l' rpy'*[178] ("he heard his voice [and] healed him").[179]

1.3.3. Asklepios/Aesculapius

Asklepios was the most prominent healing deity in the ancient Greco-Roman pantheon. Although the origins of his cult are somewhat obscure, by the fifth century B.C. his reputation as a healer was established throughout the Mediterranean region.[180] W. Jayne tentatively reconstructs the process by which the mortal physician of Thessalonica became the foremost deity of healing as well as the patron god of the medical profession as follows: (1) He first became famous as a (merely human) physician (reflected in a reference in Homer's *Iliad*); (2) was heroized after death; (3) became designated as son of

Apollo and healing god at Epidauros; (4) was recognized as a demigod and hero at Athens; and (5) was venerated as Aesculapius, the great healing god of Rome.[181]

However the veneration of Asklepios did not stop with his healing cult (although it would have been unthinkable for his worshipers to separate him from the realm of physical deliverance and healing beneficence). Rather, as summarized by H. C. Kee, his reputation increased and broadened in the following dimensions: "Asklepios as medical and cult healer"[182] → "Asklepios as benefactor and personal guide"[183] → "Asklepios as savior" (*sōtēr*). It was believed that "the god offered the meaning of [life], not merely a cure for a disease or disability,"[184] and thus the testimony of Aelius Arsitides, a rhetorician born in c. 117 B.C., may be taken as typical: He received relief from a disease (which hindered his career as a rhetor) and received guidance for life through a dream-vision at the Asklepion at Smyrna. Thus, for the rest of his life he was devoted to this deity, to whom he looked for periodic healings as well as spiritual sustenance.

For Aristides, the god was both doctor and savior (again, not exclusive, but complementary terms!), but with the epithet *savior*, Aristides meant "far more than one who delivers him from sickness. That deliverance does take place to some extent, but more important[ly] ... his life is divinely preserved, and his place in heaven is assured through the benefactions of the god in his behalf."[185] Nonetheless (and this was certainly the norm for most of the adherents of Asklepios): "Just as his interest in Asklepios arose out of Aristides' many and protracted ailments, so a continuing feature of his relationship to the god is as divine healer."[186] This would be in keeping with the ancient Near Eastern and OT perception of divine healers, wherein the god/God could at one and the same time be supplicated and worshiped as healer/deliverer/savior.

Indeed, this was a threefold conceptual cord not so easily broken in the ancient Near Eastern and Mediterranean mentality, and it is also relevant to the religious background of the

NT. Because the fame of Asklepios was so great and the ministry of healing so important in the world of the NT and early church, Asklepios "was regarded by the early Christians as the chief competitor of Christ because of his remarkable similarity in role and teachings to the Great Physician."[187] The preeminent "healer" of the day was also venerated as "savior"; conversely, for the early Christians (see below), Jesus the *sōtēr* (Savior) was also *iatros* (Physician).[188]

1.4. A SAMPLING OF JEWISH AND CHRISTIAN VIEWS ON HUMAN AND DIVINE HEALING

The tensions early Judaism and Christianity experienced in dealing with the relationship between human and divine healing are representative of the internal conflicts faced by religious or superstitious peoples who believe in deities and/or demons of healing and disease. A brief sampling of some of these developments provides what may be called a "retrospective historical context" for the biblical material to be discussed in the following chapters.

1.4.1. Jewish Views

Modern Jewish scholars have written quite strongly on the moral imperative for human physicians to heal as expressed in traditional Jewish sources,[189] and Rabbi E. Munk has also argued that for many years, Judaism has understood "the prophylactic effect of a series of religious laws" seen especially in light of Exodus 15:26.[190] Yet the "Judaic obligation to heal" has not been without the expected tensions, and rabbinic literature from the second to the twelfth centuries does not indicate total uniformity in Jewish religious thought.[191]

A case in point is the tradition dealing with Hezekiah's praiseworthy removal of "the book of remedies" (*sēper rᵉpû'ôt*)[192] as interpreted by Rashi and Maimonides.[193] According to the former, Hezekiah removed this book so that the people "would seek [God's] mercy" for healing (*b. Ber.* 10b), since their supposed dependence on human cures had produced instant results (*mitrappeʾîm miyyad*), thus removing the humbling effects often inherent in sickness (*b. Pes.* 56a). Yet Maimonides in his commentary to *m. Pes. 4:9* minced no words in refuting this interpretation, calling it "worthless and confused" (*qal* and *meššubbāš*), since if it were true, a man procuring food to relieve the "sickness" of hunger would then be guilty of a lack of dependence on God! Thus Hezekiah removed the controversial book because it was based on forbidden astrological healing methods clearly banned by the Torah.[194] Jakobovits is therefore correct in pointing out that Maimonides' "purely rational" system does not "require any biblical sanction for the practice of medicine."[195] In fact, in his biblical apologetic for the practice of medicine, Maimonides claimed that the concluding words of Deuteronomy 22:2—"and you will restore it to him"—made medical service *obligatory.*[196] It is not hard to see how Maimonides' rational mindset colored his scriptural exegesis.[197]

However, from the often "nonrational" viewpoint of religious faith, the issue was not so simple. For the medieval Karaites, the only legitimate biblical position was total dependence on God alone, with the consequent repudiation of all earthly physicians.[198] Even Ibn Ezra limited medical treatment to external injuries only,[199] understanding the healing of internal injuries to be a matter of divine providence (*beyad haššēm*).[200] In his opinion, the best method was to rely totally on one's Creator, since he had promised to be a *rôpēʾ* for Israel (Ex 15:26), removing sickness from their midst (Ex 23:25). Furthermore, Ibn Ezra continues, when sickness, being a divine prerogative (Dt 32:39; Job 5:18), comes about as a result of judgment, it is therefore incurable (Dt 28:27), and consultation with physicians is useless (2Ch 16:12).[201]

Thus there is some truth to the assertion of Preuss that in the radical system of divine healing, there is no place for a physician,[202] and Mueller, among others, has referred to the "Israelite idea of 'Yahweh's healing monopoly.'"[203] The famous objection posed by the anonymous farmer to R. Ishmael and R. Akiva when they prescribed medicine for a sick person who had asked their advice—viz., that since it was God who afflicted, they were thereby interfering with providence by prescribing a cure—actually expressed a profound question.[204] It is an indication of the apparent lateness of the story that the sages could dismiss the inquirer as a "fool" (*šôteh šebbā'ôlām*), offering an extremely well-developed apologetic on behalf of their previous humanitarian actions.

In point of fact, early rabbinic literature offers a wide diversity of opinion regarding the place of the physician. In the Mishnah, R. Yehudah is said to have stated that "the best physician is destined to go to hell,"[205] while, on the other hand, a later Talmudic source declares that no *talmîd ḥakam* ("Torah scholar") is permitted to dwell in a city that has no physician.[206] Of course, it can be assumed that the somewhat crude medical practices of the day negatively colored much of the discussion.[207] Nonetheless, much of the unresolved tension came, not from a lack of confidence in human medical skills, but rather from a conflict of faith. If God is the Healer and if life and death are in his hands, how then can one rely on human help?

This is not to say that there were not moderate views in even the prerabbinic literature. Ben Sira advised the afflicted to honor the physician, who had been created by God (Ecclus. 38:1), since it was the Lord who had both created the healing medicines (v. 4) as well as given men skill (v. 6).[208] The patient should "pray to the Lord" (v. 9), "leave off from sin" (v. 10), and "then give place to the physician" (v. 12), who will also pray to the Lord for success (v. 14).[209] Yet, while Ben Sira's moderation is generally written off to Hellenism's influence on developing Jewish thought,[210] it is noteworthy that Philo, who occasionally wrote kind words regarding the humanitarian actions of certain doctors, castigated those who mocked exclusive dependence on the "sole physician" (*monos iatros*).[211] Later, however, in the tradition of Ecclesiasticus 38, the Talmud could prescribe a confessional prayer before blood-letting, since God alone was the "reliable physician" (*rôpē' ne'ᵉmān*) who could cause the procedure to succeed (*b. B. Qam.* 85a; *b. Ber.* 60a).[212] And ultimately, as evidenced by the standard codes of Jewish law (cf. *Arba'ah Turim, Shulkhan Arukh,* and *Arukh HaShulkhan* at *Yoreh Deah*, 236; *Kissur Shulkhan Arukh*, 4:192), Judaism affirmed medical practice as a virtue, with luminaries such as Maimonides and Nachmanides heading the long list of Jewish scholar-physicians.[213]

1.4.2. Christian Views

In the history of the church, however, such a moderate position was slower in developing, since in a very special way, Christianity was the religion of healing.[214] Beginning with the miracle stories in the Gospels that were offered as proof of the messiahship of Jesus[215] and continuing on through the preaching of the apostles,[216] the message was always the same: God through his Son had procured and proclaimed liberty for the captives.[217] According to M. Kelsey, "the practices of healing described in the New Testament continued without interruption for the next two centuries,"[218] and the apologetic testimony of Justin Martyr is typical:

> For numberless demoniacs throughout the whole world, and in your city, many of our Christian men exorcizing them in the Name of Jesus Christ ... have healed and do heal, rendering helpless and driving the possessing devils out of the men, though they could not be cured by all the other exorcists, and those who used incantations and drugs.[219]

Even more striking is an account from the apocryphal *Acts of John*, wherein the apostle reacts with shock when he hears that, out of the women in Ephesus older than sixty years,

> "only four [are] in good bodily health; of the rest, some are paralytic, others deaf, some arthritic and others sick with divers diseases." And John on hearing this kept silence for a long time; then he rubbed his face and said, "Oh, what slackness among the people of Ephesus! What a collapse, what weakness towards God! O devil, what a mockery you have made all this time of the faithful at Ephesus! Jesus, who gives me grace and the gift of confidence in him, says to me now in silence, 'Send for the old women who are sick, and be with them in the theatre and through me heal them; for there are some of those who come to this spectacle whom I will convert through such healings as have been beneficial.'"[220]

Even Augustine, who in his early writings "stated quite specifically that Christians are not to look for continuance of the healing gift," decidedly changed his views while completing his *magnum opus*, *The City of God*.[221] Therefore he wrote:

> Once I realized how many miracles were occurring in our own day and which were so like the miracles of old and also how wrong it would be to allow the memory of these marvels of divine power to perish from among our people. It is only two years ago that the keeping of records was begun here in Hippo, and already, at this writing, we have nearly seventy attested miracles.[222]

The early rabbinic writings also preserve some indirect references to the healing prowess of the early messianic Jewish[223] believers, commending one Tannaitic sage who died before he was able to receive healing in the name of Jesus from the "schismatic" (*mîn*)[224] identified as Jacob of Kefar Sama (*t. Hul.* 2:22–23),[225] while reproving another sage who was healed by a *mîn* in Jesus' name.[226] It is also possible that Rabbi Akiva's exclusion from the world to come (*m. Sanh.* 10:1)[227] of "he who whispers over a wound [*hallôḥēš 'al hammakkâ*] and says, 'I will put none of the diseases upon you which I put on the Egyptians, for I am the Lord your Healer' (Exod 15:26)"[228] was directed against the contemporary Jewish followers of Jesus.[229] In any event, the testimony of the rabbinic sources cited here led S. T. Lachs to conclude, "In Jewish literature these disciples and those who followed them were best known through their healing activity in the name of Jesus."[230]

It is, therefore, no surprise that Jesus quickly received the designation of "physician" (*iatros*),[231] Ignatius even calling him "the one physician of flesh and spirit."[232] And in apparent contrast to the human, and therefore imperfect, medical profession, the Syriac church called Jesus "the good physician" (*'āsyā' ṭābā'*),[233] Aphrahat referring to him as "the wise physician" and Ephrem reserving "physician" as "his favourite title of all for Christ."[234] Moreover, according to Mueller, "It is practically a hallmark of the miracle-healing genre to speak of the failure of the physicians in order to let the healing god's power shine all the more brightly."[235] Thus the emphasis on Jesus the Healer produced as a direct—but not absolutely logical—corollary a disdain for the physician's office. An additional factor was that the church placed increasing importance on the malevolent activity of demons in causing disease,[236] so that according to Augustine, "All diseases of Christians are to be ascribed to these demons."[237] Origen was therefore skeptical of the physicians' ability to properly diagnose "a manifestation of sickness of the body," since we "believe according to the gospel that this illness in those affected is caused, as is well known, by an unclean . . . spirit."[238]

This is not to say, however, that there were not broader theological views taken, and thus sickness could sometimes be viewed as a chastisement from God, a punishment for sin, or even an aid for the perfecting or humbling of a saint.[239] Basil (among others) also taught that some sickness could be the result of "faulty diet or from any other physical origin," and thus sickness could be from either divine, satanic, or natural sources. He wrote, "When we suffer the blows of calamity at the hands of God, who directs our life with goodness and wisdom, we first ask of him understanding of the reasons he has inflicted the blows; second deliverance from our pains or patient endurance of them."[240] It is important to remember, however, that for the early church, "more often than not, there was a hesitancy to attribute disease to God; rather, God was typically viewed as the regulator of disease whether it came from natural or evil sources."[241] The pronounced NT emphasis on divine healing through Jesus the Messiah was too clear to allow for a theology that would see God as the primary sender of sickness and disease, as opposed to (primarily) the Healer.

However, as far as the impact of Christianity on the medical profession is concerned, J. W. Provonsha has argued that Jesus, not Hippocrates, should be viewed as the "Father of Medicine," since Jesus "was more often engaged in acts of healing than in almost anything else ... [and it] was the humble Galilean who more than any other figure in history bequeathed to the healing arts their essential meaning and spirit."[242] And, while D. J. Guthrie and P. Rhodes could point out that "it is sometimes stated that the early Christian Church had an adverse effect upon medical progress," they conclude that "the infinite care and nursing bestowed under Christian auspices must outweigh any intolerance shown toward medicine in the early days."[243] Moreover, in the opinion of Sigerist,

> It remained for Christianity to introduce the most revolutionary and decisive change in the attitude of society toward the sick. Christianity came into the world as the religion of healing, as the joyful Gospel of the Redeemer and of Redemption. It addressed itself to the disinherited, to the sick and afflicted and promised them healing, a restoration both spiritual and physical.

Thus, "it became the duty of the Christian to attend to the poor and the sick of the community."[244]

◆ 2 ◆

Israel's Divine Healer in the Torah and Historical Books

2.1. INTRODUCTION: ONE GOD, ONE HEALER

The great event in the memory of the people of Israel was the Exodus from Egypt.[1] In it, Yahweh declared himself to be the God of all gods as well as Lord of the forces of nature. Both sacred historian and poet attested to the importance of this event. Recounting the beginning of Israel's national history, Numbers 33:3–4 relates: "The Israelites set out from Rameses on the fifteenth day of the first month, the day after the Passover. They marched out boldly in full view of all the Egyptians, who were burying all their firstborn, whom the LORD had struck down among them; *for the LORD had brought judgment on their gods*"[2] (cf. Ex 12:12: "On that same night I will pass through Egypt and will strike down every firstborn—both men and animals—*and I will bring judgment on all the gods of Egypt.* I am the LORD"). The Song of the Sea (Ex 15), one of the earliest "theological" statements in the Bible,[3] recounts Yahweh's total mastery of the wind, the sea, and the Egyptians, culminating in verse 10: "But you blew with your breath, and the sea covered them. They sank like lead in the mighty waters." In light of this, verse 11 asks: "Who among the gods is like you, O LORD? Who is like you—majestic in holiness, awesome in glory, working wonders?" For the people of Israel, it was clear: There was none like Yahweh![4] Thus it is recorded that Jethro, the Midianite priest and father-in-law of Moses, exclaimed: "Now I know that the LORD is greater than all other gods" (Ex 18:11a), and it is in the context of the Exodus that the psalmist declared, "I know[5] that the LORD is great, that our Lord is greater than all gods" (Ps 135:5).[6]

It is, therefore, not surprising to observe the frequent, strongly worded admonitions against idolatry and polytheism that occur in every phase of Israelite law and historiography:[7]

- The Decalogue begins with the assertion that Yahweh is Israel's God (or, better, that Israel is his people), since it was he who brought them out of Egyptian bondage.[8] Therefore they are to have no gods besides him (*'al pā-nāy*),[9] for he is a jealous (*qannā'*) God (Ex 20:1–6; Dt 5:6–10; cf. also Ex 20:22–23).
- The Book of the Covenant (Ex 22:19) legislates irrevocable destruction [*yāḥorām*] for anyone who offers sacrifice to any other god.[10]
- The so-called cultic decalogue[11] of Exodus 34:10–26 begins with a strong warning against the making or worship of idols (vv. 12–17), standing as they do in stark contrast to the Lord (34:6–7, 10).
- The Holiness Code[12] contains an injunction against idolatry (Lev 19:4).
- Numbers recounts the disastrous effects of the worship of Baal of Peor (Nu 25), and Deuteronomy emphasizes repeatedly the uniqueness of Yahweh over against all other gods (e.g., Dt 4:15–39), taking pains to outline how idolaters must be purged from among God's holy people (esp. 13:1–18).
- The first curse in Deuteronomy 27 (see v. 15) is pronounced against anyone who makes and erects an idol (cf. also Lev 26:1, as a prelude to the blessings and curses that follow).

- Both the division of the united kingdom and the demise of the northern kingdom of Israel are blamed on the worship of other gods (cf. 1Ki 11:29–33; 2Ki 17:7–21), while the southern kingdom of Judah was rarely free of polytheistic strains, in spite of the reforms of Hezekiah, Josiah, and others.[13]

All this, of course, is common knowledge, and the books of the prophets provide eloquent testimony as to just how intense the battle against polytheism was throughout most of biblical Israel's history.[14] What is not as commonly recognized, however, is that the Scriptures provide evidence that the battle fought over the issue of divine healing was equally pitched. Which God/god was responsible for sickness and death, infertility and drought? Which God/god could be most effectively supplicated for healing in time of calamity? Who indeed was the greatest of the gods?

Naturally, thinking of Yahweh in such terms may seem crass to some today, but it must be remembered that the Israelites were not lured away by the sublimities of the idolatrous religions as much as by the perceived or alleged power of their gods.[15] Thus Hosea depicts adulterous Israel as saying, "I will go after my lovers, who give me my food and my water, my wool and my linen, my oil and my drink.... I will go back to my husband as at first, for then I was better off than now" (2:5, 7 [7, 9]). But, the Lord laments, "she has not acknowledged that I was the one who gave her the grain, the new wine and oil" (v. 8a [10a]). In this light, the suggestion of F. I. Anderson and D. N. Freedman that the frequent occurrence of *rp'* in Hosea may be seen as a polemic against other healing deities is entirely plausible.[16]

2.2. FOUNDATIONS IN THE TORAH

Much more certain, however, are several key references in the Pentateuch. The legislation in the Book of the Covenant culminates with an exhortation to wipe out utterly the gods of the Amorites, Hittites, Perizzites, Canaanites, Hivites, and Jebusites, whose land Israel is about to occupy (Ex 23:20–24). Then follows a foundational promise (vv. 25–26): If the Israelites will worship Yahweh alone, then his blessing will be on their food and drink, he will remove sickness from their midst, none will miscarry or be barren, and all will enjoy a full life span.[17] Thus the basic concerns of human life, viz., adequate food supply, health, longevity,[18] and the ability to reproduce[19] are vouchsafed to the people of Israel if they will remain loyal to Yahweh alone. He—in and of himself—would be their sufficiency.

Similarly, Deuteronomy 7:1–6, 16–26 contains an admonition to the Israelites, in some of the strongest terms in the Torah, to annihilate totally the Canaanites and their gods.[20] Once again, it is in the context of rooting out the gods of the Canaanites and worshiping/serving Yahweh only that removal of all sickness and unfailing fertility for man, woman, and beast are promised (7:14–15).[21] In fact, if his people would be faithful, God would put these sicknesses—in particular, the dread diseases of Egypt—on Israel's enemies (Dt 7:15; 30:7); but if they proved unfaithful, he would put them on his people[22] (see Lev 26:14–16, 21–25, 39; Dt 28:18, 20–22, 27–29, 34–35, 59–63, discussed in greater detail below, 2.2.2; note again the reference to the diseases of Egypt in vv. 27 [*šeḥîn miṣrayîm*][23] and 60 [*kol-madwê-miṣrayîm*, exactly as in 7:15]).[24] In the case of Israel's apostasy, these ailments would prove incurable (Dt 28:27, 35), since the Lord, Israel's Healer, had been rejected.[25]

Striking ancient Near Eastern parallels (especially those involving Gula, the preeminent Mesopotamian goddess of healing)[26] are instructive:

- In the epilogue to Hammurabi's Law Code (c. 1700 B.C.) Ninkarrak (i.e., Gula) is invoked against any future king who refuses to adhere to Hammurabi's words:

"May Ninkarrak . . . inflict upon him in his body a grievous malady, an evil disease, a serious injury which never heals, whose nature no physician knows, which he cannot allay with bandages, which like a deadly bite cannot be rooted out, and may he continue to lament (the loss of) his vigor until his life comes to an end!"[27]

- In the curses of the Treaty of Esarhaddon with Baal of Tyre (7th cent.), it is Gula, called the great lady physician (*azugallatu*), who is specifically entreated to "[put illness and weariness in] your [hearts], and an unhealing sore [*simmu lazu*] in your body. . . ."[28] None of the other deities are so invoked, underscoring Gula's special association with smiting and healing.[29] Similarly, in the Succession Treaty of Esarhaddon (also 7th cent.), while numerous deities are entreated to send all types of plagues and diseases upon the treaty breakers,[30] it is Gula, once again invoked as *azugallatu*, who is requested to put "an unhealing wound [again, *simmu lazu*] in your body. Bathe in [blood and pus] as if in water!"[31]
- In the Treaty of Šamši-Adad V with Marduk-zakir-šumi, King of Babylon (late 9th cent.), Sin, "[whose] punishment is renowned among the gods," is asked to inflict on any treaty breakers "a severe puni[shment] which is not to be removed from his body. . . ."[32]

It is thus logical that incurable illnesses and unhealing maladies were invoked as standard penalties for breech of covenant, since as a consequence of disobedience, the offended deity, in whose hands was thought to lay the power of life and healing, death and sickness, stood implacably against the rebel. In the world of the OT, where such matters were taken with utmost seriousness, the importance of the deity *qua* healer cannot be gainsaid: their curses would bring sickness and death, while their blessings would confer healing and life. Further parallels, provided by M. Weinfeld from the blessings and curses that occurred in oaths taken in the Greek amphictyonic leagues,[33] help underscore the importance in the ancient Mediterranean mentality of receiving divine blessing on soil, body, and womb. The oath taken by members of the Greek amphictyony against Cirrha contains the formula: "If anyone—whether city, man, or tribe [cf. Dt 29:13]—abrogates this oath ... their soil will not bear fruit, their wives will not give birth ... their livestock will not foal" (Asechines, *Against Ctesiphon* 111). The oath taken at Plateia before the war against the barbarians (§7) includes the following: "If I observe what is written in the covenant, then my city will be free of disease ... my land will bear fruit ... the women will give birth ... and the cattle will give birth."[34]

These were the great concerns of life in every society. It would have been unthinkable to divorce one's religious beliefs from these everyday life and death matters. What is unique to OT religion is the fact that the Lord, *without the help or cooperation of any other so-called god*, promised to bless his obedient people with every good thing—physically, spiritually, economically, and politically—while *he alone* would take responsibility to chastise them with every necessary curse should they turn away from him.[35] Needless to say, if he could not smite and heal, punish and deliver, curse and bless, then he would have been the least of the gods rather than the greatest.[36] The observation of Sigerist, although referring to the later healing ministry of the early NT community of believers, is relevant: "At the time of Christ the healing of the sick played such an important part in all cults that the new religion could not have competed with them unless it had also held the promise of miraculous healing."[37]

2.2.1. Exodus 15:26

Foundational to the Torah's theology of healing is Exodus 15:22–27, in particular verse 26: "If you are careful to obey the LORD your God and you do what is right in his eyes, paying attention to his commands and keeping all his statutes, I will not inflict on you any of the diseases which I inflicted on the Egyptians, for I am the LORD your Healer" (my translation).[38] Source critics have posited an unusually high level of editorial activity for this section, finding evidence of the work of J, E, D, P, and other variant sources, in the space of just six verses.[39] According to Durham,

> The awkwardness of the sequence (the use of 'he' as subject four times in v 25, twice in reference to Moses, twice in reference to Yahweh, each time without qualification; the introduction of the testing motif, v 25, followed by a Deuteronomistic-style conditional promise and the somewhat out-of-place reference to Yahweh the healer, v 26) clearly suggest a composite of sources, but provide too little information for exact attribution.[40]

However, this apparent lack of literary smoothness can just as well point to a fairly ancient, "unworked" narrative, as opposed to a later compilation, since the section smacks of simplicity and is somewhat rough, rather than finely edited.[41] Childs follows E. Meyer in noting that "the connection between the 'healing' of the water and 'Yahweh your healer' (v. 26) seems to be a very ancient one and not simply redactional"[42]—an observation that I believe more accurately points to the origin of Exodus 15:22ff. than do the various etiological, *Gattungsgeschichtliche*, and folkloristic explanations that form critics have offered for the origin of this pericope.[43]

In any case, the painstaking literary-critical analysis of verses 22–27 has often supplanted the study of verse 26 in its larger context, a context that, in terms of OT theological foundations, is strategic.[44] The newly liberated nation, safely across the sea, rid for the time of the menace of Egypt, and with the memory of Yahweh's sovereign power deeply etched into its psyche, faces its first corporate test. And it is a test calculated to bring the people into the recognition that the same Lord who smote disobedient Egypt and destroyed their resources would be the one who would heal/keep obedient Israel well, supplying their every need. Moreover, as noted above (0.2), in its wider ancient Near Eastern religious context, Exodus 15:26 stands against the backdrop of the highly developed, magical-medical polytheism of Egypt—a polytheism replete with healing deities—and looks ahead to the inevitable conflict with the gods of Canaan/Syria, one of which *might* have been called "healer" (i.e., Ugaritic *rpu*),[45] and others of which were, with apparent regularity, looked to as healers (see above, 1.3). If there was to be any hope of monolatrous/monotheistic worship for the nation in its earliest formative years,[46] then it was imperative that the people learn that the Lord—not Sekhmet, not Marduk, not Baal—was their *rôpē'*.[47] While modern readers tend to understand Exodus 15:26 in terms of Yahweh's "healing monopoly" over against human physicians, in all probability it should be read primarily in contrast with dependence on any other healing deities (although as discussed above [0.2, 1.2], ancient Near Eastern medical practices were rarely disassociated from various deities or spirits and hence were, for the most part, in religious conflict with strict monotheism).[48] Exodus 23:25–26 and Deuteronomy 7:12–15, promising health and fertility to the Israelites if they would destroy the Canaanites, underscore this truth.[49]

Other factors point to the foundational character of Exodus 15:26. (1) Verse 25 records the first "decree" (*ḥoq*) and "law" (*mišpaṭ*)[50] that the Lord gave to Israel after leaving Egypt,[51] preceding the basic Sabbath legislation of chapter 16,[52] the Ten Commandments of chapter 20, and the Book of the Covenant of chapters 21–23. (2) Verse 25 also articulates, for the first time, the important motif of the Lord's trying his people in the wilderness ("there he tested them"; cf. Ex 16:4; 20:20; Dt 8:2–3, 16; 13:3).[53] (3) Verse 26 sets the pattern for all the covenant legislation that follows: If you carefully obey my statutes, you will be blessed, while disobedience will bring a curse (the latter is implied here). Thus, the first covenant stipulation for the liberated nation, the first test they experienced, and the first promise conditioned on obedience all revolved around the revelation of the Lord as Healer.[54] Regardless of one's dating of the passage in question, its importance for biblical theology must be stressed.[55]

The specific crisis of Exodus 15:22ff.—undrinkable waters for the entire nation—cannot be disassociated from the specific promise of verse 26, viz., that the Lord would not inflict his faithful people with any of the "diseases" (*kol-hammaḥ*ᵃ *lâ*, here collective in meaning)[56] with which he inflicted Egypt, the first of which was his turning the Nile into blood (Ex 7:14–22; cf. v. 9). Although *rp'* is not used here for the "sweetening" of the waters (*wayyimt*ᵉ *qû hammayim*),[57] it is used in a similar context in 2 Kings 2:21–22: "I have made this water wholesome....[58] And the water has remained wholesome to this day."[59] Compare also Ezekiel 47:8–9, 12 (with *rp'* and *t*ᵉ *rûpâ*), referring to the eschatological "making wholesome" (NIV "fresh") of the waters of the Dead Sea.[60] And contrast Ezekiel 47:9 ("Swarms of living creatures will live wherever the river flows. There will be large numbers of fish, because this water flows there and makes the salt water fresh; so where the river flows everything will live"), the direct result of the "restoring" (*rp'*) powers of the temple river, with Exodus 7:21 ("The fish in the Nile died"), the direct result of the judgment of God, who promised to be Israel's *rôpē'*.[61] Note also that in Exodus 23:25–26, the divine promise to bless obedient Israel's food and *water* (*ûbērak 'et-laḥm*ᵉ*ka w*ᵉ*'et-mêmêka*) is followed immediately by the pledge to remove all sickness and infertility.[62]

This divine pledge to be Israel's Healer in Exodus 15:26, however, raises a question: If the Lord promises *not* to put sickness and disease on his obedient people, in what sense will he be their Healer? Does it mean that he will keep them well? Does it mean that he will heal them of penally inflicted illnesses if they disobey (and then repent), but preserve their health if they obey? Or, should the promise be understood in terms of the prophylactic power of the laws of the Torah? All of these interpretations, often in combination, have been suggested in the interesting interpretative history of this verse. K. Stendahl asserted that Yahweh's revelation as Healer does not mean that he will intervene and deliver, but rather that he is the almighty preventer of disease ("allsmäktiges profylax"). Verse 25b indicates that it is obedience to his statutes that guarantees health.[63] A. B. Ehrlich based his understanding of this verse on the premise that "in Hebrew, any verb may be used to describe not merely its own action, but also the omission or prevention of an opposite action."[64] Thus, the Lord as Israel's *rôpē'* would not allow sickness to come upon his people.[65]

The rabbis offered several alternate interpretations:

> *I will put none of the diseases upon you...* : Yet if I do put them upon you, [fear not,] "for I am the Lord that heals you"; that is R. Joshua's interpretation. Another comment: Since He will not put any diseases upon them, what is the need for healing? Said R. Johanan: This text is self-explanatory, thus: If you will diligently hearken to the voice of the Lord your God [I will put none of the diseases upon you]; but if you do not hearken, I will put them upon you.[66] Nevertheless, I am the Lord that heals you.[67]

Rashi explained the plain sense of the text in completely prophylactic[68] terms: "For I am the Lord your Healer and I teach you the Torah and commandments so that you may be delivered from them [viz., the diseases], like a physician [*rôpē'*] who says to a man, 'Don't eat this thing lest it make you sick,' and so [Scripture] says, 'It will be healing [*rip'ût*] to your body' [Prov 3:8]."[69]

In light of these interpretations, which could easily be multiplied, several comments are in order. There can be no doubt that obedience to God's laws and statutes was understood to be the sure path to life[70] and that the hygienic practices legislated in the Torah were certainly beneficial.[71] Moreover, obedience to the strict prohibitions against adultery, fornication, homosexuality, and bestiality would have greatly reduced the instances of sexually transmitted diseases among the Israelites.[72] However, these factors do not seem to be primarily in view in Exodus 15:26 and the related Torah promises (viz., Ex 23:25–26; Lev 26:3–13; Dt 7:14–15; 28:1–14). Rather, the text indicates that covenantal obedience would bring about supernatural blessings of health—i.e., more than just reaping the rewards of "clean," godly living—while breech of covenant would be (supernaturally) disastrous.

While these two concepts are not mutually exclusive, the biblical emphasis is clearly on the supernatural as opposed to the prophylatic, for several reasons. (1) The immediate context makes this clear: The plagues that were inflicted on Egypt and that would not come on faithful Israel were clearly extraordinary.[73] (2) The promised covenant curses were beyond the sphere of the natural order, while the promised blessings could only be actuated through active divine involvement.[74] As Healer the Lord would *bless* his people with health, fertility (see below, 2.2.4), and long life (2.2.3). (3) God's promise to be Israel's *rôpē'* was a dynamic one; that is, he promised *not* to place sickness on his obedient children. In other words, the Lord would actively withhold these judgment diseases if his people would follow his commands.[75]

Based on these observations, it seems best to view Yahweh's function as "Healer" in a similar vein to that of the other healing gods, whose role was to both heal and keep well.[76] Thus, as Healer, he made the waters of Marah drinkable;[77] in the future, if Israel obeyed, he would keep them free from sickness. If they encountered sickness, barrenness, infertility (physical or agricultural), or undrinkable water, he would be their *rôpe'* and make these wrong conditions right.[78]

It would be a great mistake, however, to view Yahweh as just another healing god, albeit more powerful. Even as Healer, he was infinitely greater than all other gods—and radically "other."[79] It is well known that the deities of the ancient world (whether Egyptian, Mesopotamian, Canaanite, Syrian, Hittite, or Greek) were capricious, moody, lustful, immoral, and subject to weakness.[80] Nor were they free from sickness and accident. H. W. Haggard notes:

> The gods of Egypt, like men, might suffer from disease. Ra occasionally had a disease of the eye, so that there was darkness for a time—an eclipse we should call it. He nearly died when stung in the heel by a scorpion. Horus, the son of Isis, had headaches, and like Ra, nearly lost his life from a scorpion's sting. When a god was stricken with disease he turned for aid to his friends among the gods.[81]

As opposed to this, there is never a hint of the God of Israel being sick, in danger, in difficulty, overcome by weakness, or subject to hostile attack.[82] Rather, as the later prophets and poets testified, "He will not grow tired or weary, and his understanding no one can fathom" (Isa 40:28b); "he who watches over Israel will neither slumber nor sleep" (Ps 121:4). And when he arose to smite Egypt, there was nothing the stricken gods could do to stop him. Hence the emphasis in Exodus 15:26 is not just on being Israel's Healer, but on keeping his people free from the dread diseases he inflicted on his enemies. He, and no other god, put them on Egypt; he, with no thought of any other deity, would keep Israel well.

It was thus his revealed will to keep his people blessedly separate in the future,[83] just as he had done during the Exodus plagues (Ex 8:22–23; 9:4–6; 10:23; 11:4–7; 12:13; cf. also 19:5). What may be termed the Lord's "distinguishing presence" was to remain continually with his people (33:15–16)—not the least in its promised healing manifestations (cf. also 34:10).

2.2.2. Blessings and Curses

Health and long life are not specifically enumerated as rewards for obedience in the two principal Pentateuchal passages of covenant blessing and curses (Lev 26:3–13; Dt 28:1–14).[84] However, sickness and terminal disease are most definitely seen as the curses for disobedience:

> But if you will not listen to me . . . I will bring upon you sudden terror, wasting diseases and fever that will destroy your sight and drain away your life. . . . I myself will be hostile toward you and will afflict you for your sins seven times over. . . . I will send a plague among you . . . . I will . . . pile your dead bodies on the lifeless forms of your idols. . . . Those of you who are left will waste away in the lands of their enemies because of their sins. . . . (Lev 26:14–16, 24–25, 30, 39; see also 21–22)
>
> However, if you do not obey the LORD your God . . . the LORD will send on you curses. . . . The LORD will plague you with diseases until he has destroyed you from the land you are entering to possess. The LORD will strike you with wasting disease, with fever and inflammation, with scorching heat and drought, with blight and mildew, which will plague you until you perish. . . . The LORD will afflict you with the boils of Egypt[85] and with tumors, festering sores and the itch, from which you cannot be cured.[86] The LORD will afflict you with madness, blindness and confusion of mind. At midday you will grope about like a blind man in the dark. . . . The LORD will afflict your knees and legs with painful boils that cannot be cured, spreading from the soles of your feet to the top of your head. . . . The LORD will send fearful plagues on you and your descendants, harsh and prolonged disasters, and severe and lingering illnesses. He will bring upon you all the diseases of Egypt that you dreaded, and they will cling to you. The LORD will also bring on you every kind of sickness and disaster not recorded in this Book of the Law, until you are destroyed. (Dt 28:15, 20–22, 27–29, 35, 59–61; cf. also 62–63, 65–67)

With devastating clarity, these verses confirm (as well as presuppose) what may be safely described as the common biblical outlook: Destructive maladies are a curse! Painful, wasting diseases are terrible afflictions, *not* divine blessings. Health is good; illness is bad. Debilitating sickness and devastating plague are signs of God's anger, not his pleasure. *In fact, nowhere in the Bible does the Lord ever promise sickness, disease, or calamity as blessings for his obedient children. Nowhere in the Bible is sickness, in and of itself, described as a good thing.*

As simple and self-evident as these statements are, they are fundamental to a proper understanding of the OT theology of divine healing and should not be taken for granted.[87] "Suffering sickness for the glory of God" was not part of the Torah's theology of covenantal blessing and curse.[88] Rather, when the covenant curses fell on Israel, they would be expected to say, "Have not these disasters come upon us because our God is not with us?" (Dt 31:17).

Why then were health and long life not included as blessings for obedience in Leviticus 26 and Deuteronomy 28? (1) Health in and of itself is virtually never promised in the OT. Rather, the promise is presented either in general terms of "healing" with no specific reference to sickness (e.g., Pr 3:7–8; 4:20–22), in terms of sickness and disease never touching the faithful children of God (e.g., Ps 91, esp. vv. 5–10), or in terms of the reversal of a specific sickness (e.g., Ps 41:1–3). The first two of these categories underscore what has been observed (with reference to Ex 15:26; 23:25–26; Dt 7:14–15), that God's pledge to be Israel's Healer is primarily expressed in terms of *keeping them free from disease*, as opposed to *keeping them healthy*. Closely related is the fact that there is no one biblical Hebrew word whose primary meaning is "health."[89] It therefore follows that "health" is thought of as the expected, normal condition.[90] Disobedience to the covenant, on the other hand, brings divine judgment, resulting in terrible sickness and disease. This negative aspect of the covenant is spelled out clearly.

(2) The promise of health is included in the frequent Pentateuchal promise of longevity (especially common in Deuteronomy; see below, 2.2.3). Although this is never mentioned in Leviticus 26 and Deuteronomy 28, it is emphasized in so many other contexts in the first five books that it is cer-

tainly to be assumed as a fruit of covenant loyalty. Note also, once again, that Exodus 23:25–26 joins together the promise of removal of sickness (*wᵉhasirōtî maḥᵃlâ miqqirbekā*) with the guarantee of a full life span (*'et-mispar yamêkā 'ammallē'*).

2.2.3. The Promise of Long Life[91]

According to the Scriptures, with rare exception,[92] the human body deteriorates and degenerates as old age sets in; as a result, bodily functions that were once normal either cease entirely or become increasingly difficult.[93] Thus Sarah, knowing that she and her husband were "already old and well advanced in years" (Ge 18:11) found the announcement of imminent childbirth almost impossible to believe: "So Sarah laughed to herself as she thought, 'After I am worn out and my master is old,[94] will I now have this pleasure?'" (Ge 18:12; cf. 24:1). The eyes of Isaac in his old age "were so weak that he could no longer see" (Ge 27:1),[95] and, similarly, the eyes of Israel (i.e., Jacob) "were failing because of old age, and he could hardly see" (Ge 48:10; contrast Dt 34:7).[96] Nonetheless, one could enjoy a good, full life, expressed with regard to Abraham as follows (Ge 25:8) : "Then Abraham breathed his last and died at a good old age [cf. NJV's "ripe old age"], an old man full of years" (*bᵉśêbâ ṭôbâ zākēn wᵉ śābē'a*).[97] That this is regarded as a blessing from God is self-evident; in fact, it had already been vouchsafed to Abraham (then Abram) by the Lord in Genesis 15:15: "You ... will go to your fathers in peace and be buried at a good old age" (cf. also Ge 35:29 [Isaac]; contrast Jacob's description of his own life in Ge 47:9–10).[98]

Beginning with the Decalogue, longevity—both personal and national (the latter having to do with remaining in the land of Canaan)—is often linked to covenantal obedience. To both repeat and summarize: In Exodus 20:12 (Dt 5:16), honoring father and mother is the prerequisite for living long in the land; a full life span is promised for those who worship Yahweh alone (Ex 23:25–26); whoever obeys God's decrees "will live by them" (Lev 18:5; see above, n. 70). Deuteronomy 5:33 exhorts: "Walk in all the way that the LORD your God has commanded you, so that you may live and prosper and prolong your days in the land you will possess" (cf. also 4:1, 4, 40; 6:2–3, 24; 8:1; 11:9, 21; 22:7; 25:15; 30:15–16), and Moses in 30:19 offers a challenge to the people: "This day I call heaven and earth as witnesses against you that I have set before you life and death, blessings and curses. Now choose life, so that you and your children may live. . . .[99] For the LORD is your life, and he will give you many years in the land" (cf. also 32:47).

Thus, long life was recognized as a basic covenant blessing, and (premature) death as a tragic curse.[100] The prevention and/or removal of sickness was indispensable for a long and blessed life (hence the wording of the previously discussed healing promises), while plagues and wasting diseases (in the Torah, *always* explained with reference to divine judgment) were curses that threatened to cut life short. While the afterlife may be hinted at in the concept of being gathered to one's fathers/people (e.g., Ge 25:8),[101] the Torah's orientation was almost exclusively "this worldly."[102]

2.2.4. The Promise of Fertility

Both Exodus 23:25–26 and Deuteronomy 7:12–15, two of the key divine healing passages in the Pentateuch, specifically promise fertility as a blessing for covenant loyalty (see also Lev 26:3–4 [land], 9; and esp. Dt 28:4), affirming what is explicitly stated elsewhere, that infertility and barrenness were covenant curses (Dt 28:18; see above, n. 19). *It is impossible to overestimate the importance attached to fertility in the biblical world.* With striking frequency, fecundity is directly related to the blessing of God.[103] In order to feel the force of this, the following verses should be noted from Genesis:

- 1:28a: "God *blessed* them [Adam → male and female] and said to them: 'Be fruitful and increase in number; fill the earth and subdue it.'"
- 9:1: "Then God *blessed* Noah and his sons, saying to them: 'Be fruitful and increase in number and fill the earth'" (cf. 9:7).
- 12:2a: "I will make you [Abram] into a great nation, and I will *bless* you" (cf. 13:16; 15:5; 17:6 [*wᵉhiprētî 'ōtᵉkā bim'ōd bim'ōd*;[104] 17:20]).
- 22:17a: "I will surely *bless* you [Abraham] and make your descendants as numerous as the stars in the sky and as the sand on the seashore."
- 17:16: "And I will *bless* her [Sarah] and will surely give you [Abraham] a son by her. I will *bless* her so that she will be the mother of nations [lit., so that she will become nations]; kings of peoples will come from her."
- 17:20: "And as for Ishmael, I have heard you [Abraham]: I will surely *bless* him; I will make him fruitful and greatly increase his numbers [cf. 17:6]. He will be the father of twelve rulers, and I will make him into a great nation" (cf. also 16:10; 21:13, 18).
- 24:35–36: "The LORD has *blessed* my master [Abraham] abundantly. . . . My master's wife, Sarah, has borne him a son in her old age."
- 26:3–4: "Stay in this land for a while, and I will be with you [Isaac] and will *bless* you. . . . I will make your descendants as numerous as the stars in the sky."
- 26:24b: "Do not be afraid, for I am with you [Isaac]; I will *bless* you and will increase the number of your descendants for the sake of my servant Abraham."
- 28:3: "May God Almighty [*El Shaddai*] *bless* you [Jacob] and make you fruitful and increase your numbers until you become a community of peoples" (cf. also 30:30; 32:12; 35:11; 46:3; note also Isaac's belated blessing

over Esau in 28:14a: "Your descendants will be like the dust of the earth").

- 48:3a: "Jacob said to Joseph, 'God Almighty [*El Shaddai*] appeared to me at Luz in the land of Canaan, and there he *blessed* me and said to me, "I am going to make you fruitful and will increase your numbers. I will make you a community of peoples. . . ." '"
- 48:15–16: "Then he [Jacob] *blessed* Joseph and said, 'May the God before whom my fathers Abraham and Isaac walked . . . *bless* these boys [Ephraim and Manasseh] . . . and may they increase greatly upon the earth'" (cf. also 48:19–20).[105]

Later biblical history records the actualizing of this promise of exceptional fertility to Abraham's seed (e.g., 1 Ki 4:20)—stated most clearly in Exodus 1:7: "But the Israelites were fruitful and multiplied greatly and became exceedingly numerous" (cf. v. 9; also v. 20: "So God was kind to the midwives and the people increased and became even more numerous."),[106] but emphasized also in Deuteronomy, again in the context of covenantal *blessing*: "The LORD your God has increased your numbers so that today you are as many as the stars in the sky. May the LORD, the God of your fathers, increase you a thousand times and *bless* you as he has promised" (Dt 1:10–11; see 10:22; 26:5); "If you pay attention to these laws and are careful to follow them, then the LORD your God will keep his covenant of love with you, as he swore to your forefathers. He will love you and *bless* you and increase your numbers. He will bless the fruit of your womb. . . . You will be *blessed* more than any other people; none of your men or women will be childless, nor any of your livestock without young" (Dt 7:12–14; cf. 28:4, 11).[107] Indeed, an abundantly fruitful Israel—faithful to the covenant and blessed by the Lord—was presented as a prophetic ideal (e.g., Dt 30:9; Isa 48:18–19; Hos 1:10).

Bearing of children, especially after prolonged barrenness, was recognized as a blessing and gift from God (Ge 41:52; Ex 1:21; cf. esp. Ps 127:3–5; 128:3–4), often in direct answer to prayer (Ge 25:21; 30:6, 17, 22). This outlook may also be reflected in the common ancient Near Eastern and OT *rp'* names such as *r^e pā'yâ* ("Yah healed") and *rāpû'* ("healed").[108] Conception and childbirth was one of the clearest tokens of divine favor: cf. 33:5: "Then Esau looked up and saw the women and children [of Jacob]. 'Who are these with you?' he asked. Jacob answered, 'They are the children God has graciously given [*ḥanan*] your servant.'" It was also of great importance for one's social status: "When the LORD saw that Leah was not loved, he opened her womb, but Rachel was barren. Leah became pregnant and gave birth to a son. She named him Reuben, for she said, 'It is because the LORD has seen my misery. Surely my husband will love me now'" (29:31–32;[109] cf. also Ru 4:14–15; 1Sa 1:1–8, 15–16; 2Ki 4:11–18; Isa 54:1, 4ff.). Thus childlessness was viewed as a curse (Lev 20:20–21; Dt 28:18; possibly Nu 5:19–26), or at least as an unfavorable and reproachful state (Ge 11:30; 15:2; 16:1–2, 5; 30:1 ["Give me children, or I'll die!"]; 30:23 ["God has taken away my disgrace"]; cf. also Pr 30:15–16).

It is unnecessary, however, to follow J. Gray,[110] E. Lipinski,[111] M. H. Pope,[112] et al., who claim that in the context of reversing barreness and/or infertility, *rp'* specifically means "to fertilize."[113] Rather, barrenness and/or infertility were viewed as sicknesses that needed to be *healed* (as reflected in the onomastica?), or, more broadly, as defective conditions that needed to be *made whole*. This can be seen from: (1) a comparison of two parallel accounts in Genesis; (2) the wording of two key covenantal promises; (3) the biblical perspective that it is God who simply *closes* and *opens* the womb (e.g., Ge 20:18; 29:31; 30:22); (4) the evidence of cognate usage of *rp'*, coupled with the fact that *rp'* never occurs contextually with *prh* ("be, become fruitful") or *rbh* ("be, become many, great").

(1) Genesis 12:10–20 and 20:1–18 offer similar accounts regarding the duplicity of Abram/Abraham with regard to his wife Sarai/Sarah—first with the pharaoh of Egypt, and then with Abimelech king of Gerar, both of whom unknowingly took her into their palaces. In the former account, we are told that the Lord inflicted "great plagues" [*nᵉgāʿîm gᵉdōlîm*] on the pharaoh and his household (12:17), while the latter account specifies that the Lord closed every womb in Abimelech's household (20:18; v. 17 suggests that the king himself was smitten with impotence). These parallel accounts are mutually instructive: One describes God's punitive act as a plague while the other specifies the nature of the punitive act, viz., barrenness. N. Sarna is therefore probably correct in surmising that, with regard to 12:17, "Temporary sexual impotence induced by some severe inflammation or acute infection of the genital area suggests itself (cf. Gen 20:17f.)," noting also the observation of Ramban (Nachmanides) that "the plagues must have been of the kind that would somehow suggest a connection with Pharaoh's passion for Sarai. . . ."[114] If this line of reasoning is accepted, then the usage of *rp'* in 20:17 ("Then Abraham prayed to God, and God healed Abimelech, his wife and his slave girls so they could have children again") should simply be understood as the healing of a sickness (*negaʿ* in 12:17), with no specific reference to fertility (cf. also 20:7).

(2) Both Exodus 23:25–26 and Deuteronomy 7:14–15, cited often in the discussions above, couple the absence of *sickness* with the removal of *barrenness* and *infertility*: "I will take away sickness from among you, and none will miscarry or be barren in your land. I will give you a full life span"; "You will be blessed more than any other people; none of your men or women will be childless, nor any of your livestock without young [cf. also vv. 12–13]. The Lord will keep you free from every disease, . . ." Thus, as Healer (not Fertilizer!), the Lord, Israel's *rôpēʾ*, would also keep his people free from the "disease" of the inability to procreate and reproduce.

(3) Although the Hiphil of *prh* is used with regard to divine activity (e.g., Ge 17:6, 20, cited above), God's active witholding of the blessing of fertility (cf. 30:2) is expressed in terms of "closing the womb" (e.g., 20:18; 1Sa 1:5–6), while his reversing of this condition is expressed in terms of his "opening the womb" (e.g., Ge 29:31; 30:2, 22). While this does not directly impact on the semantic range of *rp'*, it does indicate that fecundity was not necessarily thought of in exclusively "fertilizing" terms. Rather, just as barrenness could be thought of as a "sick" or wrong/abnormal condition that needed to be healed, so also it could simply be explained as a "closed" womb that needed to be "opened" by the Lord.

(4) There is not a single example of the root *rp'* occurring in any Semitic language where the specific nuance of "fertilizing/fertility" or "making fruitful" is required.[115] It is evident that *rp'* and *prh* are not semantically interchangeable, belonging to semantically related, but rarely overlapping domains. Moreover, there is not a single instance in the OT where the two roots occur in the same immediate context.[116]

In summary, then, it can be stated that the divine pledge to remove barrenness and infertility from the obedient Israelites was included in the promise to remove sickness from their midst, confirmed by the fact that biblical Hebrew could use the root *rp'* (meaning "heal" and not "make fertile") to refer to the reversal of this negative condition. Thus, supernatural fecundity was vouchsafed to those who would keep the commandments of Yahweh, the *rôpē'*.

2.2.5. Deuteronomy 32:39 and Divine Smiting and Healing in the Torah

If Exodus 15:26 is the foundation of the Torah's theology of healing, then Deuteronomy 32:39 is the capstone.[117] The former verse sets the stage for the narrative of covenantal history that follows; the latter verse summarizes God's dealings with his unfaithful people in the desert, establishing this revelation of Yahweh's character and might as a token of what may be expected in the future. Exodus 15:26 looks ahead; Deuteronomy 32:39 looks back. In this regard it seems important here in Deuteronomy to follow closely the temporal sequence of the verbs[118] (as does the NIV): "See now that I myself am He! There is no god besides me. I put to death and I bring to life.[119] I *have* wounded [*māḥaṣtî*] and I *will* heal [*wa'ᵃnî 'erpā'*],[120] and no one can deliver out of my hand."

It was emphasized above that Exodus 15:26 should be read against the backdrop of the various healing deities of the day; in other words, *the Lord alone* would be Israel's Healer.[121] In the same way, Deuteronomy 32:39, one of the strongest monotheistic statements in the Torah, declares that Yahweh—and no other god—is the one who kills and makes alive, who wounds and heals. The Hebrew is emphatic, with the first person pronoun appearing at least three times more than is necessary: *'ᵃnî 'ᵃnî hû'* ("I, I am he," the second *'ᵃnî* serving for additional emphasis); *'ᵃnî 'amît . . . wa'ᵃnî 'erpa'* ("I myself put to death . . . and I myself heal," both occurrences of *'ᵃnî* serving for added emphasis). M. Korpel, presumably influenced by de Moor's position regarding the polemic nature of this verse, states: "The context renders it likely that this defiant statement was directed against claims on the part of other Canaanite gods, especially Baal, that they were able to heal [*rp'*] and to revive the dead."[122]

It may also be noteworthy that already in Deuteronomy 32, *rešep* (the [sometimes] god of pestilence[123] in Northwest Semitic religion) occurs in demythologized garb (vv. 23–24):[124] "I will heap calamities upon them and spend my arrows[125] against them. I will send wasting famine against them, consuming pestilence [*lᵉ ḥūmê rešep*] and deadly plague; I will send against them the fangs of wild beasts, the venom of vipers that glide in the dust." Moreover, the reason that God promised to pour out his wrath on his people was precisely because of their (prophesied) idolatry (see vv. 15–18). Thus, verse 39 summarizes what has been emphasized elsewhere in the Torah: Apostasy would bring about divine—and hence, by either magical, human, or idolatrous means—irreversible curses of sickness, disaster, and death; repentance, however, would secure healing and life, all from one and the same source.

F. Lindström, however, understands Deuteronomy 32:39 differently, rendering with, "I can put to death and I can restore to life; indeed, by breaking into pieces I can heal."[126] Although he admits "that the interpretation suggested here is supported by assumptions which are uncertain and difficult to verify," on the other hand, he affirms "as strenuously as I am able that there is no reason to suppose that Deut 32:39 may be taken to support a conjectural notion of divine pancausality with respect to national disaster in ancient Israel."[127] Thus, "both the imperfect *'āmît*, 'I can put to death,' and the perfect *māḥaṣtî,* 'by breaking into pieces,' imply that it is Israel's enemies who are affected by the divine action in question."[128] Indeed, this is the theme of his entire suggestive monograph, and his treatment of 1 Samuel 2:6–7 is, not surprisingly, similar to that of Deuteronomy 32:39: "It appears that the terminology employed in v. 6f. suggests that the divine activity there described is of antithetical nature, that is, has different objects. The action alluded to is a matter of defeating arrogant enemies who are oppressing someone, thus rescuing the victim of their attack."[129] For Lindström, it is important to disassociate Yahweh from evil[130] or the indiscriminate bringing of disaster on Israel.[131] However, he has taken his argument too far.

Lindström is correct in leaving open the question of the origin of evil according to the OT (i.e., it is not clearly attributed to the Lord in the Hebrew Scriptures), and he is certainly right in distancing Yahweh himself from being equated with a demonic being or personage of any kind. However, he fails to take several things adequately into account: (1) that God's judgments are righteous whether they fall on Israel's (unrighteous) enemies or on unrighteous Israel itself (in other words, he indiscriminately judges *no one*);[132] (2) that all punishments inflicted on disobedient Israel are ultimately designed to bring them back in repentance (cf., e.g., Lev 26:14–45; 2Ch 33:10–13; Hos 5:14–15); and (3) that God's judgment on the wicked is a saving act. Thus the psalmist exhorts, "Shout for joy to the LORD, all the earth, burst into jubilant music. . . . Let them sing before the LORD, for he comes to judge the earth. He will judge the world in righteousness and the peoples with equity" (Ps 98:4, 9). There is, then, no tension regarding Yahweh's goodness in Deuteronomy 32:39, and the novel translation suggested above is neither necessary nor compelling. Rather, according to this verse, the all-powerful Lord of life and death graphically taught his chosen people the lesson that although sin had tragic and painful consequences, he would fully restore.

Looking back from its present context, Deuteronomy 32:39 stands at the end of an already disastrous history of divine wounding and/or putting to death. The Lord "inflicted serious diseases on Pharaoh and his household because of Sarai" (Ge 12:17); the angels struck the aggressive homosexual mob at Sodom with blindness (*sanwērîm*)[133] as they tried to break down Lot's door (19:11); the Lord "closed up every womb in Abimelech's household because of Abraham's wife Sarah" (20:18); he put Er and Onan to death because of their wickedness (38:7–10); he smote Egypt with ten destructive and deadly plagues because of the pharaoh's refusal to release Yahweh's people (Ex 7–12; cf. the memory of this in 1Sa 4:8; 6:1–6); he struck Israel "with a plague because of what they did with the calf Aaron had made" (Ex 32:35); he consumed Nadab and Abihu with fire because of their presumption (Lev 10:1–2; Nu 3:4); he consumed the complaining Israelites with fire (Nu 11:1–3); he struck with "a severe plague" the people "who had craved other food" (11:33–34); he inflicted Miriam with *ṣāraʿat* because of her criticism of Moses (12:1–2, 9–14; Dt 24:9); he struck down the ten spies "who made the whole community grumble against him by spreading the bad report about the land" (Nu 14:36–37); he swallowed up Korah and his men with an earthquake because of their insurrection (16:31–33), consuming Korah's 250 associates with fire (16:35; 26:10) and then sending a plague on the whole community for siding with the slain rebels—through which an additional 14,700 died (16:46–49); he sent venomous, deadly snakes[134] among the people because "they spoke against God and against Moses"—"they bit the people and many Israelites died" (Nu 21:5–6; cf. Dt 8:15 and the threat in 32:24); he struck them with a plague because of their immorality and idolatry at Peor, and 24,000 died (Nu 25: 8–9, 18; 31:16; Dt 4:3).[135] See also Exodus 32:9–14; Numbers 14:11–23; 16:21–24 (cf. Dt 9:19; 10:10),[136] where only Moses' intercession stopped the Lord from wiping out the entire nation.[137] Note also that in Numbers 16:42–50 it is only the intercession of Moses coupled with the priestly ministry of Aaron that stopped the plague (see also 25:6–9, where the zealous act of Phinehas causes the plague to end).[138]

The descriptions of God's displeasure in some of these just-cited contexts is informative. Note the following expressions: the Lord's "anger burned" (Nu 11:33; 12:9; 25:3); "wrath has come out from the LORD" (16:46); "the LORD's fierce anger" (25:4; cf. also Dt 9:22 [referring to Nu 11:34]; 31:17; 32:19–22). Numbers 25:4–10 is especially noteworthy, since it stresses the Lord's anger and merely reports the fact of the plague, not even noting that he sent it![139] (Cf. also the unusual wording in Nu 31:16 [*watᵉhî maggēpâ bāʿădat yhwh*], not fully reflected in NIV's "so that a plague struck the LORD's people," where the verb "struck" is supplied.)

The results, then, of breaking faith with the Lord were catastrophic. What were the benefits of covenant obedience and/or repentance? That is, whom did God make alive and/or heal in the first five books? Reference has already been made to the good, long lives lived by Abraham and Moses (2.2.3), to the blessing of fertility on Abraham's seed (2.2.4, including the opening of the wombs of Sarah, Rebekah, and Rachel in answer to prayer), and to the cessation and/or removal of national plagues because of the intercession of Moses and others. There are, however, several other specific instances of divine healing recorded in the Pentateuch, although, compared to the number of cases of divine smiting, they are relatively few. This, however, does not reflect the essential nature of God; rather, it reflects the essential sinful nature of humanity. The chosen people (let alone humanity as a whole; cf. the *locus classicus* in the Torah, Ge 8:21)[140] have for the most part been disobedient, primarily incurring the judgment rather than the blessing of God,[141] as warned prophetically by Moses in Deuteronomy 31:29: "For I know that after my death you are sure to become utterly corrupt and to turn from the way I have commanded you. In days to come, disaster will fall upon you because you will do evil in the sight of the LORD and provoke him to anger by what your hands have made." This also sets the stage for the rest of OT historiography, where the pattern is the same (cf. Isa 30:8–9; Eze 2:3–3:7). Although the Lord longs to bless/keep healthy/heal his people (cf. Dt 5:29; Isa 48:18–19; Eze 18:23, 32; Mt 23:37),[142] their persistent sin and rebellion causes him instead to curse.[143] The promised national outpouring of divine healing anticipated by the prophets would have to await the coming of the Messiah (see below, 4.2.2, 5.1.1).

However, an important observation can be made by comparing the instances of healing recorded in the Pentateuch with those recorded in the historical books: Whereas in the former, all healings listed (with the exception of the opening of the wombs of Sarah, Rebekah, and Rachel) are specific reversals of the effects of divine judgment, in the latter there are several instances of divine healing through prophetic intervention *where no reason is given* for the prior condition of sickness or even death (see below, 2.3.2). Thus the contrast is between what may strictly be called "covenantal healing" (supernatural health for obedience; supernatural sickness for disobedience; supernatural healing upon repentance) and what may be broadly described as "prophetic healing." This builds on the foundation of covenantal healing but also provides room for sovereign demonstrations of divine grace, paving the way for the inbreaking of eschatological (and, in the sense used here, most decidedly prophetic) healing with the coming of the messianic age as described so vividly in the NT.

In keeping with these remarks, the following Pentateuchal instances of healing should be noted. After Abimelech returned Sarah to Abraham, and in response to the patriarch's prayer (cf. Ge 20:7), "God healed Abimelech, his wife and his slave girls so they could have children, for the LORD had closed up every womb in Abimelech's household because of Abraham's wife Sarah" (20:17–18).[144] The plagues on Egypt—the fruit of disobedience (cf. Ex 13:14–15)—were stayed in response to Pharaoh's pleas for mercy, followed by Moses' intercession (8:8–13, 25–31; 9:27–34; 10:16–19).[145] Miriam was healed of *ṣāra'at* after Aaron interceded with Moses, who then interceded with the Lord (Nu 12:9–15).[146] Her condition inflicted suddenly was due to her presumption in speaking against Moses,[147] thereby incurring the Lord's anger (12:1–2, 9).[148]

In Numbers 21, after the people's grumbling brought on them the judgment of serpents with deadly bites,[149] their repentance toward God (expressed again to Moses), coupled with Moses' intercession, the making of the copper[150] snake,[151] and the people's looking at the snake, produced recovery.[152] J. Milgrom discusses this account in the context of homeopathic (or, sympathetic) magic, and Harrison states, "The Lord's response was somewhat homeopathic in nature."[153] It should be noted, however, that since the nature of homeopathic magic presupposes a psychological disposition that is inclined to look to the (former) instrument of smiting as the (present) instrument of healing, the account in Numbers 21 may be explained along psychological lines just as well as along magical lines.[154]

In either case, because the Lord himself initiates the (supernatural) method of treatment for his snake-bitten people (21:8), the process is legitimate and untainted in the eyes of the biblical authors, regardless of its apparent magical parallels.[155] It was only by getting right with the One who smote them that the people of Israel could be healed. Indeed, he alone could be their Healer.

2.2.6. Infectious "Scale Diseases" and Sin in the Torah and Historical Books

Although the lengthy section on *ṣāra'at*[156] and its purification in Leviticus 13–14 does not overtly associate this condition with sin,[157] it is frequently associated with sin in the rest of the OT[158] and is thus often interpreted as a divine judgment.[159] Moreover, while the etymology of *ṣāra'at* is still disputed (see the works cited in n. 156), the phrase *nega' ṣāra'at* (cf. also *nega'* [*ṣāra'at*] *babbayit*) strongly suggests a punitive "touch" from God.[160] Those smitten with *ṣāra'at* as a divine punishment in the OT are Miriam (Nu 12:10–15; Dt 24:8–9), Gehazi and his descendants (2Ki 5:27), and Uzziah (2Ki 15:5; 2Ch 26:16–21), while David's imprecation over Joab's house includes this condition (2Sa 3:29).[161] Aaron's description of "leprous" Miriam (Nu 12:12; cf. Job 18:13) is instructive: "Do not let her be like a stillborn infant coming from its mother's womb with its flesh half eaten away,"[162] and G. J. Wenham accordingly notes, "These symptoms are clearly abnormal, and by disfiguring the appearance of man and his works, destroy the wholeness that ought to characterize the creation. For this reason these conditions are pronounced unclean."[163] Furthermore, in its contagious and contaminating aspects, these conditions served as the epitome of a state that was "not whole."[164] Thus, "the person with such an infectious disease must wear torn clothes, let his hair be unkempt [or, must uncover his head], cover the lower part of his face and cry out, 'Unclean! Unclean!' As long as he has the infection he remains unclean. He must live alone; he must live outside the camp" (Lev 13:45–46; cf. also 2Ki 7:3).[165]

In light of the foregoing and in the context of this present study, it is not inappropriate to ask why, in a covenantal system vouchsafing health and healing to the obedient, there is such detailed legislation regarding a physical condition that is clearly associated with sin. Indeed, the Lord had promised to remove *all* sickness from his faithful people (Ex 15:26; 23:25–26; Dt 7:14–15, discussed in detail above).[166] If there was any one condition that, ideally speaking, would be entirely out of place in this blessedly separate nation, it would be *ṣāra'at*.[167]

It does seem clear from the Torah legislation, however, that there would be blind, deaf, and lame Israelites (cf. Lev 19:14; 21:18),[168] even apart from specific acts of judgment (cf. Lev 26:16; Dt 28:28–29). Apparently, these conditions would have to await the eschatological outpouring of healing grace (cf. Isa 35:5–6 with Mt 11:4–5; Lk 7:21–22, discussed below, 4.2.2, 5.2.1, 5.2.2). Interestingly, there are no examples in the OT of a single blind, deaf, mute, or lame person being miraculously restored,[169] in spite of the sweeping promises of divine healing. Nonetheless, theoretically speaking, it might well be expected that, were the Israelites to keep God's covenant, there would be none among them smitten with *ṣāra'at*![170]

I would suggest, therefore, the possibility that the legislation regarding *ṣāra'at* and its purification serves as a pragmatic testimony to the expected sinfulness of the people. In other words, in its biblical context, the laws of Leviticus 13–14 are given in the same general time frame as the aforementioned covenantal agreements regarding the Lord as Israel's Healer; yet these promises of health *conditioned on obedience* are soon followed by detailed laws regarding the very disease *most associated with disobedience* in the OT. Comparable to this would be Deuteronomy 15, where, ideally speaking, the Lord's blessing on his loyal people in Canaan would bring about a situation in which "there should be no poor among you" (v. 4a). Yet verse 7 begins, "If there is a poor man among you," and verse 11a categorically states, "There will always be poor people in the land." The ideal would never be realized![171] It is true that in the case of Leviticus 13–14, the very nature of *ṣāra'at* logically called for lengthy priestly discussion (especially in light of the immediate context, chs. 11–16, and in particular, chs. 12 and 15); nonetheless, the wider issues of *ṣāra'at* and the theology of divine healing should not be ignored. The OT community of Israel would never be free of the effects of sin, in body as well as in spirit.

It is also noteworthy that no treatment for *ṣāra'at* in humans is prescribed.[172] As is universally recognized, the priests stand merely as observers.[173] Moreover, there is no direct reference to the Lord's healing activity. However, the usage of *rp'* in Leviticus 13–14 calls for comment, since it uniquely ties together both conditions treated here (i.e., *ṣāra'at* in humans and *ṣāra'at* in fabrics and houses). Both conditions render impure, both are subject to priestly inspection and purgation, and upon remission, both are pronounced *nirpā'*. How is this fixed expression to be understood?[174] Some modern translations and commentaries reflect bifurcating, Western canons of logic, dividing Leviticus 13–14 into two sections (as, e.g., the NIV's "infectious skin diseases" and "mildew"), whereas it would be more accurate from a biblical viewpoint to group both sections together under the title "Unclean Diseases."[175] Both the *nega'-haṣṣāra'at* and the *nega' babbayit* are infectious and contaminating plagues that need "healing." G. J. Wenham, however, translates 13:18 and 14:3 with "heal," 13:37 with "cure," and 14:48 with "recover,"[176] while the NIV has "heal" in 13:18, 37; 14:3, yet renders 14:48 (*kî nirpā' hannega'*) with "because the mildew is gone." On the other hand, Milgrom and the NJV render all four occurrences of *nirpā'* with the appropriate form of "heal."[177] Is it correct, however, to render *nirpā'* with "healed" with reference to mildew in the house?

There is no doubt that both the linguistic usage and biblical mentality reflected in these chapters call for consistency of translation; thus *nirpā'* should be rendered uniformly (as should the terms *nega'* and *ṣāra'at*). Nonetheless, one must not lose sight of the fact that Hebrew *rp'* does not simply mean "heal," but rather, "restore, make whole";[178] consequently, the usage of this root with regard to the remission of an infectious plague in the house is not at all forced.[179] Of course, it is true that the uniform usage of *nirpā'* in Leviticus 13–14 is partially due to the analogous categorizations of the forms and treatments of *ṣāra'at.*[180] Yet it should also be remembered that while English "heal" is fine in 13:18, 37; 14:3, but basically inappropriate in 14:48, Hebrew *rp'* is perfectly suitable in all four verses.[181] Moreover, in addition to the simple concept of "healing" (in the strict physical sense of the word), the usage of *rp'* here may also suggest a "making whole" in priestly terms of a change from unclean to clean, impure to pure, unacceptable to acceptable.[182] The restoration process for an infected house is instructive as well, since it included replacing the contaminated stones with new stones (*'ᵃbānîm 'ᵃḥerôt*) and then replastering the walls with new clay (*'āpār 'aḥēr*; Lev 14:42).[183] Consequently, the house would be restored to its original, proper condition, just as the once afflicted individual would be restored to his or her original, proper condition. In each case the *nega'* could be pronounced *nirpā'*, meaning "restored, healed, remitted."

The translator should either be consistent in using "heal, healed" or "cure, cured" all four times (although the hyperliteralism in Lev 14:48 is certainly infelicitous), or, preferrably, use "remit, remitted," since the subject in each case is the actual condition, not the affected person/house himself/itself.[184] This problem of consistent and yet accurate translations of *rp'* within a limited context will be discussed again below, with reference to 2 Kings 2:21–22 (2.3.4) and Ezekiel 47:7–12 (4.2.2).[185]

2.2.7. Exodus 4:10–12

There is one last passage in the Pentateuch that calls for special treatment, viz., the Lord's response to Moses in Exodus 4:11–12. Although it is impossible to describe precisely the speech problem of Moses,[186] the divine reply is clear: The Lord, as the one who gives man his mouth or makes him deaf or mute, seeing or blind, is more than able to help his reluctant servant speak, even pledging to teach him what to say. In fact, the promise is so decisive that Moses, completely out of excuses, simply *declines* to go.[187] Two aspects of these verses deserve comment.

(1) The listing of "seeing" (*piqqēaḥ*) alongside the otherwise totally negative grouping of deaf, mute, and blind caused Ibn Ezra to couple *śām peh* ("make [one's] mouth") with *'illēm* ("dumb"); this is exegetically acceptable, but then contrasting *piqqēaḥ* with both *ḥērēš* and *'iwwēr* ("deaf and blind") is forced.[188] Recently, S. T. Lachs sought to buttress an earlier emendation of H. Graetz (viz., reading *pissēaḥ*, "lame," for *piqqēaḥ*), appealing to (a) the common joining of *pissēaḥ* and *'iwwēr* ("the lame and the blind") as a parallel pair elsewhere in the OT (cf. below, 4.2.2 and n. 163); and (b) a well-known midrashic interpretation of this verse that applied Exodus 4:11 to the smiting of Pharaoh's imperial guard, some of whom became mute, others deaf, others blind, and others lame.[189] From this Lachs concludes that "the text before the author of the midrash read *pissēaḥ*, not *piqqēaḥ*," arguing that this answers the question that baffled commentators to the midrash—viz., how can the reference to the lame be derived from the quotation of Exodus 4:11, upon which this midrash is based? The emendation of Graetz and Lachs, however, is open to several major objections, since it is without Hebrew textual support of any kind, it is not reflected in any of the ancient versions, and even the midrashic evidence—not to mention its lateness—is slender.[190]

(2) More importantly, the emphasis in these verses is on God's "positive" power. He not only appointed[191] the deaf, mute, and blind, but he appointed man's mouth (that is, "speaking" in contrast with "mute") and makes the seeing as well as the blind. Thus, he who formed Moses *as he was*—slow of speech—could make him *as he needed to be*—the mouthpiece of God: "Now go, I will help you speak and will teach you what to say" (Ex 4:12). With regard to the question of *why* some are made deaf or mute, seeing or blind, Exodus 4:10–12 is silent. There is no thought of either personal or historic sin, nor is a "satan" even countenanced. Rather, in the spirit of Psalm 94:9, the Lord is claiming ultimate responsibility for the life of every human being, both the whole and the disabled. Issues such as retribution, curses, demons and disease, etc., are clearly beyond the purview of this section, nor should theological conclusions regarding these matters be drawn from these verses. Rather, the emphasis is again on Yahweh's all-sufficiency: He who made everyone certainly has the power to effectively use anyone.[192]

2.3. DIVINE SMITING AND HEALING IN THE HISTORICAL BOOKS

The historical books provide further testimony to the basic perspective outlined in the Torah. Long, healthy life is presupposed as the ideal, favorable condition (cf. Jdg 2:8; 8:32; 2Ch 24:15),[193] although even for those who live good, long lives, weakness and deterioration often set in with old age (see below). Outside of this expected wearing out with age, however, sickness is viewed as a negative, "unblessed" state, while sudden disease and premature death are frequently described as divine judgments. The motif of Yahweh graciously opening wombs occurs again (cf. Jdg 13; 1Sa 1–2; see also Ruth 4:13), underscoring the blessing of fertility (e.g., 2Ki 4:8–17). And divine smiting and healing are seen as proof of Yahweh's sovereignty: "The LORD brings death and makes alive;[194] he brings down to the grave and raises up" (1Sa 2:6; see the discussion of 1Sa 6, below). Note also 2 Kings 6:18–20, where the Lord blinds and then heals the Aramean army at the request of Elisha.

According to the historical authors, David "died at a good old age, having enjoyed long life" (1Ch 29:28a, *wayāmāt bᵉśêbâ ṭôbâ śᵉbaʿ yāmîm*), and God promised Solomon, "If you walk in my ways and obey my statutes and commands as David your father did, I will give you a long life" (1Ki 3:14).[195] But the house of Eli was tragically cursed: "The time is coming when I will cut short your strength and the strength of your father's house, so that there will not be an old man in your family line.... and all your descendants will die in the prime of life" (1Sa 2:31–33).[196] Nonetheless, old age itself was not without its problems: David "could not keep warm even when they put covers on him" (1Ki 1:1); the aged Eli went blind ("his eyes were becoming so weak that he could barely see" [1Sa 3:2; see also 4:15]); Barzillai the Gileadite, "a very old man" at eighty (2Sa 19:32), had virtually lost his senses of smell, taste, and hearing (19:35);[197] and the prophet Ahijah "could not see; his sight was gone because of his age" (1Ki 14:4b).[198]

Thus, human life, however blessed, has its limits. Accordingly, David described his imminent death in these words: "I am about to go the way of all the earth" (1Ki 2:2a; cf. 2Sa 14:14a); and without any apparent censure intended,[199] Elisha, whose very bones vivified the corpse of an Israelite man hastily thrown into his grave (2Ki 13:20–21),[200] is described as "suffering from the illness from which he died" (13:14), although he is still mightily used by God (13:14–19; note also that Ahijah in his blindness still had prophetic vision; see 1Ki 14:5–6).[201]

2.3.1. Sickness as a Curse/Judgment Act in the Historical Books

Much more common than the pattern of long life, aging, and death is the frequently occurring theme of God inflicting the disobedient with sickness and plague. These are curses, not blessings—tokens of judgment, not of favor. In fact, with only one *apparent* exception (the death of Abijah, son of Jeroboam, discussed below), disease, plague, and premature death are never viewed favorably. The cumulative testimony is indisputable, demonstrating again that sickness and (premature) death are viewed as tools of divine judgment. Disobedient or idolatrous leaders are regularly struck down, either by a human being (i.e., assassinated or killed in battle) or by God, as detailed below[202] (note also Ex 5:3, where Moses and Aaron inform Pharaoh that if they are not allowed to go and worship the Lord, "he may strike us with plagues or with the sword"; cf. below, 4.1, n. 6.).

God afflicted the Philistines with (malignant) tumors[203] because they seized the ark (1Sa 5:6–12; cf. v. 11b, "For death had filled the city with panic; God's hand was very heavy upon it"); he then struck down seventy[204] of the men of Beth Shemesh for looking into it (6:19–20). In answer to the prayers of Isaiah and Hezekiah (2Ch 32:20), "the angel of the LORD went out and put to death a hundred and eighty-five thousand men in the Assyrian camp" (2Ki 18:35; 2Ch 32:21; Isa 37:36), demonstrating clearly that Yahweh was the all-powerful God and that he would not be mocked (e.g., 2Ch 32:13–15; Isa 37:21–35).[205]

Within his own nation, he also displayed his destructive might against those who sinned. "The LORD's anger burned against Uzzah" for touching the ark, and so "God struck him down and he died there beside the ark of God" (2Sa 6:7; 1Ch 13:9–11). Uzziah the king was smitten with "leprosy" for pridefully encroaching on priestly duties (2Ki 15:5; 2Ch 26:16–

21).[206] The Lord fatally struck Nabal because of his insolence (1Sa 25:1–38), and he afflicted the child born of the adulterous union of David and Bathsheba, causing the infant's sickness and death, despite the king's pleas (2Sa 12:13–18; cf. also v. 22). Although David's confession of sin resulted in Yahweh's sparing his own life, the very wording of the pardon presupposes that sin inevitably leads to death: "The LORD has taken away your *sin*. You are not going to *die*. But . . . the son born to you will *die*" (12:13–14). In a similar vein, the terrified Israelites asked Samuel to "pray to the LORD your God for your servants so that we will not *die*, for we have added to all our other *sins* the evil of asking for a king" (1Sa 12:19).

David's curse of Joab's house included the wish that his descendants would "never be without someone who has a running sore or leprosy or who leans on a crutch or who falls by the sword or who lacks food" (2Sa 3:29),[207] and Gehazi and his descendants were smitten with "leprosy" because of his duplicity (2Ki 5:19b–27). Jeroboam's hand withered when he ordered the unnamed prophet to be seized (1Ki 13:4),[208] and in the end "the LORD struck [Jeroboam] down and he died" (2Ch 13:20). Elijah informed King Ahaziah that he would die because, after his injury, he consulted Baal Zebub rather then Yahweh (2Ki 1:1–17),[209] and "the LORD afflicted Jehoram with an incurable disease in his bowels" because of his idolatry (2Ch 21:18–19). The fact that his disease was "incurable" (*le'ên marpe'*)—as well as terribly painful and ultimately fatal—is in keeping with the nature of the threatened divine curses as emphasized several times above (esp. 2.2); the same phrase aptly serves as a metaphor of Judah's irreversible condition in 2 Chronicles 36:16: "But they mocked God's messengers, despised his words and scoffed at his prophets until the wrath of the LORD was aroused against his people and there was no remedy [*'ad le'ên marpe'*]." Such is the fate of a nation that continually spurns God's grace and refuses to heed his merciful warnings (cf. 36:15); its condition becomes irremediable.[210]

The narrative recorded in 2 Samuel 24 and 1 Chronicles 21 is especially instructive in terms of the judgment nature of pestilence and plague. David's foolish order to take a census,[211] attributed to God's anger in Samuel and the provocation of Satan in Chronicles,[212] leads to a further outpouring of divine wrath. The choices given to David are enlightening, in particular in the Chronicler's account:[213] "This is what the LORD says: 'Take your choice: three years of famine, three months of being swept away before your enemies ... three days of the sword of the LORD—days of plague in the land, with the angel of the LORD ravaging every part of Israel.'" (1Ch 21:11–12; cf. 2Sa 24:13). The three dire options—famine, defeat in war, or plague—each speak clearly of divine wrath and cursing (cf. above, 2.2.2).[214] Of the three choices offered to David, however, a devastating plague more directly implied the involvement of the Lord himself—note the emphasis on the "sword of the LORD"; hence the king chose to "fall into the hands of the LORD, for his mercy is great," rather than into the hands of men (2Ch 21:13; cf. 2Sa 24:14). The account is vivid: "So the LORD sent a plague. ... And God sent an angel to destroy Jerusalem. ... David looked up and saw the angel of the LORD standing between heaven and earth, with a drawn sword in his hand extended over Jerusalem" (2Ch 21:14–16).[215] In keeping, however, with the king's hope for divine mercy, after the plague had killed 70,000 people, God's grief caused him to order the destroying angel to cease, and "the LORD spoke to the angel and he put his sword back into its sheath" (2Sa 24:15–16; 2Ch 21:27).[216] Prayer and sacrifice finally stayed the judgment (2Sa 24:17–25; 2Ch 21:27–30).

Once again, certain basic conclusions are inescapable. Pestilence was viewed just as negatively as was famine, locust invasion (cf. 1Ki 8:37–40), or defeat in war. Disease and premature death were curses that one might wish upon one's enemies, not blessings to be desired for one's friends.[217] Furthermore, sickness incurred by divine wrath could only be cured by repentance, thereby reversing both God's anger and the condition that ensued. There was no "cure" or "remedy" (*marpē'*) for those who rejected the Healer. Even a "pagan" nation like the Philistines learned that the only remedy for their hemorrhoids/buboes[218] was to appease the God of Israel whose ark they had violated. In the words of their priests (1Sa 6:3b): "Then you will be healed [*'āz tērāpᵉ 'û*] and you will know why his hand has not been lifted from you."[219] Healing was for the repentant, the obedient, and the contrite, whereas *most* sickness that draws comment in the historical books (outside of that pertaining to old age and then death) is attributed directly to sin or judgment.[220]

The case of Abijah son of Jeroboam is not a true exception. The king's wife, wearing a disguise, came to ask the prophet Ahijah what would happen to their sick son. The prophet's reply was devastating: God was going to cut off every male from the house of Jeroboam, burning up his house as one burns dung. "Dogs will eat those belonging to Jeroboam who die in the city, and the birds of the air will feed on those who die in the country" (2Ki 14:10–11). For the ancient Israelite, almost no fate could be worse.[221] However, because Abijah was the only one in Jeroboam's family in whom the Lord found anything good, he would die of his illness: "All Israel will mourn for him and bury him. He is the only one belonging to Jeroboam who will be buried" (14:12–13). Thus, it was an act of mercy on God's part to allow (the apparently young) Abijah to die of sickness and be buried, sparing him the terrible fate of violent death and exposure that awaited his brothers. In fact, this is the clearest biblical example of Isaiah 57:1: "The righteous perish, and no one ponders it in his heart; devout men are taken away, and no one understands that the righteous are taken away to be spared from evil." Their premature (and relatively easy?) death is only to spare them from a far worse fate coming on the wicked, the horror of which is underscored by the fact that being "taken away" was to be preferred to this coming evil.[222]

Nonetheless, neither sickness nor death were viewed positively in and of themselves, by humans (for quite obvious reasons!) or by the Lord.[223] Rather, in certain rare cases, God might take his righteous ones out of the way before terrible devastating judgment arrived in the land. In a real sense, it was a matter of the lesser of two evils. The death of the godly King Josiah in a battle that immediately preceded Judah's brutal subjugation by the Babylonians might fit in this category as well: "I will gather you to your fathers, and you will be buried in peace. Your eyes will not see all the disaster I am going to bring on this place" (2Ki 22:20, with vv. 1–19; 2Ch 34:1–28). To die at the hands of Egyptian archers (2Ki 23:29–30; 2Ch 35:20–25)—Josiah was not yet forty—was no better than to die of sickness at that early age. But, just as Abijah's death by sickness was much to be preferred to the horrible fate that would soon befall his kin, so Josiah's death in battle was much to be preferred to suffering "the heat of [the LORD's] fierce anger, which burned against Judah because of all that Manasseh had done to provoke him to anger" (2Ki 23:26).[224]

2.3.2. Prophetic Healing in the Historical Books

There are four principal accounts of miracles of physical healing involving the prophets, viz., the raising of the widow's son in Zarephath (involving Elijah, 1Ki 17:17–24), the raising of the Shunammite's son (involving Elisha, 2Ki 4:8–36), the healing of Naaman the Aramean (involving Elisha, 2Ki 5), and the healing of Hezekiah (involving Isaiah, 2Ki 20:1–11; 2Ch 32:24–26; Isa 38:1–8).[225] It was mentioned previously that these miracles of healing and resuscitation are unique in the OT, since they do not contain the motif of the Lord first smiting a person because of disobedience and then healing because of repentance.[226] Thus, sickness is not described as the specific result of sin or as an act of judgment—although those concepts are not always far from the minds of the afflicted ones!—and restoration and resurrection come as the result of prophetic intercession and/or tearful, desperate prayer. The healings are gracious acts of God, revealing his power to make whole and demonstrating his willingness to intervene in human affairs in answer to prophetic supplication and faith.

2.3.2.1. The Raising of the Widow's Son

After the son of the widow at Zarephath succumbed to a fatal illness, the bereaved woman confronted Elijah: "What do you have against me, man of God? Did you come to remind me of my sin and kill my son?" (1Ki 17:17–18). The prophet's prayer assumes the direct involvement of God (v. 20: "O LORD my God, why have you brought tragedy also upon this widow I am staying with, by causing her son to die?") but contains no word of repentance or even a plea for mercy. Rather, Elijah engages in a simple act of intercession that bespeaks his intimacy and special standing with God.[227] Strangely, S. J. DeVries claims that the grief-stricken mother's "theology of divine judgment is so erroneous that Elijah must act to refute it. Yahweh, the God of Israel, has established no cause and effect relationship between a person's sin and the calamities of life (contra Job's friends!)."[228] The numerous OT examples already cited throughout this chapter, however, provide ample evidence that there often is, in fact, a divinely established "cause and effect relationship between a person's sin and the calamities of life."[229] Moreover, in order to support his thesis, DeVries must argue that verse 20 is "a secondary addition" containing "three mistakes," the last of which is "allowing Elijah to voice the woman's bad theology to the effect that Yahweh might actually kill little boys"![230] As for Job's friends, it may safely be stated that their basic "theological outlook" of retribution and reward reflected mainstream OT patterns; what was in error was their unbending and impersonal application of their orthodox views to Job, a man whose seemingly inexplicable sufferings defied the generally expected norm.[231] The reactions of both the mother and Elijah, as recorded in verses 17–20, were normal, and it is possible that verse 18 may reflect a somewhat standard, proverbial response to personal calamity. For the prophet, however, Yahweh, the God of Israel, could not allow the son of this faithful woman (cf. vv. 7–16) to die. As the Lord's servant and representative (cf. vv. 12, 14, 24), therefore, he appealed to his God to "let this boy's life [*nepeš*] return to him" (v. 21)—regardless of whether or not sin was the cause of the boy's death. "The LORD heard Elijah's cry, the boy's life returned to him, and he lived" (v. 22).

2.3.2.2. The Raising of the Shunammite Woman's Son

The raising of the Shunammite's son by Elisha contains similar elements. (1) In both cases, there is the tacit understanding that it is not right that the boys have died.[232] In 1 Kings 17, it is because the non-Israelite widow treated Elijah with kindness, receiving miraculous provision from the hand of Yahweh, the God of Israel. In 2 Kings 4, it is because the son himself was a special blessing bestowed in appreciation for the hospitality shown to Elisha (4:8–17); in a real sense, he was already a child of promise. (2) In seeking to resuscitate the widow's son, Elijah prayed and then stretched himself over the lad three times.[233] In the case involving Elisha, when Gehazi's intervention—in accordance with the prophet's instructions—failed to revive the boy, Elisha prayed and then "got on the bed and lay upon the boy, mouth to mouth, eyes to eyes, hands to hands. As he stretched himself out upon him,[234] the boy's body grew warm" (4:34).[235] (3) Quite naturally, in both cases the mothers were awestruck by the prophet's power and/or relationship with the Lord (1Ki 17:24; 2Ki 4:37).

In the case of the Shunammite, however, there is no mention of sin or the (smiting) hand of God. Only the mother's "bitter distress" (2Ki 4:27) and dashed hopes (v. 28) are spoken of, and Elisha's prayer is not recorded. It is interesting to note, however, just how dependent the mother was upon the prophet, choosing not to tell either her husband or Gehazi what was wrong and refusing to leave the prophet's side, her speech echoing Elisha's oath to Elijah.[236] After all, it was at Elisha's initiative that she had been promised a son, despite her unbelieving protestations (v. 16b: "'No my lord,' she objected. 'Don't mislead your servant, O man of God'"); and it was to this fact she referred in her indirect disclosure to Elisha of her son's death (v. 28—"'Did I ask you for a son, my lord?' she said. 'Didn't I tell you, "Don't raise my hopes"?'"). Thus, the woman appeals primarily to the man of God instead of to God himself. (In any case, while she might well have prayed for the boy's healing, it would be highly unlikely that she herself would have presumed to pray for his *resuscitation*.) Elisha, reflecting both the goodness as well as the power of Yahweh, was able to raise him from the dead, a fact of no small note (cf. 8:4–5).

2.3.2.3. The Healing of Naaman

A careful reading of the narrative in 2 Kings 2–5 indicates that Elisha had already been used by the Lord to make undrinkable and death-producing waters wholesome (2:21–22; see below, 2.3.4), to raise the boy from the dead, and to cause poisonous stew to lose its harmful effects (4:38–41), all before a young Israelite girl taken captive by the Arameans commented to her mistress, the wife of the "leprous" general Naaman, "If only my master would see the prophet who is in Samaria! He would cure him of his leprosy" (5:3). By this time he had gained quite a reputation (and note well the wording: "*He* [i.e., Elisha!] would cure him of his leprosy"); in many ways, the healing of Naaman is the pinnacle of the miracle ministry of Elisha.

It has been claimed that Naaman's specific skin disease (belonging to the general category of *ṣara'at*)[237] may not have been particularly severe, since he had direct access to the palace and close relations with the king.[238] Nonetheless, his condition was serious enough to be a blemish on his great reputation (2Ki 5:1) and worthy of the Israelite maiden's fervent wish that it might be cured.[239] Furthermore, it seems clear from verses 2–3 that no earthly remedy would avail, and it is implied that no foreign deity could help. Rather, only the God of Israel could reverse Naaman's condition, and he could be supplicated through his emissary Elisha. Thus, upon his visit to Israel, the general expected the prophet "to come out to me and stand and call on the name of the LORD his God, wave his hand over the spot and cure me of my leprosy" (v. 11b). Significantly, there was to be a different plan, one that brought about the same end result while also producing greater humility, probably aiding in his conversion.

Several particulars of the narrative call for comment. (1) We are informed that the Lord had already been involved in the Aramean general's life: "He was a great man in the sight of his master [i.e., the king of Aram] and highly regarded, because through him the LORD had given victory to Aram" (2Ki 5:1a). Thus, unknown to Naaman, God's hand was already on him. (2) The king of Israel, presented with the request to cure Naaman, took it as a provocation from a hostile king, knowing that only God could "kill and bring back to life" (v. 7).[240] (3) No mention is made of personal sin or repentance. Rather, only simple (and for Naaman, humbling!) obedience was required. (4) As in the legislation dealing with the remission of *ṣāra'at* in Leviticus 13–14, the verb *ṭihēr,* "to cleanse, purify," is used (cf. vv. 10, 14); the removal of the grievous skin disease also speaks of ritual purification (cf. also Mt 8:2–4 and par.). (5) The required act of obedience for cleansing consisted in dipping seven times in the Jordan, a point of interest because of the actual physical "cleansing" involved and because of the possible hint of ritual immersion implicit in the dipping.[241] (6) Naaman's healing results in his conversion.[242] It was an Israelite captive who informed him of the Israelite prophet, and it was at the prophet's direction that he was cleansed.[243] For Naaman there could be no doubt: "Now I know that there is no God in all the world except in Israel" (v. 15b). He had become a professing monotheist! Thus, as with the raising of the widow's son in 1 Kings 17, this healing serves also as a forerunner of the gospel, both in terms of the universal availability of healing grace and in terms of a specific healing act functioning as a proclamation of the greatness of Yahweh to the nations (cf. below, 5.2.6).

2.3.2.4. The Healing of Hezekiah

Hezekiah's sickness and healing are recorded in 2 Kings 20:1–11 and Isaiah 38:1–8, and (briefly) in 2 Chronicles 32:24–26.[244] He was sick "to the point of death" when Isaiah gave him the divine word: "This is what the LORD says: Put your house in order, because you will die; you will not recover" (2Ki 20:1).[245] To that point in the biblical record, the king had been an exemplary leader, and so the fact that he appealed to his former godly conduct is no surprise: "Hezekiah turned his face to the wall and prayed to the LORD, 'Remember, O LORD, how I have walked before you faithfully and with wholehearted devotion and have done what is good in your eyes.'" (vv. 2–3). That Isaiah 38, the psalm celebrating Hezekiah's healing, makes reference to his sins (Isa 38:17c, "you have put all my sins behind your back") is not necessarily contradictory; rather, it was taken for granted that serious illness was somehow related to personal sin (cf. below, 3.1.1, 3.1.5, 3.1.6, 3.1.8, for further discussion in the context of the Psalms).[246] However, in Hezekiah's case, the king could appeal to his prior righteous conduct as Israel's leader. There was a just basis for his petition![247] He had done nothing worthy of death, or, even if he had, there was ample reason to make the appeal that, in this case, mercy should override judgment. Is it also implied that it was probably in God's best interests to let him live?

Hezekiah, his face turned to the wall, "wept bitterly." *He was not yet forty years old.*[248] Moreover, he may not yet have had an heir: Manasseh was not born until three years *after* the healing, and there is no mention of other sons.[249] Thus the reason for his impassioned plea for healing might well have been twofold: He had been a godly king and was now being cut down in the prime of life (cf. the imagery used in Isa 38:10–12); even worse, he had no posterity, and hence no continued life in this world, dynastic or otherwise.[250] In immediate response to the king's prayer, and with clear evidence of the Lord's favor toward the king (cf. 2Ki 20:5, where Hezekiah is referred to as "the leader of my people"; note also the reference to "the God of your father David" in Isa 38:5), the Lord sent Isaiah back with a promise of recovery:

> I have heard your prayer and seen your tears; I will heal you.[251] On the third day you will go up to the temple of the LORD. I will add fifteen years to your life. And I will deliver you and this city from the hand of the king of Assyria. I will defend this city for my sake and for the sake of my servant David." (2Ki 20:5–6)

Thus God's covenant faithfulness to David would be extended to his successor (Hezekiah) and his city (Jerusalem). Also, healing from a terminal condition forms a fitting parallel to deliverance from a more powerful, invading army.[252] The "changing of God's mind" in response to prayer has already been noted in the context of the intercession of Moses, Aaron, and Phineas.[253]

Of special interest in this healing is the use of figs, especially since it comes at the direction of the prophet. No sooner had the divine promise to heal been given than Isaiah said, "'Prepare a poultice of figs.' They did so and applied it to the boil,[254] and he recovered" (2Ki 20:7, placed as a pluperfect at the end of the narrative in Isa 38:21). Of course, there are other examples of specific natural "means" utilized in prophetic miracles—e.g., the tree that sweetened the waters of Marah (note that it was thrown in at God's command, Ex 15:22–25); Elisha's throwing a new bowl with salt into bad water (2Ki 2:21–22; see below, 2.3.4); and his throwing flour into the pot with poisonous stew (4:38–41). Here, however, Hezekiah's healing—clearly miraculous, as indicated by the sundial sign performed by the Lord in earnest of the imminent healing—is facilitated by applying figs, which were commonly used for medicinal purposes.[255] Several interpretations are possible: (1) All of the aforementioned miracles may be explained along the lines of *efficacious magic* (i.e., the belief that the tree, the salt, the flour, or the figs actually had power when used by qualified people);[256] (2) in each case, the physical means used were simply *representative* in their power (i.e., as visible aids to faith in the invisible God, so that salt thrown into salt water was somehow related to the counteracting of the negative saline effects); (3) the use of figs in 2 Kings 20 was, in fact, thought to be medicinal (thus, Isaiah used what means were available, and the Lord worked a miracle).[257]

2.3.3. Second Kings 18:4 and *nᵉḥūštān*

Among his other reforms,[258] Hezekiah "broke into pieces the bronze snake Moses had made, for up to that time the Israelites had been burning incense to it. (It was called Nehushtan.)" (2Ki 18:4). Much discussion has taken place concerning the significance of this particular idol in Judah, because the biblical account of the origin of the bronze (or copper) snake in Numbers 21 specifically connects "Nehushtan" with healing rites, while both ancient and modern iconographic representations frequently associate snake/serpent imagery with fertility and healing.[259] Thus Niehr refers to Nehushtan as one of the healing deities in Israel,[260] while Gray (following Rowley) speculates that "it was a legacy of the pre-Israelite cult of Jerusalem," with Numbers 21:6–9 serving as an etiological myth that either indicates its antiquity or attempts to legitimize its worship.[261] Unfortunately, the text itself says little, and the elaborate theories of Rowley, Gray, and others have virtually no certain biblical support. What does seem clear, however, is that the definite associations of the snake with fertility and healing (through Nu 21 and/or common iconography) made veneration of this object especially attractive. Moreover, as T. R. Hobbs has noted, "Regardless of its early associations with Moses, it is possible that by the time of Hezekiah the symbol had become associated with Canaanite worship (see K. R. Joines, *JBL* 87 [1968]: 245–56),"[262] and thus it was to be treated as a dangerous graven image in competition with Yahweh, the invisible God and the true Healer.

2.3.4. The Root *rāpā'* in 1 Kings 18:30; 2 Kings 2:21–22; 2 Chronicles 7:14; 30:20

Considerable attention was given to the root *rāpā'* in our introductory discussion of the OT language of healing (above, 0.3.1, 0.3.2). While the verses treated here do not relate to physical healing (2Ch 30:20 may be the exception), they are important for the insights that may be gleaned in terms of the semantic range of the root *rāpā'*, and, more importantly, in terms of the varied roles played by the Lord as *rôpē'* (with the exception of 1Ki 18:30).

First Kings 18:30 has nothing to do with divine healing; however, it is important semantically. It is written of Elijah, *wayyᵉrappē' 'et-mizbaḥ yhwh hehārûs*—"and he repaired the altar of the LORD, which was in ruins."[263] Of course, the Piel of *rp'* here cannot possibly be translated with "heal."[264] However, the LXX remarkably renders with *iaomai*;[265] the Koehler-Baumgartner lexicon lists this verse under "*heilen*; to heal" (903); and in W. Holladay's widely used abridgement of KBL, 1 Kings 18:30 is the only verse cited under Piel, "to heal"![266] All this is eloquent testimony to the problems that arise when it is assumed that the basic meaning of Hebrew *rp'* is "to heal."[267] But when the proper *Grundbedeutung* ("root meaning") of "restore, make whole" is recognized, then the specific and individual nuances are more easily recognized: a broken down altar, a sick body (2Ki 20:5), and a ravaged land (2Ch 7:14) all need to be *restored* or *made whole.* Thus, "to repair" is not a meaning to be derived by analogy from the specific nuance of physical healing, nor is the reverse process to be assumed.[268] Both "to repair" and "to heal" are specific applications of one general sense.[269]

In 2 Kings 2:21 the Piel of *rp'* is again used (also with no apparent intensive or causative force), while the the Niphal occurs in 2:22. Here it is related that when Elisha and the prophets were at Jericho, the city's water supply was bad (*hammayim mārîm*), and consequently the land could not produce its crops (*wᵉhā'āreṣ mᵉšakkālet*—here "mother earth" is miscarrying).[270] Having brought some salt to the water in a new bowl, Elisha cast it in and pronounced, "This is what the LORD has said: 'I have made this water wholesome. No longer shall death and unproductivity [lit., "miscarrying"] proceed from it'" (my translation; *rippi'tî lammayim hā'ēlleh lō'-yihᵉyeh miššām 'ôd māwet ûmᵉšakkālet*); verse 22 continues, "And the water has remained wholesome to this very day" (NIV; *wayyērāpû hammayim 'ad hayyôm hazzeh*).[271] When translators persist in using "to heal," it becomes difficult to remain consistent in verses 21–22 (so NIV: "I have healed this water.... And the water has remained wholesome"; similarly NJV; KJV is consistent but incorrect: "I have healed these waters.... So the waters were healed").[272]

Although Gray classifies this section under the heading of "restoring fertility,"[273] the *water* was not unfertile; it merely produced that effect in the land. Hence the water did not need to be "refertilized." Like the undrinkable water of Exodus 15:22–25 and the former salt water of Ezekiel 47:8, which previously could not produce life, this water needed to be made wholesome (there is also the underlying notion that fresh, drinkable waters were pristine and pure; salt waters were thus candidates for "*rᵉpû'â*").[274] As for the salt remedy, it was either used symbolically because of its representative medicinal qualities, or else it was used in a "magical" sense.[275] And note again that it is the Lord, presumably as *rôpē'*, who makes the water wholesome. It was he who had power to restore both the physically and emotionally sick, as well as "sickly" water and land.

The theme of "restoring" the land occurs in 2 Chronicles 7:14, the broader context for which is 2 Chronicles 7:12–22, which relates a dream theophany following Solomon's dedication of the temple. In verses 13–14 the Lord promises that if, because of the people's sin (this is understood by what follows), he closes up the heavens so that there is no rain, and if he sends locusts and plagues against his land and people, then "if my people who are called by my name will humble themselves and pray, and seek my face and turn back from their wicked ways, then I will hear from heaven and forgive their sins and restore [*wᵉ'erpā'*] their land" (from the ravaging effects of drought and locusts; my translation).[276] There is no need here to suggest the underlying imagery of a "mother earth" whose "womb" has been shut.[277] The land was "barren" simply because of the lack of rain, and the only direct reference to the land itself in verse 13 is that of the locusts' devouring of the land (*wᵉhēn 'aṣawweh 'al-ḥāyāb le'ᵉkôl hā'āreṣ*); it is not referred to as inherently fruitless (as if *rp'* here has the nuance of "refertilize, make fertile").[278] Rather, the land is in need of restoration rather than healing. Although the phrase "I will heal their land" (KJV and most modern translations) has become famous in English-speaking religious circles,[279] and although it accurately conveys the Hebrew image of a wounded and sickly land,[280] it stretches the force of the English verb "to heal." Once again, the closest semantic equivalent to *rp'* in English is "to restore," a verb that also answers to the specific problems from which the land was suffering.[281]

Turning now to 2 Chronicles 30:20, the problem is not so much one of translation (although that may come into play), as much as interpretation. What is the exact nature of the "healing" referred to in the words, "And the LORD heard

Hezekiah and healed the people" (*wayyišma' yhwh 'el-ḥizqiyyāhû wayyirpā' 'et -hā'ām*)? Does it mean that the Lord healed the people of their sicknesses (quite tacitly implied by the context?) or that he forgave or reinstated them? According to 30:18–19, in the story of the celebration of Hezekiah's newly reinaugurated Passover Feast, "most of the people ... had not purified themselves, yet they ate the paschal lamb in violation of what was written. Hezekiah prayed for them, saying, 'The good LORD will provide atonement [*yᵉkappēr*; NIV "pardon"] for everyone who set his mind on worshiping God, the LORD God of his fathers, even if he is not purified for the sanctuary'" (NJV). According to Bertheau, as stated by Keil, "first sickness, and then even death, were to be expected as results of transgression of the law, according to Lev XV.31, and ... the people might be already regarded as being sick, or as being on the point of becoming."[282] Now, while this is certainly possible,[283] it is probably assuming far too much for the present context in which ritual/legal impurity itself is the paramount concern (cf. v. 15—*wayyitqaddᵉšû*; v. 16—*kᵉ tôrat mōšeh*; v. 17—*lō'-hitqaddāšû*; v. 18—*bᵉ lō' kakkātûb*). Moreover, there is nothing in Hezekiah's prayer that refers to a need for physical healing, but only for forgiveness (this would have included healing, had it been needed; cf. below, 3.1.3, on Ps 41).[284] However, if Bertheau is right, there is here a striking parallel to 1 Corinthians 11:27–32, wherein many Corinthians had become sick, and some had even died, because they partook of the Lord's Supper (the NT Passover!) in an unworthy fashion, i.e., spiritually or morally impure.[285]

A. B. Ehrlich thought he found the key to understanding 2 Chronicles 30:20 (as well as Ex 15:26; Isa 57:18; Hos 11:3) in his previously cited view: "In Hebrew, any verb may be used to describe not merely its own action, but also the omission or prevention of an opposite action."[286] Thus, as noted above, *'ᵃnî yhwh rōpᵉ'ekā* would mean that the Lord as Israel's *rôpē'* would not allow sickness to come upon his people (*kol-hammaḥᵃlâ 'ᵃšš̌er-śamtî bimisrayim lō'-'āśîm 'ālêkā*). Ehrlich thus translates *wayyirpā' 'et-hā'ām* with "*und verschönte das Volk*," meaning *wᵉlō' hikkâ bā'ām*—"he didn't smite the people."[287] Similarly, Rudolph[288] understands the verse in terms of *heil blieb* ("remain whole"), because the Lord did not allow any of the threatened punishments to come upon Israel. However, both Rudolph and Ehrlich seem to proceed from an overly narrow understanding of *rp'* (i.e., *rp'* must mean "to heal");[289] moreover, it seems quite clear from the words *wayyirpā' 'et-hā'ām* that the Lord is actually seen as doing something to the people, not withholding something from them (contrast however, Ex 15:26, where Ehrlich's view makes somewhat better sense; see above, 2.2.1). Curtis and Madsen,[290] while translating, "And healed the people," note, "i.e., forgave them (cf. Ps. 41:5[4]; Hos 14:3; Jer 3:22). This ceremonial transgression, like other sins, is conceived of as a disease, in the thought of its effects, to be removed by a healing remedy."[291] Yet to list these verses together is to greatly oversimplify, and hence, to cloud the issue (see the relevant discussion of these verses in 3.1.4 and 4.1.2, below). In any case, Curtis does not entirely exclude physical illness either, for he writes, "Physical sickness, or even death, may have been in the mind of the writer."

In my opinion, physical healing cannot be excluded from the context, although I have stated my reservations regarding that interpretation here. Nor would I understand *rp'* primarily in terms of forgiveness, although it is requested in Hezekiah's prayer, and naturally mercy, not punishment, was desired.[292] Rather, the fundamental problem was that this joyous Paschal celebration was being marred and tarnished by the fact that most of the people were ceremonially impure and thus unable to enjoy the full covenant fellowship of their God. Although they ate the lambs, a breech had arisen between the Lord and his people, and they were therefore not "whole." They may also have been under his wrath in some sense, although not necessarily sick. However, by overlooking their impurity and forgiving their sin, the Lord "made them whole," restoring them to acceptable standing in his holy presence. This corresponds to the biblical view that anyone (or anything) sick, impure, in sin, or, in any sense of the word, not "whole" was a candidate for *r^{e}pû'â*. Regarding the above quotes of Curtis and Bertheau, the former's remarks of "ceremonial transgression" more accurately convey this truth, although the limited information given in 2 Chronicles 30 makes it impossible to be dogmatic.

◆ 3 ◆

Israel's Divine Healer in Poetry and Wisdom Literature

3.1 THE BOOK OF PSALMS

3.1.1. Sickness and Healing in the Psalms: Overview[1]

The book of Psalms provides us with a window of insight into the experience of the sufferer.[2] Here we find detailed descriptions of both physical and mental affliction, of bodily ailments as well as spiritual maladies. The psalms remind us again of the intimate connection in the Israelite mind between sin and sickness on the one hand, and divine favor and healing on the other hand, reflecting a worldview in which physical restoration is taken as an indication of spiritual reconciliation.

The psalmist in his sickness speaks of his sense of alienation from God and of his desperation, frustration, and guilt. His healing—either as a historical reality for which he *now* gives thanks, or as a sought-after blessing for which he *will* give thanks—is always perceived as a gift from God, a direct answer to prayer.[3] Thus, the Torah's theology of divine healing is reaffirmed in the psalms of sickness and healing, even to the point of gross caricaturization: Because it was so strongly believed that the blessing of God invariably accompanied the righteous, the afflicted one could be forsaken by his friends and scorned by his adversaries,[4] since his extreme suffering apparently gave evidence of his sin and subsequent abandonment by the Lord.[5]

The comment of H. J. Kraus on Psalm 6 applies in general to much of the material under discussion here:

> For the understanding of the entire psalm the following fact is determinative: the petitioner knows that he stands under the wrath of God. This fact gives the real shape to the suffering and sighing, to the praying and the pleading.... In the physical suffering of which the petitioner speaks somewhat later, he therefore recognizes a consequence of the judicial wrath of God that avenges the violation of the covenant. And thus the prayer for averting the anger is joined to pleading for healing from sickness (v. 2). In the OT the association of guilt and sickness is indissoluble (Pss. 32:1ff.; 38:2ff.; 39:8, 11; and often. Cf. G. von Rad, *OT Theol*, 1: 274ff.). In sickness, guilt becomes manifest both as human perdition and as divine wrath. With physical distress Yahweh "chastizes" the human being (*ysr*, Pss. 38:11; 118:8).[6]

In the psalms, the one afflicted with a serious illness feels deeply that something is wrong;[7] he knows (or senses) that he has sinned and that God is disciplining, correcting, and chastising him in his wrath. He suffers greatly in body and mind because of his physical pain, the anguish and frustration of unanswered prayer, the prospect of imminent death, and the derision of his "enemies." He weeps and mourns and may even wear sackcloth;[8] his foes mock him and await his demise. Thus his healing is more than a physical recovery from impending death; it is a triumph, a vindication, a deliverance, a cause for jubilation and thanksgiving, a fitting testimony to the faithfulness of God. "He put a new song in my mouth, a hymn of praise to our God. Many will see and fear and put their trust in the LORD" (Ps 40:3[4]).[9]

3.1.2. The Classification of the Psalms of Sickness and Healing

According to R. Martin-Achard,[10] Psalms 6, 38, 41, 88, and 102 are to be classified under the general theme of psalms of sickness and healing. K. Seybold classifies Psalms 38, 41, and 88 as belonging with certainty to the theme at hand; Psalms 30, 39, 69, 102, and 103 (and Isa 38:9–20) are identified as such with relative certainty; while Psalms 6, 13, (31), 32, (35), 51, (71), and 91 are considered with uncertainty to be psalms of sickness and healing.[11] Of course, the problem of serious illness and disease provides the backdrop for various petitions, laments, and pleas throughout the psalms.[12] For the present purposes, however, it is sufficient to deal with what may be judged to be the key psalms: 6, 30, and 41, which definitely deal with the theme of physical sickness *and* healing (thus including the element of thanksgiving);[13] Psalms 38, 88, and 102, clearly psalms of sickness, with no explicit reference to healing (thus, primarily of the lament genre); Psalm 103, whose *Sitz im Leben* is best seen as thanksgiving after healing from a life-threatening illness; and Psalm 91, a graphic psalm of divine protection, especially from demons and disease. Specific verses from other psalms (esp. 13, 32, 39, 40, 69, 116) will be cited where appropriate, and Isaiah 38, the thanksgiving psalm of Hezekiah, will also be incorporated into the discussion here.

As far as the general arrangement of the relevant material in the book of Psalms, it is possible that on at least three occasions (Pss 38–41; 102–103; 146–147), psalms dealing with sickness and recovery or extolling Yahweh's healing virtues, have been intentionally placed together.[14] In the first grouping,[15] Psalms 38 and 41 without doubt belong to this class, while Psalm 39, which reflects on the frailty of human life, refers to God's scourge, rebuke, and discipline, and Psalm 40 begins with thanksgiving for divine deliverance from "the slimy pit."[16] Psalm 102 is entitled, "A prayer of an afflicted man,"[17] while

Psalm 103 is the great paean of praise for healing. Psalm 146 celebrates the Lord who "sets prisoners free" and "gives sight to the blind," while Psalm 147 extols Yahweh who "heals the brokenhearted and binds up their wounds." It may also be argued that Psalms 88 and 89 are strategically joined together: The former psalm, representing one "chapter" of life, ends with hopelessness and despair in the midst of terrible affliction; the latter begins with vibrant praise and faith (although unrelated to the issue of healing), opening up a new and brighter "chapter."[18]

3.1.3. Characteristic Elements of the Psalms of Sickness and Healing[19]

Certain recurring elements may be identified in the material under discussion, although not necessarily in the following order:

(1) *Reference to God's wrath*: for example, Psalm 8:1(2): "O LORD, do not rebuke me in your anger or discipline me in your wrath" (cf. the almost identical Hebrew wording in 6:1[2]).

(2) *Confession of and/or recognition of sin*: for example, 38:18: "I confess my iniquity; I am troubled by my sin."

(3) *Plea for mercy/healing/deliverance*: for example, 41:4(5): "I said, 'O LORD, have mercy on me; heal me, for I have sinned against you.'"

(4) *Complaint/"How long?"*: for example, 6:3(4): "My soul is in anguish. How long, O LORD, how long?" (cf. esp. 13:1–2[3–4]).[20]

(5) *Description of affliction (including weeping and frustration)*: for example, 32:3[4]: "When I kept silent, my bones wasted away through my groaning all day long" (see below, 3.1.4).

(6) *Reference to the redemptive aspect of divine chastisement*: for example, 39:11a(12a): "You rebuke and discipline men for their sin" (see below, 3.1.8).

(7) *Thanksgiving for answered prayer/praise for God's faithfulness*: for example, 103:2–3: "Praise the LORD, O my soul, and forget not all his benefits—who forgives all your sins and heals all your diseases."

(8) *"No praise in the grave"; the imminent threat of going down to the pit*: for example, 30:9(10): "What gain is there in my destruction, in my going down into the pit? Will the dust praise you? Will it proclaim your faithfulness?" (see also below, 3.1.7).

(9) *Specific reference to dying*: for example, 13:3b(4b): "Give light to my eyes, or I will sleep in death."

(10) *Reference to "enemies/evil ones"*: for example, 41:7(8): "All my enemies whisper together against me; they imagine the worst for me" (see esp. 69:26, and below, 3.1.5).

(11) *Recounting of God's promises*: for example, 41:3(4): "The LORD will sustain him on his sickbed and restore him from his illness."

It is noteworthy, however, that in Psalm 6, element 2 (confession of and/or recognition of sin) is lacking,[21] while in Psalm 30, it is not explicit. It is true that in both psalms, there is the expected reference to the anger of the Lord: "O LORD, do not rebuke me in your anger or discipline me in your wrath" (6:1[2]);[22] "For his anger lasts only a moment" (30:5a[6a]; see below, n. 39). Moreover, 30:7b(8b) makes reference to the Lord hiding his face (cf. also 6:3b[4b] with "How long . . . ?" and 6:4a[5a], with "Turn," i.e., turn back from your wrath[23]). Nonetheless, the closest thing to an overt admission of sin in either psalm is found in 30:6(7), apparently a confession of self-dependence or overconfidence: "When I felt secure, I said, 'I will never be shaken.'"[24] P. C. Craigie, seeking to explain the reference to divine wrath in 6:1(2), rejects the possibility that the psalmist has sinned in ignorance (and, hence, cannot explicitly repent).[25] Rather,

> It may be that the psalmist prays not to be rebuked or chastised for bringing this problem to God in prayer; whatever the reason for his sickness, it must either have

> been sent or permitted by God, and it might seem presumptuous of a mere mortal, albeit a suffering mortal, to complain of the experience which God has permitted to fall upon him.[26]

This explanation, however, is not satisfactory. First, it fails to reckon adequately with the standardized language of the psalms of sickness and healing, especially when they speak of divine wrath and mercy. In other words, the formulaic language utilized presupposes a fairly fixed theological understanding,[27] and it is unwise to interpret references to God's wrath (manifest in serious sickness) and pleas for mercy (tangibly answered in physical healing)[28] in radically different ways when they occur in virtually identical contexts. Thus, as Ibn Ezra noted, it is "because of iniquity [*ba'ᵃbûr he'āwôn*] the LORD reproves with sicknesses, as [it is written] in [Ps 39:11(12)], 'in rebukes because of iniquity you discipline men.'"[29] The plea for mercy tacitly presupposes this understanding, even without an overt confession of sin.[30]

Second, Craigie's view that "it might seem presumptuous of a mere mortal, albeit a suffering mortal, to complain of the experience which God has permitted to fall upon him," violates the general tenor of the whole book of Psalms. *It is expected* that the sufferer will bring his petition, lament, or even complaint before God.[31] This certainly was not a violation of Israelite piety, so long as it was reverential in tone.[32] Moreover, the proposition that Yahweh was the Healer of his people to whom they should readily come for deliverance was certainly well known, be it through the "official" cultic religion or by means of "popular/folk" beliefs,[33] regardless of the dating of the psalm.[34] Thus the seriously ill suppliant would quite naturally cry out to the Lord for healing grace. Although neither personal sin nor a request for forgiveness are mentioned in Psalm 6, both should be implicitly understood in the reference to wrath, the plea for mercy, and the prayer for healing (vv. 1–2, 9[2–3, 10]),[35] just as in 41:4(5), the request for forgiveness is included in the prayer for mercy and healing (albeit with the specific confession that "I have sinned against you"). It is, however, possible (in accordance with the suggestion rejected by Craigie) that the psalmist did actually sin in ignorance (cf. 19:12?).[36] The fact that he was stricken with a life-threatening illness suggested to him that he must have displeased the Lord. Thus the sickness is interpreted in thoroughly monotheistic terms as evidence of the wrath of Yahweh,[37] the cause of which can only be human sin, *not* divine caprice.[38]

As for the interpretation of Psalms 6:1(2) and 38:1(2), it should be noted that, since the psalmist is already experiencing God's wrath, his plea, "O LORD, do not rebuke me in your anger or discipline me in your wrath," must mean, "Please, LORD, no more! If, *in your anger alone,* you teach me everything I need to learn or pay me back fully for what I may have done, it will be more than I can bear. So please, LORD, be merciful and let up!"[39] As noted above (2.2.5, n. 120), all healing was perceived as a merciful gift (see below, 3.1.9, on Ps 103).

3.1.4. The Physical, Emotional, Spiritual, and Social Condition of the Seriously Ill Petitioner

The descriptions of human suffering in the OT are vivid. It is hard to imagine more gripping portraits of agony and despair than those painted with such graphic literary strokes by the authors of books like Lamentations and Job. The petitions of the individual sufferers in the book of Psalms are no less forceful in their evocative power. There are moving descriptions of turmoil within and without and of intense pain in body and in spirit. The suppliant's concrete and often pathetic portrayal of his sufferings underscores just how debilitating, discouraging, frustrating, and even excruciating serious illness can be.[40] It is truly life-sapping, an enemy of well-being in every sense of the word, affecting one's social status as well. H. E. Sigerist notes: "At all times disease isolates its victims socially because their lives are different from those of healthy people. The sick man is thrown out of gear with life, finds himself confined in his movements, is helpless and compelled to rely on the assistance of others."[41] Thus his life-threatening or incapacitating condition may also seriously stigmatize him.[42]

The treatment of the sick by the Kubu people in Sumatra, a tribe observed carefully by anthropologists, is enlightening. In the case of someone suffering from minor ailments, wounds, bruises, and injuries, there is no adverse cultural reaction, since none of these problems prevented one from functioning as a normal member of society. As Sigerist writes, however,

> Things are different in the case of serious diseases, more especially those involving fever such as an epidemic of smallpox invading the region, an event which happens not infrequently. Such a patient finds himself unable to take his part in the life of the tribe; he is incapacitated, and there is a sharp reaction which leads to his abandonment both by the tribe and by his own kin. All avoid him as they would a corpse, making his isolation complete. The sufferer is dead socially long before physical death has overtaken him.[43]

Moreover, if it was feared that a disease was communicable—either physically or through numinous powers—the sufferer in any society, primitive or modern, would normally experience even greater isolation.[44]

For the Israelite, there was a further dimension: Serious illness was generally taken as an indication of divine wrath, understood to be the result of personal transgression. This is expressed succinctly in Psalm 38:3[4]: "*Because of your wrath* there is no soundness in my body; my bones have no soundness *because of my sin*." Thus rebellion and sin lead to anger and wrath, resulting in prostrating and even terminal illness.[45] Kraus's comments to 38:4 bear repeating:

> The sickness is the herald of guilt; it announces a transgression which, so to speak, has erupted to the outside and become manifest. In the lamenting description of his afflic-

tion the psalm singer therefore immediately lays bare his guilt. The body which is covered from head to toe with wounds is a witness to the overwhelming transgression (v. 4) that sweeps over the sick man like a flood (cf. Pss. 69:2, 15; 124:4). Helplessly, he who is struck by the wrath of God collapses under the weight of developing guilt that reaches full growth in punishment.[46]

Repentance, however, leads to mercy resulting in healing and life:[47]

> Sing to the LORD, you saints of his;
> praise his holy name.
> For his anger lasts only a moment,
> but his favor lasts a lifetime;[48]
> weeping may remain for a night,
> but rejoicing comes in the morning. (Ps 30:4–5)[49]

As expressed by Craigie:

> *Anger* is the divine response to human sin; *favor* is the divine response to goodness, but also to repentance and contrition. The consequence of divine anger is death, for the sinner cannot live in God's presence; the consequence of favor is life.... Anger, as experienced by humans, may prompt confession and repentance; as such, it may lead into a return to the divine favor.[50]

It is important to remember, however, the extreme nature of the conditions that form the basis for lament and petition in the psalms under discussion. Minor, passing, or everyday ailments are not in question here! The petitioner was seriously ill, in some cases facing death. Note the following typical references:[51]

- "My bones are in agony.
  My soul is in anguish....
  I am worn out from groaning;
  all night long I flood my bed with tears [cf. the reference to wailing and sackcloth in 30:11]
  and drench my couch with tears.
  My eyes grow weak with sorrow;
  they fail me because of all my foes." (6:2b–3a, 6–7)

- "For your arrows have pierced me,
  . . . there is no health[52] in my body;
  my bones have no soundness. . . .
  My wounds fester and are loathsome. . . .
  I am bowed down and brought very low;
  all day long I go about mourning.
  My back is filled with searing pain;
  there is no health[53] in my body.
  I am feeble and utterly crushed;
  I groan in anguish of heart. . . .
  My heart pounds, my strength fails me;
  even the light has gone from my eyes. . . .[54]
  I am like a deaf man, who cannot hear,
  like a mute, who cannot open his mouth;
  I have become like a man who does not hear,
  whose mouth can offer no reply. . . .
  For I am about to fall,
  and my pain is ever with me." (38:3, 5–8, 10, 13–14; note also v. 9, "my longings//my sighing"; v. 11b, "my wounds")
- "I sink in the miry depths,
  where there is no foothold.
  I have come into the deep waters;
  the floods engulf me.
  I am worn out calling for help;
  my throat is parched.
  My eyes fail,
  looking for God." (69:2–3)[55]
- "For my soul is full of trouble
  and my life draws near to the grave [Sheol].
  I am counted among those who go down to the pit;
  I am like a man without strength.
  I am set apart with the dead,[56]
  like the slain who lie in the grave,
  whom you remember no more,
  who are cut off from your care.
  You have put me in the lowest pit,
  in the darkest depths.
  Your wrath lies heavily upon me;
  you have overwhelmed me with all your waves.
  You have taken from me my closest friends

and have made me repulsive to them.
I am confined and cannot escape;
my eyes are dim with grief....
From my youth I have been afflicted and close to death;
I have suffered your terrors and am in despair.
Your wrath has swept over me;
your terrors have destroyed me.
All day long they surround me like a flood;
they have completely engulfed me.
You have taken my companions and loved ones from me;
the darkness is my closest friend." (88:3–9a, 15–18)

- "For my days vanish like smoke;
my bones burn like glowing embers.
My heart is blighted and withered like grass;
I forget to eat my food.[57]
Because of my loud groaning,
I am reduced to skin and bones....
All day long my enemies taunt me;
those who rail against me use my name as a curse.[58]
For I eat ashes as my food
and mingle my drink with tears
because of your great wrath,
for you have taken me up and thrown me aside.
My days are like the evening shadow;
I wither away like the grass." (102:3–5, 8–11)

In light of these verses, it is surprising that scholars and expositors, especially in previous generations, have sometimes been guilty of over-spiritualizing the sufferings of the psalmist. Thus E. W. Hengstenberg, commenting on Psalm 30:3, wrote: "To conclude from the expression, 'Thou didst heal me,' that David had been literally ill of a bodily disease, would be as absurd as to conclude from the expression, 'Thou hast drawn me out,' of the 1st verse, that he had fallen into a well."[59] Verses such as 41:4[5], "I said, LORD, be merciful unto me; *heal my soul*, for I have sinned against thee" (AV, my emphasis) seemed to support this spiritual emphasis,[60] even when the overall context of the psalm was recognized.[61] Moreover, as noted by Anderson, the stereotyped expressions[62] used by the psalmist (such as 102:4ff.[3ff.]; 38:1–8, 11ff.) make it difficult to determine "whether he was actually suffering from a fever (or a similar illness) or whether the word-pictures were simply used to describe the feeling of God-forsakenness which had arisen on account of the affliction."[63] Tate refers to "the typical elusive quality of descriptive language in the psalms."[64]

However, it is difficult to conceive of a robust, healthy Israelite bemoaning himself in such graphic, bodily terms. The numerous references to death and/or going down to Sheol, the fact that the sufferer was stigmatized by his enemies and former friends, and the fact that, in some cases, he was clearly unable to go to the temple,[65] underscore the physical nature of his affliction. Thus Kraus was right in emphasizing the importance of recognizing the concrete nature of the petitioner's affliction: "The psalmist [in Ps 6] prays in bitter suffering. His sickness has brought him to the brink of the grave. This situation is completely lost sight of if the sufferings expressed in the psalm are understood to be an expression of 'pain of the soul' and if the added comment is made that Near Easterners have a way of depicting distress of soul with a lively fantasy."[66]

Several additional arguments can be offered in support of the fact that physical sickness and healing are often at the heart of the OT poetic literature.[67] (1) Serious illness, with all its ramifications for one's family, social status, finances, and faith, is one of the most universal problems experienced by humankind and is thus a common subject in various historical and narrative strands elsewhere in the OT.[68] It is unreasonable to think that biblical psalmody would not also contain laments, pleas, petitions, and hymns of thanksgiving whose central subject matter was sickness and healing.

(2) Ancient Near Eastern literature provides ample testimony to the *religious* relevance and importance of these subjects (see above, 1.2, 1.3). Some of the hymns, prayers, and incantations make it impossible to doubt the physical nature of the suffering involved.[69]

(3) Job describes his great suffering in language that is sometimes reminiscent of the psalms under discussion; hence, it could also be interpreted in spiritual terms, should certain hermeneutical presuppositions obtain. However, in the case of Job, the canonical context (i.e., the prose prologue) makes it impossible to deny that the poet speaks often of *physical* torment (see further below, 3.3.2.2).

(4) The context of some of the psalms in question leaves little room for misinterpretation. Thus, Psalm 41 opens with the promise[70] that Yahweh will deliver and preserve the one "who has regard for the weak," stating, "The LORD will sustain him on his sickbed and restore him from his bed of illness" (vv. 1,3[2,4]).[71] Furthermore, the afflicted psalmist laments,

> My enemies say of me in malice,
> "When will he die and his name perish?" . . .
> All my enemies whisper together against me;
> they imagine the worst for me, saying,
> "A vile disease[72] has beset him;
> he will never get up from the place where he lies." (41:5, 7–8[6, 8–9])

There can be no question, therefore, that verse 4(5) does *not* speak of "healing of the soul," and that almost all modern translations are correct in rendering it: "I said, 'O LORD, have mercy on me; heal *me* [my emphasis], for I have sinned against you'" (so, e.g., NIV).[73] There is even less reason to interpret *rp'* in spiritualizing terms in 6:2(3); 30:2(3), or to deny that serious bodily ailments are being described in verses such as 38:3, 5, 7 (for discussion of 103:1–5, which adds further evidence to the literality of the psalmist's sickness and healing, see below, 3.1.9).

Seybold, who rightly interprets the nature of the afflictions described, suggests another dimension in the psalmist's suffering. Not only was this "a society that considered the sick person to be stigmatized, or at least, marked by guilt," but it was a society "in which no remedies were known for many or almost all sicknesses. . . . To the very last, medicine appeared to the Yahweh faith as a heathen art bound in an alien religious fashion, mixed with incantations and magic, an art whose ambiguous practices it could only reject—with the exception of a few techniques of treating wounds."[74] One may question, however, just how much relief and genuine help was offered by the physicians and exorcists of the surrounding lands. Is it possible that the ancient Israelite may also have been *spared* many a superstitious (and sometimes potentially dangerous) "medical" practice because of the related restrictions that seem to have grown out of Yahwism?[75] Furthermore, if the petitioner did, in fact, find help through following the designated means of prayer and sacrifice, was his position as desperate as portrayed by Seybold? Is it possible that there really was consolation and grace obtained through one's relationship with the living God? Were the constant references to the Lord's goodness, mercy, lovingkindness, and compassion[76] merely religious figures of speech, or were they descriptions based on the actual experience of corporate and individual Israel?[77] Did Yahweh, in fact, truly heal some of his hurting people? A positive answer to any of these questions would tend to brighten the overly dark picture painted by Seybold.[78]

According to Kraus, "The sick person was not allowed to come to the temple until he was healed. Rites of expiation and cleansing were required before the restored could again take part in the celebration of the congregation and offer his *tôdâ*."[79] This too, however, is an overstatement and presents an exaggerated picture of the degree to which the sufferer was spiritually isolated. Nowhere does the OT indicate that a sick person was barred from participation in the temple cult, with the exception of someone suffering with unclean, infectious diseases (cf. Lev 12–15), which in turn were the only conditions requiring "rites of expiation and cleansing."[80]

Of course, the seriously afflicted individual might be physically unable to make the trip to the temple, underscoring his sense of rejection, alienation, and separation (discussed below, 3.1.5–7). Moreover, his very condition might make him feel "unclean" (cf. Allen's description of the sufferer in Ps 102 as "utterly demoralized" by his illness[81]), and it is possible that he would not be eager to be seen in public in such a weakened (or, even temporarily disfigured) state, while his sense of being under divine punishment might also lessen his desire to appear at the temple courts until his healing had begun. However, the Torah legislation does not state that the sick person—seriously, chronically, or other—was to be excluded from the sanctuary,[82] and Craigie has even suggested that the background to Psalm 41 is that "the sick person comes to the temple to seek divine healing, but before speaking, he must hear a statement from the priest concerning the basic character of the kind of person who could legitimately seek God's blessing and healing."[83] If Craigie is correct, this would have been a fairly common occurrence. In any case, Kraus rightly speaks of the recovered person's desire to "again take part in the celebration of the congregation and offer his *tôdâ*," and it is certainly probable that at this point, sacrifices for cleansing would often be appropriate. Then the worshiper would be fully restored and whole.[84]

3.1.5. Sin, Sickness, and the "Enemies"[85]

OT scholars have almost unanimously portrayed Israelite society as one in which it was always assumed that the sick Israelite was suffering for his sins.[86] K. Seybold speaks of the "ironclad law of behavior-consequence. Whoever is sick is himself to blame for it."[87] Virtually all commentators on the psalms make reference to "the direct link between sin and sickness."[88] But is this a totally accurate assessment? Certainly, it reflects the *general* understanding of the Torah and historical books—the infirmities of old age excepted—and it is reinforced in Psalms and Proverbs. Without doubt, *whenever known sin or habitual disobedience preceded serious sickness, it was assumed to be the cause*—hence the frequent references to divine wrath coupled with pleas for mercy. However, as observed in chapter 2, the historical books do offer a few cases wherein sickness is not linked to personal sin, and several psalms (notably Ps 73), along with Job and Ecclesiastes, question the concept that "whoever is sick is himself to blame for it."[89]

It would be interesting to know at what juncture in time the "orthodox" and "unorthodox" points of view were joined together by later shapers of the canon (i.e., by "biblical" editors). In other words, how late in the development of Israelite religion were teachings such as those found in Job incorporated? Were they reactions against an unbending orthodoxy, or do they reflect balancing, complementary truths that alike were part of Israel's early faith? Certainly, the concepts of retribution are firmly entrenched in OT doctrine: Obedience brings divine favor and blessings, including long life, fertility, and health, while disobedience brings divine anger and curses, including premature death, infertility, and disease.[90] However, not all the healthy were godly and not all the sick were sinful. Thus, one cannot be sure that every Israelite who experienced sudden and/or life-threatening illness always assumed that he was being punished, disciplined, or chastised for his sins. That the sickness itself was *not* considered a blessing is indisputable (though its benefits could afterward be recognized as blessings). But it is possible that in the (rare?) case where the sufferer was convinced that he was right before the Lord, his affliction could be viewed as a mystery, and prayers for healing—presumably without any reference to wrath—could be offered.

Why then do the psalms seem to presuppose the understanding that life-threatening or debilitating sickness is always the result of sin? (1) From the OT viewpoint, that is the normal, albeit not absolute, pattern. (2) In none of the psalms of sickness and healing does the sufferer have any question about either the cause or even fairness of the affliction[91] (see, e.g., Ps

51, possibly including references to physical suffering[92] and containing outright acknowledgment of guilt in full). In such cases, the equation of "sin plus wrath equals sickness" was fully accepted. (3) The psalms of sickness and healing that were most likely to enter the Psalter would presumably be those utilized by the cult; hence the themes of confession of sin, breach of covenant leading to wrath, divine favor bringing restoration, and, finally, thanksgiving for healing, would be most appropriate and, generally speaking, in keeping with the expected pattern of Israelite piety. However, since the Bible could freely speak of revered figures such as Jacob, David, and Elisha in their final sicknesses—some of them in full spiritual vigor even to the end—and since there does not seem to be any indication that blind, lame, or deaf Israelites were viewed as special vessels of wrath,[93] one must be careful not to make the sweeping assumption that in the OT (or in Psalms), *all sickness was always regarded as the consequence of personal sin.*[94]

This naturally leads to the question: Was the sick person invariably forsaken by his companions, or was this a further, even unexpected, indignity suffered at the hand of "false friends"?[95] Of course, the psalmist's historic enemies (the *pōʿᵃlê ʾāwen*, "workers of iniquity") would be quick to point to the sufferer's grave condition as clear evidence of his guilt, and their own health, by implication, would point to their "rightness." Also, a prolonged illness would suggest to an even wider audience that something was clearly wrong somewhere in the sufferer's life. He could thus become the proverbial "talk of the town."[96] Nonetheless, it seems that the psalmist did *not* expect to be deserted by his friends, hence the terrible shock and added pain.[97] For example, Psalm 41:8(9) expresses genuine surprise: "Even my close friend, whom I trusted, he who shared my bread, has lifted up his heel against me."[98] How different this behavior was from that of the author of Psalm 35:

> They repay me evil for good
> and leave my soul forlorn.

Yet when they were ill, I put on sackcloth
    and humbled myself with fasting.
When my prayers returned to me unanswered,
    I went about mourning
    as though for my friend or my brother.
I bowed my head in grief
    as though weeping for my mother. (vv. 12–14)[99]

One can also recall the three friends of Job who, at least in their initial intentions, came to identify with and comfort their devastatingly afflicted friend. Whether or not the sufferer had sinned was not the question; solidarity with the sick for the purpose of restoration was the higher issue. Thus, the hostile parties are censured in Psalm 69:26(27): "For they persecute those You have struck; they talk about the pain of those You have felled" (NJV).[100] Their reaction was wrong! Even if God did, in fact, smite the sick person (clearly the assumption of Eliphaz and his compatriots with regard to Job), that was no reason to persecute and malign him. Rather, one should pray for him, weep for him, mourn for him, and restore him.[101] *That* would be an expression of true friendship. Moreover, it is unreasonable to think that, in virtually all cases of serious illness, the sufferer would be forsaken by most (or all) of his friends. This conclusion is certainly not required by the evidence at hand, and thus broad statements describing the extreme nature of the sick person's isolation from society should be tempered. That this terrible isolation did, in fact, occur, even with some frequency, cannot be doubted, greatly heightening the sufferer's trauma (cf. 88:8, 18 [9, 19]).[102] But it certainly was not the only pattern to be found in Israelite society.[103]

Also noteworthy is the fact that the psalmist, *because* he was unjustly forsaken, had something on which to fall back: He was more "righteous" than his accusers![104] Thus, the suppliant of Psalm 41 can freely confess his sin to God (v. 4[5]) while at the same time asking the Lord for vindication over against his enemies, even pointing to his integrity (*tūm*; see vv.

10–12[11–13]). In context, then, we see that the psalmist had previously lived a godly life, thereby qualifying him as a recipient of the promises recounted in verses 1–3(2–4). True, he had sinned; but he was not a "sinner"![105] Rather, it was his enemies who were the "sinners."[106] Soon, he would be healed, vindicating his cause; and the hostile parties would be brought down, exposing their guilt.[107]

3.1.6. "One Foot in the Grave"

In chapter 1 (1.3.1) reference was made to the descriptions of deliverance and healing in a hymn of praise to Marduk: "The Lord took hold of me, the Lord set me on my feet, the Lord gave me life, he rescued me [from the pit,] he summoned me [from destruction . . .] he pulled me from the *Ḫubur* river.[108] . . . 'Who but Marduk restores his dead to life? . . . Marduk can restore to life from the grave.'" These references to "restoring the dead to life" and "restoring to life from the grave" are to *healing* from a serious, life-threatening illness as opposed to a future *resurrection* from the dead.[109] An ancient Egyptian hymn was also cited to the effect that "[Amun] saves whom he will, even though he were already in the underworld," with the explanation of Brunner that the underworld here "is the isolation of the individual from his surroundings, and above all sickness or living in a foreign land." It is in this context that a worshiper of Gula, the preeminent Mesopotamian goddess of healing, puts into her mouth the boast, "I am merciful, I can hear from afar, I bring up the dead from the underworld."[110] The comment of Sigerist, cited above regarding the Kubu people (3.1.4, n. 43), is also relevant: "The sufferer is dead socially long before physical death has overtaken him." Similar images and concepts are found in the OT poetry literature whenever there was a threat of death (whether by sickness or by hostile parties) or the sufferer languished in a "half-dead" state.[111]

In the context of being saved from the very real peril of mortal *enemies*, the psalmist writes:

> The cords of death entangled me;
> the torrents of destruction overwhelmed me.
> The cords of the grave [Sheol] coiled around me;
> the snares of death confronted me. (Ps 18:4–5 [5–6])

Using similar language, but more likely with reference to the peril of mortal *illness*, he writes: "The cords of death entangled me, the anguish of the grave [Sheol] came upon me" (116:3a).[112] The images of being rescued from deep waters, miry pits, and the like are also common:[113]

> He reached down from on high and took hold of me;
> he drew me out of deep waters. (18:16[17])

> I will exalt you, O LORD,
> for you lifted me out of the depths. (30:1a[2a])

> Save me, O God,
> for the waters have come up to my neck.
> I sink in the miry depths,
> where there is no foothold.
> I have come into the deep waters;
> the floods engulf me. . . .
> Rescue me from the mire,
> do not let me sink;
> deliver me from those who hate me,
> from the deep waters.
> Do not let the floodwaters engulf me
> or the depths swallow me up
> or the pit close its mouth over me. (69:1–2, 14–15 [2–3, 15–16])

> You have put me in the lowest pit,
> in the darkest depths.
> Your wrath lies heavily upon me;
> you have overwhelmed me with all your waves. (88:6–7 [7–8])[114]

Against this backdrop, the metaphors of God as "rock" and "refuge" become much more meaningful. According to one image, the desperate sufferer, inundated by the flood waters of death, battered and submerged by the crashing waves of sickness and pain, swallowed up by the torrents of wrath, and about to sink beyond hope of recovery, was rescued just in time. His God delivered him! Using another figure, the helpless suppliant in Psalm 40 was drawn out of the muck and mire into which he had inextricably fallen:[115]

> He lifted me out of the slimy pit,
> out of the mud and mire;[116]
> he set my feet on a rock
> and gave me a firm place to stand.[117]
> He put a new song in my mouth,
> a hymn of praise to our God.
> Many will see and fear
> and put their trust in the LORD. (40:2–3[3–4])

According to a related line of thought, the potentially terminal sufferer was in danger of "going down to the pit" (Ps 28:1b).[118] Deprived of all appetite, he "drew near the gates of death" (107:18b), his life drew "near the grave [Sheol]" (88:3b[4b]). Thus to be healed was literally to be rescued from the jaws of death and lifted up from Sheol:[119] "O LORD, you have brought me up from the grave [Sheol]; you spared me from going down into the pit" (30:3[4]);[120] "Though you have made me see troubles, many and bitter, you will restore my life again;[121] from the depths of the earth you will again bring me up" (71:20); "In your love you kept me from the pit of destruction" (Isa 38:17b). At the last minute, the terminal sentence was stayed.

Yet, even while living, the acute sufferer was already counted (or counted himself) among the dead (see esp. Ps 88:4–5[5–6], cited above; also 31:12a[13a]). How is this to be explained? (1) On the most basic level, the seriously ill person was hardly "alive" in the true sense of the word (see above, 0.3.3, on *hyh*). To be incapacitated (e.g., 41:8b[9b]), racked with pain (e.g., 38:7a, 17b), filled with anxiety (e.g., 13:2), a burden to family and society (e.g., 31:11–12[12–13]), moaning and groaning (e.g., Isa 38:14a), soaking the sickbed with tears (e.g., Ps 6:6b),[122] languishing by day and tormented by night (e.g., 102:3a, 7a [4a, 8a]), and tossing and turning without strength or even hunger (e.g., 32:4; Job 33:20), was hardly to be "living." This did not reflect the divine intention for his glorious creation, teeming as it did with life (see Ps 8, 65, 104). This was hardly the intent or expression of man as made in the image of God.[123] Rather, the afflicted one could only say: "My days are like the evening shadow; I wither away like grass" (102:11[12]); and, "Darkness is my closest friend" (88:18b[19b]).[124] Surely this was incipient death,[125] and in a real sense, the sufferer had already entered into the shadowy existence of the netherworld.[126] Thus, in more ways than one, he had "one foot in the grave."

(2) Being confined (cf. Ps 88:8c[9c]) meant being cut off from the sanctuary and hence unable to participate in the cult. This too was akin to already being among the dead: "With death the individual's participation in the cult was extinguished: the dead stood [outside] the orbit of the worship of Jahweh, and were therefore debarred from glorifying his deeds."[127] Also related to this was the feeling of being cut off from Yahweh's favor (because of sin resulting in wrath)—hence, as if one were already in the underworld and separated from the presence of the Lord.[128] Thus, it is with little hyperbole that Kraus, referring to the petitioner of Psalm 30, states, "In our way of thinking, we would conclude that the one speaking in Ps. 30:3 has not really died. But he *did* really die! For the reality of death struck deep into his life, in the concrete diminution of life that he experienced."[129] Healing was truly deliverance from death,[130] both incipient and impending. Thus, for the psalmist, it was Yahweh who indeed was the *muballiṭ mīti*, the one who gives life to the dead (see below, on Ps 103).[131]

3.1.7. "The Living, the Living—They Praise You" (Isaiah 38:19a)[132]

According to 2 Timothy 1:10, Jesus the Messiah and Savior "has destroyed death and has brought life and immortality to light through the gospel." Through the cross and resurrection, death and the grave have lost their sting, and physical mortality is already being swallowed up by eternal life (Jn 5:24; 1Co 15:50–57). This, however, was not the perspective of OT believers, even if there are texts that indicate there was some hope of a blessed afterlife in ancient Israel.[133] Rather, the focus was on this present life: Now was the time to eat, drink, work, procreate, and rejoice in the Creator; now was the time to instruct one's children in the fear of the Lord; now was the time to glorify him in the midst of the festive throng. In death, none of this was possible.[134]

On a wholly practical level, this meant that death would spell the end of human productivity and activity; thus mere mortals should not be so arrogant. Soon they will perish (cf. Pss 49; 146:3–4)! On a spiritual level, however—and this was the deeper concern of the psalmists—the grave meant the silencing of praise and the end of the intervention of God on behalf of his servant:

> No one remembers you when he is dead.
> Who praises you from the grave? (6:5[6])

> Do you show your wonders to the dead?
> Do those who are dead rise up and praise you?
> Is your love declared in the grave,
> your faithfulness in Destruction?
> Are your wonders known in the place of darkness,
> or your righteous deeds in the land of oblivion?
> (88:10–12[11–13])

Thus Craigie notes: "Sickness, in a sense, is an anticipation of Sheol; it was hard in sickness to rejoice in God and praise him, but in Sheol it would be impossible."[135] For the faithful worshiper of Yahweh, this was the ultimate nightmare. Praising God was the essence of life.[136] And so, Psalm 115:17–18 proclaims:

> It is not the dead who praise the LORD,
> those who go down to silence;
> it is we who extol the LORD,
> both now and forevermore.

Similarly, the grateful King Hezekiah, spared from premature death, announced:

> For the grave cannot praise you,
> death cannot sing your praise;
> those who go down to the pit
> cannot hope for your faithfulness.
> The living, the living—they praise you,
> as I am doing today;
> fathers tell their children
> about your faithfulness. (cf. Ps 22:30–31[31–32])
>
> The LORD will save me,
> and we will sing with stringed instruments
> all the days of our lives
> in the temple of the LORD. (Isa 38:18–20)

To live was to worship the living God in his temple,[137] proclaiming his faithfulness to the next generation, through whom one's own life would be continued.[138] As expressed by the Puritan commentator Matthew Henry, "A life from the dead ought to be spent in extolling the God of our life."[139]

As a result, God was encouraged to act, as it were, for his own sake, lest another praiser go down to silence:

> What gain [*mâ-beṣ́a'*][140] is there in my destruction [*bᵉdāmî*],[141]
> in my going down to the pit?
> Will the dust praise you?
> Will it proclaim your faithfulness? (Ps 30:9[10])

Moreover, if the Lord responded to the petitioner and miraculously delivered him, additional praise would accrue to him:

Rescue me from the mouth of the lions;
    save me from the horns of the wild oxen.
[Then] I will declare your name to my brothers;
    in the congregation I will praise you. (22:21–22[22–23])

Many will see and fear
    and put their trust in the LORD. (40:3b[4b])

As a result of the expected (or already experienced) deliverance, others are encouraged to not be silent (cf. also the importance of *zēker*, "memory" in 6:5[6]).

It would be a mistake, however, to think that the only reason the terminal sufferer prayed for healing was in order to continue living for the glory of God. Certainly this was of great importance; but the petitioner also wanted to live for the sake of life itself. Thus Hezekiah had thought to himself:

"I will not again see the LORD,
    the LORD, in the land of the living;
no longer will I look on mankind,
    or be with those who now dwell in this world." (Isa 38:11)

He was not ready to be cut off from fellowship with God or the companionship of humankind. He wanted to live!

Of course, it was not appropriate for *everyone* to live long on the earth. The wicked ought to be cut down prematurely; indeed, it was hoped and expected that "bloodthirsty and deceitful men will not live out half their days" (Ps 55:23b[24b]).[142] But as for the righteous, they should enjoy longevity and health. This was certainly the OT ideal.[143] Thus Hezekiah had felt deeply that his life was being cut short, that he was dying before his time. This is eloquently expressed both literally and metaphorically:[144]

I said, "In the prime of my life
    must I go through the gates of death
    and be robbed of the rest of my years?" . . .
Like a shepherd's tent my house
    has been pulled down and taken from me.
Like a weaver I have rolled up my life,

and he has cut me off from the loom;
day and night you made an end of me." (Isa 38:10, 12)[145]

This, however, due to the mercy of the Lord, was not the end of the story, and the godly king—duly humbled by his encounter with death (v. 15)—could joyfully count himself among the living (expressed energetically as *ḥāy ḥāy* ["the living, the living"] in v. 19). Divine healing had extended his life.

Of course, it was understood that one's time on earth was limited (see Pss 39:4–6[5–7]; 90:3–12[4–13]), especially in light of the eternal nature of God (cf. 90:1–2[2–3]; 102:24–28[25–29]). Thus the concept of being pilgrims and sojourners occurs already in the OT (cf. 1Ch 29:15; Ps 119:19; see Heb 11:8–16; 1Pe 1:17). This, however, did not detract from the fact that a long, full, healthy life was viewed as a particular divine blessing.[146] Certainly there was nothing "unspiritual" or illogical in this, and, in a certain sense, it is underscored by the NT revelation. For in spite of the stress on taking up the cross, losing one's life, and being called to rejection, suffering, and even martyrdom in this world—all of which must be viewed in light of eternal rewards and consequences (cf. Mt 5:10–12; Mk 8:34–38; Jn 12:24–25; Ro 8:18; 2Co 4:16–18)—there is still a tremendous emphasis in the ministry of Jesus and the apostles on healing and deliverance (cf. Ac 10:38), i.e., on relieving human suffering for the glory of God (see ch. 5). The reason the Lord calls his disciples to "die" is so that they—and others—may truly live, either in this world or in the world to come (cf. the reference to "the life that truly is life" in 1Ti 6:19b). Death itself is never the ideal; rather, it is the necessary path to resurrection. Life in and with God is the ultimate goal of both OT and NT. Moreover, sickness and pain are not glorified in the NT.[147] To the contrary, believers in both OT and NT knew intuitively that the living God conferred life on his people, and they also recognized that true life could be found only in him (cf. above, 3.1.6; see Jn 17:3).[148]

What did change, however, with the advent of the messianic age was the matter of perspective: This present life, with its difficulties, trials, and sorrows, must now be seen in light of the bright, sure promise of eternity, as opposed to being viewed (primarily) against the shadow of the gloomy, uncertain prospect of Sheol.[149] Nonetheless, even in the NT, it remains true that *now* is the time to do the work of the Lord (cf. 2Ti 4:7; Php 1:20–26) and that this life must be given wholly to his service (Ro 12:1–2).[150] In fact, Catherine Booth, the wife of Salvation Army founder William Booth, commented, "There is nothing like the light of eternity to show us what is real and what is not."[151] Thus the redeemed, who know so well that they are only passing through this world (1Jn 2:15–17), are exhorted in this manner: "Be very careful, then, how you live—not as unwise but as wise, making the most of every opportunity, because the days are evil" (Eph 5:15–16). And Jesus himself stressed, "As long as it is day, we must do the work of him who sent me. Night is coming, when no can work" (Jn 9:4; cf. 11:9–10; with different imagery, see Ro 13:11b–12; 1Th 5:4–8; 1Jn 2:8b).[152] It is the living who must work for God while there is still time,[153] entrusting his truth to each new generation. On this, all the Scriptures agree,[154] emphasizing once again the practical importance of divine healing in the lives of the people of God. Without health, it is often difficult, and sometimes even impossible, to actively fulfill his will, and premature death, especially caused by sickness or disaster (as opposed to martyrdom), cuts short one's opportunity for service in the unique arena of this present age.[155]

3.1.8. Sickness as Chastisement

The image of God as a loving Father gently disciplining his firstborn son, Israel, is grounded in the Deuteronomic revelation: "Know then in your heart that as a man disciplines his son, so the LORD your God disciplines you" (Dt 8:5). Divinely imposed hardship and chastisement are thus evidences of special interest and care (cf. Pr 3:11–12, with further elaboration in Heb 12:5–11), and so the one who is being disciplined is "blessed" (Job 5:17; Ps 94:12). This has both short-term and long-term dimensions. For the moment, it reminds the sufferer that God is treating him as his own child, even "as the son in whom he delights" (Pr 3:12b).[156] But in the long run, the present difficulties promise to produce lasting fruit, since the chastised—and corrected—child of God will now be able to avert the disaster and judgment that otherwise would surely have been his lot, had not his heavenly Father mercifully intervened and guided him back to the path of righteousness (cf. Job 5:17ff.).[157] Thus divine discipline can also be a portentous forewarning of divine judgment: "More of the same—and even worse—is coming if you don't get right!"

Given the biblical association between the blessing of God and life and health, sickness serves as an ideal form of divine chastisement, since it clearly indicates that one has strayed from the path of life.[158] It said, "Something's wrong! Turn back! You're going in the wrong direction. You're on the path that leads to death." For the Israelite whose conscience was already pricked because of known disobedience, or for the one who was imperceptibly straying, the onslaught of serious illness served as a wake-up call, designed to evoke a contrite response.

The fact that sickness and disease are literal "afflictions" reminds us again that for the ancient Israelite, Yahweh's discipline was not simply envisioned as a spiritual concept or poetic figure of speech. In terminal cases, sickness literally leads to death.[159] In chronic or temporary afflictions, it bears the mark of death. Instead of vigor there is weakness; instead of wholeness there is decay; instead of health there is disease; instead of rest there is pain. Thus sickness could not only get the attention of the straying sufferer, it could remind one vividly of the error of his or her ways. "You are losing the blessing and favor of

God and drifting from the light into darkness. Soon you will sleep in death. Turn back!"[160] This is stated most clearly in Job 33:29–30: "God does all these things to a man—twice, even three times—to turn back his soul from the pit, that the light of life may shine on him."[161] It is also affirmed by Job's three friends, as though it were a commonly accepted, widely held truth (for further discussion, see below, 3.3.2.3).[162]

Several verses in Psalms also refer to the beneficial effects of the Lord's discipline (e.g., 39:11[12]; 119:67, 71, 75).[163] However, one must not assume that every reference to "affliction" in the psalms speaks of physical illness (although it is certainly meant in Job 33 and Isa 38, as well as, most probably, in Ps 39),[164] nor is it correct to surmise that it is God's *primary* way of correction. It is certainly not countenanced in Deuteronomy 8, nor is it required by the Piel of the root *'nh*, translated "afflict" in Psalm 119:67, 71, 75.[165] Also, in cases where sickness was the means of discipline, it seems that no one would think of praising God for the sickness itself, but rather (retrospectively!) for the life-giving effects wrought by the sickness. Thus the author of Psalm 119 makes reference to the benefits gained through his affliction (whatever that affliction may have been),[166] but he does this only as he looks back from his present vantage point:

> Before I was afflicted I went astray,
> but now I obey you word....
> It was good for me to be afflicted
> so that I might learn from your decrees....
> I know, O LORD, that your laws are righteous,
> and in faithfulness you have afflicted me. (vv. 67, 71, 75)

Similarly, viewing the scene from the outside, Elihu can speak of the divine efforts to arrest the attention of the terminally ill sufferer as he nears the gates of death. But sickness in and of itself was never viewed as a good thing, and the afflicted one naturally cried out for healing, especially if he was ready to confess or acknowledge his sin.[167] The affliction was surely not to be gloried in;[168] rather, the sooner it could be looked back to as history the better.

Thus, according to the Scriptures, several things are true. (1) Sin can lead to judgment in the form of sickness; however, for the righteous, even when punitive, it can be redemptive. (2) Sin, including an unconscious straying from the path of obedience, can lead to discipline, sometimes in the form of sickness.[169] But it is a mistake to think that all sickness in the life of the believer is due to either judgment or discipline.[170] (3) Sin can lead to sickness simply because one reaps what he sows, although the biblical emphasis is more on the principle of what the rabbis called *middâ kᵉneged middâ* (i.e., *being repaid by God* "measure for measure"; cf. *b. Šabb.* 105b; *b. Ned.* 32a; *b. Sanh.* 90a). In any case, the Lord is to be praised, not as the giver of sickness, but rather as the Healer of sickness. In the Scriptures, when sickness had accomplished its task, the Lord was petitioned to remove it.

This, however, is not always sufficiently appreciated, and sometimes sickness is cast in too positive a light.[171] Thus, the nineteenth-century Anglican bishop J. C. Ryle, after acknowledging that sickness is "a rough schoolmaster" and pointing out that "myriads" of restored sufferers learn nothing from their experience of serious illness,[172] overly extols the positive benefits of sickness:

> We have no right to murmur at sickness and complain at its presence in the world. We ought rather to thank God for it. It is God's witness. It is the soul's adviser. It is an awakener to the conscience. It is a purifier to the heart. Surely I have a right to tell you that sickness is a blessing and not a curse, a help and not an injury, a gain and not a loss, a friend and not a foe to mankind. So long as we have a world in which there is sin, it is a mercy that it is a world in which there is sickness.[173]

The evaluation of S. Kim is more biblically oriented:

> [The] constructive characteristics of diseases cannot cancel out the fundamentally destructive nature of diseases.

> Diseases come from Satan [this, of course, reflects an especially NT viewpoint; see below, 3.3.2.1, 5.1.1, 5.3.1] and are evil forces which are diametrically opposed to the Kingdom of God and His wholeness that God intends for all His creation.[174]

While there are potentially positive by-products that can result from the experience of sickness and disease, the biblical writers never forgot that, fundamentally speaking, sickness is a tragic state ultimately caused by a tragic act: human sin (either corporate or individual). In itself, it remains a curse, even if its final results are salutary or even salvific.[175]

3.1.9. The Healer of All Diseases (Psalms 103; 146; 147)

Since God was the *rôpē'* of his people,[176] it is instructive to see how the root *rp'* is used in the book of Psalms.[177] There are two petitions for physical healing (6:2[3]; 41:4[5]), two grateful recountings of Yahweh's previous acts of healing (one personal and recent, 30:2[3]3; the other corporate and historic, 107:20), two hymnic participles proclaiming the Lord as the one who "heals all your diseases" (103:3) and "heals the brokenhearted" (147:3), and one petition for the *mending* of the earth's fissures after an apparent earthquake judgment (60:2[4]).[178] Of course, the participial usage of *rp'* is particularly instructive, since participles by their very nature can be declarative and descriptive.[179]

However, before discussing Psalms 103:3 and 147:3, brief attention should be given to Psalm 60:2(4), since more than any other text in the Psalter, it evidences the wider range of meaning associated with *rp'* (cf. above, 0.3.1–2; 2.3.4). Verse 1(3), begins with the acknowledgment that God in his wrath has rejected and burst forth upon his people, ending with the plea, "Now restore us!" (*tᵉšōbēb lānû*). Verse 2(4) also begins with a confession, detailing the effects of the Lord's anger ("You have shaken the land and torn it open"), turning again to a petition: "Mend its fractures, for it is quaking" (*reᵖâ šeᵇārêhā kî-māṭâ*). Clearly, the earth is not being personified as a patient awaiting medical treatment. Rather *rp'* is being used in its most basic sense of "repairing, restoring, making whole."[180] The same God who promised to restore (*rp'*) the land in 2 Chronicles 7:14 was now petitioned, quite literally, to put it back together. This was not beyond the scope of his role as *rôpē'*, set forth so forcefully in Psalms 103:1–5; 147:1–3 (cf. also 146:6–9).

The clear language of Psalm 103:3–5 should leave no doubt that the basis for praise in this psalm was recovery from a near fatal illness.[181] This is indicated by at least two things. (1) Verse 3 refers to Yahweh as he who forgives[182] all the psalmist's sins (*hassōlēaḥ lᵉkol-ʿᵃwōnēkî*)[183] and heals all his diseases (*hārôpē' lᵉkol-taḥᵃlū'āyᵉkî*)—a conceptual linking that is certainly not haphazard, given the close connection between sickness and sin, healing and forgiveness, elsewhere in the psalms.[184] (2) The psalmist describes Yahweh as he who redeems[185] the psalmist's life from *šaḥat*[186] so that his "youth is renewed like the eagle's" (vv. 4a, 5b)[187]—speaking of a deliverance from potential death and, apparently, a miraculous renewing of life (cf. Job 33:25: "Then his flesh is renewed like a child's; it is restored as in the days of youth").[188] These were some of the gracious "benefits" (v. 2; *gᵉmūlāyw*)[189] of the Lord, and for these the author stirs himself—to his very inmost being—to praise God. His life, ebbing away and already beginning to slip into the pit, was rescued, and he was restored to vitality. First and foremost, however, as the necessary precursor to all that followed, was the forgiveness of sin/guilt (*'awwōn*),[190] which, quite naturally, becomes the great continuing theme of the psalm.[191] Spiritual wholeness and physical wholeness are integrally related, and in this instance, God's healing act blotted out sin and its consequences.[192]

According to Psalm 146, the Lord

> ... upholds the cause of the oppressed
> and gives food to the hungry.

The LORD sets prisoners free,
the LORD gives sight to the blind,
the LORD lifts up those who are bowed down,
the LORD loves the righteous.
The LORD watches over the alien
and sustains the fatherless and the widow,
but he frustrates the ways of the wicked. (vv. 7–9)

Yahweh's giving sight to the blind (*pōqēaḥ ʿiwwrîm*)[193] should probably not be understood in terms of physical healing; rather, it is to be explained with reference to setting the prisoners free (*mattîr ʾᵃssûrîm*). In other words, by releasing prisoners from their dark dungeon cells, they were again able to see the light of day.[194] This is in keeping with the general context (viz., God's intervention on behalf of the poor and oppressed—here, presumably, unjustly confined prisoners), as well as the fact that nowhere in the OT did Yahweh actually open blind eyes (see above, 2.2.6); this was to await the eschaton (see below, 4.2.2, 5.1.1).

Yet there was a significant "healing" promised to the people of God even before that day, although at times it seemed impossible. The devastation wrought by the Babylonians was so great that the anguished prophet, looking upon Jerusalem, asked in Lamentations 2:13c, "Truly your breech is as great as the sea. Who can heal you?"[195] Could the people's gross sin render their Healer impotent? The author of Psalm 147 would certainly say it could not.[196] Rather, it is the Lord who "builds up Jerusalem" and "gathers the exiles of Israel" (v. 2). As for those battered and bruised within, downcast and hopeless after such a great national tragedy, Yahweh is hailed in verse 3 as *hārôpēʾ lišbûrê lēb ûmᵉḥabbēš lᵉʿaṣṣᵉbôtām*—he who "heals the brokenhearted and binds up their wounds [lit., pains]."[197] Thus, he who forgives sin and cures physical disease restores the emotionally wounded as well, and he who works righteousness for the oppressed also rebuilds Jerusalem and regathers her exiles. National recovery, bodily healing, and spiritual rejuvenation all flowed from one source: the Lord, Israel's divine *rôpē'*.

3.1.10. Psalm 91: A Psalm of Divine Protection

Although there are certain ambiguities that make it especially difficult to ascertain the background to this psalm,[198] not the least of which include the question of exactly who the different speakers are,[199] several factors point to the conclusion that Psalm 91 should primarily be read in terms of protection from sickness, demonic attack, and (possibly) personal calamity in battle. (1) The hostile forces enumerated in verses 3–6 were perceived as being real threats, capable of inflicting emotional and physical damage and destruction.[200] This was certainly the mindset reflected in both the OT and NT world.[201] In fact, verses 3–6 may contain the fullest list of demonic powers—under various descriptive figures of speech—in the OT.[202] After "the fowler's snare" (*paḥ yāqûš*) are enumerated "the deadly pestilence" (*deber hawwôt*), "the terror of night" (*paḥad lāylâ*),[203] "the arrow that flies by day" (*ḥēṣ yā'ûp yômām*),[204] "the pestilence that stalks in the darkness" (*deber bā'ōpel yahᵃlôk*), and "the plague that destroys at midday" (*qeteb yāšûd ṣāhorāyim*).[205] Note also verse 13: "You will tread upon the lion [*šaḥal*][206] and the cobra; you will trample the great lion and the serpent [*tanîn*]." Of course, this verse was not literally intended,[207] but that does not mean that the creatures spoken of were not perceived as real. Rather, they referred to malignant spiritual enemies who would be rendered powerless because of Yahweh's protection and angelic host (vv. 11–12).

(2) The one who made his abode in the divine hiding place (*sēter*)[208] was promised protection from death (in battle? see v. 7).[209] The wicked might fall by the thousands around him, but he will be protected (v. 8). Again, this cannot be reduced to a mere spiritual figure.

(3) God is spoken of as the "refuge" (*maḥseh*) and "fortress" (*m*^e *ṣûdâ*) of the worshiper (vv. 2, 4, 9), a protective covering whose truth is a "shield and rampart" (v. 4).[210] Absolute safety was found in dwelling in him (vv. 9ff.), and the Lord would personally protect, rescue, answer, deliver, and honor his faithful one (v. 14). Could this possibly exclude *literal* deliverance from hostile attack?

(4) The psalmist was assured long life; specifically, he will be satisfied "with long life" (v. 16a).[211] This, of course, requires either the preservation of health or else healing from life-threatening or debilitating illnesses; cf. also v. 16b: "[I will] show him my salvation"—and not only in the world to come![212]

(5) Thus the sweeping nature of the promises militates against any narrow interpretation that excludes physical health as a primary benefit. For example, the pledge of bodily protection can hardly be removed from verse 10:[213] "Then no harm [*rā'â*] will befall you, no disaster [*nega'*, often rendered "plague"] will come near your tent."[214] Moreover, the vivid promise of angelic help (vv. 11–12) is patterned after Exodus 23:20ff., a passage that also speaks of the removal of sickness (vv. 25–26; see above, 2.2).[215]

Psalm 91, then, may be read as the culmination of the healing promises of the OT, personally applied. There are, however, two ways in which this psalm anticipates the NT revelation of divine healing. (1) In both there is a clear association between demons and disease. In the NT this is common and is stated in a straightforward manner (cf., e.g., Mt 4:23–24; 8:16–17; 12:22–28; Lk 13:10–18; see below, 5.3.1). In Psalm 91 this association is expressed by means of somewhat hypostatized language (e.g., the stalking plague) as well as by merging together the literal language of sickness (e.g., the deadly pestilence) with apparent demonic imagery (the flying arrow).[216]

(2) Psalm 91 also anticipates the NT's vantage point in its nascent *offensive* stance. Throughout the OT, the faithful were

promised protection and/or healing from sickness by Yahweh, a state that may be termed *defensive* in nature. Nowhere were the Israelite prophets, holy men, priests, or kings ever commissioned to go and "heal the sick." That they did, on occasion, heal is not disputed. But the healings were granted after petitions for mercy or through prophetic acts of intercession; they were not part of an aggressive attack against demons and disease. However, with the inbreaking of the kingdom of God in the NT, Jesus sends forth his disciples to heal the sick and drive out demons (see Mt 10:1–8; Mk 6:7, 12–13; Lk 9:1–2; 10:9, 17–19; see below, 5.2.1, 5.3.1, for full discussion). This offensive mentality is anticipated in Psalm 91:13, which speaks of "treading upon" and "trampling" the powerful forces of evil.[217] Thus, when the disciples return jubilant from their victorious mission of deliverance and healing, exclaiming, "Lord, even the demons submit to us in your name" (Lk 10:17), Jesus seems to have Psalm 91:13 in mind:[218] "I have given you authority to trample on snakes and scorpions and to overcome all the power of the enemy; nothing will harm you" (Lk 10:19).[219] These NT reflections also underscore the literal manner in which the traditions of Psalm 91 were interpreted within the later biblical community: Demons and disease were real threats, but Yahweh's power was greater.[220]

3.1.11. The Psalms of Sickness and Healing in the Life and Liturgy of Israel[221]

There should be no question that the psalms of sickness and healing were utilized with regularity in the temple services in Jerusalem. Form critical studies spanning more than two generations of scholarship have helped to elucidate both the original setting of particular psalms as well as their place in the ongoing liturgy of Israel. With regard to the psalms under discussion here, it can be argued plausibly that their very subject matter would make them particularly appropriate for the public setting, either as petitions during personal or national times of affliction and distress, or as hymns of praise after a significant healing or deliverance.[222] However, concrete evidence for the exact usage of the Psalter in ancient Israel's liturgy is at best scant and at worst nonexistent; hence, there is great diversity in the various scholarly reconstructions. Thus, Gerstenberger exercises caution in his overall analysis:

> Summing up all this scattered [extrabiblical and biblical] information, we may conclude that individual complaints belonged to the realm of special offices for suffering people who, probably assisted by their kinsfolk, participated in a service of supplication and curing under the guidance of a ritual expert [with reference here to his *Der bittende Mensch*, 134–60]. The liturgies of such offices very likely would vary a good deal from place to place and throughout the centuries. It is important to note that individual petition rituals were apparently independent of local shrines.[223]

When dealing with specific verses, however, Gerstenberger offers more specific reconstructions. For example, he notes at Psalm 6:

> A man had fallen ill. He and his family tried all sorts of remedies, to no avail. Finally, they turned to the ritual expert, the liturgist, who knew and owned the proper prayers and rites to heal a sick man (cf. 1 Kgs 14:1–3; 2 Kgs 4:18–36; 5:11; etc.). He would prepare and conduct a service or incantation for the ailing person, and the immediate family of the patient would participate in it. The healing ritual probably consisted of a sacrifice or offering, as we know from Mesopotamian tablets ... and, most important, a prayer to be recited by the patient himself.[224]

In Seybold's view, the psalm of the individual sick person was

> spoken within the private sickroom, probably with the aid of a priest. It was very likely not to be performed by the sick person himself during a pilgrimage to a holy place, since anyone seriously sick was generally not up to the rigors of such a trip. Or the psalm belonged in the thanks-

> giving phase as a laudatory prayer and personal (sacrificial) contribution within the framework of a community meal, celebrated at the sanctuary after the successful recovery of the recovered person. This could happen to a man "twice, three times" [obviously referring to Job 33:29ff.] during the course of life. The actual, individual, and liturgically formed psalms of sickness originated in this way.[225]

As noted, however, the evidence for these reconstructions is specious, and the few verses that can be adduced as possibly relevant only highlight how little we actually know about the usage of these psalms in the cult. For example, Allen, commenting on Psalm 107:20a,[226] states, "The primary reference seems to be to a priestly oracle of healing . . . brought from the holy place to the enquirer or his proxy waiting in the temple court."[227] However, Dahood's interpretation is just as plausible and contextually more likely: "The psalmist pictures the word of Yahweh as an angel sent to heal the Israelites."[228] There is, therefore, no compelling reason to assume that the original setting of this psalm reflected some healing rite, nor can we assume that it was utilized in part of a cultic healing ceremony.

The opening verses of Psalm 41 provide more direct evidence. As noted above (n. 83), verses 1–3(2–4) have been understood as the words spoken by the priest at the bedside of the sick person. Nonetheless, some questions remain: Was Psalm 41 used in the cult, and if so, how? Were the opening words part of a larger complex of "healing promises," adapted here for use at the sickbed, or were they developed out of private or local "wisdom" traditions, incorporated here into the larger cultic system? Was it only the priest or "ritual expert" who would speak these "bedside" assurances, or would the family of the bedfast sufferer go to the cultic center to hear the priest make these standard liturgical pronouncements for the sick? Unfortunately, we cannot be sure about the answers to any of these questions. What does seem sure, however, based on verses such as Psalms 22:22ff.(23ff.); 40:9–10(10–11); et al., is that the delivered/healed worshiper would *publicly* proclaim the saving power of the Lord; thus, for example, Psalm 103 is generally interpreted against this background.[229] Nonetheless, aside from some broad general statements, all reconstruction must be recognized as highly speculative.

The agnosticism expressed here, however, does not mean that the aforementioned suggestions of scholars such as Gerstenberger and Seybold are inherently wrong or unlikely. Rather, it is only a reminder that we are dealing with limited evidence and that the various ancient Near Eastern analogies provide no conclusive paradigms.[230] That the psalms of sickness and healing played an important role in the life and liturgy of the people is certain. But exactly *how* that was played out in the cultic setting is uncertain. Moreover, we do not know the extent to which material composed for public (i.e., cultic) use was utilized privately, whether by the common Israelite or "the ritual expert," nor do we know the process by which privately composed prayers became the property of the community.[231] Judging by historic Jewish and Christian usage, however, it seems that psalms of sickness and healing, confession and forgiveness, lamentation and celebration were utilized at fixed times and in fixed ways in communal settings, while they were fully exploited by private worshipers to the extent they were known and suitable to the occasion. Needless to say, their relevance and utilization by "people of the Book" continues unabated.[232]

3.2 THE BOOK OF PROVERBS

3.2.1. Wisdom as the Path of Life and Health

The outlook of the book of Proverbs is simple and clear: The path of wisdom is the path of well-being, protection, and life; the path of folly is the path of disaster, destruction, and death. "For whoever finds me [i.e., wisdom] finds *life* and receives favor from the LORD. But whoever fails to find me harms himself; all who hate me love *death*" (Pr 8:35–36). Thus, Proverbs details the practical outworking of the Torah principles of blessings for obedience and curses for disobedience, with one notable difference: In the Torah, God was the active agent behind the blessing and curse; in Proverbs, life and well-being are primarily seen as the natural results of godly living, while death and calamity are viewed as the logical (and necessary) consequences of ungodliness and sin.

Of course, there is no tension or contradiction in this, since the Lord blesses his people for doing what is right and good, and, conversely, doing what is right and good leads to blessing. Moreover, according to Proverbs, the Lord is in fact involved in the daily affairs of humankind, as an ever-present Witness and Judge (cf. Pr 5:21; 15:3, 11; 16:2; 17:3; 20:27; 21:2; cf. also 17:5; 24:10–12), the Righteous One who straightens everything out (cf. 15:25; 22:14, 22–23; 30:6; see also 3:32–33; 6:16–19; 11:1; 12:22; 15:26; 16:5; 17:15; 20:20, 23 [contrast 16:11]), the Ruler of human affairs (16:1, 4, 9; 19:21; 20:24; 21:30–31), the faithful Protector and Provider (3:9–10, 25–26; 10:3, 28:25; 29:25; 30:5), and the reliable Guide (3:5–6; 16:3).[233] However, the decided emphasis in Proverbs is not one of active divine intervention, but rather of consequences and results (cf. 9:12; for a classic example of the natural consequences of sin, cf. 6:27–35).[234]

For the sinner, the outlook is bleak. With striking regularity these themes are drilled home: "Ill-gotten gain . . . takes away the lives of those who get it" (Pr 1:19). "For the waywardness of the simple will kill them, and the complacency of fools will destroy them" (1:32). Indeed, "the wicked will be cut off from the land, and the unfaithful will be torn from it" (2:22); for "ruin overtakes the wicked" (3:25a), and, "The LORD's curse is on the house of the wicked" (3:33a). In spite of the allurements of sin, the feet of an adulteress "go down to death; her steps lead straight to the grave. She gives no thought to the way of life" (5:5–6a); he who is seduced by her "will die for lack of discipline" (5:23a). Still, he follows after her, "little knowing it will cost him his life" (7:23c) and ignorant of the fact that "her house is a highway to the grave, leading down to the chambers of death" (7:27). So also, the simple ones who heed Folly's message ("Stolen water is sweet; food eaten in secret is delicious!") are unaware "that the dead are there, that her guests are in the depths of the grave" (9:18).

Because of the corrupt and sinful lifestyle of the "scoundrel and villain" (Pr 6:12; see below, n. 253), "disaster will overtake him in an instant; he will suddenly be destroyed—without remedy" (6:15; *wᵉ'ên marpē'*; cf. 29:1, and see discussion, below). Thus, "when the storm has swept by, the wicked are gone ... [and] the years of the wicked are cut short" (10:25a, 27b). They "will not remain in the land" (10:31b); rather, "wicked men are overthrown and are no more" (12:7a). The trouble from which the righteous man is rescued "comes on the wicked instead" (11:8), and "he who pursues evil goes to his death" (11:19b). For "the wicked have their fill of trouble" (12:21b), and "he who speaks rashly will come to ruin" (13:3b). "When calamity comes, the wicked are brought down" (14:32a); and "he who hates correction/he who is contemptuous of his ways will die" (15:10b/19:16b). Thus parents are exhorted: "Discipline your son, for in that there is hope; do not be a willing party to his death" (19:18); "punish him with the rod and save his soul from death" (23:14). For "if a man curses his father or mother, his lamp will be snuffed out in pitch darkness" (20:20), and "a man who strays from the path of understanding comes to rest in the company of the dead" (21:16). Sin does not pay! "A false witness will perish, and whoever listens to him will be destroyed forever" (21:28). Both the Lord and the king will "send sudden destruction upon [the rebellious], and who knows what calamities they can bring?" (24:21–22).

The exact opposite holds true for the righteous; in fact, "he who hates ill-gotten gain will enjoy a long life" (Pr 28:16b; contrast 1:19). For "the path of the righteous is like the first gleam of dawn, shining ever brighter till the full light of day. But the way of the wicked is like deep darkness; they do not know what makes them stumble" (4:18–19). Yes, it pays to lead a godly life! The promises of wisdom are manifold: "Whoever listens to me will live in safety and be at ease, without fear of harm" (1:33); for the upright, the Lord "holds victory . . . he is a shield . . . he guards . . . and protects . . . ; he blesses the home of the righteous" (2:7–8; 3:33b; see also 2:11–12, where it is personified "discretion" who protects, "understanding" who guards, and "wisdom" who saves; cf. further 4:6; 6:22). Thus, "the upright will live in the land, and the blameless will remain in it" (2:21), and obedience to one's father's commands "will prolong your life many years and bring you prosperity" (3:1–2).[235] Indeed, "long life is in her [i.e., wisdom's] right hand. . . . She is a tree of life[236] to those who embrace her; those who lay hold of her will be blessed" (3:16a, 18a). For "sound judgment and discernment . . . will be life to you"; keeping them always in view will insure that "you will go on your way in safety, and your foot will not stumble" (3:21–23). Yes, "understanding is a fountain of life to those who have it" (16:22a), and so the wise father urges his son: "Keep my commands and you will live. . . . Listen, my son, accept what I say, and the years of your life will be many. . . . Hold on to instruction . . . for it is your life" (4:4 [7:2a], 10, 13). "For these commands are a lamp, this teaching is a light, and the corrections of discipline are the way to life" (6:23).

Lady Wisdom calls to the foolish: "Leave your simple ways and live. . . . For through me your days will be many, and years will be added to your life" (Pr 9:6a, 11). In fact, "righteousness delivers from death" (10:2b; 11:4b), and "the teaching of the wise is a fountain of life, turning a man from the snares of death" (13:14). Thus, "he who heeds discipline shows the way to life" (10:17a), and "he who obeys instruction guards his life" (19:16a; cf. also the reference to "a life-giving rebuke" in 15:31a). Therefore, "the righteous [and their house] stand firm forever" (10:25b; 12:7b); they "will never be uprooted" (10:30a; 12:3b); their "root . . . flourishes" (12:12b). "The righteous man is rescued from trouble" (11:8a; 12:13b). "The wages of the righteous bring them life" (10:16a), and "the truly righteous man attains life" (11:19a); he "will thrive like a green leaf" (11:28b), and his fruit "is a tree of life" (11:30a).

An important element in this is "the fear of the LORD," which "adds length to life" (Pr 10:27a) and is "a fountain of life, turning a man from the snares of death" (14:27; cf. also 14:26).[237] In fact, "the fear of the LORD leads to life: Then one rests content, untouched by trouble" (19:23); "humility and the fear of the LORD bring wealth and honor and life" (22:4). Watching one's speech can also mean the difference between life and death (see esp. 18:21): "The mouth of the righteous is a fountain of life" (10:11a); "he who guards his lips guards his life" (13:3a); and "he who guards his mouth and his tongue keeps himself from calamity" (21:23).[238] Thus, in summary, it can be said that "in the way of righteousness there is life; along that path is immortality" (12:28);[239] for "the path of life leads upward for the wise to keep him from going down to the grave" (15:24; cf. 16:17). Consequently, "he who pursues righteousness and love finds life, prosperity [or, righteousness] and honor" (21:21).

3.2.2. Proverbs 3:7–8

In light of the foregoing, it is logical to find similar promises regarding *healing* and *health* as natural results of godly living. This concept finds classic expression in two key texts, Proverbs 3:7–8 and 4:20–22. Proverbs 3:7–8 can be rendered: "Do not be wise in your own eyes; fear the LORD and depart from evil. It will be healing [*rip'ût*] to your flesh [*šārrekā*][240] and tonic [*šiqqûy*] to your bones [*'aṣmôtêkā*]."[241] Many translations of this verse (e.g., AV, NASB) and most of the lexicons (e.g., BDB, GB, KBL, Ben Yehuda) render *rip'ût* with "healing," presumably based on the abstract ending (*-ût*).[242] Other modern versions, however, render *rip'ût* with a concrete noun, such as "medicine" (NEB) or "cure" (NJV), possibly based on the parallelism.[243] However, the apparently concrete noun *šiqqûy* ("tonic"?) in v. 9a does not demand that the parallel expression in v. 9b, viz., *rip'ût*, also be rendered concretely,[244] while the morphological argument based on the *-ût* of abstraction argues strongly for a translation such as "healing." This rendering, supported by the ancient versions,[245] is also contextually suitable in the West Semitic loanword *ripûtu*, occurring in EA 269:17, as well as in Ecclesiasticus 38:14.[246]

In terms of actual exegesis, there is no reason to interpret *rip'ût* and *šiqqûy* here in spiritual terms, any more than there is reason to spiritualize the references in Proverbs to such things as diligence and laziness, riches and poverty, life and death.[247] While it is true that Hebrew and Near Eastern imagery can be metaphorically rich and descriptive (as observed above, 3.1.1, 3.1.4), one might ask what words and figures the biblical author *could* have used to express himself unequivocally in physical terms, if not those used in these very verses. Moreover, even if the references to "healing" in verses such as Proverbs 3:8 and 4:22 are, in fact, "first and foremost spiritual" (a position with which I do not agree),[248] they are most certainly not *only* "spiritual." That is to say, the holistic biblical mentality evidenced throughout this study argues strongly that "spiritual healing" was thought to go hand in hand with "physical healing."[249] The former might be the precursor of the latter, but it certainly did not stand alone. Godly living and the fear of the Lord were expected to produce tangible results. As W. McKane noted, "Longevity and physical and material well-being . . . are important aspects of the man who keeps the words and sayings of the teacher."[250]

3.2.3. *marpē'* and *'ên marpē'*: "Healing, Remedy, Cure" and "Without Healing, Remedy, Cure"

Both the terse expression of the proverbial literature[251] and the wisdom tendency to categorize life's events into more or less qualitative conditions give rise to the fact that all occurrences of the root *rp'* in Proverbs are nominal (*rip'ût* in 3:8; see above, 3.2.2; *marpē'* in 4:22; 12:18; 13:17; 15:4; 16:24; *'ên marpē'* in 6:15; 29:1).[252] As just mentioned (3.2.1), the phrase *'ên marpē'*, which occurs in five out of the fifteen OT occurrences of *marpe'*, speaks of the disastrous state of those whose defiant sinfulness takes them beyond the brink of possible recovery. Both 6:15 and 29:1 contain the identical warning: he "will be suddenly destroyed—without remedy" (*peta' yiššābēr wᵉ'ên marpē'*). This will be the fate of the devious and iniquitous mischief maker[253] who is always plotting evil (6:12–15a), as well as the final end of the oft-reproved yet persistently obstinate man. When judgment overtakes him, there will be no healing cure (29:1; on the national level, cf. 2Ch 36:16).[254] Such is the state of those for whom there is no *marpē'*.

However, Proverbs 4:20–22 states: "My son, pay attention to my words; give ear to my sayings. Do not let them out of your sight, keep them deep within your heart [cf. 4:23]; for they are life to those who find them and healing [*marpē'*][255] for their entire body" (my translation).[256] Thus Israel's lawgivers, historians, poets, sages, and (as we shall see) prophets, present life, health, and when necessary, healing, as the ideal consequence of godly behavior. As Ross notes on these verses, "The health that is promised here is physical, emotional, and spiritual—the whole person. It is made possible because of God's words that bring deliverance from the evils that harm and hinder life."[257]

This broad statement also receives practical, specific articulation, with acute psychosomatic observations (see further, below, 3.2.4). Proverbs 12:18 states that whereas the indiscriminate words of a chatterbox (*bōṭē'*)[258] are like sword-thrusts, "the tongue of the wise brings healing" (i.e., from the wounds inflicted in v. 18a). Similarly, in 13:17, in stark contrast to the wicked messenger who always falls into trouble, "a trustworthy envoy brings healing" (*sîr 'ᵉmûnîm marpē'*).[259] Also, continuing on the theme of 12:18b (viz., good and proper speech), 16:24 notes, "Pleasant words are a honeycomb, sweet to the soul [*nepeš*, better rendered here "palate"] and healing to the bones."[260] In all of the above, *marpē'* seems to bring healing to a previously bad or "hurting" condition.[261] In the case of 16:24, we may assume that with the generally destructive speech patterns of most human beings (this is an a priori assumption of Proverbs) producing harmful results, there will always be situations calling for pleasant, healing words.[262]

Proverbs 15:4a ("The tongue that brings healing[263] is a tree of life"), fits into this same class, contrasting again with 15:4b, "but a deceitful tongue crushes the spirit" (*waselep bâ šeber bārûaḥ*).[264] However, the exact interpretation is uncertain. There is no compelling reason to classify this verse as another instance of *marpē'* = *marpeh*, as at Ecclesiastes 10:4 (and in all likelihood, Pr 14:30)[265]—hence, "a quiet, relaxed tongue" (cf. RSV; NEB; NASB), in spite of 15:1a ("a gentle answer turns away wrath") and 25:15b ("a gentle tongue can break a bone"), since it might be argued that the image of a "relaxed" or "quiet" tongue would have more of a passive effectiveness not likely to be equated with a "tree of life." Yet a "healing tongue," i.e., one that speaks truthful, wise, comforting, and upbuilding words is certainly a "tree of life" (cf. again *ḥayyîm* and *marpē'* in 4:22).[266]

3.2.4. Further Psychosomatic Observations[267]

Several other verses in Proverbs offer what may rightly be called psychosomatic observations, relating healing, health, and well-being to one's psychological, emotional, or spiritual state.[268] According to Proverbs 14:30, "A heart at peace[269] gives life to the body,[270] but envy rots the bones." A calm, passive, and undisturbed disposition, in contrast to the agitated state of envy,[271] is indeed "the life of the flesh."[272] As Malbim aptly noted, "Flesh and bones are only as healthy as the spirit they encase."[273] Thus, the circumstances of life can have either a positive or negative effect on one's inner being,[274] which, consequently, affects the bodily state too (note the frequent reference to the bones, as mentioned above, n. 241). So, for example, it is stated that "an anxious heart [*dᵉ'āgâ bᵉlēb 'îš*; lit., "worry, grief in a man's heart"] weighs a man down, but a kind word cheers him up" (12:25), while "hope deferred makes the heart sick, but a longing fulfilled is a tree of life" (13:12). Similarly, "A happy heart makes the face cheerful,[275] but heartache crushes the spirit" (15:13). And again, "All the days of the oppressed are wretched, but the cheerful heart has a continual feast" (15:15). There are, however, related physical consequences: "What brightens the eye gladdens the heart; good news puts fat on the bones" (15:30, NJV). More pointedly, "A cheerful heart is good medicine [*yêṭib gēhâ*],[276] but a crushed spirit dries up the bones" (17:22), and "A man's spirit sustains him in sickness, but a crushed spirit who can bear?" (18:14).[277]

Circumstances, words, and relationships impact the mind, will, and emotions, which in turn impact the body—to its very bones. Moreover, as stressed earlier (3.2.1), the Lord's guiding hand and keeping power accompany the righteous as they journey—with circumspection and wisdom—along the path of life. Such are the holistic assurances of Proverbs.

3.3. THE BOOK OF JOB

3.3.1. Overview

We turn now to the brutal honesty and almost impenetrable depths of Job. Quite naturally, no real attempt can be made to do justice to the weighty themes of this book in the few pages that follow.[278] However, the limited scope of this present study enables us to focus clearly on one question only, albeit a fundamental question to the book—that of the theology of the divine Healer in Job. Several preliminary remarks will help to lay the foundation for our discussion. (1) The general OT understanding that the righteous are blessed in this life and the wicked punished is presupposed.[279] Thus Job is pictured as an ideally righteous and thus blessed man.[280] The calamities that overwhelmed him like a flood came as total surprises. Such things were not expected for the godly! Indeed, it is only against this backdrop that the *mystery* of suffering—*a*, if not *the*, major theme of the book[281]—is really a mystery. In other words, the suffering of the wicked is no mystery; it is their lot![282] But the suffering of the righteous is mysterious.

(2) God himself refuses to afflict his loyal servant, for that would be contrary to his nature. Thus, he responds to Satan's challenge to smite Job by refusing himself to touch him; the adversary must do the dirty work (1:11–12; 2:5–6). In fact, in extremely anthropomorphic terms, the Lord is described as being provoked by Satan to destroy Job without a cause.[283]

(3) The theology of suffering espoused by Job's friends, especially Eliphaz, Bildad, and Zophar, but even Elihu too, follows the only "orthodox" options available: Either righteous Job has strayed from the path—after all, no human is perfect—and God is chastening him,[284] or else Job is positively wicked, in which case God has judged him. For the three friends, Job's intransigence, coupled with his accusations of divine injustice, forced them quickly to abandon the first option (stated in the speech of Eliphaz in chs. 4–5) and to move aggressively to the second one (see below, 3.3.2.3).

(4) While the book of Job emphatically teaches that sometimes inexplicable things do happen to the truly righteous, it ultimately reaffirms the OT's theology of the blessing of God as the expected norm for the *ṣaddîq*. It is true that Job spoke rashly, meddling with affairs that were totally beyond his

knowledge. However, after humbling himself and repenting, the Lord graciously restored his fortunes (or, turned his captivity).[285] God smiled on Job by giving him twice what he previously had in material possessions, granting him ten more children (seven sons and three splendid daughters),[286] and extending his life another 140 years.[287] The reason the friends were censured for not speaking rightly about God as had Job (42:7)—certainly in his repentance, but possibly also in his agonizing honesty—is *not* because they affirmed the orthodox OT theology. Rather, it was because their narrow and inflexible application of this theology had become a religious straightjacket, leading them to speak incorrectly about the Lord's dealing with his servant in this particular case. In point of fact, Job was neither being chastised nor judged, although his afflictions ultimately proved redemptive. Rather, his suffering was a mystery, and the friends *misjudged Job* by branding him a sinner and *misrepresented God* by presuming to speak on his behalf.

In keeping with the approach of this volume (see above, 0.2), no attempt is made to deal with the prose introduction and conclusion (chs. 1–2; 42) in isolation from the main, poetic body of the book (chs. 3–41),[288] nor are the Elihu speeches treated separately as later intrusions.[289] Rather, the text in its present form is analyzed as a whole, although it is understood that the literary history of Job is somewhat complex and that certain internal indicators (e.g., references to the person and work of Satan) point to the relatively late date of the book's final composition.[290]

3.3.2. The Main Players

3.3.2.1. God and (the) Satan: The Prologue

The opening chapters of Job unfold like a chess game. However, it is one in which the basic rules and participants are presupposed. Thus, no explanation is given as to why and how Satan (*haśśāṭān*, "the adversary, the accuser, the satan") is allowed to have access to the heavenly court. The drama quickly unfolds: Satan implicitly challenges God. When asked by the Lord, "Where have you come from?" he answers, "From roaming through the earth and going back and forth in it" (1:6–7; also 2:2). God's response, asking Satan if he has considered righteous Job, may indicate the subtle undertone of the adversary's words: "I've been going all around the earth, and it looks pretty bleak to me. I don't see too many faithful servants of the Lord!"[291] And so the Lord counters with, "What about Job?"[292]

Now there is a public, heavenly confrontation, with all the *bᵉnê ʾᵉlōhîm* ("sons of God, divine beings, angels") looking on. However, Satan's malignant response is totally unexpected:

> Does Job fear God for nothing? . . . Have you not put a hedge around him and his household and everything he has? You have blessed the work of his hands, so that his flocks and herds are spread throughout the land. But stretch out your hand and strike everything he has, and he will surely curse you to your face. (1:9–11)

The honor of God is now at stake. Is his man Job *truly* devoted, or (to use a NT figure; cf. Jn 6:26) is he only serving the Lord for the fishes and the loaves?[293] Thus, it is not that the Lord initiates Job's sufferings (putting foreknowledge aside, since it is clearly not a factor in the author's story at this point); rather, Job is a pawn in a larger, cosmic drama. Ultimately, he will emerge as a hero of the faith, God will be exalted, and the very existence of Satan (let alone any explicit references to him or his work) will not even be acknowledged. He is the true loser of the book, utterly forgotten in the revelation of God's majesty.

Regarding sickness and healing, a straightforward reading of the prose prologue presents an "orthodox" picture of the inherent nature of God and the adversary: The latter is arrogant[294] and hateful, a destroyer of the innocent, a bringer of calamity. He wipes out Job's sons and daughters, devastates his possessions (1:13–20), and then smites godly Job "with painful sores from the soles of his feet to the top of his head" (2:7). However, the Lord, who *had*, in fact, put a hedge around Job and his household, blessing the work of his hands, refuses to lay a hand on him, despite Satan's provocations (1:11–12; 2:5–6). He is deeply troubled by his servant's sufferings (2:3). This is quite important! Although, from the viewpoint of Job and the friends (cf. 42:11b), all his afflictions came from the Lord (this was the only option available to them), from the viewpoint of the heavenly court and the reader, both of whom are privy to "behind the scenes" information, God was not the prime mover and did not send Job's afflictions; he did not rejoice in them[295] and, as soon as was appropriate, he removed them.[296]

Although modern opponents of divine healing often point to Job's sufferings as proof that God sometimes wills sickness for his obedient children, that proposition cannot be supported by the text.[297] The situation is far more complex, and one in which it is Satan—in open antagonism to the beneficent character of the Lord—who is associated with sickness and wanton destruction. That he receives *divine permission* to carry out his nefarious schemes can only be explained in light of the larger heavenly stakes, as emphasized above. It cannot, however, be interpreted as broadly indicative of either the nature of God or his general plans for his people, although one could rightly argue that for the ultimate good of his servants as well as for his own glory, he might *allow* the enemy to test and attack them.[298] He will, of course, turn it for good in the end, given the continued cooperation of his children.[299]

It should also be emphasized that the revelation of Satan here is significant in the Bible's overall theology of sickness and disease, since with rare exception in the OT, Yahweh alone is seen as the Author of both health and disease, blessing and curse.[300] There is, of course, the mention of the destroyer in Exodus 12, along with the smiting messengers of 2 Kings 19:35 and Ezekiel 9 (cf. also Acts 12:23, and above, 2.3.1, n.

216).[301] But it is only in 2 Chronicles 21:1, as compared with 2 Samuel 24:1, that a significant insight is gained: Sometimes the agent of the Lord's wrath is Satan (see above, 2.3.1).[302] Job 1–2, coupled with Psalm 91 (see above, 3.1.10) adds a further insight: There are hostile powers in the spiritual realms who, on their own volition, are out to destroy and afflict the righteous (and, no doubt, the wicked). That these powers are ultimately under Yahweh's control is not disputed; nonetheless, they are not to be confused with him, either in nature or activity. Thus in the Gospels, it is Jesus, always and only doing his Father's will (Jn 5:17ff.), who frees the sick and oppressed from the tyranny of the devil, demons, and disease (as summarized classically in Ac 10:38; see below, 5.1.1, 5.2.4).

Apparently with the deepening of Judean monotheism at the time of the Exile, in the providence of God, it became possible for the biblical authors to reveal in greater depth the existence and actions of a malignant, spiritual "superpower,"[303] though without fearing that he would now become the object of worship or superstitious veneration, as had Nehushtan at an earlier time (i.e., the copper snake and healing agent, cf. 2.3.3).[304]

3.3.2.2. Job

The prologue of the book presents a man of whom the Lord could truly boast. There was none like Job—a God-fearer who shunned evil and was blameless and upright, prosperous, respected, scrupulous in his religious care for his children, and, above all, of unshakable integrity and faith.[305] His responses to the absolutely overwhelming calamities that suddenly beset him are impeccable (see 1:20–22; 2:10) and have themselves become classic expressions of spirituality.[306] Although his life had followed the "expected" pattern for decades, with the manifold blessing of God as his portion, he greeted the totally unexpected loss of possessions, children, and health with an attitude of worship and submission.

The Job of the poetic body of the text is no less a man of great faith.[307] It is *because* he is such a fervent believer that he wants to "have it out" with God; he wants a hearing![308] It is because of his deep piety that he waxes impious.[309] Indeed, while the friends are content to speak to Job about God and for God, Job only wants to speak to his Maker. The corrections, observations, revelations, and accusations of his friends are mere annoyances to be quickly dismissed. Job, for his part, is frequently engaged in a soliloquy before the Lord.[310] Moreover, he knows his innocence,[311] and at the same time, he knows that God rules over his creation. But in spite of the fact that these two irreconcilable truths produce a spiritual and psychological collision in Job, his faith at times soars; at all times it is tenacious.[312] Indeed, it ultimately draws a divine response, albeit a severe rebuke. Nonetheless it is only Job, not his comforters, who is deemed worthy of the Lord's reply. His primary concern, as Murphy correctly stresses, was not his restoration; it was his relationship with God.[313]

J. Hartley summarizes Job's physical sufferings as including the following symptoms: "painful pruritus (2:8), disfiguration (2:12), purulent sores that scab over, crack, and ooze (7:5), sores infected with worms (7:5), fever with chills (21:6; 30:30), darkening and shriveling of the skin (30:30), eyes red and swollen from weeping (16:16), diarrhea (30:27), sleeplessness and delirium (7:4, 13–14), choking (7:15), bad breath (19:17), emaciation (19:20), and excruciating pain throughout his body (30:17)."[314] Added to all this were the pain of bereavement, the devastating loss of all wealth (and with it, social standing), the estrangement of his own wife,[315] and, shortly thereafter, the accusations of his friends. But even worse was the intense spiritual conflict: How could God do such things to his faithful servant? The benign, utterly righteous Ruler of the universe has now become his enemy—for no good reason.[316]

Indeed, Clines points out that in 10:16; 16:9, for example, Job "borrows cultic language depicting enemies to apply to

God," describing the Lord's attack on him as "that of a wild beast.... It is God's anger that motivates this assault upon him ... tearing him as a lion or wolf tears its prey ... making his attack incessant ... grinding his teeth, a sure threat to the prey of its imminent devouring ... and piercing him with the sharp look of a murderous intent."[317] All this from the One whom Job worshiped, served, and revered! All this from the One who so carefully crafted him long ago (9:8–12), but who now appears monstrous! Little wonder that Job mourns in sackcloth and ashes, giving full vent to his grief. His whole world has been *shattered*.

From this new, sometimes tormented perspective, Job calls into question God's general justice in governing his earthly creation (e.g., 7:17–21), refuting what certainly would have been his old, orthodox view that the wicked suffer and the righteous prosper.[318] There is no rhyme or reason for the good life one person enjoys in contrast with the wretched existence of another, and even death fails to set things right (21:23–26). The Lord's power is both wanton and destructive (9:5ff., 15ff., esp. 22b).[319] Nonetheless, Job is constantly fleeing *from* God *to* God,[320] and his mood of despondency and despair (passim!) alternates with remarkable flights of courage, hope, and confidence.[321] In the end, when confronted with an overwhelming vision of the glory, majesty, wisdom, and infinitude of the Creator, Job shows his true colors by humbling himself, repenting, and acknowledging his ignorance and folly. He believes and worships—sickness, pain, bereavement, shame, and all—not because he now understands, but rather because he sees (1) that he cannot possibly understand, and (2) that God truly is God, the infallible Lord, worthy of unwavering faith and reverent praise.[322]

Job is in the process of spiritual and emotional restoration. His *physical* and *material* restoration—to the disappointment of some readers![323]—is soon to follow. For the rest of the story, cf. below, 3.3.3.

3.3.2.3. The Three Friends

The viewpoints of Job's comforters, no doubt true friends and men of sincerity (cf. 2:11–13), can be treated quickly, since they reflect standard beliefs articulated elsewhere in the OT. As previously mentioned, their primary error was in the *misapplication* of these truths to Job's particular situation. Nonetheless, the dialogue between Job and his comforters plays an important didactic role in the Scriptures, since these chapters underscore the fact that life is not always so simple. In other words, a straightforward, albeit superficial, reading of much of the OT indicates that everything always goes well for the righteous, while for the wicked there is only trouble and hardship (cf. Isa 3:10–11; see above, 2.2.2, 3.2.1). Of course, speaking in ultimate, eternal terms, this is affirmed as biblical truth (Pr 23:18; 24:20; Da 12:2; Mt 25:46; Jn 5:28). Moreover, as seen throughout this study, it is to be expected that "godliness has value for all things, holding promise for both the present life and the life to come" (1Ti 4:8b). The book of Job, however, reminds us that serving God cannot be reduced to a mathematical formula, as if trouble and adversity in the life of the believer never coexist.[324] This is something that Job's friends, along with many sincere believers in every subsequent generation, failed to grasp.

Eliphaz, normally viewed as the oldest and most urbane of the friends,[325] affirms Job's piety (4:6), arguing that no one, being innocent (*nāqî*), will ever perish, nor will the upright be destroyed. This is the fate of the wicked (4:7–9; 5:1–6). Nonetheless, Eliphaz has learned by revelation that no mortal is truly righteous before God (4:12ff.),[326] a theme returned to often in the ensuing chapters (e.g., 9:2b [with sarcasm]; 15:14–16). Trouble is therefore the lot for humans (5:7), yet God, in his awesome might, does rescue the lowly and needy (5:9–16). Eliphaz then counsels Job to lay his cause before the Lord (5:8), although he already has a definitive answer: *Job is being chastised.*[327] "Blessed is the man whom God corrects; so do not despise the discipline of the Almighty. For he wounds, but he also binds up; he injures, but his hands also heal" (5:17–18).[328] Thus, in terms reminiscent of Psalm 91, a presumably repentant and restored Job is vouchsafed a totally blessed future: He will be protected from famine, wild beasts, and natural disasters; his family and possessions will be secure; he will be blessed with many descendants; and he will die at a good old age (5:19–26). "We have examined this," affirms Eliphaz, "and it is true. So hear it and apply it to yourself" (5:27).

What is wrong with this speech? Certainly not the concluding promises of 5:19–26! Rather, this is what Job previously enjoyed in the past, what he would ultimately enjoy in the future, and what he *should have been* enjoying in the present. His current experience was exceptional and anomalous. Undoubtedly, there was truth in Eilphaz's revelation of the inherent weakness and sinfulness of humanity; and in this light, some kind of divine correction, even for the most godly, would be appropriate (cf. above, n. 156, to Pr 3:11–12). But not the wiping out of one's family, possessions, and health! This would be in direct contradiction to his assertion in 4:7, that the innocent/upright are never destroyed by God. Thus, there is tension and potential self-contradiction in this first, and most reasonable, speech.

Especially noteworthy is Job 5:18, with clear allusions to Hosea 6:1 and Deuteronomy 32:39,[329] here offered by Eliphaz in explanation of the supposed divine chastening through which Job is passing.[330] Yet Deuteronomy 32:39,[331] part of the ancient song of witness *against* Israel (i.e., the apostate nation) and placed contextually after the covenant curses in chapters 27–28, was a promise of potential future restoration after repentance for rebellion. Having crushed the people for their defiant, persistent sin, God was calling them to return and be healed. And so the broken Israelites take up similar words in Hosea 6:1 (see below, 4.1.2). But in Eliphaz's mouth such concepts were totally out of place. Job deserved blessing not cursing; prosperity, not disaster; and his test was not the result of divine chastening.[332]

The friends, however, were in a quandary. They knew that God's ways were impeccable; at the same time, however, they initially assumed their old friend Job was basically righteous. Thus the gentle prodding of Eliphaz was somewhat muddled, albeit well-intentioned. And given his theological options, it was a genuine attempt to affirm the greatness of the Lord, while at the same time not condemning Job. In this way, he hoped to point his afflicted friend to the path of restoration. However, as the dialogue continues and as Job begins to do the unthinkable (i.e., to question and even accuse the Lord while seeking to justify himself), the tone of the three friends quickly changes. Simply stated, Job's punishment (overwhelming, probably unprecedented divine destruction) did not seem to fit his crime (some minor secret sin or sins that merited divine chastisement). This was a problem. But the solution was near at hand. Job was a gross sinner, a criminal character! He *deserved* what he got. Thus, according to Bildad (already in his first speech and despite the promises of vv. 5ff. and 20–22), "When your children sinned against him [i.e., God], he gave them over to the penalty of their sin." Even more clearly, Zophar calls for Job's repentance (11:11, 13–15). Then Eliphaz becomes directly accusatory in the second round (e.g., 15:4ff.), while Bildad and Zophar simply reiterate the absolute and final misery and destruction of the wicked (chs. 18 and 20, a theme also sounded in their first speeches, where at least there was still a promise offered to Job, should he humble himself).[333] Finally, even Eliphaz has had it: "Is it for your piety that he rebukes you [contrast 4:6!] and brings charges against you? Is not your wickedness great? Are not your sins endless?" (22:4–5). As if to say, "Job, you are guilty! You have defrauded, oppressed, and extorted the poor, and have been merciless to widows and orphans" (cf. vv. 6–9). "That is why snares are all around you, why sudden peril terrifies you, why it is so dark you cannot see, and why a flood of waters covers you" (vv. 10–11).

This, then, is the final conclusion of the friends, although once more there is a glorious promise of restoration offered (22:21–30). For Job, however, that promise was no better than what might be offered to many prisoners of conscience suffering torture and confinement under oppressive regimes: "Confess to crimes against the state (that you *know* you never committed), and we will release you and treat you well." Integrity makes such a "compromise" impossible. Thus, for Job, until he was overpowered and overwhelmed with a personal revelation of God, he defended his ways. In fact, the approach of his friends ultimately solidified his own convictions, and his biting description of them in 13:4 as *rôpᵉʾê ʾᵉlîl* ("quack doctors") proved accurate: They had no idea what the patient was suffering from, yet they were prescribing worthless cures.

3.3.2.4. Eilhu

The range of opinions regarding the Elihu speeches is almost endless.[334] Again, however, we need focus on only one aspect of his thought, viz., that God may use serious, life-threatening illness to chastise and instruct a man. Job had asserted that God refused to speak or respond to him (cf. 33:13). Elihu claims that God does speak, and in fact *has spoken* to Job, if he would only listen:

For God does speak—now one way, now another—
    though man may not perceive it.
In a dream, in a vision of the night,
    when deep sleep falls on men
    as they slumber in their beds,
he may speak in their ears
    and terrify them with warnings,
to turn man from wrongdoing
    and keep him from pride,
to preserve his soul from the pit,
    his life from crossing the River. (33:14–18)[335]

In other words, God warns the sinner through dreams so as to spare him from disaster (cf. Jer 18:5–10; Eze 3:16–21; 18:32). The warnings are remedial and preventative.

But there is a more forceful way in which God can get his point across:

Or a man may be chastened on a bed of pain,
  with constant distress in his bones,
so that his very being finds food repulsive
  and his soul loathes the choicest meal.
His flesh wastes away to nothing,
  and his bones, once hidden, now stick out.
His soul draws near to the pit,
  and his life to the messengers of death. (33:19–22)[336]

Through terminal illness, God reproves![337] Through terrible suffering, because of which life itself no longer has any meaning, significance, or joy[338]—the sufferer is barely existing and, in the biblical sense of the word, is hardly alive (cf. 3.1.6)—the sinner's conscience will be awakened. "If the person responds to God's message, he will avoid a premature death."[339] But he needs the help of a (heavenly?) "mediator," one who will intercede with God on his behalf and point him back in the right direction (or vouch for his uprightness; cf. NJV).[340] This mediator will

. . . be gracious to him and say,
  "Spare him from going down to the pit;
  I have found a ransom[341] for him"[342]—
then his flesh is renewed like a child's;
  it is restored as in the days of his youth.
He prays to God and finds favor with him,
  he see God's face and shouts for joy;
  he is restored by God to his righteous state.
Then he comes to men and says,
  "I sinned, and perverted what was right,
  but I did not get what I deserved.
He redeemed my soul from going down to the pit,[343]
  and I will live to enjoy the light." (33:23–30)

Restoration had come![344]

Although the exact interpretation of specific phrases and terms is disputed, Elihu's message is vividly clear. In fact, verses 19–28 contain the most graphic and forceful description of restoration from serious illness anywhere in the Bible. The afflicted one goes from the edge of the pit, already in the grasp of the messengers of death, to seeing the face of God with joyful exultation. He is transformed from being a mere skeleton, with his bones protruding from his skin, to plump, youthful health and vigor.[345] It is truly a change from agony[346] to ecstasy.[347] Indeed, "God does all these things to a man—twice, even three times—to turn back his soul from the pit, that the light of life may shine on him" (33:29–30).[348] He does not want to the see the self-willed sinner die in his sin; he wants to heal him, renew him, and bless him.

Thus runs the argument of Elihu, and little fault found can be found with it. It reflects biblical truth (see above, 3.1.8); it comes close to describing Job's present, anguished state, and, in a sense, it prophesies his coming restoration. There is only one problem: It did not accurately apply to Job. He did not deserve such treatment! Although, in his final penitence he acknowledged his sin, he was not speaking of a state of guilt prior to his sufferings (contrast the confession of 33:27). In other words, the sin he was confessing was *not* the cause of his trial. Rather, he admitted to his sinful presumption in daring to speak against God *in the midst* of his trial. Thus, not even Elihu's carefully crafted proposal hits the mark; it is at best only a partial fit.[349]

3.3.3. Epilogue: The Moral of the Story

The divine speeches in Job 38–41 do not directly touch on the subject of healing and restoration.[350] They do, however, bring Job to a place of repentance and contrition, as well as into a more intimate knowledge of the Lord: "My ears had heard of you but now my eyes have seen you. Therefore I despise myself and repent in dust and ashes" (42:5–6).[351] Job caught a revelation of God's greatness, of his eternal wisdom, of his power, of his inscrutability, and of his ability to rule. This was more than enough.[352] There was no need for God to answer his specific questions. Indeed, in light of God's majesty, Job had none.[353] For his part, the Lord seems eager now to speak of Job as "my servant" (42:7–8)—with a notable hint of "parental pride." And as Job intercedes for his friends (certainly not what Eliphaz had envisioned in 22:30!), the Lord accepts his priestly ministry.

Then, while engaged in this selfless act of prayer for those who had so harshly accused him, the Lord "rehabilitated Job's position."[354] Indeed, "the LORD blessed the latter part [*'aḥᵃrît*] of Job's life more than the first [*re'šît*]" (42:12a; cf. 8:7!). Yet, as Hartley correctly notes,

> the doubling of Job's estate does not mean that he received a bountiful reward for the endurance of undeserved affliction, but rather that Yahweh freely and abundantly blessed him. The blessing proves that Yahweh is a life-giving God, not a capricious deity who takes pleasure in the suffering of those who fear him. In his sovereign design he may permit a faithful servant to suffer ill-fortune for a season, but in due time he will bring total healing.[355]

We can also learn a lesson from the fact that there is continued debate about so many of the major questions of the book, such as: Why did God have to prove anything to Satan? Aren't some of Job's arguments valid? Why is the third cycle of speeches seemingly incomplete, and how did chapter 28 make its way into the poem? And doesn't the Lord's self-revelation fail to address the heart of Job's complaints? These unanswered questions are part of the grandeur of the book. In other words, the book of Job itself remains somewhat of a mystery, refusing to fit neatly into anyone's theology.[356] However, taking all this into account, and with due caution to the danger of oversimplification, this may be stated: The book of Job affirms an essential truth of the OT, viz., that God does bless the righteous *in this life*. Clines has summarized this clearly:

> It must be admitted that the ending of the book undercuts to some extent the divine speeches of chaps. 38–41. For although the Lord has implied that questions of justice and retribution are not the central ones, the narrator's concluding word is that after all the principle of retribution stands almost unscathed by the experience of Job. By rights, according to the principle, the innocent Job should never have suffered at all; so the principle was partially defective. Yet in the end the principle becomes enshrined in the history of Job, and he functions as a prime witness to its general validity. Even if in every instance it does not explain human fates, in the main it is affirmed by the Book of Job as the truth about the moral universe.[357]

However, sometimes truly inexplicable things do happen to the righteous—things that, technically speaking, are undeserved (i.e., they are neither chastisement nor judgment) and, based on the general tenor of biblical promises (from Ex 23:25–26 to Ps 91; from Ps 103:1–5 to Pr 4:20–22), are certainly unexpected. Nonetheless, it would be an error to change one's theology based on these unexplained and seemingly contradictory occurrences. Rather, looking back, it would have been best for Job to continue his posture of worshipful submission and for the friends to continue in solidarity with him.[358] The mistake of Job and his friends was that Job radically revised his view *of God* because of his sufferings, while the friends drastically altered their view *of Job* because of his sufferings and subsequent behavior. Instead, it is best to patiently wait and trust, always believing in the goodness of God[359] and his desire to bless, walking humbly before him, and expecting that in the end, he will cause *everything* to work for the good.

Where sickness or disaster is preceded by known sin, it should immediately be confessed and forsaken (Pr 28:18; 1Jn 1:9), and mercy should be sought. Where the disciplinary hand of the Lord is sensed, there should be complete cooperation to see that this trial accomplishes its goal. In both cases, however, it should be expected that healing or restoration will generally follow repentance, submission, and/or change, although in some cases, there may still be lasting negative consequences.[360] Also, in both of these cases the suffering is not inexplicable or mysterious, although, as emphasized previously, it can still be redemptive. However, when no such convenient explanation is at hand, then unshakable, persevering faith is the only answer. And when satanic involvement is revealed or discerned[361]—this is now moving us to a NT perspective—the evil one is to be resisted.[362] All this, however, is hindsight. The book of Job, and its central character, remain something of a marvel.[363]

In terms of the subject of Israel's divine Healer, the book is of central importance, since it affirms foundational truth in an absolutely realistic way: It tackles head-on the problem of human suffering, providing no cheap answers; ultimately, it points us back to the only One who can sort everything out. That he is *good* and that he is *God* should be enough for us. In the end it makes perfect sense, as Job would surely testify.[364]

3.4. THE BOOK OF ECCLESIASTES

There is a certain cynicism or skepticism in Ecclesiastes that at times questions whether or not the righteous and wicked are, in fact, paid back in this life.[365] Note 7:15, for example: "In this meaningless life of mine I have seen both of these: a righteous man perishing in his righteousness, and a wicked man living long in his wickedness." In keeping with this, there are frequent exhortations to serve God and enjoy life while one has the opportunity (cf. the thematic statement in 5:18), before old age (12:1–7)[366] and death, the great equalizer (e.g., 9:2, 11),[367] do their work. Outside of these general statements, however, there is only one specific reference to healing, viz., 3:3, a verse that has been the subject of much discussion because of the apparently inexact parallelism felt in *hrg//rp'*, traditionally, "kill//heal."[368] C. D. Ginsburg rendered *'ēt lahᵃrôg wᵉ'ēt lirpô'* with "a time to kill and a time to save," citing in his favor the Peshitta's *lᵉmaḥᵃyē* ("to save, keep alive, restore to life") and rejecting the war imagery supplied by the Targum to elucidate the passage.[369] Sa'adiah[370] rendered the verse literally in Arabic, *waqatu lilqatl wawaqatu liššifa'*—"a time for killing and a time for healing." Similarly, E. W. Hengstenberg cited Deuteronomy 32:39 (referring also to Hos 6:1), seeing here the divine process of judgment and restoration.[371]

If the background of war is posited (when else is there a time to kill?),[372] then the text would simply mean that there is a time for killing in war and a time for healing of the wounded after war (cf. 3:8b: "a time for war and a time for peace"). If no specific background is intended, the Hebrew could be rendered "a time to kill and a time to restore,"[373] understanding *rp'* in the broadest possible terms (cf. above, 0.3.2). However, in the light of 1 Kings 18:30 (see above, 2.3.4), Ehrlich suggests the emendation, reflected in NJV's footnote, "wrecking . . . repairing" (i.e., *lahᵃrōs . . . lᵉrappē'*); this solution is attractive and admirably suits the context. There is, however, no textual evidence for this change, there is no plausible confusion of *sāmek* with *gimel* at any stage of Hebrew orthography, nor is there is a need to force greater exactness in the parallelism.[374]

This much is clear: As the text stands, Koheleth too affirms the fundamental nature of "healing, restoring" in the cycle of life: As surely as building follows tearing down, mending follows tearing up, dancing follows mourning, and laughing follows weeping,[375] healing follows killing. The "Preacher" did well to put healing last. In this case, darkness gives way to light.[376]

◆ 4 ◆

Israel's Divine Healer in the Prophetic Books[1]

4.1. THE PROPHETS AND THE RESTORATION OF ISRAEL

The hope of the prophets of Israel can be summed up in one word: *restoration*. All too often the prophets carried the heavy burden of tearing up, tearing down, demolishing, and destroying; only seldom were they privileged to build and to plant (cf. Jer 1:10).[2] The prophets saw God strike (*nkh*), smite (*ngp*), wound (*mḥṣ*), break (*šbr*), tear (*ṭrp*), and afflict (*'nh*) his people.[3] They longed for the day when he would bring healing to Israel's wounds.[4] Religious apostasy had carried sickness, death, military defeat, economic chaos, famine, and exile in its wake. Repentance and turning back (*šûb*)[5] to the Lord would bring health, life, victory, security, plenty, and resettlement to a humbled and submissive people.

How literal would God's healing be? Just as literal as his smiting had been! How could it be anything less? What the locust had eaten—and more—the blessing of God would restore. That, and nothing less, was the prophetic dream. As H. M. Wolf notes:

> The most remarkable descriptions of curse reversals in the Hebrew Bible appear in those passages in the prophets

> that deal with the restoration and rebuilding of Israel after a long period of shame and disgrace in exile. The once-battered nation now achieves a level of prosperity and blessedness that more than compensates for her great suffering and degradation. The curses of famine, disease, and war give way to unprecedented blessings of health, fruitfulness, and peace.[6]

Nowhere is this expressed more clearly than in Isaiah 30:26:

> And the light of the moon shall become like the light of the sun, and the light of the sun shall become sevenfold, like the light of seven days, when the LORD binds up his people's wounds [*bᵉyôm ḥabōš yhwh 'et-šeber 'ammô*] and heals the injuries it has suffered [*ûmaḥaṣ makkatô yirpā'*; NJV].[7]

Central to the prophetic concept of restoration was the root *rp'*, occurring twenty-nine times in verbal forms and nine times in nominal forms in the prophetic literature.[8] Clearly, this prophetic usage of *rp'* was anything but "spiritualizing," neither was it to be understood merely as a "poetic" figure of speech. In the biblical mentality, the "healing" of a devastated and broken nation (e.g., La 2:13) was no less real—and in that sense "literal"—than the healing of a sick body (e.g., Nu 12:3), nor were the reversals of divine judgment—seen as divine exploits of salvation and deliverance—conceived of as merely "spiritual" acts or "poetic" figures.[9] One could no more convince an eighth-century B.C. Israelite (or a sixth-century B.C. Judean) that his promised "healing" was to be understood "figuratively"[10] than one could convince him that the wounds and injuries inflicted on him by the fierce Assyrian (or Babylonian) army were figurative. The literality of the promised restoration would have to be just as real as the literality of the threatened judgment.

Yet this fundamental truth is often missed. An artificial dichotomy between "literal" and "figurative" healing has been constructed, a dichotomy seen in major theological dictionaries and leading biblical commentaries. Thus A. Oepke, in treating the LXX usage of *iaomai* in his article in *TDNT*, distinguishes between "God the Healer (in the literal sense)"[11] and "Healing in the Figurative Sense,"[12] grouping instances of physical healing in the OT under the first division, while virtually everything else is cited under the "figurative" heading. In fact, Oepke is so convinced of the OT origin of this latter sense that, in discussing the evolution of "The Gospel of the Healer and of Healing in the Early Church," he states: "In some measure *under Old Testament influence*, the figurative use of the terms came into its own again."[13] Actually, with regard to biblical usage, the reverse it true: When *rp'* and its synonyms occur in the Hebrew Scriptures, they primarily refer to the *literal* making whole of a broken or sickly condition, be it a body, a city, an inanimate object, or a people.[14]

4.1.1. "Sin-Sick" Israel and Its "Healing"

It is incorrect to state that in the prophetic books, sickness and pain are merely figurative expressions representing sin and alienation, as if "healing" is equated there only with forgiveness and reconciliation. Yet this view is commonly seen in biblical and theological studies. Thus, for example, in his commentary on 1 Peter, J. R. Michaels explains the usage of *iaomai* in Peter's quotation of Isaiah 53:5 (in 1Pe 2:24) by stating: "Like Isaiah before him, Peter uses physical healing as a metaphor for religious conversion."[15] This, however, oversimplifies. Rather, the metaphoric usage of "physical healing" in Isaiah—as well as in the rest of the prophetic literature—is determined by the (logically) prior metaphor of apostate Israel as a disease-ridden body: "Every head is sick and every heart is ill. From the sole of the foot to the head no spot is sound: only bruises, and wounds, and fresh open sores—not pressed out, not bound up, not mollified with oil" (Isa 1:5b–6).[16] But this was not merely a spiritualizing analogy.[17] Israel's "sin-sickness" had affected every area of life. The nation (= the corporate "body") was literally reeling from the effects of a deadly disorder: "Your country is desolate, your cities burnt with fire; your land—before your very eyes strangers devour it, and it is left desolate, as when overturned by strangers" (1:7).[18] Even Jerusalem "has become a prostitute, the faithful city once filled with justice, where righteousness used to dwell—but now murderers!" (1:21). This was the condition of the dying patient. Only God could revive her! Israel's "spiritual disease," with all of its physical, social, and national implications, required a comprehensive "healing."

4.1.2. "Healing" in Hosea[19]

Hosea depicts Israel as a body eaten by "larvae" and "decay" (Hos 5:12),[20] about to be torn by a vicious lion (5:14).[21] One need only think back to the atrocities committed by the Assyrians against their foes (as God's overzealous agents of destruction) in the eighth century B.C.—skinning their victims alive, using the heads of the slain to make frightful pyramids at the city gate, and engaging in mass deportations—to understand how great this "tearing" was.[22] According to Sargon's claims, he deported 27,290 Israelites to Upper Mesopotamia and Media; there, as stated by Bright, they were "ultimately to vanish from the stage of history."[23] H. L. Ginsberg notes that "the people of Musasisr in Armenia were driven by Sargon to such a frenzy of grief that they 'went up on the roofs of their houses and wept bitterly,'"[24] making reference also to the terrified mourning of the Moabites in light of the Assyrian onslaught as described in Isaiah 15:3//Jeremiah 48:38.[25]

Tragically, when "Ephraim saw its sickness [*ḥolyô*][26] and Judah its sores [*mᵉzōrô*],[27] then Ephraim went to Assyria and sent envoys to the great king [*melek yārēb*].[28] But," the prophet goes on to lament, "he cannot heal you [*lō' yûkal lirpō' lākem*] nor cure you of your sores [*wᵉlō'-yigheh mikem māzôr*]"[29] (Hos 5:13). It was only after much suffering that the revelation came:

Yahweh alone could heal his people, since it was he who had afflicted them. Thus the people cry out in unison in 6:1,[30] "Come, let us turn back to the LORD [*lᵉkû wᵉnāšûbâ 'el-yhwh*], for it is he who tore—but he will heal us [*kî hū' ṭārap wayyirpā'ēnû*]; he smote—but he will bind us up [*yak wᵉyaḥbᵉšenû*]."[31] Divinely inflicted maladies called for divinely provided cures. Thus, Israel had to turn back to the Lord, the nation's great Physician. Restoration would require repentance!

Once again, the stark reality of both Israel's affliction and its promised restoration cannot be overemphasized. It would be thoroughly unbiblical to translate these graphic terms—larvae, decay, sickness, sores; tear, smite, heal, bind up, and cure—into mere poetic figures, as if they did not entail real suffering, hardship, deprivation, starvation, war, disease, and exile, to be followed by real relief, resettlement, and healing. While it is true that the prophetic usage of these terms is, to a great extent, metaphorical, it should be stressed again that it is extremely misleading to reduce them to nontangible, poetic figures.

D. K. Stuart notes: "The figure of the sick person continues to describe Israel and Judah metaphorically. Both 'illness' (*ḥly*; Dt 28:59, 61) and its parallel 'sores' (*mzwr*) represent covenant plagues (see v 12), and can connote miseries afflicted by an enemy, rather than merely human illnesses (cf. Isa 1:5–6; Jer 30:12–13)."[32] Yet one must not lose sight of the fact that conditions brought about by siege and war (i.e., some of the "miseries afflicted by an enemy") lead to increased bodily illnesses as well, along with a large number of casualties (i.e., those wounded or maimed).[33] Thus, as mentioned above (n. 6), the prophets often threatened Israel with the sword, famine, and plague—three interrelated concepts—especially if the warfare was accompanied by siege. Add to this the fact that the covenant curses speak of *further* judgment plagues (cf. the verses in Deuteronomy just cited by Stuart), and the "metaphors" of sickness and sores become more graphic still.[34]

It might have been better to state that "illness" and "sores" in Hosea 5:13ff. (as well as in the prophetic literature as a whole) "can connote miseries afflicted by an enemy, *along with* merely human illnesses." That is to say, the "metaphorical" prophetic usage of *rp'* must be seen as *inclusive*, not *exclusive.* While it may not *focus* on literal healing of corporeal ailments (as a result of Israel's repentance), it certainly does not exclude that.[35] As expressed by H. K. Nielsen with reference to 6:1: "The prophet certainly spoke symbolically regarding this verse; however, the words also have validity in the case of real sickness."[36]

Moreover, one should not assume that the "metaphorical" usage discussed here had the same significance for the ancient Israelite as it might for the contemporary reader. In other words, it is probable that in the biblical mentality, societal life in general was viewed in more holistic terms than it is today, with religion, family life, political and economic stability, and general health and welfare seen as thoroughly intertwined. Thus, concepts such as *šālôm* were more wide-reaching in their import (cf. above, 0.3.3, *sub šlm*), and the idea of Israel being "sick" and in need of "healing" might not have been perceived *strictly* as metaphorical by the ancient hearer. The terms could have simply conveyed the wider concepts of suffering and affliction on the one hand, and restoration and rehabilitation on the other hand, with everything those words entailed.[37] So also in Hosea 6:11b–7:1a (the proper beginning of ch. 7; see most modern versions), the concept of turning back the captivity of Israel[38] is associated synonymously with the healing of the people (*kᵉ rōp'î lᵉ yisrā'ēl*), thus equating national restoration with the root *rāpā'*.

In the opening verses of Hosea 11, the prophet deals with Israel's infancy in Egypt (v. 1), his subsequent turning after idols (v. 2),[39] and his ultimate failure to realize that it was God who taught him to walk, taking him on his arms.[40] Yet the people of Israel did not recognize that it was he who "healed them" or "made them whole" (*wᵉ lō'-yādᵉ 'û kî rᵉ pā'tîm*—v. 3).

What exactly is intended here? The great majority of interpreters understand *rp'* to mean simply "heal,"[41] but there is no adequate explanation as to the specific condition from which (infant) Israel was *healed*. For example, David Kimchi and Keil[42] understand *r^{e}pā'tîm* with reference to the broad promise of healing in the context of Exodus 15:22–26; others refer it to the deliverance from Egypt.[43] Robinson understands *r^{e}pā'tîm* against the background of Yahweh's physician-like care for Israel in the desert.[44] Andersen and Freedman further comment, "Hosea's polemic against healers in rivalry with Yahweh makes us wonder if one of the unnamed gods was a god of healing."[45] Others see a wordplay between *r^{e}pā'tîm* and *'eprayim*,[46] though this does not explain the meaning or use of *rp'* here. Ehrlich's interpretation of 2 Chronicles 30:20 (cf. above, 2.3.4) is again marshaled by him, along with *Targ. Jon.*'s free rendition (*w^e lā' yād^e'în d^{e}min qādāmay mitrahêm '^{a} lêhôn*—"they did not know that it was from me they received mercy"), in order to support his translation "dass ich sie verschonte" ("that I spared them"). Yet he was much closer to the truth when he observed, "*rp'* not only expresses the healing of a sickness, but also the restoration or repair of a defect of any kind (cf. esp. 1Ki 18:30)."[47]

In 1985, I argued that *rp'* here gave evidence of its broader semantic range, specifically, bringing Israel to a state of wholeness from its physically immature, weak, and undeveloped condition.[48] This, of course, would be significant in terms of the semantic range of *rp'*, because a normal child learning to walk cannot be thought of as being *healed*. Rather the thought is that of bringing him from weakness and immaturity to strength and maturity. Yet, in spite of the fact that this interpretation is contextually appropriate and fits well within the bounds of the usage of *rp'* elsewhere in the OT (cf. above, 0.3.1, 0.3.2), it is found, as far as I know, only in the twelfth-century commentary of Ibn Ezra.[49]

Upon further reflection, however, it seems plausible that there is, in fact, an actual reference to *healing* sickly Israel in its infancy, with possible reference to the apposite traditions found later in Ezekiel 16:1–7. There the Lord found baby Jerusalem, pictured as an abandoned, despised, and dying infant girl kicking about in her blood, and said to her, "Live!"[50] Although the origin of this tradition is unknown,[51] it is certainly possible that it was not created wholesale by Ezekiel in the sixth century and that he drew on earlier sources. If, in fact, there were similar traditions known in Hosea's day (in this case, picturing Israel as a little boy—Hos 11:1), then the meaning of verses 1–3 would be this: "When Israel was just a sickly, weak, faltering infant, I lovingly brought him out of Egypt, taking him by the arms and teaching him to walk (through the treacherous wilderness) one step at a time.[52] But—how tragic!—he worshiped the Baals and the idols, failing to recognize that I was the one who healed him." In light of the foundational importance of Exodus 15:22–26 (see 2.2.1; note the views of Kimchi and Keil, cited above) and the Deuteronomic description of Yahweh's loving care for his frail people in the desert (cf. esp. Dt 8:1–5, again with the Father-son motif[53]), the association of the Lord as Israel's Healer—from its very infancy—is suitable, underscoring once more the theological importance of this particular revelation of Yahweh's character in the history of Israel.

In Hosea 14:5, God answers his penitent people with the promise, "I will heal[54] their backsliding [*'erpā' mᵉšûbātām*], I will love them freely, for my anger has turned away [*šab*] from them." Here, in contrast to 5:13 (with *ḥōlî*, *māzôr* and *ghh*; "sickness, sores, and cure"), 6:1 (with *ṭrp*, *nkh*, and *ḥbš*; "tear, strike, and bind up"), and 11:3 (with *trgl*; "train to walk"), there is no physical imagery. Yet once again, as in 6:1 and 6:11b–7:1a (cf. also 5:15; 11:5), the root *šûb* plays an important role: When the people turn away from their sins and turn back to God in contrition, he turns away from his wrath and turns back to his people in mercy, thus bringing healing and restoration.[55] This is the essence as well as the expression of forgiveness. Healing of the corporate heart produces healing of the corporate body.

4.1.3. "Healing" in Jeremiah

This graphic imagery of restoration and repair is found throughout the book of Jeremiah.[56] Jerusalem's "sickness and wounds" (*ḥolî ûmakkâ*) are before the Lord continually (6:7b).[57] Jerusalem is a city in distress. At present "violence and destruction are heard in her" (6:7a); soon corpses will fill the streets, and the wailing of the mourners will be almost maddening. (Read the book of Lamentations!) Indeed, when the prophet hears (in the Spirit) the sound of the imminent battle cry, he has symptoms akin to a heart attack: "My insides! My insides! I writhe. The walls of my heart! My heart moans within me; I cannot keep silent" (4:19).[58] How Jerusalem needed her Healer! Thus, in deep anguish, Jeremiah asks (8:22): "Is there no balm in Gilead? Is there no physician [*rôpēʾ*] there? For why has no healing [*ʾᵃrûkâ*] come to my poor people?"[59] Tragically, no one could be found to make Jeremiah's people well. Therefore he remonstrates with God in 14:19: "Have you utterly rejected Judah? Has your heart abhorred Zion? You have smitten us, but we have no healing [*hikîtānû wᵉʾên lānû marpēʾ*]. We wait for peace[60]—but no good comes; for a time of healing,[61] but instead there is terror." Clearly, the only *rôpēʾ* who could effectively treat the people was the Lord.[62]

Six times Jeremiah referred to the imminent *šeber gādôl*—"great collapse" (with reference to Judah: 4:6; 6:1; 14:17; 48:3; with reference to Babylon: 50:22; 51:54).[63] *šeber* ("disaster/fracture/collapse") is the central word used to describe the people's broken condition; in fact, it is so central to Jeremiah's vocabulary that over one-third of its OT occurrences are found in his book.[64] According to Holladay,

> The noun *šeber* in Jrm appears to center around three usages: the fracture of a bone (metaphorically in 6:14; 8:21; 10:19; compare Lev 21:19); the shattering of pottery (compare Isa 30:14); and the breaking of walls (compare Isa 30:13). When a village or city is destroyed, walls collapse, roof-beams fall and break pottery storage jars, and these images are here in the forefront: the nation crashes with the totality of numberless crashes and so itself collapses in a heap.[65]

The promised restoration of Judah and Israel (primarily described by *rp'*[66] and *šûb šᵉbût)* could be no less comprehensive in its overall healing effects than the tragic, devastating collapse. Once again, the prophetic word was clear: What the Lord "broke/shattered/smashed" (the root *šbr*) could only be "repaired/healed/restored" (the root *rp'*) by his hand.

In chapter 19, Jeremiah is commanded to buy a clay jar and take it with him to the entrance of the Potsherd Gate at the Valley of Ben Hinnom. There, in the presence of the elders and the priests, he gives a dire warning: This valley will soon be called "the valley of slaughter"; the people of Judah will fall by the sword before their enemies, their carcasses left as food for the birds; and in the pressure of an unrelenting siege, the inhabitants of Jerusalem will eat their own offspring (19:6–9). Then Jeremiah breaks the jar[67] and declares: "This is what the LORD of hosts has said: 'Thus I will shatter [*'ešbor*] this people and this city as one shatters [*yišbōr*] a potter's vessel, which cannot be repaired again [*'ᵃšer lō'-yûkal lᵉhērāpēh 'ôd*] and which is buried in Tophet for lack of a place to be buried.'" (19:11).

The potter's vessel now lay broken in pieces on the ground; Jerusalem would soon lie shattered too—its buildings destroyed, the temple demolished, and the people defeated and crushed. The city would be found in a state of *'ᵃšer lō'-yûkal lᵉhērāpēh*—"which could not be repaired or healed." The parallel language in Deuteronomy 28:27, 35 is instructive: Covenant disobedience would bring about physical plagues *'ᵃšer lō'-tûkal lᵉ hērāpē*—"which could not be healed."[68] And it can be argued that Jeremiah, presumably present at the covenant renewal ceremony of Josiah and with the curses of Deuteronomy etched clearly on his mind,[69] would have used the phrase *'ᵃšer lō'-yûkal lᵉ hērāpēh* as an intentionally biting reference to the imminent judgment promised in "the book of the Law."

Furthermore, the notion of sin and its consequent penalties being beyond remedy is reflected in the Chronicler's description of this very same time period as one in which "the anger of the LORD arose against his people until there was no cure [*'ad lᵉ'ên marpē'*]" (2Ch 36:16).[70] One can only imagine how great the pain and how intense the physical and spiritual suffering would have to be—both on a personal and national level—in order to evoke the hopeless cry in Lamentations 2:13c:[71] "Truly your breach [*šeber*] is as great as the sea. Who can heal you?"[72] Only the gross sin that brought on the Babylonian exile could effectively render inaccessible the only one who could possibly heal Judah's wounds. Breach of covenant, tantamount to rejecting Yahweh as Healer, meant irreparable damage. Thus the smashed jar served as a striking symbol of the great *šeber* that was to come: The city would be literally devastated and the people literally plagued. Their desperately needed "healing" would have to be just as literal. A comparison of the similar (antithetic) semantic ranges of the roots *šbr* and *rp'* in Jeremiah is illuminating:

with reference to a clay jar, "smashed-repaired";
with reference to a bone, "fractured-treated";
with reference to a body, "sick-healed";
with reference to a city, "collapsed-restored."[73]

The grievous sin of the prophets and priests (Jer 6:13) is that "they superficially treat[74] the fracture of my people [note again *šeber//rp'*] saying, 'All is well, all is well,' when nothing is well [*šālôm šālôm wᵉ'ên šālôm*]."[75] They are willingly unaware of the seriousness of the present fracture (*šeber*);[76] therefore they cannot comprehend the awfulness of the coming national collapse (*šeber gādôl*). It is this deplorable practice that is mentioned as a key factor in Jerusalem's downfall in Lamentations 2:14: "The visions of your prophets were false and worthless; they did not expose your sin to ward off your captivity. The oracles they gave you were false and misleading" (NIV).[77] They failed to diagnose the acute condition of the patient; therefore they could only offer a superficial—and ineffective—cure.

Jeremiah declares in 30:12–13: "This is what the LORD has said: 'Your fracture is grievous, your wound is incurable [again *šeber* and *makkâ*: *'ᵃnûš lᵉšibrēk naḥlâ makkatēk*; cf. also Mic 1:9]. No one pleads your cause; there is no healing for your sore, no fresh skin for you [*'ên-dān dînēk lᵉmāzôr rᵉpū'ôt tᵉ'ālâ 'ên lāk*].'"[78] According to verse 15 (this time with *šeber-mak'ōb*), the pained condition of Israel is due to its great guilt and multiplied sin. Yet the divine judgment is not without a promise, for the Lord says (v. 17a): "Surely I will bring you health, and will heal you of your wounds" (*kî 'a'ᵃleh 'ᵃrūkâ lāk umimmakkôtayik 'erpā'ēk*). And in 33:6, in the context of the future restoration of Judah, God says, "I am going to bring her health and healing [*hinnᵉnî ma'ăleh-lāh 'ᵃrūkâ ûmarpe'*], and I will heal them [*ûrᵉpā'tim*] and reveal for them an abundance of peace and truth."[79]

Now, what is interesting in Jeremiah 33:6ff. is that this divine healing translates out to the return of the Judean and Israelite captives (v. 7a),[80] the rebuilding of the cities as of old (v. 7b), and the purification from and forgiveness of past sins (v. 8).[81] Repentance would lead to the return of the wearied exiles, the rebuilding of their ruined cities, and the reconciliation of their spiritual lives (cf., similarly, 30:17–21). The fracture would be healed; the breach would be restored; "new-skin" would arise! This was the promise of divine *rᵉpū'â*. With the covenant curses lifted, the blessings of God could come. Thus the promise and call that undergirded the prophetic message is found in 3:22—*šûbû bānîm šôbābîm 'erpâ mᵉšûbōtêkem*: "Turn back, O backturning children; I will heal your backslidings."[82]

The *šeber//rp'* vocabulary was also applied (quite naturally) to Jeremiah's own experience. As an intercessor whose soul was bound up with his nation,[83] his spiritual sufferings paralleled their natural sufferings[84] and are expressed in identical terms: "Woe to me because of my injury [*šibrî*]! My wound [*makkatî*] is incurable! Yet I said to myself, 'This is my sickness [*ḥolî*], and I must endure it.'" (10:19 NIV). Because of the breach [*šeber*] of Jeremiah's poor people,[85] he himself was broken (8:21; cf. also 23:9).[86] As his people's sickness appeared to be incurable (see immediately above), so too his own wound seemed incurable and his pain endless, refusing to be healed (15:18a).[87] In fact, he felt as if God himself had deceived him (15:18b).[88] Yet for the burdened prophet as well as for the people for whose sake he suffered reproach,[89] there was still only one possible hope: "Heal me, O LORD, and I will be healed! Save me, and I will be saved![90] For You (alone) are my glory" (17:14)."[91]

4.1.4. "Healing" in Isaiah

Reference was made earlier to Isaiah's description of apostate Israel as a disease-ridden body for whom only repentance could bring a cure.[92] The Isaianic material continues to expand on this theme.[93] Isaiah 3 describes a time in which the people were reeling from a penal disaster. Note verse 6: "A man will take hold of his brother from his own household saying, 'You have a garment, you will be our chief [*qāṣîn*], and this ruin will be under your care.' [The other] will raise his voice on that day saying, 'I'm no surgeon [*lō'-'ehᵉyeh ḥōbeš*]!'"[94] Thus, the one to whom the people looked as a potential savior could crush their hopes by saying, "I'm no *ḥōbēš*!"[95] In other words, "Don't look to me to put this torn, shattered mess together! I'm no miracle worker!"

In Isaiah 6:10, the prophet is commissioned to a ministry of hardening his people,[96] lest upon their seeing, hearing, and understanding (*šāb wārāpā' lô*), "it [i.e., the nation[repents[97] and is made well."[98] Interestingly enough, *Targ. Isa.*'s interpretive rendering, *wîtûbûn weyište bēq le hôn* ("and they repent and be forgiven"; cf. Syriac), is reflected in one citation of this verse in the NT (Mk 4:12), where LXX's literal *kai iasomai autous* is not followed.[99] Also, the Talmud and the later rabbinic commentators saw here a reference to forgiveness as opposed to literal (i.e., physical) healing.[100] This is similar to the usage of *rp'* in Hosea 14:5 and Jeremiah 3:22 (see above). However, while *Targ. Isa.*'s rendering of *rp'* here, as well as in Isaiah 53:5 and 57:19, indicates that "forgiveness of sins" could be seen as a divine healing act, the overall imagery of the preceding verses in Isaiah 6 (the land desolate and destroyed and the people under judgment), coupled with the prophetic call to make Israel *more* sickly,[101] suggests the propriety of rendering *rp'* here too with "heal, become well" as opposed to "save."[102] Nonetheless, it is useful to observe how the concepts of forgiveness and restoration coalesce in the prophetic usage of *rp'*.[103]

This prophetic usage is most fully developed in Isaiah 53, where the figures of sin, sickness, and suffering are so beautifully intermingled that some Christian commentators, in applying this chapter to Jesus, have sought to read it in exclusive terms of *either* spiritual redemption *or* physical redemption, but not both.[104] Actually, however, this "either-or" tendency is ancient, and it is reflected in the AV's translation of verse 4, "Surely he hath borne our griefs and carried our sorrows" (*'ākēn ḥolāyēnû hû' nāśā' ûmak'ōbênû sebālām*). This emphasis on "griefs" and "sorrows," i.e., on a spiritualizing interpretation of *ḥolî* and *mak'ōb*,[105] follows the lead of both the LXX and *Targ. Isa.*, respectively: *houtos tas hamartias hēmon pherei kai peri hēmon odunatai*—"This man bore our sins and was pained because of them"; *bekēn 'al ḥôbāna' hû' yib'ê wa'awayatānā' bedîlēh yištabqûn*—"Then for our sins he will pray and our iniquities will be forgiven because of him." Yet in Matthew 8:17, the evangelist strikingly departed from the LXX rendering and literally translated:[106] "This [viz. the healing of the sick mentioned in v. 16] was to fulfill what was spoken through the prophet Isaiah: 'He took up our *infirmities* and carried our *diseases*.'" (NIV; my emphasis).

Some Christian expositors and proponents of divine healing have noted that from Matthew's viewpoint, Isaiah 53:5 is speaking of *physical* healing, and thus healing of the body is considered to be part of "the atonement."[107] Others, pointing to the Petrine application of *ûbaḥᵃ būrātô nirpā' lānû* (Isa 53:5, quoted in 1Pe 2:24—"and by his wounds you were healed"), have sought to establish that what is in view in Isaiah 53 is actually *spiritual* healing in "the atonement."[108] The citation in Matthew 8:17 is then explained as follows: "The Lord took away the diseases of men by healing them. He died for our sins, not for our diseases."[109] However, these divisions are completely unscriptural, and they do not do justice to the context of either Matthew 8:16–17 or Isaiah 53:4–5.[110] A. Edersheim's rebuke should have been enough for the general reader, for whom his work was intended: "I can scarcely find words strong enough to express my dissent from those who limit Is. liii. 4, either on the one hand to spiritual, or the other to physical 'sicknesses.' The promise is one of future deliverance from both, of a Restorer from all the woe which sin had brought."[111] Yet it is with these very readers that his words have gone unheeded.[112]

Isaiah 53:5 strategically joins *peša'*, *'āwōn*, *šālôm*, and *rāpā'* ("transgression, iniquity, well-being, and healing"); the servant's sufferings would produce complete restoration for his sin-sick people. As noted by Motyer, "Isaiah uses 'healing' [in 53:5] in a total sense: the healing of the person, restoring fulness and completeness, a mark of the Messianic day (19:22; 30:26)."[113] As indicated through Matthew's citation of Isaiah 53:4 and Peter's usage of 53:5, the servant came to relieve the burden of sin and sickness; his wounds make his people whole. What makes Matthew's citation especially significant is that, from the viewpoint of Christological exegesis, the servant's bearing of our sickness and pain (Isa 53:4a) *took place on the cross.*[114] Yet the evangelist refers it to the Lord's itinerant preaching and healing ministry! This is correctly interpreted by D. A. Carson, who does not fail to draw out the implications of Matthew's theology: "Jesus' healing ministry is itself a function of his substitutionary death, by which he lays the foundation for destroying sickness."[115]

Thus, for Matthew (and, from the Christian perspective, for Isaiah as well), healing cannot be conveniently divorced from "the atonement." Moreover, regardless of the NT usage, it is clear from a strictly OT viewpoint that the interpreter of Isaiah 53 should recognize the pregnant meaning of *'iš mak'ōbôt wîdû'a ḥōlî* (v. 3), both "a man of sorrows and acquainted with grief" (AV) and "a man of suffering, familiar with disease" (NJV).[116] So also the *ḥōlî* and *mak'ob* of verse 4a are rich in meaning, as seen in AV's "griefs" and "sorrows" and NJV's "sickness" and "suffering."[117] One should also note verse 12b, where instead of *ḥolāyēnû hû' nāśā'* ("our *sickness* he bore"), the text is *ḥēṭ'-rabbîm nāśā'* ("the *sin* of many he bore"), and the mixed imagery of verse 10a, where the Lord "afflicts" (*ḥlh*)[118] his servant in conjunction with the servant's offering himself as a guilt offering.

By bearing sin and iniquity the servant bore sickness and pain; by taking his people's guilt he thereby incurred their punishment;[119] and it is at the cost of his wounds that total healing has come.[120] There is no artificial dichotomy here! The whole man has been wholly healed. The straying and sickly nation has been completely restored and made well.[121] Thus the beatific vision of Isaiah 33:17ff. culminates in verse 24: *ûbal-yō'mar šākēn ḥālîtî hā'ām hayyōšeb bāh nᵉśū' 'āwōn*—"And the inhabitant will not say, 'I am sick.' For those who dwell in it [i.e., Jerusalem] will be forgiven of their sins."[122] With sin finally vanquished, sickness is utterly banished.[123]

The last reference to *rp'* in Isaiah is in 57:18–19, again following God's punitive measures against his disobedient people.[124] The Lord's mercy will cause him to turn back and say, "I have seen his ways[125] and will heal him [*w^e'erpā'ēhû*].... It shall be well, well with the far and the near—says the LORD—and I will heal him [*šālôm šālôm lārāḥôq w^e laqqārôb 'āmar yhwh ûr^{e}pā'tîw*]."[126] Hence the pronouncement of *šālôm* is the result of "I will heal him"; in other words, "I will make him whole" (thus bringing him into a state of *šālôm*—complete well-being).[127] Thus Isaiah 57 leads well into chapter 58,[128] where to those who will observe the Lord's appointed fast it is promised:

> Then your light will break forth like the dawn,
> and your healing will quickly appear [*wa'^{a}rūkāt^{e}kā m^{e}hērâ tiṣmaḥ*];
> then your righteousness will go before you,
> and the glory of the LORD will be your rear guard....
> The LORD will guide you always;
> he will satisfy your needs in a sun-scorched land
> and will strengthen your frame [*w^e 'aṣmōtêkā*—lit., "bones" (*yaḥ^{a}lîṣ*)].[129]
> You will be like a well-watered garden,
> like a spring whose waters never fail.
> Your people will rebuild the ancient ruins
> and will raise up the age-old foundations;
> you will be called Repairer of Broken Walls,
> Restorer of Streets with Dwellings.
> (58:8, 11–12 NIV; cf. the promises to the Sabbath-keepers in v. 14)[130]

4.1.5. Faithless Shepherds and the "Healing" of the Flock

Both Ezekiel 34:4 and Zechariah 11:16 speak of unfaithful shepherds (i.e., political and spiritual leaders),[131] who are so negligent that, among other failings, they do not strengthen the weak sheep (*'et-hannaḥlôt lō' ḥizzaqtem*), or treat the sick (*wᵉ'et-haḥôlâ lō'-rippē'tem*), or bind up the injured (*wᵉlanniš-beret lō' ḥābaštem*; Eze 34:4; Zec 11:16 has *wᵉhannišberet lō' yᵉrappe'*—"and he will not treat the injured").[132] Here the purely physical imagery has its obvious application in the life of the nation; according to W. Eichrodt, "This image does not need to be explained in detail; it is transparently obvious and immediately applicable to the way in which the proletariat are taken advantage of, denied their just rights and treated with injustice."[133] L. C. Allen notes: "Behind the shepherd language lies the typical royal duty of welfare of society's weaklings (cf. Jer 21:12; 22:3; Ps 72:4, 12–14)—and its absence from the royal agenda in the last decades of the kingdom (cf. Jer 22:15–17; 34:8)."[134] It was time for the Lord himself to shepherd his scattered, straying, and sickly sheep (Eze 34:11–16; cf. also Mic 4:6–7): "I will seek out the lost and bring back those driven away; I will bind up the injured and strengthen the sick [this time *ḥzq* instead of *rp'*],[135] but the fat and the strong I will destroy. I will tend the flock with justice" (Eze 34:16).[136]

4.2 THE FINAL "HEALING" OF THE NATIONS AND ISRAEL

4.2.1. The Prophets and the Nations

The images of sickness and healing are also applied by the prophets to the nations, with the concept of "incurable illness" again functioning to describe the (present or future) hopeless condition of Israel's neighbors. Whereas Israel at times appears to be terminally ill, final repentance—and thus healing—are expected.[137] This is not always the case with the nations. With reference to Egypt, Ezekiel declares (Eze 30:21): "Mortal man, I have broken the arm of Pharaoh king of Egypt, so it could not be bound up for healing, nor securely bandaged to make it strong enough to grasp a sword."[138] This means the breaking of Egypt's power and its consequent subjugation and dispersion by the Babylonians (Isa 30:22–26). Similar in thought is Jeremiah 46:11: "Go up to Gilead and procure balm, O fair maiden of Egypt; it is for naught that you have multiplied remedies [*laššawᵉ' hirbêt*—so Qere—*rᵉpu'ôt*]—there is no healing for you [*tᵉ 'ālâ 'ên lāk*]."[139]

But Egypt's broken condition was not to be permanent. In Isaiah 19, "The 'Egypt' Pronouncement" (so NJV),[140] verses 1–17 describe the imminent destruction of the Egyptian people and their ultimate subjection to the people of Judah. Then, in verse 18,[141] the prophet foresees the day when the Egyptians, subjugated by the Judeans and speaking the language of Canaan,[142] will "swear (allegiance) to the LORD of hosts." As a result of their crying out to God because of their oppressors, the Lord will send a deliverer and champion (*môš'îa warab*) and will rescue them (v. 20). Then the Egyptians will know God and worship him (v. 21). All this is summarized in verse 22: "And the LORD will smite Egypt [*wᵉnāgap yhwh 'et-miṣrayim*], smiting and then healing [*nāgōp wᵉrāpô'*];[143] when they turn back to the LORD [*wᵉšābû 'ad-yhwh*], he will be entreated by them and will heal them [*ûrᵉpā'ām*]." Significantly, the divine judgments are grouped under the heading of *yhwh nāgap*, and the bringing anew into divine favor is characterized by *rᵉpā'ām*. Also, as noted often above, the root *šûb* is integrally related to the "healing" process.

Yet, while there was hope for Judah and Israel—and, surprisingly, for Egypt—there was to be no hope for Babylon when the time of her judgment came. Jeremiah 51:8 begins with the pronouncement: "Suddenly Babylon has fallen and is shattered. Howl over her!" Sarcastically Jeremiah calls for help: "Get balm for her wounds: perhaps she can be healed" (*qᵉḥū ṣorî*—note again 8:22a: *lᵉmak'ôbah 'ûlay tērāpē'*). But alas, "We treated Babylon, but she would not heal" (*ripi'nû 'et-bābel wᵉlō' nirpātâ*).[144] While the divine Physician would soon successfully treat his people, there was no cure for the godless Babylonians.[145] In stark contrast to the prophetic prognosis offered to sickly Israel and Judah, Babylon had no hope.[146] Thus, as observed by the Talmudic sages, although the biblical prophets addressed their own people first with a message of doom, they ended with a message of hope.[147] Divine judgment and chastisement would finally issue in repentance and restoration. In the end, Israel's divine Healer would triumph for his people.

4.2.2. Israel's Eschatological "Healing"

Although it is impossible to know the relative time frame in which the prophets expected final redemption to come (cf. 1Pe 1:10–12),[148] it is clear that they did, in fact, entertain a great hope of radical, universal change for the better. The wicked would be destroyed (e.g., Mal 4:1 [3:19]), the earth would be renewed (e.g., Isa 65:17), ancient hostilities would end (e.g., 11:5–13), and the righteous would flourish (e.g., Zep 3:11–20). The kingdom of God would come! The Lord would lay bare his holy arm; he would intervene for his downtrodden people; he would establish justice. Suffering would cease! "They will neither hurt nor destroy in all my holy mountain, for the earth will be filled with devotion to the LORD, as the waters cover the seas" (Isa 11:9).

Several of the "Servant of the LORD" passages in Isaiah portray the redemption of Judah against the backdrop of its impending release from Babylonian captivity,[149] and Isaiah 40–55 as a whole pictures the return of the exiles in terms of a new creation and a second exodus.[150] In this context, there are promises of the liberation of captives from confinement: "I the LORD have called you in righteousness [or, victoriously], and I will grasp your hand and keep you and appoint you as a covenant for the people and a light to the nations, to open [*lipqōaḥ*] the eyes of the blind, to bring forth the prisoner from his cell and those who dwell in darkness from the dungeon" (Isa 42:6–7). Similarly, the prophet proclaims in 61:1, "The

Spirit of the Lord GOD is on me, because the LORD has anointed me to preach good news to the meek. He has sent me to bind up the brokenhearted, to proclaim freedom[151] for the captives and opening [of the eyes][152] for the prisoners." Clearly, the opening of the eyes (*lipqōaḥ*; *pᵉqaḥ-qōaḥ*) spoken of here describes the experience of the prisoner coming out of his dark, gloomy dungeon, once again to see the light of day.[153] Thus, while 42:7 spoke of the eyes of the *blind* being opened, 61:1 speaks of *prisoners* receiving their sight. It is thus a general promise of liberation rather than a specific promise of healing. In that sense, it is the hallmark of the public ministry of Jesus the Messiah (see below, 5.2.2): "The Servant's task, as in chs. 42 and 49, has a universal scope. God's coming is good news to *all* the poor of the earth. *All* broken hearts are to be bound up, and *all* prisoners set free."[154]

However, Isaiah 35:6 must be understood with specific reference to healing miracles.[155] The coming of God's kingdom will produce radical change; nature itself will be transformed (35:1–2, 6b–8a). Thus the feeble and fearful are encouraged to be strong and not afraid (vv. 3–4a). To them it will be said: "Behold, your God! Vengeance, the recompense of your God will come. He himself will come and save you! Then the eyes of the blind will be opened and the ears of the deaf unstopped. Then the lame will leap like a deer, and the tongue of the dumb will shout for joy. For waters will burst forth in the wilderness and streams in the desert" (vv. 4b–6). Certainly, the final establishment of the rule of God on earth will bring with it the removal of sin and its consequences (cf. 33:24), in terms of both the earth itself and humankind as a whole. Thus, outstanding miracles of healing, unprecedented throughout the OT, are anticipated with the eschaton.

It is fitting that it is primarily to this chapter in Isaiah, with allusion also to chapter 61, that Jesus points the disciples of John the Baptist when they come to inquire on behalf of their imprisoned leader, "Are you the one who was to come, or should we expect someone else?" (Lk 7:20). The deliberate record of Luke is significant:

> At that very time Jesus cured many who had diseases, sicknesses and evil spirits, and gave sight to many who were blind. So he replied to the messengers, "Go back and report to John what you have seen and heard: The blind receive sight, the lame walk, those who have leprosy are cured, the deaf hear, the dead are raised, and the good news is preached to the poor. Blessed is the man who does not fall away on account of me." (7:21–23; cf. Mt 11:2–6)[156]

Messiah the King had come![157]

It is also noteworthy that Isaiah 35 serves as a paradigm of the entire "already-not yet" eschatology of the NT.[158] The first manifestations of the kingdom are already here, viz., miraculous healings and deliverances. The captives are already being liberated. Moreover, metaphorically speaking, the prophesied terrestrial transformations are also unfolding: Streams of life-giving water are bursting forth in the desolate places, made barren by generations of spiritual darkness.[159] However, the literal restoration and renewal of the earth is still to come, awaiting the Messiah's return. Thus, while there is a firstfruits for the present age, viz., spiritual rejuvenation, deliverance from sin, and miraculous healings,[160] the "grand finale"—when sin and sickness will be no more—is still to come. Delitzsch has stated this clearly:

> The bodily defects mentioned here[,] there is no reason for regarding as figurative representations of spiritual defects.[161] The healing of bodily defects, however, is merely the outer side of what is actually effected by the coming of Jehovah (for the other side, comp. ch. xxxii. 3,4). And so, also, the change of the desert into a field abounding with water is not a mere poetical ornament; for in the last times, the era of redemption, nature itself will really share in the *doxa* which proceeds from the manifested God to His redeemed.[162]

Interestingly, "the blind and the lame," often representative of the weak, underprivileged, and oppressed,[163] will also partake of the benefits of restoration. In the eschatological context of Isaiah 35, the promise is definite: They will be made whole! However, in Jeremiah 31:8, it is simply stated that they, along with women with children and in labor, will be among the exiles returning from Babylon, while in Isaiah 33:23 it is noted that, with Zion's final triumph, "even the lame will carry off the plunder." There is, however, one significant addition in verse 24, viz., that no one living then in Zion will be sick, since all those who dwell there will have been forgiven of their sins.[164] Thus, for Jeremiah, speaking of the return of the Judean captives, the reference to the weak, handicapped exiles was positive. God will bring his hurting people back to their land. But for Isaiah, with an "end-time" vision in mind, the reference to the lame was problematic. Thus J. J. M. Roberts notes, "Finally, and as if to correct the notion suggested by the mention of the lame, Isaiah promises that the inhabitants of this purified Jerusalem will not suffer illness, for they will be a forgiven people, unlike the battered and sick Zion of the period before God's purging judgment (Isa 1: 5–6)."[165]

The prophet Ezekiel, in keeping with his priestly heritage, uses different imagery to speak of Israel's ideal future.[166] Thus Ezekiel 47:8–12, continuing the vision of the temple river,[167] states that when the river flows from the Arabah into the (Dead) Sea, the water there will become wholesome (v. 8; *wᵉnirpᵉ'û hammayim*). The fish and swarming creatures of the sea will thrive, "for [the water] will become wholesome, and everything will live wherever the river goes" (v. 9; *wᵃyērāpᵉ'û wāḥāy kol 'ᵃšer-yābô' šāmmâ hannāḥal*). This will result in a great increase of fishermen there (v. 10); yet the Sea's swamps and marshes will not become wholesome, for they will be used for salt (v. 11; *biṣṣotāw ûgᵉbā'āyw wᵉlo' yerāpᵉ'û lᵉmelaḥ nittānû*). Finally, along the banks there will be all kinds of trees for food. "Their leaves will not wither and their fruit will not fail; month by month they will produce new fruit, because the water for them flows from the temple. Their fruit will serve for food and their leaves for making whole" (v. 12).[168]

Remarkably enough, just as infectious diseases could spread their contaminating germs, so also the life-giving temple river could spread its healing force wherever it went.[169] Unusable and life-threatening saltwater would be "restored" to its healthy and proper state (*wenirpe'û hammayim*). Fish would thrive in the new abundant fresh waters. And the trees, nourished by this supernaturally invigorating stream, would not only produce consistent fruit and never-withering leaves, but these very leaves would possess "healing" qualities in and of themselves! And so this image is borrowed in the last description of God's ideal kingdom, found in the last chapter of the NT, vouchsafing, as it were, ultimate healing: "Then the angel showed me the river of the water of life, as clear as crystal, flowing from the throne of God and of the Lamb down the middle of the great street of the city. On each side of the river stood the tree of life, bearing twelve crops of fruit, yielding its fruit every month. And the leaves of the tree are for the healing of the nations" (Rev 22:1–2).[170]

It is altogether fitting that Malachi, the last canonical prophet,[171] also reaffirmed the promise of final healing (*marpe'*) for his generation, speaking of the time in which the sun[172] of righteousness (or "victory") would arise with healing in its wings (or corners of its[173]garments; 4:2a [3:20a]).[174] This time, the "healing" would be for the godly remnant,[175] the nation having been purged of the godless and hypocritical (cf. Mal 3:1–3; 4:1 [3:19]). As a result, the prophet says to the righteous, "You shall go forth and stamp like well-fed calves and you shall trample the wicked to a pulp, for they shall be dust beneath your feet on the day that I am preparing, said the LORD of hosts.... Then the offerings of Judah and Jerusalem shall be pleasing to the LORD as in the days of yore and in the years of old" (3:20b–21 [4:2b–3]; 3:4 NJV).[176] Indeed, as another prophet of Israel declared: "My Lord GOD will wipe the tears away from all faces and will put an end to the reproach of his people over all the earth—for it is the LORD who has spoken" (Isa 25:8 NJV). God's healing would be glorious! It only awaited its appointed time.

◆ 5 ◆

Israel's Divine Healer in the New Testament[1]

5.1. OLD TESTAMENT HEALING AND NEW TESTAMENT HEALING

5.1.1. Continuity and Discontinuity[2]

Anyone who has made a careful study of the biblical subject of divine healing, having systematically treated the OT material, cannot help but feel that the floodgates of healing have opened in the pages of the NT.[3] The trickle has become a deluge, the exceptional has become the norm, the occasional has become the commonplace, the hoped for has become the experienced, the longed for has become the realized. The angel Gabriel's words in Luke 1:37—following on the heels of the astonishing news that not only will the virgin Mary conceive, but that her old cousin Elizabeth is already pregnant—set the stage for the outpouring of the miraculous in the Gospels and Acts: "For nothing is impossible with God." Indeed, the glory of the One and Only Son (Jn 1:14, 18) was seen clearly in his mighty healing deeds (Jn 20:30–31), and his earthly ministry is often summed up in terms of preaching, teaching, and healing.[4] He came to set the captives free! (See below, 5.2.1, 5.2.2.)

Thus Matthew twice records: "Jesus went through all the towns and villages, *teaching* in their synagogues, *preaching* the good news of the kingdom and *healing* every disease and sickness" (Mt 9:35; cf. 4:23–25; italics added); and from the Savior's own lips, in a message for Herod, he summarized his activities by saying: "Go tell that fox, 'I will *drive out demons* and *heal* people today and tomorrow, and on the third day I will reach my goal'" (Lk 13:32; italics added). Similarly Peter, preaching to the first Gentile audience in Acts, encapsulates the Lord's ministry by describing "how God anointed Jesus of Nazareth with the Holy Spirit and power, and how he went around *doing good* and *healing* all who were under the power of the devil, because God was with him" (Ac 10:38; italics added). Likewise, when the apostles were first sent out to preach, they were given "authority to *drive out evil spirits* and to *heal* every disease and sickness" (Mt 10:1; cf. 10:7–8; Mk 6:7, 12–13; Lk 9:1–2; 10:8–9); accordingly, "they set out and went from village to village, *preaching* the gospel and *healing* people everywhere" (Lk 9:6; italics added). This pattern continued powerfully in the book of Acts, expanding beyond the ministry of the twelve apostles (e.g., Ac 8:5–8).[5]

It is impossible to think of the ministry of Jesus and the early believers without thinking of miraculous healing.[6] The kingdom of God, with its glorious transforming power, had suddenly broken into human history (see below, 5.2.1). This had profound implications, and J. D. Crossan vividly expresses the attitude of the Galilean peasants who would have heard Jesus:

> He speaks about the rule of God, and they listen as much from curiosity as anything else. They know all about rule and power, about kingdom and empire, but they know it in terms of tax and debt, malnutrition and sickness, agrarian oppression and demonic possession. What, they really want to know, can this kingdom of God do for a lame child, a blind parent, a demented soul screaming its tortured isolation among the graves that mark the edges of the village?[7]

The rest of the NT provides the resounding answer.

Certainly, the heart of God toward his people has been constant, as expressed in Jeremiah's letter to the exiles in Babylon: "For I am mindful of the plans I have made concerning you—declares the LORD—plans for your welfare, not for disaster, to give you a hopeful future" (Jer 29:11 NJV). It has always been the Father's desire to bless and not curse, to heal and not smite, to forgive and not condemn (cf. above, 2.2.2, 2.3.2).[8] However, the pattern of disobedience seen throughout the OT meant that, for the most part, Israel suffered God's wrath. Many were smitten; relatively few were healed (cf. 2.2.5, 2.3.1; note Lk 4:24–27). But the coming of Jesus into the world brought about a new day. He healed *many* (e.g., Mk 4:32–34);[9] *all* who touched him in faith were made whole (e.g., Mt 14:34–36); as stated by Luke, "He healed those who needed healing" (Lk 9:11).[10] Yet he smote no one.

It is true that his coming brought into the world fiery judgment (cf. Mt 3:11–12).[11] Moreover, in no uncertain terms, he warned his contemporaries of impending doom, since they did not recognize him as Messiah (e.g., Lk 19:41–44; 23:27–31). The stakes of rejecting God became much higher in this age of visitation than they were in previous generations (cf. Mt 11:20–24; Heb 2:1–4; 10:26–31; 12:25–29). Also, the book of Acts is not without record of divine judgments (Ananias and Sapphira in 5:1–11; Herod in 12:19b–24; Elymas in 13:6–12, all of which were accompanied with salutary effects for the early church), and the glorified Lord in Revelation threatens "Jezebel" and her followers with painful affliction and death if they will not repent (Rev 2:20–23).[12] But, in contrast to the OT account, these acts of wrath are now the exception to the glorious rule. Thus, in what may be called the "platform speech" of Jesus' ministry,[13] he read from Isaiah 61:1–2 only as far as the words "to proclaim the year of the Lord's favor," strategically stopping in the middle of the sentence and thereby omitting "and the day of vengeance of our God." He had come to proclaim the day of grace![14]

This helps to explain the free and universal offer of forgiveness and healing. *It is as if God declared general amnesty for all those who would repent and believe* (see below, 5.2.2). Now, while it is incorrect to say that, from an OT standpoint, all sickness is the result of individual sin (cf. above, 2.2.2, n. 87), it is clear that sickness is often the result of individual disobedience, and that it was the curse of God, not his blessing, that often brought about plagues and debilitating diseases (2.2.2). Moreover, in the broadest possible terms, humanity's alienation from God was the ultimate cause of its suffering. Thus, when the Messiah entered the world, the physical results of sin were everywhere. There were masses of sick and demon-possessed people suffering from every imaginable affliction. For some, their condition was specifically related to their sin (cf. Jn 5:14); for others, it was clearly unrelated to any transgression on their part (e.g., Jn 9:1–3; see below, 5.3.2). However, whether or not these sufferers were getting what they deserved (i.e., based on a strict covenantal reading of passages such as Ex 15:25b–26) was not the issue. Indeed, from a NT perspective, all were sinners and therefore deserved death and judgment (cf. Lk 13:1–6). All needed the Great Physician's touch (cf. Mt 9:9–13 with Ro 3:9b). But now it was time for unmerited favor,[15] and Jesus freely offered liberty from both sin and sickness.[16]

Another point of contrast often noted between divine healing in the OT and NT has to do with the relationship between demons and disease (cf. below, 5.3.1). In the OT, Satan and demons were only rarely associated with sickness (cf. 3.1.10). Yahweh smote and Yahweh healed (cf. 2.2.5). However, with monotheism more firmly entrenched, later OT revelation began to disclose the activity of intermediate agents of wrath (cf. 2.3.1 on 2Ch 21:1) who were, in fact, diabolical and destructive in and of themselves (3.2.1).[17] With the veil lifted in the NT,[18] and with battle lines publicly drawn between the kingdom of darkness and the kingdom of light (5.2.1, 5.3.1), it became clear that Satan and his denizens had wreaked havoc on the human race. Deliverance was therefore a cornerstone of Jesus' ministry.

To summarize: The human race as a whole—including, for the most part, even the chosen nation[19]—stood alienated from God. They were, generally speaking, under his judgment, not his favor, and they suffered the ravages of sin and Satan in body and spirit. A key task of the Messiah was to bring freedom and relief to this suffering world, spiritually and bodily. Healings flowed from his life as a natural outworking of his divine mission and character. Thus, the woman who had been bleeding for twelve years was instantly healed by simply drawing *dunamis*[20] from Jesus by faith, *without a volitional act on his part* (Mk 5:21–34). Where his direct action was called for, healing seemed to be the immediate response, virtually a "reflex reaction."[21] For example, Matthew 12:22 records, "Then they brought him a demon-possessed man who was blind and mute, and Jesus healed him, so that he could both talk and see." And Mark records, "And wherever he went—into villages, towns or countryside—they placed the sick in the marketplaces. They begged him to let them touch even the edge of his cloak, and all who touched him were healed" (Mk 6:56). To the end of his earthly ministry, such events were a matter of course: "The blind and the lame came to him at the temple, and he healed them" (Mt 21:14; cf. also Lk 22:51, the healing of Malchus's ear in the Garden of Gethsemane).[22]

5.1.2. The New Testament Vocabulary of Healing[23]

sōzō.[24] In keeping with this delivering-saving-healing emphasis, Jesus is called *sōtēr*, "Savior," approximately seventeen times in the NT (cf. also Mt 1:21, regarding the significance of the name "Jesus"). As noted earlier (cf. 1.3.3), this title was also applied to Asklepios/Aesculapius, the preeminent Greco-Roman healing deity of the age. The NT usage of the verbal root *sōzō* (basically, "to rescue, save, deliver, preserve from danger, etc.") evidences a similar inclusive meaning.[25] Thus, in the space of less than two chapters in Luke, it is used in 7:50 with reference to being *saved from sin* (see 7:36–49), in 8:36 with reference to being *saved from demons* (see 8:26–39), in 8:48 with reference to being *saved from sickness* (see 8:43–47), and in 8:50 with reference to being *saved from death* (see 8:49).[26] Jesus is a *sōtēr* who forgives, delivers, heals, and resurrects, both temporally and eternally.[27] Elsewhere in the NT, *sōzō* or *diasōzō* are found in the following healing contexts:[28] the healing of blind Bartimaeus (Mk 10:52; Lk 18:42); the disciples' comment that if Lazarus sleeps "he will get better" (Jn 11:12); the healing of the crippled beggar (Ac 4:9); the healing of the man lame from birth (Ac 14:9); the promise that the elders' prayer offered in faith will heal the sick (Jas 5:15). James 5:15 in particular provides an excellent example of the holistic usage of *sōzō* (rendered here as "save" by the AV and "make . . . well" by the NIV): The sick person will be "raised up" (*egeirō*),[29] and if he has sinned (thus assuming a potential link between his sickness and sin; cf. below, 5.3.2), he will be forgiven. While the primary emphasis is clearly on physical healing, the broader meaning of *sōzō* makes a reference to forgiveness of sin appropriate in this context.[30]

It should be noted also that there is a great deal of fluidity in the usage of the various healing words. Thus, for example, in the account of the healing of the centurion's servant, Luke uses *diasōzō* for the initial request (Lk 7:3, lacking in Matthew), then agrees with Mt 8:8 in using *iaomai* (Lk 7:7, "But say the word, and my servant will be *healed*"), and has *hugiainō* ("made well") in 7:10 for Matthew's *iaomai* (Mt 8:13, "healed").[31] One should also note the descriptions of the healing of a crippled beggar in Acts: with *sōzō* in Ac 4:9 (translated in NIV as "healed") but with *iasis* in 4:22 (translated, in conjunction with *semeion*, as "miraculously healed"; the Greek is literally, "this sign of healing"); see further John 5:6–15, with *hugiainō* ("well") four times and *therapeuō* ("heal") once (v. 10).

iaomai. With the meaning of "to heal, cure," this verb almost always renders Hebrew *rāpā'* in the LXX, even when forced (e.g., 1Ki 18:30; cf. above 0.3.1, 0.3.2, 3.4; cf. also the derivative forms *iama* [1Co 12:9, 28, 30; in the LXX, four times for *rp'*] and *iasis*, both "healing" [Lk 13:32; Ac 4:22, 30; in the LXX ten times for *rp'*]). While the primary application of *iaomai* in the NT relates to physical healing (three times in Matthew; not in Mark; eleven times in Luke; twice in John; three times in Acts), it sometimes reflects secondary OT usage of *rāpā'* in terms of bringing restoration to a "sin-sick" people (cf. above, 4.1.1). Thus for Hebrews 12:13, BAGD notes, "The figure of sin as a wound or disease is . . . plain,"[32] classifying 1 Peter 2:24 here as well[33] (cf. also the discussion of the NT's usage of Isa 6:10 above in 4.1.4; see Mt 13:15; Jn 12:40; Ac 28:27; contrast Mk 4:12).[34]

therapeuō. This verb, which originally meant "to wait upon, to serve as a *therapon* [attendant], do service to the gods" (Ac 17:25; in the LXX, the primary usage), early extended into the semantic range of healing. Hence, it came to mean "to treat medically, cure, heal, restore to health," very close in usage and meaning to *iaomai*,[35] and in this sense, it is the most common NT word for healing, occurring more than forty times in healing contexts (e.g., Mt 4:23; 10:1; Mk 3:2; Lk 8:43; Jn 5:10; the totals are Matthew—16 times; Mark—5; Luke—14; John—1; Acts—5; Revelation—2; *therapeia* occurs twice in Luke and once in Revelation, viz., 22:2; see 4.2.2). Since those suffering demonization were, in a sense, afflicted with a malady—even if not physically ill—*therapeuō* is also used for their deliverance (cf. Lk 7:21, "At that very time Jesus *cured* many who had diseases, sicknesses and evil spirits, and gave sight to many who were blind"; also Mt 15:28, on the "healing" [*iaomai*] of the demon-possessed daughter; see below, 5.3.1). It is noteworthy that *therapeuō*, used most frequently in *medical* healing contexts in contemporaneous literature, is used in the NT "in the sense of 'to heal,' and always in such a way that the reference is not to medical treatment, which might fail, but to real healing."[36] Also, while Philo could use *therapeuō* especially for the healing of the soul,[37] such figurative usage is never found in the NT, in spite of the LXX's usage of *iaomai*, reflected in several NT citations.

hugiainō. In two separate passages (Lev 13; Eze 47), the LXX renders *rp'* with *hugiazō* (cf. above, 2.2.6; 4.2.2), a form closely related to *hugiainō*, "to be sound, healthy." In the NIV, *hugiainō* is rendered eight times with "sound" (normally, "sound doctrine," e.g., 1Ti 1:10; but see Mt 12:13 for a healing context) and once each with "enjoy good health," "healthy," "safe and sound," and "well"; the related form, *hugiēs* (once in the LXX for *t^e rûpâ*), occurs eleven times in the NT, reflecting a similar range of meanings (the NIV renders with "well" four times [Jn 5:6, 11, 14, 15, in the context of the lame man who was healed]).[38]

5.2. ASPECTS OF THE HEALING MINISTRY OF JESUS THE MESSIAH

The subdivisions in this section have been chosen because they represent different, though often overlapping, aspects of NT divine healing, each of which may easily be compared with antecedent OT material.

5.2.1. Healing and the Kingdom of God[39]

According to the testimony of the evangelists, Jesus was called "King of the Jews" by the Magi at his birth (Mt 2:2) and by the Romans at his death (Mt 27:37; Mk 15:26; Lk 23:38; Jn 19:19). When he began his public ministry, he took up the message of John the Baptist: "'The time has come,' he said. 'The kingdom of God is near. Repent and believe the good news!'" (Mk 1:15; cf. Mt 4:17 with 3:2). Wherever he went, this was his theme (cf. Mt 4:23; 9:35), and his healing acts were directly linked to the inbreaking of the kingdom (cf. Lk 4:40–44; 9:10–11). Thus, when he sent his disciples out to preach the coming of the kingdom of God, he commissioned them to heal and exorcise in conjunction with this proclamation: "As you go, preach this message: 'The kingdom of heaven is near.' Heal the sick, raise the dead, cleanse those who have leprosy, drive out demons" (Mt 10:7–8a; cf. also Lk 9:2, "and he sent them out to preach the kingdom of God and to heal the sick"). Luke 10:8–9, the commissioning of the Seventy-Two, is especially clear: "When you enter a town and are welcomed, eat what is set before you. Heal the sick who are there and tell them, 'The kingdom of God is near you.'" *Miracles of healing and deliverance announced the inbreaking of the reign of God* (cf. above, 4.2.2, on Isa 35).[40]

In particular, Jesus made reference to the conflict between the kingdom of God and the kingdom of Satan in his exorcisms:[41] "If Satan drives out Satan, he is divided against himself. How then can his kingdom stand? ... But if I drive out demons by the Spirit of God, then the kingdom of God has come upon you" (Mt 12:26, 28).[42] As noted by Mueller, and reflecting the consensus of NT scholarship, these acts of deliverance were "an element in the struggle for the establishment of eschatological salvation.... His exorcism of demons, and with it the victorious struggle against Satan on earth, are visible signs of the advent of the eschatological time of salvation in which God alone will reign."[43] This concept is also found in the longer ending of Mark, where the first sign to accompany the believers is this: "In my name they will drive out [*ekballō*] demons" (Mk 16:17b), the use of *ekballō* being suggestive of the LXX's rendering of *gārēš*, "to drive out," used frequently with reference to the conquest of Canaan (e.g., Ex 23:28–30; Dt 33:27; less frequently, but in similar contexts, *ekballō* renders the Hiphil of *yrš*, "to dispossess"; e.g., Ex 34:24; Dt 11:23).[44] Thus, just as the Israelites were commissioned by Yahweh to drive out and dispossess the Canaanites, thereby taking the Promised Land, so also the disciples were commissioned by Jesus to drive out and dispossess demons,[45] thereby taking back what rightfully belonged to God and making disciples for him, the new subjects of his kingdom (Mt 28:18–20; Col 1:13; Rev 1:5b–6). This gospel of the kingdom was proclaimed by the early church (cf. Mt 24:14; Ac 8:12; 20:24–25; 28:23, 31), suggesting that there would be a continuing pattern of miracles integrally associated with the message, since the battle for the final establishment of the kingdom of God raged (and rages) on.[46]

5.2.2. Healing and the Eschatological Jubilee[47]

Closely related to the foregoing is Jesus' Jubilee proclamation in Luke 4:18–19: Spiritually speaking, it was time for all slaves to go free and all debts to be canceled.[48] Reading from Isaiah 61:1–2 (with a phrase from 58:6 included),[49] Jesus announced to the expectant congregation: "Today this scripture is fulfilled in your hearing" (Lk 4:21). Then, after escaping from the quickly infuriated crowd, he performed two miracles whose significance should not be missed, since in both (an exorcism and the healing of Peter's mother-in-law) Jesus *rebukes* the evil, intrusive presence (4:35, 39; NIV's "Be quiet!" in v. 35 is not exact and misses the important connection with v. 39).[50] These individual miracles are then followed by the healing and deliverance of many, recorded in all three Synoptics (Lk 4:40–41; cf. Mt 8:16–17; Mk 1:32–33). Having proclaimed liberty to the captives, Jesus purposefully went about setting them free.[51]

This helps to explain why there is not a single instance in the Gospels or Acts in which Jesus or his disciples directly *pray for* the healing of the sick as they address them, their sickness, or the demonic spirit behind it. Sometimes there is prayer *before* ministering to the afflicted ones (cf. Ac 9:40; 28:8, see, broadly, 4:29–30; Jn 11:41–43 hardly applies), but the sick themselves are never prayed for (contrast Jas 5:14–15). Rather, the dead are commanded to rise (Mk 5:41–42; Lk 7:14–15; Jn 11:43–44; Ac 9:40–41), the lame are commanded to get up (Jn 5:8–9; Ac 3:6–8; 8:34 [prefaced by the proclamation, "Aeneas ... Jesus Christ heals you"]; 14:8–10), the man with the shriveled hand is commanded to stretch it out (Mt 12:9–13), the ears of the deaf mute are commanded to be opened (Mk 7:31–35), the leper is commanded to be cleansed (Mt 8:1–3), and before healing the crippled woman (*bound* eighteen long years by Satan; see Lk 13:10–16; cf. further, below, 5.2.4, 5.3.1), Jesus announces to her, "Woman, you are set free from your infirmity."[52] Thus the healing and deliverance ministry of Jesus and his followers was a ministry of restoration and emancipation,[53] to culminate ultimately in the glorious liberty of the children of God (Ro 8:19–23) upon the Lord's return (1Co 15:50–55; 2Co 5:1–5; Rev 21:4; see Ac 3:19–21).[54] Our total emancipation was set in motion with Jesus' prophetic Jubilee proclamation in Luke 4, and it was purchased and secured by means of his atoning death, by which we are released from the debt of sin.[55]

5.2.3. Healing and the Holy Spirit[56]

In a well-known example of "realized eschatology" in the NT, Peter in his Pentecost sermon changes Joel's, "And *afterward*, I will pour out my Spirit" (Joel 2:28[3:1]) into, "'*In the last days*, God says, I will pour out my Spirit'" (Ac 2:17). The baptism in the Spirit, accompanied by a miraculous gift of tongues, is seen as the fulfillment of Joel's prophecy and has thus ushered in the end of the age, an era characterized by the infusion of the Holy Spirit in power (cf. Mt 3:11; Jn 7:37–39;[57] for the "last days," see 1Co 10:11; Heb 1:2a).[58]

While the Matthean logion emphasizes that Jesus drove out demons *by the Spirit* (Mt 12:28; see above, 5.2.1), it is especially Luke-Acts that connects the Spirit to the miracles of

Jesus and the disciples.[59] After the Spirit descended on him at his baptism (Lk 3:22), "Jesus, *full of the Holy Spirit*, returned from the Jordan and was *led by the Spirit* in the desert, where for forty days he was tempted by the devil" (4:1–2a).[60] After that, he "returned to Galilee *in the power of the Spirit*" (4:14a), and in the synagogue, he read from the prophet Isaiah, "*The Spirit of the Lord is on me*, because he has anointed me to preach good news to the poor. He has sent me to proclaim freedom for the prisoners and recovery of sight for the blind, to release the oppressed, to proclaim the year of the Lord's favor" (4:18–19, discussed above, 5.2.2). *It was by the Spirit that Jesus preached, healed, and delivered.*[61]

In Luke 5:17, the author writes that "the *power* [*dunamis*] of the Lord was present for him to heal the sick"; and in 6:19, the large crowd of "people all tried to touch him, because *power* was coming from him and healing them all."[62] It was this same power that came from him to heal the woman with the issue of blood (8:46) and that Jesus gave to his apostles when he sent them out to preach, heal, and exorcise (9:1; see below, 5.3.1). His closing words in Luke before his ascension were, "I am going to send you what my Father has promised; but stay in the city until you have been clothed with *power* from on high" (24:49), and this is explicitly connected with the reception of the Spirit promised in Acts 1:8: "But you will receive *power* when the *Holy Spirit* comes on you; and you will be my witnesses in Jerusalem, and in all Judea and Samaria, and to the ends of the earth."

Thus, after Pentecost, "With great *power* the apostles continued to testify to the resurrection of the Lord Jesus, and much grace was upon them all" (4:33). Indeed, Peter stated, "We are witnesses of these things, and so is the *Holy Spirit*, whom God has given to those who obey him" (5:32), while Paul reminded the Spirit-oriented Corinthians, "My message and my preaching were not with wise and persuasive words, but with a demonstration of the *Spirit's power*" (1Co 2:4; cf. also 2Co 12:12).[63]

According to this theology, the continued acts of the Holy Spirit through the disciples gave proof to the Lord's resurrection and ascension (cf. also below, 5.2.6, on the confirming nature of these miracles): "Exalted to the right hand of God, he has received from the Father the promised Holy Spirit and has poured out what you now see and hear" (Ac 2:33). J. Ruthven is thus correct in stating: "The exaltation of Jesus and the resulting overflow of the charismata through his church must be placed in the context of salvation history."[64]

The book of Acts speaks of the Spirit and his work more than sixty times,[65] and Paul's first letter to the Corinthians makes clear that the supernatural gifts they were enjoying—including healings and miracles—were manifestations of the Spirit, given freely for the common good (1Co 12:1–11; cf. also Gal 3:1–5). The prophesied time had come. No longer would the Spirit fall on only a select few prophets and servants, enabling them to perform mighty acts for God.[66] Now the Holy Spirit, who had come to indwell every believer (Ro 8:15–16; 1Co 6:19; Gal 4:6; 1Jn 2:27; cf. also Jn 14:17b), would be poured out freely on them all (Ac 2:17–18; cf. Nu 11:29). The church would be the community of the Spirit (1Co 3:16, speaking corporately; Eph 2:22).[67]

5.2.4. Healing and the Sabbath[68]

In the Exodus version of the Decalogue, the command to remember the Sabbath is grounded in creation: "For in six days the LORD made the heavens and the earth, the sea, and all that is in them, but he rested on the seventh day. Therefore the LORD blessed the Sabbath day and made it holy" (Ex 20:11). However, in the Deuteronomic version, Israel is commanded to keep the Sabbath holy in light of the Exodus: "Remember that you were slaves in Egypt and that the LORD brought you out of there with a mighty hand and an outstretched arm. Therefore the LORD your God has commanded you to observe the Sabbath day" (Dt 5:15).[69] For Jesus, the Sabbath was thus the ideal day for removing the terrible burden of sickness and demonic oppression, thereby providing true rest for the formerly enslaved (cf. Heb 4!).[70] In fact, *he went out of his way* to heal on the Sabbath, in some cases healing in spite of opposition and unbelief, in contrast to his normal pattern of ministry (see below, 5.2.5). The Sabbath was the day for doing good, and healing was a good thing (cf. Ac 4:9; 10:38; see also Jn 10:32). Thus, he challenged the religious leaders with the question: "Is it lawful to heal on the Sabbath? . . . Which is lawful on the Sabbath: to do good or to do evil, to save life or to kill?" (Mt 12:10b; Mk 3:4). Then, answering his own question, he asked rhetorically: "If any of you has a sheep and it falls into a pit on the Sabbath, will you not take hold of it and lift it out? How much more valuable is a man than a sheep! Therefore it is lawful to do good on the Sabbath" (Mt 12:11–12).[71] He then healed the man with the shriveled hand, to the consternation of the leaders (Mt 12:13–14).

In Luke 13, the two Sabbath concepts, viz., *true rest* through *emancipation*, are again combined in the healing of the crippled woman. In answer to the indignant synagogue ruler's charge to the people that "there are six days for work. So come and be healed on those days, not on the Sabbath" (13:14), Jesus answers sternly, "You hypocrites! Doesn't each of you on the Sabbath untie his ox or donkey from the stall and lead it out to give it water? Then should not this woman, a daughter of Abraham, whom Satan has kept bound for eighteen long years, be set free on the Sabbath day from what bound her?" (13:15–16). The Sabbath was *not* the day to be bound, nor was it a time for carrying heavy loads.[72]

It is also noteworthy that on at least five different occasions, Jesus *initiated* a healing on the Sabbath, each time healing just one person (Lk 14:1–6; Jn 5:1–14; 9:1–41; and the two instances just cited).[73] He was thereby declaring himself Lord of the Sabbath,[74] which includes the concept of being Lord of every word of God made into a human tradition.[75] The strategic positioning of these accounts in the Synoptics (in Mark and Luke, immediately after the parable of the new wineskins, coupled with the dispute concerning picking grain on the Sabbath [Mk 2:18–3:5;[76] Lk 5:33–6:11]; in Matthew, following Jesus' invitation to the weary and burdened to come to him, for his yoke was easy and his burden light [Mt 11:28–30])[77] and the legal controversies that followed the healings in John's gospel make this emphatically clear. Jesus as Lord of the Sabbath saved, healed, and delivered, bringing to full expression the divine purpose for the day.

5.2.5. Healing and Compassion[78]

In the OT, Yahweh's healings were perceived as acts of mercy and grace, reflective of his goodness and worthy of praise (see Pss 6:2[3]; 103, which have as their background healing a serious illness; see above, 3.1.1–3; cf. also Php 2:27). In a similar vein, it is noted several times that Jesus healed out of compassion, stated most broadly in Matthew 14:14: "When Jesus landed and saw a large crowd, he had compassion on them and healed their sick."[79] The following individual cases of healing or resurrection out of compassion (always *splanchnizomai*) are also recorded: the leper (Mk 1:40–42); the two blind men (Mt 20:29–34, in response to their cries for mercy; cf. Mk 9:22 and the request for compassion ["take pity on us"] from the father of the demon-possessed boy); and the bereaved widow (Lk 7:11–15). In similar fashion, Jesus fed the five thousand and the four thousand because he was moved by compassion for them (Mk 6:34; 8:2), and it was because of his compassion for the crowds—like sheep without a shepherd—that he urged his disciples to petition the Lord of the harvest to send forth laborers into his harvest field (Mt 9:36–37).[80] Thus these supernatural healings were not merely authenticating signs of his divinity or messiahship (see below, 5.2.6); rather, they reflected the very heart of God toward sick and suffering humanity.[81]

Based on this observation, one gains insight into the character of the Father: Jesus healed and delivered because God was with him (Ac 10:38). In curing the paralytic on the Sabbath, he was only doing what he saw his Father doing (Jn 5:16–20); in fact, it was the miracles themselves that gave proof to the fact that the Father was in him and he in the Father (10:38). Thus Jesus could say to his detractors, "Do not believe in me unless I do what my Father does" (10:37); and to Philip he could pointedly ask:

> Don't you know me, Philip, even after I have been among you such a long time? Anyone who has seen me has seen the Father.... The words I say to you are not just my own. Rather, it is the Father, living in me, who is doing his work. Believe me when I say that I am in the Father and the Father is in me; or at least believe on the evidence of the miracles themselves. (14:9–11)

As expressed in the NT letters, Jesus was "the radiance of God's glory and the exact representation of his being" (Heb 1:3a), "the image of the invisible God" (Col 1:15a)—both in power and in love. Through his words and deeds, his life and death, he made God known to humanity (Jn 1:18).[82]

5.2.6. Healing and Faith[83]

As seen throughout chapters 2 to 4, in the OT the primary requirement for healing and health was covenantal obedience, including fealty to Yahweh alone (e.g., Ex 23:24–26; Dt 7:1–16), keeping his commandments (e.g., Ex 15:25b–26), and walking in godly fear and humility (Pr 3:7–8). Obedience resulted in divine blessings, not the least of which were health and long life, while disobedience resulted in divine curses, not the least of which were terrible sickness and premature death (cf. above, 2.2.2, 2.2.3). All of this, of course, presupposed faith—in the ability of the Lord and in the truthfulness of his Word.[84] However, in keeping with the OT emphasis, obedience rather than faith was presented as the paramount issue. Not surprisingly, the NT healing accounts put a tremendous emphasis on faith.[85] For example, to the woman healed of her bleeding problem and to the cleansed leper Jesus said, "Your *faith* has healed you/made you well" (Lk 8:48; 17:19; both with *sōzō*; see above, 5.1.2), while to Jairus, after hearing the report that his gravely ill daughter has just died, Jesus made the comment, "Don't be afraid; just *believe*, and she will be healed" (Lk 8:50). When the blind men asked Jesus to have mercy on them and restore their sight, he asked them, "Do you *believe* that I am able to do this?" (Mt 9:27–28), and he assured the father of the tormented boy, "Everything is possible for him who *believes*" (Mk 9:23b).[86] Accordingly, he explained to his disciples that they were not able to drive out the demon because they had "so little *faith*," adding, "I tell you the truth, if you have *faith* as small as a mustard seed, you can say to this mountain, 'Move from here to there' and it will move. Nothing will be impossible for you" (Mt 17:18–21). Thus, he "did not do many miracles [in his hometown] because of their lack of *faith*" (13:53–58). In fact, just as he was amazed at the great *faith* of the Roman centurion (8:10; cf. also the great *faith* of the Canaanite woman, 15:28)—resulting in a miracle of healing—so also he was amazed at the lack of *faith* of his own people in his hometown—resulting in the healing of just a few sick folk, with no outstanding miracles (Mk 6:5–6).[87]

This faith emphasis continues in the book of Acts: Peter explained the healing of the lame man in terms of "*faith* in the name of Jesus. . . . It is Jesus' name and the *faith* that comes through him that has given this complete healing to him, as you can all see" (Ac 3:16). In a later incident Paul perceived that the cripple "had *faith* to be healed," so he called out to him, "Stand up on your feet!" (14:9–10). Thus, in keeping with the overall thrust of the NT revelation, everything involved in our redemption—including miracles of healing—hinges on faith in Jesus the Christ. He is looking for people to put their trust in him (cf. Isa 7:9b; 30:15–16; Jer 17:5–8), and in him alone.[88]

5.2.7. Healing and the Authentication of Jesus as Messiah[89]

Miraculous healings were part of the divine attestation of the messiahship of Jesus: "Men of Israel, listen to this," declared Peter in his Pentecost sermon, "Jesus of Nazareth was a man accredited by God to you by miracles, wonders and signs, which God did among you through him, as you yourselves know" (Ac 2:22). When questioned by the disciples of John, Jesus appealed to the testimony of these miracles (Mt 11:2–6; Lk 7:18–23; cf. also Jn 10:37–38).[90] After his resurrection and ascension, similar miracles wrought by his followers bore witness to the veracity of their message (cf. above, 5.2.3). The longer appendix to Mark states that after Jesus' ascension, "the disciples went out and preached everywhere, and the Lord worked with them and confirmed his word by the signs that accompanied it" (Mk 16:20). Similar testimony is offered by Hebrews 2:3–4: The message was not only confirmed to the new audience by eyewitnesses of the Lord during his earthly ministry, but "God also testified to it by signs, wonders and various miracles, and gifts of the Holy Spirit distributed according to his will" (cf. also 1Co 2:1–5).[91]

This was in keeping with the pattern of miraculous confirmation found throughout the OT. In spite of the possibility of counterfeit signs, wonders, and miracles (e.g., Ex 7:8–12, 22; 8:7; Dt 13:1–5; see also Mt 24:24; 2Th 2:9; Rev 13:13–14), God backed up his servants with demonstrations of his power, thus attesting to the truthfulness of their mission and calling (e.g., Ex 4:1–9, 29–31; Nu 16:28–35; 1Ki 18:36–39), and at the same time, triumphing over idolatrous and counterfeit powers (e.g., Ex 8:16–19). The ultimate demonstration of God's power in the OT, viz., taking a whole nation out of another, greater nation, through the ten plagues and splitting of the sea (cf. above 2.1), becomes the backbone of all future revelation to Israel, forming the basis for the Ten Commandments and the covenant given at Mount Sinai.[92] This may be compared with *the* great act of divine confirmation in the NT, viz., the resurrection of Jesus from the dead, followed by his ascension and demonstrated in ongoing fashion by the gifts and power of the Spirit manifested through those who proclaimed the gospel (see above, 5.2.3; cf. Ac 2:24–36; 3:15; 5:29–32; 13:32–37; 17:29–31; Ro 1:1–4; 4:25; 1Co 15:1–20; et al.).[93]

It would be a mistake, however, to follow B. B. Warfield and others who limit the miracles of Jesus and the apostles to the level of mere confirmation—that is, to bare, outward attestations of power that have little intrinsic value.[94] Rather, Ruthven is correct in citing the view of R. Brown as representing "the consensus of modern biblical scholarship," when Brown writes:

> Jesus' miracles were not only or primarily external confirmations of his message; rather the miracle was the vehicle of the message. Side by side, word and miraculous deed gave expression to the entrance of God's kingly power into time. This understanding of the miracles as an intrinsic part of revelation, rather than merely an extrinsic criterion, is intimately associated with a theory of revelation where the emphasis on the God who acts is equal to (or even more stressed than) the emphasis on the God who speaks.[95]

Thus, Jesus refused to give his critics an abstract demonstration of power, such as a sign from heaven (cf. Mt 16:1–4). He did, however, frequently and freely point to his *miracles* as proof, since they attested to the very heart of who he was and what he came to do.[96]

As Messiah, Jesus came to inaugurate the kingdom of God (5.2.1), to proclaim the eschatological jubilee (5.2.2), to usher in the era of the Spirit (5.2.3), to bring true Sabbath rest (5.2.4), to reveal the love of the Father (5.2.5), and to present himself as the object of saving faith (5.2.6).[97] His miracles were often the loudest sermon he preached. He was Israel's divine Healer in the flesh, the living Word in action, bringing at last to his covenant people what the Torah itself could not deliver because of the weakness of the flesh (cf. in general Ac 13:39; Ro 8:3–4; Heb 8:7–12 [following the reading favored by the NIV for 8:8a, as opposed to the marginal rendering[98]]; see also above, 5.2.5).

5.3. SICKNESS, SATAN, SIN, AND SUFFERING

5.3.1. Sickness and Satan, Demons and Disease[99]

Jesus' ministry of healing is inextricably linked with the ministry of deliverance from demons, and sickness is frequently associated with satanic power in the Gospels. This is in keeping with the OT view that sickness in and of itself is bad, often associated with the anger and curse of God, while healing is good, always associated with his favor and blessing (see above, 5.1.1, for references). As noted previously, however, the NT revelation of the diabolical character of much sickness, disease, and infirmity[100] goes beyond the general tenor of that which is disclosed in the OT. Yet, when understood properly, it does not *contradict* the foundations laid in the Hebrew Scriptures; rather, it *builds* on that which has been established (again, see 5.1.1). Thus it is important to stress that in healing the sick and delivering the oppressed, *Jesus was only doing the will of God* (cf. 5.2.4, 5.2.6; note again Jn 5:19 in context). According to Acts 10:38, those whom he healed (here *iaomai*) "were under the power of the devil." In that sense, every healing is a deliverance from an oppressive condition (and, sometimes, spirit; see below, Lk 13:10–16, cf. n. 100, above), while every deliverance is a healing from a demonic bondage. Likewise, both *therapeuo* and *iaomai* can be used with reference to exorcisms (see 5.1.2).

The following reiterates the relevant testimony of the Gospels and Acts: (1) Luke summarizes Jesus' earthly ministry in terms of driving out demons and healing (Lk 13:32)—cf. further Philip's ministry in Samaria: "With shrieks evil spirits came out of many, and many paralytics and cripples were healed" Ac 8:7).

(2) Often included among those whom Jesus and his disciples *healed* are the demon-possessed (e.g., Mt 4:23–24)—cf. further Acts 19:11–12: "God did extraordinary miracles through Paul, so that even handkerchiefs and aprons that had touched him were taken to the *sick*, and their *illnesses* were *cured* and the *evil spirits left* them."

(3) Conversely, Matthew 8:16 notes only that "many who were demon-possessed were brought to him," with no mention being made of the sick (contrast the Lucan parallel, Lk 4:40–41). However, the text then reads, "and he drove out the spirits with a word *and healed all the sick*." Significantly, these acts of healing and deliverance are then explained as the (quite literal) fulfillment of Isaiah 53:4: "He took up our *infirmities* and carried our *diseases*" (Mt 8:17; see above, 4.1.4).

(4) Specific conditions and illnesses are attributed to demons and/or satanic influence. Thus, the (apparent) epilepsy of the boy described in Mark 9:14–29 and parallels was caused by a demon, identified by Jesus as a "deaf and mute spirit" (Mk 9:25). "Jesus rebuked the demon, and it came out of the boy, and he was healed [*etherapeuthe*] from that moment" (Mt 17:18; cf. Lk 9:42, "he rebuked the spirit and healed the boy").[101] Other examples include: Matthew 12:22 ("a demon-possessed man who was blind and mute, and Jesus healed him so that he could both talk and see"), and Luke 13:10–17 (a woman "who had been crippled by a spirit for eighteen years," to whom Jesus said, "Woman, you are set free from your infirmity," explaining that this woman was "a daughter of Abraham whom Satan has kept bound for eighteen long years").

(5) Especially noteworthy is the fact that Jesus gave his disciples *authority* (*exousia*)[102] over demons and disease: "He called his twelve disciples to him and gave them authority to drive out evil [unclean] spirits and to heal every disease and sickness" (Mt 10:1; cf. Lk 9:1–2, "He gave them power and

authority to drive out all demons and to cure diseases, and he sent them out to preach the gospel and to heal the sick"). Clearly, sickness and demons are associated here, seen as hostile forces to be driven out.[103] Mark 6:7 speaks only of Jesus giving the Twelve "authority over evil [unclean] spirits"; later we read, however, "They went out and preached that people should repent. They drove out many demons and anointed many sick people with oil and healed them" (6:12–13; cf. Lk 10:16–19; see also Mk 16:17–18, beginning with exorcism and ending with healing).[104] This, in fact, served as a paradigm for the ministry of the early church: preaching the risen Christ and setting the captives free in his name.[105] All of this relates to the announcement of the kingdom of God and the eschatological jubilee (cf. 5.2.1–2).

5.3.2. Sickness and Sin[106]

The connection made in the OT between sickness and sin is so clear and frequent that some scholars have overstated the case, as if the Hebrew Scriptures taught that *all sickness* is traceable to specific sin.[107] Rather, it must be realized that the OT material is selective, recorded especially for spiritual and moral purposes, so that when sickness *is* mentioned (except that associated with aging), it is almost always connected with sin.[108] The lesson, however, is indisputable: Sin often does result in sickness (and both of these are bad!), while forgiveness of sin and healing of disease (both of which are good!) are intimately woven together.[109] This theme is reiterated in the NT with two qualifications: (1) Jesus' proclamation of release (*aphesis*; see 5.2.2) from sin and sickness offers reconciliation and restoration on a scale unknown in OT times; and (2) Jesus offers the most direct statement that one's sickness may be unrelated to personal or familial sin (Jn 9:1–5; see below).[110]

Interestingly, however, Jesus also offers the Bible's most decisive example of the *close relationship* between sickness and sin in his healing of the paralytic. To him he said, "Take heart, son; your sins are forgiven," before *demonstrating* his authority to forgive by saying to him: "Get up, take your mat and go home" (Mt 9:1–8).[111] His words of comfort to the paralytic ("Take heart") would be inexplicable unless the connection between the man's condition and his sin was presupposed. Similarly, no one needed to explain to the crippled man healed at the Bethesda pool the meaning of Jesus' words: "See, you are well again. Stop sinning or something worse may happen to you" (Jn 5:14).[112]

This theology is presupposed as well in James 5:15–16, where we read: "And the prayer offered in faith [by the elders] will make the sick person well [*sōsei*]; the Lord will raise him up. If he has sinned, he will be forgiven. Therefore confess your *sins* to each other and pray for each other so that you may be *healed* [*iathete*]."[113] Paul also reflects this understanding when writing to the Corinthians. The reason some of them were weak and sick while others had died ("fallen asleep") is because they had sinned against the body and blood of the Lord, eating the bread and drinking the cup in an unworthy manner and thereby bringing themselves under divine judgment (1Co 11:27–32).[114]

Therefore, just as in the OT where individual healing was coupled with forgiveness (cf. 2.2.5, 2.3.1, 3.1.5, 3.1.9), so also the healing of the paralytic in Matthew 9 and the healing of the sick in James 5:15 are associated with forgiveness. Moreover, Jesus freely, even indiscriminately, healed all who came to him in faith—regardless of the cause of their suffering—since, as we have seen, amnesty for the repentant and spiritually dependent was a foundation of his ministry. More broadly, however, it can be observed that just as the OT provides potentially suggestive examples that point to the *general* connection between atonement and/or healing liberty—Leviticus 25:8–13 (the Year of Jubilee begins on the Day of Atonement);[115] Job 33:24 (healing is secured when the "intercessor" finds a "ransom" [Heb. *kōper* = Gk. *lutron*; cf. Mk 10:45]; see 3.3.2.4); Isaiah 53:4–5 (the Servant bears sickness and pain in his substitutionary death for sin; see 4.1.4); Isaiah 33:24 (no one will be sick in beatific Zion, since all its inhabitants will be forgiven of their sins; see 4.2.2)—so also, from a NT perspective, all healing, whether it be realized in this age or the age to come, ultimately flows out of the cross.[116]

5.3.3. Sickness and Suffering[117]

The followers of Jesus are not only assured that they will suffer for his sake (Mt 5:11–12; 10:24–25; Jn 15:18–21), they are also told that doing so is a privilege (Php 1:29). Thus the apostles, after being flogged, "left the Sanhedrin, rejoicing because they had been counted worthy of suffering disgrace for the Name" (Ac 5:41), and Peter counsels those suffering persecution for the faith to "rejoice that you participate in the sufferings of Christ," adding, "you are blessed, for the Spirit of glory and of God rests on you" (1Pe 4:12–14). The simple fact is that "everyone who wants to lead a godly life in Christ Jesus will be persecuted" (2Ti 3:12), and it is to this believers are called. "So then," Peter exhorts, "those who suffer according to God's will should commit themselves to their faithful Creator and continue to do good" (1Pe 4:19).[118]

There is, however, no logical connection between suffering persecution *for* the faith and suffering sickness *in spite* of the faith—or at the least, *unrelated* to the faith. The former is the special calling of those who take up their cross and follow the Savior; the latter is common to the whole human race (saint and sinner alike). The contrasts are obvious: Suffering persecution always comes as a result of obedience; suffering sickness sometimes comes as a result of disobedience. (When disobedience is not a factor, sickness comes as a result of natural causes, the fallen state of man, demonic attack, or a larger scheme in the plan of God—cf. above, 5.3.2, with reference to

Jn 9 and 11—but not as the result of obedience.) While Jesus promised persecution to his loyal disciples, he offered healing to the sick and oppressed.

In 1 Peter 4:15–16, Peter is careful to speak of those who suffer "according to God's will," contextually meaning suffering as Christians in contrast to suffering as lawbreakers or sinners. However, it may also be stated that being sick or under the power of spirits of infirmity has nothing to do with suffering as a Christian. Rather, Jesus spent much of his time bringing relief to the very people who suffered from these life-sapping conditions (cf. above, 3.1.4, 3.1.6, 3.1.7). Simply stated, nowhere in the Bible are obedient children of God told to *expect* sickness or disease as part of their calling in life. And if OT Israelites were accustomed to cry out to their beneficent Lord for deliverance from such afflictions—especially, when necessary, in conjunction with repentance—how much more should sick and diseased Christians be inclined to ask God to heal and deliver *them*.[119]

Sickness and disease are the common lot of humanity (and as such, the lot of Christians as well); but sickness and disease are unrelated to suffering for the faith (with the exception of bodily and mental conditions that may arise out of torture, confinement, and deprivation because of our role as Christians). Believers are called to suffer as Jesus did (and he certainly did suffer): "If the world hates you," he said, "keep in mind that it hated me first" (Jn 15:18). He was rejected, slandered, and ultimately beaten and crucified. This may be the believer's lot too! But the Savior was not (literally) made sick.

Persecution is a direct result of standing with God against the world. As such it can include rejection, persecution, imprisonment, torture, loss of possessions, and even martyrdom—all at the hands of human beings (see Mt 10:17ff.; 16:21; cf. also Php 2:25–27, where Epaphroditus almost died for the work of the Lord, apparently because of his sacrificial service). Sickness, however, is wholly unrelated to standing with God against the world (unless, as just mentioned, it arises as a by-product of persecution and mistreatment). That is, there is no logical connection between a believer suffering death by the sword (for the faith) and a believer suffering death through cancer (sometimes in spite of the faith). The only common ground will be how each one handles his or her suffering, and in this, the sick Christian and the persecuted Christian can both be shining lights by enduring hardship with joy, patience, and faith. The NT pattern, however, suggests that, in the case of the believer suffering serious illness, God is especially glorified in *healing* him or her.

It is true that there are significant changes between the OT and NT in terms of the relative importance of material things, notably earthly wealth.[120] While believers in both Testaments thought of themselves as "strangers and pilgrims" (e.g., 1Ch 29:15; 1Pe 1:17), recognizing that the key to contentment was in "the fear of the LORD" (cf. Pr 15:16; 1Ti 6:6), and while there are promises of financial prosperity from the Torah to Proverbs and from the Gospels to the NT letters (e.g., Dt 28:1–14; Ps 112:3; Pr 22:4; Lk 6:38; 2Co 9:6–11), Jesus exhorts his followers not to lay up their treasures on earth, but rather in heaven (e.g., Mt 6:19–24; Lk 12:32–34).[121] We now live much more fully in the light of eternity (see above, 3.1.7), and it is our Savior who taught, "Blessed are you who are poor" (Lk 6:20; cf. Mt 5:3, with "poor in spirit").[122] But he never said, "Blessed are the sick," nor did he ever warn about the perils of health.[123] This is significant!

One can carefully comb the pages of the NT and find numerous references to the rejection, shame, reproach, or hardship Christians will endure. Sickness, however, is not part of the cross we are called to bear. The Gospels in particular are clear: Jesus came to bring healing and relief into a suffering, disease-ridden world. To these sufferers, he offered freedom. But he invited all to follow him—and this meant opposition, persecution, and even death. Thus, to die of sickness was one thing; to die for the faith another.[124]

Of course, this is not to say that Christians who are sick, diseased, or handicapped are therefore under God's wrath or in sin, or that they are unspiritual and unloved by the Lord; nor does it imply that he cannot work all things for their good—including their infirmity.[125] However, their condition is not to be assigned to "suffering for the gospel." From a NT perspective, one could well ask God for their healing. Had they been among the crowds touching Jesus in faith, they would have been made well, not told, "This is your cross to bear!"[126]

For these theological and scriptural reasons, I am inclined to see Paul's "thorn"—a favorite subject of critics of divine healing—as unrelated to sickness, a position I also find exegetically sound (this seems to be clear from a straightforward reading of 2Co 12:8–10, especially in light of 11:21b–33).[127] Whether or not Galatians 4:13 speaks of a physical infirmity from which Paul suffered is not at issue here.[128] What *is* in dispute is the view that would present his unique afflictions for the faith as some kind of physical sickness.[129] This I find contrary to the NT view of suffering, a view that exhorts Christians to be strong in the face of great difficulties for the faith (e.g., 2Ti 2:1–3), not daunted by the suffering entailed (e.g., 1:8), but a view that also offers the hope of healing to the sick (e.g., 1Co 12:1–7; Jas 5:14–16).[130]

5.4. HEALING IN THE NEW TESTAMENT AS A PARADIGM FOR THE RELATIONSHIP BETWEEN THE TESTAMENTS[131]

Although the progression and development of divine healing from OT to NT has not been a major theme pursued in biblical theology, it does, in fact, provide a general structure that is paradigmatic of the relationship between the Testaments.[132] The following areas are all worthy of further consideration: (1) The deluge of healing mercy that inundates the pages of the NT (in particular, the Gospels and Acts) as compared with the relative paucity of OT healings (cf. above, 5.1.1) is reflective of the relationship between law and grace, works and faith. (2) The NT healings also reflect the development from promise (= OT) to fulfillment (= NT), with both eschatological and messianic overtones. (3) The NT healings literally express the inbreaking of the kingdom of God and the proclamation of the prophetic jubilee. (4) The NT healings also help exhibit the universal offer of forgiveness and final atonement through the cross and faith in the name of Jesus, carrying out the OT tradition that relates healing to forgiveness. (5) Finally, the NT healings offer a more personal and intimate revelation of the character of God through faith in his Son. He now (justifiably!—cf. Ro 3:21–26) does for his people what he has always longed to do, thus providing a foretaste of the world to come.

◆ 6 ◆

Conclusions and Reflections

6.1. SUMMARY AND CONCLUSIONS

At the outset of this study, it was observed that little had been written on the subject of Israel's divine Healer despite the religious and theological importance of this biblical theme. The lack of systematic scholarly treatments was especially glaring when dealing with the OT material. This book has been written to help fill that void. Now, having treated the scriptural evidence in some depth—philologically, exegetically, historically, and theologically, including comparative evidence from the ancient Near Eastern and Mediterranean world and culminating with a survey of the relevant NT witness—it will be useful to summarize our findings and to offer some final reflections.

6.1.1. Sickness as a Curse; Healing as a Blessing

Despite the rich and varied testimony of Scripture, the overall picture that emerges concerning Israel's divine Healer is somewhat monolithic, albeit multitextured. Healing and health are good conditions, associated with the favor of God, while sickness and disease are bad conditions, associated with the disfavor of God. Never in the Bible is sickness in and of itself described as a divine blessing, nor is health in and of itself described as a divine curse. The Bible provides dozens and dozens of examples of sickness and plague as divine judgments, and an equally large number of examples of healings and cures as divine blessings. Nowhere do the Scriptures record that God "blessed" one of his obedient children with disease or "cursed" a disobedient sinner with healing and health.[1] He smote the rebellious, healed the repentant (cf. Dt 32:39), and preserved the righteous (cf. Ps 41:1–3[2–4]). Thus, health, fertility, and long life are promised as blessings for covenantal obedience, while disease, plagues, incurable illnesses, infertility, and premature death are threatened as curses for breech of covenant. In keeping with this, life and health are prayerfully desired for one's friends, while imprecations calling for serious disease and even death are reserved for one's enemies.

6.1.2. God as Healer

The ancient Near Eastern and biblical mentalities did not neatly separate the spiritual from the physical; thus the Lord (or the pagan deity in question) was expected to meet the needs of his (or her) devotees, providing them with forgiveness of sins, the ability to reproduce, adequate food and water supply, and health for their bodies (cf. Ex 23:25–26). A God/god who could not heal would not be considered worthy of the name; thus virtually all Egyptian and Mesopotamian deities were invoked at times for physical healing and help. The deity was at one and the same time viewed as healer-savior-deliverer, a threefold conceptual cord not easily broken. In this light, the OT use of the root *rp'* is especially significant, since, when Yahweh pledged himself to be Israel's *rôpē'* (Ex 15:26), his promise was comprehensive, reflective also of the fundamental sense of *rp'*, viz., "to restore, make whole." As *rôpē'*, the Lord was supplicated to make undrinkable waters fresh and wholesome (2Ki 2:21–22), to restore a locust-eaten and drought-stricken land (2Ch 7:14), to mend the earth's fissures after an earthquake (Ps 60:2[4]), to remit both infectious skin diseases and mildew (Lev 13–14), to heal barrenness and infertility (Ge 20:17), and to cure all kinds of sickness (e.g., 2Ki 20).

A similar holistic use is found in the NT word *sōzō* ("to save"). It is interesting to note that the preeminent Greco-Roman healing deity of the day, Asklepios/Aesculapius, was revered as both *sōtēr*, "savior" and *iatros*, "doctor," once again seen as thoroughly intertwined concepts. Only Jesus the Messiah, with his fame as Savior/Healer, ultimately eclipsed the Asklepios cult. Without a pronounced emphasis on physical miracles of healing, this would not have been possible.

In the ancient Near Eastern world, what distinguished the belief in Yahweh as Healer from the other purported healing deities was the OT's staunch monotheism (or at least, in the earliest times, monolatry), emphasizing clearly that it was one God who both smote and healed, and he was anything but cavalier in his actions. Worship of any other so-called god was not only forbidden, it was absolutely unnecessary. The Lord alone was sufficient. In fact, when Moses declared to his people that the Lord would be Israel's Healer, he was not primarily turning his people away from human medical help (see immediately below). Rather, he was cautioning them against looking to any other god for aid.

6.1.3. Doctors and Medical Practice

Contrary to the large body of evidence documenting medical practices in the ancient Near East, there is little evidence of widespread, specialized medical activity in ancient Israel. There are, to be sure, casual biblical references to the treating of wounds and broken bones, and in one instance, the Torah actually legislated medical treatment in the case of a serious injury suffered in a fight (Ex 21:18–19). There is no proof that village physicians treating external injuries were considered to be in opposition to Yahweh, and in a metaphorical context, the absence of a physician and healing balm was lamented (Jer 8:22).

However, since it was natural for a worshiper to look to his or her "god" in times of illness or barrenness (even atheists have been known to pray after receiving hopeless medical prognoses!), and because of the mysterious, internal nature of most sickness and disease, it was often the pagan priests who were the medical practitioners. For the people of Israel, consultation with any other deity was strictly censured (cf. 2Ki 1:2–17), and the fatal sin of Asa, king of Judah, was not primarily that of looking to doctors for help. Rather, he was guilty of consulting pagan, or at least magical or idolatrous, physicians in his time of extremity, rather than turning to the Lord (2Ch 16:1–12). When the help of the Lord alone was sought, to use other means for healing was not proscribed (cf. 2Ki 20:1–11; see also Ex 15:22–25; see further, below, 6.2).

6.1.4. Sickness, Sin, Chastisement, and Healing

There is no doubt that sickness and disease were often viewed by the Israelites as direct consequences of sin, indicative of the wrath of Yahweh. For this reason, sickness was often perceived as a form of divine chastisement, awakening the sinner's conscience and telling him clearly that something was wrong and that, to his own destruction, he was straying from the path of life. Sickness was often the first manifestation of guilt, and continued rebellion would lead to death. Not surprisingly, when serious symptoms persisted and when the sufferer was unable to participate in public worship or be an active, contributing member of his family, his detractors were quick to accuse him of being downright wicked, an enemy of Yahweh, rather than a faithful one who had sinned. The Lord seemed to be abandoning him! His subsequent healing was then viewed as the outward evidence of forgiveness and of the removal of guilt and restoration to divine favor, bringing a sense of vindication and triumph as well.

Since the biblical concept of life was "vibrant," the seriously ill Israelite was thought of as barely being "alive" in the true, full sense of the word, both because of his social and spiritual separation and because of his debilitating physical conditions—often including acute pain, disfigurement, paralysis, and exhaustion caused by constant lack of sleep. He already had one foot in the grave, and the powers of death and the netherworld had him in their grasp. His sickness was therefore a cause for mourning, and his healing the grounds for great jubilation. He was, as it were, raised from the dead, rescued from the pit of destruction and spared to be a useful member of society. More importantly, he could now publicly thank God his Healer, proclaiming the gracious acts of the Lord in the midst of the assembly. He could continue to enjoy, and testify to, the blessings of the Lord in the land of the living.

While the restored worshiper would be quick to acknowledge that it was good that he had been afflicted (e.g., Job 33:19–30; cf. also Ps 119:67, 71, 75, although the root *'nh* need not be interpreted there in terms of sickness), the affliction itself was not perceived as being a good thing. Rather, it was the necessary and fitting disciplinary tool to get him back on the path to life—both spiritually and physically (cf. Job 33:28). Thus, God may use sickness to chasten a straying child, but this again proves the rule: Sickness indicates to the sufferer that something is wrong and that he or she has gotten off the path of life and is out of the favor of God. Proper response to this discipline is confession of sin and repentance, after which, the lesson having been learned, the sickness could be healed and complete fellowship with God restored. Chastisement had served its purpose.

The book of Proverbs, in no uncertain terms, reinforces the belief that the path of sin and disobedience (= folly) is the way to death and destruction, while the path of obedience (= wisdom) leads to life. Folly cuts life short; wisdom preserves and prolongs it. In fact, the words of wisdom are healing and life to those who find them (Pr 4:20–33), and the fear of the

Lord, coupled with turning away from evil, is healing to the body and tonic to the bones (3:7–8).

Was all sickness, however, perceived to be the result of sin? Certainly not. The gradual deterioration of the body with the onset of old age was normal, and to avoid such ailments was the rare exception (cf. Ge 48:10; contrast Jos 14:10–11). Also, in spite of John 9:1–2, there is no OT evidence that handicapped Israelites were seen as "sinners." Rather, they were the subject of compassionate legislation (e.g., Lev 19:14), though their healing would have to await the eschaton. When God's kingdom came, they would be well (see below, 6.1.5) Thus, their condition, while far from ideal, was not automatically associated with sin or guilt.

More broadly, however, as far as the perceived relationship between sickness and sin is concerned, the scriptural authors were selective in their use of material, choosing to speak primarily of people and events of spiritual import. Thus, most of the examples of sickness and fatal illness mentioned in the OT illustrate Yahweh's judicial punishment of sin. There doubtless were many other examples of sickness in the daily life of the people to which little theological import was attached. However, there can be no question that when known sin preceded sickness, the affliction was perceived as a stroke from God's hand; thus prayers for healing could only be offered in conjunction with repentance from sin. When sudden sickness or tragedy struck, it was also natural to search one's heart for secret sin.

The great lesson of the book of Job is that sometimes seemingly inexplicable things do happen to the righteous—things that, scripturally speaking, do not appear to be merited or deserved. Chastisement and punishment, yes. But wholesale destruction for the godly—no! Thus, it is a terrible mistake to misjudge an afflicted person as "guilty" simply because of his great suffering. There may be more to the story than meets the eye. But it is equally wrong to misjudge God as acting contrary to his nature, accusing him of indiscriminately smiting his exemplary saints. Rather, the sufferer is called to patient endurance and unwavering faith in the light of the overwhelming, destructive assault. In the end, the Lord will turn it all for good, bringing restoration as well.

6.1.5. Prophetic Healing and the Kingdom of God

The prophets often used *rp'* metaphorically, based on the image of Israel as a sin-sick body in need of healing and restoration. However, this use was anything but spiritualizing. The "healing" that the prophets longed for must be just as literal as the divine smiting that the nation had endured, equally comprehensive in its restoring effects. Thus, while the prophetic concept of healing did not center on the curing of physical sickness, it most certainly included such concepts. Isaiah 53:5, vouchsafing healing at the cost of the servant's wounds, must be taken in its broadest possible terms. The prophetic hope was for the whole man to be wholly healed. This is underscored by the prophetic expectation of the inbreaking of the kingdom of God: Not only would righteousness and peace prevail, but sickness would also disappear (cf. Isa 33:24; 35:1–6).

6.1.6. The New Testament Continuum and Fulfillment

The OT teaching of divine healing is both underscored and advanced in the NT. It is true that our mortal existence in this world is seen more clearly in the light of eternity, bringing with it strong admonitions against greed and the hoarding of earthly possessions. Yet the beatitudes do not include "Blessed are the sick" (contrast Lk 6:20 with Mt 5:3), and sickness does not become a token of divine favor in the NT. Rather, Jesus devoted a large part of his public ministry to healing the sick and the oppressed, a pattern imitated by the early church.

There, are, however, some differences in perspective between the Testaments. Thus, whereas sickness was primarily associated with Yahweh's smiting hand in the Hebrew Scriptures, the Gospels frequently point to the work of the devil and demons in similar conditions (cf. Lk 13:10–16; Ac 10:38). Nevertheless, there is no essential difference, since both Testaments view sickness in negative terms and both promise healing for the sick. What the NT provides is further "behind the scenes" information (cf. Job 1–2; also 1Ch 21:1 with 2Sa 24:1), indicating that it is Satan and his minions who often do the "dirty work" (though cf. Ac 12:23; Rev 2:22–23). Moreover, humanity as a whole, whether or not there is a question of personal sin, suffers the attack of the evil one. Jesus offers amnesty and relief, translating out to the free proclamation of forgiveness and healing to all who desire it.

The NT also brings with it the beginning of the fulfillment of the OT hope. The messianic age has begun. The kingdom of God has broken into human history, displacing demons and disease. The eschatological jubilee has been proclaimed, announcing liberty from bondage to sin, Satan, and sickness. The Holy Spirit has been poured out, accompanied by miraculous gifts and manifestations, and the book of Acts continues the account of all that Jesus began to do and teach (Ac 1:1). Thus, naturally, healing prayer for the sick became the heritage of the early believers (cf. Jas 5:14–16). While intense persecution was commonly experienced and suffering for the Lord was viewed as a privilege, there is no indication that the general experience of being sick—the common lot of all humanity—was equated with suffering for Jesus and the gospel.

6.2. THEOLOGICAL AND PRACTICAL REFLECTIONS

It is right and fitting for the church to lead the way in ministries of mercy that seek to tangibly relieve the suffering of the human race. Such activities include feeding the poor, caring for orphans, educating the impoverished, and housing the homeless. The ministry of healing is also of great importance. However, many Christian leaders think only in terms of building hospitals, sending out medical missionaries, and improving hygiene and diet. All this is of real value, and from Genesis to Revelation, the Scriptures testify to the fundamental importance of healing and health. One can only rejoice at the huge strides that have been made in modern medical science, greatly extending the average life span of millions around the world. But what about the *primary* biblical pattern of healing? What about the ministry of prayer and the Word? What about healing as part of the proclamation of the gospel?[2] This, I believe, must lay at the foundation of the church's healing activity.

We should use all godly means available—both supernatural and natural—to alleviate the acute suffering caused by sickness, epidemic, and disease.[3] In fact, it is inconsistent for Christians to aggressively fight against malignant killers such as cancer, heart disease, and AIDS—using all medical means available—while at the same time adopting a spiritual stance of acquiescence to these health destroying conditions.[4] The same compassion that motivates the medical missionary motivates the pastor praying for the sick in his flock. It is not a matter of either-or.

To be sure, modern proponents of divine healing have often sensationalized and commercialized the "ministry" of healing of the sick, and some have been outright charlatans.[5] Public demonstrations of compassion and understanding have often been sadly lacking, and there has frequently been a corresponding lack of sound biblical exegesis. As one active in Pentecostal ministry around the globe, I can speak freely and candidly. However, as an evangelical student of the Word, I must also say candidly that modern opponents of divine healing have generally thrown out the baby with the bath water. In their zeal to correct the excesses and abuses of the "faith healing" movement, they too have misread the Scriptures, denying the reality and promise of an unbroken continuum of divine healing power. While their exposition of individual verses is often superior to that found in the popularized writings of divine healing teachers,[6] the overall thrust of the latter's message is more sound biblically in terms of its attitude toward sickness and health. The same God who heals the broken in heart today also heals the broken in body.

What then does all this mean to the seriously ill person? How does this apply to those suffering debilitating pain and disease? Certainly, if there is any subject that does not lend itself to abstract theological discussion, it is that of sickness and healing. What does a cancer-stricken child care about biblical theology? Why would an anguished minister standing by the bedside of a terminally ill mother of five want to know about ancient Near Eastern healing deities? Is there a practical value to the hundreds of pages and seemingly endless endnotes that have led up to this point? I offer an unequivocal yes. The Word of God speaks to us today.

Anyone visiting the intensive care unit of a hospital cannot help but feel a longing to see healing and relief come quickly to the sick and suffering. Such attitudes are in keeping with the Scriptures. Sickness and disease are terrible reminders of the Fall, speaking vividly and forcefully of the horrid consequences of historic, human sin. Who cannot be moved to compassion in the face of such suffering? The good news is that our God and Father is also moved to compassion. In his ultimate act of sacrificial love, he gave his Son for us, offering him up for our rebellion. Through his death, Jesus struck at the root cause of all human suffering, viz., our sins, nailing them to the cross and thereby opening the door for a profusion of healing grace to come to the whole person—spirit, soul, and body. The Scriptures offer us hope! No doubt there will be godly people who suffer from protracted diseases, along with handicapped saints who are not made physically well. Certainly there will be mysteries of suffering that will not be explained to us in this lifetime, and many will find redemptive value in their personal experience of sickness or even in the tragic death of a loved one. Yet the Word of God encourages us to come in confident and humble faith, asking the Lord for healing. He who made all things good in the beginning and who in the end will remove all suffering and pain is accessible for healing mercy even now.

Let us look back to the Word of God—to the covenant at Sinai promising healing as a blessing and dread diseases as a curse, and to the history of Israel, where God struck down the guilty but delivered those who put their trust in him. Let us bring to mind the book of Psalms with the anguished sufferer on his sickbed, ridden with guilt and pain, then wonderfully restored within and without, now encouraging us not to forget all the Lord's gracious deeds, especially forgiveness and healing. Let us remember the wisdom of Proverbs, exhorting us to walk in the fear of the Lord, which adds length of life and brings healing to the bones. And then let us consider the final end of Job.

Let us hear afresh the words of the prophets who spoke of the future restoration of their sin-sick nation, longing for the day when God's kingdom would be manifest on earth, when the lame would jump, the blind would see, and the broken-hearted wound be bound up. And let us look up to the Redeemer, whose coming into the world meant the inbreaking of that prophesied kingdom, spelling "the beginning of the end of Satan's reign," whose whole earthly ministry was a vicarious bearing of our pain and guilt, and who revealed the heart of the Father by healing the sick and oppressed. Let us look to him who promised that all who believe in him would do the works that he did, sending his Spirit to empower his people after his ascension and resulting in a glorious pattern of healings and miracles throughout the early centuries of the church. And then let us remember the words the Master spoke to the "leprous" man seeking healing from his hand: "I am willing," the Lord said, and with that the man was cured.

That is the essence of divine healing in the Bible, in history, and in the world today. It translates theology into action. It brings the divine Healer into intimate contact with suffering humanity. It produces radical change.

"But," someone might ask, "can we really expect such divine acts in our day?" As long as God is God and there is sickness and disease on the earth, the answer is certainly yes. "For no matter how many promises God has made, they are 'Yes' in Christ. And so through him the 'Amen' is sounded by us to the glory of God" (2Co 1:20). Israel's divine Healer is still at work—for his glory and for our good.

Notes

Introduction

[1]While this approach is sometimes fruitful, in my judgment it is also fraught with difficulties, since by its very nature it leans heavily on hypotheses rather than verifiable data. Cf., e.g., the detailed survey of scholarly opinion regarding the authorship, sources, and dating of the book of Genesis by V. P. Hamilton, *Genesis 1–17* (NICOT; Grand Rapids: Eerdmans, 1991), 111–38, where most of the views presented are mutually contradictory, in whole or in part, in spite of the erudition of their proponents. Even among scholars who agree on a specific Pentateuchal source like P, there is often wide disparity in dating; cf. J. Milgrom, *Leviticus 1–16* (AB; Garden City, N.Y.: Doubleday, 1992), 3–13 ("The Antiquity of P"), with special attention to the contributions of B. A. Levine and A. Hurvitz. For the "canonical" approach of this study, see immediately below; cf. also the remarks of N. M. Sarna, *Genesis* (The JPS Torah Commentary; Philadelphia: The Jewish Publication Society, 1989), xviii, regarding the first book of the Pentateuch: "Whatever the merits or demerits of this type of [documentary] analysis, it is beyond doubt that the Book of Genesis came down to us, not as a composite of disparate elements but as a unified document with a life, coherence, and integrity of its own." The same can be said of the Scriptures as a whole (cf. below, 0.2). For a defense of the diachronic, source-critical method for the purposes of exegesis, see W. D. Davies and D. C. Allison Jr., *The Gospel According to Saint Matthew*, vol. 1 (ICC; Edinburgh: T. & T. Clark, 1988), 1–7; B. A. Levine, *Numbers 1–20* (AB; Garden City, N.Y.: Doubleday, 1993), 48–50; S. Booren, "The Importance of a Diachronic Approach: The Case of Genesis–Kings," *CBQ* 51 (1985): 195–208; J. A. Fitzmyer, "Historical Criticism: Its Role in Biblical Interpretation and Church Life," *TS* 50 (1989): 244–59.

[2]Before asking, "Did it really happen?" H. C. Kee correctly observes that "the hermeneutically prior and far more important question is, 'What did the ancient writer who reported the event understand to have occurred?'" See his *Miracle in the Early Christian World* (New Haven: Yale Univ. Press, 1983), 3.

[3]J. Hempel, *Heilung als Symbol und Wirklichkeit im biblischen Schriftum* (Göttingen: Vandenhoeck & Ruprecht, 1958), originally published as *Nachrichten der Akademie der Wissenschaften in Göttingen, Philologisch-Historische Klasse*, I/3 (1958), 237–314 (the independent book form of this monograph retains its original pagination); idem, "Ich bin der Herr dein Arzt," *ThLZ* 82 (1957): 809–26. Cf. also T. Struys, *Ziekte en Genezing in het Oude Testament* (Kampen: Kok, 1968).

[4]K. Seybold, *Das Gebet des Kranken in Alten Testament: Untersuchungen zur Bestimmung und Zuordnung der Krankheits- und Heilungspsalmen*, BWANT 99 (1973); "Krankheit und Heilung: Soziale Apekte in dem Psalmen," *BK* 20 (1971): 107–11; idem and U. B. Mueller, *Sickness and Healing*, trans. D. W. Stott (Nashville: Abingdon, 1981), 9–96 (this is Seybold's contribution, treating the OT material); cf. also C. Barth, *Die Erretung vom Tode in den individuellen Klage- und Dankliedern des Alten Testament* (Zollikon: Evangelischer Verlag, 1947); F. Michaeli, "Les malades et le temple dans l'Ancien testament," *Église et Théologie* 21 (1958): 3–12; R. Martin-Achard, "La prière des malades dans le psautier d'Israël," *Lumière et Vie* 86 (1968): 25–43 (also "Approche des psaumes," *CTh* 60 [1969]: 49–65).

[5]K. Stendahl, "Gamla Testaments föreställningar om helandet. Rafa'-utsagorna i kontext och ideologi," *Svensk Exegetisk Årsbok* 15 (1950): 5–33. At the beginning of his study (5), he also notes that *rp'* has received little scholarly attention, singling out J. J. Stamm's treatment of *rp'* in his 1940 Basel dissertation, *Erlösen und Vergeben im A.T.,* as a notable exception. Stamm's treatment of *rp'*, however, is weakened by his (over)emphasis on the root's relationship to the semantic domain of "forgiveness."

[6]N. Lohfink, "'Ich bin Jahwe, dein Arzt' (Ex 15,26): Gott, Gesselshcaft und menschliche Gesundheit in einer nachexilischen Pentateuchbearbeitung (Ex 15, 25b.26)," in H. Merklein and E. Zenger, eds., *Ich will euer Gott werden: Beispiele biblischen Redens von Gott* (SBS 100; Stuttgart: Katholisches Bibelwerk, 1981), 11–73. Not surprisingly, Lohfink, who has written much on the book of Deuteronomy, gives special attention to questions of possible Deuteronomic editorial activity. On p. 14, n. 4, he writes: "Soweit ich sehe, gibt es bisher keine Arbeit, die sich thematisch mit Ex 15, 25f befasste," pointing out that Hempel's 1957 study in *ThLZ* bears Ex 15:26 only as a kind of "Mottotitel."

[7]H. Niehr, "JHWH als Arzt: Herkunft und Geschichte einer Alttestamentlichen Gottesprädikation," *BZ* 35 (1991): 3–17. Niehr traces much of Yahweh's role as Healer to solar imagery and the preeminent place of solar deities in the ancient Near East; for further discussion, see below, 2.2.5 (on Dt 32:39) and 4.1.6 (on Mal 4:2[3:20]). See more broadly, idem, *Der hochste Gott: Alttestamentlicher JHWH-Glaube im Kontext syrisch-kanaanäischer Religion des 1, Jahrtausends v. Chr.* (BZAW 190; Berlin/New York: de Gruyter, 1990). For the reconstruction of H. Rouillard, "*El Rofé en Nombres* 12, 13," *Sem* 37 (1987): 17–46, who also treats Nu 12:13 in some detail; see below, 1.3.2, n. 173; for Nu 12:13, cf. 2.2.5, n. 146.

[8]W. Ebstein, *Die Medizin im Alten Testament* (repr. München: Werner Fritsch, 1965); cf. idem, *Die Medizin im Neuen Testament und im Talmud* (repr., München: Werner Fritsch, 1975); A. Gemayel, *L'hygiène et la médecine à travers la Bible* (Paris: P. Geuthner, 1932); A. Lods, "Les idées des Israélites sur la maladie, ses causes et ses remèdes," in K. Budde, ed., *Vom Alten Testament*, 181–93 (= K. Marti Festschrift, BZAW 41; Berlin: Alfred Toppelman, 1925); P. Humbert, "Maladie et médecine dans l'Ancien Testament," *RHPhR* 44 (1964): 1–29; C. Westermann, "Heilung und Heil in der

Gemeinde aus der Sicht des Alten Testaments," *WzM* 27 (1975): 12–25; E. Neufeld, "Hygiene Conditions in Ancient Israel (Iron Age)," *BA* 34 (1971): 42–66; H. Weippert, "Bad und Baden," *BRL*², 30–33; W. T. Im der Smitten, "Patient und Arzt: Die Welt des Kranken im Alten Testament," *Janus* 61 (1974): 103–29; D. J. Simundson, "Health and Healing in the Bible," *Word & World* 2 (1982): 330–39; idem, "Mental Health in the Bible," *Word & World* 9 (1989): 140–46; D. W. Amundsen and G. B. Ferngren, "Medicine and Religion: Pre-Christian Antiquity," in M. E. Marty and K. L. Vaux, eds., *Health/Medicine and the Faith Traditions: An Inquiry into Religion and Medicine* (Philadelphia: Fortress, 1982), 53–92 (esp. 61–70); G. F. Hasel, "Health and Healing in the Old Testament," *AUSS* 21 (1983): 191–202; J. V. Kinnier-Wilson, "Medicine in the Land and Times of the Old Testament," in T. Ishida, ed., *Studies in the Period of David and Solomon* (Winona Lake, Ind.: Eisenbrauns, 1982), 337–65; D. J. Wiseman, "Medicine in the Old Testament," in B. Palmer, ed., *Medicine and the Bible* (Exeter: Paternoster, 1986), 13–42. Cf. also J. Scharbert, *Der Schmerz im Alten Testament* (BBB 8; Bonn: Peter Hanstein Verlag, 1955). For further references to literature on the Bible and medicine, see A. Oepke, "*ἰάομαι*, etc.," *TDNT* 3:194–95; A. Gelin, "Médecine dans la Bible," *DBSup* 5:957–68; and note the brief historical survey of literature in Y. Liebowitz, "רְפוּאָה," *EM* (Hebrew; Jerusalem: Bialik, 1976), 7:407–8, with bibliography (424–25) listing most of the principal journals and periodicals dealing with the history of medicine, and cf. *Koroth* 9/1–2 (1985) and 9, Special Issue (1987), as well as the bibliography compiled by M.-C. Sullivan in Marty and Vaux, *Health/Medicine*, 315–46. See also I. Jacob and W. Jacob, *The Healing Past: Pharmaceuticals in the Biblical and Rabbinic World* (Studies in Ancient Medicine, 7; Leiden: E. J. Brill, 1993), and more broadly, H. Schipperges, E. Seidler, and P. U. Unschuld, eds., *Krankheit, Heilkunst, Heilung* (München: Karl Aber, 1978).

9W. W. G. von Baudissin, *Adonis und Esmun: Eine Untersuchung zur Geschichte des Glaubens an Auferstehungsgötter und an Heilgötter* (Leipzig: Hinrichs, 1911); see especially 316–24, 385–90, and 397–402; W. A. Jayne, *Healing Gods of Ancient Civilizations* (repr., New York: AMS Press, 1979); J. C. de Moor, "Rāpi'ūma–Rephaim," *ZAW* 88 (1976), 323–45 (see esp. 336–37). Jayne does not discuss the biblical material at all.

10Representative of the primarily medical approach are R. K. Harrison, "Healing, Health," *IDB* 2:541–48; idem, "Heal," *ISBE* 2:640–47 (this contains several more paragraphs of OT theological discussion than does his earlier *IDB* article); Liebowitz, "רְפוּאָה," *EM* 7:407–25. More theologically oriented are the articles of H. Loewe, "Disease and Medicine (Jewish)," *ERE* 4:755–57, and H. C. Kee, "Medicine and Healing," *ABD* 4:659–64.

11Cf. H. J. Stoebe, "רפא–heilen," *THAT* 2:803–9; M. L. Brown, "רָפָא," *TWAT* 7:617–25; W. White, "רָפָא, heal, make healthful," *TWOT* 2:857; F. Stolz, "חלה–krank sein," *THAT* 1:567–70; K. Seybold, "חָלָה, etc.," *TDOT*, 4:399–409; C. P. Weber, "חָלָה," *TWOT*, 1:286–87; cf. also M. L. Brown, *I Am the Lord Your Healer: A Philological Study of the Root* RP' *in the Hebrew*

Bible and the Ancient Near East (Ph.D. Dissertation, New York: New York Univ., 1985).

[12]G. von Rad, *Old Testament Theology*, trans. D. M. G. Stalker (New York: Harper & Row, 1962), 1:274–76. The subject of God the Healer is not treated in G. F. Hasel's summarizing work, *Old Testament Theology: Basic Issues in the Current Debate* (4th ed., Grand Rapids: Eerdmans, 1991). According to Lohfink, "'Ich bin Jahwe, dein Arzt' (Ex 15,26)," 14, "Die beiden Verse Ex 15,25f, die unser Satz abschliesst, spielen in Darstellungen der altestamentlichen Theologie kaum eine Rolle."

[13]L. Kohler, *Hebrew Man*, trans. P. R. Ackroyd (London: SCM Press, 1956); H. W. Wolff, *Anthropology of the Old Testament*, trans. M. Kohl (Philadelphia: Fortress, 1974).

[14]Y. Kauffman, *Toledot HaEmunah HaYisra'elit*, 8 vols. (Jerusalem/Tel Aviv: Bialik/Dvir, 1955–56; English abridgement by M. Greenberg; Chicago: Univ. of Chicago Press, 1960); W. F. Albright, *Archaeology and the Religion of Israel* (5th ed., Baltimore: Johns Hopkins Univ. Press, 1968); idem, *Yahweh and the Gods of Canaan* (London: Althone Press, 1968); G. Fohrer, *A History of Israelite Religion*, trans. David E. Green (Nashville: Abingdon, 1972); H. Ringgren, *Israelite Religion*, trans. John Sturdy (Philadelphia: Fortress, 1966); W. H. Schmidt, *The Faith of the Old Testament: A History*, trans. John Sturdy (Philadelphia: Westminster, 1983).

[15]J. C. de Moor, *The Rise of Yahwism: The Roots of Israelite Monotheism* (Leuven: Leuven Univ. Press, 1990), e.g., 225; M. S. Smith, *The Early History of God: Yahweh and the Other Deities in Ancient Israel* (San Francisco: Harper & Row, 1990), e.g., 119 (with reference to Mal 3:20[4:2] and Isa 58:8). See also above, n. 5, for the monograph of H. Niehr.

[16]Cf. Kee, "Medicine and Healing," 659: "In all three sections of the Jewish Scriptures—the Pentateuch, the Prophets, and the Writings—the image of Yahweh as healer is present as a central aspect of God's relationship to the covenant people." Cf. also Hasel, "Health and Healing," 200: "The fact that the Lord is 'your healer' . . . is fundamental to biblical faith"; and note Humbert, "Maladie et médecine," 21.

[17]Ancient Near Eastern literature consistently reflects the union of religion and healing, i.e., the conceptual unity of the natural and spiritual worlds, underscoring the role of the deity as healer.

[18]The relative neglect of this concept in OT studies stands in direct contrast to the attention given to the subject of divine healing and miracles in the NT; cf. recently H. K. Nielsen, *Heilung und Verkündigung: Das Verständnis der Heilung und ihres Verhältnisses zur Verkündigung bei Jesus und in der ältesten Kirche* (Leiden: E. J. Brill, 1987), with extensive bibliography on 269–83. Of course, in the NT documents, the healing ministry of Jesus and the apostles receives tremendous emphasis; cf. below, ch. 5.

[19]This will be argued below, 2.1., 2.2.1.

[20]Seybold, *Sickness and Healing*, 86, dating Ex 15:26 much later in the biblical tradition, notes that, "The confessional statement in Exod 15:26 is a documentation of the very likely tedious struggle in this area [of conflict with

daily Canaanite life], and one notices the reflection of a taxing, difficult victory in the statement." Cf. also Niehr, "JHWH als Arzt," 3, who follows Lohfink, "'Ich bin Jahwe, dein Arzt,'" in dating Ex 15:26 late in Israelite religious history.

[21]On the broad subject of the relationship between magic, medicine, and religion, see, in general, I. Jakobovits, *Jewish Medical Ethics* (2d ed., New York: Bloch, 1975), xxxi-xxxvi, 1–44; W. H. Rivers, *Medicine, Magic and Religion* (repr. New York: AMS Press, 1985); H. W. Haggard, *Devils, Drugs and Doctors* (repr. Boston: Charles River, 1980); C. J. S. Thompson, *Magic and Healing* (repr. New York: Bell, 1989); cf. further A. D. White, *A History of the Warfare of Science with Theology* (repr. Gloucester, Mass.: Peter Smith, 1978), 2 vols.; J. Neusner, E. S. Frerichs, and P. V. M. Flesher, eds., *Religion, Science, and Magic* (Oxford: Oxford Univ. Press, 1989); S. J. Tambiah, *Magic, Science, Religion and the Scope of Rationality* (New York: Cambridge Univ. Press, 1990); J. H. Brooke, *Science and Religion: Some Historical Perspectives* (The Cambridge History of Science; New York: Cambridge Univ. Press, 1991; note esp. the bibliographic essay, 348–403).

[22]See E. K. Ritter, "Magical-expert (= *ašipu*) and Physician (= *asû*): Notes on Two Complementary Professions in Babylonian Medicine," in H. G. Guterbock and T. Jacobsen, eds., *Studies in Honor of Benno Landsberger on His 75th Birthday* (AS 16; Chicago: Univ. of Chicago Press, 1965), 299–321.

[23]See M. Stol, *Zwangerschap en geboorte bij de Babyloniers en in de Bijbel* (Medelelingen en Verhandelingen van het Vooraziatisch-Egyptisch Genootschap "Ex Oriente Lux," 23, with a chapter by F. A. M. Wiggermann; Leiden: Ex Oriente Lux, 1983).

[24]Ritter has aptly coined this "the 'two-valued' system of healing" ("Magical-expert," 299). For a broad-ranging study, see Marty and Vaux, *Health/Medicine and the Faith Traditions.*

[25]See White, *Warfare of Science with Theology*, vol. 2, for an engaging treatment of this subject as it pertains to the history of the church.

[26]For recent discussion of canonical criticism, cf. M. G. Brett, *Biblical Criticism in Crisis? The Impact of the Canonical Approach on Old Testament Studies* (Cambridge: Cambridge Univ. Press, 1991); and J. N. Oswalt, "Canonical Criticism: A Review from a Conservative Viewpoint," *JETS* 30 (1987): 317–25. For the differences between the precritical and postcritical approaches (fundamentalist vs. canonical?), cf. especially D. A. Brueggeman, "Brevard Childs' Canon Criticism: An Example of Post-Critical Naivete," *JETS* 32 (1989): 311–26; cf. also the major review of Brett by J. Barr, *JTS*, n.s. 43 (1992): 135–41; cf. further D. F. Morgan, "Canon and Criticism: Method or Madness," *ATR* 68 (1986): 83–94. My own use of the term *canonical* is general, not implying any type of thorough-going canonical criticism.

[27]*Genesis*, xviii; cf. above, n. 1. For a trenchant statement, with little appreciation for the critical method, cf. E. Berkovitz, *Man and God* (SBT; Detroit: Wayne State Univ. Press, 1969), 7: "No matter what one's opinion may be regarding the literary sources of the Bible, it would be sheer irresponsibility to maintain that the biblical text represents an accidental and haphaz-

ard conglomeration of pieces of writings without much unity and consistency between the various parts." Berkovitz also cites the more reserved observation of N. H. Snaith, *The Distinctive Ideas of the Old Testament* (London: Epworth, 1955), 89: "The literary criticism (Higher Criticism) of the Old Testament has often forgotten that those who pieced the OT together, pieced it together as we have it now" (ibid.). Cf. also D. N. Freedman, *The Unity of the Hebrew Bible* (Distinguished Senior Faculty Lecture; Ann Arbor: Univ. of Michigan, 1991).

[28]Seybold, *Sickness and Healing*, 36, gives similar reasons for dividing the OT material into: (1) Narrative Literature (36–43); (2) Psalms (43–56); (3) Wisdom Literature (56–62); (4) Prophecy (62–65). For similar approaches to the OT material, cf. A. Ho, *Ṣedeq and Ṣᵉdāqāh in the Hebrew Bible* (American University Studies: Series VII, Theology and Religion 78; New York: Peter Lang, 1991), where the OT material is divided into the genres of Narrative, Wisdom, and Prophets; G. A. Rendsburg, *Diglossia in Ancient Hebrew* (AOS 72; New Haven: American Oriental Society, 1990), 153, where the biblical data is treated under the "five literary types" identified as prophetic, poetic, legal/cultic, narrative, and orational.

[29]Cf. Seybold, *Sickness and Healing*, 85: "A portrayal of the Old Testament understanding of sickness ordered according to the various epochs proves to be impossible" (cf. previous note); note also H. Loewe, "Disease and Medicine (Jewish)," *ERE* 4:756, as well as the remarks on the Isaianic material by Stendahl, "Rafa'," 16, n. 26.

[30]As J. H. Walton has aptly remarked, "Israelite theology becomes more meaningful if we are aware of the world in which it took shape and of the tensions that were tugging at it" (*Ancient Israel in Its Cultural Context* [Grand Rapids: Zondervan, 1990], 13). On the question of religious borrowings through convergence and conflict, see ibid., 13–17, and Smith, *Early History*, xxiii-xxiv, 154–57, with the works cited on xxxiii, n. 12. Cf. also J. A. Dearman, *Religion and Culture in Ancient Israel* (Peabody, Mass.: Hendrickson, 1992).

[31]For bibliography and discussion, see A. Cooper, "Divine Names and Epithets in the Ugaritic Texts," *RSP* 3:458–60.

[32]According to S. R. Hirsch, *rōkēb bišᵉmê šᵉmê-qedem* (Ps 68:34[33]) should be interpreted to mean, "He Who still guides the worlds as He did in days of old" (*The Psalms* [Jerusalem/New York: Feldheim, 1976], 1: 470). One might question whether Baal was so conceptualized in ancient Ugarit. F. Delitzsch, *Psalms*, KD 5/2:271, following the older understanding of Hebrew *rkb ʿrbt* as "rider on the steppes," finds a contrast between *rkb bšmy šmy-qdm* and *rkb bʿrbt* in Ps 68:34(33) and 5(4), viz., "the exalted majesty of the superterrestrial One" as compared to "His immanence in history." M. E. Tate, *Psalms 51–100* (WBC; Waco, Tex.: Word, 1991), 176, believes that "the two concepts of Cloud Rider and Wilderness Rider seem likely to be merged here" [viz., in the phrase *rōkēb bāʿᵃrābôt*].

[33]Cf. D. Kidner, *Psalms 1–72* (TOTC; Downers Grove, Ill.: InterVarsity, 1973), 239, n. 1: "The title of Baal, 'rider of the clouds' (*rkb ʿrpt*), is almost identical with the Hebrew expression here, which may be a pointed re-

minder that only the Lord has a right to it"; in other words, this is an intentional polemic contrast. Cf. Tate, *Psalms 51–100*, 176: "The psalm affirms that it is not Baal who makes the rain clouds his chariot and rides across the heavens to aid the defenseless, but Yah (Yahweh) (cf. Dt 33:26; Pss 18:10; 104:3; Isa 19:1)."

[34]"Rāpi'ūma," 337; cf. also idem, *Rise of Yahwism*, 225.

[35]*Sickness and Healing*, 66, my emphasis. While one might question the interpretation of the Ugaritic material suggested by de Moor and Seybold, (cf. M. L. Brown, "Was There a West Semitic Asklepios?" *UF*, forthcoming), there should be no question as to the polemic nature of Ex 15:26. That is to say, Yahweh *alone* was to be Israel's divine Healer. For a discussion of the polemic dimensions of Dt 32:39, cf. de Moor, "Rāpi'ūma," 337 (with further references), and see below, 2.2.5. Niehr, however, questions whether the formal description of Yahweh as *rôpē'* can be traced to a borrowed epithet from either El or Baal, since, in his view, this would be unlikely in a first-millennium B.C. context, the time in which he dates this occurrence. Rather, he sees the borrowing in the context of solar deities; see "JHWH als Arzt," 15–17.

[36]Cf. the remarks of M. Harper regarding the miracles of Jesus recorded in the Gospels: "There are theological questions which it is right to ask about the healings of Jesus. We may even question whether they really took place. What we cannot question is the fact that for the gospel writers themselves, self-deceived as they may have been or naive in the light of subsequent scientific discoveries, the healings of Jesus have a message for men and women which needs to be heeded and responded to positively" (*The Healings of Jesus* [The Jesus Library; Downers Grove, Ill.: InterVarsity, 1986], 16–17).

[37]As mentioned in the preface, the nontechnical reader may choose to proceed directly to section 0.3.2.

[38]A. Even-Shoshan, *A New Concordance of the Bible* (Hebrew; Jerusalem: Kiryath Sepher, 1981), 713, lists 16 occurrences of *marpē'*, incorrectly citing Ecc 10:4 and Pr 14:30 under the definition *r^{e}pû'â* (in Ecc 10:4, *marpē'* certainly equals *marpeh*, while in Pr 14:30 it most probably equals *marpeh*). BDB lists Ecc 10:4 under *rp'* (not *rph*), but with the meaning of "composure" (951). Stoebe, "רפא," 804, groups Ecc 10:4 and Pr 14:30, 15:4 under the heading "*Gelassenheit*." For the exegesis of Pr 15:4 justifying the rendering of "healing," see below, 3.2.3.

[39]Cf. also Ecclus 38:14.

[40]For the plural form *t^{e}rûpôt*, see Ecclus 38:4. F. Buhl derived *t^{e}rûpâ* from the root *rûp*, *Wilhelm Gesenius' Hebräisches und Aramäisches Handwörterbuch uber das Alte Testament* (repr. Berlin: Springer, 1962; henceforth Gesenius-Buhl), 889, comparing the apposite form *t^{e}bû'â*. The entry for *rûp* (752) reads: "*N[eben] f[orm] zu rp'*"; *t^{e}rûpâ* is then listed. In the 1846 edition of the Gesenius *Hebrew and Chaldee Lexicon*, ed. S. P. Tregelles (repr. Grand Rapids: Eerdmans, 1949), the author opines that *t^{e}rûpâ* means "*medical powder*, from the root *rûp* to make small" (874)! For a full and detailed discussion, including *t^{e}rûpâ* in the versions, see E. Ben Yehudah, *Dictionary and*

Thesaurus of the Hebrew Language (New York: Thomas Yoseloff, n.d.), 8:7908, n. 2; see also *HALAT* 4:1649.

[41]There are seven instances of defective orthography, where the verb is treated as a *tertia-y* form (cf. GKC, 216–17nn-rr; BL, 376r): Jer 3:22 (*'erpâ*); Job 5:18 (*tirpênâ*); Ps 60:4 (*r^e pâ*); Jer 19:11 (*l^e hērāpēh*); Jer 51:9 (*nirpātâ*); 2Ki 2:22 (*wayērāpû*); Jer 8:11 (*way^e rappû*); note also the nominal form *t^e rûpâ* in Eze 47:12. In Jer 38:4 *m^e rappē'* is to be derived from *rph*; in 2Ki 2:21, *ripi'tî* is vocalized on the Piel pattern of *rph* (cf. also Jer 51:9); cf. D. Sperber, "Weak Waters," *ZAW* 82 (1970), 114–16; and see the discussion of this verse below, 2.3.4. Ecc 10:4 and Pr 14:30 (also, according to some, Pr 15:4) have *marpē'* = *marpeh*.

[42]For details of the comparative Semitic usage, see Brown, "רָפָא," 618–19; idem, *A Philological Study*, 97–160 (the discussion of the South Semitic material in the latter work is modified in the former). The root *rp'* is widely used in theophoric onomastica throughout the Semitic languages, including biblical Hebrew (cf. *r^e pā'ēl*, *r^e pāyâ*; note also *rāpā'/rāpâ*, *rapû'*, and the place name *yirp^e'ēl*); Ugaritic (e.g., *'mrpi* [equals syllabic *ammurapi*]); Amorite (e.g., ^dIM-*rapi*); Aramaic (e.g., Palmyrene *rp'l*, *bwrp'* [contracted from **b[w]lrp'*]); Old South Arabian (e.g., *'lrf'* ; cf. also Arabic *yarfa'u*); see Brown, "רָפָא," 619; *Philological Study*, 161–73, and supplement the bibliography there with M. Fowler, *Theophoric Personal Names in Ancient Hebrew: A Comparative Study* (JSOTSupp 49; Sheffield: JSOT Press, 1988); M. Maraqten, *Die semitischen Personennamen in den alt- und reichsaramäischen Inschriften aus Vorderasien* (Hildesheim: Olms, 1988); M. H. Silverman, *Religious Values in the Proper Names at Elephantine* (AOAT 217; Neukirchen: Neukirchener-Vluyn, 1985). The fact that *rp'* is so well attested in personal names, associated, as it were, with various Semitic deities, indicates once again the importance of the concept of the god as healer; see further below, 1.3; 2.2.1.

[43]I refer to this as the "prehistoric *Grundbedeutung*," i.e., a theorized proto-Semitic root meaning (based largely on a reconstruction from comparative sources). On the difficult subject of proto-Semitic, see G. Bergstrasser, *Introduction to the Semitic Languages*, trans. with notes, bibliography, and an appendix on the scripts by P. T. Daniels (Winona Lake, Ind.: Eisenbrauns, 1983), 2–24, with bibliography on 264–66; on the matter of common proto-Semitic root meanings, cf. D. Cohen, *Dictionnaire des racines semitiques ou attestées dans les langues semitiques* (The Hague: Mouton, 1970–); idem, "La lexicographie comparée," in P. Fronzaroli, ed., *Studies on Semitic Lexicography* (Quaderni di Semitistica 2; Firenze: Istituto di Linguistica e di Lingue Orientali, 1973), 183–208, with references, and cf. below, n. 53.

[44]This is based primarily on Arabic and Ethiopic usage; cf., e.g., *HALAT* 4:1187: "im asa. (?), ath. (tigr.) und ar. ist die Grdb. des vb's erhalten, aus der sich die von 'heilen' entwickelt hat"; Stoebe, "*rp'*," 803: "Das Sudsem. kennt die Wurzel *rp'* (arab., ath. rf') in der Bed. 'flicken, ausbessern, zusammennähen' (Wehr 314b; Dillmann 320; Conti Rossini 243f.) und durfte den ursprünglichen Wortsinn widergeben." Note that of the possible English ren-

derings of Stoebe's "ausbessern," "repair" and not "improve" properly translates some of the Arabic and Ethiopic cognates.

[45]I refer to this as the "historic" *Grundbedeutung*, i.e., a root meaning that can be deduced from a survey of one particular language, in this case Hebrew. The question of Semitic roots and their historical development is treated by P. Fronzaroli, "Problems of a Semitic Etymological Dictionary," in *Studies on Semitic Lexicography*, 1–24, with ample documentation. See further J. Greenfield, "Etymological Semantics," *ZAH* 6 (1993): 26–37.

[46]Cf., e.g., BDB, 950; Gesenius-Buhl, 769–70; KBL, 903; *HALAT* 4:1186–88; Ben Yehuda, *Dictionary*, 7:6670. Virtually all comparative Semitic references to Hebrew *rp'* define it with "heal," and comments such as those of D. J. A. Clines, *Job 1–20* (WBC; Waco, Tex.: Word, 1989), 281, 4.c., are the general rule: "*rp'* . . . everywhere else [in the OT] 'to heal.' "

[47]See in particular James Barr, *The Semantics of Biblical Language* (Oxford: Oxford Univ. Press, 1961), especially 100–106 and 114–16; cf. also D. A. Carson, *Exegetical Fallacies* (Grand Rapids: Baker, 1984), 26–32; M. Silva, *Biblical Words and Their Meaning: An Introduction to Lexical Semantics* (Grand Rapids: Zondervan, 1983); P. Cotterell and M. Turner, *Linguistics and Biblical Interpretation* (Downers Grove, Ill: InterVarsity, 1989), especially 106–28 (on 113, the "widespread popular view that the 'original' meaning of a word is its 'proper' meaning" is referred to as "nonsense").

[48]This is not just a modern problem; the ancient versions sometimes rendered *rp'* with forced "healing" equivalents (cf. 1Ki 18:30 with *iaomai* [LXX], or 2Ki 2:21–22 with *'sy* [*Targ. Jon.*]).

[49]Cf. M. L. Brown, "Etymology and Semantics: A Positive Assessment for Semitic Studies," delivered at the North American Conference of Afroasiatic Linguistics (1992), forthcoming.

[50]An important collection of seminal studies is W. Bodine, ed., *Linguistics and Biblical Hebrew* (Winona Lake, Ind.: Eisenbrauns, 1992); for further bibliography, cf. N. M. Waldmann, *The Recent Study of Hebrew: A Survey of the Literature with Selected Bibliography* (Cincinnati/Winona Lake, Ind.: Hebrew Union College Press/Eisenbrauns, 1989), 50–57.

[51]The watershed work is again by J. Barr, *Comparative Philology and the Text of the Old Testament* (Oxford: Clarendon, 1968).

[52]Barr's negative examples (see esp. his "Limitations of Etymology as a Lexicographical Instrument in Biblical Hebrew," repr. in the new ed. of *Comparative Philology* [Winona Lake, Ind.: Eisenbraun's, 1987], 412–36) should probably be seen as more the exception than the rule.

[53]Cf. T. Nöldeke, "Zweiradikalige Substantiva," printed in his *Neue Beitrage zur semitischen Sprachwissenschaft* (repr. with the author's *Beitrage zur semitischen Sprachwissenschaft*, Amsterdam: Philo Press, 1982), 109–78; cf. also the list of "Common-Semitic Words" compiled by Daniels in Bergstrasser-Daniels, *Introduction to the Semitic Languages*, 209–23; see also W. S. LaSor, "Proto-Semitic: Is the Concept No Longer Valid?" in E. M. Cook, ed., *Sopher Mahir: Northwest Semitic Studies Presented to Stanislav Segert* (= *Maarav* 5–6), 189–205, interacting critically with M. Liverani, "Semites," *ISBE* 4:388–92.

[54]For further details of the following discussion of *rp'* in the Semitic languages, see the references cited above, n. 42.

[55]Kohler, *Hebrew Man*, 53. Cf. Harrison, "Heal," 645: "Physicians (Hebrew *rôp^{e}'îm*, from a root meaning 'repair, stitch together') . . ."; Amundsen and Ferngren, "Medicine and Religion," 67: "The Hebrew word for physician is the participle of the verb *rapha*, the original meaning of which appears to be 'one who sews together' or 'one who repairs.'" The latter suggestion seems closer to the truth.

[56]Wolff, *Anthropology*, 143; cf. also Seybold, *Das Gebet*, 33. Gesenius-Tregelles, *Lexicon*, reflecting theories elaborated in the former's *Thesaurus*, begins the entry for *rāpā'* (775) with "prop. to sew together, to mend," comparing not just the Arabic and Ethiopic cognates, but also Greek *raptō*, German *raffen*, *rupfen*, *rauben*, and Hebrew *gārap*, *ḥārap*, *ṭārap*. It is claimed that *rp'*, "from the primary and onomatopoet. stock [Hebrew] *rp*, which has the sense of seizing and plucking, *rapiendi* and *carpendi* . . . imitates the sound of a person sewing rapidly."

[57]For this broad usage of the term Old Aramaic, see M. L. Brown, "'Is it Not?' or 'Indeed!': *hl* in Northwest Semitic," *Maarav* 4 (1987), 211, n. 51.

[58]The primary evidence for *rf'* = "heal" in South Semitic consists of two verbal occurrences in Old South Arabian (apparently missed by W. W. Muller, "Altsudarabische Beitrage zum hebräischen Lexikon," *ZAW* 75 [1963], 315, *sub rfh*, who claims that this root is attested only in proper names), a nominal form in Ge'ez (*rafa'i*, "tailor; one who heals"; cf. *rafi'*, "one who sews; one who helps"), and the very late Soqotri *terof*, "be healed" (according to W. Leslau, *Comparative Dictionary of Ge'ez [classical Ethiopic]* [Wiesbaden: Harrassowitz, 1987], 463, the Soqotri form is apparently not related to *rf'*; cf. Brown, *A Philological Study*, 160, n. 18). While these few examples indicate that the suggested semantic development of "stitch, mend" → "heal" certainly could take place, the fact that *rf'* never became a *primary* word for healing in South Semitic urges semantic caution. Note that J. C. Biella, *Dictionary of South Arabic: Sabaean* (HSS 25; Chico, Calif.: Scholars, 1982), 492–93, was tentative in her understanding of *rf'*, suggesting either "heal" or "favor" (cf. also Leslau, *Comparative Dictionary*, 463, "SAr. *rf'* 'safeguard, protect'"); the evidence for the latter, however, is specious, and A. Jamme privately communicated to me (1989) his conviction that the meaning "heal" is certain in the two verbal contexts in Old South Arabian. These two verbal occurrences of *rf'* were overlooked in *A Philological Study*, leading to an exaggerated statement as to the absence of *rp'* in the sense of "heal" in either classical Arabic or Old South Arabian (cf. 8, n. 36).

[59]Thus, according to the traditional understanding of *rp'*, the putative root meaning of "join together" explains how in Arabic *rf'* could be used in the sense of "pull a ship to shore" as well as "darn, mend," while this same proto-meaning in Hebrew could give birth to nuances such as "repair" (1Ki 18:30; Jer 19:11), "mend" (Ps 60:4[2]), and "heal," "make whole," and "restore." My own solution differs somewhat from this reconstruction; see immediately below, and note that Arabic *rf'*, "pull a ship to shore," may not be cognate with *rp'*; cf. Brown, *A Philological Study*, 150–56.

[60]So A. Dillmann, H. H. Rowley, NEB; see S. R. Driver and G. B. Gray, *The Book of Job* (ICC; Edinburgh: T. & T. Clark, 1977), 121, referring to others who fall back "on a meaning of the root unknown in Hebrew, but paralleled in Arabic and Ethiopic . . . ."

[61]This understanding is also implied in Gesenius-Buhl's definition of *rāpā'* with "heal: originally, wounds"; cf. below, n. 69.

[62]Cf. the references to "stitching" in the ancient Egyptian medical papyri, cited by Kinnier-Wilson, "Medicine," 340, although ancient Near Eastern physicians were not primarily "stitchers."

[63]The principal word for "sew, stitch" in the OT is *tāpar* (4 times).

[64]W. Leslau, *Hebrew Cognates in Amharic* (Wiesbaden: Harrassowitz, 1969), cites the forms *marfe*, "needle, injection," and *marfe*, "needle," from *raf'a*, "stitch together," comparing Hebrew *rāpā'*, "'heal' perhaps originally "bandage'" (55, 103). In his *Comparative Dictionary*, 463, he suggests a slightly different etymological explanation for lexemes representing both sewing and healing: "For the relationship between 'sew' and 'heal', cp. Ar. *šafa* (*šfy*) 'heal' and *išfa* 'awl' (Fraenkel 1898:68)." In any event, etymological theories should always be proposed with a degree of caution; cf. G. Krotkoff, "*Laḥm* 'Fleisch' und *leḥem* 'Brot,'" *WZKM* 62 (1969): 76–82.

[65]Cf. esp. A. Oepke, "*iavomai*," *TDNT* 3:203–14; cf. below, 4.1, 4.1.1. Although the discussion of M. C. A. Korpel, *A Rift in the Clouds: Ugaritic and Hebrew Descriptions of the Divine* (UBL 8; Münster: Ugarit-Verlag, 1990) regarding God as the Healer of Israel is balanced and insightful (cf., e.g., 333–66), her summarizing statements regarding the OT usage of *rp'* are incorrect. See, e.g., 310: "in most cases the verb 'to heal' is used metaphorically in the sense of 'to deliver from oppression by the enemy,' or in the meaning of 'to forgive sins and transgressions.'" Oddly enough, some verses cited under these headings, such as Pss 6:3; 30:3; 107:20 ("to deliver from oppression by the enemy") or Pss 41:5; 103:3 ("to forgive sins and transgressions") are then listed on 334 (with n. 130) as examples of God acting "as a true [i.e., literal] healer."

[66]BDB, 950–51. Falling under this second heading are most of the *rp'* verses in the prophetic texts. B. Keach, in his massive eighteenth-century work *Preaching from the Types and Metaphors of the Bible* (repr. Grand Rapids: Kregel, 1981), 161, states, "To cure, or heal, metaphorically signifies a deliverance or restoration from calamity, adversity or trouble," listing Ex 15:26 (incorrectly) among other more appropriate verses (such as 2Ch 36:16; Isa 3:7).

[67]BDB, 950.

[68]Ibid., 951. The first citation is from Jer 51:8–9, dealing with the irreparable fall of Babylon.

[69]Gesenius-Buhl, 769. Listed under the subsequent heading, "Bildl.: ein krankes Volk heilen," are, *inter alia*, Isa 6:10; Hos 5:13; La 2:13.

[70]KBL, 903.

[71]*HALAT* 4:1187 (the comparative Semitic and bibliographic data, however, are much fuller).

[72]Ben Yehudah, *Dictionary*, 7:6670.

[73]Cf. A. B. Ehrlich, *Randglossen zur hebräischen Bibel* (repr. Hildesheim: Olms, 1968), 5:200: " … allein *rp'* druckt nicht nur die Heilung einer Krankheit aus, sondern auch das Ausbessern eines Schadens irgendwelcher Art; vg. besonders 1K. 18:30"; Baudissin, *Adonis und Esmun*, 385–86: " … das Piel und Niphal werden gebraucht von der Ausbessern irgendeines Schadens [I Kon 18,30. Jer 19,11] oder von der Ausbesserung eines Zustandes [2 Kon 2,21f. Ez 47,8f. 11], ohne dass es sich um Krankheit handelt"; W. E. Vine, M. F. Unger, and W. White Jr., *An Expository Dictionary of Biblical Words* (New York: Thomas Nelson, 1984), 175: "'To heal' may be described as 'restoring to normal,' an act which God typically performs." In spite of some bizarre etymological speculation in the Gesenius-Tregelles *Lexicon* (775, and see above, n. 40), the metaphorical use of *rp'* (776, citing instances of God healing a person, people, or land) is defined with "to restore to pristine felicity."

[74]Cf. Stendahl, "Rafa'," 7, n. 4, who finds Swedish "hela, göra hel" ("heal, make whole") to be the exact equivalent of the basic meaning of *rp'*.

[75]If my understanding of the Arabic material is correct (i.e., if it can be demonstrated that the meaning of "to pull a ship to shore" is not related to *rf'*-I, or if it represents a later inner-Arabic development based on the potentially similar motion involved in mending or darning), then "to restore, make whole" should probably be recognized as the prehistoric *Grundbedeutung* of *rp'* in Semitic. In Old South Arabian, applied to a person, it means "to heal"; in Arabic and Ethiopic, applied to a garment, "to mend, sew" (from whence derive meanings such as "needle" and "tailor"); cf. Ibn Barun to *rp'* in Jer 17:14, in P. Wechter, *Ibn Barun's Arabic Works on Hebrew Grammar and Lexicography* (Philadelphia: Dropsie College for Hebrew and Cognate Learning, 1964), 120, comparing Hebrew *rp'* to Arabic *rf'*, "since mending with respect to a garment is similar to curing with respect to the body." Although Stoebe, "רפא," 803, gives "flicken, ausbessern, zusammennähen" for the South (and Proto-) Semitic meaning of *rp'*, I have argued that "zusammennähen" is really a separate (or, derived) semantic stream. In any case, a proto-meaning of "put [anything!] (back) together" → "restore, make whole" would be acceptable.

[76]Although Korpel, *A Rift in the Clouds*, 334, refers to the frequent OT usage of *rp'* "in the sense of 'to restore' from all kinds of affliction," she inaccurately refers to this as its "strictly" metaphorical usage; cf. above, n. 65.

[77]A small minority of scholars has posited a relationship between *rp'* and *rph* (e.g., Robert Gordis, "Studies in Hebrew Roots of Contrasted Meanings," *JQR* 27 [1936]: 55–56; F. Delitzsch, *Proverbs*, KD 5/1:261–62, *ad* Prov 12:18); however, the roots do not, in fact, evidence true semantic polarity (*aḍdād*), nor can any definite Proto-Semitic connection be established.

[78]Anthropologist V. Turner, cited in Milgrom, *Leviticus 1–16*, 1083, notes that "the general direction [in the semantic history of a term] is from the concrete to the increasingly abstract." However, "to restore, make whole" can be regarded as the *simple*, not abstract, meaning of *rp'*, with the earliest stages of the root corresponding to its broadest, least specialized usage. What *is*

more abstract, and hence to be regarded as a later development, is the notion of, e.g., a *corporate people* or *city* being restored/made whole.

[79]All the nominal derivatives and verbal aspects of *rp'* cited by M. Shächter-Haham, *Compound of Hebrew (In Thousand Stem Words)* (Jerusalem: Kiryat Sepher, 1982), 656–57, fall within the semantic range of healing; cf. also A. Even-Shoshan, *HaMilon HeḤadash* (Jerusalem: Kiryat Sepher, 1986).

[80]It is also interesting to observe that both medieval rabbinic commentaries and modern English versions of the Bible have had trouble in dealing with the usage of *rp'* in verses such as 1Ki 18:30 and 2Ki 2:21–22, since they clearly fall outside the semantic domain of bodily healing. See below, 2.3.4.

[81]Although Seybold claims that *rôpē'* designates "surgeon, assistant medical officer," he correctly notes that *rāpā'* means "to make whole" and states that *rôpē'* "actually [means] 'one who makes whole'" (*Sickness and Healing*, 16).

[82]De Moor, "Rāpi'ūma," 336, notes that "in many cases the 'healing' done by YHWH is clearly meant literally as 'to restore to health.' However, in a number of cases a medical meaning would seem to be out of the question. It rather indicates that YHWH comes to the rescue of harrassed nations and restores the *šālôm* on earth."

[83]For German "Heiland" ("Savior/Healer"), cf. below, 1.3.2. Hasel, "Health and Healing," 200, finds the rendering "your physician" to be "better" than "your healer," referring to Hempel's article, "Ich bin der Herr, dein Arzt." But this may be a strictly stylistic observation, since elsewhere Hasel translates *rôpē'* with reference to God as "healer" (e.g., 197, 200); cf. further Seybold, *Sickness and Healing*, 65–66, where he finds the "customary translation" of "your physician" to be "misleading . . . because there were no physicians in Israel in the modern sense; no physicians besides wound surgeons and 'patchers' until late in the Old Testament period."

[84]As a general rule, we equate healing with the body and forgiveness with the soul, applying the term *salvation* primarily to the latter. This too, however, is not entirely accurate from a biblical standpoint (see below, 5.1.2 [*sōzō*]; for the application of Isa 53:5 in 1Pe 2:24, see below, 4.1.4).

[85]Typical is the following, overly simplified comment, written to refute the idea that *rāpā'* in Isa 53:5 has any reference to physical healing: "It is common knowledge that the Hebrew word *raphah* often refers to spiritual rather than physical healing" (H. Hanegraaff, *Christianity in Crisis* [Eugene, Ore.: Harvest House, 1993], 249–50). Hanegraaff cites Jer 3:22 for support, with reference to E. Miller, *Healing: Does God Always Heal?* (San Juan Capistrano, Calif.: CRI, 1979), 3–5; cf. similarly J. F. MacArthur Jr., *Charismatic Chaos* (Grand Rapids: Zondervan, 1992), 103–4. See below, 4.1.1–4.1.4, for discussion of Isa 53:5 and Jer 3:22, as well as the sin-sick imagery in the prophetic books in general. For literal vs. spiritual "healing" in the Psalms, see 3.1.1, 3.1.4; for the influence of OT *rp'* on NT *iamoai*, see below, 5.1.2.

[86]All significant "healing" verses cited in this section are discussed more fully under the appropriate headings in chs. 2–4.

[87]See BDB, 62; the entry in D. J. A. Clines, ed., *The Dictionary of Classical Hebrew* (Sheffield: Sheffield Academic Press, 1993), 1:346–49, is exten-

sive; however, it is not particularly clear with regard to the verses treated here (see p. 347).

[88]More generally, the king of Israel, sensing a trap, asked, "Am I God? Can I kill and bring back to life [*lᵉ haḥᵃ yôt*]?" (2Ki 5:7a). See immediately below for both *ḥyh* and *šwb* as healing vocables.

[89]J. Blau and S. E. Loewenstamm, *Thesaurus of the Language of the Bible* (Hebrew-English; Jerusalem: The Bible Concordance Press, n.d.), 1:245; cf. A. B. Ehrlich, *Mikra Ki-Pheshuto* (repr. New York: Ktav, 1969), 2:343. See also Gesenius-Buhl, 55: "to take in from leprosy, that is, to introduce the sick back into human society through healing."

[90]Cf. on this, Levine, *Numbers 1–20*, 333.

[91]So most versions; cf. *Targ. Jon.*, Vulgate, and most modern versions. The LXX renders each occurrence of *'sp* in 2Ki 5 with *aposunagō* (according to LSJ, 221, "*recover* a man *from*," e.g., v. 3: *aposunaxei autov apo tēs lepras autou*), the only times this verb occurs in the LXX.

[92]Although Ugaritic *asp* (normally "to gather, carry off"; see U. Rüterswörden, R. Meyer, and H. Donner, *Wilhelm Gesenius Hebräisches und Aramäisches Handwörterbuch über das Alte Testament* [Berlin: Springer, 1987; henceforth *Handwörterbuch*], 1:83, and cf. also Akkadian *ešēpu*) in KTU 1.107:10–20 is used with reference to the removal of poison (*ḥmt*), a specific nuance of "cure, heal" cannot be deduced for the verb there, since *ḥmt*, the object of *asp*, is not "cured" but rather "removed," while other objects of the verb in the same context, such as "dark cloud" (*ǵrpl*), demand the meaning of "remove, take away." Cf. J. Sanmartín, "Zum orthographischen Problem der Verben I'," *UF* 9:261, with ref. to *UF* 7:129. See also Blau and Greenfield's rendering of ll. 19–20, cited in *UF* 7:128–29: *isp.*[sp]*s l hrm.ǵrpl. 'l arṣ.* [la]*n ḥmt.*—"Remove, O Shapash, from the mountains fog, from on the earth the strength of venom." M. Astour, cited in ibid., 128, renders *asp* with "pick."

[93]BDB, 74.

[94]Clines, *Dictionary*, 1:372, classifies Jer 30:17 and 33:6 as "of person, **healing**" (along with Isa 58:8; Jer 8:22), with no reference to the metaphorical usage; he renders *'ᵃ rûkâ* with "**restoration.**"

[95]Cf. *HALAT* 1:82; *Handwörterbuch* 1:96: "übertr[agen] bautechn[isch] Ausbesserung, Wiederherstellung." For further discussion, see the literature cited in Gesenius-Buhl, 64, especially Delitzsch, *Isaiah*, KD 7/2, 389–90 (on Isa 58:8), also with reference to Arabic *arika*, although *Handwörterbuch* 1:96 notes that the etymology is unclear.

[96]Cf. *HALAT* 4:1628, "**Überzug** *(die bei der Heilung einer Wunde sich bildende neue Fleishschicht)*" (with lit.); W. L. Holladay, *Jeremiah* 2 (Herm.; Philadelphia: Fortress, 1989), 174.

[97]Cf. the Syriac cognate; BDB, 155; *HALAT* 1:174; *Handwörterbuch* 1:204.

[98]For varied interpretations cf. Rashi; Joseph Qara (whose comments reflect the later Hiphil form); W. Rudolph, *Hosea* (KAT; Gutersloher: 1966), 125; see below, 4.1.2.

[99]Emending to *g*^{e}*wiyyâ* (cf. *BHS*) is unnecessary. Ehrlich's novel interpretation of *gēhâ* (see *Randglossen*, 6:100) is amusing but unworthy of serious consideration (cf. also below, 3.2.3.; and see Blau and Loewenstamm, *Thesaurus*, 206).

[100]According to the note in the NJV, "*Heb.* kehah [*is*] *a variant of* gehah; *see Prov 17:22.*" Cf., similarly, A. Even-Shoshan, *HaMilon HeḤadash*, 2:526, where *kēhâ* is defined with "healing, cure" (*t*^{e}*rûpâ, marpē'*) and is listed as a by-form of *gēhâ*. F. Buhl, Gesenius-Buhl 335, correctly traces this view back to Abul-Walid Ibn Jannach, the medieval Hebrew grammarian and lexicographer (see the latter's *Sepher HaShorashim*, 212).

[101]If, however, *kēhâ* is to be derived from *khh*, "to grow dim, faint," then the apparent meaning would be "lessening, alleviation" (see BDB, 462; Gesenius-Buhl, 335; *HALAT* 2:440, all of which, however, suggest the possibility of reading *gēhâ*). Cf. the serious attempts of Ibn Ezra and Radak (David Kimchi) at explaining the noun based on the root *khh*. R. L. Smith, *Micah–Malachi* (WBC; Waco, Tex.: Word, 1984), 90, simply cites *kēhâ* as a hapax, translating it as "healing."

[102]See *HALAT* 1:277.

[103]The participles are *ḥōbēš* (Isa 3:7; cf. modern Hebrew *ḥôbēš/ḥabbāš*, with meanings including "nurse, medical orderly, dresser, bandager") and *m*^{e}*ḥabbēš* (Ps 147:3).

[104]Cf. BDB, 289–90.

[105]Cf. N. C. Habel, *The Book of Job* (OTL; Philadelphia: Westminster, 1985), 553. For postbiblical Hebrew usage of *ḥbš* , "to fetter," cf. Jastrow, 423, and note that modern Hebrew *ḥôbēš* can also mean "jailer."

[106]*ḥbš* occurs together with *rp'* in Job 5:18; Ps 147:3; Isa 30:26; Eze 30:21, 34:4; Hos 6:1.

[107]E.g., E. J. Young, *The Book of Isaiah* (Grand Rapids: Eerdmans, 1965) 1:135, J. A. Alexander, *Isaiah* (repr. Grand Rapids: Zondervan, 1974), 1/1:112; O. Kaiser, *Isaiah 1–12*. trans. R. A. Wilson (OTL; Philadelphia: Westminster, 1972), 39; AV, RSV.

[108]"*Wundarzt*"; e.g., Delitzsch, KD, *Isaiah,* 7/1:133; B. Duhm, *Das Buch Jesaia* (repr. Göttingen: Vandenhoeck and Ruprecht, 1968), 45; V. Herntrich, *Der Prophet Jesaia* (*Kapitel 1–12)* (ATD; Göttingen: Vandenhoeck & Ruprecht, 1957), 44; *HALAT* 1:277.

[109]E.g., G. B. Gray, *The Book of Isaiah* (ICC; Edinburgh: T. & T. Clark, 1912), 61.

[110]H. Ringgren, "חָיָה," *TDOT* 4:337; for bibliography, see 324; the entire article covers 324–44; cf. also Baudissin, *Adonis und Esmun*, 390–97; G. Gerleman, "חיה, leben," *THAT* 1:549–57. See also the insightful survey of OT usage of *ḥyh* by A. R. Johnson, "Jonah ii, 3–10: A Study in Cultic Phantasy," in H. H. Rowley, ed., *Studies in Old Testament Prophecy* (T. H. Robinson Festschrift; Edinburgh: T. & T. Clark, 1946), 82–102; and cf. idem, *The Vitality of the Individual in the Thought of Ancient Israel* (2d ed., Cardiff: Univ. of Wales Press, 1963).

[111]See the convenient summary of *balāṭu* in Ringgren, "חָיָה," 327–30. Akkadian also uses *šullumu* (D-stem of *šalāmu*), "to make whole," and *asuta epēšu*, "to practice medicine." See Brown, "רָפָא," 617.

[112]See below, 1.3.1.

[113]Cf. also the usage of *sōzō* in the Gospels, below, 5.1.2, and cf. the definition for the Aphel of Syriac *ḥyh*, "to give life, save, keep alive, save alive; to quicken, restore to life," in R. P. Smith (J. P. Smith, ed.), *A Compendious Syriac Dictionary* (repr. Oxford: Clarendon, 1979), 139. For an example of Aramaic usage, cf. *Gen.Apoc.* 20:22.

[114]A. R. Johnson, "Jonah ii. 3–10," 89–90, notes that "the *Qal* verb, i.e., *ḥāy* or *ḥāyâ*, 'to live,' is used idiomatically, not only of '*sur*vival,' nor even simply of '*re*vival' as restoration from death in the normal sense of the latter term, but also of 'revival' as recovery from bodily weakness of any kind," since, in OT thought, "just as death in the strict sense of the term is the weakest form of life, so any weakness in life is a form of death." For further discussion, cf. below, 3.1.6, 3.1.7.

[115]Normally the Piel of *ḥyh* would be expected in similar contexts; the Hiphil usage in Isa 38:16 is unique in the OT but parallel to the Aramaic usage in the Aphel.

[116]Ringgren, "חָיָה," 334.

[117]According to N. Lohfink, 6 of the 56 occurrences of the Piel of *ḥyh* in the OT (viz., Dt 6:24; Ne 9:6; Pss 33:19; 41:3[2]; Ecc 7:12; Jer 49:11) should be understood as meaning "to maintain" (juridically or economically); see his "Deuteronomy 6:24: *lᵉ ḥayyōtēnû*, 'To maintain us,'" in M. Fishbane and E. Tov, eds., *"Sha'arei Talmon": Studies in the Bible, Qumran and the Ancient Near East Presented to Shemaryahu Talmon* (Winona Lake, Ind.: Eisenbrauns, 1992), 111–19.

[118]Cf. Johnson, "Jonah ii. 3–10," 92ff.; and cf. below, 3.1.9.

[119]N. Lohfink, "Deuteronomy 6:24: *lᵉ ḥayyōtēnû* 'To mantain us.'" For MT *wayyeḥᵉzaq* in Isa 39:1b (Hezekiah's recovery from his near terminal illness), 11QIs[a] reads *wyḥyh*; see J. W. Watts, *Isaiah 34–66* (WBC; Waco, Tex.: Word, 1987), 63, for discussion.

[120]Cf. also Tate, *Psalms 51–100*, 373.

[121]The lexicons do not always subdivide these roots; contrast BDB, 321 (*ḥlm* I = "be healthy, strong"; *ḥlm* II = "dream"; similarly Gesenius-Buhl, 234–35; for the reverse order, see Blau and Loewenstamm, *Thesaurus*, 3:159–60) with *HALAT* 1:307–8 (one root only, with the Qal, meaning 1 is given as "kraftig werden," and meaning 2 is listed as "[sexuell, dann uberhaupt] traumen"; cf. Holladay, *Lexicon*, 106). The semantic development proposed in *HALAT* is explained more fully in Blau and Loewenstamm, *Thesaurus*, 159–60: "to be strong → attain maturity → dream sexual dreams → dream" (cf. M. Ottosson, "חָלַם," *TDOT* 4:427; I concur with Ottosson that the proposed semantic "development seems a bit forced; there is much to support the hypothesis of two roots"). For brief discussion of the cognate usage in Arabic and Aramaic, cf. *HALAT* 1:307; Blau and Loewenstamm, *Thesaurus*, 160.

[122]Other nominal derivatives of *tmm* (see conveniently BDB, 1070–71) are: *tōm*, moral completeness or soundness (thus, "integrity"; cf. also *tūmmâ*); *tōm*, which can refer to both moral and physical completeness, the latter in terms of strength or beauty; and *tammîm*, which occurs 91 times and also includes moral, time-oriented (e.g., a Sabbath in its entirety), and physical completeness, the latter commonly being found with reference to the requirements for acceptable animal sacrifices (thus 47 times in the NIV as "without defect"). In Pr 1:12 *tammîm* is in parallelism with *ḥayyîm*.

[123]For most of the important lit., see *HALAT* 4:1326–31; for a concise English summary of the various usages of *šwb* in the OT, cf. W. L. Holladay, *A Concise Hebrew and Aramaic Lexcion of the Old Testament* (Grand Rapids: Eerdmans, 1971), 362–63. For discussion of the Semitic cognates (esp. Arabic *tāba*, a loan word via Aramaic), see M. L. Brown, "Man Repents and God Relents: *šûb* and Its Congeners," unpublished paper delivered at the Northeast Regional Meeting of the SBL, 1982; cf. further A. Graupner and H. Fabry, "שׁוב," *TWAT* 7:1118–77.

[124]Holladay, *Lexicon*, 362. Further support could be found in the end of v. 6: " and [the king's hand] became as it was before."

[125]For the usage and meaning of *šûb šebût*, cf. now I. Willi-Plein, "*ŠWB ŠBWT*—eine Wiederwägung," *ZAH* 4 (1991): 55–71; see also the lit. cited below, 3.3.3.3; 4.1.

[126]Cf. also the discussion of Isa 53:5, below, 4.1.4.

[127]Cf. de Moor, "Rapi'uma," 336, cited above, n. 82. Seybold, "חָלָה," 401, refers to *šalôm* as "the broadest [OT] term" for "a normal state of health," while A. M. Rodríguez, "Health and Healing in the Pentateuch" (Silver Spring, Md.: Biblical Research Institute, 1993; circulated privately), 1, claims, "There seems to be general agreement among biblical scholars on the fact that the Hebrew term *šālôm* comes closer than any other term to express the biblical understanding of health," with reference to Seybold. Cf. also Niehr, "JHWH als Arzt," 3, and see in general W. Eisenbeis, *Die Wurzel sh-l-m im Alten Testament* (BZAW 105; Berlin, Walter de Gruyter, 1969); H. H. Schmid, *Šalôm "Frieden" im alten Orient und im Alten Testament* (SBS 51; Stuttgart: KBW Verlag, 1971); G. Gerleman, "שׁלם, genug haben," *THAT* 2:919–35. For the important usage of the root *šlm* in ancient Near Eastern salutations and requests for well-being from the gods, cf. Levine, *Numbers 1–20*, 237, with relevant discussion also on 241.

[128]For references, see above, n. 4; cf. also Scharbert, *Der Schmerz im Alten Testament*; and Stolz, "חלה, krank sein."

[129]Seybold, "חָלָה," 399–402; cf. also M. Sussman, "Sickness and Disease," *ABD* 6:6–15.

[130]As far back as 1969, J. C. Greenfield felt it necessary to offer a disclaimer on bibliographical completeness in the field of Ugaritic studies alone ("Some Glosses on the Keret Epic," *EI* 9 [1969 = Albright *Festschrift*]: 60). How much more can this be said of wide-ranging comparative and biblical studies such as this! Of course, Ugaritic bibliography is no longer "at best a haphazard affair" (ibid.); however, in the last twenty years, literary output in

Ugaritic, general ancient Near Eastern studies, and the Bible has increased at an exponential rate—hence the impossibility of attaining bibliographical completeness, even in English literature alone.

[131]Cf. the apposite comments of D. K. Stuart, *Hosea–Jonah* (WBC; Word: Waco, Tex., 1987), xi: "The sheer amount of information from the ancient world and from the history of scholarship on the Bible that is relevant to a biblical commentary is greater than can be included in any commentary. To include all would distort the overall picture for the reader—by mixing the truly central with the tangential. Increasingly, therefore, commentaries represent distillations rather than compendia."

[132]In other words, where a modern commentary represents or succinctly states a consensus opinion, this single reference will generally suffice, without providing a bibliography of the history of interpretation.

[133]*Job 1–20*, xxx.

[134]Cf., e.g., T. W. Overholt, *Prophecy in Cross-Cultural Perspective: A Sourcebook for Biblical Researchers* (Atlanta: Scholars, 1986).

[135]In religious communities, the faith response to disease is, broadly speaking, fairly predictable, with different reactions largely depending upon perceptions of divine sovereignty, fatalism, and the freedom and power of malevolent forces (cf. Seybold, *Sickness and Healing,* 43, on Nebuchadnezzar's "exhomologesis" in Da 3:31–4:34). The psalms of sickness and healing should not be read in a modern, purely academic vacuum any more than they should be read in an ancient, noncomparative vacuum (i.e., as if biblical Israel had been totally isolated from its neighbors). Moreover, some Jewish and Christian survivors of plagues and epidemics have provided living exegeses of Ps 91, and where the gospel message today stands in direct competition to—and conflict with—the practice of witch doctors and cult healers, verses like 2Ch 16:12 become remarkably relevant. It is also interesting to observe how certain stock, biblical passages are used throughout the generations by those seeking divine healing. Thus, verses such as Ex 15:26; Dt 7:15; Ps 91 are "standard" texts for divine healing ministers to this day, while all of them were favorites in Aramaic incantations and formulae for healing; cf. J. Naveh and S. Shaked, *Magic Spells and Formulae: Aramaic Incantations of Late Antiquity* (Jerusalem: Magnes, 1993).

Chapter One—Human Physicians and Healing Deities

[1]Cf. F. F. Cartwright and M. D. Biddiss, *Disease and History* (repr. New York: Dorset, 1991); H. E. Sigerist, *Civilization and Disease* (Chicago: Univ. of Chicago Press, 1943), esp. 112–30, although Sigerist, 128, following Leo Tolstoy (*War and Peace*, vol. 4, pt. 10, ch. 28), downplays the overall impact on history caused by specific maladies suffered by individuals (e.g., Napoleon's cold at Borodino, Sept. 7, 1812; contrast Cartwright and Biddiss, *Disease*, e.g., 108–11). See also W. H. McNeill, *Plagues and Peoples* (Garden City, N.Y.: Doubleday, 1975).

[2]See H. W. Haggard, *Devils, Drugs and Doctors*, 3–24.

[3]Cf. W. Farber, *Schlaf, Kindchen, schlaf! Mesopotamische Baby-Beschworungen und -Rituale* (Winona Lake, Ind.: Eisenbrauns, 1989). Commenting on Lev 27:6, B. A. Levine notes, "At the age of one month, a child was considered viable and likely to survive the perils of infant mortality" (*Leviticus* [The JPS Torah Commentary; Philadelphia, Jewish Publication Society, 1989], 193). Cf. also Nu 3:15; 18:16, on which see J. Milgrom, *Numbers* (The JPS Torah Commentary; Philadelphia, Jewish Pub. Society, 1991), 153, who points out, "In Jewish law the child is not considered fully viable until that age [viz., one month; see *t. Shab.* 15:7; *Num R.* 4:3]. Therefore, neither funeral nor mourning rites are observed for the child who has not reached one month [*b. Moed Qat.* 24b]."

[4]Cf. the commentaries to Ecc 12:1–7 cited in G. A. Barton, *The Book of Ecclesiastes* (ICC; Edinburgh: T. & T. Clark, 1909), 186–96; cf. Wolff, *Anthropology*, 119–27.

[5]For a powerful eyewitness account of the devastation caused by an epidemic, cf. J. S. Amelang, ed. and trans., *A Journal of the Plague Year: The Diary of the Barcelona Tanner Miquel Parets 1651* (New York: Oxford Univ. Press, 1991).

[6]I take for granted that the first reaction of people feeling sick was often simply to rest or seek refreshment through food or drink; cf. these typical references to individuals gaining strength and being revived after eating and drinking (often after going without food or drink for some time): Jdg 15:19b; 1Sa 14:26–30; 30:11–12; cf. also J. D. Safran, "'He Restoreth My Soul': A Biblical Expression and Its Counterpart," in G. D. Young, ed., *Mari in Retrospect: Fifty Years of Mari and Mari Studies* (Winona Lake, Ind.: Eisenbrauns, 1992), 265–71.

[7]See above, 0.2 (*sub* Comparative), and cf. Sigerist, *Civilization and Disease*, 131–32:

> The primitive concept of disease was magical. It contained religious elements, to be sure, but at that stage of civilization it is difficult to draw a line between religion and magic. . . . [S]eemingly rational treatments were applied as part of a magical ritual: a drug did not act as a drug but because the ritual under which it was given, the incantation pronounced over it, gave it power to cure disease and alleviate suffering. Thus magical, religious and empirical elements are inextricably blended in primitive medicine under the common denominator of magic.

Cf. further C. S. Myers, "Disease and Medicine (Introductory and Primitive)," *ERE* 4:723–31; J. Sutcliffe and N. Duin, *A History of Medicine: From Prehistory to the Year 2020* (New York: Barnes and Noble, 1992), 8.

[8]Cf. the opinion of Abraham Ibn Ezra (commenting on Ex 21:19), that the help of physicians could be sought only in the case of external injuries; von Rad states, quite casually, "There were, of course, surgeons for external wounds in Israel (Ex. XXI.19)," *Old Testament Theology*, 1:274. The fact that the injury for which Ex 21:19 *legislated* treatment—see below, 1.2.2.2—was

inflicted by *a man* probably alleviated any religious compunctions about the propriety of some form of medical treatment. On the knowledge of anatomy and the specific functions of internal organs in the Bible, see Wolff, *Anthropology*, 7–79, 247 (end of n. 18); J. Wilkinson, "The Body in the Old Testament," *EvQ* 63 (1991): 195–210; cf. also Preuss, *Biblical and Talmudic Medicine*, 41–137.

[9]For the medical, anthropological, and philosophical distinctions between terms such as "sickness," "illness," and "disease," cf. G. P. Murdock, *Theories of Illness* (Pittsburgh: Univ. of Pittsburgh Press, 1980), along with the articles of A. Kleinman and L. Sung, A. Young, and P. Worsley (some of which treat issues of "indigenous healing") cited in J. D. Crossan, *The Historical Jesus: The Life of a Mediterranean Jewish Peasant* (San Francisco: HarperSanFrancisco, 1991), 336–37 (cf. 477, 485).

[10]Sigerist, *Civilization and Disease*, 131–32.

[11]Seybold, *Sickness and Healing*, 17, with reference to "the hand of God ... which strikes or weighs heavily upon a person" (18), for which see J. J. M. Roberts, "The Hand of Jahweh," *VT* 21 (1971), 244–51; and idem and P. D. Miller Jr., *The Hand of the Lord: A Reassessment of the 'Ark Narrative' of 1 Samuel* (Baltimore: Johns Hopkins Univ. Press, 1977). H. Wildberger, *Isaiah 1–12*, trans. T. H. Trapp (Minneapolis: Fortress, 1991), 26, notes that the word *makkâ* ("blows") "really meant various types of wretched diseases (Dt 28:59, 61; 29:21; Lev 26:21)."

[12]Ibid., 23–24.

[13]For a superstitious response, cf., e.g., R. C. Thompson, ed., *The Reports of the Magicians and Astrologers of Nineveh and Babylon in the British Museum* (repr. New York: AMS, 1977), 1:Plate 85 (#277); 2:xci ("When a foetus has eight legs and two tails, the prince of the kingdom will seize power"); cf. also the discussion of Ex 4:11, below, 2.2.7. As to whether sickness or serious birth defects can be redemptive, see below, 5.3.2, *sub* Jn 9:1–5. For traditional Jewish views on the reasons for deformities and infant deaths, see S. Klass in *The Jewish Press*, 6 Nov. 1992, 5, 48, 68.

[14]Cf. the surveys of Kinnier-Wilson, "Medicine in the Land and Times of the Old Testament"; Amundsen and Ferngren, "Medicine and Religion: Pre-Christian Antiquity," 55–61; Liebowitz, "רְפוּאָה," *EM* 7:407–26; R. D. Biggs, "Medizin. A. In Mesopotamien," *RLA* 7:623–29; idem, "Babylonien," in Schipperges et al., eds., *Krankheit, Heilkunst, Heilung*, 91–114; idem, "Medicine in Ancient Mesopotamia," in A. C. Crombie and M. A. Hoskin, eds., *History of Science* (Cambridge: Heffer, 1969), 8:94–105; I. E. S. Edwards, "Krankheitsabwehr," *LÄ* 3:750–62; H. de Meulenaere, "Arzt," *LÄ* 1:455–59; see also the works cited in Seybold, *Sickness and Healing*, 197 (nn. 26, 28, 34, 35) and 198 (nn. 41–44). More ambitious in scope is the work of P. Prioreschi, *A History of Medicine: Volume 1, Primitive and Ancient Medicine* (Lewiston: Edwin Mellen, 1991); see especially 297–419 ("Egyptian Medicine") and 421–84 ("Mesopotamian Medicine"), with references. (Prioreschi is a medical historian and not a biblical or ancient Near Eastern scholar; thus

his broad-ranging work must rely primarily on secondary sources.) See also below, nn. 16 and 35.

[15]Contrast, however, E. Thrämer, "Health and Gods of Healing (Greek)," *ERE* 6:541.

[16]There is general agreement that some of the great medical papyri, dating in their current form to the middle of the second millennium B.C., actually go back early into the period of the Old Kingdom. Cf. in general J. A. Wilson, *The Culture of Ancient Egypt* (Chicago: Univ. of Chicago Press, 1951), 56, who dates "the beginnings of formal Egyptian medicine" to the First to Fourth Dynasties of the Old Kingdom (see also n. 17). For recent studies of ancient Egyptian medicine, see n. 14 and P. Ghalioungui, *The House of Life—Per Hankh: Magic and Medical Science in Ancient Egypt* (Amsterdam: B. M. Israël, 1973); idem, *The Physicians of Ancient Egypt* (Cairo: Al-Ahram Center for Scientific Translations, 1983); E. Edel, *Ägyptische Arzte und ägyptische Medizin am hethitischen Königshof: Neue Funde von Keilschriftbriefen Ramses' II aus Bogazkoy* (Opladen: Westdeutscher Verlag, 1976); J. W. Estes, *The Medical Skills of Ancient Egypt* (Canton, Mass.: Science History Publications, 1989); for further references, supplement the listing of older works in Jayne, *Healing Gods*, 523–27, with the references in Prioreschi, *Primitive Medicine,* 394–419, especially H. Grapow, H. von Deines, and W. Westendorf, *Grundriss der Medizin der alten Ägypter,* 9 vols. (Berlin: Akademie Verlag, 1954–73); note also the works cited in de Meulenaere, "Arzt," 459.

[17]EA 49. See W. L. Moran, *The El Amarna Letters* (Baltimore: Johns Hopkins Univ. Press, 1992), 120. It is interesting to note that there is no mention of physicians among the various professional classes referred to in Ugarit (cf. T. Yamashita in *RSP* 2:41–68), nor does the root *rp'* ever occur in Ugaritic texts with reference to a human physician. (For the question as to whether *rp'* is ever used in Ugaritic with reference to divine healers, see below, 1.3.2.)

[18]O. Keel, *The Symbolism of the Biblical World*, trans. J. Hallet (New York: Seabury, 1978), 197, # 270: "A Syrian noble has come seeking treatment [from Nebamon, the chief physician].... The boat and the oxcarts in the bottom register indicate the length of the journey the man has undertaken in order to consult the famous physician. The servants of the patient bring costly vessels as remuneration.... The children may also be part of the compensation."

[19]As phrased by Moran, *The Amarna Letters*, 121, n. 5.

[20]So rendered in G. Steindorff and K. C. Seele, *When Egypt Ruled the East*, rev. by Keith C. Seele (Chicago: Univ. of Chicago Press, 1957^{2}), 129. The quotation, given there with no reference by the authors, has been taken from Herodotus, 2:84—"Medicine is practised among them on a plan of separation; each physician treats a single disorder, and no more; thus the country swarms with medical practicioners...." See *The History of Herodotus of Halicarnassus*, trans. G. Rawlinson, rev. and annotated by A. W. Lawrence (Bloomsbury: Nonesuch Press, 1935), 190.

[21]P. Prioreschi, *Primitive Medicine*, 365, states, "Although in ancient Egypt there were three classes of healers, the physician (*swnw*), the priest (of *Sekhmet*), and the magician, probably there were no well-defined barriers

between the three professions as far as healing practices were concerned. . . ."

[22]For further discussion of *ašipu* and *asû*, see below.

[23]"Medicine," 338. While the comparison of these two classes of medical men in Egypt and Mesopotamia is useful, it should be remembered that the Egyptian *swnw* was far more scientific than the Mesopotamian *asû*.

[24]For the dating and description of these papyri, see W. R. Dawson, "The Egyptian Medical Papyri," repr. in D. Brothwell and A. T. Sandison, eds., *Diseases in Antiquity* (Springfield, Ill.: C. C. Thomas, 1967), ch. 7; Jayne, *Healing Gods*, 34–38; Kinnier-Wilson, "Medicine," 337–47. Among those papyri deserving special mention are the Ebers Medical Papyrus, the Edwin Smith Surgical Papyrus, the Kahun Papyrus, the Hearst Medical Papyrus, the Berlin Papyrus 3033, the Berlin Papyrus 3038, and the London Medical Papyrus. For further details, see the works on Egyptian medicine cited above, n. 16, and cf. H. Grapow, *Untersuchungen über die altägyptischen medizinischen Papyri* (Leipzig, n.p., 1935).

[25]Cf. G. Lefebvre, *Tableau des parties du corps humain mentionnés par les Égyptiens* (Le Caire: Impr. de l'Institut Français d'Archéologie Orientale, 1952).

[26]The Edwin Smith Surgical Papyrus is well known for its entirely pragmatic surgical prescriptions, containing only "one glaring exception" to its otherwise "scientific" analyses (Wilson, *Culture*, 57; Sigerist, *Civilization and Disease*, is confident that the "incantations at the end are undoubtedly interpolations," although he admits that "the rational character [of the papyrus] may to a certain extent be due to the fact that [it] deals primarily with surgical affections"). The standard work on this important document is J. H. Breasted, *The Edwin Smith Surgical Papyrus* [Oriental Institute Publications, vol. 3; Chicago: Univ. of Chicago Press, 1930]). The Ebers Medical Papyrus is best known for its lengthy discussion of the heart, which, in spite of a fundamental misunderstanding of this organ, is totally remarkable for its time (for initial publications and studies, see Jayne, *Healing Gods*, 36). In many ways, there were no documents comparable to these two papyri until the scientific age of medicine dawned among the Greeks.

[27]Cf. Jayne, *Healing Gods*, 3–4; note the titles *swnw pr'* ("*medécins du palais royal*") and *swnw nsw* ("*medécins du roi*") cited by de Meulenaere, "Arzt," 456.

[28]According to H. W. Wolff, "In Egypt the 'house of life' which belonged to the larger sanctuaries is probably to be interpreted as a medical school" (*Anthropology*, 246–47, n. 18, with references to H. Bonnet's *Realexikon der ägyptischen Religionsgeschichte*, 417–18, and H. de Meulenaere's article, "Arzteschule," in *LÄ* 1:79–80). As P. Prioreschi, *Primitive Medicine*, 345, notes, "the influence of magic medicine was such that the word for 'prescription' or 'remedy' had also the meaning of 'potion' or 'spell,'" citing R. K. Ritner's review of Ghalioungui, *The Physicians of Ancient Egypt* in *JNES* 47 (1988): 199–201.

[29]This, of course, is a social as well as religious phenomenon, since the hierarchical system of education and the acquisition of knowledge (especially

in ancient Egypt) restricted the number and variety of "professional" classes. For references on Egyptian "priest-physicians," see Baudissin, *Adonis*, 310–11, and n. 3, and Jayne, *Healing Gods*, 51–52 (with citations from Homer, Herodotus, and Strabo). On the relationship between the scribe and the physician in Egypt, see H. Junker, "Die Stele des Hofarztes 'Irj,'" *ZÄS* 63 (1928): 53–70.

[30]See below for details. Note that the name of this goddess is often written as Sakhmet or Sachmet.

[31]The descriptions of the deities' illnesses, as well as the prescribed treatments, were a common subject of the papyri (see the Hearst Medical Papyrus for a good example of this).

[32]For examples from the Ebers Papyrus, cf. S. I. McMillen, *None of These Diseases* (rev. and expanded by D. E. Stern; Old Tappan, N.J.: Revell, 1984), 19–22 (cf., e.g., 19: "To prevent the hair from turning gray, anoint it with the blood of a black calf which has been boiled in oil, or with the fat of a rattlesnake").

[33]Cf. the statement of Grapow, as cited by Oepke: "It is obvious that Egyptian medicine degenerates into magic, not that it develops out of it" (*TDNT* 3:195).

[34]Liebowitz, "רְפוּאָה," 408. Wilson has even pointed out that in certain instances found in the Edwin Smith Surgical Papyrus, the physician, unable to cure the patient, merely recorded the progression of the illness: "He did not ascribe a hopeless case to the malignant activity of some divine or demoniac force; he did not resort to a magico-religious hocus pocus; with dispassionate scientific curiosity, he noted the succession of purely physical symptoms" (see his *Culture*, 57). Cf. also n. 26 above and Keel, *Symbolism*, 196–98: "There were, of course, many diseases and infirmities which could not be healed by medical means. In [those] cases ... the deity remained the only hope" (with ref. to #270a).

[35]Cf. F. Kocher, *Die babylonische-assyrische Medizin in Texten und Untersuchungen* (Berlin: De Gruyter, 1963–); R. Labat, *Traité akkadien de diagnostics et prognostics médicaux*, vol. 1, *Transcription et traduction*, vol. 2, *Planches* (*Collection de travaux de l'académie internationale d'historie des sciences*, no. 7; Paris: Académie Internationale d'Histoire des Sciences / Leiden: E. J. Brill, 1951). For notes on other important publications, see the references cited in Ritter's "Magical-expert"; see also the bibliographical listings in H. W. F. Saggs, *The Greatness That Was Babylon* (New York: Mentor Books, 1968), 495 (Medicine) and 496 (Chemistry), and in Prioreschi, *Primitive Medicine*, 474–84. Cf. also above, n. 14. For an interpretative analysis of Mesopotamian medicine and medical men, see A. L. Oppenheim, *Ancient Mesopotamia* (rev. ed. by E. Reiner; Chicago: Univ. of Chicago Press, 1977), 288–305, with a bibliographical supplement on 397. An older, concise survey may be found in E. Ebeling, "Arzt," *RLA* 1:164–65.

[36]This text is also interesting because it gives prescriptions only, leaving out the expected enumeration of the malady for which treatment is being prescribed. For details, see M. Civil, "Prescriptions médicales sumériennes," *RA*

54 (1960): 57–72. Cf. the additional references cited in Oppenheim, *Ancient Mesopotamia*, 385, n. 10. For a more popular discussion of this text with a representative sampling of the material, see S. N. Kramer, *The Sumerians* (Chicago: Univ. of Chicago Press, 1963), 93–99. The only other Sumerian medical text extant contains just one prescription; cf. M. Civil, "Une nouvelle prescription médicale sumérienne," *RA* 55 (1961): 91–94. This paucity of Sumerian medical texts is not only unfortunate, but quite striking as well, since the large corpus of Akkadian medical texts is replete with Sumerian medical words and phrases. In any case, these Sumerian prescriptions indicate to Prioreschi (*Primitive Medicine*, 459) that "the naturalistic paradigm of Mesopotamian medicine [alongside the supernaturalistic paradigm; see 471] goes back to early times."

[37]In terms of actual medical specialization, however, and in stark contrast to the Egyptian specialists referred to above, only the eye doctor (*asû ini*) is attested in Mesopotamian literature. Cf. Oppenheim, *Ancient Mesopotamia*, 386, n. 14, for the citation, as well for references to a woman physician and a veterinarian. In this vein, the well-known comment of Herodotus expressing his disdain for Mesopotamian physicians (3:1) contrasts with his high esteem for their Egyptian counterparts.

[38]For *āšipu*, see *CAD* A, II, 431–35; *AHW* 3:1487 ([*w*]*āšipu*); for *asû* see *CAD*, ibid., 344–47; *AHW* 1:76. On *āšiputu* and *asûtu*, see respectively, *CAD*, ibid., 435–36.; *AHW* 3:1488 ([*w*]*ašiputu*); and *CAD* A, I, 351–52; *AHW* 1:77. *āšipu*, which is to be derived from *wašāpu*, "*beschworen*" (*AHW* 3:1484), has been variously rendered as "magical-expert" (Ritter), "conjurer" (Oppenheim), *Beschworungspriester* (*AHW*), or "exorcist" (*CAD*). There is, of course, a vast corpus of literature dealing with *ašiputu* outside of a medical context. See especially *La divination en Mesopotamie ancienne et dans les regions voisines*, XIVe Recontre assyriologique internationale (Paris: Press universitaire de France, 1966), and the additional references cited in Oppenheim, *Ancient Mesopotamia*, 206–27, with nn. on 370–75. The word *asû*, of Sumerian origin (A.ZU; see S. Lieberman, *The Sumerian Loanwords in Old-Babylonian Akkadian* [HSS 22; Missoula, Mont.: Scholars, 1977], 237–38, for details), has generally been interpreted as "water knower" (cf. still *AHW* 1:76, "*Wasserkundiger*"), but this is not universally accepted (see *CAD*, A II, 347b; cf. Kaufman, *Akkadian Influences*, 37).

[39]Ritter, "Magical-expert," 301.

[40]Ibid., 302.

[41]This, again, is in contrast to the above-cited Sumerian medical text, which, according to Kramer, might conceivably be of "some practical value to modern medical research" (*The Sumerians*, 97). As summarized by Sigerist, *Civilization and Disease*, 132: "All disease came from the gods, and the task of the priest-physician was to discover and interpret the intentions of the gods so that he could placate them. Babylonian medicine included a great many magical and also empirical elements, but as a whole it was a system of religious medicine."

[42]For a representative text, see Labat, *Traité akkadienne*, 1:2–7, with lines 15–22 containing a series of prognoses based on the observation of various types of oxen (*alpu*). A judicious sampling of texts in English translation may be found in Saggs, *The Greatness*, 434–43.

[43]See *AHW* 1:245.

[44]Cf. R. K. Harrison, *The Healing Herbs of the Bible* (Leiden: Brill, 1966); for Akkadian references, see especially *AHW* 3:1156–57, *sub sammu* (in particular 1157 "*med. u. mag. Heilpflanze*"); cf. n. 56 below, on balm. According to Oppenheim, *Ancient Mesopotamia*, 292, "the term *sammu*, 'herbs,' seems often to be an equivalent for 'medicine.'" For bibliographical references on the important *Uruanna*: *mastakal* composition with its long list of herbs, animal parts, and other matter, see ibid., 378, n. 27; and for Talmudic plant remedies, see Preuss, *Biblical and Talmudic Medicine*, 433–35.

[45]See below, 1.3.1, for details.

[46]The most recent study is Prioreschi, *Primitive Medicine*, 501–36.

[47]According to Amundsen and Ferngren, "Medicine and Religion: Pre-Christian Antiquity," 67, "there is no evidence for the existence of a distinct medical profession among the Jews during the Old Testament period" (cf. also 68: "Not until the intertestamental period do we have evidence for a Jewish medical profession"). In question, of course, is exactly what is meant by a "medical profession."

[48]According to Seybold, *Sickness and Healing*, 22, "We know practically nothing about ancient Israelite medicine." He is correct in downplaying the significance of the trepanned skulls found at Lachish, arguing against G. E. Wright that they "by no means impy an 'advanced stage of medicinal art in Judea during the time of the prophet Isaiah,' since trepanation is an achievement of Stone Age culture; furthermore, in this case it could well have been practiced by the Assyrian medical officers." While the latter suggestion seems unlikely, the antiquity of trepanation cannot be disputed; see, e.g., A. S. Lyons and R. J. Petrucelli II, *Medicine: An Illustrated History* (New York: Abradale Press/Harry N. Abrams, Inc., 1987), 27, where trepanation is dated back to the Neolithic period in France; cf. also Sutcliffe and Duin, *A History of Medicine*, 11, with reference to trepanning in Neolithic Gaul, Bohemia, North Africa, Asia, Tahiti, New Zealand, and South Africa.

[49]For discussion of the nature of *ṣāra'at*, cf. below, 2.2.6.

[50]Milgrom, *Leviticus 1–16*, 888.

[51]As noted by Amundsen and Ferngren, "Medicine and Religion: Pre-Christian Antiquity," 65: "There appears to be no evidence for priests functioning as physicians and surgeons, much less as diviners and exorcists."

[52]Cf. ibid., 68: "Even though, in the Old Testament, God is represented as the only healer and God's people are to refrain from resorting to magical or pagan healing practices, the use of natural or medicinal means is not only not precluded but even employed in ostensibly miraculous healings."

[53]For discussion of the ancient Near Eastern treatment of wounds, including the use of oil and bandages, see Wildberger, *Isaiah 1–12*, 27.

[54]*haṣᵒrî 'ên bᵉ gil'ad 'im-rōpē' 'ên šam kî maddû'a lō' 'ălᵉ tâ 'ᵃ rūkat bat-'ammî*. The final phrase is literally, "Why hasn't my poor people's new skin arisen?" See above, 0.3.3, for discussion of *'ălᵉ tâ 'ᵃ rūkâ* and *tᵉ 'ālâ*.

[55]For the treatment of wounds in general in the ancient Greco-Roman world, see Preuss, *Biblical and Talmudic Medicine*, 238–39; Amundsen and Ferngren, "Medicine and Religion: Pre-Christian Antiquity," 70–90; cf. also 2Ch 28:15.

[56]On the identity and medicinal value of balm, see W. L. Holladay, *Jeremiah 1* (Hermeneia; Philadelphia: Fortress, 1986), 294; Harrison, *Healing Herbs*, 17–18; M. Zohari, "צֳרִי," *EM* 6:770–71; and cf. *HALAT* 987–88. For the religious significance of anointing with oil, cf. E. Kustch, *Salbung als Rechtsakt* (BZAW 87; Berlin: Walter de Gruyter, 1963).

[57]*rᵉpū'ôt* (always pl., and found only here and at Jer 30:13 and Eze 30:21) can mean either "medicines, remedies" (as at Jer 46:11) or their object, viz., "healing" (for the former, cf. BDB, 951, and for the latter, Gesenius-Buhl, 770). On Ecclus 3:28, cf. M. Z. Segal, *Seper ben Sira' HaŠalem* (Jerusalem: Bialik, 1971), 19–20. In light of the singular form in Ecclus, as well as Ahiqar 100 (*rp'h*, for which see Brown, "רָפָא," 619, contra the proposed derivation and interpretation of *rp'h* in Ahiqar by I. Kottsieper, *Die Sprache der Ahiqarsprüche* [BZAW 194; Berlin: De Gruyter, 1990, 232]), there is no reason to accept Ehrlich's contention that *rᵉpū'â* is in fact a ghost word nonexistent before the time of the Mishnah ("the noun *rᵉpū'â* never existed nor was it created before the language of the Mishnah"—*Mikra*, 3:240, on Jer 30:13) and that *rᵉpū'ôt* is a misvocalization of *rip'ût*. See more concisely *Randglossen*, 4:318.

[58]*rp'* in the Piel may sometimes carry the nuance of "to treat"; see below, n. 68.

[59]Cf. Hempel, *Heilung*, 238–39; for *rp' // ḥbš*, cf. above, 0.3.3, *sub ḥābaš*. In 16:4, Ezekiel uses the root *ḥtl* with regard to the normal health care of a newborn: "On the day you were born your cord was not cut, nor were you washed with water to make you clean, nor were you with rubbed with salt or wrapped in cloths" (*wᵉ hoḥtēl lō' ḥūtālt*). Cf. also Job 38:9, where the Lord made thick darkness (*'ᵃ rāpel*) a swaddling cloth for the sea. For further discussion of the practices listed in Eze 16:4–5, see M. Greenberg, *Ezekiel 1–20* (AB; New York: Doubleday, 1983), 274, who notes, "Talmudic rabbis deemed these operations on the newborn [which persist to this day in the Middle East] so vital that they expressly permitted them even in violation of the sabbath (BT *Shabbat* 129b; see commentary of R. Nissim of Gerona)."

[60]In this light, Seybold's contention that "the religious claim associated with all healing practices in antiquity was no doubt the reason behind the Yahweh religion's opposition" (*Sickness and Healing*, 23) seems somewhat overstated. While it is true that the priests of the Egyptian goddess Sekhmet were renowned for their bone-setting skills (see below, 1.3.1), there is little doubt that at least some ancient Near Eastern medical procedures were divorced from any "religious claim." Cf. also below, 3.2.2, 3.2.3, on *rip'ūt* and *marpē'* in Wisdom Literature, and note that *lᵉ hitrappē'* in 2Ki 8:29; 9:15; 2Ch 22:6 (all of which refer to the same event, viz., the recovery of Joram/

Jehoram from the wounds he received in battle at Ramoth Gilead) can be rendered "to receive treatment" instead of "to recover"; for these various meanings in rabbinic Hebrew, cf. Jastrow, *Dictionary*, 1490; B. K. Waltke and M. O'Connor, *An Introduction to Biblical Hebrew Syntax* (Winona Lake, Ind.: Eisenbrauns, 1990), 23c.

[61]Especially *b. Ber.* 60a; *b. B. Qam.* 85a-b (for translation, see below, n. 211); *m. B. Qam.* 8:1, which forms the basis for *b. B. Qam.* 85a-b, legislated that "he who injures his fellow is liable to [compensate] him on five counts: injury, pain, medical costs [*rippûî*], loss of income [lit.: loss of time], and indignity.... *Medical costs:* [If] he hit him, he is liable to provide for his medical care. From this (we see that) permission is given to the physician to heal" (following J. Neusner, *The Mishnah: A New Translation* [New Haven: Yale Univ. Press, 1988], 520); cf. also the *Mekilta* to Ex 21:19 (see J. Z. Lauterbach, ed. and trans., *Mekilta de-Rabbi Ishmael* [Philadelphia: Jewish Pub. Society, 1976], 3:51–56). For comments on the wide-ranging discussion of Ex 21:19 in *b. B. Qam.* 85a-b, see B. H. Epstein, *Torah Temimah*, 2:246–47.

[62]Cf. the assumptions of Kohler, *Hebrew Man*, 53–54, and Wolff, *Anthropology*, 145–46. This does not imply, however, that an actual physician would always be consulted, since some of the treatments referred to in the verses above were known and practiced by the populace in general. Cf. the Samaritan's treatment of the beaten stranger in Lk 10:34 (esp. in light of Isa 1:6; see also S. Spenser, "2 Chronicles 28:5–15 and the Parable of the Good Samaritan," *WTJ* 46 [1984]: 317–49); also, as noted above, it was the shepherds, not veterinarians, who were responsible for treating injured and sickly sheep (Eze 34:4; Zec 11:16).

[63]Once again, the issue is not whether the contemporary reader believes that the Book of the Covenant was divinely given. What matters is that the scriptural author/editor claims that, *by the instruction of the Lord*, in certain cases medical treatment was to be obtained. J. M. Meyers, *II Chronicles* (AB; Garden City, N.Y.: Doubleday, 1965), 95, notes regarding the healing arts, "There are hints of its approval and use in the OT (Exod xxi 19; Jer viii 22; Isa xxxviii 21). In general, however, Yahweh is the healer (e.g., Ps ciii 3b)."

[64]*raq šibtô yittēn*; cf. the LXX's *argias sou* = NJV, "his idleness."

[65]Cf. again the LXX and NJV; *Targ. Onk.* and *Targ. Ps. Jon.—wa'ᵃgar 'āsyā' yᵉšallēm* ("and he will pay the physician's fee")—are followed by Rashi, and note *b. B. Qam.* 85a; see also the commentaries of Keil, Noth, and Childs, *sub* Ex 21:19. Amundsen and Ferngren, "Medicine and Religion: Pre-Christian Antiquity," 67–68, state, "The last clause indicates that the expense of medicines, and perhaps of the one dispensing and applying them, was to be borne by the guilty party."

[66]*ANET*, 175; for further discussion of ancient Near Eastern material, see Hempel, *Heilung*, 241–43. This also parallels, in less detail, *m. B. Qam.* 8:1, cited above. On the apparent antiquity of certain laws and customs reflected in the Mishnah, see the studies of Y. Muffs, A. L. Oppenheim, and B. A. Levine cited in Y. Elman, "The Judaism of the Mishnah: What Evidence?" *Judaica Book News*, 1982, 17–24. For critical discussion of the sources and

dating of Ex 20:22–23:33, see L. Schwienhorst-Schönberger, *Das Bundesbuch (Ex 20,22–23,33): Studien zu einer Enstehung und Theologie* (BZAW 188; Berlin: de Gruyter, 1990), who finds 21:18–22:16 to be the original core.

[67]On the Piel in general, see E. Jenni, *Das hebräische Pi'el* (Zurich: EVZ Verlag, 1968); S. A. Ryder, *The D-Stem in Western Semitic* (The Hague: Mouton, 1974); J. Weingreen, "The Pi'el in Biblical Hebrew: A Suggested New Concept," *Henoch* 5 (1980): 21–29; Waltke and O'Connor, 396–417; cf. also J. Huehnergard, "Historical Phonology and the Hebrew Piel," in Bodine, ed., *Linguistics and Biblical Hebrew*, 209–29.

[68]Cf. Jer 6:14; 8:11; 51:9; Eze 34:4; Zec 11:16 (the last two referring to injured animals); 1Ki 18:30 refers to repairing a broken-down altar, and 2Ki 2:21 to making wholesome ("deadly") salt water. What Baudissin has adduced for the Piel and Niphal ("das Piel and Niphal werden gebraucht von der Ausbesserung irgeindes Schadens [I Kon. 18,30. Jer 19,11] oder von der Verbesserung eines Zustandes [II Kon 2,21f. Ez. 47,8f. 11], ohne dass es sich um Krankheit handelt," *Adonis und Esmun*, 385–86; cf. above, 0.3.2, n. 73) can in reality be adduced for virtually *all* aspects of the root (cf. Baudissin's further reference to the Qal in Job 13:4, 386, n. 1). I do not know why Ibn Jannach lists this verse (i.e., Ex 21:19) as only "possibly" to be derived from *rp'*—"to heal"; see A. M. Ibn Janach, *Sepher Haschoraschim* (Heb. tr., J. Ibn Tibbon; repr. Berlin: M'Kize Nirdamim, 1896), 484.

[69]Accordingly, *ḥōbēš* should not be considered an exact equivalent to *rōpē'*, the latter being of more general meaning. For various translations of *ḥōbēš*, see above, 0.3.3, *sub ḥbš*, where the rendering "dresser of wounds" was preferred to "surgeon" or "healer." In any event, J. Preuss was evidently correct in stating that a "separate speciality of surgeons did not exist" in ancient Israel (*Biblical and Talmudic Medicine*, 191).

[70]Cf. F. I. Andersen, *Job* (TOTC; Downers Grove, Ill.: InterVarsity, 1976), 164: "They [i.e., the three friends, in Job's estimation] cover their ignorance by diagnosing an imaginary illness in Job (his dreadful, hidden sin) and prescribing a *worthless* ['*ᵉlil*] cure (repentance, and so on)." See also ibid., where it is noted that the LXX's rendering of Job 13:4a "smearers of lies" (Heb. *tōpᵉ lê šāqer*) with *iatroi adikoi* ("unrighteous physicians") extends the medical imagery (incorrectly) to both halves of the verse, in contrast to the NEB, which removes the imagery (incorrectly) from 13:4b.

[71]The LXX here renders *rōpᵉ'îm* with *entaphiastēs* ("embalmers"); *ḥānaṭ* ("to embalm") is translated by its Greek equivalent *entaphiazō*, for which see LSJ, 575.

[72]W. Spiegelberg, "Die Beisetzung des Patriarchen Jacob (Gen 50, 2ff.) in Licht der agypt. Quellen," *OLZ* 26 (1923): 422; he refers to Herodotus 2:86 (n. 2), for which see Rawlinson and Lawrence, *History*, 191, with commentary on Egyptian embalming.

[73]Spiegelberg, "Die Beisetzung," 424. According to A. S. Yahuda, "Medical and Anatomical Terms in the Pentateuch in the Light of Egyptian Medical Papyri," *Journal of the History of Medicine*, 2 (1947): 554, "The fact that in the case of Jacob the *physicians* and not the ordinary professional embalmers

(*wetiyu*) were entrusted with the job, perfectly accords with Egyptian custom, when the deceased belonged to the higher class." Both he and Spiegelberg find further confirmation of the author's accuracy with reference to "the duration of the embalming of the body and the seventy days of mourning." (Yahuda [n. 7] points out that it was at his suggestion that Spiegelberg published his article.) For further information on Egyptian embalming, see A. T. Sandison, "Balsamierung," *LÄ* 1:610–14.

[74]Pap. Berlin 5507; see Spiegelberg, "Die Beisetzung," 423, and nn. 3 and 4.

[75]See LSJ, 1758.

[76]Normally written *swnw* or *synw*; cf. Yahuda, "Medical and Anatomical Terms," 554, and see conveniently A. Gardiner, *Egyptian Grammar* (3d ed.; London: Oxford Univ. Press, 1973), 512 (Sign-list T11). Coptic has *saein* (cf. Spiegelberg, "Die Beisetzung," 423).

[77]This could also be regarded as an instance of calque, for which see E. Y. Kutscher, "Aramaic Calque in Hebrew," (Hebrew) *Tarbiz* 33 (1964): 118–30.

[78]R. M. Good, "Supplementary Remarks on the Ugaritic Funerary Text RS 34.126," *BASOR* 239 (1980): 41.

[79]Good (ibid.) concludes, "A **rapi*' is one who has undergone that 'healing' that leads to burial; we may assume this 'healing' to have included either embalming or interment or both. The Ugaritic *rpu arṣ* are thus literally the *interred*." For discussion of the Ugaritic material, where Good's proposal, including his argument (along with that of C. L'Hereux) for a stative vocalization of the Ugaritic *rpu/m*, is rejected, see Brown, *A Philological Study*, 142–46.

[80]See the discussion in Preuss, *Biblical and Talmudic Medicine*, 22–26 (23–24 for 2 Chr 16:12); cf. Nachmanides to Lev 26:11.

[81]A. S. Lyons, *Illustrated History*, 70. Even stronger is the statement of medical historian Prioreschi, *Primitive Medicine*, 526: "[Jehovah], of course, did not need the mediation of physicians and medicinal plants to restore to health. In fact, any attempt to interfere with his will, in the field of health as in any other, would be not only useless but blasphemous. We have seen how Asa relied on physicians instead of putting his faith in God and how he died a deserved death."

[82]K. Seybold, *Sickness and Healing*, 23. "It may very well be, of course, that the Old Testament accounts are one-sidedly biased for the purpose of denigrating medicinal healing practices; but it is nonetheless noticeable that not even a trace can be found in Israel of that kind of medicine which was, to a certain extent, so highly developed and specialized in the Fertile Crescent as well as in Egypt." Thus, he tentatively concludes, "we cannot expect much beyond folk medicine." According to S. Japhet, *I & II Chronicles* (OTL; Louisville: Westminster/John Knox, 1993), 738,

> This is the only categorical statement in the Bible warning against eliciting human medical advice in case of illness, and making a man's conduct during his sickness a touchstone of his attitude towards God. The view that God is the supreme physician . . . is prevalent throughout the Scriptures, as well as the conviction that illness is divinely inflicted. The

turning to God for cure is attested abundantly throughout the Bible; *nowhere, however, do we find a negative attitude towards human medicine or human attempts to heal*. The Chronicler follows his views to their extreme conclusion—a demand of absolute exclusivity" (my emphasis).

[83]H. C. Kee, *Medicine, Miracle and Magic in New Testament Times* (SNTSMS 55; New York: Cambridge Univ. Press, 1986), 17.

[84]It should be noted that this NT verse does not *absolutely* require a disparaging view of the medical profession as a whole. One might compare the account of Diodorus Siculus in praise of Isis, who was both healer as well as helper of the physicians: "The Egyptians say that she was the discoverer of many health-giving drugs and was greatly versed in the science of healing; consequently, now that she has attained immortality, she finds her greatest delight in the healing of mankind . . . ; and many who have been despaired of by their physicians because of the difficult nature of their malady are restored to health by her . . ." (*Library*, 1.25.3, 5, cited by Kee, *Miracle in the Early Christian World*, 125–26).

[85]M. Woodworth-Etter, *A Diary of Signs and Wonders* (1916; repr. Tulsa, Okla.: Harrison House, n.d.), 202. This was her response to the question, "But is not the ministry of physicians recognized in the Bible?" Cf. also *Tobit* 2:9–10.

[86]According to J. B. Payne, "1 and 2 Chronicles," *EBC* 4:491, while the *rōpᵉʾîm* in 2Ch 16:12 "may have been pagans, Scripture usually speaks positively of those who heal (Exod 21:19; Jer 8:22); medicine is God's gift (cf. 2 Kgs 20:7)." This, however, is somewhat oversimplified, as our previous discussion would indicate.

[87]Hasel, "Health and Healing," 199, summarizes major interpretations of this verse under three headings: "(1) that the healing science of physicians is condemned because only the Lord is the physician [with reference to F. F. Bruce in *Hastings Dictionary of the Bible*, rev., 637]; (2) that Asa 'consulted only physicians, without consulting the Lord at all' [Myers, *II Chronicles*, 95]; and (3) that Asa consulted foreign-priest physicians who employed a combination of medicinal art and magic, without consulting the Lord [with reference to Rudolph, *Chronikbücher*, 249; Stoebe, *THAT* 2:806, incorrectly cited as 306]." For Hasel's view, which is not dogmatic, see 199–200.

[88]For general discussion and background, cf. C. D. Evans, "Asa," *ABD* 1:468–70; see also R. Dillard, "The Reign of Asa (2 Chronicles 14–16): An Example of the Chronicler's Theological Method," *JETS* 23 (1980): 207–18.

[89]According to C. T. Begg, "'Seeking Yahweh and the Purpose of Chronicles," *LS* 9 (1982): 128–42, seeking Yahweh is the underlying theme of all of Chronicles.

[90]For speculation on the exact nature of Asa's affliction, cf. R. B. Dillard, *2 Chronicles* (WBC; Waco, Tex.: Word, 1987), 126: "Asa's foot disease has been variously diagnosed as gangrene developing from a vascular obstruction, gout, or dropsy," with reference to H. G. M. Williamson, *1 and 2 Chronicles* (NCB; London: Marshall, Morgan, and Scott, 1982), 276–77. Dillard

notes, "For the Chronicler disease is one form that judgment can take (21:16–20; 26:16–23; contrast 32:24)." For G. R. Driver's suggestion to render *ḥlh* in 2Ch 16:12 with "gangrenous," based on South Semitic cognates meaning "rust, to become rusty," see Seybold, "חָלָה," 401. For medical discussion, see A. DeVries and A. Weinberger, "King Asa's Presumed Gout: Twentieth Century A.D. Discussion of Ninth Century B.C. Biblical Patient," *New York State Medical Journal* 75 (1975): 452–55.

[91]Cf. the account of Manasseh in 2Ch 33:10–13 (v. 12: *ûkᵉ ḥāṣēr lô hillâ 'et-pᵉnê yhwh*); see also the Apocryphal Prayer of Manasseh and the Talmudic traditions associated with his repentance (cf. Y. Y. Hasidah, *565 Biblical Personalities. As Seen by the Sages of the Talmud and Midrash* [Hebrew; Jerusalem: n.p., 1978], 263–65).

[92]According to E. Bertheau, *Die Bücher der Chronik* (KHAT; Leipzig: Hirzel, 1873), 318: "ein solcher rascher Wechsel der Construction ist in prosaischen Büchern sehr selten." The Vulgate's *et nec in infirmitate sua quaesivit Dominum sed magis in medicorum arte confisus est* distinguishes between *dāraš 'ēt* and *bᵉ*, but fails to fully grasp the point. The rendering of the (late) Targum to Chronicles, *w'wp kd mr' l' tb' 'wlpn mn qdm yhwh 'lhyn b'swwt'*, reflects either a noncognitive, slavish following of the Hebrew or else an accurate appreciation of the idiom (cf. Targumic *tb' b-* for Hebrew *drš b-* at 2 Kgs 1:2, with Targumic *tby yt* for Hebrew *drš 'et* at 2 Kgs 8:8); however, in light of the earlier wording, literally, "he didn't seek help from before Yhwh" (*l' tb' 'wlpn mn qdm yhwh*), *b'swwt'* probably just means "among the physicians," with no oracular meaning implied.

[93]The REB rendering, "he did not seek guidance of the LORD but resorted to physicians," also distinguishes between *dāraš 'ēt* and *bᵉ*, without, however, bringing out the important idiomatic meaning of the latter. *Young's Literal Translation of the Holy Bible* is more unintelligible than it is literal: "and also in his disease he hath not sought Jehovah, but among physicians."

[94]E. L. Curtis and A. A. Madsen, *The Books of Chronicles* (ICC; Edinburgh: T. & T. Clark, 1910), 390; Myers, *II Chronicles*, 95; Dillard, *2 Chronicles*, 126. The only relevant remark to 16:12 from the classical rabbinic commentaries is that of *Mesudat David*: "*lō dāraš*: to pray to the Lord; *kî bārōpᵉ'îm*: he put his trust in the physicians."

[95]C. F. Keil, *The Second Book of Chronicles*, KD, 3/2:370.

[96]Again, *dāraš bᵉ*.

[97]W. Rudolph, *Chronikbücher* (HAT; Tübingen: J. C. B. Mohr, 1955), 249; Stoebe, *THAT*, "*rapa'*," 806. G. von Rad rightly apprehended the notion of "misplaced faith" but failed to appreciate the significance of *dāraš bᵉ*; see his *Old Testament Theology*, 1:274.

[98]J. Hayford, et al., eds., *Spirit-Filled Life Bible* (Nashville: Thomas Nelson, 1991), 629; cf. also Kelsey, *Healing and Christianity*, 39–40.

[99]For an enlightening parallel, cf. *Gen Apocryphon* 20:19: (*wšlḥ*) *qr' lkwl ḥkymy mṣryn wlkwl 'špy' 'm kwl 'sy mṣryn hn ykwlwn l'sywth mn mktš' dn*—"*(So he sent) for all the wise men of Egypt, all the magicians, and all the physicians of Egypt (to see) if they could cure him of this plague.*" (Text and translation from

J. A. Fitzmyer and D. J. Harrington, *A Manual of Palestinian Aramaic Texts* [Rome: Pontifical Biblical Institute, 1978], 114–15.) Note also the comment of G. R. Driver and J. C. Miles, *The Babylonian Laws,* vol. 1 (Oxford: Oxford Univ. Press, 1952), 416–17: "The numerous surviving [Akkadian] medical texts show the intimate connection between religion, magic, and medicine . . ." (cited more fully by Hempel, *Heilung,* 241, n. 3). This, of course, restates what has been strongly emphasized above, 0.2, 1.2.1; see also below, 1.3.

[100]Payne, "1 and 2 Chronicles," 491, comes close to this view, but without recognizing the oracular nature of Asa's dependency: "The king's sin lay in having recourse to them 'only' and not seeking 'help from the LORD,' who is the ultimate healer of men's diseases (2 Kings 20:5; Ps 103:3)." Note that the word "only," emphasized by Payne and found in the NIV, does not occur in the Hebrew.

[101]Cf., e.g., Rudolph, *Chronikbücher*, 249, n. 2, with ref. to Curtis; *BHS*. For Niehr, "JWHW als Arzt," 5, 2Ch 16:12 provides an OT example "where an opposition is *established* [my emphasis] between JHWH and the *rᵉpā'îm,* who in the case of a sickness were consulted as 'healers,'" referring only to R. Liwak, "רְפָאִים," *TWAT* 7:625–36 (esp. 629), without mentioning in his own discussion that MT reads *rōpᵉ'îm* and not *rᵉpā'îm.*

[102]M. Jastrow, "Rō'eh and Ḥōzeh in the Old Testament," *JBL* 28 (1909): 49–50, n. 23.

[103]Hempel, *Heilung*, 284–85; for a different explanation of Isa 26:14 and Ps 88:11, with special reference to J. C. de Moor, "Rapi'uma," see Brown, "Was There a West Semitic Asklepios?"

[104]M. S. Smith, "Rephaim," *ABD* 5:675. Cf. more fully his *Early History*, 130: "The contrast drawn between the help of Yahweh and the aid of physicians appears forced, as seeking help from doctors is not contrary to seeking help from Yahweh. However, if the reading of the word were not *rōpᵉ'îm*, 'physicians,' but **rᵉpā'îm*, 'the dead,' the objection would be clear." Although Smith notes that "the verb *drš*, translated in this context as 'seek help,' is a regular term for divination," he fails to note the intentional, idiomatic distinction in the verse between *drš 'ēt* and *drš b*. While it is true that *drš 'ēt* can also mean "to consult" (e.g., 2Ki 8:8), the contextual usage of *drš 'ēt* requires a meaning of "to seek" in 2Ch 16:12 (cf. 2Ch 14:3; 15:12; see also 15:2; note 15:13, with *drš l-*, which provides a variant for *drš 'ēt*, but that variant is not *drš b-*).

[105]That is, either *'āsāyâ* or *'āsā'ēl*; see Rudolph, *Chonikbücher*, 249, n. 1; *HALAT* 1:70–71; *Handwörterbuch* 1:83, with reference to Akkadian *Ilumasum*, "the god is healer." Cf. more fully Fowler, *Theophoric Personal Names*, 159, 337; also 231, 291. For discussion of the ancient Near Eastern *rp'* onomastica, see above, 0.3.1, n. 42 (with lit.). Even if this was not the true etymology of the name (cf. Noth, *Israelitsche Personenammen*, 181–82, deriving from *'sp*), the Chronicler's audience probably would have thought in terms of the Aramaic meaning (i.e., "to heal"), given their linguistic milieu. Dillard cites A. Shinan and Y. Zakowitch, "Midrash on Scripture and Midrash within Scripture," *Scripta Hieroslymitana* 31 (1986): 272, who "suggest the Chroni-

cler is providing a pun based on the king's name . . ." (*2 Chronicles*, 126). See also Japhet, *Chronicles*, 738–40.

[106]2Ch 17:3–4 may provide a subtle hint regarding the idolatrous nature of Asa's sin, since it says of Jehoshaphat, son of Asa, "He did not consult the Baals [*dāraš l*ᵉ] but sought the God [again, *dāraš l*ᵉ] of his father" (i.e., David; see v. 3a).

[107]Amundsen and Ferngren, "Medicine and Religion: Pre-Christian Antiquity," 67, note: "Many biblical scholars take this as a condemnation of resorting to secular medicine as such, but a more likely explanation is that the physicians whom Asa consulted were foreign physicians whose procedures, even if empirical, would have been of a magico-religious nature."

[108]See below, n. 172.

[109]On *ṣāra'at*, see below, 2.2.6.

[110]Most notably Isaiah in 2Ki 20:7 (= Isa 38:22), where the means of healing (a poultice of figs applied to Hezekiah's malignant boil) is reminiscent of some of the folk cures alluded to in the discussion of Mesopotamian medicine (see 1.2.1, above). Of course, in the narrative of Hezekiah's illness, the Lord is clearly the Healer, and the application of the figs is not of central importance. On the prophets (in particular, Elijah and Elisha) as healers, see J. Lindblom, *Prophecy in Ancient Israel* (Philadelphia: Fortress, 1973), 201–2. For further discussion of Hezekiah's illness, see below, 2.3.2.4; for the psalm of Hezekiah (Isa 38), see below, 3.1.7.

[111]See Ex 20:26; also M. Noth, *Exodus*, trans. J. S. Bowden (OTL; Philadelphia: Westminster, 1962), 176–77.

[112]The best study to date on this subject is still Baudissin's *Adonis und Esmun*. W. Jayne's *Healing Gods of Ancient Civilizations* is more ambitious in scope (ranging from Egypt, Rome, and India to the Celts) but is of less scholarly value for the ancient Near Eastern material, the author's specialization being primarily medical as opposed to philological. For specific bibliographical notes on the various healing deities and practices, see below, and cf. M. T. Kelsey, *Healing and Christianity* (New York: Harper & Row, 1973), 33–51; M. Hamilton, *Incubation, or the Cure of Disease in Pagan Temples and Christian Churches* (London: Simpkin, Marshall, Hamilton, Kent & Co., 1906); E. Thrämer, "Health and Gods of Healing, *ERE* 6:540–56. For a general, somewhat dated, survey of ancient Semitic deities, see S. Moscati, ed., *Le Antiche Divinita Semitiche* (Studi Semitici 1; Rome: Centro di Studi Semitici, 1958); for more recent bibliography, cf. the relevant articles in *RSP* I–III.

[113]The ancient Near Eastern medical texts discussed above, 1.3, underscore the fact that the healing art—especially in the case of internal or mysterious ailments—was virtually always carried out in conjunction with the deity/deities. Without the healing and regenerative powers that are built into the human body, medical treatments are of no avail (witness the current AIDS epidemic; cf. the comments of J. W. Provonsha, cited below, 1.6, and see n. 114). To the unscientific mentality in particular, these healing processes sometimes bespeak special divine intervention and favor.

[114]Cf. Sigerist, *Civilization and Disease*, 43–86.

[115]As bemoaned by J. W. Provonsha, M.D., "The Healing Christ," in Kelsey, *Healing*, 361–64.

[116]Although the emphasis on "the salvation of the soul" to the virtual neglect of "the salvation of the whole man" has been maintained by "systematic" or "biblical" theologians, the biblical correctness of this position must be questioned. Cf. also below 6.1.2, 6.2.

[117]Cf. below, n. 213.

[118]Sigerist, *Civilization and Disease*, 134–35.

[119]Baudissin, *Adonis*, 310.

[120]For the divine epithets in Akkadian see K. L. Tallqvist, *Akkadische Götterepitheta* (Studia Orientalia edidit Societas orientalis Fennica, 7; repr. Hildesheim: Georg Olms, 1974).

[121]See Baudissin, *Adonis*, 311 ("Auf semitischen Boden weiss ich einen Speziallgott der Heilkunst mit Sicherheit nicht nachzuweisen"), and Jayne, *Healing Gods*, 52 ("Few of the many gods of ancient Egypt were prominent as healers"). Although it would certainly not be correct to equate the Mesopotamian goddess Gula with Asklepios, she is, more than any other Mesopotamian deity, identified as a healer. See below; also 2.2, above.

[122]For discussion of Asklepios, see below, 1.5.2. For a negative assessment of de Moor's claim that Baal was a West Semitic Asklepios, see below, 1.5.1, and cf. Brown, "Was There a West Semitic Asklepios?"

[123]An older but still valuable survey may be found in A. W. Shorter, *The Egyptian Gods* (repr. London and Henley: Routledge & Kegan Paul, 1978); for specifics on the healing aspects of some of these deities, see Jayne, *Healing Gods*, 52–86; for a study of the theophoric onomastica, see K. Hoffman, *Die theophoren Personennamen des alteren Ägyptens* (Leipzig: Hinrichs, 1915). For overall interpretations of Egyptian religion, see S. Morenz, *Egyptian Religion*, trans. A. Keep (London: Methuen, 1973); idem, *Religion und Geschichte des alten Ägypten: Gesammelte Aufsatze*, ed. E. Blumenthal, S. Herrmann, and A. Onasch (Cologne: Bohlau Verlag, 1975); E. Hornung, *Conceptions of God in Ancient Egypt: The One and the Many*; trans. J. Baines (Ithaca, N.Y.: Cornell Univ. Press, 1982); S. Quirke, *Ancient Egyptian Religion* (London: British Museum Press, 1992).

[124]See "The Hymn of a Thousand Stophes," III, 14–15, as translated by H. Brunner in W. Beyerlin (ed.), *Near Eastern Religious Texts Relating to the Old Testament*, trans. J. Bowden (Philadelphia: Westminster, 1978), 23. For a recent study of Amun (and Re), see J. Assman, *Re und Amun: Die Krise des polytheistichen Weltbilds im Ägypten der 18–20. Dynastie* (Orbis Biblicus et Orientalis 48; Göttingen: Vandenhoeck & Ruprecht, 1983), and see idem, *Ägyptische Hymnen und Gebete* (Zurich and Munich: Artemis Verlag, 1975), for a translation of 242 Egyptian hymns, the first 112 of which are solar hymns. Cf. also de Moor, *Rise of Yahwism*, 42–57 (note p. 49 [with references]: "Of course, it is Amun-Re who blesses parents with children because he is the life-giving god, the breath of life in the nose of every creature. . . . [He is] the Shepherd . . . . If one of his herd is afflicted by disease he manifests himself as the great Healer"). Amun Re is also hailed as "lord of life and health."

[125]See his *Preparation for the Gospel*, 10:6; cf. Jayne, *Healing Gods*, 53–54. Among other gods credited with the foundation of medicine are Thoth and Ubastet.

[126]Jayne, *Healing Gods*, 61, quoting from the Turin Papyrus.

[127]Ibid., 63.

[128]Ibid., 66–67. Jayne's citation there of the prayer to Isis found in the Ebers Papyrus is instructive in that Isis, the "great enchantress," was asked to heal the suppliant and save him from "all evil things of darkness," while at the same time Re and Osiris were called on to promote the healing manifestation in the sick man's body. Thus we have here religion, magic, and medicine (the quote, being taken as it were, from the Ebers Medical Papyrus) in one short and representative prayer. Among other prominent magician-healers, Thoth is worthy of special mention.

[129]Ibid., 69–70.

[130]Ibid., 78.

[131]For a typical example of praise and petition directed to Ptah, see Brunner's translation in *Religious Texts*, 36–37.

[132]See Jayne, *Healing Gods*, 74–76.

[133]Ibid., 76–77. For a concise but thorough discussion of Sekhmet, see H. Sternberg, "Sachmet," *LÄ* 5:323–33, with ample documentation, and note especially S.-E. Hoenes, *Untersuchungen zu Wesen und Kult der Gottin Sachmet, Habilitationschrift Dissertationsdrucke, Reihe Ägyptologie*, Heft 1 (Bonn: Habelt, 1976).

[134]Even the Ebers Papyrus, "a purely medical book dealing with internal diseases . . . begins with a prayer to Isis, just as Arabic medical books begin [with the Islamic introductory formula], 'In the Name of God the Merciful the Clement'" (Sigerist, *Civilization and Disease*, 133).

[135]Jayne, *Healing Gods*, 1217–28, lists under this same heading twelve different deities, and Baudissin refers briefly to at least eight different deities; for an overview, see Oppenheim, *Ancient Mesopotamia*, 171–227 (with a bibliographical note on 395–96), and T. Jacobsen, *The Treasures of Darkness* (New Haven: Yale Univ. Press, 1976). For details on the early evolution of the Mesopotamian deities, see J. J. M. Roberts, *The Earliest Semitic Pantheon* (Baltimore: Johns Hopkins Univ. Press, 1972).

[136]For references to other deities praised as healers in Akkadian literature, see Tallqvist, *Götterepitheta*, in particular 28 (*asû*), 67–68 (*balāṭu* II), 94 (*āšipu*), 136–38 (*nadānu*), 160 (*qâšu*).

[137]Ibid., 317; *CAD*, ibid., 529; *AHW* 1:92. Cf. the references below, 1.4.1, 1.4.2, to the LORD as "the faithful (or, reliable) physician" (*rôpē' ne'ᵉmān*) and Jesus as "the good physician" (*'āsyā' ṭābā'*). For other references to Gula, cf. Baudissin, *Adonis*, 312–13.

[138]See W. G. Lambert, "The Gula Hymn of Bulluṭsa-rābi," *Orientalia*, n.s. 36 (1967), 117, 121 (for complete text, translation, and notes, see 105–32; *Bulluṭsa-rābi* means "her healing is great"). On the importance of the healing herbs, see above, and note how closely the healing practices of the goddess reflect the healing practices of her earthly counterparts.

[139]Cf. also *qā'išat napišti, nādinat balāṭi, nādinat napišti Anim* (see Tallqvist, *Götterepitheta*). Note that in the *balāṭu* phrases, *balāṭu* means "life, vigor, good health" (cf. *CAD*, B, 46).

[140]*ša tudukkā[ša] bulluṭu* (*CAD*, B, 58); cf. Tallqvist, *Götterepitheta.*

[141]On *muballiṭat* (or, *muballiṭ*) *mīti*, a common epithet for the Mesopotamian gods, see immediately below, and cf. 3.1.6, 3.1.7.

[142]On this cf. Tallqvist, *Götterepitheta.*

[143]Cf. also the epistolary greeting formula in which it is wished that Ninib and Gula would give "soundness of heart and soundness and flesh" (*ṭūb libbi ṭūb šīri*, cited in Baudissin, *Adonis*, 312), an expression reminiscent of Ignatius' above-cited reference to Jesus as the "one physician of flesh and spirit."

[144]Tallqvist, *Götterepitheta*; cf. *AHW* 1256, *šu'ātu* III, for *šu'ētu*, "Lady" ("*Herrin*").

[145]*ša naplussa balāṭu u nashurša šalāmu*, as cited and translated in *CAD*, B, 46.

[146]For a study of the epithets and descriptions of Marduk in *Enuma Elish* VII, see J. Bottero, "Les noms de Marduk, l'écriture et la 'logique' en mesopotamie ancienne," in Ellis, ed., *Essays on the Ancient Near East*, 5–28.

[147]Tallqvist, *Götterepitheta*, 369; cf. there for *bel napišti mati, mudissu balāṭi, qa'iš balāṭi*, etc.

[148]Ibid.

[149]A.ZU-*u mudu*; see *CAD, A/2*, 346, 6'.

[150]Tallqvist, *Götterepitheta*; cf. the reference to Damu as both *asû* and *āšipu rābu* (ibid., 279).

[151]*šipat balāṭu kummu imat balaṭu kummu* (ibid., 369, with reference to Mk 7:33, 8:23; Jn 9:6).

[152]*ša bulluṭu irammu* (*CAD*, B, 58); cf. Baudissin, *Adonis*, 311.

[153]For text and translation, see W. G. Lambert, *Babylonian Wisdom Literature* (Oxford: Clarendon Press), 21–62. There are extremely graphic descriptions of the sufferer's healing on pp. 52–55. For a good collection of hymns and prayers that are comparable to much of the Hebrew material, see M.-J. Seux, *Hymnes et prières aux dieux de Babylonie et d'Assyrie* (Littératures anciennes du Proche-Orient 8; Paris: Les éditions du Cerf, 1976).

[154]Lambert, *Babylonian Wisdom Literature*, 58–59, lines 2–7.

[155]Ibid.

[156]"Danach mogen mit jenem Epitheton zum Teil die Götter bezeichnet sein als allgemein aus irgendwelcher Not errettende" (Baudissin, *Adonis*, 313).

[157]Ibid., 313; cf. H. Ringgren, *Israelite Religion*, trans. D. E. Green (Philadelphia: Fortress, 1966), 245: "The Akkadian term seems to refer primarily to healing the sick."

[158]For this word see below, 3.1.6, n. 118; cf. *Ludlul*, Tablet IV (?), 6 (Lambert, *Babylonian Wisdom Literature*, 58–59), "He summoned me [from] destruction"; see also Ringgren, *Religion*, 243ff.

[159]Baudissin, *Adonis*, 313.

[160]"[Amun] saves whom he will, even though he were already in the underworld," Brunner, *Near Eastern Religious Texts*, 23.

[161]Ibid., 23–24. Similar concepts will be discussed below, 3.1.6, 3.1.7, in the context of the biblical psalms.

[162]Cf. G. D. Young, ed., *Ugarit in Retrospect* (Winona Lake, Ind.: Eisenbrauns, 1981). It is still too early for a major assessment as to the religious importance of the Ebla texts. For a summary of the important religious texts from Canaan and its environs, see Smith, *The Early History of God*, esp. 1–40.

[163]For further references, see Niehr, "JHWH als Arzt," 4, n. 2.

[164]His seminal work on this is his 1976 study, "Rāpi'ūma-Rephaim."

[165]De Moor is in the minority in identifying *rpu* with Baal; other scholars identify *rpu* with *el*, while some maintain that he is an independent deity, simply known as *rpu* (or sometimes, *rpu mlk 'lm*). For discussion and bibliography, see M. Dietrich and O. Loretz, "Baal *RPU* in KTU 1.108; 1.113 und nach 1.17 VI 25–33," *UF* 12 (1980): 170–82; A. Cooper, "Divine Names and Epithets in the Ugaritic Texts," in *RSP* 3:460–67 (IV, #41), with bibliography on 462–63 (cf. also M. H. Pope, in ibid., 446). After surveying the literature, M. S. Smith suggests, "If *rp'u* is to be identified with any other deity [i.e., other than *rp'u* itself], the available evidence would best support an identification with Ugaritic *mlk* who dwells in Ashtaroth (*'ṯtrt*), although both *mlk* and *rp'u* could be epithets of one another or another deity" (*Early History*, 140, n. 15; see there for further references).

[166]See Brown, "Was There a West Semitic Asklepios?"

[167]Note, however, de Moor's student, M. C. A. Korpel, who avers, "The great healer [*rp'u*] among the gods is Ba'lu" (*A Rift in the Clouds*, 332). In support of this she claims that Baal: (1) could revive the dead; (2) healed the spirits of the dead; (3) could cast out demons; (4) "he is prayed to [to] stop the arrows of Rashpu" (332–33). The most specific instance in the Ugaritic texts of Baal's healing activity is KTU 1.19.III, where Baal is implored to "repair/remake" (*bny*) what he "smashed" (*ṯbr*); cf. Gordon, *UT* 373; Conrad L'Heureux, *Rank Among the Canaanite Gods: El, Ba'al, and the Repha'im* (HSM 21; Missoula, Mont.: Scholars, 1979), 12ff. The contextual emphasis, however, is more on Baal's (destructive) power than on his healing prowess. Note also that in biblical Hebrew, *šbr/rp'* (not *šbr/bny*) form a common antonymic word pair (see, e.g., Jer 6:14); thus, while *rp'* might possibly have been expected in the Ugaritic text, *bny* was used instead.

[168]At best *rpu* is seen as a dispenser of blessing and general well-being (see KTU 1.108); cf. Korpel, *A Rift in the Clouds*, 305–6, with reference to this text: "The king asks him [*rpu*, equated by Korpel with Baal] to extend his divine protection, his patronage, and his beneficial strength over the city of Ugarit. Apparently he was the national god upon whom the well-being of the nation was thought to depend." K. Spronk, *Beatific Life*, 193–96, points to KTU 1.124, where Ditanu, one of the *rpum*, is apparently involved in a healing, claiming that this establishes a clear connection between the *rpum* and healing activities. But his argument is somewhat specious; cf. again Brown, "Was There a West Semitic Asklepios?" For recent discussion (with bibliography) of the *rpum-rᵉpā'îm* question, see Liwak, "רְפָאִים," *TWAT* 7:625–35; for the latest treatment of the *rpum* texts (viz., KTU 1.20–22), see

W. T. Pitard, "A New Edition of the 'Rapi'uma' Texts: *KTU* 1:20–22," *BASOR* 285 (1992): 33–77; cf. also O. Loretz, "Die Teraphim als 'Ahnen-Götter Figur(in)en' im Lichte der Texte aus Nuzi, Emar und Ugarit. Anmerkiungen zu ilānu/ilh, ilhm/'ilhym und DINGIR. ERIN. MEŠ/ inš ilm," *UF*_24 (1992), 133–78.

[169]For de Moor, MT *r^e pā'îm* is a late revocalization for an earlier *rōp^e'îm*, "healers, physicians." For references, see Brown, "Was There a West Semitic Asklepios?"

[170]For further discussion, see Brown, "Was There a West Semitic Asklepios?"; idem, *A Philological Study*, 115–48, esp. 146–48; cf. Lohfink, "'Ich bin Jahwe, dein Arzt' (Ex 15,26)," 41–42. Note also the comment of S. Loewenstamm, "רְפָאִים," *EM* 7:406, "There is not in any [Hebrew, Phoenician, or Ugaritic *rp'm*] text a clear reference to an act of healing [*r^e pû'â*], be it healing the sick, reviving the dead, or restoring fertility to man or earth." Cf. also below, 2.2.4.

[171]See *CIS* I, 41,3 (*b'l mrp'*), a Phoenician inscription from Cyprus; for philological discussion, see Brown, "Was There a West Semitic Asklepios?"

[172]J. Gray, *I & II Kings* (OTL; Philadelphia: Westminster, 1970), 463, speculates that the (apparent) veneration of Baal Zebub of Ekron (see 2Ki 1:2 for the sole reference) as "the power giving life and health may have been established early in the Philistine settlement in Palestine, when, in the unsettled conditions of their occupation of their new homes, they suffered from new maladies of a local nature, which obliged them to placate the local god. An analogous case is the veneration of Yahweh at Bethel by the Assyrian military colony in face of local troubles." Cf. further the bibliography and discussion in Cooper, *RSP* 3:355–56 (IV 9q., on 2Ki 1:2–3, 6, 16); see also Niehr, "JHWH als Artz," where Baal Zebub, the *r^e pā'îm*, and *n^e ḥûštān* (see above, 1.3.2) are viewed as healing deities in Israel.

[173]H. Rouillard, "*El Rofé*," believes that *rapi'u* was first an epithet of El, then a function of Baal, before possibly becoming an independent healing deity. He sees this reflected in OT texts where Yahweh has coalesced with El (e.g., Nu 12:13; cf. below, 2.2.5) or is magnified as Healer in polemical texts against an impotent Baal.

[174]R. Whittaker, *Concordance*, cites fifteen occurrences of *ḥrn* in the corpus extant to him. Cf. Korpel, *A Rift in the Clouds*, 333; Cooper, *RSP* 3:365–66; B. A. Levine and J.-M. de Tarragon, O.P., "'Shapshu Cries Out in Heaven': Dealing with Snake-Bites at Ugarit," *RB* 95 (1988): 481–518; D. Pardee, "A Philological and Prosodic Analysis of the Ugaritic Serpent Incantation UT 607," *JANESCU* 10 (1978): 73–108.

[175]Cf. E. Lipinski, "Eshmun, 'Healer,'" *AION* 23 (1973): 161–83.

[176]Jayne, *Healing Gods*, 138. Some scholars have sought to connect *'ašmannîm* in Isa 59:10 (*'ašmûnnîm*, with *wāw* in 1QIs^a and one Kennicot MS) with this deity (hence, "lively, healthy; health"; cf. *Handwörterbuch*, 109; W. F. Albright, *Yahweh and the Gods of Canaan* [Garden City, N.Y.: Doubleday, 1968], 187; N. Torczyner [Tur Sinai], in Ben Yehuda 1:424, n. 2 [this note also contains includes details on Eshmun]); however, the same meaning can

be derived from the root *šmn* (see BDB, 1032; Ehrlich, *Mikra* 3:145–46; *Randglossen* 4:211; note that Delitzsch, *Isaiah*, KD 7/2:400, discusses the name Eshmun in this context, but also as derived from *šmn*). For morphological discussion of the form *'šmn*, see the references in *Handwörterbuch*, 109; *HALAT* 1:93; for the additional *waw* in 1QIs[a], see E. Y. Kutscher, *The Language and Linguistic Background of the Isaiah Scroll* (Hebrew; Jerusalem: Magnes, 1959), 281, 294; cf. further Clines, *Dictionary*, 1:417, with reference to the root *šmn*.

[177]*KAI* 2:81, "*Führer*"; Tomback, *Lexicon*, has no root *'rḥ* and no entry *m'rḥ*; *DISO*, 24, cites *m'rḥ* under *'rḥ*, treating it as a participle (so *KAI*) and tentatively translates with "*guide?*". The Latin and Greek translations (or better here, transliterations) read *Merre* and *Merre*, respectively (cf. *PPG*, 67, §143). On Eshmun, the Punic equivalent of Asklepios (so the Latin and Greek transcriptions) as a healer, cf. *KAI*, 2:81, with reference to Baudissin, *Adonis und Esmun*, 243; note Jayne, *Healing Gods*, 135–41. In de Moor's opinion, Eshmun "might be regarded as a relatively late offshoot of the Baal-cult." See "Rāpi'ūma," 329, n. 43, and C. Virolleaud, "Les Rephaim," *RES-Babyloniaca* (1940), 78, for an earlier statement of this view.

[178]Tomback, *Lexicon*, reads [*q*]*l* in place of [*q*]*l'*.

[179]For the Phoenician deity Shadrapa (*šdrp'*), presumably associated with healing, see B. Peckham, "Phoenicia and the Religion of Israel: The Epigraphic Evidence," in P. D. Miller Jr., P. D. Hanson, S. D. McBride, eds., *Ancient Israelite Religion: Essays in Honor of Frank Moore Cross* (Philadelphia: Fortress, 1987), 81, 91 (nn. 26, 28). For an example of a petition for health and blessing in an Aramaic-Akkadian text, cf. Tell Fekheriye, ll. 1–10 (Aramaic) and 1–14 (Akkadian) with the deity Hadad. Once again, this should remind us that in the ancient Near East, although there were "specialists," any god could be petitioned for the basic needs of life.

[180]See E. J. Edelstein and L. Edelstein, eds., *Asclepios: Testimonies* (Baltimore: Johns Hopkins Univ. Press, 1945), for the inscriptional evidence from the healing shrines, and H. C. Kee, *Miracle in the Early Christian World* (New Haven: Yale Univ. Press, 1983), 78–104, for a survey of recent scholarship. Even though Imhotep, the statesman, architect, and physician of Djoser in the Third Dynasty (for the chronology see Sir A. Gardiner, *Egypt of the Pharaohs* [Oxford: Oxford Univ. Press, 1961], 72ff.), underwent a similar deification process, sometimes being referred to as the Egyptian Aesculapius, the Imhotep healing cult arose late in Egyptian history; for references, see Baudissin, *Adonis und Esmun*, 310 and n. 2, and Jayne, *Healing Gods*, 62–64.

[181]See Jayne, *Healing Gods*, 240–303; Kee, *Miracle*, 78, n. 2. Kee cites the slightly different reconstruction of C. Kerenyi, *Asklepios: Archetypal Image of the Physician's Existence* (New York: Pantheon/Bollingen Foundation, 1959), xiii–xviii, who "wants to reject the divinization of a hero-physician from Thessaly, supposing rather that Homer has passed over in silence an older cult." In any case, it is important to note that as chief healer, Asklepios could also be the patron of the medical profession, as at Cos near Rhodes, the home of both a major medical school and a major Asklepion temple.

[182]At this stage, the emphasis is on sacred sleep and dream-visions (with a healing lick from the tongue of a dog or snake), miraculous (instantaneous) cures, and the active agency of the priests (see Kee, *Miracle*, 83–88).

[183]At this stage, according to Kee, "although the god is given ultimate credit for the cure, the therapy seems to have been largely self-administered.... The beneficiary is grateful for the improvement in his health, but there is no miraculous healing at a stroke" (ibid., 89; see 88–93).

[184]Ibid., 93. Note that Asklepios did not offer guidance and direction *instead of* physical healing; rather, these blessings were *in addition* to his healing activities.

[185]Ibid., 93–94. He also attributes his phenomenal success as an orator to Asklepios.

[186]Ibid., 94.

[187]Amundsen and Ferngren, "Medicine and Religion: Pre-Christian Antiquity," 80.

[188]The Old German *Heiland*, used as an epithet for Christ, is noteworthy, in that its meaning includes both "savior" and "healer" (cf. de Moor, "Rāpi'ūma–Rephaim," 323).

[189]See, e.g., D. M. Feldman, *Health and Medicine in the Jewish Tradition* (New York: Crossroad, 1986), 1–21; J. D. Bleich, "The Obligation to Heal in the Judaic Tradition: A Comparative Analysis," repr. in F. Rosner and J. D. Bleich, eds., *Jewish Bioethics* (Brooklyn: Hebrew Pub. Co., 1979), 1–44; F. Rosner, *Modern Medicine and Jewish Law* (New York: Bloch Pub. Co., 1972), 11–24.

[190]Cited in Jakobovits, *Jewish Medical Ethics,* xxi, with a catalog of medieval Jewish scholars cited on 295, n. 2, in support of this position. According to F. Rosner, "There are a multitude of interpretations of the scriptural phrase *for I am the Lord that healeth thee* indicating that this verse is not to be understood literally," *Medicine in the* Mishneh Torah *of Maimonides* (New York: Ktav, 1984), 61, with reference to idem, "The Physician and the Patient in Jewish Law," repr. in *Jewish Bioethics*, 45–55. For further discussion of Ex 15:26, see below, 2.2.1.

[191]For more thorough discussion see J. Preuss, *Biblical and Talmudic Medicine*, trans. F. Rosner (New York: Hebrew Pub. Co., 1978), 18–31; H. Friedenwald, *The Jews and Medicine* (repr. with an introduction by G. Rosen; New York: Ktav, 1967), 5–68; and I. Jakobovits, *Jewish Medical Ethics*, 1–23. There is also a convenient collection of original sources in M. Asaf, ed., *HaRefu'a BaMekorot* (Jerusalem: Rubin Mass, Ltd., 1982). For the early rabbinic period, see I. Jacob and W. Jacob, *The Healing Past: Pharmaceuticals in the Biblical and Rabbinic World*; S. S. Kottek, *Medicine and Hygiene in the Works of Flavius Josephus* (Studies in Ancient Medicine 9; Leiden: Brill, 1994). For the rabbinic responsa from the twelfth to the nineteenth centuries, see H. J. Zimmels, *Magicians, Theologians, and Doctors: Studies in Folk-medicine and Folklore as Reflected in the Rabbinic Responsa* (London: Edward Goldston & Son, 1952). The leading medical respondent today is Rabbi E. Y. Waldenberg; see his *Ṣiṣ Eliezer* (16 vols. to date); note also that both journals

and series of studies on the subject of medicine and Jewish law (*halakah*) continue to appear.

[192]*M. Pes.* 4:9; cf. *b. Pes.* 56a, *b. Ber.* 10b; for *sēper r^epû'ôt*, the Yerushalmi (*y. Sanh.* 1, 18d, bot.) reads *ṭablâ šel r^epû'ôt*. Note that authorship of this book was traditionally ascribed to Solomon (cf. Josephus, *Antiquities*, VIII, 2, 5; see M. Hengel, *Judaism and Hellenism*, trans. J. Bowden [Philadelphia: Fortress, 1974], 241). For additional rabbinic traditions relating to Hezekiah's stopping up of the spring of Gihon and his destruction of the bronze serpent, see L. Ginzberg, *Legends of the Jews* (Philadelphia: The Jewish Publication Society of America, 1928), 6:369, n. 90.

[193]Cf. Jakobovits, *Jewish Medical Ethics*, 304, n. 8; H. Albeck, *Shishah Sidrei Mishneh* (Jerusalem: Mosad Bialik, 1959), 156, 448–49; P. Kehati, *Mishnayot Mebu'arot* (Jerusalem: Hosa'at Heykal Shlomo, 1977), 3:325–26; Ginzberg, *Legends*.

[194]For further discussion and later rabbinic critiques of Maimonides' logic, see F. Rosner, "The Illness of King Hezekiah and 'The Book of Remedies' which He Hid," *Koroth* 9/1–2 (1985): 191–93.

[195]Jakobovits, *Jewish Medical Ethics*, 304.

[196]See Rosner, *Medicine in the* Mishneh Torah, 63, citing Maimonides' decisive comment on *m. Ned.* 4:4: "It is obligatory from the Torah for the physician to heal the sick, and this obligation is included in the explanation of the scriptural phrase *and thou shalt restore it to him*, meaning to heal his body." See also Jakobovits, *Jewish Medical Ethics*, 4, and Asaf, *HaRefu'a*, 149–54, for further details.

[197]For the influence of "medieval religious rationalism" on the Mishneh Torah in general, see I. Twersky, *Introduction to the Code of Maimonides* (New Haven: Yale Univ. Press, 1980), 86–88.

[198]See Jakobovits, *Jewish Medical Ethics*, 2, 5, 303 (n. 5), 305 (n. 29); and Friedenwald, *The Jews and Medicine*, 9.

[199]Cf. Ibn Ezra on Ex 21:19, *w^erappō' y^erappē'*; see above, n. 8.

[200]For the varied rabbinic views on the extent to which Providence could be invoked as the cause of disease, see especially Jakobovits, ibid., 2ff.

[201]Cf. below, 2.2.1, 2.2.2, 2.2.5, 3.3.2.3, and above, 1.2.2.3, for the exegesis of the verses cited in Ibn Ezra's comments to Ex 21:19. On the omission of Ex 21:19 from Maimonides' discussion, see B. H. Epstein, cited in Rosner, *Medicine in the* Mishneh Torah, 62.

[202]Preuss, *Biblical and Talmudic Medicine*, 23; cf. above, 1.2.2.3, on 2Ch 16:12.

[203]Mueller, *Sickness and Healing*, 105. For Philo's reference to God as *monos iatros*, see below.

[204]See *Midrash Samuel*, iv. 1, cited in Asaf, *HaRefu'a*, 60, and translated, *inter alia*, in Jakobovits, *Jewish Medical Ethics*, 303–4 (n. 7), and Rosner, *Modern Medicine*, 12.

[205]*M. Qid.* 4:14 (= *b. Qid.* 82b—*ṭôb šebbārôp^e 'im l^e gēhinām*); cf. the similarly worded remark in *Abot de Rabbi Nathan* 36:5 that "the best physician" (again, *ṭôb šebbārôp^e 'îm*) was one of the seven who had no part in the world to come

(cf. S. Schechter, ed., *Aboth de Rabbi Nathan* [New York: Philip Feldheim, 1945], 108, for another reading of the latter passage, as well as for bibliographical notes; see also below, n. 229). For various apologetic comments seeking to mollify these statements, see Friedenwald, *Medicine*, 11–13.

[206]*B. Sanh.* 17b; cf. the other positive Talmudic citations collected in Asaf, *HaRefu'a*, 51–53.

[207]Cf. Preuss, *Biblical and Talmudic Medicine*, passim, for examples from every aspect of medical treatment.

[208]Cf. the words of Oral Roberts, arguably the most well-known contemporary proponent of divine healing: "Respect your doctor. Respect medicine. Don't divide God's healing power. Some people will pray and never take medicine, and some will take medicine and never pray. I don't know about them, but I take it all from God myself." See *A Daily Guide to Miracles* (Tulsa, Okla.: Pinoak, 1975), 360, quoted in R. G. Witty, *Divine Healing* (Nashville: Broadman, 1989), 17.

[209]For a recent treatment of Ben Sira's comments in Ecclus. 38:1–15, see P. W. Skehan, *The Wisdom of Ben Sira* (AB; New York: Doubleday, 1991), 438–43; add D. Flusser, "The Role of the Doctor According to Ben-Sira," (Heb.), *Mahanayim* 122 (1970): 48–55, to the studies of A. Sovic, H. Duesberg, A. Stöger, P. C. Beentjes, and J. T. Nelis, cited in Skehan's commentary, 443. Although Smend, Peters, Box-Oesterley, and Duesberg-Fransen prefer the reading: "he [viz., the sinner] will be delivered into the hands of the doctor" for Ecclus. 38:15b, Skehan seems to be correct that "this reading, which puts the doctor in an unfavorable light, hardly is in keeping with the tone of the rest of the poem" (ibid.).

[210]For an evaluation of Ben Sira's encounter with Hellenism, especially in its more liberal aspects, see Hengel, *Judaism*, 131–53. For an appreciation of Ben Sira's wisdom as an early representation of Jewish moderation and sanity, see Friedenwald, *The Jews and Medicine*, 6–8, 17; see also Wolff, *Anthropology*, 146–47. According to Kee, *Medicine, Miracle and Magic*, 19, Ben Sira's attitude toward physicians is "a radical shift" from the OT perspective.

[211]For the former, see Philo's *Concerning the Sacrifice of Cain and Abel*, 123; for the latter, see ibid., 70; for further details, see Oepke, *TDNT* 3:202, and Mueller, *Sickness and Healing*, 106.

[212]The relevant text, as translated by J. Neusner (*The Talmud of Babylonia: An American Translation. I: Tractate Berakhot* [Chico, Calif.: Scholars, 1984], 406, LXXXII) reads: "He who goes in to have blood let says, 'May it please you, Lord my God, that this procedure serve as healing for me, and that you may heal me. For you are a God who heals faithfully, and your healing is truth. For in point of fact mortals do not have the power to heal, but they merely do what is customary.'" Note that the propriety of this prayer is challenged by Abayye, based on *rappō' ye rappē'* (Ex 21:19), since the biblical injuction mandates medical treatment, thus implying that physicians do, in fact, heal. See above, 1.2.2.2, on Ex 21:19. The ninth benediction of the Shemoneh Esreh, the prayer par excellence of the synagogue, is the petition for healing: "Heal us, O Lord, and we will be healed; save us, and we will be

saved. For You are our praise [Jer 17:14]. Bring about complete healing for all our afflictions, for You are God, King, the faithful and compassionate Healer. Blessed are You, O Lord, Who heals the sick of Your people Israel."

[213]See in general, Friedenwald, *The Jews and Medicine*. On Judaism's emphasis that its physicians ultimately depend on "the Healer of all flesh," see Jakobovits, *Jewish Medical Ethics*, 22–23; cf. the collection of the physician's oath and prayers collected in Asaf, *HaRefu'a*, 49–53.

[214]See especially Kelsey, *Healing and Christianity*; cf. also Jakobovits, *Jewish Medical Ethics*, 1. As stated by Sigerist, *Civilization and Disease*, 140, "Medicine was faith healing in the early Christian community."

[215]Cf. J. D. G. Dunn, *Jesus and the Spirit* (Philadelphia: Westminster, 1975), 69–76; see below, ch. 5, for further discussion and bibliography.

[216]Cf. the sources gathered in E. Frost, *Christian Healing: A Consideration of the Place of Spiritual Healing in the Church of Today in the Light of the Doctrine and Practice of the Anti-Nicene Church* (London: A. R. Mowbray & Co., 1940), and, more concisely, Kelsey, *Healing*, 104–99. Mueller states, "Not only did Jesus heal the sick and drive out demons, the early church as a whole was a movement which turned its attention to the situation of the sick in a significant way" (*Sickness and Healing*, 182).

[217]See H. C. Kee, *Miracle*, 146–73, for the apocalyptic significance of miracles of deliverance; see also Mueller, *Sickness and Healing*, 116–19; cf. below, 5.2.2, on the Jubilee pronouncement in the gospel of Luke.

[218]Kelsey, *Healing and Christianity*, 129, n. 1.

[219]*Second Apology to the Roman Senate*, cited in ibid., 136. Out of many similar testimonies that could be cited, see Tertullian, *To Scapula* 4 (in ibid., 137): "And how many men of rank (to say nothing of common people) have been delivered from devils, and healed of diseases!"

[220]Trans. by K. Schäferdieck, in W. Schneemelcher, ed., *New Testament Apocrypha*, trans. R. McL. Wilson (Louisville: Westminster/John Knox, 1992), 2:177. Regardless of the authenticity of this account, it does, of course, reflect the attitude that for the NT church, divine healing was thought of as an expected norm. Cf. further P. J. Achtmeier, "Jesus and the Disciples as Miracle Workers in the Apocryphal New Testament," in E. S. Fiorenza, ed., *Aspects of Religious Propaganda in Judaism and Early Christianity* (Notre Dame: Univ. of Notre Dame Press, 1976), 149–86.

[221]See Kelsey, *Healing and Christianity*, 184–88.

[222]Augustine, *City of God*, 22.8, cited in Kelsey, ibid., 185. See also the important statement in Augustine's *Retractions*, 1.13.7 (also 1.14.15), cited in ibid., wherein he specifically revises his earlier views.

[223]G. Boccaccini has recently argued that "Christianity" be recognized as a "Judaism" (see his *Middle Judaism: Jewish Thought, 300 B.C.E. to 200 C.E.* [Minneapolis: Fortress, 1991], with some strictures in the foreword by J. H. Charlesworth, xviii), citing the judgment of scholars who underscore the "Jewishness" of early Christianity (see esp. 13–18; see also the challenge of G. Vermes, *Jesus and the World of Judaism* [Philadelphia: Fortress, 1983], 87–88, for a new "Schürer-type *religious* history of the Jews from the Maccabees

to AD 500 that fully incorporates the New Testament data." For further bibliography of related works, cf. M. L. Brown, *Our Hands Are Stained with Blood: The Tragic Story of the "Church" and the Jewish People* [Shippensburg, Pa.: Destiny Image, 1992], 233–34, 237–38). Because Christianity quickly developed into a predominantly Gentile religion, at times hostile to its Jewish roots, I believe scholarly references to "Jewish Christianity" may present an unnecessary oxymoronic problem. Terms such as "Messianic Jew/ish" and "Messianic Judaism" may be more appropriate, descriptive, and in fact accurate when applied to the first followers of Jesus.

[224]Although dated, the standard collection of the relevant rabbinic material is R. T. Herford, *Christianity in Talmud and Midrash* (London: Williams & Northgate, 1903); for more recent discussion, cf. L. H. Schiffman, *Who Was a Jew? Rabbinic and Halakhic Perspectives on the Jewish-Christian Schism* (Hoboken, N.J.: Ktav, 1985); C. J. Setzer, *Jewish Responses to Early Christians: History and Polemics, 30–150 C.E.* (Minneapolis: Augsburg Fortress, 1994).

[225]Cf. Schiffman, *Who Was a Jew?*, 68–71 (on the scurrilous name "Yeshu' ben Pantira," see the literature cited on pp. 100–101, n. 5).

[226]See below, nn. 228–229; cf. also *t. Hul.* 2:21, cited in Schiffman, *Who Was a Jew?*, 64: "We are not healed by them, neither healing of property nor healing of life." (According to one view, this means neither healing of animals nor healing of humans; the other view interprets the phrases in question—*rippûi mamôn* and *rippûi nepašôt*—to refer to healing in cases where there is no mortal danger vs. healing in cases involving mortal danger; see p. 99, n. 79.) It is not clear whether miraculous healings by the *minnîm* are included here, or whether the prohibition only countenances medical treatment by the *minnîm*. To this day, the Orthodox rabbinic community has strongly discouraged Jews from receiving ministry from Christian "faith healers" (including *Gentile* Christian faith healers), seeing that faith in Jesus would be involved. Note the end of a relevant responsum of Rabbi Y. Y. Weiss: "How right were our sages in forbidding us to be cured by a cleric in an unnatural way, even in life-threatening situations. May God send a complete recovery to all the sick in Israel" (see A. Y. Finkel, *The Responsa Anthology* [Northvale, N.J.: Jason Aronson, 1990], 178). Weiss states emphatically that the Jew "should use only qualified physicians, prayer to God, and charity," rather than utilize the services of a minister such as Rev. Tony Agapo of Manila, who, according to Rabbi Weiss's questioner, "cures all diseases and plagues and performs surgery without making incisions, just with his hands."

[227]This seems to be a later addition; cf. Schiffman, *Who Was a Jew?*, 41–46, who identifies the core of *m. Sanh.* 10:1 as a pre-A.D. 70 censure primarily directed against Sadducees.

[228]*T. Šab.* 12:10; *b. Šab.* 101a (cf. also *b. Šebu.* 15b; *Abot R. N.* ch. 36, end; *y. Sotah* 81, Halakha 4) add *w^{e}rôkēk*—"and spits." For subsequent rabbinic codification (with no reference to *minnîm*), see *Shulhan Arukh, Yoreh Deah*, 179:8 (and cf. Epstein, *Torah Temimah*, 2:156, n. 44). Stendahl, with reference to L. Ginzberg, "Some Observations on the Attitude of the Synagogue Towards the Apocalyptic-Eschatological Writings," *JBL* 41 (1922): 123–24, claims that

the usage of Ex 15:26 was especially significant for the followers of Jesus (whom Stendahl sees as the object of R. Akiva's censure), since the last words of the verse correspond by Gematria to 391 (388 for the consonants plus one for each of the three words), the numerical equivalent of the name Yeshu'a (actually, Yehoshua); see Stendahl, "*Rafa'*," 9, n. 8. In Ginzberg's view, the early Jewish followers of Jesus might have quoted Ex 15:26 in place of Jesus' name so as to retain secrecy.

229*Y. Šab.* 14:4 (14d) and *y. Avod. Zar.* 2:1 (40d–41a), both of which contain the account of Jacob of Kefar Sama found in *t. Ḥul.* 2:22–23, record an instance where a certain man came to the sick grandson of Joshua ben Levi and "whispered over him" (*w^e laḥaš lēh*; or, "whispered an incantation over him") in the name of Yeshu ben Pandera. His grandfather reproved him over this, telling him it would have been better to have died. According to H. Albeck, *Shishah Sidrei Mishnah* (Jerusalem: Mosad Bialik/Dvir, 1977), *Seder Neziqin*, 455, top, "It is known that the early *minnîm* used to whisper over wounds and perform miracles" (*'ôsîm ma'^a seh nissîm*). More generally, however, J. Goldin, ed. and trans., *The Fathers According to Rabbi Nathan* (New Haven: Yale Univ. Press, 1983), 212, n. 35, refers the exclusion from the world to come to those who practice "magical healing by incantation," with reference to J. Trachtenberg, *Jewish Magic and Superstition* (New York: Atheneum, 1939), 120–21. According to Ginzberg, "Some Observations," 123, "The severe condemnation by Rabbi Akiba of the use of Exod 15, 26 in connection with medication is certainly directed against Christian healers, as has been felt by many scholars, though they were unable to explain why just this Biblical verse was so opprobrious to the Rabbis."

230S. T. Lachs, *A Rabbinic Commentary on the New Testament. The Gospels of Matthew, Mark and Luke* (Hoboken/New York: Ktav/Anti-Defamation League of B'nai Brith, 1987), 178, on Mt 10:1; see H. Strack and P. Billerbeck, *Kommentar zum Neuen Testament aus Talmud und Midrasch* (München: C. H. Beck, 1928), 1:38. For convenient English translations of most of the relevant material, see Herford, *Christianity in Talmud and Midrash.* For a structural-genre analysis of the Talmudic and NT healing stories, cf. D. Noy, "The Talmudic-Midrashic 'Healing Stories' as a Narrative Genre," *Koroth* 9, Special Issue (1988): 124–46.

231See G. Dumeige, "Le Christ médecin dans la littérature chrétienne des premiers siècles," *Rivista di archeologia cristiana* 48 (1972): 115–41; J. Ott, "Die Bezeichnung Christi als *iatros* in der urchristlichen Literatur," *Der Katholik* 90 (1910): 454–58; cf. G. W. H. Lampe, ed., *A Patristic Greek Lexicon* (Oxford: Oxford Univ. Press, 1961), 662; BAGD 368–69; Oepke, *TDNT* 3:214–15. According to de Moor, "Rāpi'umā–Rephaim," 323, n. 2: "In the early church the epithets ἰατρός and *medicus* were quite common" (see there for further references).

2321 Eph 7:2 (*eis iatros estin sarkikos kai pneumatikos*). It is possible to render the whole line as, "There is one physician, who is flesh and spirit," understood with reference to the dual nature of Jesus. For this view, see J. B. Lightfoot, *The Apostolic Fathers* (repr. Hildesheim: Olms, 1973), 2/2:47–48, who seeks to demonstrate the validity of this translation by means of the contextual references to the hypostatic union of Christ. However, in light of the context, it is also possible to see Ignatius' designation as a double entendre in which Jesus, who is flesh and spirit, is the Physician of flesh and spirit. In any case, the reference to Jesus as "the one physician" is beyond dispute. For full discussion, cf. W. R. Schoedel, *Ignatius of Antioch* (Herm.; Philadelphia: Fortress, 1985), 59–60. While Schoedel notes that a contrast with pagan healing deities might lie in the background (as per Ott, "Die Bezeichnung Christi"), he prefers to read the text in terms of a contrast with the bite of the mad dogs (i.e., false teachers). See further 1 Eph 20:2b, translated by Schoedel, 95, as "breaking one bread, which is the antidote preventing death, but leading to life in Jesus Christ forever."

[233]See Payne-Smith, *Thesaurus*, 289; Jesus is also *m'assyānā'*, "healer" (see *Acts of Judas Thomas*, 65, 143, 156 ['*asāyā*']; 10, 37, 42, 156 [*m'assyānā'*]). Cf. R. Murray, *Symbols of Church and Kingdom: A Study in Early Syriac Tradition* (Cambridge: Cambridge Univ. Press, 1975), 199–203.

[234]See Murray, *Symbols*, 200, who continues: "It is a constant refrain in the Diatessaron commentary." See also Ephrem's important statement, summarized by Murray, 201. In the rich Syriac literature, both Jesus and the apostles (and bishops) were healers of human bodies and souls; cf. *Acts of Judas Thomas*, 95, 155 (regarding Jesus); and Marutha, *Homily* 11, *OrChr* 3, 408.12–17 (for the apostles); cf. again Murray, 200–201.

[235]Mueller, *Sickness and Healing*, 106.

[236]For the varied Jewish views on this subject, see Jakobovits, *Jewish Medical Ethics*, 24–44; Preuss, *Biblical and Talmudic Medicine*, 139–41; cf. further Strack-Billerbeck, 4/1:501–35. On the attribution of sickness to demons in the ancient Near Eastern world, see below; cf. also Hempel, *Heilung*, 260–71.

[237]Augustine, *De Divinatione Daemonum*, ch. 3, as cited by White, *History*, 27–28; cf. Haggard, *Devils*, 298, and Jakobovits, *Jewish Medical Ethics*, 28.

[238]Origen, *Commentary on Matthew*, 13:8, cited in Mueller, *Sickness and Healing*, 137; see 130–38 for further NT perspectives. Cf. White, *History*, 27–30, 97–167, for extensive discussion of developments in the history of the church.

[239]For a good summary, see D. W. Amundsen and G. B. Ferngren, "Medicine and Religion: Early Christianity Through the Middle Ages," 93–131.

[240]Cited in ibid., 99.

[241]Ibid., 98.

[242]Provonsha, "The Healing Christ," 361, 363. Provonsha contends that the Hellenistic body-soul dichotomy, which strongly influenced the post-NT church, brought about a decreased emphasis on the importance of ministry to one's physical needs, noting also that "the Post-Apostolic Church often saw the healing ministry of Jesus, and that committed to the Church, as radically opposed to the methodology of 'pagan' physicians of the period. It was miracle against scientific method—Christ's healings were miraculous, not scientific! But the early Church often failed to distinguish between 'miracle'

and 'magic'" (363). On the tendency to disdain proper care of the body in certain wings of the church, see White, *History*, 67–96.

[243]"Medicine," *Encyclopaedia Britannica*, 23:890. In fact, outside of that portion of the contemporary church that emphasizes the importance of divine healing for today, Christian healing practices have steadily moved *away* from miraculous healing by faith—the primary pattern for the NT and early church!—becoming identified instead with compassionate medical practice (e.g., building hospitals, sending out medical missionaries, training many Christian doctors and nurses, etc.). It is my conviction that, from a biblical perspective, the two emphases go hand in hand. Cf. also Kelsey, *Healing*, 8: "Most modern Christian churches believe that they have nothing to do officially with healing the sick.... Oddly enough, this constitutes an about-face in Christian belief."

[244]Sigerist, *Civilization and Disease*, 69. In the words of D. J. Seel, "Early in my manhood I said I could not be a physician unless I were first a disciple of Jesus Christ.... *Jesus healed.* It follows that the gospel of Jesus cannot be complete without that compassionate ministry. Jesus demonstrated that our God is compassionate, that He is moved by human suffering. And therefore Christ's disciples must seek to be instruments of healing, in one or more of the various avenues available for medical ministry. Christian medicine must be above all else an exhibit, a demonstration, of the character of God" ("The Imperative of a Christian Approach to Healing," *The Proceedings of the Consultation on the Study Program of Healing Ministry, October 30-November 1, 1980* [Seoul: Asian Center for Theological Studies and Mission/Korea Christian Medico-Evangelical Association, n.d.], 3, 5).

Chapter Two—Israel's Divine Healer in the Torah and Historical Books

[1]Cf. Y. Zakovitch, *"And Tell it to Your Son ...": The Concept of the Exodus in the Bible* (Jerusalem: Magnes, 1991); note D. L. Christensen, *Deuteronomy 1–11* (WBC; Waco, Tex.: Word, 1991), li: "The central event in the shaping of the epic story of the Hebrew Bible is the deliverance of the people of Israel from slavery in Egypt." See also S. E. Loewenstamm, *The Evolution of the Exodus Tradition* (Jerusalem: Magnes, 1992); P. Doron, "The Motif of the Exodus in the Old Testament," *Scripture Bulletin* 13 (1982): 5–8; contrast J. Van Seters, "The Plagues of Egypt: Ancient Tradition or Literary Invention?" *ZAW* 98 (1986): 31–39.

[2]Cf. A. Niccacci, "Yahweh e il Faraone. Teologia biblica ed egiziana a confronto," *BN* 38/39 (1987): 85–102; J. K. Hoffmeier, "The Arm of God Versus the Arm of Pharaoh in the Exodus Narratives," *Bib* 67 (1986): 378–87. For the cosmic dimensions of the plagues on Egypt, see T. E. Fretheim, "The Plagues as Ecological Signs of Historical Disaster," *JBL* 110 (1991): 385–96.

[3]In the opinion of D. N. Freedman, "'Who Is Like Thee Among the Gods?' The Religion of Early Israel," in *Ancient Israelite Religion*, 327, "In this poem ... we are confronted with Mosaic Yahwism, in its pristine original form, the faith by which the lawgiver led his people from slavery in

Egypt to freedom in the wilderness." See ibid., 315–35, for the dating and theological significance of Exodus 15 in the context of early Israelite religion; cf. also de Moor, *Rise of Yahwism*, 210–11, who dates the poem "to the united monarchy," claiming that "the polytheistic formula in v. 11, which is unique in the entire Old Testament, forbids a low date." For a postexilic dating, cf. M. L. Brenner, *The Song of the Sea: Ex. 15:1–21* (BZAW 195; Berlin: Walter de Gruyter, 1991), and cf. the review of Brenner by W. Brueggeman in *JBL* 112 (1993): 126–28.

[4]Cf. R. L. Smith, *Old Testament Theology: Its History, Method, and Message* (Nashville: Broadman & Holman, 1993); 164–233 ("Who Is a God Like Yahweh?"), with no specific section, however, devoted to God's role as Healer.

[5]It is probably better to render, "Surely [*kî*] I know . . ."; cf. the commentaries of H. J. Krauss and M. Dahood, ad loc. (rendering with "Indeed").

[6]The fact that the psalmist mentions other gods does not necessarily mean that his viewpoint is monolatrous as opposed to monotheistic (cf., e.g., 2Ki 19:17–19), although Ex 18:11, which Ps 135:5 echoes, is best understood as monolatrous. For Yahweh as the highest God, cf. H.-J. Kraus, *Psalms 1–59,* trans. H. C. Oswald (Minneapolis: Augsburg, 1988), 83–84.

[7]For studies on the meaning and nature of polytheism and idolatry, see M. Habertal and A. Margalit, *Idolatry*, trans. N. Goldblum (Cambridge, Mass.: Harvard Univ. Press, 1992); J. Faur, "The Biblical Idea of Idolatry," *JQR* 69 (1978): 1–15; see also T. Jacobsen, "The Graven Image," in *Ancient Israelite Religion*, 15–32.

[8]For bibliographical references dealing with the antiquity and/or foundational importance of the Decalogue, see the literature cited in Christensen, *Deuteronomy 1–11*, 105–8; M. Weinfeld, *Deuteronomy 1–11* (AB; New York: Doubleday, 1991), 236–327; B.-Z. Segal, ed., *The Ten Commandments in History and Tradition,* trans. G. Levi (Jerusalem: Magnes, 1990). According to Weinfeld, 262: "At the dawn of Israelite history the Decalogue was promulgated in its original short form as the foundation scroll of the Israelite community, written on two stone tablets, which were later called 'the tablets of the covenant' or 'tablets of the testimony.'" See also C. M. Carmichael, *The Origins of Biblical Law: The Decalogues and the Book of the Covenant* (Cornell: Cornell Univ. Press, 1992).

[9]For a detailed discussion of *'al pānāy*, cf. Weinfeld, *Deuteronomy 1–11,* 276–77.

[10]For *ḥrm*, see N. Lohfink, *TDOT* 5:180–98.

[11]See the works cited by J. I. Durham, *Exodus* (WBC; Waco, Tex.: Word, 1987), 455–56.

[12]According to Rabbi Levi (cited in *Lev Rabbah*, 24), the reason that Lev 19 was to be read before the whole assembly was "because the Ten Commandments are embodied in it." See Levine, *Leviticus*, 124–25, for explanation and comment.

[13]It would seem that the polytheism of Solomon (1Ki 11:1–8) was hardly ever fully uprooted from the royal household, evidenced by the fact that less than one hundred years after Hezekiah's reforms, every kind of detestable

and idolatrous rite was being practiced in the temple (2Ki 23:4–7; cf. also vv. 8–15). Cf. also Dearman, *Religion and Culture*, 36–39 (with references on 36, n. 111); S. Ackerman, *Under Every Green Tree: Popular Religion in Sixth-Century Judah* (HSM 46; Atlanta: Scholars, 1992); J.-M. van Cangh, "Les origines d'Israël et de la foi monothéiste: Apports de l'archéologie et de la critique littéraire," *RTL* 22 (1991): 305–26, 457–87; P. Hayman, "Monotheism—A Misused Word in Jewish Studies?" *JJS* 42 (1991): 1–15; N. Fujita, "Biblical Monolatry," *TBT* 30 (1992): 246–50; J. Blenkinsopp, "Yahweh and the Other Deities: Conflict and Accommodation in the Religion of Israel," *Int* 40 (1986): 354–66. Dearman (p. 8) notes that "neither biblical text nor material culture gives evidence of a golden age where Israel's faith was practiced in cultural isolation and Israel was free from the influence of competing world views or immune to the possibility of internal corruption." For a more wide-ranging discussion, see O. Keel, ed., *Monotheismus im Alten Israel und seiner Umwelt* (Biblische Beiträge 14; Fribourg: Schweizerisches Katholisches Bibelwerk, 1980), and N. Lohfink, "Das Alte Testament und sein Monotheismus," in K. Rahner, ed., *Der eine Gott und der dreieine Gott* (Munich: Schnell & Steiner, 1983), 28–47.

[14]In general, I would follow the assessment of M. S. Smith and others (see the *Early History*, xx, with xxxii, n. 6.), as opposed to J. H. Tigay and others (see Tigay's *You Shall Have No Other Gods: Israelite Religion in the Light of Hebrew Inscriptions* [HSS 31; Atlanta: Scholars, 1986]), with regard to the pervasive presence of idolatry in ancient Israel.

[15]Another appealing factor in some of the competing ancient Near Eastern faiths is the lower standards of holiness (note the frequent connection between immorality and idolatry in the OT, as at Peor, Nu 25:1–3), especially when fertility rites were viewed as an act of worship. For the importance attached to fertility in the ancient Near East, cf. below, 2.2.4, and see J. P. Healey, "Fertility Cults," *ABD* 2:791–93.

[16]F. I. Andersen and D. N. Freedman, *Hosea* (AB; Garden City, N.Y.: Doubleday, 1980), 581: "Hosea's polemic against healers in rivalry with Yahweh makes us wonder if one of the unnamed gods was a god of healing." Cf. below, 4.1.2, for discussion of the healing texts in Hosea, and note the apposite comment of H. C. Kee, *Medicine, Miracle and Magic*, 13: "Throughout Hosea . . . the implicit question is raised: who will heal Israel?"

[17]The specific promise in Ex 23:26 (*'et-mispar yāmêkā 'ᵃmallē'*) is literally: "I will fulfill the number of your days." For the blessing of long life, see below, 2.2.3 and 3.1.10, 3.2.1.

[18]Note this curse from Esarhaddon's Succession Treaty in S. Parpola and K. Watanabe, eds., *Neo-Assyrian Treaties and Loyalty Oaths. State Archives of Assyria*, vol. 2 (Helsinki: Helsinki Univ. Press, 1988), 45, 414–16: "May Aššur . . . not gr[ant yo]u long-lasting old age and the attainment of extreme old age." Cf. further below, 2.2.3.

[19]Cf. this vivid curse from ibid., 46, 437–39: "May Belet-ili, the lady of creation, cut off birth from your land; may she deprive your nurses of the cries of little children in the streets and squares."

[20]On the whole chapter, cf. R. H. O'Connell, "Deuteronomy vii 1–26: Assymetrical Concentricity and the Rhetoric of Conquest," *VT* 42 (1992): 248–65.

[21]Dt 7:15 should be rendered, "And the LORD will remove from you every sickness and all the dread diseases of Egypt, which you knew [so well]. He will not inflict them on you, but will put them on all those who hate you." Contrast NIV and cf. Dt 28:60–61. For an unusual interpretation of the difference between *ḥŏlî* and *madwê* (rendered here as "sickness" and "disease"), see the comments of the Vilna Gaon, *Adderet Eliyahu*, 2:605 (to Dt 7:15).

[22]Put simply, he would either destroy his (obedient) people's enemies or destroy his (disobedient) people (summarized in Dt 8:19–20), although Israel's own destruction would not be total (cf. Jer 30:11).

[23]Kinnier-Wilson, "Medicine," 362, identifies this with certainty as the Oriental (or, Tropical) Sore, "known medically as cutaneous Leishmaniasis" and called by the names of "Aleppo Boil," "Baghdad Boil," and "Delhi Boil" in those localities; for an etymological discussion, cf. Y. Elman, "An Akkadian Cognate of Hebrew *šᵉḥin*," *JANESCU* 8 (1976): 33–34.

[24]P. C. Craigie, *Deuteronomy* (NICOT; Grand Rapids: Eerdmans, 1976), 181 (also Christensen, *Deuteronomy 1–11*, 164, virtually verbatim), thinks that the diseases of Egypt probably referred to "elephantiasis, various types of boils, and afflictions of the eyes and bowels [which] were particularly common and unpleasant." (Both Craigie and Christensen make further reference to F. Marti-Ibanez, ed., *A Pictorial History of Medicine* [1965], 33–51, 283–84.) However, Craigie correctly notes (334) that the reference to the "Egyptian boil" in Dt 28:27 points back to the Lord's specific judgment on the Egyptians immediately before the Exodus (Ex 9:19).

[25]Malbim, *HaTorah veHaMitsvah*, commenting on the *Mekilta* to Ex 15:26, states that the diseases that God inflicted on the Egyptians were extraordinary (lit., "out of the sphere of nature") and therefore incurable. Thus these same diseases inflicted on disobedient Israel could not be cured by natural means.

[26]See above, 1.3.1.

[27]*ANET*, 180, 49ff., my emphasis; cf. *CAD, A/2*, 346, 6'.

[28]Parpola and Watanabe, *Neo-Assyrian Treaties*, 27, iv:3–4; cf. *ANET*, 534 (iv). The Akkadian for "unhealing sore," *simmu lazu*, literally means a "persisting, unremitting sore/wound."

[29]Of Ishtar it is asked that she "[. . . not grant] you [mercy and forgiveness]"; Melqart and Eshmun are supplicated to "deliver your land to destruction and your people to deportation . . ."; Astarte is invoked to "break your bow in the thick of battle, and have you crouch at the feet of your enemy. . ." (ibid.).

[30]E.g., Anu (ibid., 45, ll. 418A-C: "May Anu, king of the gods, let disease, exhaustion, malaria, sleeplessness, worries, and ill health rain upon all your houses"), Sin (45, ll. 419–20: "May Sin, the brightness of heaven, clothe you with leprosy. . ."), and Shamash (45, ll. 422–24: "May he remove your eyesight. Walk about in darkness!"). Cf. also *ANET*, 538 (see above, nn. 18–19).

[31]Ibid., 48, ll. 461–63; cf. *ANET*, 538–39, 52.

[32]Ibid., 5, ll. 10–11.

[33]M. Weinfeld, *Deuteronomy 1–11*, 372–73. According to him, Dt 7:13–15 is dependent on Ex 23:25–26; he states further, "This genre of blessings and curses apparently has its origin in the tribal federation of the period of Judges; hence the similarity to the blessings and curses of the amphictyonic league in ancient Greece" (373, with reference to idem, "Zion and Jerusalem as Religious and Political Capital, Ideology and Utopia," in R. E. Friedman, ed., *The Poet and the Historian: Essays in Literary and Historical Biblical Criticism* [HSS 26; Chico, Calif.: Scholars, 1983], 79–84). Thus Weinfeld sees these formulae as dating back to Israel's earliest years as a nation in their land. For the dependence of Dt 7 on Ex 23:20–33, see M. Fishbane, *Biblical Interpretation in Ancient Israel* (Oxford: Clarendon, 1988), 201.

[34]For further discussion of fertility, see below, 2.2.4.

[35]While medical historian A. S. Lyons, *Medicine: An Illustrated History*, 70, opines that "the biblical Hebrews may have inherited a number of their beliefs from ancient Mesopotamian cultures, among them a conviction that disease was divine punishment and therefore a mark of sin." He further notes, "The biblical Hebrews, although they believed in supernatural causation of disease, did not envision the world as filled with demons and spirits.... To the ancient Hebrew, it was essentially Jehovah, God Himself, who was to be placated as the giver and taker of health."

[36]In the words of missionary and divine healing minister John G. Lake (1870–1935): "A God without power to heal a sick heathen's body is a poor recommendation of His ability to save his soul" (*The John G. Lake Sermons on Dominion over Demons, Disease and Death*, G. Lindsay, ed. [repr. Dallas: Christ for the Nations Inst., 1982], 68).

[37]Sigerist, *Civilization and Disease*, 138. See further 1.3.1, where Sigerist was also cited ("All ancient gods had the power of healing").

[38]According to L. Hogan, "A Note on Healing and Ignorance in the Bible," *Koroth* 9/1–2 (1985): 109, "Exodus 15,26 is the key text on healing in the Heb. Scr." For Lohfink, "'Ich bin Jahwe, dein Arzt' (Ex 15,26)," 14, it is the "Schlusssatz," while Witty (*Divine Healing*, 30–31), who calls this verse a "vital message," exclaims: "What a significant self-revelation concerning both God's nature and also concerning disease and healing!" According to the Talmud (*b. Ber.* 5a), based on Ex 15:26, every school boy knows that the Torah shields the observant (with the assumption that even young boys had already read through the Torah; so Rashi).

[39]Cf. the discussions in B. S. Childs, *The Book of Exodus* (OTL; Philadelphia: Westminster, 1974), 266–68; Durham, *Exodus*, 211–12. See N. Lohfink, "'Ich bin Jahwe, dein Arzt,'" 11–73, for an extensive literary-critical treatment.

[40]Durham, *Exodus*, 212; contrast Childs, *Exodus*, 267. See also W. Fuss, *Die deuteronomistische Pentateuchredaktion in Exodus 3–17* (BZAW 126; Berlin: Walter DeGruyter, 1972).

[41]Note, however, that B. P. Robinson, "Symbolism in Exod 15:22–27 (Marah and Elim)," *RB* 94 (1987): 376–88, finds these verses to be a carefully

structured literary unit, while Lohfink, "'Ich bin Jahwe, dein Arzt,'" 20, n. 21, suggests the possibility of a palindrome in Ex 15:24–27 as follows (note, however, that this is not obvious):

The People
(Moses)
Yahweh
(Moses)
Water
(Moses)
(Yahweh)
(Moses)
(The People)

[42]Childs, *The Book of Exodus*; cf. also J. Wellhausen, *Prolegomena zur Geschichte Israels* (repr. Berlin: Walter DeGruyter, 1981), 342, cited in Lohfink, "'Ich bin Jahwe, dein Arzt,'" 29–30, n. 48 (cf. also 32, end of n. 53).

[43]Cf. again Childs, *The Book of Exodus*, 267–68. Korpel, *A Rift in the Clouds*, 333–34, n. 127, following Eissfeldt, finds v. 26 to be "a deuteronomistic revision of an older source," noting, "It seems not unlikely that the ephithet *rp'* belonged to the older source as a continuation of the preceding story about the bitter water. In that case too the epithet has a medical meaning." She rightly rejects the view of Struys, *Ziekte et Genezing*, 398, that the usage of *rp'* is entirely metaphorical here; there is, in fact, no justification for Struys' suggestion.

[44]Durham, *Exodus*, 214–15, provides a useful analysis of the more narrow, immediate context (viz., vv. 22–27). Kee, *Medicine, Miracle and Magic*, 12, correctly observes that the position of Ex 15:26 "in the book of Exodus is highly significant," noting that it is "one of the crucial passages in which the term [i.e., healer] appears."

[45]See above, 1.3.2.

[46]As opposed to N. P. Lemche, "The Development of the Israelite Religion in the Light of Recent Studies on the Early History of Israel," in J. A. Emerton, ed., *Congress Volume: Leuven, 1989* (VTSupp. 43; Leiden: E. J. Brill, 1991), 97–115, who sees little emphasis on monotheism until the postexilic period, I argue that the OT evidence points in the direction of monolatry moving toward monotheism from the beginnings of Israelite history. For interaction with Lemche's major 1985 study, cf. H. Seebass, "Dialog über Israels Anfänge. Zun Evolutionsmodel von N. P. Lemche, Early Israel, VTS 37, Leiden (1985)," in J. Hausmann and H.-J. Zobel, eds., *Altestamentliche Glaube und Biblische Theologie: Festschrift für Horst Dietrich Preuss zum 65. Geburtstag* (Stuttgart: Kohlhammer, 1992), 11–19. See also above, nn. 6, 13.

[47]While I largely agree with Korpel's observation that the OT's "heavy emphasis on YHWH's role as the sole healer was doubtlessly dictated by the desire to eliminate the corresponding role of other deities in Canaan," I am not convinced that "it is for this reason that the vocalization of the Hebrew word for the spirits of the dead was changed so that it no longer meant 'heal-

ers, saviours' but 'weak ones'" (*A Rift in the Clouds*, 335). See my "Was There a West Semitic Asklepios?" for further discussion.

[48]See, in particular, the treatment of 2Ch 16:12, above, 1.2.2.3.

[49]Note that Weinfeld (*Deuteronomy 1–11*, 373) saw Dt 7:14–15 as dependent on Ex 23:25–26. I suggest that the latter is dependent on Ex 15:26: The initial promise at Marah looks ahead to the Sinai legislation and conditions the blessing of divine healing on obedience to the Lord's laws; Ex 23 looks ahead to the (iconographic) conquest of Canaan and conditions divine healing on Israel's successful uprooting of the idolatrous inhabitants of the land.

[50]So NIV; for full discussion, with reference to NJV's rendering of *ḥōq* and *mišpaṭ* as a hendiadys ("a fixed rule"), see Lohfink, "'Ich bin Jahwe, dein Arzt,'" 20–21, n. 22; idem, "Noch einmal *ḥōq ûmišpaṭ* (zu Ps 81,5f)," *Bib* 73 (1992): 253–54. The rendering of A. Kaplan, *Living Torah: The Five Books of Moses* (Brooklyn: Maznaim Pub. Co., 1981)—"It was there that [God] taught them survival techniques and methods"—following Nachmanides and R. Yaakov ben Asher, has little warrant; cf., however, O. Eissfeldt, "Zwei verkannte militärtechnische Termini," *VT* 5 (1955): 232–38 (esp. 235–38).

[51]It is not surprising, given the ancient rabbinic propensity to project a Talmudic mentality back on the biblical characters (beginning with Adam, who according to *Gen Rab* 3 kept the "statutes of the earth" [*ḥuqqôt hā'āreṣ*]; see E. Levi, *Yesodot HaHalakha* [Heb.; Tel Aviv: Sinai Pub., 1985], 10), that there was great speculation as to exactly what commandments were given at Marah. Suggestions include the following: *ḥōq* refers to the Sabbath law while *mišpaṭ* refers to the commandment to honor one's parents; *ḥōq* refers to forbidden sexual relations while *mišpaṭ* refers to laws regarding rape, penalties, and injuries; more generally, the Israelites were given the so-called Seven Noachide Laws, plus the laws of Sabbath, honoring parents, and social justice (or, additionally, the law of the red heifer). See *Torah Anthology*, 204–5, #157; note also the commentary in ibid.

[52]Although Yahweh's provision of the manna and quail cannot be tied directly to his revelation as Healer, it is still noteworthy that this revelation came *before* the miraculous provision of ch. 16. Note also Ex 15:27, the first example of abundant provision.

[53]Cf. L. Ruppert, "Das Motiv der Versuchung durch Gott in vordeuteronomischer Tradition," *VT* 22 (1972): 55–63.

[54]For an emphasis on the covenantal nature of v. 26, see Durham, *Exodus*, 213–14; he feels that the "covenantal overtones" of Yahweh's self-revelation as Healer "may be louder than [the] Deuteronomistic ones" often noted by other scholars (214).

[55]For an attempt to reconstruct the literary history and dating of Ex 15:22–18:27, cf. A. Schart, *Mose und Israel im Konflikt: Eine Redaktionsgeschichtliche Studie zu den Wüstenerzählungen* (OBO 98; Frieburg, Schweiz: Universitäts-Verlag/Göttingen: Vandenhoeck & Ruprecht, 1990).

[56]According to Rashbam (Rabbi Samuel ben Meir), *maḥ*^{a}*lâ* here refers to the illness suffered by the Egyptians when their waters were turned to blood; the promise of healing refers to the sweetening of the waters at Marah. For

extensive discussion of the usage of *maḥ*ª*lâ* here, cf. Lohfink, "'Ich bin Jahwe, dein Arzt' (Ex 15,26)," 26, n. 37 (citing B. Baentsch), and 38, n. 79.

[57]Traditional Jewish and Christian exegesis of Ex 15:25 provides an interesting sidelight: Where the rabbis tend to see the Torah everywhere, the church fathers tend to see Jesus everywhere. Thus, according to the rabbis, the tree that Moses cast into the water symbolized the Torah ("a tree of life" according to Pr 3:18), noting also the similarity between *tôrâ* and MT *wayyōrēhû* (interpreted as "and he instructed him," as opposed to *wayyar'ēhû*, "and he showed him," as in the LXX and the Sam Pent.; cf. Lohfink, "'Ich bin Jahwe, dein Arzt,'" 17, n. 14). For the church fathers, however, the tree spoke of the cross (for a related interpretation, cf. R. Mayo, "Delivered by Christ from the Fear of Death," in *Puritan Sermons 1659–1689* [repr. Wheaton, Ill.: Richard Owen Roberts, 1981], 4:257). See also the relevant rabbinic and Christian exegesis of Pr 8:22–36 (preexistent wisdom is the Torah or Jesus). Cf. the traditions reflected in *Targ. Yerushalmi* and *Targ. Pseudo-Jonathan* to Ge 1:1 ("In/with wisdom the Lord created . . ."), where wisdom is once again the Torah, which serves as "the blueprint of creation" (for which concept see *The Blueprint of Creation: The Chofetz Chaim on Torah Study* [Jerusalem: Bais Yechiel Publications, 1990]) with Jn 1:3; 1Co 8:6; Col 1:16; Heb 1:2, where it is the Son through whom all things were made. For another example of the rabbinic emphasis on Torah even within this passage, cf. *Mekilta* to Ex 15:22: For those who interpret the Torah metaphorically, finding no water means that "they found no words of Torah, which is compared to water" in Isa 55:1. See conveniently, *Torah Anthology*, 202, no. 147. Cf. also Robinson, "Symbolism in Exod 15:22–27."

[58]My translation of *rippitî lammayim hā'ēlleh*; contrast NIV, "I have healed this water."

[59]*w*ᵉ*nirp*ᵉ*'û hammayim*; correctly, NIV. For further discussion, see below, 2.3.4.

[60]See below, 4.2.2.

[61]*rōp*ᵉ*'ekā* can be rendered as either "your Healer/Physician" (so LXX, *ho iomenos se; Targ. Onk.*, *Targ. Ps. Jonathan*) or "who heals you" (so *Targ. Yerushalmi*; cf. Hempel, *Heilung*, 281, "Ich, Jahve, bin der dich heilende"; Lohfink, 22, "Denn ich bin Jahwe, der dich heilende"; and see NIV and other versions and commentaries for both positions). On the basis of such parallel expressions as "for I am the LORD your God" (*kî 'ª nî yhwh 'ᵉ lōhêkā/'ᵉ lōhêkem*—e.g., Ex 6:7), where the nominal rendering alone is possible, I prefer the former translation. It might also be argued that if the verbal meaning of *rōp*ᵉ*'ekā* were intended, *rōp*ᵉ*' l*ᵉ*kā* (or pausal *lāk*) would have been expected, not *rōp*ᵉ*'ekā* (cf., e.g., Nu 12:13; 2Ki 20:5; Pss 103:3; 147:3, all with *rp'* in the Qal followed by *lāmed* + the indirect object). But the usage is not absolutely uniform (cf. Ge 20:17, with *rp'* in the Qal + direct object). In any case, verses such as "for I am the LORD who sanctifies you/your Sanctifier" (*kî 'ª nî yhwh m*ᵉ*kaddiškem*—Ex 31:13) remind us that we are dealing largely with an English translation problem of Hebrew participles, as opposed to any real ambiguity in the Hebrew itself. See also Lohfink, 22 (n. 23), 25; Hempel,

Heilung, 281–82 (and cf. the title of his earlier study, "Ich bin der Herr, dein Arzt: Ex. 15:26"); Durham, *Exodus,* 214; and note the excursus in J. E. Hartley, *Leviticus* (WBC; Dallas, Tex.: Word, 1992), 291–93, on "The Phrase 'I am Yahweh (Your God).'"

62Cf. also Ex 23:26: "none will miscarry or be barren in your land" (*lō' tiheyeh mešakkelâ be'arṣekā*) with 2Ki 2:19, 21: "the land is unproductive" (lit., "the land miscarries" [*wehā'āreṣ mešakkelet*]); and, "Never again will [the water] cause death or make the land unproductive" (lit., "Never again . . . will there be miscarrying"). These somewhat parallel passages, coupled with Ex 15:22–26, suggest the possibility that a key function of the Lord as Healer was not simply to make unwholesome and undrinkable waters wholesome so that the Israelites would have an adequate supply of water, but also so that they would have a *healthy* water supply, i.e., water to drink that would not make them sick (cf. also above, n. 56). The theme of abundant or miraculous supply of water is found in Ex 15:27 (Nu 33:9); 17:1–7; Nu 20:1–11.

63Stendahl, "Rafa'," 9; cf. Baudissin, *Adonis,* 310.

64A. B. Ehrlich, *Randglossen,* 1:192, as translated by R. Gordis, "Some Hitherto Unrecognized Meanings of the Verb SHUB," *JBL* 52 (1933): 153 = *The Word and the Book* (New York: Ktav, 1976), 218 (I have corrected the apparent typographical error of "maybe" to "may be"). Ehrlich first discussed this principle in his comments to Ge 38:23, where he interpreted *tiqqaḥ lāh* as meaning *'al tāšîb waye hî leyādāh* (cf. NIV "let her keep what she has"); see *Mikra* 1:104; he also applies this principle to the interpretation of *rp'* in 2Ch 30:20; Isa 57:18; Hos 11:3, all of which are discussed in this and the next chapter.

65See *Mikra* 1:165 ("I will not allow them to come upon you"); *Randglossen* 1:323.

66*B. Sanh.* 101a. This explanation is in keeping with the common rabbinic practice of overinterpreting the Hebrew infinitive absolute (here *'im šāmô'a tišma'*); cf., e.g., *y. Sanh.* 6:1 on Ex 34:7 (*we naqqeh lō'-ye naqqeh*). Cf. also the midrashic explanation offered by Rashi: "If I do put [these diseases] upon you [because of disobedience], it will be as if they were not put on you [i.e., if you repent]." For the exact nuance of the infinitive absolute in Ex 15:26 ("a slight emphasis"), cf. P. Joüon and T. Muraoka, *A Grammar of Biblical Hebrew* (Rome: Pontifical Biblical Institute Press, 1991), 423 (§123g). According to Epstein, *Torah Temimah,* 2:156, n. 45, the meaning of the passage in *b. Sanh.* 101a is that, contrary to the incurable plagues that were put on Egypt, any diseases that will come on Israel will be curable.

67See Kasher, *Torah Anthology,* 208; cf. also the comments of R. Isaac: "I will put none of the diseases upon you—in this world; and if I do, I am the Lord that heals you—in the Hereafter" (*Sifre Num* 136). The dichotomizing comment of R. Menachem HaMeiri (13th cent.) to R. Akiva's much-discussed prohibition from the world to come of those "who whisper over a wound" and recite Ex 15:26b (*b. Sanh.* 90a; see above, 1.4.2) apparently follows the Talmudic prohibition against quoting words of the Torah for physical healing (cf. *b. Šeb.* 15b; *y. Šab.* 67a, top; see also Ginzberg, "Some

Observations," 123–24): Those who do such things are "deniers of the Torah, for the Torah is not for the healing of the body, but of the soul." Meiri does, however, permit a healthy person to recite verses so as to protect himself from disease, since this is likened to prayer.

[68]In his popular book *None of These Diseases* (more than one million copies sold as of 1984), 15, S. I. McMillen, M.D., asks (re: Ex 15:26):

> Was this a trustworthy promise? Could submitting to a code of "restrictive" rules lead to freedom from sicknesses? Could this promise remain pertinent even in the twentieth century? Yes! Medical science is still discovering how obedience to the ancient prescriptions saved the primitive Hebrews from the scourges of epidemic plagues; and medical research is constantly proving the timeless potency of the divine prescription for modern diseases. Yes! Obedience to biblical precepts is still the most effective way to prevent many of the afflictions of mankind.

Cf. similarly E. A. Josephson, *God's Key to Health and Happiness* (Grand Rapids: Revell, 1992), with special emphasis on the benefits of following the Torah's dietary laws. Josephson, still alive as of 1992, attributes his miraculous recovery from terminal cancer in 1936 to his discovery of the therapeutic powers of adherence to these laws.

[69]For the exegesis of Pr 3:7–8, cf. below, 3.2.2; for an apposite rabbinic comment to Ex 15:26 (citing also Pr 4:22), cf. Kasher, *Torah Anthology*, 208. This, of course, is in keeping with the rabbinic view of the Torah as a "tree of life" (see above, n. 57). Interestingly, however, Judaism has not explained the dietary laws (*kashrut*) from a *primarily* medical, health-related perspective. Cf. S. R. Hirsch, *Horeb: A Philosophy of Jewish Laws and Observances*, trans. I. Grunfeld (New York: Soncino, 1981), 317, "God did not regulate your eating by these laws in order that you do not sicken physically: His word itself explains their meaning to you. . . . If you have eaten them . . . you may be more nourished and better fed: but the animal instinct will be aroused more strongly within you, and your body becomes more blunted as an instrument of the spirit." Contrast the works cited immediately above, n. 68, as well as the official position of the Seventh-Day Adventists (cf. E. G. White, *The Ministry of Healing* [repr. Boise, Ida.: Remnant Pub., 1988], 194–209, emphasizing vegetarianism as God's original ideal). Of course, many rabbinic authorities believed that certain foods were prohibited because they were injurious to health; for references, see A. Chill, *The Mitzvot: The Commandments and Their Rationale* (Jerusalem: Keter Books, 1974), 176–77 (contrast, however, Abrabanel, cited in ibid., 179). For full discussion, see Grunfeld's introduction to Hirsch's *Horeb*, lii–lxxxi, xcviii–cvi; and idem, *The Jewish Dietary Laws* (New York: Soncino, 1982), 1:3–25.

[70]Cf. the *locus classicus*, Lev 18:5 (and see W. C. Kaiser Jr., "Leviticus 18:5 and Paul: 'Do This and You Shall Live' [Eternally?]," *JTS* 14 [1971]: 19–25); note also Dt 30:15, 19–20, and esp. 32:47 ("They are not just idle words for you—they are your life. By them you will live long in the land you are cross-

ing the Jordan to possess"); cf. below, 2.2.3, 3.2.1. Levine, *Leviticus*, 119, cites the well-known rabbinic dictum—"That one may live by them, not that one should die because of them" (*t. Shabb.* 15:17; *b. Yoma* 85b)—which forms the justification for the principle that "in situations directly threatening human life, one should set aside the commandments [excluding the prohibitions against idolatry, murder, and immorality] in order to preserve life." More broadly, Wenham, *Leviticus*, 253, explains: "What is envisaged is a happy life in which a man enjoys God's bounty of health, children, friends, and prosperity. Keeping the law is the path to divine blessing, to a happy and fulfilled life in the present (Lev 26:3–13; Deut 28:1–14)." For discussion of the contemporary application (and misapplication) of these verses in a NT context, cf. below, 3.2.1, n. 235; 5.3.3, nn. 120–123.

[71]It is not uncommon for medical historians to point to the "Hebrew laws of hygiene" as important (and, extremely advanced) medical breakthroughs; cf., however, the discussion in Prioreschi, *Primitive Medicine*, 518–21; according to F. Rosner, *Medicine in the Bible and Talmud* (New York: Yeshiva Univ. Press, 1977), 9 (cited in *Primitive Medicine*, 533, n. 86): "Of the 613 biblical commandments and prohibitions, no less than 213 are health rules imposed in the form of rigorously observed ceremonial rites."

[72]Although I am not aware of a general tendency to stress this point in the context of Lev 18:5ff., it is noteworthy that the various prohibitions against forbidden sexual connections in Lev 18 follow this important OT verse.

[73]Attempts to downplay the totally supernatural nature of these plagues are somewhat forced; contrast K. A. Kitchen, *Ancient Orient and Old Testament* (Downers Grove, Ill.: InterVarsity, 1973), 157–58, who, citing with approval the work of G. Hort in *ZAW* 69 and 70 (1957–58), argues that the first nine plagues were "a sequence of unusually severe natural phenomena which began with an unusually *high* inundation of the Nile (not low, as often thought)." Of course, this fails adequately to explain the supernatural *timing* of each plague at the specific moment of Moses' announcement and/or intercession. Cf. further Z. Zevit, "Three Ways to Look at the Ten Plagues," *BibRev* 6 (1990): 16–23, 42, 44.

[74]Durham, *Exodus*, 213–14, is surely right in emphasizing the covenantal (and, hence, reciprocal) nature of Ex 15:25–26.

[75]The OT wisdom material (in particular, Proverbs) is especially rich in what may be called "cause and effect" wisdom: Folly leads to death while wisdom leads to life. However, the book of Proverbs frequently offers these admonitions and directives as proven principles as opposed to actions that require divine intervention (although that intervention *is* vouchsafed to the wise/righteous). See below, 3.2.1.

[76]Ehrlich's interpretation is, from the viewpoint of semantics, also possible, and practically speaking, not greatly dissimilar; the rabbinic exegesis in *b. Sanh.* 101a, while forced, ultimately approaches a proper understanding. Note also Korpel, *A Rift in the Clouds*, 334: "The participle has the nuance of keeping away diseases."

[77]Cf. Ehrlich, *Mikra* 1:165: "I am an expert physician, just as I demonstrated to you when I healed the waters of Marah."

[78]Could this also hint that, just as they were tested at Marah, they would be tested again in the future? They must therefore continue to listen to the Lord, for he would meet their every need.

[79]Obviously, I do not concur with the extreme OT rejectionist views of scholars like Friedrich Delitzsch (son of the OT scholar Franz Delitzsch; see J. Bright, *The Authority of the Old Testament* [Grand Rapids: Baker, 1975], 65–69), nor am I in harmony with recent evaluations of, e.g., R. P. Carroll, *The Bible as a Problem for Christianity* (Valley Forge, Pa.: Trinity, 1991), who, to say the least, is not overly impressed with the God of the Hebrew Scriptures.

[80]An oft-cited contrast between Yahweh and the gods of Mesopotamia is found in the Babylonian account of the Flood. The reason these deities regretted bringing a deluge on the earth was because, without human sacrifices, they were starving! And so, when Utnapishtim (the Babylonian "Noah") presented his offerings, the gods hovered around their long-awaited food like flies. Contrast, e.g., Ps 50:9–13; cf. the standard works of A. Heidel, *The Babylonian Genesis* (2d ed., Chicago: Univ. of Chicago Press, 1951), and *The Gilgamesh Epic and Old Testament Parallels* (2d ed., Chicago: Univ. of Chicago Press, 1949). Comparison between the Mesopotamian account of creation—with a bloody battle royale between the warring deities—and the utterly monotheistic account of Ge 1 once again highlights the "otherness" of Yahweh. In a private communication, W. H. Shea noted to me, "Enlil in particular was thought of as capricious and malevolent and could break out in this kind of behavior at any time for any unexplained reason." Cf. T. Jacobsen, "Formative Tendencies in Sumerian Religion," in G. E. Wright, ed., *The Bible and the Ancient Near East* (Garden City, N.Y.: Doubleday, 1965), 267–78.

[81]H. W. Haggard, *The Doctor in History* (repr. New York: Dorset, 1989), 44–45. On sickness and calamity in the Ugaritic pantheon, see Korpel, *A Rift in the Clouds*, e.g., 318–20, 332, 338–39.

[82]Korpel, *A Rift in the Clouds*, 337: "In contrast to the Ugaritic gods, the God of Israel is never subjected to fate." Note also p. 341: "The idea that God might be overpowered by disease is not found in the Old Testament.... On the contrary, the strength of God's arms and his never ending power is frequently stated."

[83]Cf. Weinfeld's comments on *sᵉgūllâ* (Dt 7:6), in *Deuteronomy 1–11*, 368, with special reference to S. Loewenstamm's 1983 study (in Hebrew), "*ʿām sᵉgūllâ*," in *Meḥqĕrey lashon: Festschrift Z. Ben Hayyim*, 321–28.

[84]For the important literature on this subject, cf. F. C. Fensham, "Malediction and Benediction in Ancient Near Eastern Vassal-Treaties and the Old Testament," *ZAW* 74 (1962): 1–9; D. R. Hillers, *Treaty Curses and the Old Testament Prophets* (BibOr 16; Rome: Pontifical Biblical Institute Press, 1964); D. J. McCarthy, *Treaty and Covenant: A Study in Form in the Ancient Oriental Documents and in the Old Testament* (AnBib 21A; Rome: Pontifical Biblical Institute Press, 1981). For further bibliography, cf. Hartley, *Leviticus*, 451.

[85]See above, 2.2 and n. 23.

[86]Note also v. 35, and see above, nn. 25, 27–28, 66.

[87]P. Masters, a prominent British pastor, is adamant in his objection to the exaggerated OT viewpoint which, he claims (in overly simplified terms), holds that "sickness only came upon people when they were sinful" (*The Healing Epidemic* [London: The Wakeman Trust, 1988], 58–59). While the statement with which he differs is obviously too broad, this may be said in reply: (1) The vast majority of specifically recorded afflictions in the OT are explained in terms of divine judgment; (2) sickness, in and of itself, is never viewed as a blessing; (3) the potentially redemptive aspects of the results of suffering sickness are generally not stressed in the OT, although they are mentioned several times. See below, 5.3.2, 5.3.3, for discussion of each of these points.

[88]Kelsey, *Healing and Christianity*, 90, stakes out a similar position regarding the NT's theology of sickness and healing: "The 'Christian' attitude that glories in sickness is completely alien to that of Jesus of Nazareth; it is aligned on the side of what he was fighting against.... Sickness is a destructive and evil phenomenon, and Christ as the incarnation of creativity was dead set against it." For further discussion, see below, ch. 5.

[89]The NIV does translate *'ᵃrûkâ* (Jer 30:17; 33:6), *rip'ût* (Pr 3:8), *marpē'* (Pr 4:22), and *mᵉtōm* (Ps 38:3,7[4,8]) with "health." However, *'ᵃrûkâ* certainly speaks of *recovery* from a wound (as opposed to general health; the NIV probably rendered it "health" because *marpē'* ["healing"] occurs in the same verses); *rip'ût* means either "medicine" or "healing," and *marpē'* is best rendered with "healing" (although if any one biblical Hebrew word could mean "health," it would be *marpē'*; for full discussion, see below, ch. 3); *mᵉtōm* is not so much a general term for health as a specific term for "soundness" (there is a discernible difference; see also above, 0.3.2, 0.3.3). While the NIV also renders *šālôm* with "health" at 1Sa 25:6 (*bis*), there can be no question that *šālôm* does not *primarily* mean "health." Proverbs 15:30b ("and good news gives health to the bones") is literally, "and good news *puts fat* on the bones" (*tᵉdaššēn 'āṣem*); cf. NJV.

[90]Cf., e.g., Simundson, "Health and Healing in the Bible," 330–39, who notes that health and wholeness are thought of as a person's normal condition.

[91]For the emphasis on long life in the wisdom and poetry literature, see below, 3.2.1. According to A. C. Custance, a former physiologist known for some novel theological proposals, Adam and Eve (and hence the human race), along with the animal kingdom, were not originally created so as to die. Thus, immortality, before the Fall, was inherently possible; cf. "The Theological Necessity of the Physical Immortality of the First and Last Adam," *JETS* 21 (1978): 297–303; contrast Y. Marzel, "The Tree of Knowledge of Good and Evil—Recognition of Life and Death (Genesis 2–3)," *Beth Mikra* 29 (1983/84): 352–60 (Hebrew).

[92]See Dt 34:7 (Moses; but see 31:1) and Jos 14:11–12 (Caleb); cf. also the blessing to the tribe of Asher in Dt 34:25. Cf. further Kohler, *Hebrew Man*, 41–46; Wolff, *Anthropology*, 119–27.

[93]See J. G. Harris, *Biblical Perspective on Aging* (OBT; Philadelphia: Fortress, 1987); R. Z. Dulin, *A Crown of Glory: A Biblical View of Aging* (Mahwah, N.J.: Paulist, 1988); note also above, 1.1, n. 4, and cf. J. Zias, "Death and Disease in Ancient Israel," *BA* 54 (1991): 147–59, for a paleopathological survey of diseases in ancient Israel. See also R. N. Jones, "Paleopathology," *ABD* 5:60–69, and Witty, *Divine Healing*, 29, with reference to Jacob. According to Hanegraaff, *Christianity in Crisis*, 259, "We live in a cursed creation, with aging the primary sickness of humanity." P. Zerafa, O.P., "The Old Testament Life Span," *Angelicum* 65 (1988): 99–116, argues, "The literary biblical evidence uniformly endorses Ps 90,10 [and hence, a seventy-year life expectancy] as a realistic statement" (116). For a different conclusion, cf. Wolff, *Anthropology*, 119–20, who notes that, with the sole exception of David (cf. 1Ch 29:28), none of the other Davidic kings reached the age of seventy.

[94]For the question of Abraham's having children through Keturah, cf. Sarna, *Genesis*, 172, with reference to rabbinic discussion.

[95]It is interesting to note that this called for comment from the rabbis, who explained Isaac's condition in light of midrashic traditions according to which Isaac, who was thirty-seven (!) years old at the time of his binding on Mount Moriah (Ge 22), was temporarily blinded by the ministering angels that appeared at the last moment to stop Abraham from killing him. For references and discussion, see G. Vermes, "Redemption and Genesis xxii: The Binding of Isaac and the Sacrifice of Jesus," in his *Scripture and Tradition in Judaism* (Studia Post-Biblica 4; Leiden: E. J. Brill, 1961), 193–227; for critical interaction regarding the dating of the rabbinic sources cited, see B. D. Chilton, *Targumic Approaches to the Gospels: Essays in the Mutual Definition of Judaism and Christianity* (Studies in Judaism: Lanham, Md.: Univ. Press of America, 1986), 39–49. For rabbinic speculation regarding the (sinful) cause of Elisha's terminal illness (2Ki 13:14), cf. below, n. 199. For other references to sickness and aging in the historical books, see below, 2.3.1.

[96]The fact of Jacob's final illness is also recorded (Ge 48:1). Note that Witty, *Divine Healing*, 29, although being "certain" that he has covered all references to sickness, disease, or disability in Genesis, omits any reference to the failing eyesight of either Isaac or Jacob (making reference only to Jacob's illness in Ge 48:1); this, however, does not affect his overall conclusions.

[97]The Talmud (*b. Bav. Mesia* 87a), following a literal reading of the Scriptures, claims that "until Abraham there was no old age." In a similar vein it is stated that "until Jacob there was no illness." For convenient translation and discussion in English, see A. Steinsaltz, *The Talmud: The Steinsaltz Edition*, vol. 5 (New York: Random House, 1991), 167; see the surprisingly similar statement of Witty, *Divine Healing*, 26–30. For the vivid talmudic description of Sarah's rejuvenation (cf. Ge 18:12), see Steinsaltz, 164.

[98]On questions of longevity, cf. A. Malamat, "Longevity: Biblical Concepts and Some Ancient Near Eastern Parallels," *AfO* 19 (1982): 215–24; M. A. Dandamayev, "About Life Expectancy in Babylonia in the First Millennium B.C.," in B. Alster, ed., *Death in Mesopotamia* (Copenhagen: Akademisk Forlag, 1980), 183–86; Rodríguez, "Health and Healing in the Pentateuch,"

10–11; see also M. A. Knibb, "Life and Death in the Old Testament," in R. E. Clements, ed., *The World of Ancient Israel* (Cambridge: Cambridge Univ. Press, 1989), 395–415; D. Grossberg, "Number Harmony and Life Spans in the Bible," *Semitics* 9 (1984): 49–57.

[99]The taunting offer of the commander of the Assyrian army in 2Ki 18:32, "Choose life and not death!" underscores just how literally these words were understood. No one would have dreamed of "spiritualizing" the Deuteronomic concepts of "life and death, blessings and curses."

[100]For Isa 57:1–2 and the death of Abijah, son of Jeroboam, in 2Ki 14, see below, 2.3.1.

[101]See Milgrom, *Numbers* 407–8; cf. G. Madamana, "Afterlife in the OT," *Biblehashyam* 11 (1985): 5–9 (with reference also to burial customs); contrast Westermann, *Genesis 12–36*, 397; see further below, 3.1.7, especially n. 133.

[102]Traditional Judaism, while emphatically believing in both an afterlife and a final resurrection, has maintained an emphasis on "this world" (Heb. *'ôlām hazzeh*); see conveniently, M. Angel in L. Klenicki and G. Wigoder, eds., *A Dictionary of the Jewish-Christian Dialogue* (New York: Paulist, 1984), 3–6.

[103]See D. S. Shapiro, "Be Fruitful and Multiply," in Rosner and Bleich, *Jewish Bioethics*, 59–79. After summarizing the biblical evidence (60–61), he notes: "The great blessing, then, for the human species is fertility." As stated in Ps 107:38a, "He blessed them, and their numbers greatly increased." Cf. also C. Westermann, *Genesis 1–11*; trans. J. J. Scullion, S.J. (Minneapolis: Augsburg, 1984), 140: "Interpreters are unanimous about the meaning of the blessing in the primeval story: blessing is the power of fertility. . . . Gen 1:22 shows P to be the heir of a tradition in which the blessing that confers the power of fertility is inseparable from creation where the creator is the one who blesses and the created living being has the power to reproduce itself because of the blessing. . . . To speak of life and its dynamism is to speak of the effective action of the creator." Cf. further J. Scharbert, "ברך," *TDOT* 2:279–308, esp. 302–8; C. W. Mitchell, *The Meaning of BRK "To Bless" in the Old Testament* (Atlanta: Scholars, 1987); J. Pedersen, *Israel: Its Life and Culture* (repr. Atlanta: Scholars, 1991), 1:182–212.

[104]*bim'ōd bim'ōd* can almost be rendered "in the extreme."

[105]Note Jacob's blessing over Joseph in 49:22–25, especially vv. 22 (*bēn pōrat yôsēp*) and 25 (*wîbārᵃ kekā . . . birkōt šadāyim warāḥam*), although the translation of the former is disputed; see the commentaries. Cf. also de Moor, *Rise of Yahwism*, 225, who cites 49:25 as early evidence that Yahweh already "has the functions of El as the blessing deity, especially as the one who blesses parents with children" (with n. 9, which finds confirmation for this in the theophoric, pre-Davidic personal names that preponderate with El over YHWH; see ibid., 32–33).

[106]According to Westermann, *Genesis 1–11*, 140–41, the use of the formulaic word pair "be fruitful/multiply" serves for P "as a link between parts of his work: the blessing of living beings at the creation, the promise of increase to the patriarchs, the beginning of the story of the people [Ex 1:7]." For a

sociological explanation of the extreme fecundity of Ex 1:7 (viz., extensive wet-nursing, thus resulting in less lactational amenorrhea and higher fertility rates), cf. M. I. Gruber, "Breast-Feeding Practices in Biblical Israel and in Old Babylonian Mesopotamia," *JANESCU* 19 (1989): 61–83.

[107]Cf. also 1Ch 26:4–5, where, after listing the eight sons of Obed-Edom, the author notes (parenthetically in the NIV), "For God had *blessed* Obed-Edom" (cf. 1Ch 13:14).

[108]In other words, these names might indicate that the Lord was effectively supplicated for the healing of a previously barren or frequently miscarrying female, or even an impotent male. Other possibilities (assuming that the significance of these names, at least in their earliest usage and at special commemorative times, would be recognized) include: giving thanks to the Lord for the healing of someone other than the parent; for healing the parent of some other disease; thanking the Lord as Healer for providing a new child after a previous one had died (although this seems less likely). See also above, 0.3.1, n. 42, with special attention to the literature on name-giving.

[109]The entire Leah-Rachel childbirth section (29:31–30:24) provides eloquent testimony to the importance of childearing to both mother and father (especially the former), as well as to the perceptions of divine favor on the fertile.

[110]According to Gray, "*DTN* and *RPUM* in Ancient Ugarit," *PEQ* 84 (1952): 40, "It has long been a commonplace to anthropologists that the dispensation of fertility was an important element in the power of the king." Gray's basic premise is that the *rpum* as a royal aristocracy "were a guild connected with the provision or restoration of fertility to the crops in emergency." According to this understanding, *mt rpi* would mean "the dispenser of fertility" ("*DTN*," 41). Note, however, that Gray translates *rpi arṣ* with "congregation of the land," even though he finds it "tempting to translate *rpe arṣ* as 'dispensers of fertility'" (*The Legacy of Canaan* [2d ed., Leiden: Brill, 1965], 146 with n. 5). He finds support for his fertility hypothesis "in the cult and liturgy of Mesopotamia and Egypt, in the OT, especially Messianic passages, and in Greek literature" (ibid.). In *Legacy*, 146, n. 5, he also refers to "modern primitives in Africa" for further comparative anthropological support. He cites Ge 20:17 and 2Ki 2:21–22 in favor of the "fertilizing" nuance of Hebrew *rāpā'* (ibid.); cf. also B. Z. Luria, "In the Land of Samaria," *Beth Mikra* 28 (1983): 211–22 (Hebrew).

[111]Lipinski, "Ditanu," in Yitschak Avishur and Joshua Blau, ed., *Studies in The Bible and the Ancient Near East* (Jerusalem: Rubinstein's, 1978), 95, points to the "belief that the bodies buried in the earth are sources of fertility and fecundity," stating that this belief "is widely attested among agricultural peoples and no doubt existed also in ancient Syria." In spite of this statement, however, most of the evidence that he cites is from Greek sources (ibid.). Thus, with Gray, he would see the Ugaritic *rpum* as fertilizers.

[112]Pope, "Notes on the Ugaritic Rephaim Texts," in M. de Jong Ellis and Maria de Jong Ellis, eds., *Essays on the Ancient Near East in Memory of Jacob Joel Finkelstein* (Memoirs of the Connecticut Academy of Arts and Sciences,

19; Hamden, Ct.: Archon, 1977), 167, seeks to bolster this position with appeals to an Akkadian interpretation of the name Hammurapi (in a reading cited in *CAD* as "extensive family") as an additional "connection of the root RPA with fertility," along with the "old Arabic blessing for newlyweds, *bi'r-rifa'i wa'l-banina*, 'with health (?) and children.'" While Pope's wide-ranging discussion of the fertility/death parallels is interesting (ibid., 163–82), the linguistic evidence he adduces from Akkadian and Arabic is incorrect; see Brown, "Was There a West Semitic Asklepios?"

[113]For full discussion, see Brown, "Was There a West Semitic Asklepios?"

[114]Sarna, *Genesis*, 96. On the rabbinic concept of divine judgment being *middâ k^{e}neged middâ* ("measure for measure," or, "let the punishment fit the crime"), see below, 3.1.8.

[115]For the dismissal of the cognate evidence produced by Pope, see above, n. 112.

[116]Isa 57:18–19 (with *rp'* in v. 18 and *p^{e}rî* in v. 19) is clearly not germane.

[117]With reference to both of these verses, H. C. Kee, *Medicine, Miracle and Magic*, 13, notes, "It is the figure of healing which is used here to depict God's relationship to his people, in both judgment and vindication."

[118]F. Lindström, *God and the Origin of Evil: A Contextual Analysis of Alleged Monistic Evidence in the Old Testament* (ConBOT 21; Lund: CWK Gleerup, 1983), 175, follows D. Michel, *Tempora und Satzstellung in den Psalmen* (Abhandlungen zur evangelishen Theologie 1; Bonn: Bouvier, 1960), 95ff., in arguing that "a perfect following an imperfect does not emphasize or stress; it provides an *explicative* fact" (his emphasis; for his subsequent translation, see below). While this is certainly possible, I prefer to read *māḥaṣtî* and *'erpā'* sequentially.

[119]Cf. the discussion above, 1.3.1, on the Akkadian divine epithet *muballiṭ mīti* ("he who raises the dead" = "heals the seriously ill"); note also Ecc 3:3a: *'ēt lah^{a}rōg w^{e} 'ēt lirpō'* (discussed below, 3.4). The sweeping claims of divine sovereignty in Dt 32:39, spoken in the first person, may be unique in ancient Near Eastern literature.

[120]*RS* 25.460:34' (Ug. 5:267), *[ša] im-ḫa-ṣa-an-ni ù i-ri-mi-ina*—"It is he who smote me and it is he who showed me mercy" (see *RSP* 2:393, #34)—provides an interesting ideological parallel in that "show mercy" is used in the Akkadian text whereas "heal" is used in the biblical text (cf. also Job 5:18; Isa 30:26; Hos 6:1; see *RSP* 2:398, #46). While there is no question here of either literary dependence or a "fixed" literary formula, the Akkadian and Hebrew texts in conjunction indicate that the deity's act of healing was viewed as a mercy; cf. also Pss 6:2[3], 41:4[5]; Php 2:26–27.

[121]The final alternative rendering of Dt 6:4 provided in the NIV marginal apparatus, "Hear, O Israel: The LORD is our God, the LORD alone" (cf. NJV, with ref. to Rashbam, Ibn Ezra, and Zec 14:9; note also RSV margin), most accurately conveys the meaning of Hebrew *'eḥād*. Cf. Ehrlich, *Mikra* 1:322 (with ref. to Jos 22:20; 1Ch 29:1 [where the meanings "only, alone" are appropriate], as well as to Ge 2:24; Ex 36:13 [where *'eḥād* cannot refer to absolute unity, hence mitigating against the rendering of "one" in that

sense]). M. Weinfeld, *Deuteronomy 1–11*, 337–38, translates "YHWH our God is one YHWH," arguing that "in Deuteronomy the phrase *YHWH 'lhynw* never occurs as subject and predicate but *'lhynw* always stands in apposition to *YHWH*"; he does, however, follow Ehrlich's understanding of *'eḥād* with "alone," noting also that "oneness in reference to a god involves aloneness," with ref. to Akkadian, Ugaritic, and Greek parallels. See also de Moor, *Rise of Yahwism*, 172, who notes that "it was typical of the religious spirit of the Late Bronze Age to put so much emphasis on the oneness of the deity who was exalted above others"; compare further the description of Allah as *aḥad* or *waḥid* (from *waḥida*, "to be one, alone, unique") in the Koran (cf. Sura 112:1; 6:19 with parallels; see also R. Paret, *Der Koran: Kommentar und Konkordanz* [Stuttgart: W. Kohlhammer, 1980], 530, 136; A. I. Katsh, *Judaism in Islam* [New York: Sepher-Hermon, 1980], 17–18). Cf. further D. Christensen, *Deuteronomy 1–11*, 143, with literature. For the "monotheistic flavor" of Dt 6:4, cf. Weinfeld, 350; note, however, N. Lohfink and J. Bergman, "אֶחָד," *TDOT* 1:194–97, esp. Lohfink on 197: "the idea that 6:4 can be interpreted in the sense of theoretical monotheism [i.e., denying even the existence of other gods] is out of the question." See also M. Peter, "Dtn 6, 4—ein monotheistischer Text?" *BZ* 24 (1980): 252–62.

[122]Korpel, *A Rift in the Clouds*, 328–29; cf. above, 0.2, n. 34, for de Moor's statement on the polemic nature of this verse. Note W. G. E. Watson, *Classical Hebrew Poetry: A Guide to Its Techniques* (JSOTSupp. 26; Sheffield, JSOT, 1986), 311, who makes reference to the irony in Dt 32:37–38, "common in idol polemic" (citing Isa 46:1–2; Jer 2:27; Zep 1:18).

[123]For literature on *rešep*, cf. Korpel, *A Rift in the Clouds*, 339–41; *RSP* 3:413–14; Smith, *Early History*, 68–69, n. 43.

[124]On the "generization of West Semitic deities for common nouns," cf. Smith, *Early History*, 69, n. 44 (with lit.); for discussion of *'ešmannîm/'ešmûnîm* in Isa 59:10, cf. above, 1.3.2, n. 176. According to Cooper, *RSP* 3:415, "There is no direct connection between the Ug. *Ršp* and the biblical *ršp//ršpm*," noting also the opinion of D. Conrad ("Der Gott Rescheph," *ZAW* 83 [1971]: 157–83), who claims that *ršp* in the OT "nur noch eine depotenzierte Form des alten Gottes ist." Cooper also cites W. J. Fulco (*The Canaanite God Rešep* [New Haven: American Oriental Society, 1976]), "who speaks of the 'demythologization' of *ršp* in the OT," while observing "that in most contexts where the term occurs, 'it is not difficult to trace the literary trope back to its mythological roots.'" See also next note.

[125]For the arrows of *rešep*, cf. KTU 1.82:3 (*b'l ḥẓ ršp*), 1.14:I.19, 1.103:40 (note *ršp ḥṣ* in a Phoenician inscription [*KAI* #32:3], with no reference, however, to his destructive acts); see also Ps 76:3; Job 5:7; SS 8:6. In Dt 32:23–24, God's arrows are mentioned in v. 23 while *rešep* occurs in v. 24 as a common noun (not a demon, *pace* Smith, ibid., 69, n. 44, who also cites Hab 3:5 under this heading, referring to *rešep* in these texts "as part of a theophanic vanguard" [68, n. 43]). According to Korpel, *A Rift in the Clouds*, 341, with reference also to Dt 32:23–24; Hab 3:4–5, "The pathogenic gods of the Canaanite pantheon are reduced to the status of executioners of the will of

YHWH." Cf. also J. Day, "New Light on the mythological background of the allusion to Resheph in Habakkuk iii 5," *VT* 29 (1979), 353–55, and see also n. 124, immediately above. The sometimes sudden, often bitingly painful nature of certain illnesses lent itself well to the divine arrow imagery (e.g., Job 6:4; cf. also Dt 32:42; 2Sa 22:15 [= Ps 18:14(15)]; Ps 7:13[14]; et al.), since the ancient Near Eastern sufferer immediately attributed his distressing condition to the (smiting) hand of the god/God or demon. Cf. also the Talmudic discussion of some of these *rešep* verses in *b. Ber.* 5a.

[126]F. Lindström, *God and the Origin of Evil*, 175. For his discussion of this verse, see 167–77.

[127]Contrast E. Noort, "JHWH und das Böse. Bemerkungen zu einer Verhältnisbestimmung," *OTS* 23 (1984): 120–36.

[128]Lindström, *God and the Origin of Evil*, 177.

[129]Ibid., 129 (and see 121–37).

[130]Cf. his discussion of Isa 45:7, ibid., 178–99.

[131]Cf., e.g., the treatments of Am 3:6 (ibid., 199–214), or La 3:38 (ibid., 214–36).

[132]Cf. Abraham's plea to the Lord in Ge 18:25, "Far be it from you to do such a thing—to kill the righteous with the wicked, treating the righteous and the wicked alike. Far be it from you! Will not the Judge of all the earth do right?" Note that Abraham had no argument with God slaying the wicked; his complaint was that the Lord might slay the righteous along with the wicked.

[133]On *sanwērîm* as temporary blindness (Ge 19:11; 2Ki 6:18), cf. W. von Soden, "Hebräische Problemwörter," *UF* 18 (1986): 341–44.

[134]*nᵉhāšîm śᵉrāpîm*; cf. LXX's "deadly" and Targum Onkelos' "burning" (cf. KJV's "fiery"); see also below, n. 149.

[135]I have not included here Ge 3:16, where Eve was cursed with the pangs of childbirth because of her transgression. Nor have I cited Ge 32:25–32, the dislocating of Jacob's hip, since this injury may be thought of as a "battle scar" or even as a divine "badge of honor" (cf. Keil, *Genesis*, KD 1:1/306; Ramban)—this is not a true instance of divine judgment or a condition for which Jacob would have requested healing. Commenting on the words, "The sun rose upon him" (32:21), N. Sarna, *Genesis*, 228, notes: "In light of Mal 3:20 [EV 4:2], the rising sun may also betoken the healing of Jacob's injury." However, since literary dependence of Ge 32 on Malachi is out of the question, the suggested idiomatic usage seems too subtle to have been intended by the author. For further interaction with the traditional Jewish interpretations, cf. D. E. Fass, "Jacob's Limp," *Dor le Dor* 17 (1988–89): 222–29. On the broader issues of "authorial intent" and "reader response," cf. W. C. Kaiser and M. Silva, *An Introduction to Biblical Hermeneutics: The Search for Meaning* (Grand Rapids: Zondervan, 1993).

[136]See also Ex 33:5; Dt 6:15; 7:4; 8:19–20.

[137]Cf. Ps 106:23 (cited also by Rabbenu Hananel in his commentary to *b. B. Mes.* 59b, *niṣṣᵉḥûnî bānāy*, "My sons have defeated me," with reference as well to the homonymic root *nsḥ* in the superscription of the psalm,

lamᵉ naṣṣēaḥ mizmōr lᵉ dāwid; see B. Ashkenazi, *Shittah Mekubbeset*, 5:285); the ultimate fate, however, of the unbelieving generation is recounted in Dt 2:15: "The LORD's hand was against them until he had completely eliminated them from the camp."

[138]On priestly intercession, the root *kpr*, and turning away God's wrath, see Milgrom, *Numbers*, Excursus 19, "Levitical 'Kippur,'" 369–71; Excursus 61, "The Apostasy of Baal-Peor (25:1–18)," 476–80; idem, *Leviticus*, 1079–84; B. A. Levine, *In the Presence of the Lord* (Leiden: E. J. Brill, 1974); B. Janowski, *Sühne als Heilsgeschehen* (Neukirchen-Vluyn: Neukirchener Verlag, 1982); and see the references and discussion in M. L. Brown, "The Root *Kippēr* and Atonement in Isaiah," forthcoming in the *Festschrift* for B. A. Levine. On prophetic intercession, see the insightful study of Y. Muffs, "Who Will Stand in the Breach?: A Study of Prophetic Intercession," in his *Love & Joy: Law, Language and Religion in Ancient Israel* (New York: Jewish Theological Seminary, 1992), 9–48.

[139]A. Noorditz, *Numbers*, trans. E. van der Maas (SBC; Grand Rapids: Zondervan, 1983), 96, notes that the phrase "his anger was aroused" (Nu 11:1) is "an anthropomorphism that is found in numerous places and speaks of impending punishment."

[140]The NIV marginal rendering of *kî* (as "for" as opposed to "even though") is to be preferred. It is *because* humankind is so sinful that God promises not to bring another flood on the earth. Otherwise he would be destroying the world continually! Cf. J. Calvin, cited in G. von Rad, *Genesis*, trans. J. Marks (OTL, rev. ed.; Philadelphia: Westminster, 1976), 123; note, however, that von Rad renders *kî* with "although."

[141]In keeping with this, the curses for disobedience in Lev 26 and Dt 28 greatly preponderate over the blessings, but this is typical of the ancient Near Eastern covenant treaty genre as a whole.

[142]For a discussion of these verses in the context of strict Calvinism, cf. the brief study of J. Murray and N. B. Stonehouse, *The Free Offer of the Gospel* (Nutley, N.J.: Presbyterian and Reformed, 1977), wherein the authors conclude that, based on scriptural statements such as these, God does not ordain everything he desires. Thus they state:

> We have found that God himself expresses an ardent desire for the fulfillment of certain things which he has not decreed in his inscrutable counsel to come to pass. This means that there is a will to the realization of what he has not decretively willed, a pleasure towards that which he has not been pleased to decree, [which] is indeed mysterious. (26)

[143]On the final victory of God's grace, cf. Jas 2:13b; see also J. G. McConville, *Grace in the End: A Study of Deuteronomic Theology* (SOTBT; Grand Rapids: Zondervan 1993).

[144]On the usage of *rp'* in 20:17, see above, 2.2.4.

[145]These are not, strictly speaking, "healings"; but the principle of divine judgment followed by divine respite still applies.

[146]B. A. Levine, *Numbers 1–20*, 333, renders the first half of Moses' prayer for healing in Nu 12:13 as, "No more, I beseech you!", repointing *'ēl nā'* ("Please, God") to *'al nā'* ("Do not, I pray!"); he notes, "In biblical Hebrew, *nā'* never directly follows a noun," and cites *'al nā' tihyeh*, "let her not be" (from v. 12), for further support. Any such emendation is strongly opposed by Rouillard, "*El Rofé*," not only because of the evidence of the ancient versions, medieval commentaries, and grammatical and literary arguments, but also because it would remove the reference to Hebrew *'ēl* (= Canaanite El, here as El Rapi'u; cf. above, 1.5.1).

[147]As noted by Milgrom, *Numbers*, 93: "The verb *va-tedabber* [12:1] is in the feminine singular, indicating that Miriam was the principal instigator of the gossip (note also that Miriam is mentioned ahead of Aaron, the reverse of the normal order, cf. vv. 4,5). This would therefore account for the fact that she and not Aaron was punished" (with reference to *Sifre Numbers* 99 and *Aboth de Rabbi Nathan* 9, 39). Cf. further B. P. Robinson, "The Jealousy of Miriam: A Note on Num 12," *ZAW* 101 (1989): 428–32.

[148]Milgrom, *Numbers*, 97, makes the common observation that "leprosy was considered a punishment for offenses against the Deity in Israel (and elsewhere in the ancient Near East)," referring to his *Cult and Conscience: The ASHAM and the Priestly Doctrine of Repentance* (Leiden: E. J. Brill, 1976), 80–82. For further discussion, see below, 2.2.6; cf. Dt 24:8: "In cases of leprous diseases be very careful to do exactly as the priests, who are Levites, instruct you.... Remember what the LORD your God did to Miriam along the way after you came out of Egypt."

[149]The designation of the snakes as *śᵉrāpîm* (NIV "venomous") is generally understood with reference to "the venomous bites of the snakes, and the burning inflammation produced" (so P. J. Budd, *Numbers* [Waco, Tex.: Word, 1984], 234, who translates *nᵉḥāšîm śᵉrāpîm* with "fiery snakes," noting, however, that the adjective might simply be "a description of the creatures themselves." See also Milgrom, *Numbers*, 174, who describes the "seraph figure" as a "winged snake similar to the winged Egyptian uraeus [cobra]"); cf. further "שָׂרָף," in *EM* 8:394–96 (with illustrations); H. H. Rowley, "Zadok and Nehushtan," *JBL* 58 (1939): 113–41; K. R. Joines, "The Bronze Serpent in Israel," *JBL* (1968): 245–56; idem, *Serpent Symbolism in the Old Testament* (Haddonfield, N.J.: Haddonfield House, 1974); R. K. Harrison, *Numbers* (WEC; Chicago: Moody, 1990), 277–78; Wildberger, *Isaiah 1–12*, 264–65; U. Rüterswörden, "שָׂרָף," *TWAT* 7:882–91; *HALAT* 4:1266–68. Cf. further the discussion of 2Ki 18:4, below, 2.3.3.

[150]Cf. Milgrom, *Numbers*, 175, 459–60 (Excursus 52, "The Copper Snake"; with rabbinic comments on Nu 21 and ancient Near Eastern examples of homeopathic magic); Harrison, *Numbers*, 277.

[151]For the serpent as an image of fertility and healing in the ancient world (most notably as a symbol of Asklepios, who is discussed above, 1.3.3), cf. Noorditz, *Numbers*, 187, with reference to B. Renz, *Der Orientalische Schlangendrache: Ein Beitrag zum Verständnis der Schlang im biblischen Paradeis* (Augsberg: Haas und Grabher, 1930); see also the works cited in previous note. Cf.

further L. K. Handy, "Serpent (Religious Symbol)," *ABD* 5:1113–16. For the suggestion that *nᵉḥūštān* (cf. 2Ki 18:4) was regarded as a healing god in the Israelite-Judean cult, cf. below, 2.3.3.

[152]On the meaning of *ḥyh* (Nu 21:8–9), cf. above, 0.3.3. For the usage of 21:4–9 in Jn 3:14–15, see J. D. M. Derret, "The Bronze Serpent," *EstBib* 49 (1991): 311–29; and note the references in T. R. Ashley, *Numbers* (NICOT; Grand Rapids: Eerdmans, 1993), 406, n. 25. For Nu 21 in Wis Sol 16, cf. H. Maneschag, "Gott, Erzieher, Retter und Heiland seines Volkes. Zur Rein-Interpretation von Num 21,4–9 in Weish 16,5–14," *BZ* (1984): 214–29.

[153]Milgrom, *Numbers*, 459–60; Harrison, *Numbers*, 277. According to R. S. Boraas, "Of Serpents and Gods," *Dialog* 17 (1978): 273–79, the use of the serpent as a healing device was "possibly borrowed from Egyptian models" and was "quasi-magical." Cf. also below, 2.3.3.

[154]Handy, "Serpent (Religious Symbol)," 1114, notes, "The naga serpents of India are often evil and bite people, causing death; but they also use their poisons to save lives," with reference to J. P. Vogel, *Indian Serpent-Lore or the Nagas in Hindu Legend* (repr. Varanasi: Prithivi Prakashan, 1972; cited from the London, 1926 ed.), 17–18.

[155]Cf. similarly Kee, *Medicine, Miracle and Magic*, 136, n. 4, with reference to the "technique of throwing a tree in the water" in Ex 15:22–25; for further discussion, see below, 2.3.1–2.3.4 on the healing and restoring techniques of Elijah and Elisha; cf. Cogan and Tadmor, *II Kings*, 149, commenting on 2Ki 13:14–25: "Although this act and many others performed by Elisha resemble non-Israelite magical practices, and are not accompanied by explicit invocation of YHWH, they should not be regarded as a violation of biblical law or circumvention of the divine will." Cf. also E. Neufeld, "Residual Magic in the Bible," *Dor le Dor* 17 (1988–89): 229, 255–59.

[156]For recent studies on the precise nature and proper translation of this word (with reference to the important earlier literature), cf. R. K. Harrison, "Leprosy," *IDB* 3:111–13; idem, "Leprosy," *ISBE* 3:103–6 (with a chart on 105 comparing Hansen's disease—i.e., what today is called leprosy—and the biblical description of *ṣāra'at*); J. Tas et al., "צָרַעַת," *EM* 6:774–78; D. P. Wright and R. N. Jones, "Leprosy," *ABD* 4:277–82; Milgrom, *Leviticus 1–16*, 768–901 (esp. 816–26); Levine, *Leviticus*, 75–92; Hartley, *Leviticus*, 187–89; J. Zias, "Lust and Leprosy: Confusion or Correlation?" *BASOR* 275 (1989): 27–31. Note also J. Wilkinson, "Leprosy and Leviticus: The Problem of Description and Identification," *SJT* 39 (1977): 153–69; idem, "Leprosy and Leviticus: A Problem of Semantics and Translation," *SJT* 31 (1978): 153–66; J. G. Andersen, "Leprosy in Translations of the Bible," *BT* 31 (1980): 207–12. For sociological dimensions of *ṣāra'at*, cf. J. J. Pilch, "Biblical Leprosy and Body Symbolism," *BTB* 11 (1981): 108–13.

[157]The one reference to divine judgment is found in Lev 14:34: "When you enter the land of Canaan, which I am giving you as a possession, and I put a spreading mildew [*wᵉ nātatî negaʿ ṣāra'at*] in a house in that land. . . ." However, the need for expiation in the purification/healing process (see Lev 14) no more implies sin than does the need for expiation after childbirth (Lev

13) imply a sinful condition. Rather, the issue is primarily one of cultic cleansing from impurity; cf. Milgrom, *Leviticus 1–16*, 763–68, with literature, and see above, n. 138. For a more general but related discussion, cf. A. S. Darling, "The Levitical Code: Hygiene or Holiness," in Palmer, ed., *Medicine in the Bible*, 85–99.

[158]For the *ṣāra'at* of Naaman, which may be an exception, see below, 2.3.2.3; cf. also Ex 4:6–7, where the emphasis is simply on the demonstration of the Lord's power. For general discussion of the OT material, cf. Seybold, *Sickness and Healing*, 67–74.

[159]Cf. Wright and Jones, "Leprosy," 279–80, with comparative anthropological references; Milgrom, *Leviticus 1–16*, 820–24. For the relationship between sin, evil spirits, and skin disease in the DSS, cf. J. M. Baumgarten, "The 4Q Zadokite Fragments on Skin Disease," *JJS* 41 (1990): 153–65; E. Qimron, "Notes on the 4Q Zadokite Fragments on Skin Disease," *JJS* 42 (1991): 256–59. Wright and Jones, 279 (with reference to *CAD* 8:133 and R. Caplice "An Apotropation Against Fungus," *JNES* 33 [1974]: 345–49) note, "Akkadian texts shows [*sic*] that fungal growths [comparable to the *ṣāra'at* in fabrics and walls] were portents of evil in Mesopotamia."

[160]According to Milgrom, *Leviticus 1–16*, 776, "In the Bible, God is always the author of *nega'* (cf. 14:34). It is invariably a divine punishment" (with numerous OT examples cited). Levine, *Leviticus*, 76, notes: "Literally, it means 'touch' and reflects the widespread, ancient belief that gods afflicted persons by their touch.... The 'touch' of divine beings thus became a general term for affliction, and it expressed the belief that one suffered disease as a punishment from God." Levine, 206, n. 4, and Milgrom, 776, further compare Akkadian *lapātu*, "to touch" (also, "attack by demons") and *liptu*, "touch; plague, disease, discolored spot." In the ancient Near Eastern conception, the afflicting "touch" could also have come from a demon, although this is never stated or even implied in the OT with regard to *ṣāra'at*. For the NT emphasis on the frequent connection between demons and disease, see below, 5.3.1.

[161]For further discussion of the incidents concerning Joab, Gehazi, and Uzziah, see below, 2.3.

[162]Cf. the explicit medical description of Wright and Jones, "Leprosy," 278: "A fetus that has died in the womb takes on a reddish color which lasts for the first few days after death. After this period it becomes an odd brown-gray. As it continues to become macerated in utero before finally being expelled, the skin is shed in large sheets." For rabbinic discussion, cf. A. Cooper, "The 'Euphemism' in Numbers 12:12—A Study in the History of Interpretation," *JJS* 32 (1981): 56–64.

[163]*Leviticus* (NICOT; Grand Rapids: Eerdmans, 1979), 192.

[164]Cf. Wright and Jones, "Leprosy," 281: "Against the norm of whole, healthy skin, skin diseases are abnormal; hence they are shunned." Others (cf. Milgrom, *Leviticus*, 819–20) have also emphasized the connection between *ṣāra'at* and death (even "living death"), helping to explain further the reasons for this complex of diseases being classified as "unclean." Note also Lev

22:4: "If a descendant of Aaron has an infectious skin disease [so NIV consistently for *ṣāra'at*] or a bodily discharge, he may not eat the sacred offering until he is cleansed" (cf. 21:16–23); see Milgrom, 766–68 (re: the impurity of bodily discharges, with extensive documentation).

[165]While the scholarly consensus today is that *ṣara'at* does not refer to Hansen's disease, the condition (or conditions) so designated was (or were) viewed with some degree of horror, as witnessed by these verses, coupled with the aforementioned imprecations calling down *ṣara'at* on the households of Joab and Gehazi. Truly, *ṣāra'at* was viewed as a cursed condition; cf. also Hartley's translation of *ṣāra'at* with "grievous skin disease" (*Leviticus*, 189: "for 'skin disease' is an accurate description of the ailment, and the term 'grievous' conveys the emotional dimension of *ṣr't* without suggesting any of its clinical properties"; see more broadly 187–89). Commenting on Hansen's disease, Sigerist notes, "No disease has ever had more dire consequences for the patient's life than *leprosy*.... Of all diseases [it is] the one that has the most serious social consequences" (*Civilization and Disease*, 71, 75).

[166]Again, questions of authorship or literary sources are not at issue here. Rather, these questions regarding Lev 13–14 are being raised in light of their overall canonical context in the Torah.

[167]Skin diseases are listed among the curses for disobedience in Dt 28 (cf. vv. 27, 35), but *ṣāra'at* is not specifically mentioned by name. On the blessings and curses, see above, 2.2.2.

[168]For discussion of the phrase "the blind and the lame," see below, 4.2.2. For birth defects and Ex 4:11, see below, 2.2.7. On the general subject of physical deformities in the Hebrew Bible and Jewish literature, cf. L. Holden, *Forms of Deformity* (JSOT 131; Sheffield: JSOT Press, 1991); for a general biblical perspective on human physiology, cf. J. Wilkinson, "The Body in the Old Testament," *EvQ* 63 (1991): 195–210.

[169]Examples such as 2Ki 6:18–20, the reversal of the temporary blinding of the Aramean army, are not really exceptions.

[170]Significantly, two of the divine healings in the OT involved cases of *ṣāra'at*—Miriam and Naaman.

[171]C. F. Keil's attempt to explain away this tautology is unconvincing; cf. *Deuteronomy*, KD 1/3:370–71.

[172]W. H. Shea points out in a private communication, however, that Lev 13–14 must be treated in the larger context of Lev 11–15, warning against an oversimplification of the laws of uncleanness. Thus, he notes that it is not just *ṣara'at* for which no sinful origins or causes are ascribed, rather, "no sinful situations are described as the origin of anything in the uncleanness laws of Lev 11–15." Moreover, there are not "any treatments prescribed for any of the states of Lev 11–15, not just leprosy." Thus, statements regarding either the sinful causes of *ṣara'at* and/or its uniqueness must be tempered, at least according to Leviticus.

[173]It was suggested above (1.2.2.3) that the priests could function only as observers and hygienists, *not* healers, so as to relegate all supernatural healing

to Yahweh's hand alone, in contrast to the general ancient Near Eastern pattern, where the (pagan) priests were often physicians.

[174]Cf. Lev 13:18, *wᵉnirpā'*; 13:37; 14:3; 14:48, *nirpā'*, without *wāw*; the first three refer to skin disease, the last refers to the plague in the house. On the somewhat fixed style of the priestly literature, cf. the eloquent (but negative) description of R. H. Pfeiffer, *Introduction to the Old Testament* (New York: Harper & Brothers, 1948), 208–9, who speaks of its "juristic lucidity," noting that its style is a "stereotyped style, repetitious, intolerably explicit, pedantic, erudite, colorless, and schematic." Note also that the three occurrences of *rp'* in Ez 47 (vv. 8, 9, 11), clearly a chapter characterized by priestly usage, are also in the Niphal.

[175]So, e.g., Wenham, *Leviticus*, 189 (chs. 11–16 are termed by him "Uncleanness and Its Treatment"); Milgrom, *Leviticus*, 768, terms 13:1–59 "Scale Disease," while 14:1–57 is summarized by "Purification After Scale Disease" (chs. 11–16 are "The Impurity System"); Levine, *Leviticus*, 75, groups 13:1–14:57 under "Purification of Skin Diseases" (note, however, that the adjective "skin" is inappropriate for *ṣāra'at* in fabrics and houses).

[176]Wenham, *Leviticus*, 190, 204, 191, and 206, respectively.

[177]Milgrom, *Leviticus*, 769–70, 827, 829. In this they agree with the rendering of *Targ. Onk.*, which consistently uses *'sy*.

[178]This was argued at length, above, 0.3.1, 0.3.2.

[179]Note also that in Eze 47, the subject of *rp'* is the salt waters that have been made fresh (cf. also 2Ki 2:21–22), see below, 2.3.4, 4.2.2.

[180]Cf. the remarks of Levine, *Leviticus*, 90, on 14:35 (NJV: "Something like a plague has appeared upon my house"): "The appearance of what the owner observed reminded him of a disease of the skin." Cf. further S. Meier, "House Fungus: Mesopotamia and Israel (Lev 14:33–53)," *RB* 96 (1989): 184–92; P. T. Crocker, "Archaeology, Mildew, and Leviticus 14," *BurH* 26 (1990): 3–11.

[181]The LXX rendered both verses in Lev 13 with the appropriate forms of *hygiazō* but translated 14:3, 48 with *iaomai*. Elsewhere in the LXX *hygiazō* was used to translate *rp'* in Eze 47 (3 times); otherwise, this word rendered the Qal or Piel of *ḥyh*. The Greek words *hygeia* (or *hygia*, *hygieia*) translated *ḥāy* (Ge 42:15, 16) and *nepeš* (Est 9:31); the other equivalents are unclear. See Hatch and Redpath, *Concordance*, 2:1380b.

[182]See below, 2.3.4, on 2Ch 30:20; cf. Wenham, *Leviticus*, 8–25. Note, however, Stoebe's critique of Stendahl in *THAT* 2:805–6, for emphasizing this aspect of the semantic range of *rp'* to the virtual exclusion of physical referents: "Es erscheint deswegen als zu eng wenn K. Stendahl, *Svensk Exegetisk Årsbok* 15, 1950, 5–33, dem Begriff *rp'* jeden Bezug auf körperliche Heilung abspricht und ihn auf das durch kultische Mittel zu erreichende Heilsein beschränkt, denn dann wird eine wesentliche biblische Erkenntnis nivelliert."

[183]On the purification of the disinfected house, with special reference to the priestly terminology, see Levine, *In the Presence of the Lord*, 73, n. 51 (cf. 83–84).

[184]In Lev 13:18 it is the *šᵉḥîn*; in 13:37, the *neteq*; in 14:3, the *negaʿ haṣṣāraʿat min-haṣṣarûʿa*; and in 14:48, the *negaʿ*. Thus the relevant portion of 14:3 should not be rendered "the leper has been healed of his scaly disease" (so, e.g., NJV; cf. Milgrom, *Leviticus*, 827), but rather, "the affliction of a serious skin disease has healed in the affected man" (Wenham, *Leviticus*, 204), or, "has remitted in the affected man."

[185]Versions such as the NIV, which translate Lev 14:48 differently than the first three occurrences, would do well to render 14:48 with "remitted," indicating in a marginal note that the Hebrew for "remit, remitted," is the same word as that translated "heal" in 13:18, 37; 14:3. The NIV's rendering of 14:48, "the mildew is gone," is inexact, also losing the continuity of thought and expression supplied by the fourfold usage of *rp'*. Most recently, Hartley, *Leviticus*, renders the first three verses with "heal" (13:18, "it heals"; 13:37, "the scruffy patch is healed"; 14:3, "the afflicted person has been healed of the grievous skin disease") and 14:48 with "cure" ("the growth is cured"). Again, it would have been better to have rendered all four instances with "cure."

[186]If, in fact, there actually was any kind of impediment; the Hebrew is literally, "I am not a man of words . . . but I am heavy of mouth and heavy of tongue" (cf. also 6:30, "Look, I am of uncircumcised lips"). For recent discussion, cf. D. Gewalt, "Der 'Sprachfehler' des Mose," *Dielheimer Blätter zum Alten Testament und seiner Rezeption in der Alten Kirche* 27 (1991): 8–16; L. Gruber, "Moses: His Speech Impediment and Behavior Therapy," *Journal of Psychology and Judaism* 10 (1986): 5–13; J. H. Tigay, "'Heavy of Mouth' and 'Heavy of Tongue': on Moses' Speech Difficulty," *BASOR* 231 (1978): 57–67; L. I. Rabinowitz, "Moses the Inarticulate," *Dor le Dor* 12 (1983/84): 121–22. On the speech impediment of the Hittite king Mursili, viewed as a divinely inflicted punishment that the god(s), if placated, could reverse, cf. A. Goetze and J. Pedersen, *Mursilis Sprachlähmung* (Copenhagen: Levin Nad Munksgaard, 1934); see also Milgrom, *Leviticus*, 933.

[187]Cf. Childs, *Exodus*, 78–79, for a sensitive literary and contextual treatment.

[188]According to *Exod. Rab.* 3:20, *piqqēaḥ* refers to hearing as well as seeing, i.e., "open" ears as well as eyes, a meaning reflected in later Hebrew usage.

[189]S. T. Lachs, "Exodus iv 11: Evidence for and Emendation," *VT* 26 (1976): 249–50.

[190]The versions of the midrash that make reference to the lame read *hgrym*, not *psḥym*, with only one exception, while most of the versions omit "lame" altogether (see ibid., 250, n. 6). Even if the midrashic author had a stray Torah text that read *pisseaḥ*, that would only prove that he had at his disposal an aberrant copy, *not* a true copy of the original.

[191]For the dimensions of *śîm*, cf. F. Vanoni, "שִׂים," *TWAT* 7:761–81.

[192]Not surprisingly, Ex 4:11 is often marshaled by critics of the contemporary divine healing movement; cf., e.g., J. MacArthur, *Charismatic Chaos*, 217: "God made the disabled and the infirm. Babies are born every day with defects. Many children grow up with congenital deformities. Some people have illnesses that last for years. While it is unexplainable according to our

human logic, it is all God's plan and a gift of God's love." This, however, goes far beyond the simple statement of Ex 4:11.

[193]Long life in and of itself, however, is not necessarily a proof of divine blessing, as evidenced by the fifty-five-year reign of Manasseh, the most notorious king in Judean history, yet with the longest regency of any king. (He did begin his reign, though, at age twelve, and we are not told at what age he humbled himself and repented, as recorded in 2Ch 33:10–19.) Also, certain godly kings, uncensured by the historians, died at a young age (e.g., Jotham, who began his reign at age twenty-eight and died sixteen years later; see 2Ki 15:33–38; 2Ch 27:1–9). With regard to Manasseh, however, some scholars view the Chronicler's account of this notorious king's repentance as a literary fiction, created to justify his longevity, while others, who accept the basic historicity of the narrative, tend to see Manasseh's change of heart as contributing to his long reign. In any case, it is difficult to date these events with precision; hence no conclusions can be drawn as to whether the Chronicler intended us to view the king's repentance as standing in direct relationship to his fifty-five year royal tenure; cf., briefly, C. D. Evans, "Manasseh, King of Judah," *ABD* 4:496–99, esp. 498.

[194]Although the Hebrew verbs for 1Sa 2:6a are identical to those in Dt 32:39 (Hiphil of *mût* and Piel of *ḥyh*), the NIV translates the latter with "put to death" and "bring to life," whereas here they are rendered, "brings death and makes alive." Consistency in translation would have been preferable, probably with "puts to death and makes alive" in both.

[195]Note the stock phrase, "Long live the king!" (lit., "May the king live"; cf. 1Sa 10:24; 2Sa 16:16 [*bis*]; 1Ki 1:25, 34, 39; 2Ki 11:12; 2Ch 23:11; Ps 72:15; also 1Sa 25:6); note also the hyperbolic expression of Bathsheba to the aged King David, "May my lord King David live forever!" (1Ki 1:31), commonly used in the ancient Near East (cf. Da 2:4; 3:9; 5:10; 6:22; Neh 2:3; see Keil, *I & II Kings*, KD 3/1:21–22; J. E. Goldingay, *Daniel* [WBC; Waco, Tex.: Word, 1989], 32–33, n. 4.b).

[196]The Hebrew for NIV's "prime of life" is not clear, simply stating, "they will die [as] men" (cf. NJV's tentative, "as [ordinary] men"; P. K. McCarter Jr., *I Samuel* (AB; Garden City, N.Y.: Doubleday, 1980), 88, follows the LXX and 4QSam[a], both of which read, "you will fall by the swords of men." See also Ehrlich, *Mikra* 2:107; *Randglossen* 3:177.

[197]For varied interpretations of the words, "Can I tell the difference between what is good and what is not?" cf. P. K. McCarter Jr., *II Samuel* (AB; Garden City, N.Y.: Doubleday, 1984), 422 (idiomatic for "childlike" [cf. Dt 1:39] and hence lacking in sexual vigor), and Rashi (unable to distinguish between good and bad food).

[198]In rabbinic lore, Ahijah's life (extending to 500 years!) impossibly spanned numerous generations, and he was actually thought to have been a contemporary of Amram, father of Moses; see *b. B. Bat.* 121b. According to Hasidic legends, he also appeared to and taught the Baal Shem Tov (founder of the modern Hasidic movement in the eighteenth century); see conveniently, "Ahijah the Shilonite," *EJ* 2:459–60. Note also *Gen. Rab.* 65:10,

which attributes Ahijah's blindness to the fact that he raised up Jeroboam, a wicked disciple.

[199]But note *b. B. Mes.* 87a: "Until Elisha came, there was nobody who became ill and recovered. Elisha came [and] prayed, and recovered, as it is said; 'And Elisha fell ill with the illness from which he was to die.' [This implies] that he had been ill with other illnesses. Our Rabbis taught: 'Elisha was ill with three illnesses: One, because he pushed Gehazi away with two hands; and one, because he incited bears against children; and one, from which he died.'" For translation and commentary, cf. Steinsaltz, *The Steinsaltz Talmud*, 5:166 (cf. also above, n. 97). See further Y. L. bar D. Ginsberg, *Musar HaNevi'im* (Jerusalem: Philip Feldheim, 1986), 2:420–21 (Hebrew; his note fails to treat Nu 21 and healing from the fatal bites of the venomous serpents).

[200]See Y. Zakovitch, "'Elisha died ... he came to life and stood up' (2 Kings 13:20–21): A Short 'Short Story' in Exegetical Circles," in M. Fishbane and E. Tov, eds., *"Sha'arei Talmon": Studies in the Bible, Qumran and the Ancient Near East Presented to Shemaryahu Talmon* (Winona Lake, Ind.: Eisenbrauns, 1992), 53*–62* (Hebrew).

[201]M. Cogan and H. Tadmor, *II Kings* (AB; New York: Doubleday, 1988), 149, point out that "the story of [Elisha's] death is set nearly half a century ... [after] his first appearance toward the end of the reign of Ahab." Hence like Jacob, the prophet died at an old age from illness.

[202]According to Dillard, *2 Chronicles*, 76–81, the Chronicler in particular holds to the "theology of immediate retribution," viz., the "conviction that reward and punishment are not deferred, but rather follow immediately on the heels of the precipitating events" (76). Cf. even more broadly Japhet, *Chronicles*, 737, "In the Chronicler's philosophy of history, every misfortune is regarded as a chastisement." See also below, n. 229.

[203]On 1Sa 5–6, see J. B. Geyer, "Mice and Rites in I Sam v-vi," *VT* 31 (1981): 293–304; note also McCarter, *I Samuel*, 117–39. On the nature of the plague and the meaning of *'ōpālîm*, cf. ibid., 123; *HALAT* 3:814; R. W. Klein, *I Samuel* (WBC; Waco, Tex.: Word, 1983), 50–51; L. I. Conrad, "The Biblical Tradition for the Plague of the Philistines," *JAOS* 104 (1984): 281–87; J. Wilkinson, "The Philistine Epidemic of I Samuel 5 and 6," *ExpTim* 88 (1977): 137–41; M. Eichler, "The Plague in I Samuel 5 and 6," *Dor le Dor* 10 (1982): 157–65. Notice also that here too, just as in the Exodus (see above, 2.1), the divine judgment is understood to be against the people and their gods (1Sa 5:1–7; 6:5–7).

[204]Cf. D. M. Fouts, "Added Support for Reading '70 men,' in 1 Samuel vi 19," *VT* 42 (1992): 394.

[205]Although this account might be discussed under the heading of Yahweh as a warrior, it is not inappropriate to treat it here since, strictly speaking, the deaths of the Assyrian soldiers could not be classified as battle casualties (contrast Jos 10:11), but rather as direct victims of the wrath of God—in keeping with the rest of the instances cited in this section. Cf. also Elijah's calling down fire from heaven on the king's messengers (2Ki 1:9–12; note

"the fire of God" in v. 12), Elisha's cursing the mocking youths of Bethel in the name of the Lord, after which forty-two of them were mauled by bears (2:23–24); see also 17:25, where God sent lions to kill some of the new, idol-worshiping settlers of Samaria.

[206]For the meaning of *bêt haḥopšî*, cf. W. Rudolph, "Ussias 'Haus der Freiheit,'" *ZAW* 89 (1977): 418; cf. also O. Loretz, "Die Hebräischen Termini *ḤPŠJ* 'Freigelassen, Freigelassener,' und *ḤPŠH* 'Freilassung,'" *UF* 9 (1977): 163–67; N. Lohfink, "חָפְשִׁי," *TDOT* 5:114–18 (with literature).

[207]Cf. S. W. Holloway, "Distaff, Crutch or Chain Gang: The Curse of the House of Joab in 2Sa iii 29," *VT* 37 (1987): 370–75.

[208]It was restored in answer to the prophet's intercession (1Ki 13:6–7; cf. above, 0.3.3, on the usage of *šwb*).

[209]Cf. O. H. Steck, "Die Erzählung von Jahwes Einschreiten gegen die Orakelbefragung Ahasjas (2 Kön 1,2–8, 17)," *EvT* 27 (1967): 546–56.

[210]On the fate of Jehoram as typifying that of the nation, cf. C. T. Begg, "Constructing a Monster: The Chronicler's *Sondergut* in 2 Chonicles 21," *AusBR* 37 (1989): 35–51; note also the comment of David Kimchi to 2Ch 36:16: Because "they multiplied transgressions so, repentance, which is *marpe'*, was withheld from them." On the metaphorical usage of sickness and healing in the prophetic books, see below, ch. 4. For further usages of *'ên marpē'*, cf. Pr 6:15; 29:1; see the discussion of *marpē'* in Jeremiah, below, 4.1.3.

[211]Cf. McCarter, *II Samuel*, 512–14; Milgrom, *Numbers*, 264–65; Ashley, *Numbers*, 599–600.

[212]See J. H. Sailhamer, "1 Chonicles 21:1—A Study in Inter-Biblical Interpretation," *TrinJ* 10 (1989): 33–48; for discussion of the OT–NT perspectives on God, Satan, sickness, and healing, cf. below, 3.1.10, 3.3.2.1, 5.1.1, 5.3.1.

[213]For a general treatment of the Chronicler's usage of earlier material, cf. T. Sugimoto, "The Chronicler's Techniques in Quoting Samuel-Kings," AJBI 16 (1990): 30–70.

[214]Similarly, Solomon in his temple prayer grouped together famine and plague, blight and mildew, locusts and grasshoppers, and an enemy besieging Jerusalem as disastrous circumstances that would cause the people to cry out to God for mercy (1Ki 8:37–40; note 8:38b, "each one aware of the afflictions of his own heart," or, as in 2Ch 6:29b, "each one aware of his afflictions and pains"). Cf. also Jehoshaphat's recounting of Solomon's prayer in 20:9, and note that David's aforementioned imprecation against Joab (2Sa 3:29) consists of the wish that Joab's house never be without sickness, death in battle, and famine. Note also Jer 28:8, "From early times the prophets who preceded you have prophesied war, disaster and plague against many countries and great kingdoms."

[215]For a frightfully graphic depiction of the plague as a destroying angel/demon, see the painting by Arnold Böcklin entitled, "The Plague," printed in Sigerist, *Civilization and Disease*, facing 116.

[216]On the relationship between God and the destroying angel(s), see Ex 12:12–13, 23, 29; 2Ki 18:35 and par.; Eze 9:1–11. On Ex 12, see also Lindström, *God and the Origin of Evil*, 55–71; note also Ps 78:49, in the context of the ten plagues: "He unleashed against them his hot anger, his wrath, indignation and hostility—a band of destroying angels."

[217]Contrast 1Sa 25:6; 3Jn 2 with 1Sa 2:31–34; 2Sa 3:29; Ps 109:8ff.

[218]See above, n. 203.

[219]The significance of Geyer's remark, "Mice and Rites," 294, n. 5—that "*rp*' [i.e., in 1Sa 6:3] refers to the act of divination . . . not to the return of the ark"—escapes me.

[220]P. Masters, *The Healing Epidemic*, 59, asks, "How can charismatic healers say so dogmatically that sickness in the Old Testament was *always* the result of personal sin?" citing as exceptions to this (over)statement the sickness and death of Abijah in 1Ki 14 and the child healed by Elijah. The preponderance of OT evidence, however, merely *qualifies* the position that Masters finds "amazing" and "groundless," that sickness in the Old Testament is *generally* described as the result of personal sin. Cf. also Levine, *Numbers 1–20*, 332: "In ancient Israel it was believed that *ṣara'at* was a punishment from God, as was believed of illnesses generally." Of course, the Scriptures frequently discuss sickness and disease in a spiritual context; hence, most illnesses actually referred to in the Bible are mentioned because there is normally a reason for the condition. In other words, while it would be somewhat of an overstatement to say, "According to the Old Testament, most sickness is the result of personal sin," it is correct to say, "Most sickness recorded in the Old Testament is understood to be the result of personal sin." Cf. also above, n. 87.

[221]Cf. Isa 14:18–20; Jer 8:1–2; Eze 29:5.

[222]In an amazing oversight, Witty, *Divine Healing*, 43, claims that God's smiting of Azariah in 2Ki 15:5 is another unexplained example of a good person being struck with disease; he forgets, however, that Azariah is Uzziah (2Ch 26:16–21), treated by him earlier, in ibid., 38–39! For discussion of Isa 57:1–2, cf. Delitzsch, *Isaiah*, KD 7/2:368–69.

[223]Cf. 2Sa 14:14; Eze 18:23, 32.

[224]In view of 2Ch 35:20–22, which indicates that Josiah's death could have been averted, it is possible to argue that God's wrath might have been held back until the time of his death, even had he lived to old age. Thus his death in battle might *not* be a true parallel to that of Abijah, son of Jeroboam. In any case, it was an act of foolishness on Josiah's part (cf. 2Ch 35:22) that led to his death in battle; circumspection on his part could have prolonged his life, at least theoretically.

[225]The psalm of Hezekiah (Isa 38:9–20), utilized here for corollary information, is also treated in 3.1.7. The other accounts of prophetic miracles, with the exception of 2Ki 21–22 (the making wholesome of undrinkable waters, discussed below, 2.3.4), will not be discussed here. For further discussion on the prophets as miracle workers, cf. below, n. 256.

[226]The Lord's opening of barren wombs might also be considered to be an exception to this; see above, 2.2.4.

[227]Cf. Muffs, "Who Will Stand in the Breach?"

[228]S. J. DeVries, *1 Kings* (WBC; Waco, Tex.: Word, 1985), 221.

[229]See also above, n. 202, with reference to Dillard's description of the Chronicler's theology of immediate divine retribution; cf. further D. Kraemer, "The Classical Biblical Position: Retributive Suffering," in his *Responses to Suffering in Classical Rabbinic Literature* (Oxford: Oxford Univ. Press, 1995), 18–22.

[230]DeVries, *1 Kings*, 222. The first two "mistakes" are: (1) "calling the woman a widow" (for DeVries, the woman is not the widow of Zarephath); and (2) "saying that the boy is dead" (according to DeVries, the boy was lifeless, but not dead).

[231]For discussion of sickness and healing in Job, see below, 3.3.1–3.3.3.

[232]The popular eighteenth- and nineteenth-century geographical and travel account of M. Park, *The Travels of Mungo Park* (repr. New York: E. P. Dutton, 1927), 77, contains this account of an African mother's reaction to the (ultimately fatal) shooting of her herdsman son by a Moor: "His mother walked on before, quite frantic with grief, clapping her hands, and enumerating the good qualities of her son. *Ee maffo fanio* (he never told a lie), said the disconsolate mother, as her wounded son was carried in at the gate;—*Ee maffo fanio abada* (he never told a lie; no never)."

[233]I agree with DeVries, *1 Kings*, 222, that this "is not magic, but a typical symbolic act familiar to the prophetic movement in Israel." Cf. also above, n. 155, and see further, below, n. 256. Note also Prioreschi, *Primitive Medicine*, 517 (with references on 532–33): "Some have interpreted this episode, obviously meant to be miraculous, as a case of mouth-to mouth resuscitation, of closed-chest cardiac massage, and of hypothermia with resuscitation by re-warming. This in spite of the similarity of this case with the one of Elijah . . . which underlies the miraculous nature of the cure."

[234]See Cogan and Tadmor, *II Kings*, 58, "and crouched upon him."

[235]The degree to which Elisha is portrayed as Elijah's disciple may be seen in the use of the phrase, "As surely as the LORD . . . lives, whom I serve" (*'ᵃšer 'āmadtî lᵉpānāyw*), found just four times in the OT, twice in the mouth of Elijah (1Ki 17:1; 18:15) and twice in the mouth of Elisha (2Ki 3:14; 5:16).

[236]According to T. R. Hobbs, *2 Kings* (WBC; Waco, Tex.: Word, 1985), 48, this "is a touch of literary genius, and irony."

[237]For discussion of *ṣara'at*, cf. above, 2.2.6.

[238]Cf. Cogan and Tadmor, *II Kings*, 63. According to Keil, however, the fact that Naaman was not excluded from his society only indicates that the Arameans treated those with *ṣāra'at* differently than did the Israelites (*I-II Kings* KD 3/1:317). J. Black and A. Green, *Gods, Demons and Symbols of Ancient Mesopotamia: An Illustrated Dictionary* (Austin, Tex.: Univ. of Texas Press, 1992), 68, state, "One achievement of the Babylonians in the field of medicine was their recognition of the transmissibility of leprosy: sufferers

were exiled from the community." See further V. H. Matthews and D. C. Benjamin, "The Leper," *TBT* 29 (1991): 292–97.

[239]No specific Hebrew root for "heal, cure, make whole" occurs in this passage. Rather the root *'āsap* ("to gather") is used, apparently as an ellipsis for "to remove/heal his leprosy and hence regather him to his people." For discussion, see above, 0.3.3, *sub 'āsap*. Since his condition apparently did not require total separation, it is possible that the usage of *'āsap* is simply idiomatic (i.e., in the context of the healing of *ṣāra'at*) and not to be pressed too literally here. Note that in vv. 10, 14, the root *šwb* occurs ("your flesh will be restored"; "his flesh was restored"); see also above, 0.3.3, *sub šwb*.

[240]Cf. Jacob's response to Rachel's demand for children in Ge 30:1–2.

[241]J. A. Montgomery and H. S. Gehman, *A Critical and Exegetical Commentary on the Books of Kings* (ICC; Edinburgh: T. & T. Clark, 1951), 375, note that the Greek versions translate Hebrew *ṭābal* ("dip") in v. 14 with "baptize" (*baptizomai*)—of obvious significance to the Christian reader of the LXX!—observing that the waters of the Jordan have special sanctity in the NT as well as in Mandaic tradition. Interpretations of the significance of the number "seven" fall along expected lines; cf. Keil, *I-II Kings*, KD 3/1:319: "*Seven times*, to show that the healing was a work of God, for seven is the stamp of God"; Gray, *I-II Kings*, 506: "The sevenfold immersion recommended by Elisha reveals the saga-form of the tradition."

[242]Cf. Cogan and Tadmor, *II Kings*, who entitle this chapter "The Conversion of Naaman."

[243]Note also that it was in an Israelite river that he bathed! Cf. Montgomery and Gehman, *Kings*, 375: Naaman is "disgusted that the muddy waters of Israelite Jordan are prescribed, and not the pure, cool streams of the Damascus oasis."

[244]References are generally made to 2Ki 20 except in the case of important variants.

[245]It is clear that *ḥyh* here should be translated "recover" (so NIV, etc.) and not "live"; see v. 7. The ideas, of course, overlap; cf. above, 0.3.3, *sub ḥyh*.

[246]Note also Isa 38:12–13, where it is assumed that God was behind the attack on Hezekiah's body.

[247]This may be referred to as "relative righteousness"; cf., e.g., Ps 18:19–27(20–28), wherein the psalmist points to his godly living (in obvious contrast to his enemies, from whom he has been delivered) as the cause for his victory over his foes.

[248]According to 2Ki 18:2 (2Ch 29:1), he was twenty-five years old when he became king, and he reigned in Jerusalem twenty-nine years. Since, according to the account of his healing, his life was extended fifteen years, he would not have been forty when he almost died.

[249]Cf. J. N. Oswalt, *Isaiah 1–39* (NICOT; Grand Rapids: Eerdmans, 1986), 675–76, 689.

[250]On the importance of posterity in the biblical mentality, cf. above, 2.2.2, 2.2.4. Oswalt, ibid., 676, correctly notes, "No good Hebrew could view being cut off childless in midlife as anything but a most severe judgment from

God" (with reference to Ge 15:2–3; Lev 20:20; 1Sa 1:10–11; Pr 30:15–16; Isa 53:8; 54:1; Lk 1:7, 25). Note also the interpretations of *kārēt*—being "cut off"—in Milgrom, *Numbers*, 405–8 (Excursus 36: "The Penalty of 'Karet'") and Levine, *Leviticus*, 241–42 (Excursus 1: "That Person Shall Be Cut Off"); cf. further the usage of *'aḥ^a rît* (lit., "that which comes after") in the sense of "posterity"; see BDB, 31, meaning d; *HALAT* 1:36 ("Nachkommenschaft"); Gesenius-Meyer, *Handwörterbuch* 1:42 ("Nachkommen, Nachkommenschaft," with lit.); Clines, *Dictionary* 201, meaning 4.a ("descendants, posterity"). The fact that individuals were known as X son of Y (e.g., Joshua Ben Nun, Simon Bar Jonah) indicates how strongly the father's identity was continued in the son; note also the Arabic custom of the father changing his name after the birth of his firstborn son, as, e.g., Abu Walid (i.e., father of Walid). Thus, from that time on he is primarily known as his son's father.

[251]Only in the account in 2Ki 20 does the verb *rāpā'* occur, found in vv. 5 and 8. Isaiah 38 records only the promise of fifteen additional years of life (however, in v. 16, Hezekiah's psalm, the verbs *ḥlm* and *ḥyh* are used, for which see above, 0.3.3; see further, below, 3.1.7, on the root *ḥyh* in Hezekiah's psalm); 2Ch 32 makes reference only to a miraculous sign performed in answer to prayer, emphasizing also the graciousness of God in healing the king (vv. 24–25). The end of Isa 39:1 reads *wayyišma' kî ḥālâ wayyeḥ^e zaq*, lit., "because he [the king of Babylon] heard that he [Hezekiah] was sick and became strong," whereas 2Ki 20:12 reads *kî šāma' kî ḥālâ ḥizqiyyāhû*, "because he heard that Hezekiah was sick," providing an interesting textual variation between *wayyeḥ^e zaq* and *ḥizqiyyāhû*. Note also that Isa 39:1 is the only context in which *ḥzq* is used in the context of physical healing. Since 2Ch 32:31 understands that the Babylonian emissaries came "to ask him about the miraculous sign," it seems fair to surmise that the common tradition claimed that the emissaries came, not because of Hezekiah's sickness (a *possible*, but not compelling deduction from 2Ki 20:12), but because of his healing. Thus, a fuller text might have read *kî ḥālâ ḥizqiyyāhû wayyeḥ^e zaq*, "because he heard that Hezekiah was sick and had recovered."

[252]For a similar example, but in "reverse," cf. Ps 106:24–42, where it is recounted that God first sent a plague and wasting disease on his rebellious people and later gave them over to the hand of their enemies.

[253]See above, 2.2.5; note also J. Jeremias, *Das Reue Gottes: Aspekte alttestamentlicher Gottesvorstellung* (BibS 65; Neukirchen: Neukirchener Verlag, 1975); Ashley, *Numbers*, 477–78; Hamilton, *Genesis 1–17*, 274–75; cf. also C. Pinnock, ed., *The Openness of God: A Biblical Challenge to the Traditional Understanding of God* (Downers Grove, Ill.: InterVarsity, 1994), for a wide-ranging theological exploration.

[254]The exact nature of the boil, and its possible relation to the king's terminal illness (i.e., was the boil actually the source of the illness, or was it simply the clearest symptom of the illness?) have been much discussed; suggestions include a bubo (i.e., related to a plague); a simple abcess; a furuncle or carbuncle; cf. Sussman, "Sickness and Disease," *ABD* 6:6; R. K. Harrison, "Boil," *ISBE* 1:532. Regarding the carbuncle, Harrison notes that it "is a

more extensive inflammation of the skin, usually attended by a lowering of the bodily resistance, and it can prove fatal." Most recently, S. Levin, "Hezekiah's Boil," *Judaism* 42 (1993): 214–17, has suggested that the *š^{e}ḥîn* might have been an abscessed tubercolotic rash (scrofula).

[255]Cf. J. D. W. Watts, *Isaiah 34–66* (WBC; Waco, Tex.: Word, 1987), 52: "Figs were used as medicine throughout the ANE, in Ugarit with horses ... in Mesopotamia for human toothache and lung problems ... in Old Egypt for constipation, in Arabia for the plague, and in Turkey even in modern times"; see also Oswalt, *Isaiah 1–39*, 691.

[256]As emphasized above (2.2.5, end, *sub* Nu 21), the idea of "magic" still must be somewhat redefined even in these contexts, since it is in the name of the Lord and, presumably, at his behest, that these acts are carried out. Also, the use of means makes it evident that the prophet *alone* is not the miracle worker. For a good summary of miracles in the OT, cf. Y. Zakovitch, "Miracle (Old Testament)," *ABD* 4:845–56; note especially 850 ("Miracle and Magic").

[257]For further discussion of Hezekiah's psalm, see below, 3.1.7.

[258]For discussion of the various theories regarding the reason for Hezekiah's reforms (i.e, political and/or spiritual), cf. Hobbs, *2 Kings*, 251–52.

[259]See above, nn. 149–51, for bibliographic references; cf. also Montgomery and Gehman, *Kings*, 481; Gray, *I-II Kings*, 670–71; Hobbs, *2 Kings*, 241–42; M. Haran, "נְחֻשְׁתָּן," *EM* 5:826–27; H. J. Fabry, "נָחָשׁ," *TWAT* 5:394–95; idem, "נְחֹשֶׁת," *TWAT* 5:407–8; Niehr, "JHWH als Arzt," 4, with reference to O. Keel, *Jahwe-Visionen und Siegelkunst* (SBS 84/85; Stuttgart: KBW Verlag, 1977), 81–83; L. K. Handy, "Serpent, Bronze," *ABD* 5:1117. To this day, the symbol of the doctor is the serpent on a pole (a representation, however, of Asklepios, not "Nehushtan"; i.e., not directly related to the account in Nu 21). According to Ashley, *Numbers*, 406, it was in reaction to the temptation to treat the serpent in a magical sense (as per 2Ki 18:4) "that the author of Wis. 16:5–7 asserted that it was not the serpent that saved the Israelites, but God." Cf. also above, n. 152.

[260]Niehr, "JHWH als Arzt," 4; cf. Haran, "נְחֻשְׁתָּן," 826.

[261]Gray, *I-II Kings*, 670–71.

[262]Hobbs, *2 Kings*, 251–52. The reconstruction of G. Garbini, "Le Serpent d'Airain et Moïse," *ZAW* 100 (1988): 264–67, is quite imaginative.

[263]Stendahl translates *way^{e}rappē'* with "*restaurerade*" ("Rafa'," 9).

[264]According to a comment in the thirteenth century midrashic compilation *Yalqut Shimoni* (cited in Ginsburg, *Musar HaNevi'im*, 2:306), the words *wayy^{e}rappē' 'et-mizbaḥ yhwh hehārûs* mean, "He healed them, and brought them from the evil path to the good path by means of the miracles he performed for them." Ginsburg (ibid., 306–7), however, asks why the object of *rippē'* is *the altar* if the verb actually deals with "the healing of the soul [*hannepeš*] of the people." The answer is that, when Israel does the will of the Lord, the Shekinah rests on each individual as if it were the altar of the Lord; thus, "when he turned the hearts of the people back to their heavenly Father,

in this he built the spiritual altar that was destroyed in that generation" (cf. also Rashi). All this underscores just how strongly the verb *rp'* was associated in the minds of the commentators with the semantic domain of healing.

[265]*Targ. Jon.* renders *ûbᵉnā'*, followed by most of the rabbinic commentators; cf. also below, n. 267.

[266]W. L. Holladay, *A Concise Hebrew and Aramaic Lexicon of the Old Testament* (Grand Rapids: Eerdmans, 1971), 344. This is corrected in *HALAT* 4:1188.

[267]Note, however, J. Lust, E. Eynikel, and K. Hauspie, *A Greek-English Lexicon of the Septuagint, Part I, A-I* (Stuttgart: Deutsche Bibelgesellschaft, 1992), 211, who seem to exaggerate the semantic range of *iaomai* in the LXX, rendering 2Ch 7:14 with "to deliver," 2Ch 30:20 with "to forgive," Isa 30:26 with "to soothe (of pain)," and 2Ki 2:21 with "to purify" (note also 4Mc 3:10 with "to quench").

[268]Cf. Ibn Barun's note on Jer 17:14, cited below, 4.1.3, n. 91.

[269]Cf. Stendahl's note on Swedish "*hel*," "Rafa'," 7, n. 4; cf. above, 0.3.1, on the South Semitic usage of *rf*, where a similar pattern may be observed. In classical Arabic, the root was especially applied to clothes, hence "to mend, darn"; in Old South Arabian, it was used with reference to people, hence "to heal"; for further details, see the works cited in 0.3.1, n. 41.

[270]Cf. D. J. Wiseman, *1 & 2 Kings* (TOTC; Downers Grove, Ill.: Inter-Varsity, 1993), 197.

[271]J. Gray cites recent geological and hydrological surveys of the wilderness of Judah south of Jericho, wherein it was discovered that certain springs affected by radioactivity have been the cause of sterility (*I-II Kings*, 477–78). "The apparently sudden contamination and clearing of the water may have been due to geological shifts in that notoriously unstable area in the great rift valley, or even to such a slight factor as the shift of a water-table in a drought" (478). Of course, even if the "clearing of the water" did admit a natural explanation, the fact that it occurred precisely at the moment of Elisha's symbolic action and prophetic pronouncement would classify it as a bona fide biblical miracle. See further Wiseman, *1 & 2 Kings*, 197 (with references in nn. 1, 2).

[272]The LXX has *Iamai to hudata tauta . . . kai iathesan to hudata heos tēs hemeras tautēs. Targ. Jon.* reads *'asêtî lᵉmayā' ha'ilen . . . wᵉ'itasi'û mayā' 'ad yōmā' hāden.* D. Sperber, "Weak Waters," *ZAW* 82 (1970): 114–16, argues that the versions correctly rendered the consonantal text of *rippi'tî* but that the Masoretic pointing of *rippi'tî* (instead of *rippē'tî*), as well as the defective orthography of *wayērāpû* (without *'ālep*), are a "Midrashic" allusion to the "weakening" of the waters (as if from *rph*), i.e., their sweetening or desalination. However, while his observations as to the grammar and punctuation are correct, and as Sperber notes, recognized already by David Kimchi, his argument and assumptions are too subtle to merit acceptance; cf. Hobbs, *2 Kings*, 23–24, who also surveys the orthographic data.

[273]Cf Gray, *I-II Kings,* 479. On 477 Gray translates, "I have refertilized the water. . . . So this water was refertilized." It is preferable to interpret it in the

already established sense of "making whole[some]," in spite of the reference to *hā'āreṣ m[e] šakkelet*; see above, 2.2.4.

[274]This basic notion of "wholeness" is more acceptable here than is Sperber's theory that "pure, non-saline water is called weak water, and the desalination of water might be spoken of as the weakening of water, i.e., of its powers of buoyancy" ("Weak Waters," 115). In spite of his parallels from Herodotus (*hudor asthĕnēs*), China (*Jo-shui* = "weak water"), and the Tosefta (*Sukka* 3:9), his theory fails to take in the wider range of meaning of Hebrew *rp'* and does not recognize the force of the virtually exact parallel usage in Eze 47:8–9, 11, where the properly vocalized and nondefective Niphal of *rp'* occurs throughout.

[275]Cf above, nn. 155, 233, 256.

[276]De Moor's claim that the Ugaritic "expression *rp'u 'arṣ* . . . bears great resemblance to 2Ch 7:14" seems overstated ("Rāpi'ūma," 324; see also his reference to *CTA* 23, no. 2.15, for "a similar Babylonian phrase," cited according to him, in *CAD*, A, I, 346b, although I was unable to locate this citation there). On p. 336 de Moor states that the verse under discussion "indicates that YHWH comes to the rescue of harassed nations and restores the *šālôm* on earth. In 2Ch 7:14 YHWH promises that he will 'heal' the country of the Israelites." Cf. below. 4.1.4 on Isa 57:19.

[277]Cf. Tur Sinai's note in Ben Yehuda, 7:6654, *sub r[e] 'îmâ*. Actually, what had been "shut" was the sky!

[278]De Moor correctly rejects Gray's overemphasis on the idea of "refertilizing" ("Rāpi'ūma," 324–25, n. 13), with reference to the latter's *Keret*, 59–60; for detailed treatment, cf. above, 2.2.4.

[279]In English, one does not "heal" land; the KJV rendering of 2Ch 7:14 is yet another example of a Hebraism borrowed into English via the KJV; cf. in general C. S. Lewis, *The Literary Impact of the Authorized Version* (repr. Philadelphia: Fortress, 1963).

[280]Cf. Dt 29:22–24[21–23], especially v. 22[21]: "Your children who follow you in later generations and foreigners who come from distant lands will see the calamities [*makkôt*; cf. NJV's "plagues"] that have fallen on the land and the diseases [*taḥ[a] lû'êhâ*] with which the Lord has afflicted [*ḥillâ*] it." See also v. 27[26].

[281]That is, the "plagues" and "sicknesses" with which it was afflicted were metaphorical "diseases" as opposed to bodily diseases. Nonetheless, the "holistic" nature of Hebrew thought is again evident, as was observed in the discussion regarding *ṣāra'at* in people and houses (above, 2.2.6), both of which were termed *nega'*, while the remission of both was termed *nirpā'* (Niphal of *rp'*, best rendered in Lev 13–14 with "remitted").

[282]See Keil, *I-II Chronicles*, KD, 3/2, 465.

[283]See Baudissin, *Adonis und Esmun*, 386; Hempel more confidently lists this verse under "Heilung . . . des Volkes," *Heilung*, 240, n. 2.

[284]According to Dillard, *2 Chonicles*, 245, "Though no physical illness is suggested in the passage, the Chronicler goes out of his way to introduce the

term *heal* (30:20), a direct allusion to 2Ch 7:14." He accordingly translates with "he healed the people" (239).

[285]Could it be that confronted with the ugly situation at Corinth, the apostle found OT confirmation for his conclusion, viz., that the unexpected illness and deaths were caused by a violation of holy communion? For an anticipation of this view over fifty years ago, see F. F. Bosworth's comment in his sermon, "Did Jesus Redeem Us From Our Diseases When He Atoned for Our Sins," reprinted in his *Christ the Healer* (Old Tappan, N.J.: Revell, 1973), 14–39, esp. 15–16.

[286]Cf. above, 2.2.1.

[287]*Mikra* 2:466, equivalent to *Randglossen* 7:377. Ehrlich is now followed by Japhet, *Chronicles*, 953: "We must understand 'heal' as a preventative rather than corrective measure.... The immanent danger involved in the desecration of the holy by eating it in a state of uncleanness was averted, and it did not result in a plague among the people."

[288]Rudolph, *Chronikbücher*, 302.

[289]In favor of this "narrow understanding," however, it might be argued that where the *object* of *rp'* is a person or people, it should be translated with "heal"; all the instances in which a different rendering is appropriate refer to an inanimate object (other than physical sickness, which, of course, is "healed"); thus, e.g., 2Ch 7:14 (*restore* the land); 2Ki 2:21–22 (*make wholesome* the water); 1Ki 18:30 (*repair* the altar); Lev 14:48 (the mildew is *remitted*); Ps 60:2[4] (*mend* the earth's fissures). This argument, however, fails ro take into account the prophetic usage of *rp'*, where the semantic range is broader (cf. below, 4.1, 4.1.1).

[290]Curtis and Madsen, *Chronicles*, 475.

[291]Cf. Keil, *II Chronicles*, KD, 3/2:465: "The use of the word (*rp'*) is explained by the fact that sin was regarded as a spiritual disease so that *rp'* is to be understood of healing the soul (as Ps. xli. 5), or the transgression (Hos XIV. 5; Jer iii, 22)." Cf. also Payne, "1–2 Chronicles," *EBC* 4:537, where "healed" is simply explained as "pardoned."

[292]Cf. also the discussion of *wārāpā' lô* in Isa 6:10, below, 4.1.4.

Chapter Three—Israel's Divine Healer in Poetry and Wisdom Literature

[1]The key work on sickness and healing in the Psalms is Seybold's *Das Gebet des Kranken*; note also C. Barth's important study, *Die Errettung vom Tode*, and the articles cited in 0.1, n. 4. Due to the massive amount of diversified literature on the Psalms, I have relied especially on (1) the major modern commentaries and (2) studies dealing with sickness, affliction, healing, and deliverance in the poetry and wisdom literature. See also above, 0.5.

[2]Cf. Seybold, *Sickness and Healing*, 43: "The situation of the sick person from the inner perspective of an individual's own experience is expressed in the Old Testament's literature of prayer." Cf. also E. S. Gerstenberger, *Der bittende Mensch* (WMANT 51; Neukirchen-Vluyn: Neukirchener Verlag,

1980); J. Thuruthumaly, "The Praying Man in Psalms of Lament," *Biblebhashyam* 5 (1979): 119–32.

[3]Cf. ibid., 47, where it is observed that since all (seemingly miraculous) healing was perceived as the result of divine intervention, it became "a model for divine intervention in general." Cf. above, 2.3.2.4 (re: the deliverance of Hezekiah and Jerusalem).

[4]A. A. Anderson observes that "sin brings disease and misfortune in its train, but not every illness and tragedy is the result of the sufferer's *own* actions, although many were tempted to argue along these lines" (*Psalms 1–72*, 241, his emphasis). It should be noted, however, that in most cases (e.g., Pss 32 and 41) the sufferer is only too glad to acknowledge his personal sin as the cause of his affliction. What is incorrect, however, is the *conclusion* drawn by the "enemies," viz., that the life-threatening condition gives proof to the utter and final rejection of the sufferer by the Lord in his wrath. Cf. M. Dahood, *Psalms 1–50* (AB; Garden City, N.Y.: Doubleday, 1965), 234: "The common belief that illness was a punishment for sin was an unexcelled opportunity to the psalmist's enemies, ever eager to slander, to speculate on the nature of the guilt." See below, 3.1.5, for further discussion.

[5]This perception, however, does not *have to* derive from biblical or theological antecedents; similar views were common in the ancient Near East, as well as in other societies. See below, 3.1.4–6, for further discussion.

[6]Kraus, *Psalms 1–59*, 161; for a literary and stylistic treatment of Ps 6, cf. H. W. M. van Grol, "Literair-stilistische analyse van Psalm 6," *Bijdragen: Tijdschrift voor Filosofie en Theologie* 40 (1979): 245–64; see below, n. 88, for a challenge to the general scholarly consensus, supported in this monograph, that there is often an "indissoluble" connection between sickness and guilt in the OT.

[7]This fact should be underscored. A serious physical ailment almost invariably suggested an underlying, serious spiritual problem. It is important to remember that (1) "The concept of disease as a biological process is relatively young, and disease can be and has been interpreted in very different ways" (Sigerist, *Civilization and Disease*, 131), and that (2) "A medical diagnosis means nothing to [the sufferer] because he views his own case in a different context . . ." (Seybold, *Sickness and Healing*, 45).

[8]Such behavior was also in keeping for those friends who remained faithful to the sufferer; cf. Ps 35:13–14: "Yet when they were ill, I put on sackcloth and humbled myself with fasting. When my prayers returned to me unanswered, I went about mourning as though for my friend or brother. I bowed my head in grief as though weeping for my mother." On the typical behavior of the seriously ill, cf. Seybold, *Sickness and Healing*, 45, "Thus he reacts *as prescribed* . . ." (my emphasis). On the "prescribed" (i.e., somewhat standardized, fixed) nature of Near Eastern mourning rites (in particular for the dead), cf. A. Baumann, "אָבַל," *TDOT* 1:44–48 (with further references); see also the summaries in J. B. Payne, "Burial," *ISBE* 1:557, 560. Craigie, *Psalms 1–50*, 287, explains the actions described here in Ps 35:13–14 as "typical of those stipulated in international treaties. The sickness of a fellow

monarch, linked by treaty relationship, evoked acts of fasting and sorrow in the king."

[9]Cf. J. W. McKay, "The Experiences of Dereliction and of God's Presence in the Psalms: An Exercise in Old Testament Exegesis in the Light of Renewal Theology," in P. Ebert, ed., *Faces of Renewal: Studies in Honor of Stanley M. Horton Presented on His 70th Birthday* (Peabody, Mass.: Hendrickson, 1988), 3–13.

[10]R. Martin-Achard, "Approche des psaumes," 49; see Kraus, *Psalms 1–59*, 160.

[11]K. Seybold, *Das Gebet des Kranken*, 98–164; see Kraus, *Psalms 1–59*, 52–53, 160–61.

[12]Cf. Seybold, *Sickness and Healing*, 43.

[13]Of course, there is not universal consensus here; cf., e.g., W. VanGemeren, "Psalms," *EBC* 5:96, who follows J. Ridderbos and Rogerson/McKay in understanding "the language of physical suffering [in Ps 6] as a metaphor for the anguish of abandonment." VanGemeren, does, however, interpret the afflictions of Pss 30 and 41 as literal sickness (pp. 258, 327).

[14]On the editing of the Psalter, cf. J. C. McCann, *The Shape and Shaping of the Psalter* (Sheffield: Sheffield Academic Press, 1993); G. H. Wilson, *The Editing of the Hebrew Psalter* (SBLDS 76; Chico, Calif.: Scholars, 1985). For recent discussion of "linking" and the "inner hermeneutics" of the Psalms, see N. Lohfink, "Psalmengebet und Psalterredaktion," *Archiv für Liturgiewissenschaft* 34 (1992): 1–22.

[15]Cf. M. Dahood, *Psalms 1–50*, 234, 239, 245, 249, who understands the background of Pss 38–41 in each case to be serious illness (Ps 38: "the psalmist is afflicted by a grave disease"; Ps 39: "the psalmist prays for healing from a serious sickness"; Ps 40: "thanksgiving for healing from a mortal illness"; Ps 41: "A prayer for healing from sickness"). Seybold, *Sickness and Healing*, 53, also places Pss 42–43 in this class ("the poems of someone forced to remain in a foreign country because of broken limbs [42:11?]"), though he recognizes that they "have Zion as their main motif."

[16]For discussion of this concept and its possible relationship to sickness, see below, 3.1.6.

[17]According to L. C. Allen, *Psalms 101–150* (WBC; Waco, Tex.: Word, 1983), 14, "A desperately sick man turns to Yahweh as his only hope.... Fever wracks his body and has left him utterly demoralized. It has stolen his appetite and capacity for sleep, and now he is nothing but skin and bones."

[18]For thoughts relative to Ps 88, see Y. Hoffman, "The Transition from Despair to Hope in the Individual Psalm of Lament" (Hebrew), *Tarbiz 55* (1985/86): 161–72; also J. G. McConville, "Statement of Assurance in Psalms of Lament," *IBS* 8 (1986): 64–75; for Ps 89 in and of itself, cf. M. H. Floyd, "Psalm lxxxix: A Prophetic Complaint About the Fulfillment of an Oracle," *VT* 42 (1992): 442–57.

[19]For a slightly different listing, cf. E. Gerstenberger, *Psalms Part 1, with an Introduction to Cultic Poetry* (FOTL 14; Grand Rapids: Eerdmans, 1988), 12; H. Gunkel and J. Begrich, *Einleitung in die Psalmen* (repr. Göttingen: Van-

denhoeck & Ruprecht, 1984), 212–50; S. Mowinckel, *The Psalms in Israel's Worship*, trans. D. R. Ap-Thomas (New York: Abingdon, 1962), 2:9–11; for a discussion of the recurring elements in the wider categories of psalms of praise and lament, see C. Westermann, *Praise and Lament in the Psalms*, trans. K. R. Crim and R. N. Soulen (Atlanta: John Knox, 1981). For the presence (or absence) of similar elements in related ancient Near Eastern literature, cf. Walton, *Ancient Israelite Literature*, 135–66 (and see esp. 144, n. 33, with reference to the works of W. W. Hallo, G. Widengren, and K. van der Toorn). Walton (144) broadly observes that "the similarities of subject matter, while unquestionably present, demonstrate only that people everywhere tend to approach their gods with the same sorts of problems and to praise them for many of the same sorts of activities. This reflects the common nature of humanity, not literary dependence." Cf. also above, 0.5, n. 134.

[20]According to Gerstenberger, *Psalms Part 1*, 84, "The rhetorical question 'How long?' (*'ad-'ānâ* or *'ad-mātay*) belongs to the stock expressions of ancient Near Eastern psalmography" (with references; cf. esp. G. Widengren, *The Accadian and Hebrew Psalms of Lamentation* [Stockholm: Atkielbolaget Thule, 1937], 93–257).

[21]This has often been noted, since in church tradition, Ps 6 has formed the first of the so-called Seven Penitential Psalms. See, e.g., Delitzsch, *Psalms*, KD 5/1:130, "Because the Psalm contains no confession of sin, one might be inclined to think that the church has wrongly reckoned it as the first of the seven ... *Psalmi pœnitentiales* (vi. xxxii. xxxviii. li. cii. cxxx. cxliii.)"; Delitzsch, however, does not concur with that negative assessment; see also Kraus, *Psalms 1–59*, 161, 164–65. For a classic (seventeenth-century) exposition of the Seven Penitential Psalms, cf. Sir R. Baker, Knight, *Meditations and Disquisitions upon Certain Psalms* (repr. Harrisonburg, Va.: Sprinkle Publications, 1988), 95–299.

[22]On this verse, Craigie, *Psalms 1–50*, 92, writes

> One way of understanding it is to suppose that the psalmist perceived an intimate relationship between sin and sickness; thus his experience of sickness presupposed acts of sin, which in turn suggested that sickness itself was an act of divine chastisement and rebuke. But nowhere does this psalmist explicitly confess to sin; in this, Ps 6 differs from Ps 38, which opens with an identical plea, but which continues to a confession of sin. Here, there is no confession of sin and there is no explicit statement of penitence.

[23]Cf. M. L. Brown, "Man Repents and God Relents: *šûb* and Its Congeners."

[24]Delitzsch, *Psalms*, 377, refers to the psalmist's former attitude as "self-confidence" and "carnal security," noting, "Instead of confiding in the Giver, he trusted in the gift, as though it had been his own work." Craigie, *Psalms 1–50*, 254, states, "He had not been a righteous sufferer, but suffered as a consequence of his sinful self-confidence." Cf. C. H. Spurgeon, *The Treasury*

of David (repr. Grand Rapids: Zondervan, 1966), 1/2:45, who warns the reader to "beware lest the same fumes of intoxicating success get into our brains and make fools of us also."

[25]Commenting on the reference to divine wrath in Ps 102:11, Allen, *Psalms 101–150*, 14, interestingly observes, "The psalmist feels the victim of omnipotent violence. He leaves unexplained his reference to divine wrath, not linking it with personal wrongdoing but mentioning it virtually as an amoral force."

[26]Ibid., 92.

[27]The fact of the formulaic nature of the language, is, however, noted by Craigie (*Psalms 1–50*, 91) with reference to R. C. Culley, *Oral Formulaic Language in the Biblical Psalms* (Toronto: Univ. of Toronto, 1967); see also n. 22, above, where Craigie compares the virtually identical opening verses of Pss 6 and 38. See further Gerstenberger, *Psalms Part 1*, 61–62; Kraus, *Psalms 1–59*, 162: "The prayer in sickness was probably spoken according to fixed formularies." Cf. also Delitzsch, *Psalms*, 130: "We recognise here the language of penitently believing prayer, which has been coined by David. Compare ver. 2 with xxxviii. 2; 3 with xli. 4; 5 with cix. 26; 6 with xxx. 10; 7 with lxix. 4; 8 with xxxi. 10; 11 with xxxv. 4, 26." See further, below, 3.1.11 (on Ps 107:20).

[28]Cf. W. Eichrodt, *Theology of the Old Testament,* trans. J. A. Baker (OTL; Philadelphia: Westminster, 1967), 2:457–58.

[29]This interpretation follows the literal understanding of the psalm, presented as the first alternative by Ibn Ezra; his second view is to read it prophetically concerning the nation of Israel as whole, "that in the exile are like sick people."

[30]When the psalmist was "in the right" (e.g., in a dispute with his enemies, or in terms of his general obedience to the Lord), he did not hesitate to use this in his favor; cf., e.g., 17:1–2: "Hear, O LORD, my righteous plea; listen to my cry. Give ear to my prayer—it does not rise from deceitful lips. May my vindication come from you; may your eyes see what is right." Note that in all of Ps 17 there is not a single plea for mercy. See further Ps 18:19–27(20–28), and note especially J. A. Alexander, *The Psalms Translated and Explained* (repr. Grand Rapids: Baker, 1977), 31, on Ps 6:1(2):

> Such a petition, while it indicates a strong faith, at the same time recognises the connection between suffering and sin. In the very act of asking for relief, the psalmist owns that he is justly punished. This may serve to teach us how far the confident tone of the preceding psalms is from betraying a self-righteous spirit, or excluding the consciousness of personal unworthiness and ill-desert. The boldness there displayed is not that of self-reliance, but of faith.

[31]See above, n. 27, where it was noted that prayers for healing were apparently offered along fixed (liturgical) lines, thus presupposing that these confessions and petitions were the *expected* response of the sufferer. Cf. also Seybold, *Sickness and Healing*, 43–44.

[32]In contrast, Job's agonized laments quickly became searching accusations. On this aspect of "piety," cf. below, 3.3.2.2.

[33]On the difficulty of separating these two concepts, cf. Smith, *Early History*; Dearman, *Religion and Culture*; see also above, 2.1, n. 13, and cf. R. Albertz, *Persönliche Frömmigkeit und offizielle Religion* (Stuttgart: Calwer, 1978). According to Niehr's construction, "JHWH als Arzt," 14–15, Yahweh originally was just one of the various family deities who could be consulted for healing; later, through official religious circles, Yahweh-worship was merged with worship of the solar deity, hence reinforcing his healing role. (For the question of solar imagery in Yahweh worship, see below, 4.2.2, to Mal. 4:2[3:20].)

[34]According to Kraus, *Psalms 1–59*, 161, "It is hardly possible to date the psalm"; nonetheless, its formulaic nature makes its association with the temple cult (and hence, with "official Israelite religion") likely. For a general study, cf. H. C. Knuth, *Zur Auslegungsgeschichte von Psalm 6* (Tübingen: Mohr, 1971).

[35]Cf. the words of Kraus, cited above, 3.1; see also Delitzsch, *Psalms*, 130.

[36]Cf. A. Murray, *Divine Healing* (repr. Fort Washington, Pa.: Christian Literature Crusade, n.d.), 100–101, who observed in his practical, pastoral teaching:

> It is not that the one who is sick is necessarily a greater sinner than another who is in health. On the contrary, it is often the most holy among the children of God whom He chastens .... The first step which the sick one has to take in the path of divine healing will be, therefore, to let the Holy Spirit of God probe his heart and convince him of sin, after which will come, also, humiliation, decision to break with sin, and confession.

For discussion of "sinning in ignorance" in the OT and ancient Near East, cf. esp. Walton, *Ancient Israelite Literature*, 151–56 (with literature); N. Kiuchi, *The Purification Offering in the Priestly Literature* (JSOTSup 56; Sheffield: JSOT, 1987; see the discussion there on *šᵉgāgâ*, e.g., 26); J. Milgrom, "The Cultic *Šᵉgāgâ* and Its Influence in Psalms and Job," *JQR* 58 (1967): 73–79; idem, *Leviticus 1–16*, 228ff.; Hartley, *Leviticus*, 58ff. Cf. also Oswalt, *Isaiah 1–39*, 687, who notes with reference to Isa 38, "Whatever may have been Hezekiah's spiritual condition, the truth may be affirmed that a sense of unforgiven sin is a killer which often bars the way to physical and emotional healing. The corollary of this truth is that the confidence that our sins are buried in the sea of God's grace is frequently the key to healing in these areas (Ps. 103:3, 4)." See also below, 3.1.9.

[37]As opposed to demonic attack or the stroke of another, hostile deity; cf. above, 1.2.1, and below, 3.3.2.1 and 5.3.1. As noted by Allen, *Psalms 101–150*, 14 (re: Ps 102), "A strong sense of providence combined with monotheism compelled Israel to trace suffering directly back to Yahweh." Cf. also Seybold's observation, "All 'theology of sickness' in ancient Israel proceeded on

the basis of the *solus* Yahweh, and saw Yahweh's providence in the situation of the sick person" (*Sickness and Healing*, 96).

[38]If no sin was involved, then this would be an example of an unhealthy *monism*, not a healthy *monotheism*; cf. the monograph of Lindström, *God and the Origin of Evil*, cited in the discussion to Dt 32:39, above, 2.2.5. (This stands in marked contrast to the perceived arbitrariness of the Mesopotamian gods; cf. Walton, *Ancient Israelite Literature*, 152, citing Mowinckel.) Craigie, *Psalms 1–50*, 92, suggested that "the psalmist first prays that God not be angry with him for raising a problem, namely his sickness, for which God may have a good reason." However, it is foreign to the general biblical teaching on sickness and disease (see above, 2.2.2) to suggest that God "may have a good reason" for sending sickness on one of his servants *even when no disobedience is involved*, while it is absolutely untenable to suggest that God might pour out *his wrath* on one of his obedient servants. In any event, it seems that Craigie was not entirely happy with the equation that sickness often resulted from sin; cf. ibid., 321 (on Ps 41:4[5]): "In the sick person's mind, the sin and sickness appear to be interrelated. In reality, there may have been no interrelationship; that is the advent of sickness was not necessarily a direct consequence of sin." He does, however, continue: "But the words of the prayer are nevertheless entirely appropriate, for full healing must encompass both body and soul."

[39]According to Delitzsch, *Psalms*, 131–32, "David, like Jeremiah (ch. x. 24), does not pray for the removal of the chastisement, but of the chastisement *in wrath*, or what is the same thing, of the judgment proceeding from wrath [*Zorngericht*]." (Note that Jer 10:24, cited by Delitzsch, is a fitting parallel.) Cf. also Spurgeon, *Treasury of David*, 1/1:56, "If thou remindest me of my sin, it is good; but, oh, remind me not of it as one incensed against me, lest thy servant's heart should sink in despair." See also Ps 143:2, "Do not bring your servant into judgment, for no one living is righteous before you."

[40]Cf. H. Schmidt, *Die Psalmen* (Tübingen: Mohr, 1934), 10–11.

[41]H. E. Sigerist, *Civilization and Disease*, 66.

[42]Cf. Seybold, *Sickness and Healing*, 45–47, discussed below. E. Gerstenberger, *Psalms Part 1*, 63, makes reference to "an unjust society that ignores the weak." See, however, idem and W. Schrage, *Suffering*, trans. John E. Steely (Nashville: Abingdon, 1980), 122–25.

[43]Sigerist, *Civilization and Disease*, 67. Cf. below, 3.1.6.

[44]Speaking of the sufferings brought about by the 1651 plague in Barcelona, Miquel Parets observed:

> I say that it is quite right to flee in order not to suffer from this disease, for it is most cruel, but it is just as right to flee in order not to witness the travails and misfortunes and privations that are suffered wherever the plague is found, which are more than any person can stand. One saw that whenever anyone fell sick he lost all touch with friends and relatives, as there was no one who would risk contact with him, just the person nursing him. And it would have to be someone very close or related to him who would dare to take care of him, like a wife to a hus-

band or a mother to a son or a sister to a brother, and even among these many fled or did not want to stay, for the plague was so evil and of such a bad sort that everyone fled. (Amelang, *A Journal of the Plague Year*, 59)

[45]Of course, not *all* sickness was perceived as a direct judgment because of sin. However, whenever sickness *followed* a specific sin, it was definitely perceived as judgment; thus sin plus wrath equals serious sickness. For further discussion, see below, 3.3.1, 3.3.3, 6.1.4.

[46]Kraus, *Psalms 1–59*, 412. Sigerist, *Civilization and Disease*, 68, calls the view that disease is a punishment for sin "a concept of pitiless logic and of the clearest simplicity." See above, nn. 22 and 38, with reference to the views of Craigie on Pss 6 and 41.

[47]For the relationship between forgiveness and healing, cf. Seybold, *Sickness and Healing*, 64; and below, 3.1.9; 4.1.4 (to Isa 53); 5.3.2. For representative statements from nineteenth- and twentieth-century adherents of divine healing cf., e.g., Murray, *Divine Healing*, 1–5, 99–102; Bosworth, *Christ the Healer*, 14–39; J. Wimber with K. Springer, *Power Healing* (San Francisco: Harper & Row, 1987), 74–76. For caveats—not all of which are well taken—cf. below, 5.3.2.

[48]Kraus, *Psalms 1–59*, 353, n. 5b, suggests that literally, one would have to translate, "Indeed, only briefly (does he act) in his wrath, but for a lifetime in his grace." Craigie, *Psalms 1–50*, 250, renders, "For his anger is death, but in his favor is life," following Dahood's interpretation of *rega'* suggested initially by its parallelism with "life" (*ḥayyîm*); see 251, n. 6.a. This is attractive; however, to date, it has not been buttressed with sufficient philological support to merit acceptance.

[49]If the sufferings described in Ps 32 are to be taken literally, as seems likely (see vv. 3–4, "When I kept silent, my bones wasted away through my groaning all day long. For day and night your hand was heavy upon me; my strength was sapped as in the heat of summer," and cf. Seybold, *Das Gebet*, 159–63; H. Schmidt, cited in Kraus, *Psalms 1–59*, 368; note, however, Craigie, *Psalms 1–50*, 266–67), then one should assume that the forgiveness celebrated in vv. 1–2, 5 was manifest in the psalmist's healing. Cf. the discussion to Ps 41, below; n. 51 below.

[50]Craigie, *Psalms 1–50*, 254. Cf. Murray, *Divine Healing*, 102: "When the soul has consented to make a sincere confession and has obtained pardon, it is ready to lay hold of the promise of God; it is no longer difficult to believe that the Lord will raise him up." See also below, 3.1.9.

[51]While there is no question that almost all of the descriptions here of physical pain and suffering are to be interpreted literally, in some cases they may serve as metaphors for psychological suffering as well. On the relation between the two, cf. Alexander, *The Psalms*, 31; see below, 3.2.3.

[52]More accurately, "soundness," or even "wholeness"; see the discussion of *mᵉtōm*, above, 0.3.3.

[53]See previous note.

[54]See the discussion in Davies and Allison, *Matthew 1–7*, 635–37 (with extensive references to primary Jewish and ancient sources), on the intromission theory of sight (i.e., that "light enters the body through the eye"—universally adopted in the West only for about the last 500 years) vs. the extramission theory (i.e., "that the eye contains its own light," representing the biblical, nonscientific outlook).

[55]Tate, *Psalms 51–100*, 196, notes: "The apparently terminal situation has produced great grief for the suppliant, expressed in the weariness of crying and the dry throat of the one terrified, plus the dimmed vision of the exhausted and sick (v. 4)."

[56]For *ḥopšî*, cf. above, 2.3.1, n. 206, with further discussion in Tate, ibid., 396, n. 6a, 402.

[57]The suggestion of Dahood to connect Hebrew *škh* here with Ugaritic *ṯkḥ*, in the sense of "waste, wither" (*Psalms 101–150*, 11–12, with reference to his earlier treatments), is problematic, both contextually (cf. Allen, *Psalms 101–150*, 9, n. 5.b), as well as philologically, since the Ugaritic evidence is open to dispute (cf. *HALAT* 4:1381–82, *sub škḥ* II; J. J. M. Roberts, "*niškaḥtî . . . millēb*, Ps XXXI 13," *VT* 25 [1975]: 797–801).

[58]Cf. Ps 69:12, "Those who sit at the gate mock me, and I am the song of the drunkards," and cf. again Tate, *Psalms 51–100*, 192: "The status of the speaker is so Job-like (cf. Job 19) that it has become the talk of those in the gate and the subject of the drunkards' songs."

[59]E. W. Hengstenberg, *Commentary on the Psalms*, Part One (bound as *The Works of Hengstenberg, 5*; reprint with no information as to translator or original publication and date; Cherry Hill, N.J.: Mack Pub. House, n.d.), 486.

[60]Of particular importance are the words *r^{e}pā'â napšî* (lit., but incorrectly, "heal my soul"), followed by "for I have *sinned*," as opposed to "for I am *sick*." Thus, the requested "healing" was incorrectly equated with forgiveness of sins alone, while the principle that confession of the sin, which was viewed as the *cause* of the sickness, would bring about healing of the body, was missed. Of course, physical healing presupposed spiritual reconciliation (cf. below, 3.1.9, on Ps 103), and thus the request for "healing" encompassed both; cf. especially below, 5.3.2.

[61]Cf. Keil on 2Ch. 30:20, cited above, 2.3.4, n. 291. Alexander, while recognizing that a bodily disease was in question in Ps 41, still proceeded from an incorrect understanding here of *nepeš* (*The Psalms*, 184): "The prayer for the healing of his soul may be considered as including that for the removal of his bodily disease, which seems to be referred to in this psalm as a mere consequence of inward agony." Similarly, the comment of the medieval rabbinic exegete David Kimchi is correct in terms of the connection in the psalmist's mind between sin and sickness; however, it also too literally interprets *nepeš*: "He says, 'Heal my soul,' and not, 'Heal my body,' because the reason for his sickness is his sins, and if God heals the soul of its sicknesses—i.e., atoning for [its] sins—the body will be healed."

[62]In a different context, some have argued that the prophetic descriptions of personal grief and horror (such as Isa 21:3–4; Jer 4:19) should not be

interpreted too closely, since they reflected standardized, common, ancient Near Eastern expressions. However, these very expressions presuppose or reflect certain types of behavior and emotional reaction, and thus, should not be interpreted so as to *exclude* those very expressions of shock and dismay.

[63]Anderson, *Psalms 73–150*, 706.

[64]Tate, *Psalms 51–100*, 399. With reference to Ps 88 he notes: "There is no difficulty in associating the psalm with serious and chronic (v 16) illness, but the metaphorical backdrop is wider than sickness and can encompass any severe distress or life-threatening situation (see *Form/Structure/Setting* of Ps 69)." See ibid., 401.

[65]Added to this spatial limitation, of course, was the *feeling* of alienation from God.

[66]Kraus, *Psalms 1–59*, 161. Cf. Seybold, *Sickness and Healing*, 44: "As has been shown, the psalms do speak about sickness and healing and not just about suffering of a general nature."

[67]The fact that these physical sufferings were almost always accompanied by (or even caused by!) spiritual and mental anguish only adds to the overall picture. It does not diminish the physical realities. Cf. Job 2:13b, "No one said a word to him, because they saw how great his suffering [*kᵉʾēb*; lit., "pain"] was." Cf. BDB, 456: "כְּאֵב," "*pain*, mental and physical" (citing here Job 2:13; 16:6; as well as, possibly, Ps 39:3).

[68]See above, 2.2.6; cf. J. J. Pilch, "Healing in Mark: A Social Science Analysis," *BTB* 15 (1985): 142–50; idem, "The Health Care System in Matthew: A Social Science Analysis," *BTB* 16 (1986): 102–6, for the sociological impact of serious illness in the world of the NT.

[69]K. van der Toorn, *Sin and Sanction in Israel and Mesopotamia*, 62–67 (cited by Walton, *Ancient Israelite Literature*, 144, n. 33), finds the four major subjects of laments in Israel and Mesopotamia to be physical suffering, social adversity, divine disapproval, and mental discomfort. Of course, these are often interrelated.

[70]Craigie (*Psalms 1–50*, 319) and others interpret vv. 1–3(2–4) as the "introductory words of the priests," presumably spoken by the priest at the bedside of the sick. For further discussion, see below, 3.1.11.

[71]While there is some dispute as to the exact meaning of *hapakta* (NIV "restore"), the significance of "sickbed" (*ʿereś dᵉwāy*) and "bed of illness" (*ḥolyô*, lit., "his illness") is clear, with both *dᵉwāy* and *ḥolî* belonging to the OT vocabulary of sickness (cf. above, 0.4, and see, e.g., Dt 7:15, 28:60–61). For discussion of the second person *hāpaktā* (lit., "you overturned, reversed, changed"; a third person verb would have been expected, but there is little textual support for this), cf. Craigie, *Psalms 1–50*, 320, who suggests "the metaphor is that of God the nurse, who constantly changes the bedclothes and provides the sick person with some comfort and consolation." Most translations (cf. NJV's tentative rendering: "You shall wholly transform his bed of suffering") understand *hpk* to refer to a changing of the sick person's *condition*, as opposed to the changing of the sickbed itself. Cf., however, v. 3a(4a), where the Lord supports the sufferer on his sickbed.

[72]The Hebrew, *dābār bᵉliya'al*, is literally, "a vile, base thing"; for *bᵉliya'al*, cf. below, n. 253.

[73]As could be expected, the ancient versions render the expression with "heal my soul" or the like. Kraus, however, notes, that *nepeš* here "does not denote the 'soul' but weak, frail life which is in need of healing" (*Psalms 1–59*, 432). See further idem, *Theology of the Psalms*; trans. K. Crim (Minneapolis: Augsburg, 1986), 145 (for discussion of the *nepeš* as the totality of the person, hence, "I, me"), and more fully, Wolff, *Anthropology*, 10–25.

[74]Seybold, *Sickness and Healing*, 46, 95. Note, however, 95: "Perhaps all this looked totally different in daily life. The official theology, however, all the way into the Hellenistic period, was not able to develop a positive relationship with medicine (cf., however, Sir. 38)."

[75]This, of course, is not to deny that there *was* access to certain "forbidden" medical practices (as discussed above, 1.2.2.3). However, since Israel apparently did not develop the type of medical "science" attested in Egypt and Mesopotamia (see above, 1.2.1), Seybold's emphasis on the lack of medical alternatives available seems well taken. Nonetheless, as indicated by Job 13:4 (*rōpᵉ'ê 'ᵉlîl*), even ancient Israel must have had its share of medical "practitioners," including "quacks" of proverbial fame.

[76]Cf. Bosworth (*Christ the Healer*, 62–79), commenting on Ps 145:8–9, for the relationship between compassion and healing; also see below, 5.2.4.

[77]Of course, there are many beautiful, panegyric descriptions of the other "gods" of the ancient world as well; one classic example out of many would be the Babylonian Hymn to Shamash (see *BWL*, 121–38). The question is, did worshiping the sun *really* help the worshiper? The prophets of Israel would surely say, "No!"

[78]See especially Seybold, *Sickness and Healing*, 94–96; note p. 94, "The social situation of the sick person in Old Testament times was lamentable." Cf. also idem, "Krankheit und Heilung: Soziale Apekte in dem Psalmen."

[79]Kraus, *Psalms 1–59*, 53.

[80]If one argues that the sufferer's sickness presupposed his sin, hence requiring rites of expiation and cleansing, that still would not preclude his presence in the sanctuary. Why could not the sick person come at the very outset of the illness or in the midst of the illness, when, presumably, private prayers of repentance and petitions for mercy had already been offered?

[81]See above, n. 17.

[82]In contrast, clear restrictions are given regarding the priests; cf. Lev 21:16–23; 22:4 (see 21:23, "because of his defect, he must not go near the curtain or approach the altar and so desecrate my sanctuary. I am the LORD who makes them holy").

[83]Craigie, *Psalms 1–50*, 320. With regard to Ps 41, however, it might be objected that, in this case, the sufferer was bedfast and hence *not* able to go to the temple (cf. vv. 3, 8, 10 [4, 9, 11]); thus, the opening words of the psalm would have been spoken at the patient's bedside. See below, 3.1.11.

[84]Note Seybold, *Sickness and Healing*, 47: "The recovered person would generally set out to regain his integrity at the holy place and let it be publicly

affirmed, an integrity that, within the guilt-punishment system of thought, had apparently been endangered or lost." See also his comment (47) on *ṣᵉdāqâ* ("salvation") in Job 33:26.

[85]For summary and discussion of the "enemies" in the Psalms (with ample bibliography), cf. Kraus, *Psalms 1–59*, 95–99; idem, *Theology*, 125–36; Tate, *Psalms 51–100*, 60–64. For relevant sociological observations, see Gerstenberger, *Psalms* I, 30–34; Keel, *Symbolism of the Biblical World*, 78–100; R. Gordis, *The Book of God and Man* (Chicago: Univ. of Chicago Press, 1956), 135–56; Jakobovits, *Jewish Medical Ethics*, 1.

[86]Note the discussion, above, 2.2.2, 2.2.5, 2.3.1; cf. J. Z. Baruch, "The Relation Between Sin and Disease in the Old Testament," *Hanas: Revue internationale de l'histoire des sciences* 5 (1964): 295–302; see also below. 5.3.2.

[87]Seybold, *Sickness and Healing*, 95.

[88]So, e.g., Allen, *Psalms 101–150*, 18, 3.b. (on Ps 103:3); see the discussion above, 3.1.4 (on Ps 6). Similar statements are commonplace but have now been challenged in a major new monograph by F. Lindström, *Suffering and Sin: Interpretations of Illness in the Individual Complaint Psalms* (*CB*, OTS 37; Stockholm: Almqvist & Wiksell, 1994), which arrived too late to be considered here in detail. However, in spite of important contributions that his study certainly makes, his overall argument has at least three fundamental flaws and must therefore be rejected. (1) He is forced to rely on major reconstructions of the text, since many of the psalms in their current form clearly *do* see sickness as the direct result of disobedience and sin. Thus Lindström must claim that the various psalms in their original *Gattung*—i.e., before being expanded by later, theologically motivated editors—saw no certain connection between suffering and sin; see, e.g., his treatment of Ps 41 (298–323). (2) The covenantal backdrop of blessings for obedience and curses for disobedience, which by any dating of the relevant texts must surely have influenced some of the material in question, is virtually ignored. (3) The wisdom dictum that godliness leads to life while wickedness leads to death is not adequately factored into the discussion. For interaction with Lindström's previous monograph on denying monism in the OT, cf. above, especially 2.2.5.

[89]Cf. R. Dewey, "Qoheleth and Job: Diverse Responses to the Enigma of Evil," *Spirituality Today* 37 (1985): 314–25.

[90]Cf. above 2.2.1, 2.2.5, 2.3, and below, 3.2.1.

[91]Contrast, e.g., Ps 44, which, in my view, must be interpreted as the intercessory prayer of the righteous remnant on behalf of the nation. Normally, prophetic intercession took upon itself the guilt of the people (e.g., Ezr 9:6–15; Ne 1:5–7; Da 9:4–19). In the case of Ps 44, the reverse seems to be true; i.e., the psalmist pleads for the nation based on the righteousness of the remnant, who, in fact, suffered the same terrible fate as did the people as a whole. Cf. Craigie, *Psalms 1–50*, 334–35, who clearly senses the problem—apparently a breach in covenant theology!—without coming to the solution proposed here.

[92]Cf. Tate, *Psalms 51–100*, 22.

[93]Cf. Lev 19:14 and Dt 27:18, both of which demand that the handicapped *not* be taken advantage of or mocked; note the exemplary behavior of which Job boasts: "I was eyes to the blind and feet to the lame" (Job 29:15; in v. 16, the underprivileged whom Job aided are the "needy" and "stranger"). For further discussion of "the blind and the lame," see below, 4.2.2, n. 163.

[94]Cf. above, ch. 2, nn. 87 and 220, for interaction with the position of Masters.

[95]Seybold, *Sickness and Healing*, 46, identified three classes of "hostile parties": "the false friend, the hypocritical visitor and acquaintance, and the group of enemies 'abroad' whose talk and plans the sick person hears." Cf. also Keel, *Symbolism*, 78–100, for a list of the potential enemies of the individual.

[96]Cf. Tate, above, n. 58, on Ps 69:12; cf. Ps 102:8(9).

[97]Cf. L. R. Fisher, "Betrayed by Friends," *Int* 18 (1964): 20–38, for further dimensions of the problem.

[98]Some could even be rejected by their own families; cf. Ps 69:8; also Job 19:13–19.

[99]Again, this contrasts with the behavior of the false friends: "But when I stumbled, they gathered in glee; attackers gathered against me when I was unaware. They slandered me without ceasing" (Ps 35:15).

[100]For discussion of text and translation, cf. Tate, *Psalms 51–100*, 190–91, 199; see BHS.

[101]Cf. also Job 6:14 (with commentaries); 16:4–5; 42:11 (although this consolation comes *after* Job's restoration).

[102]The psalmist laments in 38:11: "My friends and companions avoid me because of my wounds; my neighbors stay far away." This, however, need not be related to religious compunctions, but rather to the fickle nature of human beings, who often find serious or disfiguring illness to be so repulsive that they shun the sufferer, even if it be a friend. Moreover, people sometimes avoid those seriously ill because, quite simply, they do not know what to say. The fact that rabbinic Judaism developed detailed guidelines for when to visit the sick, how long to stay, what to say, etc., testifies to the importance as well as the potential difficulties involved in showing solidarity with the sick; cf. "בִקּוּר חוֹלִים," *Talmudic Encyclopedia* (Hebrew; Jerusalem: Talmudic Encyclopedia Inst., 1947–), 4:158–62. Craigie, *Psalms 1–50*, 305, observes, "The foundations of life, in Hebrew theology, rested upon two fundamental relationships, the first with God and the second with fellow human beings. Disease, in its promulgation, began to undermine these two relationships," as the sufferer was (experientially) forsaken by God and other humans.

[103]Nonetheless, Sigerist, *Civilization and Disease*, 69 (see above, 1.4.2, end), is correct in emphasizing that it was only with the advent of the healing ministry of Jesus that radically positive developments ensued in the treatment of, solidarity with, and care for the sick.

[104]This may be described as the "relative righteousness" of the sufferer: guilty before God (38:4–5, 18; 41:4; 69:5), yet more righteous than the former friends/present enemies (38:19–20; 41:10–12; 69:4); cf. also Ps 18:16–27

(17–28); see Kraus, *Psalms 1–59*, 262–63, for a refutation of the idea that the psalmist in Ps 18 is guilty in the verses cited of a "'Deuteronomistic,' if not even a Jewish-nomistic, relapse into all kinds of self-righteous reflections."

[105]See also Isa 38:3, where Hezekiah pleads with the Lord for healing, appealing to his former, godly life, whereas in v. 17c he makes reference to his sins, apparently in direct relation to his sickness.

[106]In the Psalms, as throughout the OT, "sinners" (*ḥōṭᵉ'îm*) are synonymous with "the wicked" (*rᵉšā'îm*); as such they are the enemies of God (cf., e.g., Ps 1:1, 4–6; Jn 9:31).

[107]In Ps 41:10(11), the psalmist asks to be raised up so that *he* might repay his foes. Kraus, *Psalms 1–59*, 432–33, however, makes a good case for the understanding that "the 'retribution' must consist of the thought that the slanderers may through the saving intervention of Yahweh be revealed as *rš'ym* and may in shame and disgrace suffer a judgment of God to come over them."

[108]In some traditions, the Ḥubur River was thought of as the river by which the underworld was reached (see Black and Green, *Gods, Demons and Symbols*, 155), comparable to Greek mythology's Styx and, based on Job 33:18; 36:12 (cf. the NIV's marginal renderings), Hebrew *šelaḥ*; for discussion (with references also to Ugaritic *šlḥ*), cf. L. L. Grabbe, *Comparative Philology and the Text of Job: A Study in Methodology* (SBLDS 34; Missoula, Mont.: Scholars, 1977), 103–4; J. E. Hartley, *The Book of Job* (NICOT; Grand Rapids: Eerdmans, 1988), 441, n. 9; *HALAT* 4:1405–6 (*šelaḥ* IV).

[109]For a classic juxtapositioning of these two aspects of divine power, cf. Jn 11, especially vv. 21–27.

[110]Lambert, "The Gula Hymn of Bulluṭsa-Rābi," 128–29.

[111]See the illuminating material collected by Keel, *Symbolism of the Biblical World*, 62–109; cf. Anderson, *Psalms 1–72*, 241: "Sheol was not so much a geographical location as a sphere of influence: wherever one finds the characteristics of Sheol, such as weakness, disease, misery, forsakenness, etc., there is Sheol also."

[112]Cf. Ac 2:24; also Ps 89:48b ("the power of the grave [Sheol]"); 55:4b(5b) ("the terrors of death assail me"); cf. further M. H. Pope, *The Song of Songs* (AB; Garden City, N.Y.: Doubleday, 1977), 668–75; Kraus, *Theology*, 167: "In Israel the aggressive power of Sheol was depicted with an unprecedented challenge to the imagination." Cf. also Barth, *Die Erreitung vom Tode*, 93ff., regarding the concept that "anyone who even to the slightest degree has entered in to the realm of Sheol is totally within its power" (Kraus, ibid., 166). For recent discussion of Sheol (with bibliography), cf. G. Gerleman, "שְׁאוֹל, Totenreich," *THAT* 2:837–41; L. Wächter, "שְׁאוֹל," *TWAT* 7:902–10; *HALAT* 4:1274–75. More broadly, cf. N. J. Tromp, *Primitive Conceptions of Death and the Netherworld in the Old Testament* (Rome: Pontifical Biblical Institute Press, 1969), with Assyriological strictures from W. von Soden, "Assyriologische Erwägungen zu einem neuen Buch über die Totenreichvorstellungen im Alten Testament," *UF* 2 (1970), 331–32.

[113]Cf. Tate, *Psalms 51–100*, 194 (to Ps 69): "The speaker is sinking down into the watery depths, as in the great cosmic sea, down to the netherworld of the dead"; Anderson, *Psalms 1–72* (to Ps 40): "even one who is ill is already in the process of being overwhelmed by the deep waters of the netherworld...." The "Spheres of Death" treated by Keel, *Symbolism of the Biblical World*, 62–78, are: the Grave; Prison, Cistern and Pitfall; Torrent and Sea; the Desert; and the Night.

[114]Most of the verses cited here seem to be in the context of serious illness; for similar images with definite reference to earthly foes, cf. Ps 124:4–5 (where the floodwaters speak of the wrath of Israel's enemies); 144:7 (where "the mighty waters" is in parallelism to "the hands of foreigners"). It is true that Jnh 2:2–9(3–10), Jonah's prayer from the belly of the fish, is patterned after the typical language of the psalms of deliverance from imminent death; cf. H. W. Wolff, *Obadiah and Jonah*, trans. M. Kohl (Minneapolis: Augsburg, 1986), 128–29; L. C. Allen, *Joel, Obadiah, Jonah and Micah* (NICOT; Grand Rapids: Eerdmans, 1976), 182, where it is also observed that "the 'drowning' vocabulary is a standard metaphor for deliverance from any plight." However, some of the expressions (e.g., v. 5c[6c], "seaweed was wrapped around my head") clearly go beyond the norm, hence indicating their specific composition or adaptation for the unique context of Jonah's ordeal; cf. J. D. Magonet, "Form and Meaning: Studies in Literary Techniques in the Book of Jonah" (Dissertation; Heidelberg, 1973); G. M. Landes, "The Kerygma of the Book of Jonah," *Int* 21 (1967): 3–31. See also Johnson, "Jonah ii, 3–10: A Study in Cultic Phantasy."

[115]The psalmist's persistence in prayer is underscored by the infinitive absolute in v. 1a(2a), *qawwōh qiwwêtî yhwh*, rendered by the NIV as "I waited patiently for the LORD." The phrase *wayyēṭ 'ēlāy* in v. 1b(2b) should probably be understood as a misvocalization of *wayyaṭ 'ēlāy*, short for *wayyaṭ 'oznô 'ēlāy*, "he inclined his ear to me" (cf. Rashi, although his comment makes one wonder if his text did, in fact, read *wayyaṭ* and not *wayyeṭ*). However, *wayyeṭ* may be correct, in which case NIV's "he turned to me" (cf. KJV) is fine, although NEB's vivid "he bent down to me" and NAB's "he stooped toward me" (highlighting God's amazing condescension, for which cf. Ps 113:4–9; Isa 57:15) are possible.

[116]With different metaphors, but similar language, cf. Ps 140:10(11), regarding the final end of the wicked.

[117]Cf. Anderson, *Psalms 1–72*, 334, on 42:9, who suggests, "It is not improbable that the present usage [of God as Rock] contained an implicit contrast to the mire and waters of the underworld (cf. Driver, *CML*, p. 103a)." For the broader applications of God as rock, refuge, and fortress, cf. Keel, *Symbolism of the Biblical World*, 179–83; see Ps 18:2a(3a), "The LORD is my rock, my fortress and my deliverer; my God is my rock, in whom I take refuge," in the context of deliverance from foes.

[118]For "going down to the pit" (*y-r-d bōr*), cf. Isa 38:18; Eze 26:20 (*bis*); 31:14; 32:18, 24–25, 29–30; Ps 28:1; 85:4(5); 143:7; Pr 1:12. For the meaning and etymology of *šaḥat*, also rendered "pit" (cf. Isa 38:17, with *šaḥat b*ᵉ*lî*),

see M. Held, "Pits and Pitfalls in Akkadian and Biblical Hebrew," *JANESCU* 5 (1973): 173–90; cf. further Tromp, *Primitive Conceptions*, 19, 33, 67, 69–71; *HALAT* 4:1365–66; and the articles on שְׁאוֹל by Gerleman and Wächter, cited above, n. 112.

[119]Cf. Barth, *Die Erretung von Tode*, 124ff.

[120]According to Kraus, *Theology*, 166, the "pit" (*bōr*) here refers to that "which has been dug for the corpse." Others (e.g., Anderson, *Psalms 1–72*, 241) understand *bōr* here to be synonymous with Sheol. On being "spared from going down into the pit," cf. below on Job 33:24 (3.3.2.4); see also Pss 16:9–11; 49:5–15(6–16).

[121]For discussion of the textual difficulties in MT, cf. *BHS*; Tate, *Psalms 51–100*, 210.

[122]The Hebrew is literally "making the bed swim," viz., with tears; Craigie, *Psalms 1–50*, 90, renders: "Every night, I soak my bed, I dissolve my couch with tears."

[123]For dimensions of this concept, cf. the important study of D. J. A. Clines, "The Image of God in Man," *TynBul* 19 (1968): 53–103; see also the treatments (with bibliography) in Westermann, *Genesis 1–11*, 147–60; Wenham, *Genesis 1–15*, 26–32; Matthews, *Genesis 1–17*, 132–38. See also Johnson, *The Vitality of the Individual in the Thought of Ancient Israel*.

[124]For the association of light with life and darkness with death, see Job 33:30 (note the expression *'ōr haḥayyîm*, "the light of life"); Ps 36:9(10) (cf. also Jn 1:4); Ps 56:13(14); and contrast the description of Sheol in Job 10:21–22: "before I go to the place of no return, to the land of gloom and deep shadow, to the land of deepest night, of deep shadow and disorder, where even the light is like darkness." (Gordis, *The Book of Job*, 116, notes that Milton, in *Paradise Lost*, "intuitively grasped the sense of our passage: 'The light in that region is no light, but rather darkness visible.'") See further S. Aalen, "אוֹר," *TDOT* 1:147–67 (esp. 154); H. Ringgren, et al., "חָשַׁךְ," *TDOT* 5:245–59 (esp. 255–56, where it is demonstrated that darkness "becomes a poetic name for Sheol").

[125]Cf. Craigie, *Psalms 1–50*, 95: "In sickness, the body does not function properly; in death it ceases to function altogether. Thus it is that the psalms conceived on the sickbed are marked by a profound sense of pathos, for though they contain the words of the living, they are haunted by the shadow of dying." Cf. also the concept of "sickness unto [or, not unto] death" in Jn 11:4.

[126]Cf. Johnson, "Jonah ii. 3–10," 85ff. According to S. P. Raphael, *Jewish Views of the Afterlife* (Northvale, N.J.: Jason Aronson, 1994), 56, "Life and death were seen as poles of a continuum of vital energy. In life, the energy, or *nefesh*, was dynamically present; in sickness, it was weakened; and in death, there was a maximum loss of vitality. As Johs. Pederson puts it: 'Life and death are not sharply distinguished spheres, because they do not mean existence or nonexistence. Life was something which one possesses in a higher or lower degree. If afflicted by misfortune, illness, or something else . . . then one has only little life, but all the more death. He who is ill or other-

wise in distress may say that he is dead, and when he recovers, he is pulled out of death' (*Israel* 1:153)."

[127]Von Rad, *Old Testament Theology* 1:369, cited in Kraus, *Theology*, 165; see also below, 3.1.7.

[128]See Pss 13:1(2); 88:5(6). A. A. Anderson, *Psalms 1–72*, 241, commenting on Ps 30:3(4), notes that the phrase "restored me to life" means "to a full life or existence which is not marked by God-forsakenness (the essence of Sheol-existence)." In light of the verses that indicate Sheol lies open before the Lord (cf. Ps 139:8; Pr 15:11), Kidner, *Psalms 1–72* (TOTC; Downers Grove, Ill.: InterVarsity, 1973), 62, is correct in explaining the concept that God no longer remembers the dead (88:5[6]) as meaning, "He brings to an end His saving interventions (88:12; for with God to remember is to act: *cf.*, *e.g.*, Gn. 8:1; 30:22)."

[129]Kraus, *Theology*, 166. Cf. Craigie, *Psalms 1–50*, 253 ("he had been so close to death that it was as if he were already dead").

[130]Cf. especially Barth, *Die Erreitung vom Tode*.

[131]For related concepts, cf. H. Birkeland, "The Belief in the Resurrection of the Dead in the Old Testament," *ST* 3 (1949), 60ff. It is interesting that although Hebrew *rāpā'* was used with reference to healing the terminally ill—and thus, in the sense indicated above, already "dead"—the Hebrew language would not tolerate the expression *rôpē' mētîm*. Rather, in later Jewish liturgy, God is extolled as *rôpē' ḥôlîm*, "the one who heals the sick," and *mᵉḥayyeh mētîm*, "the one who gives life to the dead"—the former referring to physical healing and the latter to final resurrection. He is also lauded as *rôpē' ḥayyîm*, "the one who heals the living." Cf. J. Heinemann, *Prayer in the Talmud*, trans. R. S. Sarason (Berlin: De Gruyter, 1977), 58, 98, 101, 160.

[132]Although virtually all NT reflection will be postponed until chs. 5 and 6, there are certain elements germane to the present subheading that are best discussed here, especially since they are not among the main points that will be treated in ch. 5.

[133]For a recent survey with discussion of earlier literature, cf. Spronk, *Beatific Afterlife*; E. Bloch-Smith, *Judahite Burial Practices and Beliefs About the Dead* (Sheffield: JSOT Press, 1993); cf. also L. R. Bailey, Sr., *Biblical Perspectives on Death* (OBT; Philadelphia: Fortress, 1979), and the concise survey (with ample bibliography) in VanGemeren, "Psalms," 560–73 ("Sheol-Grave-Death in the Psalms"). For arguments in favor of belief in an afterlife, especially from the Psalms, cf. the frequent remarks of Dahood, *Psalms 1–50, 51–100, 101–150*, many of which need to be balanced (for this, see esp. Craigie, *Psalms 1–50* ; note already E. B. Smick, "Ugaritic and the Theology of the Psalms," in J. B. Payne, ed., *New Perspectives in the Old Testament* [Waco, Tex.: Word, 1970], 105–10); L. Ramaroson, "Immortalité et résurrection dans les Psaumes," *ScEs* 36 (1984): 287–95; B. Vawter, "Intimations of Immortality and the Old Testament," *JBL* 91 (1972): 158–71; L. Bronner, "From Death to Life in Light of the Ugaritic Texts" (Hebrew), *Beth Mikra* 25 (1980): 202–12; T. D. Alexander, "The Psalms and the Afterlife," *IBS* 9 (1987): 2–17. For arguments against interpreting "seeing God" in the Psalms

as referring to life after death, taking issue in particular with the interpretation of key verses in the Psalms, cf. M. S. Smith, "'Seeing God' in the Psalms: The Background to the Beatific Vision in the Hebrew Bible," *CBQ* 50 (1988): 171–83, with reference to the doctoral dissertation of L. Dorn; R. van de Walle, "Death and Beyond in the Sapiential Literature," *Bibelbhashyam* 4 (1978): 312–21. In my judgment, there was some hope of continued *true life* after death (i.e., not just a shadowy semi-existence), along with, at a later time, an expectation of future resurrection; however, this hope was somewhat veiled and, apparently, often distant. The primary emphasis was on this present life. As noted by Oswalt, *Isaiah 1–39*, 688, n. 33, "It is true that intimations of eternal bliss appear (e.g., Ps. 23:6; Isa 26:19, etc.).... But these do not seem to represent developed, consciously held points of view." For a groundbreaking study arguing that both the immortality of the soul and bodily resurrection are concepts native to the Hebrew Bible, cf. J. Barr, *The Garden of Eden and the Hope of Immortality: The Read-Tueckwell Lecture for 1990* (London: SCM, 1992); see also J. Strange, "The Idea of Afterlife in Ancient Israel: Some Remarks on the Iconography in Solomon's Temple," *PEQ* 117 (1985): 35–40.

[134]Cf. the *locus classicus*, Ecc 9:5–6, often cited by modern cults to support the doctrine of "soul sleep." The text, however, is unrelated to speculation concerning the afterlife; its whole concern has to do with matters performed "under the sun," i.e., in this world, during this lifetime (cf. below, 3.4). According to VanGemeren, "Psalms," 99, verses such as those in Ps 6 do not indicate "that the OT denies life after death, but rather it puts the emphasis on the present life as the most important stage in man's relationship with God. The psalmist believes that there is *still* life to live and that there is therefore still time to praise the Creator."

[135]Craigie, *Psalms 1–50*, 96.

[136]Cf. Kraus, *Theology*, 165: "Just as for Old Testament faith, praise is the characteristic mode of life, so too the silencing of praise is characteristic of the realm of death."

[137]For the importance of the temple in Israelite worship, cf. H. H. Rowley, *Worship in Ancient Israel* (Philadelphia: Fortress, 1967), and, more broadly, M. Haran, *Temple and Temple-Service in Ancient Israel: An Inquiry into the Character of Cult Phenomena and the Historical Setting of the Priestly School* (Oxford: Clarendon, 1978); see Rowley for the use of the Psalms in worship; cf. also Mowinckel, *The Psalms in Israel's Worship*, and below, 3.1.11.

[138]Cf. above, 2.3.2.4, n. 250.

[139]Matthew Henry, *Matthew Henry's Commentary on the Whole Bible* (repr. McLean, Va.: MacDonald Pub. Co., n.d.), 3:340.

[140]D. Kidner, *Psalms 1–72*, 129, notes regarding the word *besa'*: "*Profit* is a sharply commercial word here, and the argument is—for the moment—quite down to earth. 'You will gain nothing, and lose a worshiper!'"

[141]NJV renders this as "death," noting that the Hebrew is literally "blood" (cf. Anderson, *Psalms 1–72*, 244). Craigie, *Psalms 1–50*, 250–51, points as

dommî, rendering with "my weeping" (cf. Dahood, *Psalms 1–50*, 183–84, with reference to consonantal *bdmy* in Isa 38:10). I prefer to follow NIV (apparently deriving consonantal *dmy* from *dmh*, "to destroy"), although it is possible that the root in question is actually *dmm*, "to be silent" (hence, "What gain is there in my being silenced?"); cf. Ps 94:17, where the NIV renders *dūmâ* with "the silence of death"; cf. LXX's *to hadē* and Vulgate's *in inferno*. This would work well with 30:12(13): "that my heart may sing to you and not be silent" (*wᵉ lō' yiddōm*).

[142]The clearest expression of this doctrine is found in Eze 18: Those who act righteously will surely live; those who act wickedly will surely die. Cf. also Kaiser, "Exodus," *EBC* 2:447, on Ex 23:25–26.

[143]Cf. 3.1.10, 3.2.1. It was baffling to the author of Ps 73 that the wicked could be so healthy and secure; his tension over this, however, was resolved along the lines of the wisdom of Ps 37: He considered their final end (*'aḥᵃ rît*); cf. 73:16ff. with 37:37–38. For the perspectives of Ecclesiastes and Job, cf. 3.3.1, 3.3.3, 3.4.

[144]For discussion of difficulties in text and translation, cf. the commentaries of J. A. Alexander, F. Delitzsch, O. Kaiser, H. Wildberger, J. D. W. Watts, and J. N. Oswalt, ad loc.

[145]Compare also Ps 102:23–24(24–25), where the afflicted one thought that God had "cut short" (*qiṣṣar*) his days and taken him away "in the midst" (*baḥᵃ sî*; cf. 55:23b[24b]) of his days.

[146]Cf. Johnson, "Jonah ii. 3–10," 98, 102.

[147]It is important to make the distinction between suffering for the cause of the Lord and simply being sick (especially as a result of personal sin or negligence); cf. below, 5.3.3.

[148]According to Johnson, "Jonah ii. 3–10," 94, Yahweh is "nothing if not the 'Living God' and the Giver of Life"; cf. 98ff. (with 98, n. 89, on Yahweh as the "Living God").

[149]Cf. Oswalt, *Isaiah 1–39*, 687–88, for a Christian perspective on the OT concept that "the dead do not praise the LORD"; note also Hengstenberg, *The Psalms*, 3:lxxxii-xc, "The Doctrine of Eternal Life,"and see above, n. 133.

[150]In keeping with Ps 150:6a ("Let everything that has breath praise the LORD"), devoted Christians through the ages have felt it their duty to use virtually every waking hour for divine purposes, seeing that they will have all eternity to enjoy and reap the rewards of their labor, yet one short life to sow in the fields of humanity. Cf. M. L. Brown, *How Saved Are We?* (Shippensburg, Pa.: Destiny Image, 1990), 105–11. George Whitefield, the great eighteenth-century revivalist, said, "It is better to wear out than to rust out," while Henry Martyn, the nineteenth-century Cambridge scholar turned missionary, inscribed in his diary upon arriving in India, "Now let me burn out for God."

[151]See ibid., 105.

[152]Cf. the exegesis of B. F. Westcott, *The Gospel of John* (repr. Grand Rapids: Baker, 1980), 1/2:32–33.

[153]Of course, from a NT perspective, they will, however, have all eternity to *praise* him (cf., e.g., Rev 7:9ff., 22:3–5); see G. A. Smith, *The Book of Isaiah: I-XXXIX* (rev. ed., New York: Harper & Brothers, 1927), 402–6.

[154]J. G. McConville, *Grace in the End*, 149, is correct in pointing out that "the contrast between the OT as 'worldly' and the NT as 'spiritual' is a false one. The OT's theology of creation, according to which God made a 'good' earth and put human beings in it to enjoy it (Ge 1), is never quite lost in the NT." Cf. further, ibid., 145–50; note also the reference to the God "who richly provides us with everything for our enjoyment" in 1Ti 6:17, occurring in a context that warns against the pursuit of earthly riches, urging us to be content with godliness and the basic necessities of life (1Ti 6:6–19).

[155]Again, this is not to deny that some of the great leaders in church history (as well as in both secular and religious history) have been cut down at tender ages. One thinks of shining Christian examples like Henry Martyn (see above, n. 150), who died at 31; Robert Murray M'Cheyne, the Scottish pastor legendary for his piety, taken away in his 30th year; or David Brainerd, famous for his journal and finally overtaken by tuberculosis at the age of 29. In Jewish mysticism there is Isaac Luria, known as the divine Rabbi Isaac (Hebrew, the Ari), fatally stricken at the age of 28; and in world history, need we look beyond Alexander the Great (356–323 B.C.)? Then, of course, there is the most influential life of all, that of Jesus, who gave himself over to death at approximately 33. Clearly, life can not be measured in terms of quantity of years alone. Nonetheless, for the most part—and this is presupposed as the biblical norm—a blessed life is thought of as a long and full one (see below, 3.1.10, 3.3.3). The statement of K. H. Richards, "Death, Old Testament," *ABD* 2:109, summarizes what has been demonstrated elsewhere in this present study: "A 'good' death is portrayed when an individual dies with sufficient offspring and at an old age (Gen 25:8; 46:30)."

[156]Cf. also Ps 11:5, where God "tries [*yibḥan*] the righteous," whereas "the wicked and those who love violence his soul hates." For a rich treatment of Pr 3:11–12, cf. C. Bridges, *Proverbs* (repr. Carlisle, Pa.: Banner of Truth, 1987), 27–31.

[157]It is often observed that the concept of discipline is implied in the reference to the divine Shepherd's rod and staff in Ps 23:3 (one for protection or the shepherd's support, the other to keep sheep from wandering off the path), the presence of which bring comfort and assurance (cf., e.g., Luther; Delitzsch, *Psalms*, KD 5:1/130). Craigie, *Psalms 1–50*, with reference to E. Power, "The Shepherd's Two Rods in Modern Palestine and Some Passages of the Old Testament," *Bib* 9 (1928): 434–42, especially 435, states: "The Palestinian shepherd normally carried two implements, a *club* (or rod) to fend off wild beasts and a *crook* (or staff) to guide and control the sheep." Note also that Yahweh not only leads his sheep into green pastures and beside still waters (v. 1), but in paths of righteousness as well (v. 2), possibly implying disciplinary measures.

[158]The statement of Murray, *Divine Healing*, 111, that "sickness is always a discipline which ought to awaken our attention to sin," is somewhat over-

stated. However, if the word "often" is substituted for the word "always," and, if one thinks in terms of serious maladies, his proposition is biblically correct. Cf. also *b. Ber.* 5a, "Said Raba, and some say, R. Hisda, 'If a person sees that sufferings afflict him, let him examine his deeds'" (as rendered by Neusner). Even J. F. MacArthur Jr., a strident critic of modern charismatic healing, teaches, "When one is sick, every area of life should be checked for unconfessed sin," urging caution, however, in making "inquiries or accusations about sin in the life of someone else. . . ." He goes on, "It may well be that in some cases a person is sick because of sin, and God is chastening him or her. But is that *always* the problem? By no means." See *Charismatic Chaos*, 217–18.

[159]Cf. the grateful remark of the recovered sufferer in Ps 118:17–18: "I will not die but live, and will proclaim what the LORD has done. The LORD has chastened me severely, but he has not given me over to death."

[160]See below, 3.3.1. According to S. Kim, "The Concepts of Health, Disease and Healing: Theological Perspective," in *The Proceedings of the Consultation on the Study Program of the Healing Ministry*, 29–30, "In so far as illness reminds us of our sin [i.e., as members of a corporately fallen race] and warns us with the idea of God's punishment, it has the constructive aspect of calling us to repentance. If it functions positively to call us to repentance, it may be regarded as God's chastisement for us to keep a right relationship to Him and God's trial of our faith for an ever stronger faith."

[161]According to Gerstenberger, *Psalms, Part 1*, 14, Job 33:14–30 may hint "at a ritual process indicated in case of God-given disease or misfortune," with reference to Seybold, *Das Gebet*, 60–62, 91–92, and J. F. Ross, "Job 33:14–30: The Phenomenology of Lament," *JBL* 94 (1975): 38–46.

[162]The image of Yahweh smiting and healing in the prophetic books is somewhat different. There the Lord brings down his sinning nation (Israel-Judah) with terrible judgments, promising, however, to restore them in the end. See below, 4.1.

[163]The NIV's rendering of Isa 38:17a, "Surely it was for my benefit that I suffered such anguish" (*hinnēh lᵉ šālôm mār-lî mār*) is far from certain, as even a glance at the ancient translations of this verse indicates (the clause is actually lacking in the LXX; note also the rabbinic traditions reflected in Targum, Talmud, and medieval commentary). The primarily literary, nontheological rendering of T. Carmi, ed. and trans., *The Penguin Book of Hebrew Verse* (New York: Penguin Books, 1981), 164, underscores the ambiguity of the Hebrew: "'O give me peace, my lot is bitter!'" or, "My great bitterness was transformed into peace." Nonetheless, the NIV's understanding reflects what Oswalt calls the majority reading (*Isaiah 1–39*, 687), rendering (680): "Behold, for well-being my bitterness was bitter."

[164]Ps 39:11a(12a) should be interpreted in light of v. 10b(11b): "Remove this scourge [*nega'*]; I am overcome by the blow of your hand." Verse 11b(12b), "you consume their wealth like a moth—each man is but a breath," contains an additional thought. Note also the comment of Alexander on v. 11a(12a) (which he renders, "*With rebukes for iniquity thou dost chasten man*"): "He here

presents his new and more correct view of God's providential strokes which he has learned to regard as the punishment of sin.... The past tense of the verb implies that what he suffers is but one link in a long chain of consistent uniform experiences. He is looking not at what has happened once or for the first time, but at something which has always been so. It is God's accustomed mode of dealing with his sinful creatures" (*Psalms*, 176).

[165]In particular, the idiom *'innâ nepeš* (lit., "to afflict the soul") primarily means "to fast" (cf. Lev 16:29; Ps 35:13; Isa 58:3, 10; note also Ibn Ezra to Lev 16:29 and Levine, *Leviticus*, 109), indicating the fairly wide semantic domain associated with the root *'nh* III; cf. BDB, 776–77; *HALAT* 3:808–9.

[166]The primary "affliction" spoken of in Ps 119 is the slander and rejection of leaders and friends (cf. vv. 22–23, 50–51, 61, 69 [this is found in the immediate context of two "affliction" verses, viz., 67 and 71], 78–79, 84–85, 87, 95, 110, 115, 122, 139, 150, 153–155, 161). While this could have been due to a serious or protracted illness (see above, 3.1.5), it is certainly not apparent from the context, although critics of some modern Christian healing movements simply assume sickness to be spoken of in these verses; cf., e.g., Hanegraaff, *Christianity in Crisis*, 267: "Three thousand years ago, King David gave proof that [Kenneth] Copeland and the Faith teachers are dead wrong. God does indeed chastise his own," viz., with sickness, quoting Ps 119:71, 75 for support. Of course, there are other verses in the psalms that would have better supported Hanegraaff's argument, as cited elsewhere in this chapter.

[167]According to Gerstenberger (commenting on Ps 6, *Psalms, Part 1*, 62), the ill person would "turn to the ritual expert, the liturgist, who knew and owned the proper prayers and rites to heal a sick man" only after "he and his family tried all sorts of remedies, to no avail." This assumption, however, may reflect a nonbiblical, rationalistic mentality, not to mention the fact that the sufferer might have simply turned *to God in prayer*, without the aid of a "ritual expert" (cf. below, 3.1.11). This is a simple, natural, and often first response for the religious person.

[168]This mentality, while often associated with deep spirituality, is not exegetically precise, although it is found in much inspirational literature (cf. the practical and edifying sermon of the much-heralded Cambridge preacher, Charles Simeon [1758–1836], "Afflictions, the Fruit of God's Love," in *Evangelical Preaching* [Portland, Ore.: Multnomah, 1986], 217–23; note also the popular study of P. Brand and P. K. Yancey, *Pain: The Gift Nobody Wants* [Grand Rapids: Zondervan, 1993]). This is probably due to the fact that verses such as Ro 5:3; 8:18; et al., are understood against the backdrop of sickness and disease instead of, as the context would suggest, hardships and difficulties encountered because of the faith (as, e.g., Ac 14:22). Cf. MacArthur, *Charismatic Chaos*, 219, where Ro 8:18; Jas 1:2–4; 1Pe 1:6–7; 5:10 are applied to not being healed from sickness and are cited in support of the (otherwise, largely correct) proposition that "after all, adversity is for our good in time." Contrast my chapter entitled "The Gospel of Suffering" in *How Saved Are We?* 85–94. See also below, 5.3.3.

[169]In an argument common to proponents of divine healing, it is asked, "But if we are convinced the [particular] sickness is God's discipline, then, should we see a doctor and seek recovery through other medicinal means? Let us not pull away from the corrective lash. If a disease is divine chastening, it generally will be cured only as the individual confesses his sin and begins a new obedience unto God" (Josephson, *God's Key to Health and Happiness*, 29). Of course, theroretically speaking, one might seek medical help *after* repentance. Cf. above, 1.4.1 on Ecclus 38, n. 207.

[170]Cf. above, n. 158.

[171]Of course, there is another exaggerated viewpoint, viz., that God *never* chastises/instructs/disciplines his people with sickness. For a contrast in extremes, cf. the view of the contemporary "Word-Faith" teacher, K. Copeland, with that of last century's "Prince of Preachers," C. H. Spurgeon. According to Copeland (most likely overreacting to a traditional notion that sickness and poverty are the hallmark of spirituality): "The religious idea that God chastises His own with sickness and disease and poverty is the very thing that has caused the church to go 1500 years without the knowledge of the Holy Spirit." But Spurgeon (who suffered terribly from gout) wrote: "I am certain that I never did grow in grace one-half so much anywhere as I have upon the bed of pain." For references, see Hanegraaff, *Christianity in Crisis*, 267, 406, nn. 11–12; see further, below, n. 173. Note, however, Spurgeon's moving account of his fervent prayer for relief from the agony of gout—a petition that was granted!—"pleading [God's] Fatherhood in real earnest" ("I could not bear to see my child suffer as Thou makest me suffer; and if I saw him tormented as I am now, I would do what I could to help him. Wilt Thou hide Thy face from me, my Father? Wilt Thou still lay on me Thy heavy hand, and not give me a smile from Thy Countenance?"). See A. Dallimore, *Spurgeon: A New Biography* (Carlisle, Pa.: Banner of Truth, 1988), 138–39. Modern teachers of healing would certainly be at home with Spurgeon's remarks: "Faith mastered it [viz., the pain] by laying hold upon God in His own revealed character—that character in which in our darkest hour, we are best able to appreciate Him.... We can still say, 'Our Father,' and when it is very dark, and we are very weak, our childlike appeal can go up, 'Father, help me! Father, rescue me!'" (ibid., 139).

[172]J. C. Ryle, *Sickness* (repr. Choteau, Mont.: Gospel Mission, 1980), 7, 9.

[173]Ibid., 10. One wonders whether a Christian physician or medical missionary would wholly subscribe to such sentiments. See above, 1.4.2, n. 243. Surely some of Ryle's adulatory language does not mesh with the portrayal of various bodily afflictions as curses in, e.g., Dt 28 (see above, 2.2.2; cf. also the prophetic trilogy of judgment, viz., sword, famine, and plague, none of which are "blessings"!—see below, 4.1). It is not in harmony with the anguished descriptions of sufferings coupled with pleas for healing found in the psalms (studied earlier in this chapter (3.1.3–7), nor is it in keeping with the fact that masses of sick and afflicted ones succesfully sought Jesus for healing (in other words, they were only too eager to be *free* from their conditions, generally perceived as being restrictive, binding, and oppressive; cf.

Lk 13:10–17; see below, 5.3.1). It is *because* sickness is (to use the terms Ryle rejects) a curse, an injury, a loss, a foe, etc., that it can help turn people back to the path of life. Contrast again Spurgeon: "I think that health is the greatest blessing that God ever sends us, except sickness, which is far better" (because of the potential growth of character and spirit through suffering); cited in T. Carter, ed., *Spurgeon at His Best* (Grand Rapids: Baker, 1988), 190, #1307.

[174]S. Kim, "The Concepts of Health, Disease and Healing," 31. A more precise, biblical statement might have been: "Diseases are ultimately the result of sin and often come as judgments from and/or afflictions from Satan."

[175]It is possible that 1Co 5:1–5 provides an example: An incestuous man is to be turned "over to Satan, so that the sinful nature [Gk. *sarx*; flesh] may be destroyed and his spirit saved on the day of the Lord." Cf. G. D. Fee, *The First Epistle to the Corinthians* (NICNT; Grand Rapids: Eerdmans, 1987), 198–214, for discussion and review of scholarly opinions. According to Fee, 210, "Most scholars understand this phrase [viz., 'the destruction of the flesh'] to refer at least to physical suffering, and most likely to death itself," although Fee himself does not concur. I would understand the phrase to refer to serious, most likely painful and even debilitating sickness from Satan's hand (cf. Job 2!). Following on the heels of exclusion from the church, this would serve to convict, awaken, and warn the straying believer, also making it difficult, if not impossible, for him to enjoy the sexual aspects of his incestuous relationship. However, I agree with Fee, 211ff., in not seeing death as intended by the word "destruction."

[176]In the Psalms, there is no reference or allusion of any kind to physicians, not even to mention that their help is/was vain or that consulting them was tantamount to leaning on the flesh (contrast Mk 5:25–26; Tob 2:10). Also, although the context of Ps 103:3 is healing from a life-threatening illness, to the Israelite, all healing was perceived as "from the Lord." Thus, even the "natural" healing process of any sickness was probably attributed to Yahweh. In our day, the AIDS pandemic reminds us of the fundamental importance of the body's (God-given) ability to fight off disease and heal itself, since the breakdown of the immune system leads to virtually certain, premature death.

[177]For a brief summary of the usage of *ḥyh* in Psalms, cf. above, 0.3., *sub ḥyh.*

[178]Regarding the superscription of the psalm, cf. Tate, *Psalms 51–100*, 104–5; U. Kellermann, "Erwägungen zum historischen Ort von Psalm LX," *VT* 28 (1978): 56–65.

[179]Cf. further Joüon-Muraoka, *Grammar of Biblical Hebrew*, 2:418 (§121.r).

[180]There is no reason to follow Dahood's rendering, *Psalms 51–100*, 75, 78: "Weak from its fractures, much did it totter," deriving *rᵉpâ* from *rph*. This fails to recognize the connection between *tᵉšōbēb lānû* and *rᵉpâ* and forces an unlikely agreement between *rᵉpâ* (taken by Dahood as fem. sing. perfect instead of imperative) and *šᵉbārêhā* (fem. pl.). Also, according to *BHS*, *rᵉpā'* occurs in a few MSS.

[181]So, e.g., Anderson, *Psalms 73–150*, 712 (with reference, however, to his caution expressed at Ps 102:3); Allen, *Psalms 101–150*, 19–22; Seybold, *Das Gebet*, 142–45; see already Ibn Ezra.

[182]Or, "the Forgiver"; so also the following hymnic participles in vv. 3–5.

[183]The possessive suffixes are almost universally recognized as Aramaisms; cf. GKC, §91e; Joüon-Muraoka, *Grammar of Biblical Hebrew*, §94h-i; Max Wagner, *Die lexicalische und grammatikalische Aramaismen im alttestamentlichen Hebräisch* (BZAW 96; Berlin: Alfred Topelmann, 1966), 130, §15.2; G. A. Rendsburg, *Linguistic Evidence for the Northern Origin of Selected Psalms* (SBLMS; Atlanta: Scholars, 1990), 83, with further references. Note that *nepeš* in vv. 1–2, referred to in the possessive suffixes, once again does not mean "soul" in a spiritualizing sense, as if the deliverances for which the Lord is praised are exclusively *internal*; see Delitzsch, *Psalms*, KD 5/3:120–21, who, while not limiting *taḥ^{a}lû'îm* to "merely bodily diseases," understands it to mean "all kinds of inward and outward sufferings" (see above, n. 73). Hengstenberg, rejects the view of "many expositors [who] suppose that *moral* infirmities are meant," since it "clearly will not suit the connection . . . [of] the fundamental passage." Nonetheless, he still states that "the *sickness* figuratively refers to *sufferings*," citing Ex 15:26; Dt 29:22 in support (*Psalms*, 3:226–27, his emphasis); cf. also VanGemeren, "Psalms," 652: "The 'diseases' may be forms of sickness (cf. Mark 2:7); but more likely it is a metaphor for adversities or setbacks (cf. Deut 29:22; Jer. 14:19; 16:4), similar to punishment ('sins')." D. Kidner's comment on Ps 103:3 (*Psalms 73–150*, 364–65) misses the point of the narrative to which he refers in 2Sa 12:

> For all the similarity of these two phrases, there is a difference between God's handling of *iniquity* and of *diseases*, which was made plain in David's own case when he repented of his sin with Bathsheba. Forgiveness was immediate; but healing was denied, in spite of seven days of prayer and fasting (2 Sa. 12:13–23). If relationship with God is paramount, this makes good sense, for sin destroys it while suffering may deepen it (Heb. 5:8; 12:11). Yet we 'wait for . . . the redemption of our bodies' (Rom. 8:23), and enjoy already many foretastes of it [his emphasis].

However, the distinction in 2Sa 12 is not primarily between God's handling of iniquity and disease; it is the difference between sin and the consequences of sin.

[184]Cf. Oswalt, *Isaiah 1–39*, 687, with reference to Hezekiah's psalm (in particular, Isa 38:17): "As Calvin remarked, and as Jesus demonstrated (Luke 5:17–26), forgiveness of sins and recovery from illness are two sides of God's saving power. Hezekiah apparently felt that had he died this untimely death it would have been in punishment for sin, perhaps the sin of pride. Now the fact that he is recovering is evidence that God has turned away from Hezekiah's sins and turned to Hezekiah." See also below, n. 190; cf. further 5.3.2.

[185]For discussion of *gô'el*, cf. H. Ringgren, "גָּאַל," *TDOT* 2:350–55.

[186]On the meaning of *šaḥat* in the psalms, cf. above, n. 118, and the discussion in 3.1.6.

[187]For the imagery involved, cf. Allen, *Psalms 101–150*, 18, n. 5.c; see also Isa 40:31 (note the interpretation of *Targ. Isa*, cited in Watts, *Isaiah 34–66*, 88, n. 31.a). As expressed devotionally by Knight (*Meditations and Disquisitions upon Certain Psalms*, 400), and with eternity in view, "the life that God hath in store for them that fear him, not only shall be always, but shall be always youth, and no defect of age shall be able to take hold of it." He contrasts this with the description of aging in Ecc 12.

[188]The language used in Ps 103:4b, "and crowns you with love and compassion," while not necessarily related to healing, is certainly suitable in that context; v. 5a, translated by the NIV as "who satisfies your desires with good things" (*hammaśbi'a baṭṭôb 'edyêk*), is of uncertain meaning; cf. Allen, *Psalms 101–150*, 18, n. 5.a. For further discussion of Job 33:24ff., see below, 3.3.2.4.

[189]Cf. K. Seybold, "גָּמַל," *TDOT* 3:30ff. (note the bibliography on 23); cf. also M. Rottenberg, "Towards the Meaning of the Verb *gml*," *Leš* 48–49 (1985): 281–83 (Hebrew).

[190]See also Wolff, *Anthropology*, 147–48 ("Yahweh's forgiving consolation is also the first step in his recovery"). Both Wolff and Allen, *Psalms 101–150*, 18, n. 3.b., list Pss 32:3–5; 107:17–20; Mk 2:5–12; the latter also refers to Jas 5:15–16; note also *b. Ned.* 41a: "The sick person does not rise from his illness until all his sins are forgiven him" (cited often in similar contexts; cf. Jakobovits, *Jewish Medical Ethics*, 303, n. 3; S. T. Lachs, *A Rabbinic Commentary*, 166; P. H. Davids, *The Epistle of James* [NIGTC; Grand Rapids: Eerdmans, 1982], 194).

[191]Cf. vv. 8–14, the revelation of Yahweh's ways to Moses (see v. 7), and note the references to the Lord's gracious actions on behalf of frail humanity (e.g., vv. 6b, 13–18).

[192]Cf. J. G. Lake's homiletical statement, "Healing is simply the salvation of Jesus Christ, having its divine action in a man's flesh, the same as it had its divine action in man's soul, or in the spirit of man" (*The John G. Lake Sermons on Dominion over Demons, Disease and Death*, ed. G. Lindsay [repr. Dallas: CFNI, 1975], 17). Commenting on Ps 103:3, Allen, *Psalms 101–150*, 18, n. 3.b., notes, "The obviously synonymous parallelism is striking: healing is a tangible result of divine forgiveness (cf. 32:3–4; Mark 2:10–11)." Allen cites H. McKeating, "Divine Forgiveness in the Psalms," *SJT* 18 (1965): 69–74, with reference also to Ps 107:17; 1Co 11:30; Jas 5:15–16. For reflections on the fact that those whose sins are remitted sometimes remain sick, see below, 6.2.1.

[193]The Hebrew is literally "opens the blind," the object "eyes" being understood; cf. Anderson, *Psalms 73–150*, 942.

[194]Cf. the discussion of Isa 42:7, below, 4.2.2 and note the comment of NJV to 42:7a ("Opening eyes deprived of light"): "An idiom meaning 'freeing the imprisoned'; cf. 61:1." See also G. W. Grogan, "Isaiah," *EBC* 6:255. Anderson, *Psalms 73–150*, 942, takes the description in Ps 146 figuratively: "Yahweh is able to help even the most helpless"; cf. also H.-J. Kraus, *Psalms*

60–150, trans. H. C. Oswald (Minneapolis: Augsburg, 1989), 552, who simply refers to Ps 145:14. Such comments indicate that a strict healing interpretation is not appropriate here, although from a retrospective canonical reading, the words do anticipate things to come.

[195]*kî-gādôl kayyām šibrēk mî yirpā'-lāk*, my translation. For discussion, cf. below, 4.1.3.

[196]Cf. N. Mendcki, "Jahwe Erbauer Jerusalems und Sammler der Zerstreuten in Ps 147, 2–3," *Collectanea Theologica* 56 (1986): 85–88.

[197]Isa 61:1 has *laḥbôš lᵉnišbᵉrê-lēb* ("to bind up the brokenhearted"). Cf. Hempel, *Heilung*, 239, n. 2, for other parallel expressions (Ex 34:4; Lam 2:13; Zec 11:16; also Job 5:18; Isa 30:26; Hos 6:1); note also Stoebe, "Rafa'," 805.

[198]Cf. Kraus, *Psalms 60–150*, 221–22. According to Tate, *Psalms 51–100*, 453, "Ps. 91 has its own validity as a literary entity without regard to a historical setting-in-life." For Tate's own interpretation, see 452–53; also next note.

[199]See the summary of recent scholarship in Tate, 450–53; for a full-length study, see P. Hugger, *Jahwe meine Zuflucht: Gestalt und Theologie des 91. Psalms* (Münsterschwarzacher Studien, 13. Münsterschwarzachen: Vier-Turma-Verlag, 1971). This psalm has been categorized (with some overlap between interpretations) as: (1) a royal psalm (hence "the speaker would be a priest or a prophet addressing the king"; Tate, 451); (2) a psalm to ward off demons; (3) a psalm written by a pious person after being healed; (4) part of a liturgical rite in which the priest would speak "to someone who seeks protection for himself and for his family in the onslaught of pestilence" (ibid.); (5) a psalm of conversion of a former devotee to Elyon-Shaddai who is now turning to Yahweh (Eissfeldt's unique view, rightly questioned by Tate, 451–52); cf. also Seybold, *Das Gebet*, 164.

[200]Cf. Kraus, *Psalms 60–150*, 223: "In vv. 5 and 6 we will have to think not only of poetic personifications (thus F. Nötscher) but also of demonic powers (cf. also L. Köhler, *Hebrew Man* [1956] 135f.)." Cf. also É. Puech, "11QPsApᵃ: un ritual d'exorcismes. Essai de reconstruction," *RevQ* 14 (1990): 377–408 (including a Qumran Ps 91 recension for apparently magical purposes).

[201]For useful surveys of biblical demonology, with bibliographies, see T. H. Gaster, "Demon, Demonology," *IDB* 1:817–24; D. E. Aune, "Demon, Demonology," *ISBE* 1:919–23; J. K. Kuemmerlin-McLean and D. G. Reese, "Demons," *ABD* 2:138–42; S. Loewenstamm, "שֵׁדִים," *EM* 7:524–25; see also G. H. Twelftree, "Demon, Devil, Satan," in J. B. Green and S. McKnight, eds., *Dictionary of Jesus and the Gospels* (Downers Grove, Ill.: InterVarsity, 1992), 163–72. The older treatment of Eichrodt, *Theology of the Old Testament*, 2:223–28, still retains value; see further below, 5.3.1, and J. Baumgarten, "Concerning the Qumran Psalms Against Evil Spirits," *Tarbiz 55* (1985/86): 442–46 (Hebrew).

[202]Cf. in general M. A. M. Juárez, O.S.A., "El diablo y los demonios. La fe del antiguo Israel," *Biblia y fe* 56 (1993): 36–54; H. Duhm, *Die bösen Geister*

im Alten Testament (Tübingen and Leipzig: Mohr and Siebeck, 1904), 51–52; J. de Fraine, "Le 'démon du midi' (Ps 91,6)," *Bib* 40 (1959): 372–83; A. Caquot, "Sur quelques démons de l'Ancien Testament: Reshep, Qeteb, Deber," *Sem* 6 (1956): 53–68. See also previous note.

[203]The rendering of Dahood, *Psalms 51–100*, 331, "the pack of night," interpreting *paḥad* with reference to "the pack of wild dogs that marauds at night," with recourse to Ugaritic and biblical parallels, is interesting, but his understanding of *paḥad* has been rightly questioned (cf. Craigie, *Psalms 1–50*, 145, n. 5.a. [on Ps 14:5a]).

[204]For the possible connection between *ḥēṣ* and *rešep*, cf. above, 2.2.5, n. 125. See also Dahood, *Psalms 51–100*, 331–32. Kraus, *Psalms 60–150*, 223, says that "the 'arrows that fly in the daytime' are destructive forces that cause sickness."

[205]For discussion of *yāšûd*, cf. Tate, *Psalms 51–100*, 448, n. 6.c. and the LXX, Vulgate, and Targum to v. 6b; note also *HALAT* 4:1318. According to Tate, 454, the fourfold dangers listed in vv. 5–6, which "alternate between action in periods of darkness and light . . . [have] the appearance of a merism, i.e., dangers which may occur at anytime, day or night; a comprehensive statement of the perils of life." Kraus, *Psalms 60–150*, 223, makes reference to Gunkel's "History-of-religions parallels adduced in great numbers," thus reminding us that the images of noon and night, day and darkness should also be interpreted specifically (which Tate does not fail to do; see ibid., 454–55). Note also the lively description of Kraus, ibid., "Thus v. 6 speaks of times that are pregnant with disaster."

[206]On the controversy concerning the rendering of *šaḥal* ("lion" or some kind of serpent or reptile), cf. the detailed discussion in Tate, *Psalms 51–100*, 449–50, n. 13.a; see also "שַׁחַל," *HALAT* 4:1355–56.

[207]Cf. Kraus, *Psalms 60–150*, 224: "We may here recall that in ancient Near Eastern representations the gods were sometimes depicted as conquerors of frightful monsters; they stand on demonic beasts as on a pedestal. A strength that conquers all dark powers is promised to those who are entrusted to God's protection." Cf. also Keel, *Symbolism*, 50ff., 87, 97.

[208]Tate, *Psalms 51–100*, 453, notes on v. 1, "The protective function of the 'shade of the king' is a widespread metaphor in the ideology of ancient Near Eastern kingship. . . . The 'shade' or 'shadow' [*ṣēl*] is that of the divine king, the Almighty One." According to Kraus, *Psalms 60–150*, 221, "The situation of the psalm becomes clear in vv. 1–2. A person who has entered the protective area of Yahweh, the sanctuary, is called on to make a thankful confession (v. 2, cf. Ps. 107:10ff.—there too the participial beginning, as in v. 1)." Thus the promises of protection are localized to the sanctuary (ibid., 223). This, however, is too narrow an interpretation, in light of the comprehensive nature of the promises given, many of which clearly refer to threats and attacks that would take place *away* from the tabernacle/temple area. Note, however, that Kraus, commenting on vv. 11–12 (ibid., 224), rightly emphasizes: "Even outside of the protective area of the holy place is Yahweh's shielding power active (vv. 11f.)."

[209]It is equally possible that vv. 7–8 referred to death by plague or famine, terrible fates often associated with battle and siege (cf. below, 4.1), but not always.

[210]Tate, *Psalms 51–100*, 446, renders this, "shield of protection"; cf. ibid., 448, n. 4.d., with reference to A. A. Macintosh, "Psalm XCI 4 and the Root *sḥr*," *VT* 23 (1973): 56–62. Cf. also J. Blau, "Concerning the Qumran Text of Ps 91," *Leš* 42 (1978): 308–9 (Hebrew).

[211]The Hebrew for "long life" is *'ōrek yāmmîm*, literally "length of days" (cf. Dt 30:20; Job 12:12; Pss 21:5; 23:6; 93:5; Pr 3:2, 16; see also La 5:20). For *śāba'*, "to be satisfied, to satisfy," often used with regard to bodily appetites, cf. Even-Shoshan, *Concordance*, 1106–7. The various renderings of the NIV include "filled, get enough, have enough, have abundant, feast on, gorge, have more than enough, satisfy fully" (see E. W. Goodrick and J. R. Kohlenberger, III, eds., *The NIV Exhaustive Concordance*, Grand Rapids: Zondervan, 1990), 1623 (#8425; cf. #'s 8426–30).

[212]See next note.

[213]The spiritualizing, other-worldly interpretation, classically expressed by Spurgeon, is wholly out of place in the OT mentality: "It is impossible that any ill should happen to the man who is beloved of the Lord; the most crushing calamities can only shorten his journey and hasten him to his reward. Ill to him is no ill, but only good in a mysterious form. Losses enrich him, sickness is his medicine, reproach is his honor, death is his gain. No evil in the strict sense of the word can happen to him, for everything is overruled by good" (*Treasury of David*, 2:93). Contrast, however, Spurgeon's experience of protection from the plague, cited below, n. 220.

[214]According to Tate, *Psalms 51–100*, 456, "the 'tent' is the 'home/habitation/dwelling place' of the faithful person—wherever he/she may be," with reference to Kraus, *Psalms 60–150*, 224; see Hugger, *Jahwe meine Zuflucht*, 226–29, for a treatment of *'hl* in the psalms (the biblical references are cited by Tate). Note that in Arabic, *ahl* can also mean "family."

[215]Surprisingly, the close affinity between Ps 91:11 and Ex 23:20 (esp. "to keep you in the way/your ways") is often missed by commentators.

[216]According to Eichrodt, *Theology of the Old Testament*, 2:226, n. 4, "the concept of demons [in Job 18:13; 19:12; Ps 91:5–6] serves rather as a poetic personification of plague and disease."

[217]Cf. further *T. Sim.* 6:6; *T. Zeb.* 9:8, and the discussion in I. H. Marshall, *The Gospel of Luke* (NIGTC; Grand Rapids: Eerdmans, 1978), 429. Cf. also Luther, cited in Kraus, *Psalms 60–150*, 224, n. 1, with reference to Ps 91: "This is the most distinguished promise and consolation: you will not only be secure, but you will go forth and conquer all evils."

[218]Cf. Kraus, *Psalms 60–150*, 224; Marshall, *Luke*, 429; P. Grelot, "Étude critique de Luc 10,19," *RSR* 69 (1981): 87–100; however, according to J. A. Fitzmyer, *The Gospel According to Luke X–XXIV* (AB; Garden City, N.Y.: Doubleday, 1985), 863, who differs here with Grelot, "it is a farfetched allusion."

[219]The last clause of Lk 10:19 ("nothing will harm you") echoes the spirit of Ps 91:10a, although there are no words in common here between the LXX of Ps 90:10a and Lk 10:19. Thus, Lucan commentators tend to make no reference to Ps 91 at this point.

[220]For the use of this psalm in rabbinic tradition, cf. *b. Shebu'ot* 15b (incorrectly printed in Tate, *Psalms 51–100*, 451, as *Sheboth* 15b); see Hugger, *Jahwe meine Zuflucht*, 331–33; for complete references, see A. Hyman and A. B. Hyman, *Torah HaKetubah VeHaMessurah* (2d ed.; Tel-Aviv: Dvir Pub. Co., 1979), 3:64–65. From a Christian perspective, Spurgeon recounts the supernatural confidence and protection he received through Ps 91 while ministering daily to the afflicted in the midst of an invasion of "Asiatic cholera" in London, 1854 (*Treasury of David*, 2:92; cf. also the "Explanatory Notes and Quaint Sayings" appended to this psalm on pp. 94–114).

[221]Because this section touches on the wider subject of the origin and editing of the Psalter, along with the complex question of worship in ancient Israel (both popular and cultic), treatment can only be brief. For references in addition to those cited below, see Seybold, *Das Gebet*, 77–98; J. H. Eaton, "The Psalms and Israelite Worship," in G. W. Andersen, *Tradition and Interpretation* (Oxford: Clarendon, 1979), 238–73; Mowinckel, *The Psalms in Israel's Worship*; Rowley, *Worship In Ancient Israel*; H.-J. Kraus, *Worship in Israel*, trans. G. Buswell (Richmond: John Knox, 1966). See also W. L. Holladay, *The Psalms Through Three Thousand Years: Prayerbook of a Cloud of Witnesses* (Philadelphia: Augsburg/Fortress, 1993). J. C. McCann's *A Theological Introduction to the Book of Psalms: The Psalms as Torah* (Nashville: Abingdon, 1993), with its deemphasis on the cultic background to Psalms, came to my attention too late to be incorporated into the discussion.

[222]Gerstenberger, *Psalms, Part 1*, 62, notes, "Since there were many possible causes of a person's misfortune (e.g., sickness; slander; sin; rejection by the community; bad omens), such prayers [i.e., similar to Ps 6] were certainly used as well in other than strictly medical cases. Later, when incorporated into the collection of written psalms, the prayer reached a much larger audience and came to be used in more situations than simply formal worship." On the connection between individual healing and national deliverance, cf. above, 2.3.2.4.

[223]Ibid., 14.

[224]Ibid., 62.

[225]Seybold, *Sickness and Healing*, 44. He also states that "long-practiced customs, not only in the behavior of the person concerned, but also in the liturgical-cultic needs and variations in ritual, no doubt consolidated and expanded this sequence into, as it were, a traversable path."

[226]"He sent forth his word and healed them; he rescued them from the grave," rendered by Allen as "sending his message of healing to rescue them from their Pit" (*Psalms 101–150*, 57).

[227]Ibid., 59, n. 20a, with reference to Kraus.

[228]Dahood, *Psalms 101–150*, 85. For a broad discussion of Ps 107, see Walter Beyerlin, *Werden und Wesen in 107 Psalms* (BZAW 153; Berlin: de Gruyter, 1979).

[229]See Seybold, *Das Gebet*, 142–45; A. Weiser, *The Psalms: A Commentary*, trans. H. Hartwell (OTL; Philadelphia: Westminster, 1962), 658; Anderson, *Psalms 73–150*, 712; Allen, *Psalms 101–150*, 19; Kraus, *Psalms 60–150*, 290: "He has experienced forgiveness of all his guilt, has been rescued from the distress of sickness and death (*šḥt*), and now praises Yahweh 'before the great congregation' (Ps 22:23ff.)—as it was customary at the thankoffering in the worship of Israel."

[230]For references to relevant ancient Near Eastern literature, cf. Gerstenberger, *Psalms, Part 1*, 2–4, 12, 14.

[231]Cf. G. W. Anderson, "'Sicut Cervus': Evidence in the Psalter of Private Devotion in Ancient Israel," *VT* 30 (1980): 388–97.

[232]For a small but representative sampling of some practical reflections on the use of the Psalter for today's believer, see J. F. Craghan, *The Psalms: Prayers for the Ups, Downs, and In-Betweens of Life* (Wilmington, Del.: Michael Glazier, 1985); B. W. Andersen, *Out of the Depths: The Psalms Speak for Us Today* (Philadelphia: Westminster, 1983); W. Brueggeman, *Praying the Psalms* (Winona, Minn.: St. Mary's, 1982); E. H. Peterson, *A Year with the Psalms: 365 Meditations and Prayers* (Waco, Tex.: Word, 1979); *Rage! Reflect! Rejoice! Praying with the Psalmists* (Philadelphia: Westminster, 1977); D. W. Vogel, *Psalms for Worship Today* (St. Louis: Concordia, 1974); D. Bonhoeffer, *Psalms: The Prayer Book of the Bible* (Minneapolis: Augsburg, 1970); T. Merton, *Praying the Psalms* (Collegeville, Minn.: Liturgical Press, 1956); *The Psalms and Their Meaning for Today* (Indianapolis: Bobb-Merrill, 1952). Note also that a substantial part of the *Siddur*, the Jewish prayer book, is made up of various psalms; cf. Heinemann, *Prayer in the Talmud*, for aspects of the historical development.

[233]Cf. R. E. Murphy, *The Tree of Life* (ABRL; New York: Doubleday, 1992), 111ff. (note esp. 125: "In short, the wisdom experience is to be described as a faith experience. The shaping of Israel's views of the world, and of the activity of God behind and in it, was done in an ambience of faith, and was characterized by trust and reliance upon God"). Cf. L. Boström, *The God of the Sages: The Portrayal of God in the Book of Proverbs* (ConBOT 29; Stockhom: Almqvist & Wiksell, 1990); A. Meinhold, "Gott und Mensch in Proverbien iii," *VT* 37 (1987): 468–77; W. C. Kaiser Jr., "Wisdom Theology and the Centre of Old Testament Theology," *EvQ* 50 (1978): 132–46.

[234]Cf. G. von Rad, *Wisdom in Israel*, trans. J. D. Martin (Nashville: Abingdon, 1973), 124–37, for discussion of the "act-consequence" relationship. In his brief treatment of the relevant texts in Proverbs, Seybold, *Sickness and Healing*, 56–57, claims that the "older proverbial sayings only touch sporadically on the topic of sickness [because this] was considered to be so much the domain of religion and magic that Wisdom would not dare approach it." Rather, it can be argued that the pragmatism of Wisdom literature (cf. Seybold's reference, 57, to "several examples [in Proverbs] with a remarkable

insight into elements touching on the anthropological problem"), coupled with the understanding that "the fear of God is beneficial to health" (p. 58), produced a fairly full and clear statement on some basic issues of sickness and healing. Again, it must be emphasized that, for the Wisdom authors, godly living was considered to be a literal matter of life and death. Moreover, in general terms, to what extent could one divorce the concept of "religion" from Wisdom literature in the OT? Cf. again Murphy, *Tree of Life*, 125, who claims that "the sages penetrated into the divine mystery in a manner that even the prophets never equaled."

[235]Although the NIV here renders *šālôm* with "prosperity" (cf. also Pss 72:3, 7; 73:3; Isa 45:7; Jer 29:7), the primary emphasis in these verses is not financial abundance. A translation such as "well-being" (so NJV at Pr 3:2) would more accurately convey the sense. However, there are many promises of financial blessing in the book of Proverbs (e.g., 3:9–10, 16b; 22:4), since it is affirmed that God blesses the generous but withholds from the stingy. Moreover, ethical, hard, honest work leads to wealth, while dishonest, undisciplined, slovenly work leads to poverty (e.g., 10:4). It is interesting to note that this cycle of godly living leading to wealth presented a problem for some Christian leaders; note the Latin saying quoted with approval by the Puritan author, Cotton Mather, *Religio perperit Divitas, et Filia devoravit Matrem* ("Religion brought forth prosperity, and the daughter destroyed the mother"), and cf. the more famous words of John Wesley, that "true scriptural Christianity has a tendency, in the process of time, to undermine and destroy itself"—because of financial prosperity coming to now hard-working Christians who before their conversion were of a much lower economic class, often due to their profligacy (see D. Willard, *The Spirit of the Disciplines* [San Francisco: Harper & Row, 1988], 196–97). In any case, the question of financial blessing is not entirely unrelated to that of physical healing (since both were promised as material benefits of covenant obedience in the Torah), and some modern proponents of divine healing also espouse what is disparagingly called the "health and wealth" gospel. For critique and discussion, including both balanced and polemical works, see B. Baron, *The Health and Wealth Gospel* (Downers Grove, Ill.: InterVarsity, 1987); G. Fee, *The Disease of the Health & Wealth Gospels* (Beverly, Mass.: Frontline Pub., 1985); W. C. Kaiser Jr., "The Old Testament Case for Material Blessings and the Contemporary Believer," *TrinJ* 9 (1988): 151–69; D. L. Larsen, "The Gospel of Greed Versus the Gospel of Grace," *TrinJ* 9 (1988): 211–20; cf. also the historical Christian perspective of W. DeArteaga, *Quenching the Spirit: Examining Centuries of the Moving of the Holy Spirit* (Lake Mary, Fla.: Creation House, 1992), 165–75 ("Prosperity as Spirituality"); see further J. L. González, *Faith & Wealth: A History of Early Christian Ideas on the Origin, Significance, and Use of Money* (San Francisco: HarperSanFrancisco, 1990). For poverty and riches in Proverbs, cf. R. N. Whybray, *Wealth and Poverty in the Book of Proverbs* (Sheffield: JSOT Press, 1990); J. D. Pleins, "Poverty in the Social World of the Wise," *JSOT* 37 (1987): 61–78; G. A. Chutter, "Riches and Poverty in the Book of Proverbs," *Crux* 18 (1982): 23–28. See also

below, 5.3.3, nn. 120–123, and cf. J. D. Pleins and T. D. Hanks, "Poor, Poverty," *ABD* 5:402–24 (with lit. on 414, 423–24), although Hanks' treatment of the NT material lays undue stress on issues of liberation theology.

[236]Cf. the title of Murphy's volume on wisdom literature, *Tree of Life*; see H. N. Wallace, "Tree of Knowledge and Tree of Life," *ABD* 6:656–60, on the tree of life imagery in the Bible and ancient Near East; see further Westermann, *Genesis 1–11*, 211–14.

[237]According to Kraus, *Theology*, 162, "The confession of faith in the prayers of the Old Testament is concentrated in the exclamation, 'With thee is the fountain of life!' (Ps 36:9). Yahweh is the origin of all life." Kraus also cites Barth, *Die Erretung von Tode*, 48: "Life of whatever sort has its origin in God and is therefore to be found where God appears and shows that his presence is near. Whoever is in need of life will strive to go into God's presence. There he knows that he is in the atmosphere in which life flourishes." The wisdom application of these cultic truths says that life is found in following God's ways, and to walk in that path is to be "in the atmosphere in which life flourishes" (cf. Pr 12:28; 15:24).

[238]On the power of words in Proverbs, cf. D. Kidner, *Proverbs* (TOTC; Downers Grove, Ill.: InterVarsity, 1964), 46–49; see also M. Margalis, *Lashon u-refuah ba-Tanakh* (Tel Aviv: Vaadat ha-Yovel shel Irgun Rofe Kupat Holim Amamit, 1949).

[239]Cf. R. L. Harris, "אַחֲרִית," in *TWOT* 1:34. For a precritical treatment of Pr 12:28, cf. Bridges, *Proverbs*, 149–50; for recent discussion, contrast W. McKane, *Proverbs* (OTL; Philadelphia: Westminster, 1975), 230, 450–52 (emending v. 28b to read "but the *way of folly leads* to death") with M. Dahood, "Immortality in Proverbs 12.28," *Bib* 41 (1960): 176–81 (arguing for, "And the treading of her path [i.e., the path of righteousness] is immortality").

[240]For an ample discussion of *šārrekā*, without emending to *šᵉʾērekā*, see McKane, *Proverbs,* 293. In the context of the rabbinic exhortation, "Busy yourself in the Torah, for it is healing (*rᵉpûʾâ*) for the whole body," Pr 3:8a is adduced in order to demonstrate that it works for the navel (*ṭibbûr*) as well (*Midr. Tanhuma*, Yithro 8).

[241]For the bones in the context of sickness and health, see Pss 6:3; 31:11; 32:3; 38:4; Pr 15:30a; 16:24b; 17:22b; Isa 58:11; La 1:13; note also the conjectural reading of Aramaic *ʿaṭmôtêkā* in Ahiqar 100 (with *rpʾh*; Brown, *A Philological Study*, 110; J. Lindenberger, *The Aramaic Proverbs of Ahiqar* [Baltimore: Johns Hopkins Univ. Press, 1983], 79, 238, n. 194). For the negative effects on the bones of envy (*qinʾâ*) and a "hussy" (following McKane's lively rendering of *mᵉbîšâ*, *Proverbs*, 228), cf. Pr 12:4b; 14:30b. See also J. K. Eakins, "Human Osteology and Archaeology," *BA* 43 (1980): 89–96. The rendering of *šiqqûy* (assumed to be from *šqh*, "to drink") with "tonic" is not certain. I take *šiqqûy* to be a medicinal drink of some kind, hence "tonic"; the NIV's "nourishment" apparently sees *šiqqûy* as a nutritious drink.

[242]For a recent survey of this form, cf. S. Bolozky and O. Scharzwald, "On the Derivation of Hebrew Forms with the +*ût* Suffix," *HS* 33 (1992): 51–69.

[243]Slightly different is the NIV's "health" (cf. *HALAT* 4:1188, "Genesung," although a rendering with "Heilmittel," as proposed there for Ecclus 38:14, is also suggested as a possibility).

[244]Cf. A. Berlin, "Parallelism," *ABD* 5:154–62 (with lit.); cf. also D. J. A. Clines, "The Parallelism of Greater Precision," in E. Follis, ed., *Directions in Biblical Hebrew Poetry* (JSOTSupp. 40; Sheffield: JSOT Press, 1987), 77–100, for instances of the second stich being more specific than the first.

[245]E.g., Targ.'s *'asyûtā'* and LXX's *iasis*.

[246]For a discussion of EA 269:17, see Brown, "רָפָא," 619. (It is possible that Amarna Akkadian *ripûtu* is cognate with Hebrew *rᵉpû'ôt*, for which see above, 1.2.2.1, n. 57, although the identification with Hebrew *rip'ût* remains attractive.) In Ecclus 38:14, *rp't* occurs in parallelism with *mḥyh*.

[247]According to Delitzsch, *Proverbs*, KD 6/1:88, *rip'ût* in Pr 3:8 does "not [have] the meaning of restoration from sickness, but the raising of enfeebled strength, or the confirming of that which exists." But, in light of the OT's uniform testimony that promises health and healing to the godly, why shouldn't *rip'ût* mean exactly that here? Moreover, Delitzsch's etymological view connecting *rp'* and *rph* has little to commend it; cf. above, 0.3.2, n. 76. For further discussion relative to *rip'ût*, cf. Humbert, "Maladie et médecin," 8.

[248]Cf. A. P. Ross, "Proverbs," *EBC* 5:917, who states: "The healing that the fear of the Lord and avoidance of evil brings is first and foremost spiritual. Scripture often uses the physical body to describe inner spiritual or psychical feelings" (with reference to Johnson, *The Vitality of the Individual*, 67–68). Ross's comment on Pr 4:20–22, however, sees "healing" there in quite comprehensive terms (see below, 3.2.3).

[249]Malbim understands Pr 4:22 in terms of "a vigor that is both spiritual ('life') and physical ('healing')"; see *Malbim on Mishley*, abridged and adapted in English by C. Wengrov (Jerusalem/New York: Feldheim, 1982), 46.

[250]McKane, *Proverbs*, 310.

[251]Cf. the simple definition of A. Marzal, *Gleanings from the Wisdom of Mari* (Studia Pohl 11; Rome: Pontifical Biblical Institute, 1976), 2: "A proverb is a brief statement, founded on experience and containing a truth." For a judicious selection of ancient Near Eastern proverbial literature, cf. McKane, *Proverbs*, 51–208; see further Murphy, *Tree of Life*, 151–79.

[252]*marpē'* in 14:30 should probably be derived from *rph*; cf. below, 3.2.4.

[253]*'ādām bᵉlîya'al 'îs 'āwen*; on *bᵉlîya'al*, cf. G. R. Driver, "Hebrew Notes," *ZAW* 52 (1934): 52–53; D. W. Thomas, "*bᵉlîya'al* in the OT," in J. N. Birdsall and R. W. Thomson, eds., *Biblical and Patristic Studies in Memory of R. P. Casey* (Freiburg/New York: Herder, 1963), 11–19. For further literature, cf. B. Otzen, "בְּלִיַּעַל," *TDOT* 2:131–36; Gesenius-Rüterswörden, *Handwörterbuch*, 152–53. Otzen, ibid., 135–36, follows Mowinckel (*Psalmenstudien*, 1:24–25) in seeing the culprit of Pr 6:12ff. as being guilty of cultic abuses. For further discussion of "anti-social magic" (here on *ḥōrēš rā'*), see Mowinckel, *The Psalms in Israel's Worship*, 1:199–200.

[254]The use of *'ên marpē'* underscores the fact that *marpē'* should be rendered with "healing, cure, remedy" as opposed to "health"; see next note.

[255]Although *marpē'* is best rendered with "healing, cure, remedy" (see n. 254; also 2.3.1, n. 210), the parallelism here with *ḥayyîm* has probably contributed to the broader rendering of "health," as in the NIV (cf. also AV, NASB, and NEB; RSV and NJV have "healing"). Cf. also the LXX's *iasis* and Sa'adiah's *šifa'* ("healing, cure, remedy").

[256]The Hebrew of this verse reads: *kî-ḥayyîm hēm lemôṣᵉ'êhem ûlᵉ kol-bᵉśārô marpē'*. Ehrlich is probably right in suggesting an original *bᵉśārām marpē'*, the final *mēm* being deleted by haplography and the *wāw* arising as a later incorrect clarification (*Randglossen*, 6:25); cf. *BHS*. On *lᵉmôṣᵉ'êhem*, note *b. Erub.* 54a, "Do not read *lᵉmôṣᵉ'êhem* but rather *lᵉmôṣî'ehem*" (i.e., to those who clearly recite [lit., "bring out"] their prayers and lessons); on the principle of *'al tiqrē'* ("Do not read this [viz., what is written in the traditional text or vocalization], but read that [viz., a novel, homiletical interpretation]"), cf. *Talmudic Encyclopedia* 2:1–2 (Hebrew); for an extensive (and comprehensive?) listing of rabbinic sources, cf. M. Sabar, *Miklol HaMa'amarim WeHaPitgamim* (Jerusalem: Mossad HaRav Kook, 1987), 145–50.

[257]Ross, "Proverbs," *EBC* 5:925–26.

[258]Cf. NIV's "Reckless words"; see also Gesenius-Rüterswörden, *Handwörterbuch*, 138; Lowenstamm and Blau, *Thesaurus* 2:53 ("speak rashly and inadvisedly").

[259]Rashi curiously notes here that the *sîr 'ᵉmūnîm* (faithful envoy) is none other than *môšeh rabbênû* (Moses our teacher)!

[260]For *nepeš* as "palate, gullet, throat" cf. Wolff, *Anthropology*, 11–15.

[261]Once again, there seems to be an overlap between "healing, cure, remedy" and that which brings it about, viz., "medicine" (cf. Ger. *Heilmittel*). Cf. also above, 1.2.2.1, n. 57; below, 4.2.2, n. 170.

[262]See above, n. 238.

[263]Cf. AV ("a wholesome tongue"); NJV ("a healing tongue"). Delitzsch's theory, grouping *rph* and *rp'* together with meanings ranging from mitigating and mildness to healing and refreshing (*Proverbs*, KD 6/1:261–62), must be rejected; for discussion, see above, 0.3.2, n. 76.

[264]*šeber barûaḥ* has been interpreted quite literally by S. R. Hirsch, *From the Wisdom of Mishle*, trans. K. Paritzky-Joshua (Jerusalem/New York: Feldheim, 1976): "One vacillating word . . . can cause a lasting split in personality" (177).

[265]On Pr 14:30, see below; on Ecc 10:4, see Brown, *A Philological Study*, 52–53; R. E. Murphy, *Ecclesiastes* (WBC; Dallas: Word, 1992), 96, 98, n. 4.c, 101. For the classification of Pr 15:4, cf. McKane, *Proverbs*, 482–83, who cites KBL, Toy, Gemser, Ringgren, Scott, Barucq, and RSV in favor of a derivation from *rph* (hence, "a conciliatory tongue"). McKane himself, however, agrees with LXX's *iasis* (according to him, "therapy") in deriving from *rp'*. Targum (*'asyûtā' dᵉlišānā'*) and Ibn Ezra also derive *marpē'* from *rp'*, but Ralbag derives it from *rph*. Sa'adiah's paraphrastic *ṣidqu-lilsān* ("truth of the

tongue") is explained in his commentary with reference to *šifa'*—"remedy, cure" (see above, n. 255).

266According to Ross, "Proverbs" (commenting on 12:18), "The words are healing because they are faithful and true, gentle and kind, and uplifting and encouraging." He states that *marpē'* (in 12:18) "is metonymy of the effect, showing the opposite of the cutting, irresponsible words." The principal difficulty of 15:4a, regardless of the derivation of *mrp'*, has to do with the word order, as *l ͤšôn marpē'* ("a tongue of healing," meaning "a healing tongue") would have been expected, as opposed to MT's *marpē' lašôn* (lit., "the healing of the tongue"). It is possible, but unlikely, that 15:4a consists of two classes, i.e., the tongue can be a healing cure, a tree of life; cf. Ehrlich's: "*Ein Segen kann die Zunge sein, ein Lebensbaum*" (*Randglossen*, 6:83); for 15:4b he reads *behiššaber b ͤ rîaḥ*—"*doch, nicht im Zaume gehalten, ist sie ein Ungluck.*" Rather, *marpē' lāšôn* should be seen as a construct phrase (meaning the tongue's healing powers are a tree of life (cf. LXX's *iasis glossēs* and Targum's *'asyûtā' dᵉlišānā'*), or *marpē' lāšôn* is simply equivalent to *lāšôn marpē'*. My basis for preferring the last view is simply that in Proverbs, the tongue itself can *either* kill or give life (cf. the *locus classicus,* 18:21). To say that the tongue itself is a healing cure, or to speak of "the tongue's healing," seems inaccurate. Of course, the *positive* use of the tongue could be implied, hence, "the healing powers [of a *godly*] tongue are a tree of life."

267Cf. the relevant lectures of D. M. Lloyd-Jones (who was first a medical doctor and then a noted biblical expositor), delivered to the Christian Medical Fellowship, British Medical Association, and Royal Commonwealth Society, and published in the U.S.A. as *Healing and the Scriptures* (Nashville: Oliver-Nelson, 1988)—especially 41–51 ("On Treating the Whole Man") and 141–73 ("Body, Mind and Spirit").

268According to Josephson, who cites Pr 14:30; 15:13; 17:22; and 18:14 (*God's Key to Health and Happiness*, 29–30), "Right attitudes encourage and refresh the soul and strengthen the moral spirit; actually, then the blood and the sympathetic nervous system are rejuvenated, which makes for good cell construction and builds healthy body tissues. Wrong relationships and attitudes depress the mind and fill the blood with alkaloid poison. The involuntary sympathetic nerve system actually causes a malformation of cell construction and tissue arrangement." He cites medical tests to support his statements.

269Deriving *marpē'* here from *rph*. Key versions, both ancient and modern (e.g., LXX ["doctor of the heart"], Targ., AV), as well as several classic and modern commentaries (e.g., Rashi, Ibn Ezra, B. Gemser, H. Ringgren) derive *marpē'* from *rp'*, and *ḥayyîm* is again in close proximity (cf. above, 3.2.2, on 15:4a). However, it seems redundant to speak of a "healing heart" (or "mind, disposition") as the life of the body; cf. McKane, *Proverbs*, 472.

270The plural *b ͤ šārîm* (lit., "fleshes, bodies"; only here in the OT) should be understood intensively; according to Delitzsch, *Proverbs*, KD 6/1:311, it signifies "the bodily life in the totality of its functions, and in the entire manifoldness of its relations" (cf. 4:22b; n. 256).

[271]Cf. Kidner, *Proverbs*, 111.

[272]Cf. McKane, *Proverbs*, 472: "If this is so, the modernity of the verse is striking, since its observation has to do with psycho-somatic relationships—it states that the mind is the seat of health or illness." Cf. already Rashi and Ibn Ezra (deriving *marpē'* from *rp'*) and Ralbag (deriving it from *rph*) for similar insights.

[273]*Malbim on Mishley*, 152 (on Pr 14:30).

[274]This is not the place to discuss in depth the terms *lēb* ("mind, heart, will") or *rûaḥ* ("spirit, disposition"). See the appropriate entries in the major theological dictionaries and lexicons, with bibliography.

[275]Cf. the modern research of P. Ekman, W. V. Friesen, and R. Davidson, building on the earlier work of the nineteenth-century French neurologist Guillame Benjamin Amand Duchenne de Boulogne, regarding human emotions and smiles and the physiological/psychological effects of both, as summarized by J. Schwartz, "Putting a Certain Face on Emotions: Right Sort of Grin May Spark Brain Response," *The Washington Post*, Monday, 8 November 1993, A3 (and note the chart entitled "Does Smiling Make You Feel Better?"); see also B. Siegel, "Healing of the Spirit and Curing of the Body," *Studies in Formative Spirituality* 12 (1991): 143–47.

[276]Although the NJV claims that the meaning of the Hebrew is uncertain, offering as an alternative "a cheerful face," there is no strong reason to depart from a rendering similar to that of the NIV. A. B. Ehrlich's interpretation is certainly unique, viz., that a merry heart makes the buttocks fat! Cf. *Randglossen*, 6:100–101, where *ghh* is compared to Arabic *jhwy*, "buttocks" (see ibid., 101, for J. Barth's suggestion to connect *ghh* with the Arabic word for face, thus to be compared with the NJV's marginal rendering). See further 0.3.3, sub *ghh*.

[277]For an attempt to interpret spiritually the apparent gender switch in the use of *rûaḥ* (with the masculine *yᵉkalkēl* in 14a but, as usual, with feminine *nᵉkē'â* in 14b, cf. Delitzsch, *Proverbs*, KD 6/2, 9–10 (although *yᵉkalkēl* is probably to be explained by the association of *rûaḥ* with *'îš* in 14a). See further McKane, *Proverbs*, 517: "It is a man's spirit which enables him to 'contain' his illness.... It is a sickness of spirit which is mortal, for when this inner citadel of resistance has been crushed and all zest for the warfare of life has departed, no man can endure."

[278]Commentators devoting hundreds of pages to the study of Job commonly express their inability to plumb its majestic depths; see N. C. Habel, *The Book of Job* (OTL; Philadelphia: Westminster, 1985), 9; Clines, *Job 1–20*, xi-xii.

[279]Although Job and his friends are portrayed as (to use an anachronistic term) "non-Israelites," the author/editor of the book writes as a thoroughgoing OT believer; cf., however, D. Wolfers, "Is Job After All Jewish?" *Dor le Dor* 14 (1985): 39–44.

[280]For detailed exegesis of the key terms in 1:1–2, cf. Clines, *Job 1–20*, 11–13. In S. Mitchell's rendering, *The Book of Job* (2d ed.; San Francisco: North Point Press, 1987), 5, Job is a man of "perfect integrity."

[281]Cf. Gordis, *The Book of God and Man*, 135–56; see the relevant discussions in the commentaries, monographs, and books devoted to Job.

[282]Cf. Ge 18:25. Abraham had no problem with God slaying the wicked, for that would be only fair and right. But it would be out of character for the Lord to sweep away the righteous with the wicked. Cf. also the commentary to Ge 18:25 of the sixteenth-century rabbinic commentator Obadiah Sforno, who notes that if God, as the Judge of the all the earth, were to judge the whole world based on the majority, then without doubt he would always destroy it, since the majority of human beings are evil.

[283]In 2:3, the word *ḥinnām* can mean "without cause" or "to no purpose" (cf. BDB, 336; S. R. Driver and G. B. Gray, *The Book of Job* [ICC; repr. Edinburgh: T. & T. Clark, 1977], 1/1:21, 1/2:12). Both meanings should probably be understood here; cf. Clines, *Job 1–20*, 42–43, for discussion. Job himself uses *ḥinnām* in 9:17b, claiming that even if God gave him a hearing, he would "multiply my wounds for no reason." On this verse M. Greenberg comments: "Ironically, Job has unwittingly stumbled on the true reason for his suffering." See "Job," in R. Alter and F. Kermode, eds., *The Literary Guide to the Bible* (Cambridge, Mass.: Harvard Univ. Press, 1987), 289; cf. Murphy, *Tree of Life*, 39, 47, n. 6.

[284]As expressed by Clines, *Job 1–20*, xl, "Even the most innocent of humans, like Job, must expect to suffer deservedly on occasion."

[285]On the meaning of *šûb šᵉbût/šᵉbît*, see below, 3.3.3.

[286]Although there is an ancient tradition that interprets the unusual form for "seven" (*šib'ānâ*) as a dual, hence "fourteen" (so *Targ.* and many interpreters since), it is best to simply read it as an archaic form (cf. E. Dhorme, *A Commentary on the Book of Job,* trans. H. Knight [Nashville: Thomas Nelson, 1965], 651–52; Hartley, *Job*, 542); in light of the reading "fourteen," it has been suggested that God gave Job twice the amount of original sons (a great blessing!) but only the same number of daughters, the girls being of lesser value (yet note that it is *the daughters* who are singled out in 42:14–15; cf. Gordis, *Job*, 498; cf. 1Ch 25:5). Otherwise, it is generally understood that the reason Job received double in possessions but only the same amount of children is that "the value of human life is so much greater than the value of property"—hence, irreplaceable—although the hint of either future resurrection or life after death (so that Job's first children were waiting for him on "the other side") has also been suggested (cf. Hartley, *Job*, 542).

[287]According to the LXX (42:16), which makes Job seventy years old at the time of his trial, God granted him 170 additional years. More importantly, Job was granted a deeper, more personal revelation of the Lord; see below, 3.3.3.

[288]For a classic example of this exercise, cf. H. L. Ginsberg, "Job the Patient and Job the Impatient," *ConsJud* (1967), 12–28; see also ibid., *Congress Volume: Rome 1968* (VTSupp.; Leiden: E. J. Brill, 1969), 88–111. For the overall flow and development of the book, cf. C. Westermann, *The Structure of the Book of Job*, trans. C. A. Muenchow (Philadelphia: Fortress, 1981), although Westermann's description of Job as a lament is somewhat forced; cf. R.

Ahroni, "An Examination of the Literary Genre of the Book of Job," *Tarbiz* 49 (1979/80): 1–13 (Hebrew).

[289]Contrast Mitchell, *The Book of Job*, who completely omits the Elihu speeches (along with other, shorter sections and isolated verses) from his translation.

[290]Cf., however, Hartley, *Job*, 17–20, for a balanced, evangelical assessment of the dating of Job.

[291]Satan's reply to the Lord, however, is subject to widely varied interpretations; see the standard commentaries; on the repetition in 2:2, see Clines, *Job 1–20*, 41.

[292]Habel's view that "Yahweh's hidden fears about Job are the counterpart to Job's inner fears about his sons" (*Job*, 89) must be rejected.

[293]Cf. Habel, *Job*, 90, who notes that Satan challenges not only Job's personal piety, but also "a basic tenet of wisdom theology which assumes an inevitable nexus between reward and righteousness." Thus, Satan infers that "righteousness is the result of divine blessings, not vice versa."

[294]Cf. Gordis, *Job*, 15, to 1:7; Hartley, *Job*, 73, to 1:11; Dhorme, *Job*, 5, to 1:6 ("Among the sons of God Satan has insinuated himself"); otherwise, Clines, *Job 1–20*, 19.

[295]Contrast, with intended irony, Dt 28:63a (AV; it is softened in the NIV).

[296]Hartley, *Job*, 72–73, notes that the "author [of Job] has a doubly difficult task throughout his work: continually to characterize Job as innocent and not to characterize Yahweh as demonic."

[297]The book of Job is actually a favorite of the critics of modern healing movements; cf. Masters, *Healing Epidemic*, 58. Job also presents a problem for strict adherents of the concept that "it is always God's will to heal"; thus, in their view, Job somehow must be held responsible for opening the door to Satan. Explanations include: Job married the wrong woman; he was walking in fear; he blasphemed (*sic* !) the Lord in 1:21. For documentation of some of these, see Hanegraaff, *Christianity in Crisis*, 97–102. Note, however, that in spite of Hanegraaff's refutation of Job's contemporary "comforters," he is also guilty of making Job fit too neatly into his own theology (pp. 101–2). Once again, Job defies narrow categorizations! Interestingly, even the *Test. Job* concocts an elaborate story of Job's heroic stand against idolatry as the provocation for Satan's attack; cf. *OTP* 1:840ff.

[298]It is not clear from Lk 22:31–32 as to whether Satan *obtained permission from God* to sift the disciples like wheat, or whether he simply *sought an opportunity*; cf. J. A. Fitmyer, *Luke X–XXIV* (AB; Garden City, N.Y.: Doubleday, 1985), 1420–28; J. Nolland, *Luke 18:35–24:43* (WBC; Dallas: Word, 1993), 1068–74. For the position of NT believers vis-à-vis the devil, especially in light of the resurrection of Jesus (Mt 28:18; Eph 1:18–23), cf. Eph 6:10–18; Jas 4:7; 1Pe 5:8–9; see also Lk 10:19, and below, 5.2.1, 5.3.1.

[299]Romans 8:28 in the AV is often quoted to demonstrate that "all things work together for good" in the life of the believer who loves the Lord. But a noncontextual quoting of this verse can possibly lead to theological misunderstanding. Do potential setbacks such as sin, rebellion, and backsliding, or

extreme hardships such as cancer, depression, and economic collapse *in and of themselves* actually work for the good? Rather, following the majority of textual critics (reflected in, e.g., the NIV), it is better to understand that in all things *God* works for the good of the committed believer (contrary to J. D. G. Dunn, *Romans 1–8* [WBC; Waco, Tex.: Word, 1988], 466, n. i, and 481, who argues for the minority view as reflected in AV). The NIV's rendering certainly held true for Job.

[300]Cf. above, 2.1, 2.2.2, and 2.2.5.

[301]Cf. Lindström, *God and the Origin of Evil.*

[302]Although Hartley, *Job*, 18, states, "The term *the Satan* in the prologue [of Job] functions as a title, not as a proper name as in the late books of Chronicles and Zechariah," it is nonetheless significant that his malignant nature (cf. Zec 3) and his association with sickness and death (cf. 2Ch 21:1, where, for the only time in the OT, "Satan" appears as a proper name without the definite article) are most clearly articulated in Job 1–2. If Hartley's dating is accepted (cf. above, n. 290), this indicates a relatively early (i.e., preexilic) understanding that *another*, heavenly power was sometimes the author of sickness and calamity. If a postexilic date is preferred (cf. the concise discussion of the problems of fixing the date of the book in Habel, *Job*, 40–42), it is still quite significant that, for as much as half a milennium *before* the NT era, this "Satan" was associated with disease and death. See also the discussion on Ps 91, above (3.1.10), and more fully, 5.3.1; cf. V. P. Hamilton, "Satan," *ABD* 5:985–89; K. Nielsen, "שָׂטָן," *TWAT* 7:745–51. Note, however, Clines, *Job 1–20*, 20, who cautions against projecting the later, fully developed image of the Satan of Jewish and Christian theology back into the opening chapters of Job. The reference to a *satan* (without the definite article) in Ps 109:6 is best rendered "an adversary, accuser," as is commonly done here; it is not a reference to a personal "Satan" (*contra* Hamilton, "Satan," 986, who argues for a "terrestrial satan" here). See also W. D. Reyburn, *A Handbook on the Book of Job* (UBS Handbook Series; New York: United Bible Societies, 1992), 39; cf., in general, P. Day, *An Adversary in Heaven: Satan in the Hebrew Bible* (Atlanta: Scholars, 1988); E. L. Fernández, "'Satán,' de nombre común a nombre propio. Historia de una palabra," *Studium Ovetense* 17 (1989):, 25–93; note the interesting perspective of S. P. Rao and M. P. Reddy, "Job and His Satan—Parallels in Indian Scripture," *ZAW* 91 (1979): 416–22.

[303]Speaking of Satan's subservience to God and in obvious contrast to Christian theology, Gordis, *Job*, 14, states: "There is no Hebrew equivalent for the phrase 'the kingdom of Satan.'" There is, however, a pervasive demonology in rabbinic Judaism, especially in the traditional and mystical sources, and Satan is active; cf. D. R. Hillers, L. I. Rabinowitz, and G. Scholem, "Demons, Demonology," *EJ* 5:1521–33; see also T. H. Gaster, "Satan," *IDB* 4:227; Hamilton, "Satan," 988.

[304]The view stated here is based on my (conservative) belief in progressive revelation—and thus, ultimately, the providential superintending of the biblical books—as opposed to a bare historical explanation, viz., that the unveiling of Satan in 2Ch 21; Zec 3; and Job 1–2 is simply due to the influence

of, e.g., Zoroastrian dualism; cf. in general J. Barr, "The Question of Religious Influence: The Case of Zoroastrianism, Judaism, and Christianity," *JAAR* 53 (1985): 201–35.

[305]Job's "oath of innocence" (see ch. 31) underscores his extraordinary piety. For ch. 31 as a legal challenge, cf. especially M. B. Dick, "The Legal Metaphor in Job 31," *CBQ* 41 (1979): 37–50; cf. Habel, *Job*, 423–40; also 54–57.

[306]I do not follow here the argument of J. G. Janzen, *Job* (Interpretation; Atlanta: John Knox, 1985), 51–53, who believes that the affirmation of faith in 2:10a is not on the same level as that of 1:21–22 (cf. already Ibn Ezra to 2:10; see *b. B. Bat.* 16a, with Rashi). See Erhlich, *Randglossen*, 6:187, followed by Gordis, *Job*, 22, both with reference to Ps 39:1(2), indicating that Job did not sin with his lips (2:10b) because he had not sinned with his heart.

[307]Has anyone articulated this more powerfully than Søren Kierkegaard?

> Job! Job! Job! Job! Didst thou indeed utter nothing but these beautiful words, "The Lord gave, the Lord hath taken away, blessed be the name of the Lord?" Didst thou say nothing more? ... No, thou who in the ripeness of thy days wast a sword for the oppressed, a cudgel to protect the old, a staff for the decrepit, thou didst not fail men when all was riven asunder—then thou wast a mouth for the afflicted, and a cry for the contrite, and a shriek for the anguished, and an assuagement for all who were rendered dumb by torments, a faithful witness to the distress and grief a heart can harbor, a trustworthy advocate who dared to complain "in anguish of spirit" and to contend with God. Why do people conceal this? ... Does one perhaps not dare to complain before God? ... Thee I have need of, a man who knows how to complain aloud, so that his complaint echoes in heaven where God confers with Satan in devising schemes against a man.

See *Repetition*, trans. W. Lowrie (Princeton: Princeton Univ. Press, 1941), 110–11, quoted in Murphy, *Tree of Life*, 38–39. See also below, nn. 309 and 319.

[308]Regardless of one's understanding of Job 13:15a (contrast the classic expression of the AV, articulated eloquently by Delitzsch, *Job*, KD 4/1:213ff.—although he does not in the end accept that understanding of the verse—with the interpretation of Forher, *Hiob*, 234, 238, 251), it is clear that he is willing to put himself in jeopardy and take his life into his own hands (13:14) to argue his case before the Lord. The translation of N. H. Tur Sinai, *The Book of Job: A New Commentary* (Jerusalem: Kiryath Sepher, 1957), 224–25, "If he slay me—I am waiting for it, but I will reprove his ways to his face," based on his claim that *dᵉrākāy* ("my ways") is a "scribal correction" for *darkô* or *dᵉrākāyw* ("his way/s"), goes too far and is unsupported by the ancient versions as well as the general context. Note that this verse, with its classic Kere-Qetib *crux*, contributes to the Talmudic discussion of whether Job served God out of love or fear; see *m. Sot.* 5:5; *b. Sot.* 27b; for *b. Sot.* 31a,

cf. R. Gordis, *The Biblical Text in the Making: A Study of the Kethib-Qere* (2d ed., New York: Ktav, 1971), 51, n. 27.

[309]For further examples of great faith taken beyond the breaking point—without "breaking"—see the boldly passionate poem composed by Richard Wurmbrand, a Jewish Christian Romanian pastor, in the midst of his three years in solitary confinement and torture (part of fourteen years in prison): *In God's Underground* (Bartlesville, Okla.: Living Sacrifice Books, n.d), 66–68; also the moving Holocaust prayer written by Zvi Kolitz and imaginatively placed on the lips of Yossel Rakover, a Hasidic Jew killed in the Warsaw Ghetto uprising: "Yossel Rakover's Appeal to God," in A. Friedlander, ed., *Out of the Whirlwind: A Reader of Holocaust Literature* (New York: Schocken, 1976), 390–99.

[310]Although, from a technical standpoint, R. E. Murphy, *Wisdom Literature* (FOTL; Grand Rapids: Eerdmans, 1981), 15, classifies only Job 3 and 29–31 under the heading of "Job's soliloquy," it is commonly recognized that much of his speaking is addressed only to God; cf. p. 26: "throughout the speeches he addresses God at least obliquely."

[311]Cf. Clines, *Job 1–20*, xlii. Of course, he does not claim perfection (cf. 7:21; 9:20; 10:6; 13:26), but it is unthinkable to him that a man of his devotion and godliness should suffer so horribly by the will and pleasure of God.

[312]Cf. Jas 5:10, which speaks of the final end (*telos*) of Job in the context of patient endurance (*makrothumia*) in the midst of suffering.

[313]See Murphy, *Tree of Life*, 40.

[314]Hartley, *Job*, 82; cf. also S. M. Paul, "An Unrecognized Medical Idiom in Canticles 6, 12 and Job 9, 21," *Bib* 59 (1978): 545–47 (that Job was "out of his mind" with sorrow). See Hartley, ibid., for speculation and caveats concerning the exact nature of Job's disease(s); cf. also Clines, *Job 1–20*, 48–49.

[315]Her response, however, can be analyzed differently; for the extreme characterization of Job's wife as *adiutrix diaboli* ("the helper of the devil"; cf. Augustine) and "Satan's tool" (cf. Calvin), as well as for the view that her *survival* was a further satanic trial for Job (cf. Thomas Aquinas and T. K. Cheyne), see Gordis, *Job*, 21 (with reference to his *Book of God and Man*, 10–11, 71–72, 223); Clines, *Job 1–20*, 51. For a sympathetic discussion, cf. Clines, ibid., 50–53, and note especially *T. Job*, 21–25, where she is presented as a remarkably sacrificial, loyal partner. Moreover, in the canonical Job, she is (apparently) the unmentioned wife of the epilogue, part of his blessed, post-calamity life, and the mother of his second set of children.

[316]Hartley, *Job*, 82–83, n. 4, notes that, in light of Dt 28:35, the specific reference to Job's being struck with boils indicates that he "was smitten with a repulsive disease that not only tormented but also symbolized that he was encountering the wrath of God." Of course, this is the insight of the later reader, as opposed to something Job would necessarily have perceived; yet the hint may have been intended by the author.

[317]Clines, *Job 1–20*, 382; see there for scriptural references illuminating all the above. Note also Habel, *Job*, 268 (with a chart showing the powerful chiastic flow of 16:9–14). As for the friends, Habel, 272, states that Job depicts

them in 16:10–11 as "a pack of scavengers, like starving jackals, [who] attend God's savage raids on his victim and intensify the plight of his prey (cf. Rowley)."

[318]See especially Job 21, with the summary of Gordis, *Job*, 223.

[319]Just as the sorely afflicted, long-suffering reader of the Scriptures finds comfort in the agonized "How long?" laments and prayers of the psalmists (cf. above, 3.1.1–4)—seeing that he or she is not the only one to wait, seemingly endlessly, for the Lord's intervention—so also many readers have found solidarity with "Job the impatient." Here, their gnawing doubts, deep questions, and even unspoken grievances against the Lord are articulated by Job, a hero of the faith and one whose final end is known to be blessed. It is important, however, to journey with Job until the end of the book; otherwise faith is shipwrecked on the shallow shores of incomplete revelation. Cf. Clines, *Job 1–20*, xxxix: "Viewed as an answer to the problem of suffering, then, the argument of the Book of Job is: By all means let Job the patient be your model so long as that is possible for you; but when equanimity fails, let the grief and anger of Job the impatient direct itself and yourself toward God, for only in encounter with him will be [*sic*] the tension of suffering be resolved." See also above, n. 307.

[320]Borrowing the concept from the great medieval poet, Solomon Ibn Gabirol, and his poem, "The Royal Crown" (see further Gordis, *Job*, 527).

[321]For the progression of faith from Job 9 to 16 to 19, see ibid., 526–28 ("Special Note 15: Arbiter–Witness–Redeemer–Job's Three Levels of Faith"). Note that Clines, however, has brilliantly challenged these views (see *Job 1–20*, ad loc.; cf. Habel, *Job*, 302–9, to 19:21–29). Note also Delitzsch, *Job*, KD 4:300, to 17:8–9: "These words of Job (if we may be allowed the figure) are like a rocket which shoots above the tragic darkness of the book, lighting it up suddenly, although only for a short time." For the question of Job's affirmation (or denial) of the afterlife and/or resurrection, see the commentaries on 7:21; 14:5–22; 16:22; 19:23–27. The proposed renderings of M. L. Barré, "A Note on Job xix 25," *VT* 29 (1979): 107–10, in particular connecting 19:25a with healing ("I know that my redeemer can [or will] restore [my] life/health"), have not gained much support.

[322]Cf. Clines, *Job 1–20*, xxxvii–xlvii.

[323]The happy ending is often considered too neat, virtually undermining the whole theme of the book; cf. R. Dedmon, "Job as Holocaust Survivor," *Saint Luke's Journal of Theology* 26 (1983): 165–85 (the divine speeches and prologue are "unsatisfying and unconvincing"). But that, in fact, is to misunderstand a final theme of Job, viz., that God *will* bless and vindicate his people in the end; see also Lk 18:7–8 and the application of Job's sufferings in Jas 5:7–11, discussed below. Ultimately, the book of Job affirms the theology of Ps 37; it almost exactly parallels that of Ps 73, often called "the little Job" (cf. Tate, *Psalms 51–100*, 226–39).

[324]I am not here speaking of *suffering for the gospel* (cf. below, 5.3.3; above, n. 168), which *is* to be expected (e.g., 2Ti 3:12) and *is* a part of the equation that every prospective believer must factor in (e.g., Lk 14:25–33). Although,

in a sense, Job suffers "for righteousness' sake" (cf. Mt 5:10; 1Pe 4:12–19), it was not, on his part, a voluntary "taking up of his cross" (as in Mt 16:26).

[325]So, e.g., Gordis, *Job*, 46.

[326]Cf. the rendering of 4:17 in RSV, JB, NJV, as well as in the commentaries of Driver and Gray, Gordis, Pope, and Clines; contrast AV, ASV, NEB, and NIV, all of which understand the point to be that no man is *more righteous* than God. But does this even need to be argued? See the commentaries cited, ad loc., for ample philological and contextual discussion.

[327]Cf. F. I. Anderson, *Job* (TOTC; Downers Grove, Ill., InterVarsity, 1976), 121–22, especially 121, n. 2, where he states that the idea of divine chastening suggested by Job's friends is "the nearest that any of them can come to a solution to Job's problem."

[328]For a comparative study, which potentially relegates some of El Shaddai's discipline to divine caprice, although ultimately for the sufferer's benefit, cf. J. B. Burns, "The Chastening of the Just in Job 5:17–23: Four Strikes of Erra," *Proceedings, Eastern Great Lakes and Midwest Bible Societies* 10 (1990): 18–30.

[329]This is recognized by Driver and Gray, *Job*, lxviii; 1:55 (noting Isa 30:26b as well); according to Dhorme, *Job*, 68–69, "The ideas and the style of Eliphaz are inspired by Dt. 32:39 . . . as also by Hos 6:1. Cf. the use of *ḥbš*, *mḥṣ*, and *rp'* in Is. 30:26." On the general issue of biblical quotations in Job, cf. the convenient chart, with discussion, in Hartley, *Job*, 11–15 (dealing here with further parallels with Isaiah); see also R. Gordis, *The Book of God and Man*, 169–89, "The Use of Quotations in Job," and idem, "Virtual Quotations in Job, Sumer and Qumran," *VT* 31 (1981): 410–27. I do not concur with W. F. Albright's view (as stated by D. N. Freedman, "Orthographic Peculiarities in the Book of Job," *EI* 9, *43) that there is in Job a "total absence of quotations from Scripture, the closest being a few word sequences and common themes." In addition to finding numerous intentional Scriptural allusions in Job, I also follow Gordis in reading verses such as 9:2b as (sometimes sarcastic) quotations of the friends (cf. 4:17; 8:3) or of other dialogues; cf. Gordis, *Job*, 102 (on 9:2), 231 (on 21:19), 345 (on 31:2–4), 492 (on 42:3–4, which clearly refer back to words of the Lord).

[330]It is possible in light of Job 5:17 (cf. Pr 3:11) that the wording of 5:18 (*kî hû' yak'îb weyeḥbāš yimḥaṣ wᵉyādāyw tirpênâ*) substantiates the assumed LXX reading of Prov 3:12 (*mastigoi de* = *wᵉyak'îb*—so *BHS*—instead of MT *ûkᵉ'ab*). This suggestion, referring to Job 5:18, was anticipated already by *BHK* (if not even earlier). Cf. also the observation of D. Yellin, *Ḥiqre Miqra—Iyyob* (Hebrew; repr. Jerusalem: Reuven Mass, 1983), cited by Gordis, Job, 57, that 5:16–18 are clearly drawn from other biblical passages: 16b = Ps 107:42; 17a = Ps 94:12; 17b = Pr 3:11; 18a = Hos 6:1; 18b = Dt 32:39, demonstrating again that it was the author of Job who intentionally borrowed from extant sacred writings, not the reverse.

[331]On the early dating of Dt 32, cf. above, 2.2.5.

[332]It should be noted here that the question of internal biblical quotations is not merely a matter of literary style or relative dating. Rather, it cuts to

the core of the book of Job's message. In other words, exactly how much irony, sarcasm, and biblical tension was intentional on the part of the author? For example, is Job 7:17ff. a parody on Ps 8? (Gordis actually hails this passage as "unsurpassed in world literature" for its irony; *Job*, 82.) Does Job 5:18 have Dt 32:39 and Hos 6:1 in mind? The recognition of intentional borrowing heightens the stakes involved, since, in a sense, it sets Job *against* the Scriptures, represented and repeated—at times literally but not appropriately—by the friends.

[333]Of course, the friends were not merely asserting the rightness of the orthodox theology, openly questioned and attacked by Job; they were also indicting him, believing that he was wicked and was suffering the well-deserved consequences (see Habel, *Job*, 331–42).

[334]From 1984 to 1987, scores of students submitting papers to me on Elihu were equally divided in their opinions, and always to opposite extremes: Either Elihu was an anointed spokesman of the Lord, or he was an arrogant youth. This, I thought, might have reflected an intended textual ambiguity, part of the book's abiding mystery. However, in 1987, at a different institute, three students of mine submitted papers on Elihu *independently* and came to the same conclusion, viz., that he was an Elijah/John the Baptist-type figure who suddenly appeared and disappeared, preparing the way for the Lord. Moreover, they arrived at this understanding before finding confirmation in Gordis, who had long ago presented this view, also pointing out that Elihu and Elijah are consonantly identical in Hebrew (both *'lyh*; see his *Book of God and Book of Man*, 115–16). In any case, my still tentative views regarding Elihu do not materially affect this section. For an exhaustive survey of scholarship on these speeches, see H.-M. Wahl, *Der Gerechte Schöpfer: Eine redaktions- und theologiegeschichtliche Untersuchung der Elihureden—Hiob 32–37* (BZAW 207; Berlin/New York: de Gruyter, 1993).

[335]The end of v. 18 follows the NIV note (cf. Pope, *Job*, 246).

[336]There are many difficult words in this section; for discussion, cf. especially the commentaries of Delitzsch, Driver and Gray, Dhorme, Pope, Fohrer, Gordis, Habel, and Reyburn, *Handbook on Job*, ad loc.

[337]Note v. 19, *wᵉhûkaḥ*, from the root *ykḥ*, "to reprove, rebuke"; cf., foundationally, 5:17a; see also Ps 94:10a; Pr 3:11–12.

[338]Cf. Hartley, *Job*, 444, for a clear, succinct summary.

[339]Ibid. Of course, it is illogical to think that God would give a sinner over to death by disease in order to keep him from sin—which leads to death. Rather, Elihu's argument is that God may hasten and intensify the effects and consequences of sin so as to bring the sinner to repentance before he wastes even more years, falls under even greater judgment, causes even more damage, and then, in the end, dies for his sin anyway.

[340]Once again, almost every word in vv. 23ff. is subject to widely different interpretations. For summaries, cf. ibid., 444–47. But regardless of the specific interpretations followed, the overall sense is clear.

[341]The concept derived by later expositors from this verse, viz., that *healing* was connected with (the) *atonement* (here *kōper,* rendered "ransom"; cf.

Gk. *lutron*) of Christ, played a key role in the instantaneous physical healing and deliverance from drug addiction of Lilian B. Yeomans, M.D., as related in her *Healing from Heaven* (rev. ed., Springfield, Mo.: Radiant Books/Gospel Pub. House, 1973), 7–16. She subsequently went on to be a prominent practitioner and teacher of divine healing. Similar testimonies relative to Job 33:24 and the issue of healing and the atonement are common; cf. also below, 5.2.2, 5.3.2. For Hebrew *kōper*, "ransom, *Lösegeld*," cf. G. Fohrer, *Das Buch Hiob* (KAT: Gütersloh: Gerd Mohn, 1963), 460.

[342]Alternatively, as reflected in the NJV, it is God who "has mercy on him and decrees, 'Spare him from descending to the Pit, for I have obtained his ransom.'"

[343]Cf. *pādâ* with *šaḥat* here in 33:28a and *gā'al* with *šaḥat* in Ps 103:4a; note also *ḥayyâ* in Job 33:28b and Ps 103:4a.

[344]Note the usage of the root *šûb* in vv. 25b, 26c, 30a.

[345]For the meaning of *rûṭāpāš* in 33:25, cf. Grabbe, *Comparative Philology*, 107–8; F. E. Greenspahn, *Hapax Legomena in Biblical Hebrew* (SBLDS 74; Chico, Calif.: Scholars, 1984), 157–58; *HALAT* 4:1141.

[346]Cf. 33:19 as rendered by Pope, *Job*, 246: "Or one may be chastened on a bed of pain, with ceaseless agony."

[347]Cf. the *tᵉrû'â*—shout of joy—in 26b; see *HALAT* 4:1647–49.

[348]For the "light of life" imagery, cf. above, n. 124; see also 2.1.

[349]Cf. also 36:8–15, where Elihu further develops the theme that God speaks to human beings in their affliction.

[350]For recent studies of these speeches, in addition to the commentaries, cf. J. G. William, "Job's Vision: The Dialectic of Person and Presence," *HAR* 8 (1984): 259–72; idem, "Deciphering the Unspoken: The Theophany of Job," *HUCA* 49 (1978): 59–72; H. P. Müller, "Gottes Antwort an Hiob und das Recht religiöser Wahrheit," *BZ* (1988): 210–31; H. Rowold, "Yahweh's Challenge to Rival: The Form and Function of the Yahweh-Speech in Job 38–39," *CBQ* 47 (1985): 199–211; A. Brenner, "God's Answer to Job," *VT* 31 (1981): 129–37; M. V. Fox, "Job 38 and God's Rhetoric," *Sem* 18 (1981): 53–61; Y. Tsmudi, "God's Answer to Job," *Beth Mikra* 34 (1988–89): 302–11 (Hebrew). For an overall interpretation, including the meaning of the divine speeches, cf. D. Bergant, C.S.A., "Why Do I Suffer?" *TBT* 20 (1982): 341–46.

[351]The translation of this verse is open to widely variant interpretations; cf. J. B. Curtis, "On Job's Response to Yahweh," *JBL* 98 (1979): 497–511; D. J. O'Connor, "Job's Final Word—'I Am Consoled . . .' (42:6b)," *ITQ* 50 (1983/84): 181–97; W. Morrow, "Consolation, Rejection, and Repentance in Job 42:6," *JBL* 105 (1986): 211–25; C. Muenchow, "Dust and Dirt in Job 42:6," *JBL* 108 (1989): 597–611; more broadly, B. L. Newell, "Job: Repentant or Rebellious?" *WTJ* 46 (1984): 298–316; note also L. J. Kaplan, "Maimonides, Dale Patrick, and Job xlii 6," *VT* 28 (1978): 356–57, who points out that the interpretation of D. Patrick put forth in the latter's "A Translation of Job xlii 6," *VT* 26 (1976): 369–71 (viz., that Job would no longer wallow in dust and ashes), was anticipated already by Maimonides in his *Guide to the Perplexed*, 3:23.

[352]Cf. McKay, "The Experience of Dereliction," 10: The sufferer "does not want reasoned explanations such as Job's comforters might care to offer. The only answer he is prepared to accept is complete restoration, which, he knows, and as Job also discovered, is to be found in the vision of the face of God and there alone. *He seeks not explanations, not consolations, not even cures, but God himself*" (his emphasis). Cf. also D. O'Connor, "The Futility of Myth-Making in Theodicy: Job 38–41" *Proceedings of the Irish Biblical Association* 9 (1985): 81–99.

[353]The interpretation of the divine speeches—both philosophically and exegetically—is possibly *the* most disputed of all the sections in the book; cf. above, n. 350.

[354]So Dhorme, *Job*, 649; for detailed textual discussion, cf. ibid., 649–50; see further M. Ben-Yashar and M. Zipor, "שְׁבִית/שְׁבוּת," *TWAT* 7:958–65 (with lit.); J. M. Bracke, "*šûb š^{e}bût*: A Reappraisal," *ZAW* 97 (1985): 233–44; *HALAT* 4:1289–90; for additional bibliography, see further below, 4.1.2, n. 38.

[355]Hartley, *Job*, 540. It is noteworthy that, as dark as Job's trial was, it seems to have been relatively brief in endurance (possibly only a matter of weeks?), underscoring the fact that his whole life, with the exception of this one dark spot, was blessed with the light of God's life. Contrast the biblical account with *Test. Job*, where he suffers for more than seventeen years (cf. *Test. Job*, 26:1), ultimately losing his faithful wife.

[356]Cf. D. N. Freedman, "Is It Possible to Understand the Book of Job?" *BibRev* 4/2 (April 1988): 26–33, 44; note also the "conclusions" of E. M. Good, *In Turns of Tempest: A Reading of Job, with a Translation* (Stanford, Calif.: Stanford Univ. Press, 1990), who claims that "the truth about Job ... cannot be found" (178), and "that the book remains open and multiple, its 'meaning' indeterminate and undecidable" (394). According to D. E. Gowan, "God's Answer to Job: How Is It an Answer?" *HBT* 8 (1986): 85–102, "God's failure to explain Job's suffering is not a flaw in the book, but it is rather the genius of the piece" (89).

[357]Clines, *Job 1–20*, xlvii; on the significance of Job's restoration, cf. Fohrer, *Hiob*, 542–43.

[358]Of course, had this been done, we would have no book of Job! I am speaking here, however, of retrospective lessons to be learned.

[359]Note that in the Scriptures, the "goodness of God" is not a bare theological maxim; rather, his goodness is evident, reasonable, and praiseworthy; cf. the frequent exhortation *hôdû layhwh kî ṭôb* ("Give thanks to the LORD, for he is good") in the Psalms (e.g., Ps 107), the rational appeal of Eze 18 (contrasting the ways of the Lord with Israel's ways), and verses such as Mt 7:9–11. The reasonable goodness of God is also a common theme in Arminian polemic against Calvinism; cf. J. Wesley, "Predestination Calmly Considered," reprinted in *Wesley's Works* 10:204–59 (Baker edition), especially 215–29.

[360]Cf. above, n. 183.

[361]Cf. below, 5.3.1, for a NT perspective.

[362]Cf. the commission to "drive out demons" (Mt 10:8; Mk 16:17); note Ac 16:16–18; Eph 6:12ff.; Jas 4:7; 1Pe 5:8–9; cf. also F. F. Bruce, *1 & 2 Thessalonians* (WBC; Waco, Tex.: Word, 1982), 58 (comparing 1Th 2:18 with Ac 16:6–7).

[363]Has any book generated a diverse bibliography such as that assembled in Clines, *Job 1–20*, lxiv-cxv (and note esp. the listing under "Job and Its Influence," civ-cxii)? For a slight indication of the varied ways in which this profound book has been read, cf. N. Sarna, *The Dimensions of Job* (New York: Schocken, 1969).

[364]Cf. Jas 5:10–11; note the reputation of Job in Eze 14:12–14, for which see Greenberg, *Ezekiel 1–20*, 257–58.

[365]For overall discussion and theological assessment of the book, along with interaction with recent scholarship, cf. most recently T. Longman, III, *The Book of Ecclesiastes* (NICOT; Grand Rapids: Eerdmans, 1994).

[366]The reading of *bôr'ekā*, "your Creator," as opposed to "your vigor" (cf. NJV, based on post-biblical Hebrew *bôrî*), should be retained in 12:1. The latter understanding seems too hedonistic, although it is not lacking in textual and interpretive support (cf. H. L. Ginsberg, *Koheleth* [Hebrew; Tel Aviv/Jerusalem: M. Newman, 1961], 129).

[367]On "time and chance" as a euphemism for death in 9:11, cf. the note to NJV's rendering "time of mischance" (cf. Ginsberg, ibid., 116).

[368]Cf. already Ibn Ezra.

[369]C. D. Ginsburg, *The Song of Songs and Coheleth* (repr. New York: Ktav, 1970), 1/2:305. Rashbam finds vv. 2–8 all referring to peace and war; cf. ibid. The Targum (*'iddān bᵉ ḥîr lᵉ qaṭālā' biqrābā' lᵉ 'iddān bᵉ ḥîr lᵉ 'assā'ā šᵉ kîb mᵉ rā'*) may be rendered: "there is an appointed time for killing in battle, and an appointed time for healing the seriously ill."

[370]According to G. Vajda, *Deux commentaires Karaites sur L'Ecclésiaste* (Leiden: Brill, 1971), 1, n. 1, the *commentary* attributed to Sa'adiah in J. Qapah's ed. of Sa'adiah's *Hameš Megillot* is actually that of Isaac Ibn Gayyat.

[371]E. W. Hengstenberg, *A Commentary on Ecclesiastes* (repr.; Minneapolis: James and Klock, 1977), 96–97.

[372]Cf. 1Ch 5:22; for Christian reflection on the broader question of killing and war, cf. W. Klassen, "War in the New Testament," *ABD* 6:867–85 (with lit.); G. F. Hershberger, *War, Peace, and Non-Resistance* (3d ed., Scottdale, Pa.: Herald Press, 1969).

[373]Cf. Ginsburg, *Coheleth*, ad loc.; Delitzsch, *Ecclesiastes*, KD 6/3: 256–57.

[374]Cf. above, 3.2.2, and n. 244.

[375]Cf. G. A. Anderson, *A Time to Mourn and a Time to Dance: The Expression of Grief and Joy in Israelite Religion* (University Park, Pa.: Penn State Univ. Press, 1991).

[376]For the exegesis of the cyclical concepts listed in 3:1–8, not all of which are "darkness followed by light," cf. concisely Murphy, *Ecclesiastes*, 28–34. For the final, triumphant viewpoint of the Scriptures as a whole, see Rev 22:1–5, as well as below 4.2.2; note also the exposition of Ps 30:5(6) in Spurgeon, *Treasury of David*, 1/2:45.

Chapter Four—Israel's Divine Healer in the Prophetic Books

[1]As explained in the preface, unless otherwise noted, all translations of OT verses in this chapter are my own; for the NT, the NIV is used, as throughout the rest of this book (unless indicated otherwise).

[2]On the integrity of the MT at Jer 1:10, see W. McKane, *Commentary on Jeremiah, Vol. 1: I–XXV* (ICC; Edinburgh: T. & T. Clark, 1985), 10–11.

[3]In fact, the prophets who proclaimed peace were suspect; the message of judgment was presumed (Jer 28:5–9); cf. also Mic 3:5–6 for another example of the so-called *šālôm* prophets. See T. W. Overholt, *The Threat of Falsehood: A Study in the Theology of the Book of Jeremiah* (SBT 2d series; Naperville, Ill.: Allenson, 1970).

[4]According to W. Rudolph (as restated by McKane), "there is a temporal order of doom and then salvation: the prophet is instructed that first he must destroy false ideas and corrupt institutions; lies must be exposed and wrongs rooted out. It is a time for demolition, or a time for drastic action to kill the weeds and clean the ground. Rebuilding can only be done from the foundations, or a time of barrenness must be endured before there can be a return to fruitfulness" (*Jeremiah*, 11). Although McKane finds this interpretation of Jer 1:10 "too tidy to be true," I believe that it is both exegetically as well as historically accurate. The titles of the recent volumes on Jeremiah by W. Brueggeman in the ITC series reflect a similar understanding: *Jeremiah 1–25: To Pluck Up, To Tear Down* and *Jeremiah 26–52: To Build and To Plant* (Grand Rapids: Eerdmans, 1988, 1991); cf. further Jer 24:6; 31:28; 42:10. Cf. further "Homily 1" of Origen's homilies on Jeremiah, delivered c. A.D. 242 (see *Homélies sur Jérémie*, ed. and trans. P. Nautin [Paris: Les Éditions du Cerf, 1976], 15–21), brought to my attention and supplied to me in English translation by my editor, V. D. Verbrugge; Origen emphasizes the point in Jer 1:10 that before God can allow the prophet "to build and to plant," he must first "uproot and tear down, destroy and overthrow" (see 1.15).

[5]On the important covenantal usage of *šûb*, see W. L. Holladay, *The Root Šûbh in the Old Testament* (Leiden: E. J. Brill, 1958); for more general studies cf. J. J. Stamm, *Erlösen und Vergeben im Alten Testament* (Dissertation: Basel, 1940); G. Fohrer, "Umkehr und Erlosung beim Propheten Hosea," *ThZ* 11 (1955): 161–85. Stendahl, "Rafa'," 13, n. 17, referring to E. K. Dietrich's 1936 Tübingen Dissertation *Die Umkehr im Alten Testament und im Judentum*, states that *šûb* is often associated synonymously with *rāpā'*.

[6]H. M. Wolff, "The Transcendent Nature of the Covenant Curse Reversals," in A. Gileadi, ed., *Israel's Apostasy and Restoration* (Grand Rapids: Baker, 1988), 321. Wolff's reference to "the curses of famine, disease, and war" is in keeping with the "trilogy" of judgment ("the sword, famine, and plague [*nega'*]") spoken of throughout the book of Jeremiah; cf. Jer 14:12; 21:6–9; 24:10; 27:8, 23; 29:17–18; 32:24–36; 34:17; 38:2; 42:17; 44:13; cf. also Jer 28:8; Eze 5:12, 17; 6:11–12; 7:15; 12:16; 14:19; 28:23; 33:27; 38:22. Ezekiel adds a fourth dreadful judgment element: "wild beasts" (cf. 14:21). See

further, below, 4.1.2; and cf. Zec 14:12–18, which graphically describes the plagues of judgment God will pour out on the disobedient nations after Israel's final deliverance; cf. on this R. L. Smith, *Micah-Malachi*, WBC (Waco, Tex.: Word, 1984), 290–91. As in the covenant curses of Lev 26 and Dt 28 (see above, 2.2.2), and as attested throughout the OT historical books (2.2.5, 2.3), the "plague" was a frightful judgment of God, sent only on the rebellious and impious. Note also Amos 4:6–11, where the divine judgments against sinful Israel include famine, drought, blight and mildew, locusts, plagues, defeat in battle, and wholesale destruction.

[7]Note *rp'* ("heal/restore") and *ḥbš* ("bind up") opposite *šbr* ("break/shatter), *nkh* ("strike"), and *mḥṣ* ("wound"). For *māḥaṣ//rāpā'* cf. Dt 32:39; Job 5:18; for *ḥābaš//rāpā'*, cf. Job 5:18; Hos 6:1; cf. also above, 2.2.5, 3.3.2.3. The possessive suffix in the phrase *maḥaṣ makkatô* (lit., "the wounding of his/its smiting") is best understood with reference to God (as opposed to Israel as rendered here in the NJV); cf. NIV's "the wounds he inflicted."

[8]This represents the largest concentration of occurrences of this root in any one literary genre in the Hebrew Bible. Distribution is as follows: verbal—16 Qal (Isa 6:10; 19:22 [2x]; 30:26; 57:18, 19; Jer 3:22; 8:22; 17:14; 30:15; 33:6; Hos 5:13; 6:1; 7:1; 11:3; 14:5); 8 Niphal (Isa 53:5; Jer 15:18; 17:14; 51:8, 9; Eze 47:8, 9, 11); 5 Piel (Jer 6:14; 8:11; 51:9; Eze 34:4; Zec 11:16); nominal—*marpē'*, 5 times (Jer 8:15; 14:19 [2x]; 33:6; Mal 3:20); *rᵉpū'â* (3 times, all pl. (Jer 30:13; 46:11; Eze 30:21); *tᵉrûpâ* is found only in Eze 47:12. The occurrences of *rp'* in Eze 47–48 evidence the prophet's priestly heritage; cf. below, 4.2.2.

[9]Cf. the semantic studies on *yš'* by J. F. A. Sawyer (see, concisely, J. F. A. Sawyer and H. J. Fabry, "ישׁע," *TDOT* 6:441–63); cf. J. C. Filteau, "La racine *yš'*. Une des expression du salut dans l'Ancien Testament hébraïque," *LTP* 37 (1981), 135–59, and below, n. 100.

[10]See BDB, 950b, "רָפָא," Qal, meaning 2, where relevant texts from the prophetic books are classified. Of course, what is meant by BDB's classification is "metaphorical" healing as opposed to "physical" healing. This, however, fails to take into account the wider semantic range of *rāpā'*, and it has also contributed to the common but erroneous idea that for the prophets "healing" referred to something entirely spiritual. This will be discussed throughout this chapter.

[11]A. Oepke, "ἰάομαι," *TDNT* 3:201–2. With the exception of Eze 47–48, where the LXX renders *rp'* with related forms of *hugiazō* (see below, 4.2.2), *rp'* is elsewhere rendered with *iaomai* or its derivatives (cf. Hatch-Redpath, *Concordance*, 2/2:264).

[12]Ibid., 203. Under this heading, Oepke states: "The crucial thing is the restoration of fellowship with God, with all the comfort which flows from this and all the help that derives from it." Many commentators and theologians have erred by somehow imagining that in the biblical mentality, it would be possible to separate "the restoration of fellowship with God" from all the physical, tangible blessings that would consequently follow. In other

words, *rp'* is rarely, if ever, used in an exclusively spiritual context; see below, 4.1.2–3 for Hos 14:5 and Jer 3:22.

[13]Ibid., 214, my emphasis. It should be noted here that Oepke's words may also suggest that such "figurative" concepts of healing were foreign to the apostolic church as well, since the development of which he speaks post-dates the NT believing community.

[14]Cf. above, 0.3.1–2, for general discussion of the usage and meaning of *rāpā'*.

[15]J. R. Michaels, *First Peter* (WBC; Waco, Tex.: Word, 1988), 149.

[16]Hempel, *Heilung*, 238, begins his study with this section, stating, "Durch brutale Schlage kann ein Korper gar übel zugerichtet." For treatment of the key terms here, cf. Wildberger, *Isaiah 1–12*, 19, 26–27.

[17]J. MacArthur, *Charismatic Chaos*, 103, fails to understand this. He asks (with reference to Isa 53:5), "Was Isaiah talking about physical healing?" answering with the claim, "A study of the book of Isaiah shows that the prophet was talking about the *spiritual* healing that Israel needed so desperately" (his emphasis). For proof of this he cites Isa 1:4–6, obviously with no reference to the following verses.

[18]For the period in question, cf. B. S. Childs, *Isaiah and the Assyrian Crisis* (SBT, 2d ser.; London: SCM, 1967); M. Cogan, *Imperialism and Religion: Assyria, Judah and Israel in the Eighth and Seventh Centuries B.C.E.* (Missoula, Mont.: Scholars, 1974); idem, "Judah Under Assyrian Hegemony: A Re-examination of Imperialism and Religion," *JBL* 112 (1993): 403–14; J. Bright, *A History of Israel* (3d ed.; Philadelphia: Westminster, 1981), 269–309; H. Spieckermann, *Juda unter Assur in der Sargonidenzeit* (FRLANT 129; Göttingen: Vandenhoeck & Ruprecht, 1982). In the opinion of J. H. Hayes and S. A. Irvine, *Isaiah the Eighth-century Prophet: His Times and His Preaching* (Nashville: Abingdon, 1987), 70, "The opening speech of Isaiah has as its background the devastating earthquake that struck Palestine during Uzziah's reign (Amos 1:1; Zech. 14:5) . . . the catastrophe that had wreaked havoc in the land." For defense of the MT's *mahpēkat zārîm* in Isa 1:7b, cf. J. A. Motyer, *The Prophecy of Isaiah* (Downers Grove, Ill.: InterVarsity, 1993), 44, n.1.

[19]Cf. A. M. Sweet, "A Theology of Healing," *TBT* 20 (1982): 145–49, dealing specifically with Hosea.

[20]For *'āš* and *rāqāb*, see F. I. Andersen and D. N. Freedman, *Hosea* (AB; Garden City, N.Y.: Doubleday, 1980), 411–12; for studies of the larger context of Hos 5:8–6:6, cf. M. C. Lind, "Hosea 5:8–6:6," *Int* 38 (1984): 398–403; W. Schütte, "Eine originale Stimme aus dem syrisch-ephraimitischen Krieg. Zu Hos 5,8–6,6," *ZAW* 99 (1987): 406–8.

[21]H. W. Wolff has observed that, "when the God of salvation becomes the judge of his covenant-breaking people, the prophet's imagery demands the listeners' attention and is intentionally unambiguous" (*Hosea*, trans. G. Stansell [Herm.; Philadelphia: Fortress, 1974], 115).

[22]Cf. E. Bleibtreu, "Grisly Assyrian Record of Torture and Death," *BAR* 17 (1991), 52–61, 75.

[23]Bright, *History of Israel*, 275. For discussion of the various theories regarding the so-called "lost tribes" of Israel, cf. L. I. Rabinowitz, "Ten Lost Tribes," *EJ* 15:1003–6.

[24]H. L. Ginsberg, "Reflexes of Sargon in Isaiah after 715 B.C.E.," in W. W. Hallo, ed., *Essays in Memory of E. A. Speiser* (AOS 53; New Haven, Conn: American Oriental Society, 1968), 47, n. 6 (Ginsberg is quoting D. D. Luckenbill, *Ancient Records of Assyria*, 2:94).

[25]Ibid.

[26]Wolff, *Hosea*, 115, notes: "Naturally Ephraim could not fail to recognize his 'sickness' (*ḥly*), since, after the coastal plain was taken, both Galilee and Transjordan were overthrown. Similarly, Judah had already seen itself dangerously wounded from the siege laid to Jerusalem by the troops of the Syro-Ephraimite coalition."

[27]On the parallelism of *ḥolî* with *māzôr*, Andersen and Freedman, *Hosea*, 413, note, "Together the words indicate an infected, running wound," although they define *māzôr* as "an ulcer or a boil."

[28]For discussion of *melek yārēb*, cf. ibid., 413–14.

[29]On *ghh*, cf. 0.3.3.

[30]I concur with the view that understands Hos 6:1–3 "to be a song which the prophet composed and attributed to the people as a sign of their fleeting repentance" (Wolff, *Hosea*, 116, with n. 78; on this cf. Jer 3:22ff.). Wolff, however, believes "that these verses are a penitential song the priests sung during these very times of danger" (ibid., 116–17 and n. 80). On Jer 3:22ff., cf. R. Mosis, "Umkehr und Vergebung—eine Auslegung von Jer 3,21–4,2," *TTZ* 98 (1989): 39–60.

[31]There is a clear echo of Dt 32:39, for which see above, 2.2.5; in contrast to Eliphaz's "application" of Dt 32:39 in Job 5:17b (see 3.3.2.3), the verse is properly applied here. For an interesting comparative study, cf. M. L. Barré, "Bulluṭsa-rābi's Hymn to Gula and Hosea 6:1–2," *Or* 50 (1981): 241–45; cf. also O. Loretz, "Tod und Leben nach altorientalischer und kanaanäisch-biblischer Anschauung in Hos 6, 1–3," *BN* 17 (1982): 37–42.

[32]D. K. Stuart, *Hosea-Jonah* (WBC; Waco, Tex.: Word, 1987), 105.

[33]Cf. above, 3.4, on Ecc 3:3.

[34]Although Stoebe speaks of the "metaphorical" use of *rāpā'*, he is careful to point out, "Über den rein metaphorischen Gebrauch hinaus bekommt *rp'* dort, wo Jahwe Subjekt ist, noch einen tieferen Gehalt" ("רפא—heilen," *THAT* 2:808–9).

[35]For further treatment of this theme, see below on Isa 53:4ff. Note also the comments on *rp'* in Psalms, above, 3.1.9. Cf. also Stoebe's critique of Stendahl for overly spiritualizing the usage of *rp'* (above, 2.2.6, n. 182).

[36]H. K. Nielsen, *Heilung und Verkundigung*, 36, n. 106. Note, however, that Nielsen's study is focusing particularly on the NT's theology of sickness and healing.

[37]To give a contemporary example, in American evangelical Christianity, 2Ch. 7:14 is often used by national repentance movements in the sense that if America "turns back to God," then he will "*heal* our land." This "national

healing" translates to the recovery of traditional morality and family life; the end of abortion on demand and militant homosexualism; a radical decrease in violence and pornography, drug and alcohol abuse; the election of God-fearing leaders; the restoration of our educational system; justice for the poor and oppressed; the elimination of our national debt; and the healing and/or cessation of diseases such as AIDS. While I have argued that it is better to translate the end of 7:14 with "I will *restore* their land" (above, 2.3.4), that is, in fact, what is understood automatically by the contemporary Christian reader. Why? Because, through the influence of the AV's literalism—perpetuated here by virtually all modern English versions—readers are unconsciously thinking Hebraically! Thus, they are not consciously interpreting a metaphor; rather, they are understanding the concept of healing "holistically."

[38]Or, "restoring the fortune of Israel" (*bᵉ šûbî šᵉ bût ʿammî*); on the various interpretations of this phrase, see above, 3.3.3, n. 354; note also the earlier studies of E. L. Dietrich, *Shub Shebut. Die Endzeitliche Wiederherstellung bei den Propheten* (BZAW 40; Giessen: A. Topelmann, 1925); E. Baumann, "*Shub Shebut.* Eine exegetische Untersuchung," *ZAW* 47 (1929): 17–44; R. Borger, "Zu *Shub Shebw/yt*," *ZAW* 66 (1954): 315–16. See also the literature cited in Rudolph, *Hosea*, 143; for details on the Hebrew textual variations of *šbwt/šbyt*, see Gordis, *The Biblical Text in the Making*, 122b.

[39]See Rudolph (*Hosea*, 209) and Wolff (*Hosea*, 190–91) for the discussion of the textual problems in v. 2.

[40]Reading *wᵉʾanōkî tirgaltî lᵉʾeprayim qāḥām ʿal-zᵉrôʿōtāy* with the final *wāw* being a dittograph from the following *wᵉlōʾ-yādᵉʿû*. According to *BHS*, this (viz., *zᵉrôʿōtāy* in place of MT *zᵉrōʿôtāyw*) is read by a few MSS as well as by the Peshitta, Vulgate, and possibly, LXX.

[41]So, e.g., LXX, AV, RSV, NIV; Andersen and Freedman, *Hosea*, 575; Rudolph, *Hosea*, 208, renders it, "dass ich ihr Arzt war" ("that I was their physician").

[42]Kimchi and Keil, *Hosea*, KD 10/1:138.

[43]E.g., Wolff, *Hosea*, 199; on 191 he translates *rpʾ* with, "I care for them." Cf. NJV's, "My healing care"; see *Targ. Jon.* and Ehrlich, below.

[44]Th. Robinson (and F. Horst), *Die zwolf Kleinen Propheten* (HAT; Tübingen: J. C. B. Mohr, 1964), 26, on Hos 7:1, with reference to Jer 51:8–9 (cited by Wolff, *Hosea*, 199).

[45]Andersen and Freedman, *Hosea*, 581.

[46]In fact, Rudolph, *Hosea*, 209, resists any alterations of *rᵉpāʾ tîm* because of this wordplay.

[47]"Allein *rpʾ* druckt nicht nur die Heilung einer Krankheit aus, sondern auch das Ausbessern eines Schadens irgendwelcher Art; vg. besonders 1K. 18:30" (*Randglossen*, 5:200); cf. above, 0.3.2, with Baudissin's comments (n. 73). Wolff (*Hosea*, 199) claims that there are only two occurrences of *rpʾ* in the Pentateuch, both in the wilderness traditions, thus serving as backdrop for Hos 11:1–3. Yet this theory, already tenuous, is further obviated by the fact that Ge 20:17, the *third* occurrence of *rpʾ* in the Pentateuch and not belong-

ing to the wilderness traditions, has been overlooked (cf. also Baudissin, *Adonis und Esmun*, 387, for related verses).

48M. L. Brown, *A Philological Study*, 66–68.

49"And this is the same as healing, to strengthen the child [*hanna'ar*] until he is able to walk." For Hebrew *na'ar* in the sense of an infant, newborn, or very young child, cf. Ex 2:6 (Moses!); 1Sa 1:24; 4:21; see BDB, 654–55.

50For defense of the longer reading of Eze 16:6, with the repeated final clause, cf. Greenberg, *Ezekiel 1–20*, 275–76.

51Cf W. H. Brownlee, *Ezekiel 1–19* (WBC; Waco, Tex.: Word, 1986), 219–22.

52Note that Ps 105:37, "He brought out Israel, laden with silver and gold, and from among their tribes no one faltered" (NIV), is sometimes cited by modern proponents of divine healing to demonstrate that every single Israelite was completely healed upon leaving Egypt (see T. L. Osborn, *Healing the Sick* [Tulsa, Okla.: Harrison House, n.d.], 15). This, however, clearly goes beyond the meaning of *kōšēl*, which simply means "stagger, falter"; a possible parallel to Ps 105:37b might be Lev 26:13: "I the LORD am your God who brought you out from the land of the Egyptians to be their slaves no more, who broke the bars of your yoke and made you walk erect [*qōmᵉmîyût*]" (NJV; cf. NIV's "with heads held high").

53Cf. S. T. Sohn, *The Divine Election of Israel* (Grand Rapids: Eerdmans, 1991), 67–73; for a different metaphor, cf. H. Schüngel-Straumann, "Gott als Mutter in Hosea 11," *TQ* 166 (1986): 119–34 (in English, cf. idem, "God as mother in Hosea 11," *TD* 34 [1987]: 3–8). See also the views of Wolff and Robinson, cited above, n. 44.

54According to Wolff, *Hosea*, 123, with n. 155 (referring to Stamm, *Erlosen*, 81), "'To heal' (*rp'*) includes the meaning of 'forgive' (cf. 14:5), for which concept Hosea uses no other word." But this statement is inaccurate; in Hos 1:6, *nś' lᵉ* is probably used elliptically for *nś' lᵉ 'āwōn* (or *nś' 'āwōn*), "to forgive iniquity" (although this is disputed). Then, even more clearly, it is found in Hos 14:2(3)—*kol-tiśā' 'āwōn*: "Forgive all guilt" (NJV, although Wolff renders otherwise, ibid., 231; for the possible influence of Hos 14:4[5] on Jer 3:22, cf. below, n. 82; for an unnecessary emendation, cf. W. von Soden, "'Die Südenlast' in Hosea 14, 3," *ZAH* 2 [1989]: 91–92). While "forgive" is certainly a *possible* rendering of *rp'* in these two instances, doing no great injustice to our proposed semantic categories, it is better to retain "heal," with "backslidings" being viewed as a spiritual sickness needing healing (see again below, n. 82). On Greek *iaomai* in the sense of "forgive," see Oepke, "ἰάομαι," *TDNT* 3:201; cf. also 1QH 2:8, where the Qumran sectary claimed that he was "healing [*marpe'*] to those who repent."

55Cf. Brown, "Man Repents and God Relents: *šûb* and Its Congeners."

56Cf. J. Muilenberg, "The Terminology of Adversity in Jeremiah," in H. T. Frank and W. L. Reed, eds., *Translating and Understanding the Old Testament: Essays in Honor of Herbert Gordon May* (Nashville: Abingdon, 1970), 42–63. On p. 61, he notes, "Closely related to the terminology of sickness, pain, and indeed every manner of affliction is the pervasive motif of healing and of Yahweh as Israel's Physician."

[57]On the questions of versification, translation, and interpretation, see W. L. Holladay, *Jeremiah 1* (Herm.; Philadelphia: Fortress, 1986), 202–9.

[58]Commenting on 4:19–20, W. Brueggemann, *The Prophetic Imagination* (Philadelphia: Fortress, 1978), 53, notes, "His [i.e., Jeremiah's] grief is expressed as a public, visible event—the actual invasion and slaughter of his people. He describes with remarkable vividness a near play-by-play of the disaster as it reaches his own bedroom. Nevertheless, that public event is matched by an internal wrenching in which his heart quakes and storms in fear and his very bowels are gripped by terror."

[59]I agree with those who see the prophet, not God, as the speaker here; see the commentaries for discussion.

[60]For *šlm* in parallelism with or proximity to *rp'*, see above, 0.3.3, *sub šlm*.

[61]As in 8:15, but here the orthography is not defective: *marpē'*.

[62]Cf. above, 1.2.2.3, on 2Ch 16:12; note also Hempel, *Heilung*, 303–4.

[63]On the possible borrowing of *šeber gādôl* from Zephaniah (cf. Zep 1:10), cf. Holladay, *Jeremiah 1*, 153 ("one wonders whether Jrm took it over from Zephaniah"), and Keil, *Jeremiah*, KD 8/1:108.

[64]It is used 15 out of 44 times. When the 5 occurrences of this word in Lamentations are added in, then almost half of all occurrences are represented in Jeremiah-Lamentations. (The text of Jeremiah represents approximately 7.1% of the Hebrew Scriptures; Jeremiah-Lamentations amounts to 7.6%.) The comparative proportion of *verbal* occurrences of *šbr* found in Jeremiah (almost 18%—26 out of 148, including the only Hophal usage of the root), is significant, although not as striking. Note also that 1 out of the 2 occurrences of *šibārôn* is found in Jeremiah.

[65]Holladay, *Jeremiah 1*, 153.

[66]The root *rp'* is found 18 times (13 verbal and 5 nominal) in Jeremiah, more than in any other biblical book. It is found in its highest relative proportion in Hosea (5 times, all verbal). See above, n. 8.

[67]J. Bright notes, "By the mind of the day such an action was not understood merely as the dramatic illustration of a point, or play acting, but as the actual setting in motion of Yahweh's destroying word" (*Jeremiah* [AB; Garden City, N.Y.: Doubleday, 1965], 133).

[68]Cf. the comments of Malbim, ch. 2, n. 24, on the extraordinary—and hence incurable—nature of divinely inflicted diseases. As noted by W. L. Holladay, *Jeremiah 1*, 167, with reference to Hillers, *Treaty-Curses*, 64–66, "The incurable wound is a traditional curse." Cf. further above, 2.2.2.

[69]Cf. H. H. Rowley, "The Prophet Jeremiah and the Book of Deuteronomy," in *Studies in Old Testament Prophecy*, 157–74; J. A. Thompson, *The Book of Jeremiah* (NICOT; Grand Rapids: Eerdmans, 1981), 59–67, "Jeremiah and the Covenant"; cf. also Bright, *Jeremiah*, XXXVIII–XLV.

[70]Cf. the discussion of this verse in 2.3.1.

[71]The verses leading up to La 2:13 are overwhelming: "My eyes fail from weeping, I am in torment within, my heart is poured out on the ground

because my people are destroyed, because children and infants faint in the streets of the city. They say to their mothers, 'Where is the bread and wine?' as they faint like wounded men in the streets of the city, as their lives ebb away in their mothers' arms" (La 2:11–12 NIV). See further M. S. Moore, "Human Suffering in Lamentations," *RB* 90 (1983): 534–55.

[72]*kî-gādôl kayyām šibrēk mî yirpā'-lāk.* On the textual and interpretative problems of v. 13a and b, cf. W. Rudolph, *Das Buch Ruth, Das Hohe Lied, Die Klagelieder* (KAT; Gutersloher: Gerd Mohn, 1962), 220; R. Gordis, *The Song of Songs and Lamentations* (New York: Ktav, 1974), 164–65; and *BHS*. Gordis, *The Song of Songs and Lamentations,* sees the use of *talḥin* (a rhetorical device in which "the author's choice of a particular word instead of a synonym is dictated by his desire to suggest both meanings simultaneously to the consciousness of the reader") in the play on *šeber* suggesting *mišbar* (thus "breakbreaker, wave") in proximity to *yām*. For the Jeremianic usage of *šbr*, cf. above, n. 64. On the authorship of Lamentations, cf. below, n. 77.

[73]In light of this, one can well ask whether the last use—with reference to a city, "collapsed-restored"—should really be classified as *metaphorical*. In the ancient Israelite mind, was this truly metaphorical language, or was it simply evidence of an expanded understanding of the nature of wholeness? Cf. above, 4.1.1.

[74]*wayerappᵉ'û 'et-šeber 'ammî 'al-nᵉqālâ le'mōr šālôm šālôm wᵉ'ên šālôm.* Thompson, *Jeremiah*, 45, translates, "Yet they treat my people's fracture with nostrums" (p. 48: "*With nostrums.* Literally 'lightly, superficially'"). Cf. further McKane, *Jeremiah 1–25*, 144, "They treat my people's wounds on the surface, saying You are cured, when there is no cure" (see also 147); contrast Holladay, *Jeremiah 1*, 210–11, 216–17 (with political, rather than medical imagery). Note that the Piel of *rp'* sometimes means "to treat" (cf. 1.2.2.2, n. 68). For the sense of the passage, see Thompson, *Jeremiah*, 258, along with the other commentaries cited; cf. the reference to Job 13:4 (Holladay, *Jeremiah 1*, 217), above, 0.3.1, n. 59; and 3.3.2.3.

[75]Or, as traditionally rendered, "'Peace, peace,' when there is no peace." For the connection between *šālôm* and *šeber*, cf. J. Pedersen, *Israel: Its Life and Culture, I–II*, 313: "Evil is in its strongest form a breach, *shebher*, an infringement upon the whole, which is peace," further noting that, "Breaches are most frequently mentioned in the prophets, in particular Jeremiah."

[76]In this context, Muilenberg, "The Terminology of Adversity," 46, prefers to render *šeber* with "wound," noting, however, "The noun may be rendered *fracture*, *breach*, *shattering*, *crash*, *blow*, and so, in a more extended sense, *disaster* or *destruction*."

[77]The fact that this verse immediately follows the image of v. 13c, "Truly your breach is as great as the sea; who can heal you?" (cf. Jer 6:14), may provide clear evidence of the Jeremianic influence on, if not actual authorship of, Lamentations. On this point, see the standard OT introductions; cf. most recently D. R. Hillers, *Lamentations* (AB; 2d ed., New York: Doubleday, 1992), 10–15, rejecting Jeremianic authorship.

[78]This verse is difficult to translate, especially in light of the Masoretic accents. BDB, 267, cites Ewald, Gesenius, and Giesebrecht, as well as AV and RV, in favor of the Masoretic division; only Graf, Cheyne, and the RV marg. follow a rendering similar to ours; cf. also NIV. There is no textual justification for deleting *'ên-dān dinēk*, as do Bright, *Jeremiah*, 271; Thompson, *Jeremiah*, 558; see further Holladay, *Jeremiah 2*, 151, and cf. *BHK* (its proposed changing of the accents is more acceptable). The proposed emendation of *BHS*, altering *dān-dinēk* into "*rikkûkîm* cf. Jes. 1, 6" is a truly *conjectural* emendation; Ehrlich's suggestion to read *lāmô* in place of *l ͤmāzôr* (with a supposed dittography of *r* from the following *r ͤpū'ôt*, which still does not explain the origin of the *z*), yielding, "there is no one to plead your cause for them" (?), is not compelling, ; see *Randglossen*, 4:318. If MT is followed, *māzôr* must mean "pressing out, binding up" (of a wound)—so David Kimchi and others cited above in BDB. My rendering, faithful to the Hebrew text but not MT's accents, understands the pronominal suffix of *dînēk* as "double duty" for *māzôr*, thus "your sore"; both *r ͤpū'â* and *t ͤ 'ālâ* (for the syntax of these words without *wāw*, see Kimchi) are dependent on the final *'ên-lāk*, with the pronominal *lāk* reinforcing the double-duty *-ek* of *dînēk*. Both *HALAT* 2:535, and Gesenius-Buhl, 411, understand *māzôr* as a wound or sore (cf. Hos 5:13 for a similar context and expression). As to Ehrlich's contention that MT *r ͤpū'ôt* is always a wrong vocalization of *rip'ût*, see above, 1.2.2.1, n. 57.

[79]The *hapax 'ateret*, rendered here as "abundance," has been a crux; cf. the textual apparatus in *BHS*. For the rendering "abundance," cf. NIV, NJV, and R. P. Carroll, *Jeremiah* (OTL; Philadelphia: Westminster, 1986), 632–33; note, however, Holladay, *Jeremiah 2*, 223.

[80]On *šûb šebût*, see the references cited above, n. 38.

[81]On *ṭihēr//salaḥ*, "purify/forgive," cf. B. A. Levine, *In the Presence of the Lord* (Leiden: E. J. Brill, 1974), 63–67.

[82]Cf. Bright's translation, *Jeremiah*, 20. He rightly remarks (p. 23): "The words seem to be drawn from Hos XIV.1,4 (vss. 2,5h)." It is possible that Jer 3:22 and Hos 14:4(5) exhibit the only two instances where *rp'* means "to forgive" (cf. also above nn. 12, 54). However, NJV's rendering of *m ͤ šûbôt* as "afflictions" should be compared with the comment of Ehrlich on Jer 2:19, where he states that "*m ͤ šûbôt* that is mentioned here means 'sicknesses'" (*Mikra* 3:182; lacking in *Randglossen* 5:210), thus picturing the *m ͤ šûbôt* as a spiritual malady in need of healing. In other words, *rp'* colors the meaning of *m ͤ šûbâ*, not the reverse. Keil's remark (cited above, 2.3.4, end) regarding sin as a "spiritual disease," while rejected in that context (viz. 2Ch 30:20), is certainly apposite here, and again explains the use of *rp'*.

[83]On the prophet's identification with his people, cf. Muffs, "His Majesty's Loyal Opposition." Note also Pedersen, *Israel: Its Life and Culture, I-II*, 313: "[Jeremiah's] soul is scarred with breaches (10:19) because his people are broken."

[84]Some of Jeremiah's descriptions indicate that his sufferings were both spiritual and physical (and, of course, emotional); see Wolff, *Anthropology*,

41–42, on Jer 4:19 (see above, n. 76, Muilenberg). The personal suffering endured by the prophets included such hardships as imprisonment (Jer 37; cf. also ch. 38, where Jeremiah is thrown into a cistern) and stoning (2Ch 24:21; cf. Mt 5:12; 23:33–37), as well as inner turmoil (as noted by A. J. Heschel, *The Prophets* [New York: Harper & Row, 1962], 1:xv: the prophet "was often compelled to proclaim the very opposite of what his heart expected"), misunderstanding (Am 7:10ff.), deprivation because of unusual requirements (e.g., Jer 16:1–3; Eze 3:24–27), and unique losses because of their function as "signs and portents" (cf. Isa 8:18) to the people (cf. Eze 24:15–27 and the death of Ezekiel's wife).

[85]So NJV's translation of *bat 'ammî*. For a study of *bat* in similar phrases, see H. Haag, "בַּת," *TDOT* 2:333ff.

[86]*hošbartî*, the only Hophal occurrence of the root *šbr*.

[87]Jeremiah 15:18a may underlie Paul's description of himself as having "great sorrow and unceasing anguish" (NIV) in his heart for his Jewish brothers who did not acknowledge Jesus as Messiah (Ro 9:2). However, there is only one word in common between the LXX and the NT text (respectively, *lupountēs* and *lupēs*).

[88]Cf. also Jer 20:7ff.; see especially D. M. Gunn, "'You tried to persuade me' and 'Violence! Outrage!' in Jeremiah XX 7–8," *VT* 28 (1978): 20–27; Heschel, *The Prophets*, 1:103–39. On the "faithless waters" imagery (15:18b), cf. Gordis, *Job*, 74, on Job 6:15.

[89]According to Muilenberg, "The Terminology of Adversity," 62, "The profuse terminology of adversity in Jeremiah is to be explained, at least in part, by the interior conflicts within the prophet himself."

[90]*rᵉpā'ēnî yhwh wa'ērāpē' hōši'anî wᵉ'iwwaša'*. According to Kugel, *Biblical Poetry*, 18, n. 41, referring also to M. Held's article, "The Action-Result (Factitive-Passive) Sequence of Identical Verbs," in *JBL* 84 (1965): 272–82, the phrase *rᵉpā'ēnî wa'ērāpē'* "certainly does not mean 'Heal me and I will be healed' (implied sequence) but 'Heal me, let me be healed,' or more faithful to the spirit, 'Heal me and make me healthy.'" While AV, RSV, NEB, NASB, and NIV all follow the traditional rendering, only NJV anticipates Kugel's "let me be healed" clause (his "make me healthy" has, in my opinion, nothing in particular to commend it). I have retained "I will be healed/saved" because of Jeremiah's emphasis on the efficacy of the divine Physician's cure alone; hence, "If you save/heal, I will be saved/healed indeed." Otherwise, Held's grammatical observations would have influenced my understanding of the verbal sequences.

[91]Ibn Barun's quaint comment here, that Hebrew *rāpā'* "may be similar to [Arabic] *rafa'*, 'to mend (clothes),' since mending with respect to a garment is similar to curing with respect to the body," accurately grasps the *Grundbedeutung* of the root on a simple and unsophisticated level; see P. Wechter, *Ibn Barun's Arabic Works on Hebrew Grammar and Lexicography* (Philadelphia: Dropsie, 1964), 120.

[92]J. A. Alexander's comment on Isa 53:4 is correct: "Healing is a natural and common figure for relief from suffering considered as wound or mal-

ady" (*The Prophecies of Isaiah* [repr. Grand Rapids: Zondervan, 1974], 1/2:296). However, it should be noted that comments like this have often been read as if both the "healing" and "suffering" involved could not be physical and literal!

[93]No major distinction has been made between the various strands of Isaianic material because (1) the use of *rp'* throughout the book is in keeping with the general prophetic usage noted heretofore; (2) no diachronic development was observed according to the various proposed dates for the different sections of Isaiah; and (3) unless there are definite indications to the contrary, our approach will continue to be "holistic." For the use of "holistic" in a similar context, cf. Greenberg, *Ezekiel 1–20* , 18–27; cf. further B. S. Childs, *Introduction to the Old Testament as Scripture* (Philadelphia: Fortress, 1979), 311–38; for Stendahl's rationale in classifying all Isaiah texts together ("Rafa'," 16–19), see ibid., 16, n. 26, and cf. Motyer, *Isaiah*, 30–33; C. A. Evans, "On the Unity and Parallel Structure of Isaiah," *VT* 38 (1988), 129–47.

[94]Literally, "I'm no dresser of wounds!" Cf. above, 0.3.3, *sub ḥbš*, for discussion of *ḥōbeš* in Isa 3:6. Note also the reference in 1:6b to the wounds that were not bound up (*ḥūbšû*), in 30:26 (cited above, 4.1) with *ḥābōš* and *šeber*, and in 61:2, "to bind up [*laḥbôš*] the brokenhearted [*lᵉ nišbᵉ rê-lēb*]." Note that *ḥbš* and *rp'* are interchanged in Eze 34:4 and Zec 11:16 with the same object, viz., the *nišberet* ("the injured"; cf. below, 4.1.5).

[95]Cf. Hempel, *Heilung*, 240–41.

[96]For an acceptable theological discussion of this concept, see Delitzsch, *Isaiah*, KD 7/1:199–201; cf. the references in Kaiser, *Isaiah 1–12*, 83, n. b.

[97]Others have understood *šab* as meaning "once again"; see Kaiser, *Isaiah 1–12*, 72; Gray, *Isaiah 1–27*, 110–11, who reads *wᵉ šāb* as opposed to *wašāb*: "*—And it be healed once more*] as it had been wont to be healed by Yahweh (Hos 6[1])"; for full textual discussion, cf. Wildberger, *Isaiah 1–12*, 250, n. 10c-c.

[98]NJV's "save itself" (with the note, "Lit. 'heal'") is not to be preferred (cf. also Wildberger, *Isaiah 1–12*, 248, "then it would return and be saved"; but note 250, n. 10c-c). On the grammar of *rāpā' lô*, cf. Nu 12:3; 2Ki 2:21; 20:5, 8; note also Isa 53:4 (with Niphal). It is correct to interpret the unexpressed third person sing. subject in Isa 6:10 as indicating the impersonal passive (cf. Jouon-Muraoka, 2:577–78, §155b; GKC 144d), thus, "one heal it/make it well" = "it is healed/made well"; cf., Delitzsch, "*Isaiah*," KD 7/1, 200; Gray, *Isaiah 1–27*, 111.

[99]Cf. Alexander, *Isaiah*, 1/1:153 (citing David Kimchi as well; see next note); M. Black, *An Aramaic Approach to the Gospels* (3d ed., Oxford: Clarendon, 1967), 211–12. R. Guelich, *Mark 1–8:26* (WBC; Waco, Tex.: Word, 1989), 210, observes, "The Hebrew and Greek [i.e., LXX] text have the verbs in the second person; Mark and the Targum have the third person. And only the Targum has the participial equivalents of *blepontēs* and *akouontēs*." This is one of three instances of *Targ. Isa.* where *rp'* is rendered with *šbq* as opposed to *'sy* (the other verses being 53:5; 57:18). On the interpretative history of Isa 6:9–10, see C. A. Evans, *To See and Not Perceive: Isaiah 6:9–10 in Early*

Jewish and Christian Interpretation (JSOTSupp. 64; Sheffield: Sheffield Academic Press, 1986). For the theology of *Targ. Isa.*, see B. D. Chilton, *The Glory of Israel: The Theology and Provenience of the Isaiah Targum* (JSOTSupp. 23; Sheffield: Sheffield Academic Press, 1983). For the variations from Mark in John's citation of Isa 6:10, cf. M. J. J. Menken, "Die Form des Zitates aus Jes 6,10 in Joh 12,40. Ein Beitrag zum Schriftgebrauch des vierten Evangelisten," *BZ* 32 (1988): 189–209.

[100]See especially *b. Meg.* 17b, where in answer to the question regarding the placement of *r*ᵉ*pû'â* (the eighth benediction in the Shemoneh Esreh) it is stated that "*rāpā' lô* is not a healing [*r*ᵉ*pû'â*] of sicknesses, but it is a healing through forgiveness [*r*ᵉ*pû'â dislîḥâ*]." Cf. Jastrow, *Dictionary*, 1489: "This is not healing referring to diseases, but a healing (from sin) through forgiveness." According to David Kimchi, "*w*ᵉ *rāpā'*: [means] healing of the soul; and this is forgiveness, as it is written, 'Heal my soul for I have sinned against You.'" For an earlier treatment of Ps 41:4(5), cited here by Kimchi (cf. also immediately above, n. 99) in this same understanding, cf. above, 3.1.4 (with n. 61), and see also above, 4.1.2, on Hos 14:4(5) and Jer 3:22.

[101]Cf. Kaiser, *Isaiah 1–12*, 83: "If the people can be described metaphorically as already sick, a prophet will not only not heal them, but make them more and more like a sick man, whose fatty heart only beats slowly, whose ears are deaf and whose eyes are closed up with a cataract."

[102]For the broad concept of salvation in the OT, as well as in the prophetic books in particular, cf. above, n. 9, and see T. V. Farris, *Mighty to Save: A Study in Old Testament Soteriology* (Nashville: Broadman/Holman, 1993); C. Westermann, *Prophetic Oracles of Salvation*, trans. K. Crim (Philadelphia: Westminster/John Knox, 1991); note also the comprehensive article on "salvation" (from the ancient Near East to the NT) by A. Bouchard, E. Laroche, É. Beaucamp, P.-Poirer, J. Laporte, J. Delorme, M. Carrez, É. Cothenet, and M. Morgen, "Salut," *DBSup* 11:513–740.

[103]Baudissin, *Adonis*, 387, cites this verse as a definite example "vom Heilen des Volkes." Because of the semantic range of German *Heilen*, Baudissin could express in one word the basic equivalent of NJV's text and accompanying footnote. Again, however, "made well" or the like is more accurate in English. For another discussion of the whole passage, see Stendahl, "Rafa'," 16–17, with reference to Stamm, *Erlosen*, 83.

[104]For the history of the Christian exegesis of this chapter, cf. H. H. Rowley, *The Servant of the Lord and Other Essays on the Old Testament* (2d ed., Oxford: Blackwell, 1965), 1–94; C. R. North, *The Suffering Servant in Deutero-Isaiah* (2d ed., Oxford: Oxford Univ. Press, 1965). The standard collection of Jewish texts is found in S. R. Driver and Ad. Neubauer, eds. and trans., *The Fifty-Third Chapter of Isaiah According to the Jewish Interpreters*, 2 vols. (repr. New York: Ktav, 1969).

[105]Cf. Alexander's comment quoted above, n. 92, with accompanying text. Note also K. Seybold, "חָלָה," *TDOT* 4:398–407, esp. 406–7. For an extremely spiritualizing translation, see F. A. Aston, *The Challenge of the Ages* (rev. ed., Wilmington: Great Christian Books, 1977), 6, and n. 3.

[106]Cf. R. Longenecker, *Biblical Exegesis in the Apostolic Period* (Grand Rapids: Eerdmans, 1975), 147–48. On Matthew's quotation style in general, see R. H. Gundry, *The Use of the Old Testament in Saint Matthew's Gospel* (Leiden: E. J. Brill, 1967).

[107]See T. J. McCrossan, *Bodily Healing and the Atonement*, ed. and repr. by R. Hicks and K. E. Hagin (Tulsa, Okla.: Faith Library, n.d.), for what may be called the traditional view of proponents of divine healing.

[108]MacArthur, *Charismatic Chaos*, 103, rightly observes that, with little attention to context, "Charismatics often use 1 Peter 2:24 to support their strong emphasis on the gift of healing...." In fact, MacArthur's "often" could easily be "almost always," as seen in the great majority of popular, charismatic books on divine healing.

[109]*The New Scofield Reference Bible* (Oxford: Clarendon Press, 1967), 759, n. 1. Although this is a popular study help, it expresses in a simplified form the seasoned views of some accepted Christian scholars. Note also A. A. Macrae, *The Gospel of Isaiah* (Chicago: Moody, 1977), 136.

[110]MacArthur, *Charismatic Chaos*, 104, n. 15, cites at length the (somewhat forced) interpretation of Mt 8:17 offered by W. Hendricksen (*The Gospel of Matthew* [Grand Rapids: Baker, 1973], 400–401), in order to refute the idea that Isa 53:5 means that Jesus bore our physical sickness, claiming (p. 104) that Jesus "does not get our diseases, but he sympathizes with the pain that we have in them." However, the logic of both Hendricksen and MacArthur is faulty here. (1) While clearly affirming the intimate connection between sin and sickness in the Scriptures, they fail to carry this truth to its logical conclusion: by bearing sin on the cross, the Servant of the Lord struck at the root cause of disease, hence breaking its stranglehold over humanity and paving the way for a profusion of both divine forgiveness *and* healing (cf., in popular form, Bosworth, *Christ the Healer*, 31–35). (2) Jesus no more needed to become sick with the sick person's sickness than he needed to become sinful with our sins. His whole ministry was vicarious and substitutionary. (3) The very argument of Hendricksen against the proponents of divine healing, viz., that Jesus healed "by means of his *vicarious suffering for sin*" (his emphasis), is actually the strongest argument *for* their position. If, in fact, Matthew cited Isa 53:5 in Mt 8:17 because "whenever [Jesus] saw sickness or distress he experienced Calvary, *his own* Calvary" (Hendricksen's emphasis)—and this vicarious suffering procured physical healing—then, a fortiori, his actual death on the cross—his ultimate vicarious act!—would certainly procure similar, universal results. See further, n. 112, below.

[111]A. Edersheim, *The Life and Times of Jesus the Messiah* (repr. Grand Rapids: Eerdmans, 1971), 488, n. 1. He calls Matthew's quotation of Isa 53:4 "most truly a N.T. 'Targum' of the original." He also notes Symmachus' translation, similar to the LXX's quoted above.

[112]For the broader subject of physical healing *in* the atonement vs. *through* the atonement, as well as discussion as to *when* the full benefits of the atonement will be realized, cf. Wimber/Springer, *Power Healing*, 152–56; for specific reference to Isa 53 in this context, cf. W. K. Bokovay, "The Relationship

of Physical Healing to the Atonement," *Didaskalia* 3 (1991): 24–39. MacArthur, *Charismatic Chaos*, 103–4, represents the standard cessationist view: "When Isaiah 53 talks about the suffering servant by whose stripes Israel will be healed, it is talking about spiritual healing, not physical.... Ultimately, the atonement will cure all our diseases when it has wrought its final work of glorifying our bodies. Thus there *is* healing in the Atonement [his emphasis], but only in its ultimate aspect of eternal glory in heaven (cf. Rev. 21:4)." For challenges to the cessationist view of the gifts and manifestations of the Spirit, cf. below, 5.2 and 6.2–6.2.1.

[113]Motyer, *Isaiah*, 436; see also above, 3.1.9, on *rp'* in Psalms. More than ten years of continued reflection on the Hebrew usage of *rp'* have convinced me that, from a biblical perspective, it would be virtually impossible to countenance a stricken and afflicted people rejoicing that they were "spiritually healed" (i.e., of their sins) while at the same time their disease-ridden bodies continued to waste away, their limbs were wracked with searing pain, their cities were broken down and desolate, their temple was destroyed, and many of them languished in exile. Rather, as emphasized throughout this chapter, the "healing" would have to be just as comprehensive as was the "disease" from which the people suffered.

[114]This is indicated clearly by Isa 53:4b–5: He bore our sickness and pain (53:4a), but when we saw him suffering, we thought it was for his own sins (53:4b). Actually, it was for *our* sins he was dying (53:5)! In other words, when we saw him on hanging on the cross, we thought he was getting his well-deserved penalty as a malefactor; little did we know that he was suffering for our sins and carrying our pains! On the "I, we, they" dynamic of the poem, cf. D. J. A. Clines, *I, He, We and They: A Literary Approach to Isaiah 53* (JSOTSupp.; Sheffield: Univ. of Sheffield Press, 1976).

[115]D. A. Carson, *Matthew* (*EBC*; Grand Rapids: Zondervan, 1984), 8:205; cf. also the apposite remarks of Delitzsch, *Isaiah*, KD 7/2:315–16. C. L. Blomberg, *Matthew* (NAC; Nashville: Broadman, 1993), 144, n. 21, cites R. H. Gundry, *Matthew: A Commentary on His Literary and Theological Art* (Grand Rapids: Eerdmans, 1982), 150, "'The healings anticipate the passion in that they begin to roll back the effects of the sins for which Jesus came to die.' Some think Isaiah spoke only of sins, but physical well-being was also thought to characterize the messianic age (Isa 29:18; 32:3–4; 35:5–6). 'We therefore do well to follow Matthew's literalism.'" Cf. similarly C. S. Keener, *The IVP Bible Background Commentary: New Testament* (Downers Grove, Ill.: InterVarsity, 1993), 67–68, who concludes his comments on Mt 8:16–17 by noting, "Jesus inaugurates the messianic era, making some of its benefits available even in advance of the cross." For the interrelatedness of sin and sickness, cf. the discussion of 2Ch 30:20, above, 2.3.4, with reference to the sermon of F. F. Bosworth, "Did Jesus Redeem Us from Our Diseases When He Atoned for Our Sins?" See further, 3.1.1, 3.1.4–5, 5.3.2. Note, however, D. A. Hagner, *Matthew 1–13* (WBC; Dallas: Word, 1993), 210–11, who strongly downplays the significance of physical healing in Isa 53, claiming also (with U. Luz) that the reference to the Servant's death in "the Isa 53 pas-

sage and the notion of vicarious suffering are not yet evident in the Gospel" of Matthew by ch. 8.

[116]D. W. Thomas's theories on *yd'* II ("to humble, afflict") are reflected in R. Loewe's rendering of this phrase in his prolegomenon to the reprint of Driver and Neubauer, *Isaiah 53*, 5: "a man in the grip of pain and brought low by sickness;" cf. also his v. 11a, "when the righteous one shall have received his full measure of humiliation," ibid., 6. For a different view, cf. M. Dahood, "Phoenician Elements in Isaiah 52:13–53:12," in H. Goedicke, ed., *Near Eastern Studies in Honor of William Foxwell Albright* (Baltimore: Johns Hopkins Univ. Press), 67.

[117]According to Blomberg, *Matthew*, 144, "it is probable that Isaiah had both sin and sickness in view in his original prophecy."

[118]Seybold, "חָלָה," 405, rightly rejects any emendation of *heḥelî*.

[119]Note v. 8: *kî nigzar mē'ereṣ ḥayyîm mippeša'ammî nega' lāmô*—"For he was cut off from the land of the living through the sin of my people, who deserved the punishment" (NJV). In the first edition of the NJV to Isaiah (published separately in 1973), the text read, "My people," i.e., God's people.

[120]Cf. the translation of C. R. North, *The Second Isaiah* (Oxford: Clarendon, 1964), 64; note also Motyer, *Isaiah*, 436. Delitzsch, *Isaiah*, KD 7/2, 319–20, has eloquently expressed this divine transaction: "We were sick unto death because of our sins; but He, the sinless One, took upon Himself a suffering unto death, which was, as it were, the concentration and essence of the woes that we had deserved; and this voluntary endurance, this submission to the justice of the Holy One, in accordance with the counsels of divine love, became the source of our healing." One need not share his Christology in order to appreciate his spiritual sensitivity.

[121]I do not enter here into a further discussion of the vicarious (so Seybold, "חָלָה," 405–6) or nonvicarious (so, polemically, H. M. Orlinsky, *The So-called "Servant of the Lord" and "Suffering Servant" in Second Isaiah*, reprinted in *Studies on the Second Part of the Book of Isaiah* [Leiden: E. J. Brill, 1977], 1–133) nature of the servant's sufferings portrayed in this chapter. I can only note that R. N. Whybray's attempt to read Isa 53 without any reference at all to vicarious suffering seems to obviate the cumulative force of the verses and phrases that he dissects (see his *Thanksgiving for a Liberated Prophet* [JSOTSupp. 4; Sheffield: Univ. of Sheffield Press, 1978], 29–76). I find inescapable the simple conclusion that "when he [i.e., the subject of Isa 52:13–53:12] was smitten, we were healed" (Alexander, *Isaiah*, 1/2:296). The selections from the Zohar cited by Driver and Neubauer in *Isaiah 53* (1:15–16; 2:15–16—both under the heading "*pinḥaš*") are extremely interesting in this context. For a study that seeks to refute the theory (prevalent since Duhm) that the "Servant Songs" were written in isolation from the orginal context of Isa 40–55, see T. N. D. Mettinger, *A Farewell to the Servant Songs: A Critical Examination of an Exegetical Axiom* (Lund: Gleerup, 1983). He argues for one "servant" throughout, viz., collective Israel. However, in my opinion, it must be recognized that at least in some passages (e.g., 49:1ff.; 52:13–

53:12), the servant is an idealized individual who fulfills the purpose of Israel, thus paving the way for a messianic interpretation.

[122]Cf. Oswalt, *Isaiah*, 605, n. 14, "As in ch. 53, forgiveness of sin and healing from disease are related. This is not to say that all disease can be related to specific sins committed by the ill person. But neither can we say no relation exists between the two. Disease is in the world because of sin." For further treatment of this verse, cf. below, 4.2.2, where the eschatological promise of healing miracles in Isa 35 will be treated, along with other references to the healing ministry of the Servant of the Lord.

[123]Cf. further below, 5.3.2.

[124]See v. 17, again with the root *nkh* (*we'akkēhû*); once more, God's "smiting" was not just "spiritual."

[125]Ehrlich disagrees with the majority view that Israel's "ways" here are penitent; rather, it is because Israel will *not* repent that God refrains from punishing them further and instead forgives them. *rp'* is then understood here as at 2Ch 30:20, where Ehrlich's translation was "*und verschonte das Volk.*" See *Mikra* 3:140–41; more concisely, *Randglossen*, 4:206: "*wᵉ'arpā'ēhû* [*sic*] = *und ich will ihn in Ruhe lassen.*"

[126]For the background and exegesis of this passage, see C. Westermann, *Isaiah 40–66*, trans. D. M. G. Stalker (OTL; Philadelphia: Westminster, 1969), 326–31. It is not clear why he translates the end of v. 19 with "and I heal him (?)" (p. 326); on p. 330 he calls this "the metaphorical 'I will heal him.'"

[127]For the borrowing of this imagery in Ephesians 2:17, with rabbinic parallels, cf. Strack-Billerbeck 3:585–92. For discussion of *šālôm* in the context of healing, cf. above, 0.3.3.

[128]For the inclusion of Isa 58:6b in the Lucan (Lk 4:18–19) citation of Isa 61:1–2, cf. below, 5.2.2, n. 49.

[129]On *yaḥᵃlîṣ*, cf. *HALAT* 1:308–9; for the frequent recurrence of "bones" in healing contexts, cf. above, 3.2.2, n. 241.

[130]Interestingly, Isa 58 is often cited by those who believe in the therapeutic (supernatural or natural) benefits of fasting.

[131]On the "shepherd" as the political leader, see J. Jeremias, "ποίμην," *TDNT* 6:486–88, with literature. Note also K. Galling on Isa 44:28a (*hā'ōmēr lᵉ kôrēš rō'î*), *Deutero Jesaja 40,1–45,7* (*BK*; Neukirchen: Neukirchener, 1970–78), 474ff.; cf. also below, n. 136.

[132]It seems evident here that the Piel of *rp'* means "to treat," being in the immediate context of *ḥizzēq* ("to strengthen") and *ḥābaš* ("to bind up"). It was the shepherd's obligation to *treat* the sickly sheep; he could not, however, guarantee its *healing*. Thus it seems better to translate here as "treat" instead of "heal"; cf. also the discussion of Ex 21:19, above, 1.2.2.2. On the shepherd's responsibility for the physical care of the sheep, cf. Hempel, *Heilung*, 239–41, 254.

[133]W. Eichrodt, *Ezekiel*, trans. C. Quinn (OTL; Philadelphia: Westminster, 1975), 470.

[134]L. C. Allen, *Ezekiel 20–48* (WBC; Waco, Tex.: Word, 1990), 161; note the bibliography of key studies on 155, especially. W. H. Brownlee, "Ezekiel's Poetic Indictment of the Shepherds," *HTR* 51 (1958): 191–203; H. Reventlow, *Wächter über Israel* (BZAW: Berlin: Töpelmann, 1962), 44–50; B. Willmes, *Die sogenannte Hirtenallegorie Ez 34: Studien zum Bild des Hirten im Alten Testament* (BBET; Frankfurt: Peter Lang, 1984).

[135]The NIV, apparently influenced by the reference to "strengthen [*hzq*] the weak" in Eze 34:4, incorrectly renders this verse with "strengthen the weak" instead of "the sick."

[136]For the image of God as Shepherd, cf. G. Wallis, "רָעָה, רֹעֶה," *TWAT* 7:566–76 (with literature); see also E. Hoffmann, "Das Hirtenbild im Alten Testament," *Fundamentum* (4, 1987): 33–50; note the Jewish mystical title of God as *ra'yā' m*^{e}*hēmnā'*, "the Faithful Shepherd." In the NT, Jesus is identified as the Good, Great, and Chief Shepherd (Jn 10:14; Heb 13:20; 1Pe 5:4); cf. Jeremias, "*ποίμην*," 490–97.

[137]See below, n. 145

[138]*ben-'ādām 'et-z*^{e}*rô'a par'ōh melek-miṣrayim šābartî w*^{e}*hinnēh lō'-ḥūbb*^{e}*šâ lātēt r*^{e}*pū'ôt lāśûm ḥittûl l*^{e}*ḥobšāh l*^{e}*ḥozqāh litpōś beḥāreb*. Cf. Hempel, *Heilung*, 238–39; on *r*^{e}*pu'ôt*, cf. next note.

[139]For *r*^{e}*pu'ôt*, "medicines, remedies" or their object, viz., "healing," cf. above, 1.2.2.1, n. 57.

[140]For the *Gattung* of this chapter, cf. Y. Hoffmann, *The Prophecies Against the Foreign Nations in the Bible* (Hebrew; Tel Aviv: Hosa'at HaQibuts HaMe'uhad, 1977); cf. also G. R. Hamborg, "Reasons for Judgment in the Oracles Against the Nations of the Prophet Isaiah," *VT* 31 (1981): 145–59.

[141]Verses 16–24 are entitled "The Conversion of Egypt" by O. Kaiser, *Isaiah 1–39*, trans. R. A. Wilson (OTL; Philadelphia: Westminster, 1974), 104 (see his discussion, 104–12). Cf. also J. F. A. Sawyer, "'Blessed Be My People Egypt (Isaiah 19:25). The Context and Meaning of a Remarkable Passage," in J. D. Martin and P. R. Davies, eds., *A Word in Season: Essays in Honour of William McKane* (JSOTSupp. 42; Sheffield: Sheffield Academic Press, 1986), 57–71.

[142]Cf. O. Loretz, "Der ugaritische Topos *b'l rkb* und die 'Sprache Kanaans,' in Jes 19, 1–25," *UF* 19 (1987): 101–12; see also A. Saénz-Badillos, *A History of the Hebrew Language* (New York: Cambridge Univ. Press, 1993).

[143]Kaiser, *Isaiah 13–39*, 104, renders v. 22, "And Yahweh will smite Egypt with healing blows . . ."; cf. also G. Fohrer, *Das Buch Jesaja* (ZBK; 2d ed.; Stuttgart: Zwingli, 1966), 1:231: "Und der Herr wird Ägypten mit heilsamen Schlage schlagen," justifying the last phrase with ref. to GKC 113a. However, the sequential translation of, e.g., NJV ("first afflict . . . then heal") seems preferable.

[144]Cf. Bright's translation (*Jeremiah*, 346): "Though we treated her, Babylon mends not"; Thompson (*Jeremiah*, 748) has, "We wanted to heal . . . "; AV, RSV, NEB, NIV all render, "We would have healed. . . ." For *rp'* in the Piel meaning "to treat," see above n. 132.

[145]This, of course, is another way of saying that God will preserve a remnant of his people but will utterly destroy Israel's enemies (the *locus classicus* is Jer 30:11). See R. de Vaux, "'The Remnant of Israel' According to the Prophets," repr. in *The Bible and the Ancient Near East*; trans. D. McHugh (Garden City, N.Y.: Doubleday, 1971), 15–30 (for the French original, see *RB* 42 [1933]: 526–39); G. Hasel, *The Remnant: The History and Theology of the Remnant Idea from Genesis to Isaiah* (Andrews University Monographs 5; Berrien Springs, Mich.: Andrews Univ. Press, 1974).

[146]Cf. also Na 3:19, which offers a similar "incurable" prognosis for Assyria's prophesied condition (see above, 0.3.3, *sub ghh*, for discussion).

[147]Cf. *y. Ber.* 8d, 5:1; *b. Ber.* 31a; see also H. N. Bilalik and Y. H. Ravnitzky, eds., *The Book of Legends: Sefer Ha-Aggadah*; trans. W. G. Braude (New York: Schocken, 1992), 478, #90.

[148]Cf., in general, D. E. Gowan, *Eschatology in the Old Testament* (Philadelphia: Fortress, 1986). With specific reference to Isaiah, cf. L. Stachowiak, "Das Problem der Eschatologie im Buch Jesaja," *Collectanea Theologica* 53 (1983): 133–45; J. Begrich, "Die eschatologische Periode in der Botschaft Deuterojesajas," ed. W. Zimmerli, *Studien zur Deuterojesaja* (Theologische Bücherei; München: Chr. Kaiser Verlag, 1969), 96–114.

[149]From an evangelical perspective, I believe that this is important for understanding the whole complex of messianic prophecy in its historical context: The Messiah is seen as coming on the immediate horizon of history. I hope to develop this theme in a future monograph devoted to the subject of the messianic hope in the OT, in light of later rabbinic and NT interpretation.

[150]Cf. further B. W. Anderson, "Exodus and Covenant in Second Isaiah and Prophetic Tradition," in F. M. Cross, W. E. Lemke, and P. D. Miller Jr., eds., *Magnalia Dei: The Mighty Acts of God. Essays on the Bible and Archaeology in Memory of G. Ernest Wright* (Garden City, N.Y.: Doubleday, 1976), 339–60.

[151]For the Year of Jubilee background (*liqrô' derôr*) and the application of this passage in the NT, cf. below, 5.2.2; cf. also Jer 34:8, 15, 17.

[152]The meaning of *p^eqaḥ-qōaḥ* has been disputed; does it mean "opening *of the eye*" or "opening *of the prison*"? For older discussion, cf. Alexander, *Isaiah* 1/2:397; Delitzsch, *Isaiah*, KD 7/2:426 ("we adhere to the strict usage of the language, if we understand by *p^e qachqoach* the opening up of the eyes [as contrasted with the dense darkness of the prison]"); for more recent treatment and textual discussion, including DSS^Isa, cf. J. D. W. Watts, *Isaiah 34–66* (WBC; Waco, Tex.: Word, 1987), 300, 1.b., 1.c. While NJV translates only in terms of "liberation to the imprisoned," NIV captures both concepts with its "release from darkness for the prisoners." The LXX (cf. Lk 4:18), reflecting an understanding similar to that of Delitzsch and possibly a different textual reading, has "blind" instead of "prisoners," thus rendering *p^eqaḥ-qōaḥ* with "opening the eyes" (see Watts, ibid.). Cf. also above, 2.2.7, on Ex 4:11–12.

[153]Cf. North, *Second Isaiah*, 112, on Isa 42:7, who rightly notes that this "refers most naturally to the physical privations of the exiles (cf. xlvii. 6)," before making broader application to release from spiritual darkness. Cf.

Mic. 7:8–9: "Do not gloat over me, my enemy! Though I have fallen, I will rise. Though I sit in darkness, the LORD will be my light. . . . He will bring me out into the light; I will see his righteousness" (NIV).

[154]J. D. Smart, *History and Theology in Second Isaiah: A Commentary on Isaiah 35, 40–66* (Philadelphia: Westminster, 1965), 261. Smart, however, identifies the Servant here as Israel. For a political understanding of Isa 61:1, cf. Watts, *Isaiah 34–66*, 303: "The new restoration of rights and buildings in Jerusalem will be received as release from a long prison sentence."

[155]While it is possible to see here an *additional*, spiritual application (cf. *Targ. Isa.*), the physical, literal application is primary (see below, n. 157).

[156]For the reference to "the dead being raised," cf. M. O. Wise and J. D. Tabor, "The Messiah at Qumran," *BAR* 18 (1992): 60–63, 65, who find a parallel expression in a recently published fragment from Qumran. Previous commentators often made reference to Isa 26:19, a passage, however, that clearly refers to future, final resurrection.

[157]Cf. Oswalt, *Isaiah 1–39*, 623–34: "That this prophecy was at least partially fulfilled in the ministry of Jesus Christ may be seen in the way in which he appropriated these figures to himself (Luke 7:22; Mark 7:37). As Delitzsch well says [see below], and as Jesus' ministry shows, the references to physical healing are not merely typological of spiritual healing. Rather, the physical healing is the outer side of a totality."

[158]See the discussion of the kingdom of God in the NT below, 5.1.1, 5.2.1–2.

[159]Cf. the exposition of E. J. Young, *The Book of Isaiah* (Grand Rapids: Eerdmans, 1970), 2:448, "The picture, in other words, is symbolic of the great change that God's grace will introduce, and in the performance of this work the true beauty, glory, and honor of the God of Israel will be made manifest."

[160]For the impact of this on the cessationist argument, cf. below, 5.2.1, 5.2.6, 6.1.6–6.2.1.

[161]Contrast *Targ. Isa.*, cited in Oswalt, *Isaiah 1–39*, 624; see above, n. 157.

[162]Delitzsch, *Isaiah*, KD 7/2:78.

[163]Cf. Lev 21:18; 2Sa 5:6–8; Job 29:15 (note also Dt 15:21; Mal 1:8, regarding unacceptable sacrifices); see J. Krašovec, *Der Merismus im Biblisch-Hebräischen und Nordwestsetmitischen* (BibOr 33; Rome: Pontifical Biblical Institute Press, 1977), 128, #176. For Israel as a blind, deaf servant in Isa 40–55, cf. 42:18–20; 43:8; 56:10; 59:10, and see P. Stern, "The 'Blind Servant' Imagery of Deutero-Isaiah," *Bib* 75 (1994): 224–32.

[164]Cf. above, n. 122.

[165]"Isaiah 33: An Isaianic Elaboration of the Zion Tradition," in C. L. Myers and M. O'Connor, eds., *The Word of the Lord Shall Go Forth: Essays in Honor of David Noel Freedman in Celebration of His Sixtieth Birthday* (Winona Lake, Ind.: Eisenbrauns, 1983), 15–25 (here quoting 23); for the chapter as a whole, see H. Gunkel, "Jesaja 33, eine prophetische Liturgie: Ein Vortrag," *ZAW* 42 (1924): 177–208. For a purely historical reading, cf. Hayes and Irvine, *Isaiah*, 360–70.

[166]Cf. in general M. Greenberg, "The Design and Themes of Ezekiel's Program of Restoration," *Int* 38 (1984): 181–208.

[167]For the temple mountain vision in general, cf. J. D. Levenson, *Theology of the Program of Restoration of Ezekiel 40–48* (Missoula, Mont.: Scholars, 1976), 5–53. For a discussion on the relationship between Ezekiel and priestly sources, see A. Hurvitz, *A Linguistic Study of the Relationship Between the Priestly Source and the Book of Ezekiel* (Paris: Gabalda, 1982). He does not compare the usage of *rp'* in Eze 47 to its usage in Lev 13–14, although there are certain affinities to be found (cf. above, 2.2.6).

[168]My translation of verse 12 approximates that of NJV, except that NJV has rendered *wᵉ ʿālēhû litrûpâ* as "and their leaves for healing," as opposed to "and their leaves for making whole." My decision for this rendering was made strictly on the basis of the contextual use of *rp'* beginning in 47:7, thus preserving the consistent (and holistic) imagery of the Hebrew. Otherwise, *tᵉrûpâ* should be rendered "healing." For Rev 22:2, see below. As for the versions, LXX's rendering of vv. 8–9, 11–12 is excellent (*kai hugiasei ta hudata* ...; *kai hugiasei kai zēsetai*...; *me hugiasosin* ...; *kai anabasis auton eis hugieian*). Elsewhere *hugiazō* was used to translate *rp'* in Lev 13:18, 37 (see above, 2.2.6); otherwise, it rendered the Qal or Piel of *ḥyh*. *hugeia* (or *hugia*, or *hugieia*) translated *ḥāy* (Ge 42:15, 16) and *nepeš* (Est 9:31); but the other equivalents are unclear. See Hatch and Redpath, *Concordance*, 2:1380b. *Targ. Jon.*'s consistent use of *'sy* (Ithpael in vv. 8–9, 11; *'ᵃsûtā'* in v. 12), while acceptable for *tᵉ rûpâ*, is forced for the other verses. Again, as in 2Ki 2:21–22 (cf. above, 2.3.4), this is consistent literality to a fault.

[169]Note also that the biblical *hapax terûpâ* occurs again in Ecclus. 38, the section on physicians (see above, 1.4.1). Thus, v. 4a asserts that *'ēl mē'ēres môṣî' tᵉ rûpôt*: "God brings out medicines [so NEB] from the earth"; cf. further the LXX's *kurios ektisen ek gēs pharmaka*. The reference in v. 5 to the tree that sweetened Israel's waters makes it clear that Ben Sira is closely following Ezekiel's reference to healing *leaves*; i.e., natural medicaments. Both Segal, *Ben Sira*, 245, and I. Levi, *The Hebrew Text of the Book of Ecclesiasticus* (Leiden: Brill 1909), 44, note the marginal *bārā' śammîn* (= *śammîm*), and both refer to *Gen. Rab.* 10 (Levi has 10): "God brought out *śammîn* [drugs] from the earth." Segal, ibid., further cites from *Yalqut Iyyob*: "Bar Sira said: 'God brought out *śammîm* from the earth.'" On the semantic overlap from "healing" to "medicine," cf. above, n. 139; on *tᵉ rûpâ*, cf. nn. 168–69, above; for *śām*, "drugs, poison," cf. Jastrow, *Dictionary*, 998.

[170]Instead of the LXX's *eis hugieian* (cf. n. 168, above), Rev 22:2 has *eis therapeian + ton ethnon* (K. P. Darr, "The Wall around Paradise: Ezekelian Ideas about the Future," *VT* 37 [1987]: 271–79, excludes the nations from Ezekiel's paradise, seeing it as only national in scope). The LXX's "healing" (= *therapeia*) is, outside of the context of Eze 47:8–12, a more appropriate rendering of *tᵉ rûpâ* than "making sound, whole" (= *hugieia*). For the need of "healing" in such a paradisaical vision, cf. Rashi, David Kimchi, *Yalqut Shim'oni*; and R. H. Mounce, *The Book of Revelation*, (NICNT; Grand Rapids: Eerdmans, 1977), 387. Delitzsch, *Proverbs*, KD 6:262, has noted on

Pr 12:18 (for which see 3.2.3) that *marpē'* "means healing (the remedy) and at the same time (cf. *therapeia*, Rev. xxii. 2) the preservation of health. . . ." Once again, this is reminiscent of Ehrlich's theory, cited above at Ex 15:26 (2.2.1) and often thereafter, that *rp'* can mean to keep free from sickness. Is this true then of *therapeia* (and *therapeuō*?), or is it only an ancient equivalent to our "preventative medicine"?

[171]For the paradise vision of the minor prophets, cf. I. Cornelius, "Paradise Motifs in the 'Eschatology' of the Minor Prophets and the Iconography of the Ancient Near East. The Concepts of Fertility, Water, Trees, and 'Tierfrieden' and Gen 2–3," *JNSL* 14 (1988): 41–83.

[172]Special attention has been given recently to the question of solar imagery and Yahweh worship; cf. J. G. Taylor, *Yahweh and the Sun: Biblical and Archaeological Evidence for Sun Worship in Ancient Israel* (JSOTSupp. 111; Sheffield: Sheffield Academic Press, 1993); H. P. Stähli, *Solare Elemente im Jahwehglauben des Alten Testaments* (OBO 66; Frieburg: Universitätsverlag/ Göttingen: Vandenhoeck und Ruprecht, 1985); Smith, *Early History*, 115–24; Dearman, *Religion and Culture*, 96; for the iconography, see O. Keel and C. Uehlinger, *Göttinnen, Götter and Gottessymbole: Neue Erkenntnisse zur Religionsgeschichte Kanaans und Israels aufgrund bislang unerschlossener Quellen* (QD 134; Freiburg/Basel/Wien: Herder, 1992). Moreover, in the specific context of healing, the sun (or, solar deity) played a well-known therapeutic role; cf. M. Green, *The Sun-Gods of Ancient Europe* (London: Hippocrene Books, 1991), 107–21. However, there is nothing particularly syncretistic about the description in Malachi, since the "sun," frequently associated with healing and life, was a common royal epithet in the ancient Near East (cf. Krauss, *Psalms 60–150*, 170; Tate, *Psalms 51–100*, 361) and could easily be used with reference to either Yahweh (see next note) or the king (cf. Smith, ibid., 119). Cf. further Ps 84:11(12), where Yahweh is praised metaphorically as both a *sun* and a *shield*, who gives grace and glory; and Smith, *Micah-Malachi*, 339, who claims, "Surely the rays of the sun must be behind the expression 'the Lord make his face to shine upon you' in the priestly blessing (Nu 6:24–26)." (On this last observation, cf. the forthcoming study of C. Cohen, cited by Levine, *Numbers 1–20*, 236ff.)

[173]If, in fact, the "sun" is used here with reference to the ideal future king (see previous note), or even to the Lord, this suffix might be best translated more personally with "his" instead of "its." On the relationship between healing and the reign of the idealized king, cf. Isa 32:1–4; for the belief in the therapeutic power of the touch of the king in medieval Europe (as well as in other cultures), cf. Sigerist, *Civilization and Disease*, 126–27.

[174]*wᵉzārᵉḥâ lākem yir'ê šᵉmî šemeš ṣᵉdāqâ ûmarpē' bikᵉnāpêhā*. Delitzsch and Dahood see a similarity of expression in Ps 112:4 (*zāraḥ baḥôšek 'ôr layᵉšārîm*—"light dawns in the darkness for the upright"), the former stating that God "is the Sun of righteousness with wings of rays dispensing 'grace' and 'tender mercies'" (*Psalms*, KD 5/3:200), the latter finding reference to God as the (rising) sun in Ps 139:11; Job 24:13; Isa 51:6 as well (*Psalms 101–150*, 127–28). On F. Vattioni's discussion of Mal 3:20 in the context of

Phoenician *yrḥ mrp' (m)* and *yrḥ zbḥ šmš*, see his "Mal. 3,20 un mese del calendrio fenicio," *Biblica* 40 (1959): 1012–15; cf. also Brown, "Was There a West Semitic Asklepios?"

[175]The godly, to whom "healing" is promised, are styled here "you who revere my name"; for the connection between "the fear of the LORD" and healing, cf. Pr 3:7–8 and above, 3.2.2.

[176]Cf. the lively rendering of Mal 4:2 (3:20) by I. G. Matthews, "Malachi," *An American Commentary* (Philadelphia: Judson Press, 1935), 34: "But to you, true worshipers of mine, the triumphant sun with healing in his rays will break out, and freed, you will go out like stall-fed calves and sport riotously" (cited by Smith, *Micah-Malachi*, 339–40).

Chapter Five—Israel's Divine Healer in the New Testament

[1]This chapter provides only a thumbnail sketch of healing and miracles in the NT, emphasizing in particular specific points of comparison, contrast, and fulfillment between the OT and NT relative to the subject of Israel's divine Healer. Key bibliographical works will be cited at the beginning of each section heading, focusing as much as is possible on the specific subject at hand. As for the appropriateness of this chapter title, note that for the first-century Jewish followers of Jesus as Messiah, there was no question that *in him*, the great expectations of the Hebrew prophets were now being realized. For these Jews, this was not the beginning of a new religion called "Christianity." Thus, after witnessing Jesus' healings in Mt 15:30–31, the crowds "praised the God of Israel" (v. 31b), and after he raised the widow's son from the dead (Lk 7:11–15), "They were all filled with awe and praised God. 'A great prophet has appeared among us,' they said. 'God has come to help his people'" (v. 16).

[2]Cf. Witty, *Divine Healing*, 53–80; for general perspectives on the theological relationship between the OT and NT, cf. below, 5.4.1. See also F.-E. Wilms, *Wunder im Alten Testament* (Regensburg: Putset, 1979).

[3]For general overviews, with bibliography, cf. C. L. Blomberg, "Healing," *Dictionary of Jesus and the Gospels*, 298–307; F. Graber and D. Müller, "Heal," *NIDNTT*, 2:163–72; A. Oepke, "ἰάομαι, ἴασις, ἴαμα, ἰατρός," *TDNT* 3:194–215; D. Wenham and C. L. Blomberg, eds., *Gospel Perspectives 6: The Miracles of Jesus* (Sheffield: JSOT Press, 1986). More recent monographs of interest, also with extensive bibliography, include H. K. Nielsen, *Heilung und Verkündigung*; R. Latourelle, *The Miracles of Jesus and the Theology of Miracles*, trans. M. J. O'Connell (New York: Paulist, 1988); cf. also Kee, *Miracle and Magic*, 1–2; Harper, *The Healings of Jesus*, 15–17; Mueller, *Sickness and Healing*, 130–48 (all with reference to the central role played by the miraculous in the Gospels and NT), and Kelsey, *Healing and Christianity*, 54, n. 3, who observes, "Out of the 3779 verses in the four Gospels, 727 relate specifically to the healing of physical and mental illness and resurrection of the dead." See also below, n. 6; cf., more generally, A. Suhl, ed., *Die Wunderbegriff im Neuen Testament* (Darmstadt: Wissenschaftliche Buchge-

sellschaft, 1980); contrast Hagner, *Matthew 1–13*, 211, regarding Matthew: "Given the entire sweep of the Gospel, the healing pericopes become relatively insignificant." I concur with A. J. Saldarini, *Matthew's Christian-Jewish Community* (Chicago: Univ. of Chicago Press, 1994), 179, who observes that for Matthew, "after teaching, Jesus' most frequent activity in the gospel is healing" (see further 178–81, 290–91, nn. 54ff.).

[4]For the intimate connection between preaching and healing (thus, between proclamation and deed), cf. especially Nielsen, *Heilung und Verkündigung*; see also G. S. Grieg and K. N. Springer, eds., *The Kingdom and the Power* (Ventura, Calif.: Regal Books, 1993), 359–92 ("Appendix 1—Power Evangelism and the New Testament Evidence").

[5]Cf. the programmatic statement in Jn 14:12: "Truly, truly, I say to you, he who believes in me will also do the works that I do; and greater works than these will he do, because I go to the Father" (RSV). While some have disputed the meaning of the "greater works," it is difficult not to conclude that *whoever believes* in the Son will also perform miraculous signs. This is indicated by: (1) the immediate context (viz., 14:9–11, with the emphasis on miracles as the *works* done by Jesus); (2) the universality of the promise (*ho pisteuōn eis eme*; cf. 3:16, 18, 36; 6:35; 11:25 for similar phraseology, rendered uniformly by the NIV in John *except* at 14:12); (3) the assurance that follows, guaranteeing the efficacy of prayer to the Father in Jesus' name. Cf. Grieg and Springer, *The Kingdom and the Power*, 393–97 ("Appendix 2—John 14:12—The Commission to All Believers to Do the Works of Jesus"). Note also W. R. Bodine, "Power Ministry in the Epistles: A Reply to the Cessationist Position," in ibid., 203–4, n. 8; and cf. C. Dietzfelbinger, "Die grösseren Werke (Joh 14. 12f.)," *NTS* 35 (1989): 27–47.

[6]According to J. Jervell, *The Unknown Paul: Essays on Luke-Acts and Early Christian History* (Minneapolis: Augsburg, 1984), 95: "Without miracle the gospel is not gospel but merely word, or rather words," cited in J. Ruthven, *On the Cessation of the Charismata* (Journal of Pentecostal Theology, Supp3; Sheffield: Sheffield Academic Press, 1993), 118, n. 1 (see 1Co 4:19–20). Harper, *The Healings of Jesus*, 15–16, notes: "In Mark's gospel ... 209 verses out of 666 are about the miracles of Jesus, just over thirty-one percent. If we look at the first ten chapters and omit the long passion narrative, there are 200 out of 425 verses, which is about forty-seven percent. Although the proportion in the other gospels is not so high, we are bound to conclude that the writers, however we may interpret what they have written, regarded them as crucially important. It is impossible to think of the gospels without them." E. P. Sanders, *Jesus and Judaism* (Philadelphia: Fortress, 1985), 6, notes that M. Smith—certainly not a fundamentalist!—argued that "the first and surest fact about Jesus is that he is a miracle worker, and [Smith] is confident that in Jesus' own ministry it was healing which attracted the crowds to whom he preached" (with reference to Smith's *Jesus the Magician* [New York: Harper & Row, 1978], 11, 14). For Crossan, *The Historical Jesus*, 310–11, the gospel miracle stories, rather than being later accretions, were problematic and controversial for both Jesus' enemies *and* friends, and thus "at a very

early stage, [were] being washed out of the tradition and, when retained, were being very carefully interpreted" (with reference to J. M. Hull, *Hellenistic Magic and the Synoptic Tradition* [SBT 2/28; Naperville, Ill.: Allenson, 1974]). While I concur with Crossan's assessment as to the fundamental nature of the miracles and healings, I would see them clearly as being a great *asset* for Jesus' "friends" (cf. below, 5.2.6) and a problem only for his enemies. On the centrality of the supernatural ministry of the Spirit in Acts, cf. Dunn, *Jesus and the Spirit*; see also Kelsey, *Healing and Christianity*, 117–28, for a brief summary of healings and miracles in Acts; G. W. H. Lampe, "Miracles in the Acts of the Apostles," in C. F. D. Moule, ed., *Miracles: Cambridge Studies in Their Philosophy and History* (London: Mowbray, 1986), 165–78.

[7]Crossan, *The Historical Jesus*, xi.

[8]Cf. Matthew Henry, *Commentary on the Whole Bible,* on La 3:33: "For he does not willingly bring affliction to the children of men."

[9]Mark's use of "many" does not suggest that there were some Jesus did not heal among those who came to him, rather, it quantifies the "all": the "all" who were healed were "many." Cf. Mk 10:45 (that the Son of Man gave his life as a ransom for "many"), and the usage of "many" in Isa 53:11–12; Da 12:2 ("many" will arise in the final resurrection), and the DSS (cf. J. Jeremias, "πολλοί," *TDNT* 6:536–45).

[10]Due to the large number of parallel accounts of Jesus' healing in the Gospels, parallels are cited only when relevant. Otherwise, the choice of which text should be cited was dictated by either context, key vocabulary, or perceived familiarity, with little reference to source-critical questions. It is beyond my scholarly expertise to offer any new insights into such matters, and the concise nature of this chapter does not allow for such digression. For a critical analysis of the Gospel record of Jesus' *acts*, cf. Sanders, *Jesus and Judaism*, 3–13, 157–73; see also Latourelle, *The Miracles of Jesus*, 70–238. In keeping with my conservative presuppositions (cf. above, 0.2), I view Jesus as the Messiah *already while in the flesh*, and thus not as a mere "charismatic miracle worker" (see G. Vermes, *Jesus the Jew: A Historian's Reading of the Gospels* [Philadelphia: Fortress], 1981) elevated to messianic status after his death (and resurrection). On this, contrast P. M. Casey, *From Jewish Prophet to Gentile God* (Philadelphia: Westminster/John Knox, 1991), with M. J. Harris, *Jesus as God* (Grand Rapids: Baker, 1992); cf. also L. W. Hurtado, *One God, One Lord: Early Christian Devotion and Ancient Jewish Monotheism* (Philadelphia: Fortress, 1988); B. Witherington III, "Lord," *Dictionary of Jesus and the Gospels*, 484–92.

[11]Some have claimed that Jesus' failure to bring judgment was the reason for John the Baptist's later questioning of whether or not he was the "one to come" (Lk 7:18–23); see Lachs, *Rabbinic Commentary*, 190–91: "John preached the coming of one who would execute judgments (cf. Matt. 3.11), whereas Jesus speaks of mercy and loving-kindness; he preferred to heal rather than to destroy the wicked," with reference to T. Manson, *The Sayings of Jesus* (London: SCM, 1949), 66; note also the wording of Mt 11:2. This interpretation, however, is unlikely, unless it is argued that it was his failure to

bring *immediate* judgment on the wicked that troubled John; cf. J. Nolland, *Luke 1–9:20* (WBC; Waco, Tex.: Word, 1989), 339–40; for the element of judgment as a result of Messiah's coming, cf. D. Wells, *No Place for Truth* (Grand Rapids: Eerdmans, 1993), 276: "In the Gospels, God's kingdom has two foci—salvation and judgment"; see also Mal 3:1–5; Jn 5:22; 9:39.

[12]For 1Co 5:1–5, cf. above, 3.1.8, n. 175.

[13]Cf. C. H. H. Wright, "Jubilee, Year of," *ABD* 3:1028, who makes reference to the "Nazareth manifesto" (cf. U. Busse, *Das Nazareth-Manifest: Eine Einführung in das lukanische Jesubild nach Lk 4:16–30* [SBS 91; Stuttgart: Katholisches Bibelwerk, 1978]); see also Nolland, *Luke 1–9:20*, 195, who notes that "Luke 4:16–30 is widely regarded as a programmatic text for Luke's whole enterprise"; J. G. Lake, "The Platform of Jesus" (Sermon #17 in the privately distributed collection, "The Unpublished Sermons of John G. Lake").

[14]While it is possible that "the day of vengeance [*nāqām*] of our God" was also positive as far as Israel was concerned (i.e., it was a day of vengeance against Israel's *enemies*; cf. the use of *nāqām* in Isa 35:4, for which see above, 4.2.2; on *nāqām* in Isa 61:1–2, cf., however, O. H. Steck, "Der Rachetag in Jesaja lxi 2: Ein Kapitel redaktionsgeschichtlicher Kleinarbeit," *VT* 36 [1986]: 323–38), the purpose and intent of Luke's reading is clear: Jesus came "to proclaim the year of the Lord's favor" (Lk 4:19). R. B. Sloan, "Jubilee," *Dictionary of Jesus and the Gospels*, 397, argues that "there can be little doubt that further references in Luke to 'preaching the gospel' must be read with jubilary significance." For in-depth treatment, cf. the works cited below, 5.2.2.

[15]Of course, the theme of "unmerited favor" was by no means absent from the OT; see McConville, *Grace in the End*. Nonetheless, Jn 1:17 does imply a contrast, and it is written as a paradigmatic statement regarding the relative emphases of Moses and Jesus; cf., however, D. P. Fuller, *Gospel and Law: Contrast or Continuum?* (Grand Rapids: Eerdmans, 1980), for caveats.

[16]According to Nolland, *Luke 1–9:20*, 202, "Jubilee release is not spiritualized into forgiveness of sins, but neither can it be resolved into a program of social reform. It encompasses spiritual restoration, moral transformation, rescue from demonic oppression, and release from illness and disability." See also below, 5.2.2.

[17]It is fitting for God to use such agents to carry out his wrath; cf. his utilization of the ruthless Assyrians and cruel Babylonians to punish Israel and Judah (e.g., Isa 10:5–19; Jer 27). However, due to their tyranny and pride, they went too far (cf. Isa 10:5–7; Zec 1:14–15). How much more has Satan "run amuck" (cf. 1Pe 5:8–9; Rev 12)!

[18]Cf. 2Ti 1:10; 2Co 3:16; for intertestamental developments in beliefs in demons, angels, and the spirit world in general, cf. the references cited above, 3.1.10, nn. 201–2, and below, 5.3.1, n. 99.

[19]Although statements such as Jn 8:44, addressed to some Jews, have been judged anti-Semitic, the position of the NT is that everyone—Jew or Gentile—who does not acknowledge Jesus as Lord is under the power of the evil

one (1Jn 5:19) and blinded by him (2Co 4:4); see Brown, *Our Hands Are Stained with Blood*, 179–80, n. 11.

[20]In Luke, this word denotes especially *miraculous* power; cf., in general, W. Grundmann, "δύναμαι, δύναμις, etc." *TDNT* 2:284–317; G. Friedrich, "δύναμις," *EDNT* 1:355–58, both with key literature; see below, n. 63.

[21]Cf. Kelsey, *Healing and Christianity*, 99, who notes that, "it was [Jesus'] nature to be hostile to illness and to have mercy on the sick; it appears almost as if he could not help himself. As the representative of God, he had the authority and power to heal; it was his task—very nearly the obligation he had to accept, if he was to fulfill and be himself." For a sense in which the healings of Jesus were not "automatic," cf. J. Deere, *Surprised by the Power of the Spirit* (Grand Rapids: Zondervan, 1993), 58–64.

[22]Cf. H. Bonar, *Christ the Healer* (repr. Grand Rapids: Baker, 1977), 80: "In his blessed path as the healer, he is ever willing to be arrested by the sons of men; counting this no detention, no trouble, no hindrance, but the true fulfillment of his heavenly mission."

[23]For a convenient listing of the key words in NT healing contexts, cf. Kelsey, *Healing and Christianity*, 110, n. 5 (there are, however, some incorrect citations; e.g., Acts 3:11 under *iaomai, iama, iasis*); for the relevant semantic domains, cf. Louw and Nida, *Greek-English Lexicon*, 1:238–76 (in particular, 268–74), and note the relevant articles in *TDNT*, *NIDNTT*, *EDNT*, and C. Spicq, O.P., *Theological Lexicon of the New Testament*, trans. J. Ernest (Peabody, Mass.: Hendrickson, 1994); see further W. Schrage, "Heil und Heilung im Neuen Testament," *EvT* 43 (1986), 197–214; cf. also W. K. Hobart, *The Medical Language of St. Luke* (repr. Grand Rapids: Baker, 1954), and R. J. Knowling, "The Medical Language of St. Luke," *BW* 20 (1902), 260–70, 370–79, both of which should be read in the light of C. J. Hemer, "Medicine in the New Testament World," in *Medicine and the Bible*, 43–83; cf. further J. J. Pilch, "Sickness and Health in Luke-Acts," in *The Social World of Luke-Acts*, J. H. Neyrey, ed. (Peabody, Mass.: Hendrickson, 1991), 181–209, for sociological definitions and dimensions (and see above, 3.1.4, n. 68).

[24]As the LXX equivalent of Hebrew *yš'*, *sōzō* was not primarily used in what may be called "Christian" soteriological contexts (cf. above, ch. 4, nn. 9 and 100, for *yš'*). That is to say, most of the "saving" done by the Lord in the OT was physical and earthly (e.g., being saved from one's enemies or from mortal distress), including saving from death that might come as a result of sickness. The NT use of *sōzō* certainly includes such meanings (in addition to the verses cited below with regard to healing, see Mt 14:30), *adding* a deeper emphasis on eternal salvation from sin and damnation.

[25]Louw and Nida, *Greek-English Lexicon*, 2:240, subdivide NT usage of *sōzō* under the general headings of "rescue," "save," and "heal" and treat *sōtēr* under the headings "rescuer" and "Savior"; cf. also Brown, "רָפָא," 623–24, where it is noted that in the biblical and ancient Near Eastern mind, viewing the deity as savior, healer, and deliverer, was part of one inclusive concept.

[26]More broadly, W. Radl, "σώζω," *EDNT* 3:319–21 (here 319–20), notes: "That from which one is saved ... include [*sic*] mortal danger, death, disease, possession, sin and alienation from God, and eternal ruin." The Lucan usage just cited suggests that one English word be utilized in translating *sōzō* in these chapters, thus helping the reader grasp the vital connection that links together Jesus' *saving* acts (cf. also above, 2.2.6, 2.3.4, 4.2.2, regarding the appropriate renderings of *rp'* in certain contexts). Cf. further Spicq, *Theological Lexicon* 3:346–47.

[27]Cf. Schrage, "Heil und Heilung im Neuen Testament."

[28]Note that *sōzō* was used for "heal" in Mk 6:56, cited above; so also Mt 14:36.

[29]Louw and Nida, *Greek-English Lexicon*, 269, #23.141, understand *egeirō* in such contexts as meaning "to restore a person to health and vigor (somewhat equivalent to the English idiom 'to get him on his feet again')."

[30]For the exegesis of Jas 5:14–16, emphasizing clearly that it is the *prayer* offered in faith, *not* the oil, that brings healing, cf. R. P. Martin, *James* (WBC; Waco, Tex.: Word, 1988), 206–10; P. H. Davids, *The Epistle of James* (NIGTC; Grand Rapids: Eerdmans, 1982), 192–95; see below, n. 113. While the NT as a whole seems to have a positive attitude to basic medicinal treatment (cf. the metaphor of the sick needing a doctor [Mt 9:12 and parallels], with no hint of disparagement; the mention of "Luke the doctor" [Col 4:14]; the actions of the Good Samaritan, bandaging the beaten man's wounds and pouring in oil and wine [Lk 10:34–35]; and Paul's counsel to Timothy to drink a little wine for his stomach problems [1Ti 5:23]), the context in Jas 5 clearly suggests that the usage of the oil is primarily symbolic, not medicinal (see the commentaries cited for a review of the debate). Cf. further Kee, *Miracle, Medicine, and Magic*; Hemer, "Medicine in the New Testament World"; see the works cited in 0.1, n. 8. Remarkably, C. R. Swindoll, in his popular pastoral book, *Flying Closer to the Flame* (Dallas: Word, 1993), 205, adduces the following from Jas 5:14–16: "In other words, 'See your doctor and follow his instructions.' That comes first. *Then*, after appropriate medical attention, there is to be prayer." Swindoll does, however, affirm that God still heals today in response to prayer.

[31]Some have argued that the variation in Lk 17:15, 19 is significant, the former (*iaomai*) being used with reference only to the leper's physical healing, the latter (*sōzō*) with reference to his full restoration after returning to Jesus to give thanks; cf. I. H. Marshall, *The Gospel of Luke* (NIGTC; Grand Rapids: Eerdmans, 1978), 652: "His faith has been the means of his cure—and of his salvation." See also G. Schneider, *Evangelium nach Lukas* (Gütersloh: Gerd Mohn, 1977), 352, cited in J. A. Fitzmyer, *Luke X–XXIV*, 1156. But in light of the Lucan usage of *sōzō* elsewhere in his Gospel, this may be reading too much into the text (but see Nolland, *Luke 1–9:20*, 420; G. E. Ladd, *A Theology of the New Testament*, rev. D. A. Hagner [Grand Rapids: Eerdmans, 1993], 75).

[32]BAGD, 368, "ἰάομαι,' 2.5. According to R. Leivestad, "ἰάομαι," *EDNT* 2:170, "The imagery in Heb 12:13 is more ethical-parenetic"; cf. similary Oepke, "ἰάομαι," 214.

[33]See also below, n. 113, where it is noted that BAGD classifies Jas 5:16 here too, thus listing all occurrences of *iaomai* (not *iama*; see above) in the letters as "figurative" healing. It should be remembered, however, that OT usage of *rāpā'* is rarely, if ever, exclusively spiritual (cf. above, 0.3.1, 0.3.2, 1.4, 4.1, 4.1.1), hence verses such as 1Pe 2:24b, pointing back to the believers' whole conversion experience—focusing on death to sin and life to righteousness through the cross—might well be translated, "by his wounds you have been restored." While the clear emphasis is on redemption from sin (cf. 1Pe 2:25), thus picturing sin as a malady needing to be healed (cf. above, 4.1.2, on Jer 3:22; Hos 14:5), Peter's audience doubtless included those whose lives had been restored from every kind of affliction—spiritual, physical, and mental. The "healing" to which they looked back would have been equally inclusive (cf. above, 4.1, 4.1.1, on the "metaphorical" usage of *rāpā'*). Interpreters tend to understand 1Pe 2:24 in terms of either spiritual healing (which is primarily in mind contextually) or physical healing (primarily not in mind here, contra most divine healing teachers; cf. above, 4.1.4, n. 108), whereas the readers of 1 Peter would have looked back to their conversion through the cross as the source of their healing in the widest possible terms. Thus a translation with "restored" seems plausible. For the NT citations of Isa 53, cf. K. D. Litwak, "The Use of Quotations from Isaiah 52:13–53:12 in the New Testament," *JETS* 26 (1983): 385–94.

[34]Since Matthew primarily uses *therapeuō* for healing, his usage of *iaomai* in 13:15 probably reflects the LXX; cf. Gundry, *The Use of the Old Testament in Saint Matthew's Gospel*, 149.

[35]Cf Lk 9:11, he "healed [*iaomai*] those who needed healing [*therapeia*]." The semantic development is clear; note Louw and Nida, *Greek-English Lexicon*, 268 (#23.139): "to cause someone to recover health, often with the implication of having taken care of such a person." Both *therapeuō* and *therapeia*, commonly used in the LXX, occur in healing contexts only in the apocryphal literature; cf. Tob 2:10, 12:3. Wis 16:12; Ecclus 18:19; 38:7; see also LSJ, 792–93, for the varied meanings of the root. According to MM, 289, 297, the primary distinction between *therapeuō* and *iaomai* is that the former, "used as a medical term, means strictly 'treat medically' rather than 'heal'" (289), whereas "*iaomai* denotes 'heal'" (297). Cf. further G. A. Lindeboom, "Luke the Evangelist and the Ancient Greek Writers on Medicine," *Janus* 52 (1965): 143–48.

[36]H. W. Beyer, "θεραπεία, θεραπεύω, θεράπων," *TDNT* 3:128–32 (here, 129).

[37]Ibid.

[38]Cf. Goodrick and Kohlenberger, *Concordance*, 1800. The noun *ischuō*, meaning "strong," is twice rendered "healthy" by the NIV (Mt 9:12; Mk 2:17; contrast Lk 5:31 with *hugiainō*); cf. also *apokathistēmi*, "to restore" (8 times, 5 with reference to healing; e.g., Mk 3:5); *anablepō*, "to look up, receive

sight" (e.g., Lk 7:22); *holoklēria*, "wholeness, health" (Acts 3:16). Other verbs used have no specific healing nuance (e.g., *anoigō*, "to open," rendered "restored" [i.e., "sight"] at Mt 9:30).

[39]Recent surveys on the kingdom of God, with bibliographies of key monographs and articles, include: D. C. Duling, "Kingdom of God, Kingdom of Heaven," *ABD* 4:49–69; C. C. Caragounis, "Kingdom of God/Kingdom of Heaven," *Dictionary of Jesus and the Gospels*, 417–30; U. Luz, "βασιλεία," *EDNT* 1:201–5; B. Klappert, "King, Kingdom," *NIDNTT* 2:372–90; cf. also the full bibliographical notes in Ruthven, "A Biblical Doctrine of the Kingdom of God Is Inimical to Cessationism," *Cessation*, 115–23; note the older article of K. L. Schmidt, "βασιλεία," *TDNT* 1:579–93, which still retains value; more popularly, but with specific reference to healing, cf. Harper, *The Healings of Jesus*, 157–67. For varied approaches to the kingdom of God in the Synoptic Gospels, cf. Ladd and Hagner, *Theology*, 42–132 (concisely, G. Ladd, "Kingdom of God," *ISBE* 3:23–29); Crossan, *Historical Jesus*, 225–416 (see also ibid., 457–60); Sanders, *Jesus and Judaism*, 123–241. For an example of a serious study of the kingdom of God with *no* emphasis on healing, cf. G. R. Beasley-Murray, *Jesus and the Kingdom of God* (Grand Rapids: Eerdmans, 1986), in spite of his section on "Signs of the Presence of the Kingdom of God."

[40]Cf. W. Kelber, *The Kingdom in Mark* (Philadelphia: Fortress, 1974), 17: "Exorcisms and healings are the two principal approaches used to translate the kingdom program into action. In both cases Jesus intrudes upon enemy territory, challenges and subdues the forces of evil which are in the way of the fulfillment of the kingdom of God" (cited in Ruthven, *Cessation*, 116–17, n. 3). Cf. similarly Grundmann, "δύναμις," *TDNT* 2:302.

[41]According to R. H. Fuller, *Interpreting the Miracles* (Philadelphia: Westminster, 1963), 40 (cited in Ruthven, *Cessation*), "Jesus interprets his exorcisms as the beginning of the end of Satan's reign."

[42]The significant Lucan variant in 11:20 ("finger of God" for Matthew's "Spirit of God") points back to Ex 8:19, as is widely recognized (cf. Fitzmyer, *Luke X–XXIV*, 922). For the ten plagues and the Exodus as a conflict between kingdoms, cf. above, 2.1, n. 1; for healing and the Holy Spirit, see below, 5.2.3; for further discussion of Mt 12:28 and Lk 11:20, cf. Nielsen, *Heilung und Verkündigung*, 28–46.

[43]Mueller, *Sickness and Healing*, 117–18; for the uniqueness of this concept, cf. ibid., 118–19; note Mueller's reference (p. 117) to Satan's *future* downfall expected in *As. Mos.* 10:1 in contrast with his *present* downfall according to Lk 10:18–19; note, however, Ro 16:20. See further, below, 5.2.2.

[44]See Hatch-Redpath, *Concordance*, 420–21. I am not aware of any Hebrew translations of the NT that render *ekballō* in Mk 16:17 with *lᵉ gārēš*.

[45]Cf. Ladd and Hagner, *Theology*, 65: "The enemies of God's kingdom are now seen not as hostile evil nations as in the Old Testament but spiritual powers of evil."

[46]Cf. H. Alford, *The Greek Testament* (with rev. by E. F. Harrison; Chicago: Moody, 1968), who regards Mark 16:9–20 as "*an authentic* [but non-Marcan]

fragment, placed as a completion of the Gospel in very early times" (1:438); he states regarding vv. 17–18: "This promise is *generally* made, without limitation to the first ages of the Church. *Should occasion arise for its fulfillment*, there can be no doubt that it will be made good in our own or any other time" (1:436–37, his emphasis throughout). He claims, however, that "we must remember that *semeia* are not needed where Christianity is *professed*," adding in woefully antiquated sentiments, "nor by missionaries who are backed by the influence of powerful Christian nations [*sic*]" (1:437, again, his emphasis). Nonetheless, he freely admits, "There are credible testimonies of miraculous powers having been exercised in the Church considerably after the Apostles' time" (ibid.). For a textual evaluation of the longer ending of Mark, cf. B. M. Metzger, *A Textual Commentary on the New Testament* (London/New York: United Bible Societies, 1975), 122–28; for continuing miracles in association with the proclamation and expansion of the kingdom, cf. below, 6.2.

[47]Cf. Wright, "Jubilee," 1025–30; Sloan, "Jubilee," 396–97; idem, *The Favorable Year of the Lord: A Study of Jubilar Theology in the Gospel of Luke* (Austin, Tex.: Schola, 1977); G. K.-S. Shin, *Die Ausrufung des endgültigen Jubeljahres durch Jesus in Nazaret: Eine historisch-kritische Studie zu Lk 4, 16–30* (Bern: Peter Lang, 1989); S. H. Ringe, *Jesus, Liberation, and the Biblical Jubilee* (OBT; Philadelphia: Fortress, 1985); W. Zimmerli, "Das 'Gnadenjahr des Herrn,'" in A. Kuschke and E. Kutsch, eds., *Archäologie und Altes Testament: Festschrift K. Galling* (Tübingen: Mohr, 1970), 321–32. The standard sociological work is R. North, *The Sociology of the Biblical Jubilee* (Rome: Pontifical Biblical Institute, 1954); see also N. P. Lemche, "The Manumission of Slaves—the Fallow Year—the Sabbatical Year—the Jobel Year," *VT* 26 (1976): 38–59. Note the works listed in J. A. Fitzmyer, *The Gospel According to Luke I–IX* (AB; Garden City, N.Y.: Doubleday, 1981), 539–40; and Nolland, *Luke 1–9:20*, 188–90. For the concept of an eschatological jubilee in related early Jewish literature, cf. *Jub.* 1:21–25; 11Q Melch; and *b. Sanh.* 97b. For the possibility that Jesus began his public ministry during a Jubilee year (26–27), cf. Marshall, *Luke*, 132–34, 184 (although not accepted by him).

[48]It is significant that the Greek for "forgiveness of sins" (*aphesis harmatiōn*; e.g., Lk 24:47) is literally "release [from the debt] of sins," with *aphesis* serving as the LXX's rendering of Hebrew *d*ᵉ *rôr* (for which see next note) in a number of relevant OT texts. For the connection between Jesus' proclamation of forgiveness of sins (a spiritual amnesty) and supernatural healings (a physical amnesty), cf. below, 5.3.2. Sloan, "Jubilee," 397, claims that "the Sabbath/Jubilee Year import of the Nazareth sermon would have been lost on no one in Jesus' or Luke's audience familiar with either the Mosaic traditions or the then popular eschatological text of Isaiah 61."

[49]It is clearly the LXX's rendering of *ḥopšî* ("free") with *aphesis* in Isa 58:6 that caused its inclusion in the reading from Isa 61, recounted in Lk 4:18. As noted above, 4.2.2, Isaiah's *liqrō' d*ᵉ *rôr* ("proclaim liberty") is to be compared with Lev 25:10 (*ûq*ᵉ *rā'tem d*ᵉ *rôr*; cf. also Jer 34:8, 15, 17): "Consecrate the fiftieth year and proclaim liberty throughout the land. It shall be a jubilee for you; each one of you is to return to his family property and each to

his clan." See North, "דְּרוֹר," 265–69, who notes (p. 265) that the usage of *dᵉ rôr* by Jeremiah, Isaiah, and Ezekiel (see Eze 46:17) "represents the spiritualizing of an 'emancipation' originally regarded as economic." Thus, regardless of one's dating of Lev 25, it is recognized that the *social* dimensions of *dᵉrôr* preceded the spiritual application; cf. Zimmerli, "Das 'Gnadenjahr des Herrn,'" 327; North, "דְּרוֹר," 269; and Wright, "Jubilee"; note also the Akkadian usage of the cognate *andurāru*, well attested already in the third millennium B.C. in the sense of "remission of (commercial) debts," "manumission (of private slaves)," and "the canceling of services illegally imposed on free persons" (North, "דְּרוֹר," 266, with reference to *CAD*, A/2, 115, 117; and cf. *AHW* 1:50–51). See J. Lewy, "The Biblical Institution of *dᵉ rôr* in the Light of Akkadian Documents," *EI* 5:21–31. For LXX's *aphesis* and Hebrew *dᵉ rôr*, see North, "דְּרוֹר," 267; Wright, "Jubilee," 1028; more fully, Sloan, *The Favorable Year of the Lord.*

[50]Among the Synoptics, only Luke states that Jesus "rebuked" the fever of Peter's mother-in-law (Lk 4:39; see Mt 8:14–15; Mk 1:29–31). For the significance of this usage, cf. Fitzmyer, *Luke I–IX*, 546, who notes (with reference to H. C. Kee, *NTS* 14 [1967–68]: 232–46), "It is part of the vocabulary belonging to the description of the final defeat of Belial and his minions." The glossary to Wimber's *Power Healing*, 240, contains the entry "**prayer of rebuke:** a prayer in which demons are cast out or their power is broken (Mark 9:25)." Cf. also Nolland, *Luke 1–9:20*, 212: "Illness, too, is a demonic force from which Jesus brings release. This healing and the exorcism anticipate concretely the evening healings and exorcisms to follow and all together clarify the fuller scope of what is meant for Jesus to be preaching the kingdom of God in the synagogues of the Jews (cf. [4:]14–15, 43–44)."

[51]Cf. Ruthven, *Cessation*, 116, who observes that "miracles manifest the essential core activity of [Jesus'] mission: to displace the physical and spiritual ruin of the demonic kingdom by the wholeness of the kingdom of God." Contrast R. Gaffin, *Perspectives on Pentecost: Studies in New Testament Teaching on the Gifts of the Holy Spirit* (Grand Rapids: Baker, 1979), 45.

[52]In other instances, the request for healing is simply granted (e.g., Mt 15:28; cf. also Jn 4:50); note the convenient charts in Wimber, *Power Healing*, 245–46; Kelsey, *Healing and Christianity*, 55–57, listing all the Gospel healings with the method or methods involved in each instance.

[53]According to Nolland, *Luke 1–9:20*, 202, "Jubilee release is not spiritualized into forgiveness of sins, but neither can it be resolved into a program of social reform. It encompasses spiritual restoration, moral transformation, rescue from demonic oppression, and release from illness and disability."

[54]Cf. Wright, "Jubilee," 1028–29: "Jesus announced the inbreaking of the eschatological reign of God. He claimed that the hopes of restoration and messianic reversal were being fulfilled in his own ministry. . . . Likewise in Acts the jubilary concept of eschatological restoration is found in the otherwise unique idea of *apokatastasis*. It occurs in Acts 1:6 and 3:21, related to God's final restoration of Israel and all things." Wright also notes, 1029, how the early church "responded to this hope at the level of economic mutual

help." For the NT view of history compared with that of the OT, cf. the diagrams in Ruthven, *Cessation*, 120; Ladd and Hagner, *Theology*, 66–67.

[55]The fact that the levitical Year of Jubilee was to be proclaimed every fiftieth year *on the Day of Atonement* (Lev 25:8–12) has not been missed by proponents of divine healing; see below, 5.3.2.

[56]See M. M. B. Turner, "Holy Spirit," *Dictionary of Jesus and the Gospels*, 341–51; G. F. Hawthorne, *The Presence and the Power* (Dallas: Word, 1991); J. D. G. Dunn, *Jesus and the Spirit*; D. A. Carson, *Showing the Spirit* (Grand Rapids: Baker, 1987); S. Schatzmann, *A Pauline Theology of the Charismata* (Peabody, Mass.: Hendrickson, 1987); H. Gunkel, *The Influence of the Holy Spirit: The Popular View of the Apostolic Age and the Teaching of the Apostle Paul*, trans. R. A. Harrisville and P. A. Quanbeck (Philadelphia: Fortress, 1979); cf. also Ruthven, *Cessation*, 114–15 ("A Biblical Doctrine of the Holy Spirit Is Inimical to Cessationism"), also 123–87; more broadly, see G. Fee, *God's Empowering Presence: The Holy Spirit in the Letters of Paul* (Peabody, Mass.: Hendrickson, 1994).

[57]For this passage, cf. M. M. B. Turner, "The Significance of Receiving the Spirit in John's Gospel," *VoxEv* 10 (1977): 24–42, and see the works listed in G. R. Beasley-Murray, *John* (WBC; Waco, Tex.: Word, 1987), 100–101.

[58]For the meaning of, "He will baptize you with the Holy Spirit and fire" (Mt 3:11), cf. Davies and Allison, *Matthew 1–7*, 316–18; J. D. G. Dunn, "Spirit and Fire Baptism," *NovT* 14 (1972): 81–92; for the Lucan connection between the Spirit and power, cf. Lk 1:35; 4:14 (note also 1:17); Ac 1:8; 10:38. For a concise discussion of "realized eschatology," cf. D. C. Allison Jr., "Eschatology," in *Dictionary of Jesus and the Gospels*, 206–9, with references; note also the references in Ladd and Hagner, *Theology*, 758 (see under "Eschatology, realized").

[59]Cf. M. M. B. Turner, "The Spirit and the Power of Jesus' Miracles in the Lucan Conception," *NovT* 33 (1991): 124–52; idem, "Jesus and the Spirit in the Lucan Perspective," *TynBul* 32 (1981): 3–42; note also the Lucan emphasis on the Spirit in the infancy narratives: Lk 1:15, 35, 41, 67; 2:25, 27 (see also Hawthorne, *The Presence and the Power*, 53–96).

[60]Although the etymological meaning of *mašîaḥ/christos* was not necessarily paramount in the minds of Jesus' audience, certainly many of his hearers were conscious of the fact that the Messiah/Christ was the Anointed One (Heb. *mašaḥ*; Gk. *chrio*, "to anoint")—in particular, anointed by the Spirit (cf. Isa 61:1–2); cf. S. Talmon, "The Concept of *Mašîaḥ* and Messianism in Early Judaism," in J. H. Charlesworth, ed., *The Messiah* (Minneapolis: Fortress, 1992), 79–115.

[61]There is no hint in the Gospels that Jesus performed any miracles before the Spirit came on him at his baptism in the Jordan. (If the meaning of Jn 3:34 is that God gave the Spirit to Jesus without limit, as in the NIV, this certainly points back to the Jordan experience.) Based on this, divine healing teachers stress the fact that Jesus, emptied of his divine prerogatives (the *kenosis*), performed his miracles by the Spirit's power, just as his disciples did; cf. A. B. Simpson, *The Holy Spirit*, cited in Hawthorne, *The Presence and*

the Power, 234–35. I concur with Hawthorne, who sees the ministry of the Spirit in the life of Jesus as "the key to the kenosis" (199–225); cf. p. 218: Because of the Son of God's deliberate self-emptying, "he depended upon the Holy Spirit for wisdom and knowledge and for power to perform the signs and wonders that marked the days of his years" (thus establishing the paradigm for the Spirit-empowered believer to this day; 227–44). Cf. also the works cited in n. 56; note again Ac 10:38, grounding Jesus' ministry of healing and deliverance in the anointing of the Spirit's power. Thus, Acts 1:8 makes this paradigmatic for succeeding generations of believers (cf. 2:38–39). For a strenuous evangelical objection to the idea that Jesus completely emptied himself of all deity at his incarnation (kenotic theology), cf. R. Rosenbladt, "Who Do TV Preachers Say That I Am?" in M. Horton, ed., *The Agony of Deceit* (Chicago: Moody, 1990), 106–20 (esp. 114–16).

[62]Cf. E. May, "'... For Power Went Forth from Him ...' (Luke 6,19)," *CBQ* 14 (1952): 93–103.

[63]Note that the plural of *dunamis*, *dunameis*, is commonly rendered with "miracles" (sixteen times in the NIV), sometimes joined together with "signs" (*semeia*) and "wonders" (*terata*); cf. Ac 2:22; 2Co 12:12. On the significance of the use of *dunameis*, cf. Grimm, "θεραπεύω," *EDNT* 2:144: "The acts of healing are not described as interruptions of causal connections within natural law, but rather as manifestations of the kingdom of God in the struggle of the powers (cf. esp. Matt 11:2–6; 12:28). Thus they are repeatedly called *dunameis* (Matt 11:20ff.; 14:2; Mark 6:2, 5, 14; 9:39; Acts 2:22)."

[64]Ruthven, *Cessation*, 119.

[65]It is especially noteworthy that in Ac 21:11, the standard prophetic formula, "The Lord says," becomes, "The Holy Spirit says" (cf. also 8:29; 13:2; 20:22–23); this is the era of the Spirit; cf. D. E. Aune, *Prophecy in Early Christianity and the Ancient Mediterranean World* (Grand Rapids: Eerdmans, 1983), 263–34, with regard to NT prophecy with "the Holy Spirit says" vs. OT prophecy with "YHWH says."

[66]For the Holy Spirit in the OT, with reference also to prophetic ministry, cf. F. W. Horn, "Holy Spirit," *ABD* 3:262–63 (with general bibliography on 278–80); C. Westermann, "Geist im Alten Testament," *EvT* 41 (1981): 223–30; K.-D. Schunck, "Wesen und Wirken des Geistes nach dem Alten Testament," *SLAG* 18 (1979): 7–30; W. Bieder, "πνεῦμα, πνευμάτικος," *TDNT* 6:359–75; some of the works cited above, n. 56, are also relevant.

[67]An interesting insight into the eschatological dimension of the outpouring of the Spirit is found in the *magnum opus* of the ninth-century Jewish philosopher Sa'adiah Gaon, entitled *Emunot weDeot* ("Beliefs and Opinions"), ch. 8, end. He explains there that one of the signs of the messianic age will be that the spirit of prophecy will be on all the Israelites.

[68]Representative studies with discussion and bibliography relevant to the subject at hand include: S. Westerholm, "Sabbath," *Dictionary of Jesus and the Gospels*, 716–19; E. P. Sanders, *Jewish Law from Jesus to the Mishnah* (London/Philadelphia: SCM/Trinity, 1990), 6–23 (for methodological differences, contrast J. Neusner, *Judaic Law from Jesus to the Mishnah: A System-*

atic Reply to Professor E. P. Sanders [Atlanta: Scholars, 1993]); J. D. G. Dunn, *Jesus, Paul and the Law* (Louisville: Westminster/John Knox, 1990), 10–36; I. M. Zeitlin, *Jesus and the Judaism of His Time* (New York: Polity, 1988), 73–77; P. Sigal, *The Halakha of Jesus of Nazareth According to the Gospel of Matthew* (Lanham, Md.: University Press of America, 1986), especially 119–53; D. A. Carson, "Jesus and the Sabbath in the Four Gospels," in idem, ed., *From Sabbath to Lord's Day: A Biblical, Historical, and Theological Investigation* (Grand Rapids: Zondervan, 1982), 57–97; R. Banks, *Jesus and the Law in the Synoptic Tradition* (SNTSMS 28; Cambridge: Cambridge Univ. Press, 1975); D. Daube, *The New Testament and Rabbinic Judaism* (repr. Salem, N.H.: Ayer, 1984), 67–71; cf. also the relevant sections of Lachs, *Rabbinic Commentary*; in popular form, J. Neusner, *A Rabbi Talks with Jesus: An Intermillennial, Interfaith Exchange* (New York: Doubleday, 1993), 58–74. For further discussion of the Jewish legal background, cf. E. P. Sanders, *Judaism: Practice & Belief 63 BCE–66 CE* (London/Philadelphia: SCM/Trinity, 1992), 208–11; Schürer, Vermes, Miller, and Black, *History of the Jewish People* 2:424–27, 447–54, 467–75; L. H. Schiffman, *The Halakhah at Qumran* (SJLA; Leiden: E. J. Brill, 1975). For specific studies on the healings of Jesus and the Sabbath, cf. the works cited in J. Nolland, *Luke 9:21–18:34* (WBC; Dallas: Word, 1993), 721; Guelich, *Mark 1–8:26*, 130–31.

[69]Cf. Weinfeld, *Deuteronomy 1–11*, 301–9.

[70]For the connection between Sabbath, Sabbatical year, and the Year of Jubilee, cf. C. H. H. Wright, "Sabbatical Year," *ABD* 5:857–61, with literature.

[71]For legal analysis, cf. Sigal, *The Halakhah of Jesus of Nazareth*, 119–53 (although his identification of the Pharisees is not convincing); see Str-B 1:610–30, for an uncritical but useful gathering of later sources; note also Dunn, "Pharisees, Sinners, and Jesus," in *Jesus, Paul, and the Law*, 61–88; Schiffman, *The Halakhah at Qumran*.

[72]See Jer 17:19–27, developed in *great* length and detail in *b. Šabb.*

[73]This is the answer to the question often asked by critics of modern divine healing, Why did Jesus heal just one paralytic at the pool of Bethesda (Jn 5:1–14)? *It was a specific sign-healing on the Sabbath.* No one else came to him, nor is it recorded that he refused to heal anyone. The normal pattern was that immediately after the Sabbath, when the sick could be carried to Jesus, he ministered to the crowds (Mk 1:32–34 and par.).

[74]Most of the important literature on this concept is cited in the recent commentaries of Guelich, *Mark 1–8:26*, 117–18, 125–27; Nolland, *Luke 1–9:20*, 251–52, 257–58; and Hagner, *Matthew 1–13*, 326, 330.

[75]Cf. Kelsey, *Healing and Christianity*, 66.

[76]Cf. Dunn, *Jesus, Paul and the Law*, 27–29.

[77]On the religious meaning of "yoke" in rabbinic literature, cf. Lachs, *Rabbinic Commentary*, 196; note also the works cited in Hagner, *Matthew 1–13*, 322.

[78]Cf. the literature cited in N. Walter, "σπλάγχνον," *EDNT* 3:265 (and see 265–66, including idem, "σπλαγχνίζομαι," on 265); Kelsey, *Healing and Christianity*, 52–103, is especially strong on this point; for a popular treat-

ment, cf. Bosworth, *Christ the Healer*, 62–79; for the concept of God suffering with his people in the OT, with references to relevant literature, cf. T. E. Fretheim, *The Suffering of God: An Old Testament Perspective* (OBT; Philadelphia: Fortress, 1984); for a typical example of a major Christology that lays no emphasis on Jesus as Healer—thus missing out on an important element of his character—cf. O. Cullmann, *The Christology of the New Testament* (rev. ed., Philadelphia: Westminster, 1963).

[79]It is commonly noted that Matthew here (and in 19:2) has "heal" for Mark's "teach"; cf. A. Plummer, *An Exegetical Commentary on the Gospel According to St. Matthew* (repr. Grand Rapids: Baker, 1982), 203, n. 2; E. Schweizer, *The Good News According to Matthew*, trans. D. E. Green (Atlanta: John Knox, 1975), 319. Though J. A. Alexander, *The Gospel According to Matthew* (repr. Grand Rapids: Baker, 1980), has a good treatment of *splanchizomai* (274–75, on Mt 9:36), he notes strangely on 14:14, "What excited his divine and human sympathy was not of course their numbers or their physical condition, but their spiritual destitution" (p. 394). Why must it be *either* their physical *or* spiritual condition that aroused the Lord's sympathy?

[80]Cf. Deere, *Surprised by the Power of the Spirit*, 279–80, n. 2.

[81]This insight would suggest strongly that, just as it is right and fitting for the church to lead the way in performing acts of mercy for the hungry, impoverished, and socially and politically oppressed, so also it is right and fitting for the church to lead the way in the ministry of healing for the sick—both by natural and supernatural means. See below, 6.2, n. 3, and above, 1.4.2. See also J. Wilkinson, "The Mission Charge to the Twelve and Modern Medical Missions," *SJT* 27 (1974): 313–28.

[82]Cf. Kelsey, *Healing and Christianity*, 89: "The healing ministry of Jesus is the logical result of the incarnation: God so loved the world that he gave his only begotten Son; Jesus so loved that he healed. His healings were the authentication of his mission and his person. They flowed naturally from him because he was what he was."

[83]Cf. Mueller, *Sickness and Healing*, 158–65; Harper, *The Healings of Jesus*, 168–78; see more broadly R. T. France, "Faith," *Dictionary of Jesus and the Gospels*, 223–26 (with literature). The emphasis in modern healing ministry on the connection between faith and healing has resulted in these teachers being dubbed "faith healers"; cf. D. E. Harrell, Jr., *All Things Are Possible: The Healing and Charismatic Revivals in Modern America* (Bloomington, Ind.: Indiana Univ. Press, 1975).

[84]Cf. S. Erlandsson, "Faith in the Old and New Testaments: Harmony or Disagreement?" *Concordia Theological Quarterly* 47 (1983): 1–14; note also G. Braulik, "Law as Gospel: Justification and Pardon According to the Deuteronomic Torah," *Int* 38 (1984): 5–14.

[85]This, however, should not be taken to mean that the NT authors downplayed the importance of obedience; rather, they saw holiness of heart and actions as the necessary *proof* of living faith; see Ro 1:5; 6:17–18; Gal 5:24; Heb 12:14; Jas 2:14–26.

[86]His response in Mk 9:24b, "I do believe; help me overcome my unbelief!" was not an excuse for unbelief, but rather a plea for mercy to help a true believer conquer the nagging doubts that assaulted him (and the disciples too; cf. Mt 17:20a). Nonetheless, the story emphasizes the compassion of the Savior, who healed the man's son rather than castigated him for his weakness. The NT, however, does have strong words for the double-minded (e.g., Jas 1:5–7; see also Heb 11:6).

[87]Cf. Oepke, "ἰάομαι," 211.

[88]Although D. H. Stern's translation of *pisteuō* and *pistis* with "trust" (verb and noun) instead of with "believe" and "faith" may be open to objection on various grounds (cf. his *Jewish New Testament* [Jerusalem/Clarksville, Md.: Jewish New Testament Publications, 1989]), it has the merit of rendering the same Greek root, nominally and verbally, with the same English word, and it underscores the aspect of dependence—as opposed to an abstract, religious concept called "faith"—demanded by the Lord. Of course, there are times when God acts, delivers, and heals in spite of unbelief, simply because in his goodness he chooses to bestow blessing. But there is no overt, clear NT reference where the Lord refused to meet the need of those who came to him in dependent faith. God simply wants his people to trust him.

[89]Cf. Latourelle, *The Miracles of Jesus*, 281–98; D. C. Duling, "The Therapeutic Son of David: An Element in Matthew's Christological Apologetic," *NTS* 24 (1978): 392–410; cf. also W. S. Green, "Palestinian Holy Men: Charismatic Leadership and Rabbinic Tradition," *ANRW* 2.19 (1979): 619–47; B. M. Bokser, "Wonder-Working and the Rabbinic Tradition: The Case of Hanina Ben Dosa," *JSJ* 16 (1985): 42–92; see also, more broadly, G. S. Grieg, "The Purpose of Signs and Wonders in the New Testament: What Terms for Miraculous Power Denote and Their Relationship to the Gospel," in idem and Springer, eds., *The Kingdom and the Power*, 133–74; D. M. Lloyd-Jones, *The Sovereign Spirit: Discerning His Gifts* (Wheaton, Ill.: Harold Shaw, 1985), 15–33.

[90]Cf. Nielsen, *Heilung und Verkündigung*, 57–65; for discussion as to the exact nature of John's question (specifically, the meaning of Greek *ho erchomenos*, "the one who is to come"), cf. Fitzmyer, *Luke I–IX*, 666–67.

[91]Although the manifestations of the Spirit were part of the initial confirmation of the divine origin of the gospel (as seen in the texts from Heb 2 and 1Co 2), it is clear from 1 Corinthians they continued as part of the heritage of the believing community "for the common good" (1Co 12:7); cf. further Ruthven, *Cessation*, 124–31, on 1Co 1:4–8. Cf. also F. Delitzsch, *The Epistle to the Hebrews*, trans. T. L. Kingsbury (repr. Minneapolis, Klock & Klock, 1978), 1:100–101, n. 1, who cites Theodore of Mopsuestia, "There [i.e., under the law], miracles were wrought in cases of necessity only, but under the gospel many heathens have been healed by us from all manner of diseases: we possess such a fulness of miraculous power, that even the dead are raised; and ofttimes, when it must be so, we bring individuals to a sense of their wrong-doing by striking them with blindness through a mere threat, or inflict sudden death on the malevolent," adding, "What an intensity of

Christian consciousness at so late a period (the boundary line of the fourth and fifth centuries), and in the mouth of a Theodore!" Even if one judges some (or much) of this account to be legendary, there must be a stratum of the miraculous that underlies it, especially when one considers that it is an account given by an apparent eyewitness of events purported to be contemporary (cf. also above, 1.4.2).

[92]On the pivotal role of the Exodus and Mount Sinai for the OT canon, see above, 2.1.

[93]Cf. A. Richardson, "Christianity is the religion of miracle, and the miracle of Christ's Resurrection is the living centre and object of Christian Faith," quoted in Harper, *The Healings of Jesus*, 71.

[94]For B. B. Warfield's classic exposition of this theme, cf. his *Counterfeit Miracles* (New York: Charles Scribner's Sons, 1918), restated concisely by C. E. Koop, "Faith-Healing and the Sovereignty of God" in Horton, ed., *The Agony of Deceit*, 175: the miracles, "no doubt, authenticated Christ's claims and His mission. Thereafter, He invested His twelve apostles with these same healing capabilities in order to authenticate this 'new' religion, which we call Christianity. But after serving their purpose, these gifts ceased." Recently, the cessationist view has come under increasing criticism; for releases in 1993, cf. Grieg and Springer, eds., *The Kingdom and the Power*; Ruthven, *Cessation* (based on his Ph.D. dissertation, Marquette University, 1989); Deere, *Surprised by the Power of the Spirit* (written for a popular audience by an OT scholar and former cessationist); cf. also DeArtega, *Quenching the Spirit* (1992), for a broader and more philosophically oriented treatment; see further I. G. Wallis, "Christ's Continuing Ministry of Healing," *ExpTim* 104 (1992): 42–45, reflecting the most recent affirmations of the Church of England; see below, 6.2–6.2.1. The fundamental problem with statements such as those of Koop is their failure to understand the purpose of miraculous healings and the revelation of the nature of God made manifest in the miracles.

[95]R. Brown, *JBC*, 787; see Ruthven, *Cessation*, 116. A further problem for the "mere confirmation" assessment of the miracles of Jesus is found in the proofs Jesus gave to the disciples of John, for not only did he point to his healings of the sick and resurrections of the dead, but he adds: "The good news is preached to the poor. Blessed is the man who does not fall away on account of me" (Lk 7:18–23, here vv. 22b–23). Would anyone classify "preaching the good news to the poor" among "first-century confirming signs" that are thus not applicable to today? Rather, both his miracles and preaching were part and parcel of his messianic work of redemption and mercy. As Marshall, *Luke*, 178, notes (on Lk 4:16ff.), "The era of salvation has arrived; it is the year of the Lord's favour, characterised by the preaching of the good news to the needy and the performance of mighty works."

[96]Cf. also Kelsey, *Healing and Christianity*, 99:

> Far from using his healings as signs of power, he seemed embarrassed by them and told people not to speak of them. At times he even gave the impression that he would rather not have performed miracles, from a tactical point of view. But it was his nature to be hostile to illness and

to heal the sick.... If Jesus saw himself as the Messiah, then he represented the essential nature of God himself and was his specific messenger, and his healings therefore sprang from the essential nature of God.... By dealing with them as the Messiah, the agent of God, Jesus laid the attitude of God toward sickness out on the counter where all could see it.

[97]According to Latourelle, *The Miracles of Jesus*, 293–94, "in the Scriptures the miracles of Christ are regarded first of all as manifestations of the power and love of God the Savior." Second, they signify "that the prophesied kingdom has come at last and that Jesus of Nazareth is the awaited Messiah; the miracles fulfill the Scriptures." Third, they signify "that he is God's envoy." Fourth, "they accredit Christ as Son of God." Finally, "they give an anticipatory glimpse of the glorious order introduced by the resurrection of the body and the transformation of the cosmos at the end of time."

[98]Cf. Metzger, ed., *Textual Commentary*, 667.

[99]Cf. G. H. Twelftree, *Jesus the Exorcist* (Peabody, Mass.: Hendrickson, 1995); idem, "Demons, Devil, Satan"; H. Bietenhard, "Demon," *NIDNTT* 1:449–54; see also, above, 3.1.10, nn. 201–2; 3.3.2.1.

[100]Contrast the nature of Satan (associated with lies, darkness, and death) with the nature of the Son of God (associated with truth, light, and life; cf. Jn 8:31–47; 1Jn 1:4–7; et al.). In connection with this, it is Satan who is thus associated with sickness and disease and Jesus who is associated with healing and deliverance. Cf. also Beyer, "θεραπεύω," 130–31: "The essential feature [of Jesus' miracles] is that in a wonderful 'already' the light shines in which Jesus will perfect His victory over all dark, Satanic powers."

[101]For discussion of the exact condition of the boy, cf. J. Wilkinson, "The Case of the Epileptic Boy," *ExpTim* 79 (1967): 39–42; Nolland, *Luke 9:21–18:34*, 505–11.

[102]This is stressed in modern literature on divine healing; cf. Osborn, *Healing the Sick*, 185–219; for the relationship between "authority"and "power," cf. G. S. Shogren, "Authority and Power," *Dictionary of Jesus and the Gospels*, 50–54.

[103]Cf. above, 5.2.1.

[104]Note that it is *the Twelve* who preach, drive out demons, anoint the sick, and *heal* them—by the authority given them. Note also Ac 6:8, *Stephen*, full of God's grace and power, *did great wonders and miraculous signs*; 8:6, the crowds heard *Philip* and saw the *miraculous signs he did*; 28:7, *Paul*, after prayer, placed his hands on Publius's father *and healed him.* Cf. also Mt 10:8b ("Freely you have received, freely give") with Ac 3:6a ("what I have I give you"; see also 2:43; 5:12). Although these people were not the healers, they healed by the authority and power granted them; cf. Deere, *Surprised by the Power of the Spirit*, 269, n. 3.

[105]See S. M. Burgess, "Proclaiming the Gospel with Miraculous Gifts in the Postbiblical Early Church," in Grieg and Springer, eds., *The Kingdom and the Power*, 277–88; R. A. N. Kydd, *Charismatic Gifts in the Early Church* (Peabody, Mass.: Hendrickson, 1984); A. J. Gordon, *The Ministry of Healing:*

Miracles of Cure in All Ages (Harrisburg, Pa.: Christian Publications, 1982); cf. also n. 91; 1.4.2, nn. 214, 216.

[106]Cf. P. H. Davids, "A Biblical View of the Relationship of Fruit and the Fruits of Sin: Sickness, Demonization, Death, Natural Calamity," in Grieg and Springer, eds., *The Kingdom and the Power*, 111–32; Mueller, *Sickness and Healing*, 126–27, 165–68; Kelsey, *Healing and Christianity*, 92–97.

[107]Cf. Kelsey, *Healing and Christianity*, 94, "Deuteronomic Judaism affirmed that all sickness was the result of sin—that it was one of God's punishments for disobedience to his will." Elsewhere Kelsey is more careful (cf. above, 2.2.2, n. 87); of course, the second half of his statement here is accurate. The odd comment of Koop errs to the opposite extreme: "Contrary to what many televangelists will tell you, there is no connection [*sic*!] between specific sin and the judgment of God, in the sense of retributive justice" ("Faith-Healing and the Sovereignty of God," 177).

[108]Cf. above, 2.2.5, 2.3.1, 3.1.1–3, 3.1.5.

[109]Cf. the sections cited in previous note; also note the frequent connection between repentance and restoration in the prophets (esp. with the roots *šûb* and *rāpā'*; see ch. 4).

[110]This, of course, is an unspoken lesson taught in the book of Job; cf. above, 3.3.3. Also, in total harmony with the OT, it is not through the blind's man *blindness* that the work of God is manifest, but rather through his *healing* (for the meaning of Jn 9:3, see Westcott, *John*, 1/2:32; R. Schnackenburg, *The Gospel According to St. John* [New York: Crossroad, 1979], 2:240–41), a function of Jesus' being the Light of the world (Jn 9:5; cf. 11:9–10). So also, in 11:4, it is not the *sickness* and *death* of Lazarus that bring glory to God, but rather his *resurrection* from the dead (cf. 11:40, "Did I not tell you that if you believed, you would see the glory of God?"). Note also 11:4, "This sickness will not end in death. No, it is for God's glory so that God's Son may be glorified through it." The implication is obvious: If the sickness ended in death, not healing, it would not have been for God's glory.

[111]For treatment of this much-discussed pericope, with literature, cf. Guelich, *Mark 1–8:26*, 80–96.

[112]But cf. Beasely-Murray, *John*, 74, with reference to E. C. Hoskyns, *The Fourth Gospel*, ed. F. N. Davey (2d ed., London: Faber & Faber, 1947), 253.

[113]There can be no question that Jas 5:15 speaks of *physical* healing and then forgivness of sins; cf. above, 5.1.2, *sub sōzō*. By contextual implication, this would seem to be the meaning of v. 16, *iaomai* being just as clear as *sōzo* (but note BAGD, 368, "ἰάομαι," 2.5, "Pass. of sin Js 5:16"); F. Vouga, *L'épître de s. Jacques* [CNT; Geneva: Labor et Fides, 1984], 143, where *iaomai* is interpreted in terms of healing the breaches in the community). See also 1Pe 2:24 (but see above, n. 33); J. Wilkinson, "Healing in the Epistle of James," *SJT* 24 (1971): 326–45.

[114]Cf. Fee, *First Corinthians*, 531–67.

[115]Cf. Bosworth, *Christ the Healer*, 16–17.

[116]On this all Christians can agree, be they ardent cessationists or divine healing proponents; see above, 4.1.4, n. 112. For a statement of the differences

between healing in the "present kingdom" age as compared to the kingdom "in its future manifestations," cf. Ladd and Hagner, *Theology*, 74.

[117]Cf. especially P. H. Davids, *The Book of First Peter* (NICNT; Grand Rapids: Eerdmans, 1990), 30–44; on a popular level, note that K. E. Hagin, the father of the modern Word-Faith movement, comes to the same conclusions (viz., distinguishing between suffering persecution and suffering sickness); see his *Must Christians Suffer?* (Tulsa, Okla.: Faith Library, 1982); cf. more generally, D. J. Simundson, *Faith Under Fire: Biblical Interpretations of Suffering* (Minneapolis: Augsburg, 1980); Gerstenberger and Schrage, *Suffering*.

[118]Cf. Brown, *How Saved Are We?* 85–94; idem, "The Gospel of Martyrdom Vs. the Gospel of Success," distributed privately, 1994.

[119]The a fortiori argument stated here should be self-evident, based on the material presented throughout this chapter.

[120]Cf. P. H. Davids, "Rich and Poor," *Dictionary of Jesus and the Gospels*, 701–10 (with literature); M. Hengel, *Poverty and Riches in the Early Church* (London: SCM, 1974); T. E. Schmidt, *Hostility to Wealth in the Synoptic Gospels* (JSNTSupp. 15; Sheffield: JSOT Press, 1987); J. B. Adamson, *James: The Man and His Message* (Grand Rapids: Eerdmans, 1989), 228–58; see also above, 3.2.1, n. 235.

[121]According to Adamson, *James*, 230, "The NT never asserts or implies that it is a sin to be rich; but, unlike the OT, it never tires of warning us of the constant spiritual dangers of wealth or of condemning some who have given way, or are giving way, to its temptation." For OT warnings relative to riches, see Dt 8:10–20; Pr 23:4–5.

[122]See the commentaries on Matthew and Luke, *ad loc.*; cf. the works cited in Davids, "Rich and Poor," 709–10, and the relevant commentary discussions on Lk 16:19–31, the parable of the rich man and Lazarus. Nolland, *Luke 1–9:20*, 283, correctly observes, "There is no glorifying of poverty involved in the beatitudes [cf. Lk 6:20–21]. To be poor, hungry, and weeping is not at all the situation that Luke envisages in the ideal state of Christian existence (Ac 2:43–47; 4:34).... The beatitude of the poor connects naturally in the Gospel not with the renunciation material but rather with the reversal motif (cf. at 1:52–53; 16:25; note also the 'afflicted state' of 1:48) and more particularly with the announcement of good news to the poor (4:18; 7:22)."

[123]It is unfortunate that some contemporary charismatic ministers preach the so-called "health and wealth" gospel, as if the two logically go hand in hand or are benefits of the cross to be enjoyed in this life. While Jesus went about making people well, he did not make them wealthy. Cf. above, 3.2.1, n. 235; note also the title of the balanced review of Haneggraff's *Christianity in Crisis* by B. Barron, "Sick of Health and Wealth," in *Christianity Today* (22 November 1993): 27–28; contrast, O. Roberts, *How I Learned Jesus Was Not Poor* (Altamonte Springs, Fla.: Creation House, 1989). Needless to say, the NT offers a strong work ethic (e.g., Eph 4:28) and exhorts toward generous giving, with the goal of each believer becoming an ongoing channel of blessing to

those in need (e.g., 2Co 9:6–11). And as far as health is concerned, the NT does not teach that all believers will always be free from sickness and pain.

[124]Cf. Davids, *First Peter*, 43–44: "The need today is to recapture the biblical tension. It is the need to meet illness with prayer . . . and to meet persecution with endurance."

[125]The best-known contemporary Christian example is probably that of Joni Eareckson Tada (cf. idem with J. Musser, *Joni* [Minneapolis: World Wide Publications, 1976]), whose testimony has brought encouragement and strength to many handicapped people; it would be incorrect, however, to base a theology of healing solely on her experience.

[126]This is reflected throughout Kelsey's *Healing and Christianity*. Critics of the "health and wealth" gospel often fail to recognize this, supposing that references to suffering for the Lord in the NT have in mind suffering sickness; cf. M. Horton, "The TV Gospel," in idem, ed., *The Agony of Deceit*, 126–27; his general objections, however, are, by and large, well taken (pp. 122–50).

[127]For a survey of historical opinions on this subject through the nineteenth-century, cf. J. B. Lightfoot, "St. Paul's Infirmity in the Flesh," in *The Epistle of St. Paul to the Galatians* (repr. Grand Rapids: Zondervan, 1975), 186–91; for a recent survey, see R. P. Martin, *2 Corinthians* (WBC; Waco, Tex.: Word, 1986), 410–18; see also Mueller, *Sickness and Healing*, 171–82; G. H. Twelftree, "Healing, Illness," in G. F. Hawthorne and R. P. Martin, eds., *Dictionary of Paul and His Letters* (Downers Grove, Ill.: InterVarsity Press, 1994), 378–81 (specifically, 379). For aggressive attacks against the position that Paul's thorn was sickness, see Bosworth, *Christ the Healer*, 190–206; Osborn, *Healing the Sick*, 273–91.

[128]So, explicitly, NIV, along with most modern versions and commentaries; cf. R. K. Y. Fung, *The Epistle to the Galatians* (NICNT; Grand Rapids: Eerdmans, 1988), 196–97; cf. also Davids, *First Peter*, 39, n. 59.

[129]Nonscholarly readers may be unaware that the interpretation of Paul's thorn as sickness is not, and has not been, the consensus view of the church (although many interpreters through the years have suggested various maladies from which the apostle allegedly suffered, from opthalmia to epilepsy to a speech defect); cf. the surveys of Lightfoot and Martin, noted above, n. 127.

[130]I have no sympathy for the views of some divine healing proponents, represented in particular among some extreme elements in the Word-Faith camp, who hold that suffering of *any kind* for the Christian—including persecution—does not have to be "accepted," or, worse still, is the result of lack of faith. (I have even heard this applied to Paul's thorn and Stephen's martyrdom!) It is to be hoped that such positions have now been abandoned.

[131]I am not aware of any major study devoted specifically to this topic. On the broad level of a comprehensive theology of the both Testaments, cf. B. S. Childs, *Biblical Theology of the Old and New Testaments* (Minneapolis: Fortress, 1992), with extensive bibliographies (and cf. H. Strauss, "Theologie des Alten Testaments als Bestandteil einer biblischen Theologie," *EvT* 45 [1985]: 20–29). Important monographs include: D. L. Baker, *Two Testaments, One Bible: A Study of the Theological Relationship Between the Old and New*

Testaments (rev. ed., Downers Grove, Ill.: InterVarsity, 1991); J. Goldingay, *Approaches to Old Testament Interpretation* (rev. ed., Downers Grove, Ill.: InterVarsity, 1990; cf. on this M. J. Evans, "The Old Testament as Christian Scripture," *VoxEv* 16 [1986]: 25–32); C. Westermann, ed., *Essays on Old Testament Hermeneutics* (Richmond: John Knox, 1963). A sampling of relevant articles includes: M. K. Karlberg, "Legitimate Discontinuities between the Testaments," *JETS* 28 (1985): 9–20; P. A. Verhoef, "The Relationship Between the Old and the New Testaments," in Payne, ed., *New Perspective on the Old Testament*, 280–303; see also D. L. Bock, "Evangelicals and the Use of the Old Testament in the New," Parts 1 and 2, *BSac* 142 (1985): 209–23, 306–19; J. Blekinsopp, "Old Testament Theology and the Jewish-Christian Connection," *JSOT* 28 (1984): 3–15; H. Hübner, "Biblische Theologie und Theologie des Neuen Testaments," *Kerygma und Dogma* 27 (1981): 2–19.

[132]For a restatement of the popular charismatic argument that a "newer and better covenant" should by definition include an *increase* in healing grace, cf. M. L. Brown, *Whatever Happened to the Power of God: Is the Charismatic Church Slain in the Spirit or Down for the Count?* (Shippensburg, Pa.: Destiny Image, 1991), 45–47.

Chapter Six—Conclusions and Reflections

[1]For the question of the suffering of Job, cf. below, 6.1.4, and above, 3.3.1.–3.3.3; for the death of Abijah and Paul and his thorn in the flesh, see 2.3.1, 5.3.3, respectively.

[2]For a typical case study, cf. J. V. Sterk, "Evangelism with Power: Divine Healing in the Growth of the Tzotzil Church," *Missiology* 20 (1992): 371–84 (in spite of persecution, a large number of the Tzotzil in Chiapas, Mexico, became evangelical believers because of divine healing); see also Wallis, "Christ's Continuing Ministry of Healing," regarding the positive stance of the Church of England concerning the ongoing ministry of divine healing.

[3]Among those making special efforts to combine both medical and spiritual means of healing, joining together biblical, anthropological, missiological, and medical perspectives, mention should be made of the Asian Center for Theological Studies (ACTS) and the Korea Christian Medico-Evangelical Association (KCMEA), the former being a seminary with a department of healing ministry; see *A Collection of Abstract[s] 1983–1993: Department of Healing Ministry* (Seoul: Asian Center for Theological Studies and Mission, 1993); *The Proceedings of the Consultation on the Study Program of Healing Ministry*, October 30–November 1, 1980; other relevant studies include *Healing and Wholeness: The Churches' Role in Health. The Report of a Study by the Christian Medical Commission, World Council of Churches* (Geneva: Christian Medical Commission, WCC, 1990); cf. also *Brethren Life and Thought* 33 (1988), for discussion of the varied facets of the healing ministry of the church; and see the articles of T. A. Droege ("Congregations as Communities of Health and Healing"); J. T. Carroll ("Sickness and Healing in the New Testament Gospels"); J. P. Wind ("A Case for Theology in the Ministry of Healing"); and A. R. Evans ("The Church as an Institution of Health: Making It Happen") in

Int 49 (1995). See further H. Bouma III, D. Diekema, E. Langerak, T. Rottman, and A. Verhey, eds., *Christian Faith, Health, and Medical Practice* (Grand Rapids: Eerdmans, 1989); see also B. Waltke, "Relating Human Personhood to the Health Sciences: An Old Testament Perspective," *Crux* 25 (1989), 2–10, for a somewhat different, though not unrelated, approach.

[4]Cf. K. Blue, *Authority to Heal* (Downers Grove, Ill.: InterVarsity, 1987), 25–26, who observes, "When we get sick or hurt, we go to the doctor and expect him to help us. We never question whether or not it is God's will for us to go. We presume that it is proper to get medical help and for that help to be effective. Why then are we reluctant to seek help through spiritual means?"

[5]I have often addressed these and related subjects in popular form; see *The End of the American Gospel Enterprise* (Shippensburg, Pa.: Destiny Image, 1989), 91–97; *How Saved Are We?* 43–50; *Whatever Happened to the Power of God?* passim. Regarding the question of faith vs. medicine, healing ministers of the last 50 years have generally not spoken against the use of doctors or medicine, arguing instead that both medical science and ministers praying for the sick have a common enemy (viz., that which destroys health) and a common goal (healing and physical well-being). It is generally argued, however, that divine healing is the best and most biblical way to health, and, certainly in terminal or incurable cases, the only way. For a fair survey of the main personalities involved in the modern healing movement (through the 1970s), cf. Harrell, *All Things Are Possible*.

[6]I would not classify the works cited above, 5.2.6, end of n. 94, as belonging to this popularized, often exegetically loose class of writings.

◆ Select Bibliography ◆

The following listing excludes virtually all general references, including commentaries, lexicons, theologies, histories of religion, etc. It is limited to works specifically dealing with sickness and healing, both from religious, theological, and biblical viewpoints and from medical and sociological viewpoints. Where pertinent, studies dealing with the interpretation of key verses are also included. Some popular, contemporary literature is also listed.

A Collection of Abstract[s] 1983–1993: Department of Healing Ministry. Seoul: Asian Center for Theological Studies and Mission, 1993.

Achtmeier, P. J. "Jesus and the Disciples as Miracle Workers in the Apochryphal New Testament." Pp. 149–86 in E. S. Fiorenza, ed., *Aspects of Religious Propoganda in Judaism and Early Christianity.* Notre Dame: Univ. of Notre Dame Press, 1976.

Amelang, J. S., ed. and trans. *A Journal of the Plague Year: The Diary of the Barcelona Tanner Miquel Parets 1651*. New York: Oxford Univ. Press, 1991.

Amundsen, D. W., and G. B. Ferngren. "Medicine and Religion: Pre-Christian Antiquity." Pp. 53–92 in M. E. Marty and K. L. Vaux, eds., *Health/Medicine and the Faith Traditions: An Inquiry into Religion and Medicine*. Philadelphia: Fortress, 1982.

Asaf, M., ed. *HaRefu'a BaMekorot.* Jerusalem: Rubin Mass Ltd., 1982.

Bailey, Sr., L. R. *Biblical Perspectives on Death.* OBT. Philadelphia: Fortress, 1979.

Baron, B. *The Health and Wealth Gospel.* Downers Grove, Ill.: InterVarsity, 1987.

Barré, M. L. "Bulluṭsa-rābi's Hymn to Gula and Hosea 6:1–2." *Or* 50 (1981): 241–45.

Barth, C. *Die Erreitung vom Tode in den individuellen Klage- und Dankliedern des Altes Testament*. Zollikon: Evangelischer Verlag, 1947.

Baruch, J. Z. "The Relation Between Sin and Disease in the Old Testament." *Hanas: Revue Internationale de l'historie des sciences* 5 (1964): 295–302.

Beyer, H. W. "θεραπεία, θεραπεύω, θεράπων." *TDNT* 3:128–32.

Biggs, R. D. "Babylonien." Pp. 91–114 in H. Schipperges et al., eds., *Krankeit, Heilkunst, Heliung*.

________. "Medicine in Ancient Mesopotamia." Pp. 94–105 in A. C. Crombie and M. A. Hoskin, eds., *History of Science*, vol. 8. Cambridge: Heffer, 1969.

________. "Medizin. A. In Mesopotamien." *RLA* 7:623–29.

"בִּקּוּר חוֹלִים." *Talmudic Encyclopedia*. Jerusalem: Talmudic Encyclopedia Inst., 1947–, 4:158–62.

Bleich, J. D. "The Obligation to Heal in the Judaic Tradition: A Comparative Analysis." Pp. 1–44 in F. Rosner and J. D. Bleich, eds., *Jewish Bioethics*. Brooklyn: Hebrew Pub. Co., 1979.

Bloch-Smith, E. *Judahite Burial Practices and Beliefs About the Dead*. Sheffield: JSOT Press, 1993.

Blomberg, C. L. "Healing." Pp. 298–307 in *Dictionary of Jesus and the Gospels*. Downers Grove, Ill.: InterVarsity, 1992.

Blue, K. *Authority to Heal*. Downers Grove, Ill.: InterVarsity, 1987.

Bokovay, W. K. "The Relationship of Physical Healing to the Atonement." *Didaskalia* 3 (1991): 24–39.

Bokser, B. M. "Wonder-Working and the Rabbinic Tradition: The Case of Hanina Ben Dosa." *JSJ* 16 (1985): 42–92.

Bosworth, F. F. *Christ the Healer*. Old Tappan, N.J.: Revell, 1973.

Bouchard, A., and E. Laroche, É. Beaucamp, P. Poirer, J. Laporte, J. Delorme, M. Carrez, É. Cothenet, M. Morgen. "Salut." *DBSup* 11:513–740.

Bouma III, H., and D. Diekma, E. Langerak, T. Rottman, A. Verhey, eds. *Christian Faith, Health, and Medical Practice*. Grand Rapids: Eerdmans, 1989.

Brand, P., and P. K. Yancey. *Pain: The Gift Nobody Wants*. Grand Rapids: Zondervan, 1993.

Breasted, J. H.. *The Edwin Smith Surgical Papyrus*. Oriental Institute Publications, Vol. 3. Chicago: Univ. of Chicago Press, 1930.

Brooke, J. H. *Science and Religion: Some Historical Perspectives*. The Cambridge History of Science. New York: Cambridge Univ. Press, 1991.

Brown, M. L. "Was There a West Semitic Asklepios?" *UF* (forthcoming).

———. "רָפָא." *TWAT* 7:617–25.

———. *Whatever Happened to the Power of God: Is the Charismatic Church Slain in the Spirit or Down for the Count?* Shippensburg, Pa.: Destiny Image, 1991.

———. *I Am the Lord Your Healer: A Philological Study of the Root* rp' *in the Hebrew Bible and the Ancient Near East*. Ph.D. Dissertation. New York: New York Univ., 1985.

Burns, J. B. "The Chastening of the Just in Job 5:17–23: Four Strikes of Erra." *Proceedings, Eastern Great Lakes and Midwest Bible Societies* 10 (1990): 18–30.

Busse, U. *Das Nazareth-Manifest: Eine Einführung in das lukanische Jesubild nach Lk 4:16–30*. SBS 91. Stuttgart: Katholisches Bibelwerk, 1978.

Carson, D. A. *Showing the Spirit*. Grand Rapids: Baker, 1987.

Cartwright, F. F., and M. D. Biddiss. *Disease and History*. Repr. New York: Dorset, 1991.

Civil, M. "Une nouvelle prescription médicale sumérienne." *RA* 55 (1961): 91–94.

———. "Prescriptions médicales sumériennes." *RA* 54 (1960): 57–72.

Custance, A. C. "The Theological Necessity of the Physical Immortality of the First and Last Adam." *JETS* 21 (1978): 297–303.

Dandamayev, M. A. "About Life Expectancy in Babylonia in the First Milennium B.C." Pp. 183–86 in B. Alster, ed., *Death in Mesopotamia*. Copenhagen: Akademisk Forlag, 1980.

Davies, Steven L. *Jesus the Healer: Possession, Trance, and the Origins of Christianity*. New York: Continuum, 1995.

Dawson, W. R. "The Egyptian Medical Papyri." Pp. 98–111 in D. Brothwell and A. T. Sandison, eds., *Diseases in Antiquity*. Springfield, Ill.: C. C. Thomas, 1967.

de Meulenaere, H. "Arzt." *LÄ* 1:455–59.

———. "Arzteschule." *LÄ* 1:79–80.

de Moor, J. C. "Rāpi'ūma—Rephaim." *ZAW* 88 (1976): 323–45.

Deere, J. *Surprised by the Power of the Spirit*. Grand Rapids: Zondervan, 1993.

DeVries, A., and A. Weinberger. "King Asa's Presumed Gout: Twentieth-Century A.D. Discussion of Ninth-Century B.C. Biblical Patient." *New York State Medical Journal* 75 (1975): 452–55.

Dewey, R. "Qoheleth and Job: Diverse Responses to the Enigma of Evil." *Spirituality Today* 37 (1985): 314–25.

Dietzfelbinger, C. "Die grösseren Werke (Joh 14. 12f.)." *NTS* 35 (1989): 27–47.

Dulin, R. Z. *A Crown of Glory: A Biblical View of Aging*. Mahwah, N.J.: Paulist, 1988.

Duling, D. C. "The Therapeutic Son of David: An Element in Matthew's Christological Apologetic." *NTS* 24 (1978): 392–410.

Dumeige, G. "Le Christ médecin dans la littérature chrétienne des premiers siècles." *Rivista di archeologia cristiana* 48 (1972): 115–41.

Dunn, J. D. G. *Jesus and the Spirit*. Philadephia: Westminster, 1975.

Dupont-Sommer, A. "Exorcismes et guérisons dans les éscrits de Qoumran." VTSupp 7 (1960), 246–61.

Eakins, J. K. "Human Osteology and Archeology." *BA* 43 (1980): 89–96.

Ebstein, W. *Die Medizin im Alten Testament*. Repr. München: Werner Fritsch, 1965.

________. *Die Medizin im Neuen Testament und im Talmud*. Repr. München: Werner Fritsch, 1975.

Edel, E. *Ägyptische Arzte und ägyptische Medizin am hethitischen Königshof: Neue Funde von Keilschriftbriefen Ramses' II aus Bogazkoy*. Opladen: Westdeutscher Verlag, 1976.

Edelstein, E. J., and L. Edelstein, eds. *Asclepios: Testimonies*. Baltimore: Johns Hopkins Univ. Press, 1945.

Edwards, I. E. S. "Krankheitsabwehr." *LÄ* 3:750–62.

Eisenbeis, W. *Die Wurzel* sh-l-m *im Alten Testament*. BZAW 105. Berlin: de Gruyter, 1969.

Elman, Y. "An Akkadian Cognate of Hebrew *šᵉḥin*." *JANESCU* 8 (1976): 33–34.

Erlandsson, S. "Faith in the Old and New Testaments: Harmony or Disagreement?" *Concordia Theological Quarterly* 47 (1983): 1–14.

Estes, J. W. *The Medical Skills of Ancient Egypt.* Canton, Mass.: Science History Publications, 1989.

Fee, G. *God's Empowering Presence: The Holy Spirit in the Letters of Paul.* Peabody, Mass.: Hendrickson, 1994.

———. *The Disease of the Health and Wealth Gospels.* Beverly, Mass.: Frontline Pub., 1985.

Feldman, D. M. *Health and Medicine in the Jewish Tradition.* New York: Crossroad, 1986.

Fensham, F. C. "Malediction and Benediction in Ancient Near Eastern Vassal-Treaties and the Old Testament." *ZAW* 74 (1962): 1–9.

Filteau, J. C. "La racine *yš'*. Une des expression du salut dans l'Ancien Testament hébraïque." *LTP* 37 (1981): 135–59.

Fisher, L R. "Betrayed by Friends." *Int* 18 (1964): 20–38.

Flusser, D. "The Role of the Doctor According to Ben-Sira" (Hebrew). *Mahanayim* 122 (1970): 48–55.

Foerster, W., and G. Fohrer, "σώζω, etc." *TDNT* 7:965–1024.

France, R. T. "Faith." Pp. 223–26 in *Dictionary of Jesus and the Gospels.* Downers Drove, Ill.: InterVarsity, 1992.

Fretheim, T. E. "The Plagues as Ecological Signs of Historical Disaster." *JBL* 110 (1991): 385–96.

Friedenwald, H. *The Jews and Medicine.* Repr. with an introduction by G. Rosen. 3 vols. New York: Ktav, 1967.

Friedrich, G. "δύναμις." *EDNT* 1:355–58.

Frost, E. *Christian Healing: A Consideration of the Place of Spiritual Healing in the Church of To-day in the Light of the Doctrine and Practice of the Anti-Nicene Church.* London: A. R. Mowbray & Co., 1940.

Fuller, R. H. *Interpreting the Miracles.* Philadelphia: Westminster, 1963.

Gaffin, R. *Perspectives on Pentecost: Studies in New Testament Teaching on the Gifts of the Holy Spirit.* Grand Rapids: Baker, 1979.

Gelin, A. "Médecine dans la Bible." *DBSup* 5:957–68.

Gemayel, A. *L'hygiène et la médecine à travers la Bible.* Paris: P. Geuthner, 1932.

Gerleman, G. "חיה, leben." *THAT* 1:549–57.

———. "שלם, genug haben." *THAT* 2:919–35.

Gerstenberger, E. S. *Der bittende Mensch.* WMANT 51. Neukirchen-Vluyn: Neukirchener Verlag, 1980.

________, and W. Schrage. *Suffering*. Trans. J. E. Steeley. Nashville: Abingdon, 1980.

Ghalioungui, P. *The Physicians of Ancient Egypt*. Cairo: Al-Ahram Center for Scientific Translations, 1983.

________. *The House of Life—Per Hankh: Magic and Medical Science in Ancient Egypt*. Amsterdam: B. M. Israël, 1973.

Good, R. S. "Supplementary Remarks on the Ugaritic Funerary Text RS 34.126." *BASOR* 239 (1980): 41–42.

Gordis, R. "Studies in Hebrew Roots of Contrasted Meanings." *JQR* 27 (1936): 55–56.

Gordon, A. J. *The Minstry of Healing: Miracles of Cure in All Ages*. Repr. Harrisburg, Pa.: Christian Publications, 1982.

Graber, F., and D. Müller. "Heal." *NIDNTT* 2:163–72.

Grapow, H. *Untersuchungen über die altägyptischen medizinischen Papyri*. Leipzig: n.p., 1935–36.

________, and H. von Deines, W. Westendorf. *Grundriss der Medizin der alten Ägypter*. 9 vols. Berlin: Akademie Verlag, 1954–73.

Green, W. S. "Palestinian Holy Men: Charismatic Leadership and Rabbinic Tradition." *ANRW* 2.19 (1979): 619–47.

Grelot, P. "Étude critique de Luc 10,19." *RSR* 69 (1981): 87–100.

Grieg, G. S., and K. N. Springer. *The Kingdom and the Power*. Ventura, Calif:: Regal Books, 1993.

Grimm, W. "θεραπεύω." *EDNT* 2:143–44.

Grossberg, D. "Number harmony and life spans in the Bible." *Semitics* 9 (1984): 49–57.

Grundmann, W. "δύναμαι, δύναμις, etc." *TDNT* 2:284–317.

Haggard, H. W. *The Doctor in History*. Repr. New York: Dorset, 1989.

________. *Devils, Drugs and Doctors*. Repr. Boston: Charles River, 1980.

Hagin, K. E. *Must Christians Suffer?* Tulsa, Okla.: Faith Library, 1982.

Handy, L. K. "Serpent, Bronze." *ABD* 5:1117.

Hamilton, M. *Incubation, or the Cure of Disease in Pagan Temples and Christian Churches*. London: Simpkin, Marshall, Hamilton, Kent & Co., 1906.

Hanegraaff, H. *Christianity in Crisis*. Eugene, Ore.: Harvest House, 1993.

Haran, M. "נְחֻשְׁתָּן." *EM* 5:826–27.

Harper, M. *The Healings of Jesus*. The Jesus Library. Downers Grove, Ill.: InterVarsity, 1986.

Harrell Jr., D. E. *All Things Are Possible: The Healing and Charismatic Revivals in Modern America*. Bloomington: Indiana Univ. Press, 1975.

Harris, J. G. *Biblical Perspective on Aging*. OBT. Philadelphia: Fortress, 1987.

Harrison, R. K. "Heal." *ISBE* 2:640–47.

________. "Healing, Health." *IDB* 2:541–48.

________. *The Healing Herbs of the Bible*. Leiden: Brill, 1966.

Hasel, G. F. "Health and Healing in the Old Testament." *AUSS* 21 (1983): 191–202.

Hawthorne, G. F. *The Presence and the Power*. Dallas: Word, 1991.

Healey, J. P. "Fertility Cults." *ABD* 2:791–93.

Healing and Wholeness: The Churches' Role in Health. The Report of a Study by the Christian Medical Commission, World Council of Churches. Geneva: Christian Medical Commission, WCC, 1990.

Held, M. "Pits and Pitfalls in Akkadian and Biblical Hebrew." *JANESCU* 5 (1973): 173–90.

Hemer, C. J. "Medicine in the New Testament World." Pp. 43–85 in B. Palmer, ed., *Medicine and the Bible*. Exeter: Paternoster, 1986.

Hempel, J. *Heilung als Symbol und Wirklichkeit im biblischen Schriftum*. Göttingen: Vandenhoeck & Ruprecht, 1958.

________. "Ich bin der Herr dein Arzt." *ThLZ* 82 (1957): 809–26.

Hillers, D. R. *Treaty Curses and the Old Testament Prophets*. BibOr 16. Rome: Pontifical Biblical Institute, 1964.

Hobart, W. K. *The Medical Language of St. Luke*. Repr. Grand Rapids: Baker, 1954.

Hoenes, S.-E. *Untersuchungen zu Wesen und Kult der Gottin Sachmet, Habilitationschrift Dissertationsdrucke, Reihe Ägyptologie*. Heft 1. Bonn: Habelt, 1976.

Hoffman, Y. "The Transition from Despair to Hope in the Individual Psalm of Lament" (Hebrew). *Tarbiz* 55 (1985/86): 161–72.

Hoffmeier, J. K. "The Arm of God Versus the Arm of Pharaoh in the Exodus Narratives." *Bib* 67 (1986): 378–87.

Hogan, L. "A Note on Healing and Ignorance in the Bible." *Koroth* 9/1–2 (1985): 107–12.

Holloway, S. W. "Distaff, Crutch or Chain Gang: The Curse of the House of Joab in 2 Sam iii 29." *VT* 37 (1987): 370–75.

Hugger, P. *Jahwe meine Zuflucht: Gestalt und Theologie des 91. Psalms.* Münsterschwarzacher Studien 13. Münsterschwarzachen: Vier-Turma-Verlag, 1971.

Humbert, P. "Maladie et médecine dans l'Ancien Testament." *RHPhR* 44 (1964): 1–29.

Im der Smitten, W. T. "Patient und Arzt. Die Welt des Kranken im Alten Testament." *Janus* 61 (1974): 103–29.

Jacob, I., and W. Jacob. *The Healing Past: Pharmaceuticals in the Biblical and Rabbinic World.* Studies in Ancient Medicine 7. Leiden: Brill. 1993.

Jakobovits, I. *Jewish Medical Ethics.* 2d ed. New York: Bloch, 1975.

Jayne, W. A. *Healing Gods of Ancient Civilizations.* Repr. New York: AMS Press, 1979.

Johnson, A. R. *The Vitality of the Individual in the Thought of Ancient Israel.* 2d ed. Cardiff: Univ. of Wales Press, 1963.

________. "Jonah ii, 3–10: A Study in Cultic Phantasy." Pp. 82–102 in H. H. Rowley, ed., *Studies in Old Testament Prophecy. Festschrift for T. H. Robinson.* Edinburgh: T. & T. Clark, 1946.

Jones, R. N. "Paleopathology." *ABD* 5:60–69.

Josephson, E. A. *God's Key to Health and Happiness.* Grand Rapids: Revell, 1992.

Junker, H. "Die Stele des Hofarztes 'Irj." *ZÄS* 63 (1928): 53–70.

Kaiser Jr., W. C. "The Old Testament Case for Material Blessings and the Contemporary Believer." *TrinJ* 9 (1988): 151–69.

Kee, H. C. "Medicine and Healing." *ABD* 4:659–64.

________. *Medicine, Miracle and Magic in New Testament Times.* SNTSMS 55. New York: Cambridge Univ. Press, 1986.

________. *Miracle in the Early Christian World.* New Haven: Yale Univ. Press, 1983.

Keel, O. *The Symbolism of the Biblical World.* Trans. T. J. Hallet. New York: Seabury, 1978.

Kelsey, M. T. *Healing and Christianity.* New York: Harper & Row, 1973.

Kerenyi, C. *Asklepios: Archetypal Image of the Physician's Existence.* New York: Pantheon/Bollingen Foundation, 1959.

Kim, S. "The Concepts of Health, Disease and Healing: Theological Perspective." Pp. 27–35 in *The Proceedings of the Consultation on the Study Program of the Healing Ministry.*

Kinnier-Wilson, J. V. "Medicine in the Land and Times of the Old Testament." Pp. 337–65 in T. Ishida, ed., *Studies in the Period of David and Solomon.* Winona Lake, Ind.: Eisenbrauns, 1982.

Knibb, M. A. "Life and Death in the Old Testament." Pp. 395–415 in R. E. Clements, ed., *The World of the Ancient Israel.* Cambridge: Cambridge Univ. Press, 1989.

Knowling, R. J. "The Medical Language of St. Luke." *BW* 20 (1902): 260–70, 370–79.

Kocher, F. *Die babylonische-assyrische Medizin in Texten und Untersuchungen.* Berlin: de Gruyter, 1963–.

Koop, C. E. "Faith-Healing and the Sovereignty of God." Pp. 169–81 in M. Horton, ed., *The Agony of Deceit.* Chicago: Moody, 1990.

Korpel, M. C. A. *A Rift in the Clouds: Ugaritic and Hebrew Descriptions of the Divine.* UBL 8. Münster: Ugarit-Verlag, 1990.

Kottek, S. S. *Medicine and Hygiene in the Works of Flavius Josephus.* Studies in Ancient Medicine 9. Leiden: Brill. 1994.

Kraemer, D. *Responses to Suffering in Classical Rabbinic Literature.* New York: Oxford Univ. Press, 1995.

Kydd, R. A. N. *Charismatic Gifts in the Early Church.* Peabody, Mass.: Hendrickson, 1984.

L'Heureux, C. *Rank Among the Canaanite Gods: El, Ba'al, and the Repha'im.* HSM 21. Missoula, Mont.: Scholars, 1979.

Labat, R. *Traité akkadien de diagnostics et prognostics médicaux*; vol. 1, *Transcription et Traduction*; vol. 2, *Planches*. Collection de travaux de l'académie internationale d'historie des sciences 7. Paris: Academie internationale d'histoire des sciences / Leiden: Brill, 1951.

Lambert, W. G. "The Gula Hymn of Bulluṭsa-rābi." *Orientalia*, n.s. 36 (1967): 105–32.

Latourelle, R. *The Miracles of Jesus and the Theology of Miracles.* Trans. M. J. O'Connell. New York: Paulist, 1988.

Lefebvre, G. *Tableau des parties du corps humain mentionnés par les Égyptiens.* Le Caire: Impr. de l'Institut Francais d'Archeologie Orientale, 1952.

Leivestad, R. "ἰάομαι, ἴαμα, ἴασις." *EDNT* 2:169–70.

________. "ἰατρός." *EDNT* 2:171.

Levin, S. "Hezekiah's Boil." *Judaism* 42 (1993): 214–17.

Levine, B. A., and J.-M. de Tarragon, O.P. "'Shapshu Cries Out in Heaven': Dealing with Snake-Bites at Ugarit." *RB* 95 (1988): 481–518.

Liebowitz, Y. "רְפוּאָה." *EM* 7:407–25.

Lindeboom, G. A. "Luke the Evangelist and the Ancient Greek Writers on Medicine." *Janus* 52 (1965): 143–48.

Lindsay, G., ed. *The John G. Lake Sermons on Dominion over Demons, Disease and Death*. Repr. Dallas: Christ for the Nations Inst., 1982.

Lindström, F. *Suffering and Sin: Interpretations of Illness in the Individual Complaint Psalms*. OTS 37. Stockholm: Almqvist & Wiksell, 1994.

________. *God and the Origin of Evil: A Contextual Analysis of Alleged Monistic Evidence in the Old Testament*. ConBOT 21. Lund: CWK Gleerup, 1983.

Lipinski, E. "Eshmun, 'Healer.'" *AION* 23 (1973): 161–83.

Litwak, K. D. "The Use of Quotations from Isaiah 52:13–53:12 in the New Testament." *JETS* 26 (1983): 385–94.

Liwak, R. "רְפָאִים." *TWAT* 7:625–36.

Lloyd-Jones, D. M. *Healing and the Scriptures*. Nashville: Oliver-Nelson, 1988.

________. *The Sovereign Spirit: Discerning His Gifts*. Wheaton, Ill.: Harold Shaw, 1985.

Lods, A. "Les idées des Israélites sur la maladie, ses causes et ses remèdes." Pp. 181–93 in K. Budde, ed., *Vom Alten Testament: K. Marti Festscrhift*. BZAW 41. Berlin: Alfred Toppelman, 1925.

Loewe, H. "Disease and Medicine (Jewish)." *ERE* 4:755–57.

Loewenstamm, S. "רְפָאִים." *EM* 7:406.

Lohfink, N. "*Deuteronomy 6:24:* lᵉḥayyōtēnû, *'To mantain us.'*" Pp. 111–19 in M. Fishbane and E. Tov, eds., *"Sha'arei Talmon": Studies in the Bible, Qumran and the Ancient Near East Presented to Shemaryahu Talmon*. Winona Lake, Ind.: Eisenbrauns, 1992.

________. "'Ich bin Jahwe, dein Arzt' (Ex 15,26). Gott, Gesselshcaft und menschliche Gesundheit in einer nachexilischen Pentateuchbearbeitung (Ex 15, 25b.26)." Pp. 11–73 in H. Merklein and E. Zenger, eds., *Ich will euer Gott werden: Beispiele biblis-*

chen Redens von Gott. SBS 100. Stuttgart: Katholisches Bibelwerk, 1981.

Loretz, O. "Tod und Leben nach altorientalischer und kanaanaäisch-biblischer anschauung in Hos 6, 1–3." *BN* 17 (1982): 37–42.

MacArthur Jr., J. F. *Charismatic Chaos*. Grand Rapids: Zondervan, 1992.

Malamat, A. "Longevity: Biblical Concepts and Some Ancient Near Eastern Parallels." *AfO* 19 (1982): 215–24.

Margulis, D. S. *Lashon u-refuah ba-Tanakh*. Tel Aviv: Vaadat ha-Yovel shel Irgun Rofe Kupat Holim Amamit, 1949.

Martin-Achard, R. "Approche des Psaumes." *Cahiers théologiques* 60 (1969): 49–65.

————. "La prière des malades dans le psautier d'Israël." Lumière et Vie 86 (1968): 25–43.

Marzel, Y. "The Tree of Knowledge of Good and Evil—Recognition of Life and Death (Genesis 2–3)" (Hebrew). *Beth Mikra* 29 (1983/84): 352–60.

Masters, P. *The Healing Epidemic*. London: The Wakeman Trust, 1988.

Matthews, V. H., and D. C. Benjamin. "The Leper." *TBT* 29 (1991): 292–97.

May, E. "'... For Power Went Forth from Him ...' (Luke 6,19)." *CBQ* 14 (1952): 93–103.

McCarthy, D. J. *Treaty and Covenant: A Study in Form in the Ancient Oriental Documents and in the Old Testament*. AnBib 21A. Rome: Pontifical Biblical Institute, 1981.

McConville, J. G. "Statement of Assurance in Psalms of Lament." *IBS* 8 (1986): 64–75.

McCrossan, T. J. *Bodily Healing and the Atonement*. Ed. and repr. R. Hicks and K. E. Hagin. Tulsa: Faith Library, n.d..

McKay, J. W. "The Experiences of Dereliction and of God's Presence in the Psalms: An Exercise in Old Testament Exegesis in the Light of Renewal Theology." Pp. 3–13 in P. Ebert, ed., *Faces of Renewal: Studies in Honor of Stanley M. Horton Presented on His 70th Birthday*. Peabody, Mass.: Hendrickson, 1988.

McKeating, H. "Divine Forgiveness in the Psalms." *SJT* 18 (1965): 69–74.

McMillen, S. I. *None of These Diseases.* Rev. and expanded D. E. Stern. Old Tappan, N.J.: Revell, 1984.

McNeill, W. H. *Plagues and Peoples.* Garden City, N.Y.: Doubleday, 1975.

Mendcki, N. "Jahwe Erbauer Jerusalems und Sammler der Zerstreuten in Ps 147, 2–3." *Collectanea Theologica* 56 (1986): 85–88.

Michaeli, F. "Les malades et le temple dans l'Ancien Testament." *Église et Théologie* 21 (1958): 3–12.

Miller, E. *Healing: Does God Always Heal?* San Juan Capistrano, Calif.: CRI, 1979.

Mitchell, C. W. *The Meaning of BRK "To Bless" in the Old Testament.* Atlanta: Scholars, 1987.

Mosis, R. "Umkehr und Vergebung—eine Auslegung von Jer 3,21–4,2." *TTZ* 98 (1989): 39–60.

Moule, C. F. D., ed. *Miracles: Cambridge Studies in Their Philosophy and History.* London: A. R. Mowbray & Co., 1986.

Muilenberg, J. "The Terminology of Adversity in Jeremiah." Pp. 42–63 in H. T. Frank and W. L. Reed, eds., *Translating and Understanding the Old Testament: Essays in Honor of Herbert Gordon May.* Nashville: Abingdon, 1970.

Murdock, G. P. *Theories of Illness.* Pittsburgh: Univ. of Pittsburgh Press, 1980.

Murray, A. *Divine Healing.* Repr. Fort Washington, Pa.: Christian Literature Crusade, n.d.

Myers, C. S. "Disease and Medicine (Introductory and Primitive)." *ERE* 4:723–31. Also in J. Sutcliffe and N. Duin, *A History of Medicine: From Prehistory to the Year 2020.* New York: Barnes and Noble, 1992.

Naveh, J., and S. Shaked. *Magic Spells and Formulae: Aramaic Incantations of Late Antiquity.* Jerusalem: Magnes, 1993.

Neufeld, E. "Hygiene Conditions in Ancient Israel (Iron Age)." *BA* 34 (1971): 42–66.

Neusner, J., and E. S. Frerichs, P. V. M. Flesher, eds. *Religion, Science, and Magic.* Oxford: Oxford Univ. Press, 1989.

Niccacci, A. "Yahweh e il Faraone. Teologia biblica ed egiziana a confronto." *BN* 38/39 (1987): 85–102.

Niehr, H. "JHWH als Arzt. Herkunft und Geschichte einer altestatmentlichen Gottesprädikation." *BZ* 35 (1991): 3–17.

———. *Der hochste Gott: Alttestamentlicher JHWH-Glaube im Kontext syrisch-kanaanäischer Religion des 1, Jahrtausends v. Chr.* BZAW 190. Berlin/New York: de Gruyter, 1990.

Nielsen, H. K. *Heilung und Verkündigung: Das Verständnis der Heilung und ihres Verhältnisses zur Verkündigung bei Jesus und in der ältesten Kirche.* Leiden: Brill, 1987.

Noy, D. "The Talmudic-Midrashic Healing Stories as a Narrative Genre." *Koroth* 9, Special Issue (1988): 124–46.

Oepke, A. "ἰάομαι, ἴασις, ἴαμα, ἰατρός." *TDNT* 3:194–215.

Osborn, T. L. *Healing the Sick.* Tulsa, Okla.: Harrison House, n.d.

Ott, J. "Die Bezeichnung Christi als *iatros* in der urchristlichen Literatur." *Der Katholik* 90 (1910): 454–58.

Ottosson, M. "חָלַם." *TDOT* 4:426–32.

Palmer, B., ed. *Medicine and the Bible.* Exeter: Paternoster, 1986.

Pardee, D. "A Philological and Prosodic Analysis of the Ugaritic Serpent Incantation UT 607." *JANESCU* 10 (1978): 73–108.

Parpola, S., and K. Watanabe, eds. *Neo-Assyrian Treaties and Loyalty Oaths. State Archives of Assyria,* vol. 2. Helsinki: Helsinki Univ. Press, 1988.

Paul, S. M. "An Unrecognized Medical Idiom in Canticles 6, 12 and Job 9, 21." *Bib* 59 (1978): 545–47.

Pilch, J. J. "Healing in Mark: A Social Science Analysis." *BTB* 15 (1985): 142–50.

———. "The Health Care System in Matthew: A Social Science Analysis." *BTB* 16 (1986): 102–06.

———. "Sickness and Health in Luke-Acts." Pp. 181–209 in J. H. Neyrey, ed., *The Social World of Luke-Acts.* Peabody, Mass.: Hendrickson, 1991.

Pitard, W. T. "A New Edition of the 'Rapi'uma' Texts: KTU 1:20–22." *BASOR* 285 (1992): 33–77.

Preuss, J. *Biblical and Talmudic Medicine.* Trans. F. Rosner. New York: Hebrew Pub. Co., 1978.

Prioreschi, P. *A History of Medicine.* Vol. 1, *Primitive and Ancient Medicine.* Lewiston, N.Y.: Edwin Mellen, 1991.

Provonsha, J. W. "The Healing Christ." Pp. 361–64 in Kelsey, ed., *Healing and Christianity.* New York: Harper & Row, 1973.

Puech, É. "11QPsApa: un ritual d'exorcismes. Essai de reconstruction." *RevQ* 14 (1990): 377–408.

Radl, W. "σώζω." *EDNT* 3:319–21.

Ringe, S. H. *Jesus, Liberation, and the Biblical Jubilee*. OBT. Philadelphia: Fortress, 1985.

Ringgren, H. "חָיָה." *TDOT* 4:324–44.

Ritter, E. K. "Magical-expert (=*ašipu*) and Physician (=*asû*). Notes on Two Complementary Professions in Babylonian Medicine." Pp. 299–321 in H. G. Guterbock and T. Jacobsen, eds., *Studies in Honor of Benno Landsberger on his 75 Birthday*. AS 16. Chicago: Univ. of Chicago Press, 1965.

Rivers, W. H. *Medicine, Magic and Religion*. Repr. New York: AMS Press, 1985.

Roberts, J. J. M. "niškaḥtî … millēb, Ps XXXI 13." *VT* 25 (1975): 797–80.

________. "The Hand of Jahweh." *VT* 21 (1971): 244–51.

________, and P. D. Miller Jr. *The Hand of the Lord: A Reassessment of the "Ark Narrative" of 1 Samuel*. Baltimore: Johns Hopkins Univ. Press, 1977.

Roberts, O. *A Daily Guide to Miracles*. Tulsa, Okla.: Pinoak Press, 1975.

Robinson, B. P. "Symbolism in Exod 15:22–27 (Marah and Elim)." *RB* 94 (1987): 376–88.

Rodríguez, A. M. "Health and Healing in the Pentateuch." Silver Spring, Md.: Biblical Research Institute, 1993 (circulated privately).

Rosner, F. "The Illness of King Hezekiah and 'The Book of Remedies' Which He Hid." *Koroth* 9/1–2 (1985): 191–93.

________. *Medicine in the Mishneh Torah of Maimonides*. New York: Ktav, 1984.

________."The Physician and the Patient in Jewish Law." Pp. 45–55 in idem and J. D. Bleich, eds., *Jewish Bioethics*. Brooklyn: Hebrew Pub. Co., 1979.

________. *Medicine in the Bible and Talmud*. New York: Yeshiva Univ. Press, 1977.

________. *Modern Medicine and Jewish Law*. New York: Bloch Pub. Co., 1972.

Rouillard, R. "El Rofé en Nombres 12,13." *Sem* 37 (1987): 17–46.

Ruthven, J. *On the Cessation of the Charismata*. Journal of Pentecostal Theology, Supp3. Sheffield: Sheffield Academic Press, 1993.

Ryle, J. C. *Sickness*. Repr. Choteau, Mont.: Gospel Mission, 1980.

Safran, J. D. "'He Restoreth My Soul': A Biblical Expression and Its Counterpart." Pp. 265–71 in G. D. Young, ed., *Mari in Retrospect: Fifty Years of Mari and Mari Studies*. Winona Lake, Ind.: Eisenbrauns, 1992.

Sandison, A. T. "Balsamierung." *LÄ* 1:610–14.

Saydon, P. P. "Disease and Healing in the Bible." *Melita Theologica* 15 (1963): 12–27

Sawyer, J. F. A., and H. J. Fabry. "ישע." *TDOT* 6:441–63.

Scharbert, J. "ברך." *TDOT* 2:279–308.

Scharbert, J. *Der Schmerz im Alten Testament*. BBB 8. Bonn: Peter Hanstein Verlag, 1955.

Schatzmann, S. *A Pauline Theology of the Charismata*. Peabody, Mass.: Hendrickson, 1987.

Schipperges, H., and E. Seidler, P. U. Unschuld, eds. *Krankheit, Heilkunst, Heilung*. München: Karl Aber, 1978.

Schmid, H. H. *Šālôm: "Frieden" im Alten Orient und im Alten Testament*. SBS 51. Stuttgart: KBW Verlag, 1971.

Schrage, W. "Heil und Heilung im Neuen Testament." *EvT* 43 (1986): 197–214.

Schwartz, J. "Putting a Certain Face on Emotions: Right Sort of Grin May Spark Brain Response." *The Washington Post*, Nov. 8, 1993, A3.

Seel, D. J. "The Imperative of a Christian Approach to Healing." Pp. 3–12 in *The Proceedings of the Consultation on the Study Program of the Healing Ministry*.

Seybold, K. "חָלָה, etc." *TDOT* 4:399–409.

________. *Das Gebet des Kranken in Alten Testament: Untersuchungen zur Bestimmung und Zuordnung der Krankheits- und Heilungspsalmen*. BWANT 99. Stuttgart: Kohlhammer, 1973.

________. "Krankheit und Heilung. Soziale Aspekte in den Psalmen." *BK* 20 (1971): 107–11.

________, and U. B. Mueller. *Sickness and Healing*. Trans. D. W. Stott. Nashville: Abingdon, 1981.

Shapiro, D. S. "Be Fruitful and Multiply." Pp. 59–80 in F. Rosner and J. D. Bleich, *Jewish Bioethics*. Brooklyn: Hebrew Pub. Co., 1979.

Shin, G. K.-S. *Die Ausrufung des endgültigen Jubeljahres durch Jesus in Nazaret: Eine historisch-kritische Studie zu Lk 4, 16–30*. EH 23. Bern: Peter Lang, 1989.
Shogren, G. S. "Authority and Power." Pp. 50–54 in *Dictionary of Jesus and the Gospels*. Downers Grove, Ill.: InterVarsity, 1992.
Siegel, B. "Healing of the Spirit and Curing of the Body." *Studies in Formative Spirituality* 12 (1991): 143–47.
Sigerist, H. E. *Civilization and Disease*. Chicago: Univ. Of Chicago Press, 1943.
Simeon, C. "Afflictions, the Fruit of God's Love." Pp. 217–23 in idem, ed., *Evangelical Preaching*. Portland, Ore.: Multnomah, 1986.
Simundson, D. J. "Mental Health in the Bible." *Word & World* 9 (1989): 140–46.
________. "Health and Healing in the Bible." *Word & World* 2 (1982): 330–39.
________. *Faith Under Fire: Biblical Interpretations of Suffering*. Minneapolis: Augsburg, 1980.
Sloan, R. B. "Jubilee." Pp. 396–97 in *Dictionary of Jesus and the Gospels*. Downers Grove, Ill.: InterVarsity, 1992.
________. *The Favorable Year of the Lord: A Study of Jubilary Theology in the Gospel of Luke*. Austin, Tex.: Scholars, 1977.
Smith, M. S. "Rephaim." *ABD* 5:674–76.
Speigelberg, W. "Die Beisetzung des Patriarchen Jacob (Gen 50, 2ff.) in Licht der ägypt. Quellen." *OLZ* 26 (1923): 421–24.
Spenser, S. "2 Chronicles 28:5–15 and the Parable of the Good Samaritan." *WTJ* 46 (1984): 317–49.
Sperber, D. "Weak Waters." *ZAW* 82 (1970): 114–16.
Stamm, J. J. *Erlösen und Vergeben im Alten Testament*. Dissertation: Basel, 1940.
Stendahl, K. "Gamla Testaments föreställningar om helandet. Rafa'-utsagorna i kontext och ideologi." *Svensk Exegetisk Årsbok* 15 (1950): 5–33.
Sterk, J. V. "Evangelism with Power: Divine Healing in the Growth of the Tzotzil Church." *Missiology* 20 (1992): 371–84.
Sternberg, H. "Sachmet." *LÄ* 5:323–33.
Stoebe, H. J. "רפא, heilen." *THAT* 2:803–9.
Stöger, A. "Der Artz nach Sir (38, 1–15)." *Artz und Christ* 11 (1965): 3–11)

Stol, M. *Zwangerschap en geboorte bij de Babyloniers en in de Bijbel.* Medelelingen en Verhandelingen van het Vooraziatisch-Egyptisch Genootschap "Ex Oriente Lux" 23. With a chapter by F. A. M. Wiggermann. Leiden: Ex Oriente Lux, 1983.

Stolz, F. "חלה, krank sein." *THAT* 1:567–70.

Struys, T. *Zietke en Genezing in het Oude Testament.* Kampen: Kok, 1968.

Suhl, A., ed. *Die Wunderbegriff im Neuen Testament.* Darmstadt: Wissentschaftliche Buchgesellschaft, 1980.

Sullivan, M.-C. "Bibliography." Pp. 315–46 in Marty and Vaux, eds., *Health/Medicine and the Faith Traditions: An Inquiry into Religion and Medicine.* Ann Arbor: University Microfilms International (Books on Demand).

Sussman, M. "Sickness and Disease." *ABD* 6:6–15.

Sweet, A. M. "A Theology of Healing." *TBT* 20 (1982): 145–49.

Tallqvist, K. L. *Akkadische Götterepitheta.* Repr. Studia Orientalia edidit Societas Orientalis Fennica 7. Hildesheim: Georg Olms, 1974.

Tambiah, S. J. *Magic, Science, Religion and the Scope of Rationality.* New York: Cambridge Univ. Press, 1990.

The Proceedings of the Consultation on the Study Program of Healing Ministry, October 30-November 1, 1980. Seoul: Asian Center for Theological Studies and Mission/Korea Christian Medico-Evangelical Association, n.d.

Thompson, C. J. S. *Magic and Healing.* Repr. New York: Bell, 1989.

Thompson, R. C., ed. *The Reports of the Magicians and Astrologers of Nineveh and Babylon in the British Museum.* 2 vols. Repr. New York: AMS, 1977.

Thrämer, E. "Health and Gods of Healing (Greek)." *ERE* 6:540–56.

Thuruthumaly, J. "The Praying Man in Psalms of Lament." *Biblebhashyam* 5 (1979): 119–32.

Ties, A. *Jahwe als Artz.* Dissertation, Rome, 1964–65.

Turner, M. M. B. "The Spirit and the Power of Jesus' Miracles in the Lucan Conception." *NovT* 33 (1991): 124–52.

———. "Jesus and the Spirit in the Lucan Perspective." *TynBul* 32 (1981): 3–42.

Twelftree, G. H. *Jesus the Exorcist.* Peabody, Mass.: Hendrickson, 1995.

Unger, M. F. "Divine Healing." *Bibliotheca Sacra* 128 (1971): 234–44.

Van Seters, J. "The Plagues of Egypt: Ancient Tradition or Literary Invention?" *ZAW* 98 (1986): 31–39.

Vattioni, F. "Mal. 3,20 e un mese del calendario fenicio." *Bib* 40 (1959): 1012–15.

von Baudissin, W. W. G. *Adonis und Esmun: Eine Untersuchung zur Geschichte des Glaubens an Auferstehungsgötter und an Heilgötter*. Leipzig: Hinrichs, 1911.

Waldenberg, E. Y. *Ṣiṣ Eliezer*. Jerusalem: n.p., 1985–.

Wallis, I. G. "Christ's Continuing Ministry of Healing." *ExpTim* 104 (1992): 42–45.

Waltke, B. "Relating Human Personhood to the Health Sciences: An Old Testament Perspective." *Crux* 25 (1989): 2–10.

Warfield, B. B. *Counterfeit Miracles*. New York: Charles Scribner's Sons, 1918.

Weber, C. P. "חָלָה." *TWOT* 1:286–87.

Weippert, H. "Bad und Baden." *BRL*[2] 30–32.

Wenham, D., and C. L. Blomberg, eds. *Gospel Perspectives 6: The Miracles of Jesus*. Sheffield: JSOT Press, 1986.

Westermann, C. "Heilung und Heil in der Gemeinde aus der Sicht des Alten Testaments." *WzM* 27 (1975): 12–25.

White, A. D. *A History of the Warfare of Science with Theology*. 2 vols. Repr. Gloucester, Mass.: Peter Smith, 1978.

White, E. G. *The Ministry of Healing*. Repr. Boise, Ida.: Remnant Publications, 1988.

White, W. "רָפָא." *TWOT* 2:857.

Widengren, G. *The Accadian and Hebrew Psalms of Lamentation*. Stockholm: Atkielbolaget Thule, 1937.

Wilkinson, J. "The Body in the Old Testament." *EvQ* 63 (1991): 195–210.

________. "The Mission Charge to the Twelve and Modern Medical Missions." *SJT* 27 (1974): 313–28.

________. "Healing in the Epistle of James." *SJT* 24 (1971): 326–45.

________. "The Case of the Epileptic Boy." *ExpTim* 79 (1967): 39–42.

Wilms, F.-E. *Wunder im Alten Testament*. Regensburg: Putset, 1979.

Wimber, J., and K. Springer. *Power Healing*. San Francisco: Harper & Row, 1987.

Wiseman, D. J. "Medicine in the Old Testament." Pp. 13–42 in B. Palmer, ed., *Medicine and the Bible*. Exeter: Paternoster, 1986.

Witty, R. G. *Divine Healing*. Nashville: Broadman, 1989.

Woodworth-Etter, M. *A Diary of Signs and Wonders*. Repr. Tulsa, Okla.: Harrison House, n.d.

Yahuda, A. S. "Medical and Anatomical Terms in the Pentateuch in the Light of Egyptian Medical Papyri." *Journal of the History of Medicine* 2 (1947): 549–74.

Yates, K. M. *The Theological Significance of Healing in the Old Testament*. Dissertation, Southern Baptist Theological Seminary, 1955.

Yeomans, L. B. *Healing from Heaven*. Rev. ed. Springfield, Mo.: Radiant Books/Gospel Pub. House, 1973.

Zerafa, P., O.P. "The Old Testament Life Span." *Angelicum* 65 (1988): 99–116.

Zevit, Z. "Three Ways to Look at the Ten Plagues." *BRev* 6 (1990): 16–23, 42, 44.

Zias, J. "Death and Disease in Ancient Israel." *BA* 54 (1991): 147–59.

Zimmels, H. J. *Magicians, Theologians, and Doctors: Studies in Folk-Medicine and Folklore as Reflected in the Rabbinic Responsa*. London: Edward Goldston & Son, 1952.

Zimmerli, W. "Das 'Gnadenjahr des Herrn.'" Pp. 321–32 in A. Kuschke and E. Kutsch, eds., *Archäologie und Altes Testament: Festschrift für K. Galling*. Tübingen: Mohr, 1970.

Zohari, M. "צֳרִי." *EM* 6:770–71.

Name Index

The references in this index refer to discussions of these authors in the text, not in the endnotes.

Subject Index

Wisdom: and health, 157–61; preserves life, 240; promises of, 160
Word of God, 246. *See also*, Scriptures.
Wrath, 103, 117, 124, 134, 190; of God, 120, 122, 127, 234; of the Lord, 170; pour out his, 88; torrents of, 139; of Yahweh, 239. *See also*, Chastisement, Curse, Discipline, Judgment, Smiting.
Yahweh, 106–8; the all-powerful, 101; all-sufficiency of, 99; as the Author of, 169; character of, 190; declared himself, 67; faithful worshiper of, 142; as he who forgives, 150; as Healer, 23, 76–77, 124, 238; healing virtues of, 121–22; as *rôpē'*, 24–25; smiting hand of, 243; sovereignty of, 99–100; wrath of, 125. *See also*, Lord.

◆ Scripture Index ◆

All Old Testament entries refer to the English text, not the Hebrew text